Ricardo on Money

Despite his achievements, David Ricardo's views on money have often been misunderstood and underappreciated. His advanced ideas had to wait until the twentieth century to be applied, and most historians of economic thought continue to consider him as an obsolete orthodox. The last book devoted in tribute to Ricardo as a monetary economist was published more than 25 years ago.

Ricardo on Money encompasses the whole of Ricardo's writings on currency, whether in print, unpublished notes, correspondence, or reported parliamentary speeches and evidence. The aim of the book is at rehabilitating Ricardo as an unorthodox theorist on money and suggesting his relevance for modern analysis. It is divided into three parts: history, theory and policy. The first describes the factual and intellectual context of Ricardo's monetary writings. The second part puts the concept of standard centre stage and clarifies how, according to Ricardo, the standard regulated the quantity – and hence the value – of money. The final part shows that Ricardo relied on the active management of paper money rather than on flows of bullion and commodities to produce international adjustment and guarantee the security of the monetary system.

Published to coincide with the 200th anniversary of the publication of *On the Principles of Political Economy, and Taxation*, this book will be of great interest to all historians of economic thought and scholars of monetary economics.

Ghislain Deleplace is Emeritus Professor of Economics at University Paris 8 at Saint-Denis, France. His fields of research are the history of monetary thought (Steuart, Ricardo, Marx, Keynes, Sraffa), the history of the international monetary system (sixteenth century, nineteenth century), and the post-Keynesian theory of money.

Routledge Studies in the History of Economics

For a full list of titles in this series, please visit www.routledge.com/series/SE0341

187 The Political Economy of Latin American Independence
Edited by Alexandre Mendes Cunha and Carlos Eduardo Suprinyak

188 Jean-Baptiste Say and Political Economy
Jean-Baptiste Say
Gilles Jacoud

189 Economists and War
A heterodox perspective
Edited by Fabrizio Bientinesi and Rosario Patalano

190 Great Economic Thinkers from the Classicals to the Moderns
Translations from the series *Klassiker der Nationalökonomie*
Bertram Schefold

191 Business Cycles in Economic Thought
A History
Edited by Alain Alcouffe, Monika Poettinger and Bertram Schefold

192 Economics, Ethics, and Ancient Thought
Towards a Virtuous Public Policy
Donald G. Richards

193 Ricardo on Money
A Reappraisal
Ghislain Deleplace

Ricardo on Money

A Reappraisal

Ghislain Deleplace

LONDON AND NEW YORK

First published 2017 by Routledge

2 Park Square, Milton Park, Abingdon, Oxfordshire OX14 4RN
52 Vanderbilt Avenue, New York, NY 10017

Routledge is an imprint of the Taylor & Francis Group, an informa business

First issued in paperback 2019

British Library Cataloguing in Publication Data
A catalogue record for this book is available from the British Library

Library of Congress Cataloging in Publication Data
Names: Deleplace, Ghislain, author.
Title: Ricardo on money : a reappraisal / Ghislain Deleplace.
Description: Abingdon, Oxon ; New York, NY : Routledge, 2017.
Identifiers: LCCN 2016048743| ISBN 9780415661584 (hardback) |
ISBN 9781315207872 (ebook)
Subjects: LCSH: Ricardo, David, 1772-1823. | Money. | Monetary policy.
Classification: LCC HB103.R5 D45 2017 | DDC 332.401--dc23
LC record available at https://lccn.loc.gov/2016048743

ISBN: 978-0-415-66158-4 (hbk)
ISBN: 978-0-367-86783-6 (pbk)

Typeset in Times New Roman
by Sunrise Setting Ltd, Brixham, UK

To the memory of Charles (1921–2012) and Simonne (1921–2015) Deleplace
To Nathalie, Aurélien, Raphaël

Ricardo's Memorial in Hardenhuish churchyard

Contents

Tables

Acknowledgements

The numerous quotations from Ricardo are taken from *The Works and Correspondence of David Ricardo*, edited by Piero Sraffa with the collaboration of Maurice H. Dobb, and originally published in 11 volumes between 1951 and 1973 by Cambridge University Press for the Royal Economic Society. These texts are now published online by Liberty Fund, freely available for academic purposes.

Parts of various chapters of the book have been published in the entries "Bullionist Controversy", "Monetary Theory", and "Papers on Money and Banking" which I wrote for *The Elgar Companion to David Ricardo*, edited by Heinz D. Kurz and Neri Salvadori in 2015. I thank the editors and Edward Elgar Publishing for granting permission to reproduce these extracts.

Part of Chapter 6 and Ricardo's letter quoted in full in Appendix 6 have been published in G. Deleplace, C. Depoortère and N. Rieucau (2013) "An unpublished letter of David Ricardo on the double standard of money", *The European Journal of the History of Economic Thought*, 20 (1), February: 1–28. I thank my co-authors, the editors of the journal, and Routledge for granting permission to reproduce this extract and the letter.

For 25 years I have passionately discussed with Maria Cristina Marcuzzo and Annalisa Rosselli about how Ricardo on money was different from what he was usually believed to be; this scientific complicity has been invaluable. For even longer Carlo Benetti and Jean Cartelier have been for me a source of inspiration by their unorthodox approach to money and I tried to convince them that Ricardo could unexpectedly have something to do with such an approach. They read and commented on Part II of the book, and helped me to improve its presentation. My understanding of the historical background of Ricardo's monetary writings has much benefited from a research on international bimetallism implemented during more than twenty years with Marie-Thérèse Boyer-Xambeu and Lucien Gillard. Discussions with my co-authors on Ricardo, Nathalie Sigot for one article, Christophe Depoortère and Nicolas Rieucau for another, have contributed to the shaping of some of the propositions contained in this book.

I am grateful to those who commented on my presentations in conferences on Ricardo on money and finance organised by the University of Paris 8 at Saint-Denis (2006), the Ricardo Society of Japan in Kyoto (2012), SOAS, University of London (2016), and in other international conferences organised in Thessaloniki

(2009), Istanbul (2011), Saint Petersburg (2012), Paris (2016) by the European Society for the History of Economic Thought, in London (2010) by the City University of London, and in Cambridge (2012) by Gonville and Caius College. I thank those who raised many interesting points on these occasions, particularly (in addition to those already mentioned) Christian Bidard, Sylvie Diatkine, Jan Kregel, Luigi L. Pasinetti, Ajit Sinha and Susumu Takenaga.

Some of the ideas contained in the book have been tested on the successive generations of students attending the seminar "Money and exchange from Ricardo to Keynes" in the Master's program "History of economic thought" of the University Paris 1 – Panthéon-Sorbonne, and on Christophe Depoortère during the preparation of his doctorate thesis "Ricardo's method in his theories of value and money" at the University Paris 8 at Saint-Denis. Their reactions were most helpful.

During all these years I have benefited from the financial support of the Laboratoire d'Economie Dionysien (LED) of the University Paris 8 at Saint-Denis. Nathalie Sigot and Alexandre Reichart contributed to the preparation of the manuscript, and the production of the book benefited from the expertise of Katharine Bartlett, Sarah Cook, Karen Greening and Laura Johnson.

Finally, I would like to thank my kids, Aurélien and Raphaël, for having so often asked "Tu l'as bientôt fini ton livre?" ("Will you soon finish your book?"), and my wife, Nathalie Sigot, for having accepted for so many years a ménage à trois with dear old David.

Introduction

1. Why a book on Ricardo on money?

Money is what made Ricardo become an economist. The publication in 1810 of *The High Price of Bullion, a Proof of the Depreciation of Bank Notes* established him as a leading figure in the economic debates of the time, and, more than on public finance or free trade, his monetary ideas gained him celebrity during the whole of his lifetime, for better or worse. In his own eyes, the adoption of the Ingot Plan by Parliament in 1819 was "the triumph of science and truth in the great councils of the Nation", but it was also about money that one of his opponents dubbed him ironically "the Oracle by excellence".

Revaluation

For the past two centuries, money has also played a singular part in the evaluation of Ricardo as an economist. This singularity lies in a paradox: Ricardo's monetary theory is usually exposed on the basis of his contributions to the debates around the *Bullion Report* of 1810, as if his subsequent theory of value and distribution contained in *On the Principles of Political Economy, and Taxation* (1817–1821) had not affected in any way his monetary views. A mere chronological gap makes the starting point become *ipso facto* the ending point of the story: Ricardo's theory of money pre-exists his theory of value and distribution, hence the former is independent of the latter. To use a modern phrase: the "dichotomy" between his "real" theory of value and his "monetary" analysis is complete. A variant of this approach to Ricardo on money is to acknowledge that *Principles* might have affected Ricardo's theory of money, but just to lock it into inconsistency or contradiction: advocating a paper money anchored to a metallic standard, Ricardo would be trapped in the impossible task of reconciling a commodity-theory of money – in which the value of money determines its quantity – and a quantity theory of money – in which the causality runs the other way round.

The present book aims at challenging this view by arguing that Ricardo's theory of money is neither independent from nor contradictory with his theory of value and distribution. But this requires looking *also* at his monetary writings *after* he started inquiring into the determination of the rate of profit – that is, after *An*

Essay on the Influence of a low Price of Corn on the Profits of Stock (1815) – not only *before*. I will contend that the most elaborate expression of Ricardo's theory of money – again using a modern phrase, one that integrates his monetary analysis in his theory of value and distribution – is to be found in his late monetary writings (of 1819–1823), *not* in his early ones. The publication of *Proposals for an Economical and Secure Currency* in 1816 and of the three successive editions of *Principles* in 1817–1821 gave a theoretical foundation to Ricardo's views on money in the 1819–1823 papers, by putting the notion of monetary standard centre-stage. The bicentenary of these two books thus offers the opportunity of revaluing Ricardo on money by shifting the cursor from the early to the mature monetary writings.

Rehabilitation

Such revaluation leads to a rehabilitation. In modern times, the dominant evaluation of Ricardo on money has been negative. It will not be asked in the book since when and why it is so. Surely Keynes's statement in *General Theory* that "Ricardo conquered England as completely as the Holy Inquisition conquered Spain" (Keynes 1936: 32) played a role, although it was strictly addressed to "Ricardo's doctrine that it was impossible for effective demand to be deficient" (ibid). It seems that in academic circles Schumpeter's judgement in *History of Economic Analysis* was decisive, both for its negative tone and the affirmation that it was useless to dig into Ricardo's numerous writings on money and banking. Listing the published ones, he wrote:

> Other items might be added. Ricardo's theory of money, credit, and banking gains on acquaintance, and in perusing his letters as well as his evidence before the Committees on the Usury Laws and on Resumption, one discovers more and more fragments that might be combined into a spacious structure. No attempt will be made, however, to do so.
>
> (Schumpeter 1954: 689n)

Their author having died in 1950, these words had been written before the publication by Piero Sraffa of the *Works and Correspondence of David Ricardo*, which started in 1951. Although this publication added many more "other items" related to this field, it did not, however, give rise to any attempt at building the "spacious structure" suggested by Schumpeter. Several books that will be mentioned here have aimed at providing a comprehensive view of Ricardo's works, but money has always been treated as only a piece of them. Leaving collections of essays aside – such as *Ricardo on Money and Finance*, edited by Yuji Sato and Susumu Takenaga in 2013 – the only book devoted entirely to money in Ricardo was published twenty-five years ago (in 1991) by Maria Cristina Marcuzzo and Annalisa Rosselli and it was an important source of inspiration for the present research. However, as indicated by its title – *Ricardo and the Gold Standard. The Foundations of the International Monetary Order* – it mainly aimed at integrating theoretical analysis and historical reconstruction in order to account for a particular question: international adjustment. Thus, although a rough calculation indicates that more than one half of what Ricardo wrote in economics was devoted to money and banking, no book covers this topic as a consistent whole.

It may thus be worthwhile to take up the challenge suggested by Schumpeter, all the more so since the reason why he did not do it himself – and possibly why it was not done since – is to be found in his negative evaluation of Ricardo's theory of money. The above quotation continues as follows:

> We shall have to be content with a few features of Ricardo's analysis that are of major importance to doctrinal history. The reader is warned that this may involve some injustice to his performance as a whole. But the impression the reader is bound to get, that Ricardo did not contribute much that was both true and original, agrees with Viner's judgment, and so does, I believe, my opinion that as an analyst of money and credit Ricardo was inferior to Thornton.
>
> (Schumpeter 1954: 689n)

The distinction between "doctrinal history" and what should be expected from "an analyst of money and credit" speaks for itself. A few pages further, Schumpeter is even clearer:

> In matters of monetary as of general theory, Ricardian teaching is a detour and it slowed up the advance of analysis, which could have been much quicker and smoother had Thornton's lead been followed – had Ricardo's force not prevailed over Thornton's insight.
>
> (ibid: 704n)

This opinion, it seems, only gained in force during the last sixty years and this may explain the lack of comprehensive study on Ricardo on money: why should "a spacious structure" be built to accommodate the whole of Ricardo's writings in this field if it is to tell the story of "a detour [having] slowed up the advance of analysis"? In contrast with Sraffa's "Introduction" to *Works* (Sraffa 1951a) that launched a heated and ongoing debate on the logical structure of Ricardo's theory of value, distribution, and accumulation, nothing of the kind exists for Ricardo's theory of money, and it might be that nothing could exist, if Schumpeter was right in his evaluation. On the contrary, I will try to show that, on money too, there is an original and coherent theory of money to be found in Ricardo, provided the whole of his monetary writings is taken into account. This is why the second object of the present book is to rehabilitate Ricardo as a first-rank monetary theorist.

Completeness

The dominant negative evaluation of Ricardo on money is also to be related to the paradox mentioned at the beginning. On the one hand, it usually overemphasises his doctrinal extremism. For Schumpeter, "here as elsewhere Ricardo was a prisoner to once-for all conceived ideas. In this case he had pinned his colors to the mast of a rigid quantity theory" (ibid: 724). He was "espousing a hard-line version of it [the quantity theory]" (Blaug 1995: 31) and held an "extreme bullionist" position (Viner 1937: 106; Laidler 1987: 290) On the other hand, as noted above, commentators usually draw exclusively on what Sraffa called "the Bullion Essays" of 1809–1811 to ascertain Ricardo's theory of money, in spite of the fact that these writings were mostly concerned with a monetary regime in which, due to the then inconvertibility of the Bank of England note, the quantity of money was *not* regulated by a standard (to use Ricardo's words). In contrast, his theory of money in *Proposals for an Economical and Secure Currency* (1816) and beyond dealt with a monetary regime endowed with such regulation:

> The only use of a standard is to regulate the quantity, and by the quantity the value of the currency.
>
> (*Proposals*; IV: 59)[1]

The centrality of the standard in Ricardo's mature theory of money was not only a matter of historical context – the perspective of the resumption of convertibility. Parallel was Ricardo's elaboration of a theory of value and distribution that would apply to all commodities produced in competitive conditions – including the standard of money: gold bullion – and end up in the search for an invariable standard of value. As we will see, this "real" line of inquiry had important consequences for the theory of money. Before attributing a quantity theory of money to Ricardo – and *a fortiori* an extreme version of it – it seems thus prudent to account for the writings dealing explicitly with a currency regulated by a standard: not only *Proposals* and *Principles* but also the 1819–1823 papers, whether published, in manuscript form, or reported. This prudence should also apply to other negative evaluations of Ricardo's theory of money, which less emphasise its extremism than its contradiction with the theory of value and distribution contained in *Principles*. A third object of the present volume is to demonstrate, on the basis of *all* Ricardo's monetary writings, that there is neither extremism nor contradiction, but an idiosyncratic theory, which is neither a quantity theory of money nor a commodity-theory of money, and which integrates money into Ricardo's theory of value and distribution.

Relevance

Assessing a theory of money that focuses on the standard could as well be for Ricardo the kiss of death. Against the old accusation of abstract reasoning, modern commentators have mostly relied on Ricardo's knowledge of facts and practices to revaluate him: for Davis (2005: 100) he was "an empirical economist", and for King (2013: 81) "he reveals himself to be above all a practical economist". This judgement is particularly applied to monetary matters: the only qualifications to an overall negative evaluation that may be found in modern literature are Ricardo's defence of an exclusive paper circulation and of an independent central bank regulating the issue by open-market operations. In contrast, emphasising Ricardo's *theory* of money and shifting it towards the understanding of a currency anchored to a standard seems to be a sure recipe to bury it in the gone-away times of the gold standard.

However, theorising on money did not mean for Ricardo neglecting adjustment processes and feasible plans. And there are two levels at which his theory of money may appeal to modern readers. First it has been long acknowledged that the Ingot Plan was the forerunner of the gold-exchange standard, hence of any monetary system where the domestic currency is anchored to a foreign currency – a still-debated issue today. Second, one lesson to be drawn from Ricardo is that the standard may "regulate the quantity, and by the quantity the value of the currency" thanks to private arbitrage between its market price and its legal price. This adjustment process does not require necessarily a metallic standard but solely any marketable asset that is legally convertible into money and into which money is legally convertible at a fixed price. Such asset might as well be a public bond purchased and sold for money by a central bank at a fixed price – a situation not far from that of our modern economies.

The reasons why the present book was started are thus four: it aims at providing a comprehensive study of Ricardo on money, rehabilitating him as a theorist, accounting for all his monetary writings, and suggesting his relevance for modern analysis.

2. An evolution in Ricardo's theory of money

The relation with the theory of value and distribution

Money in Ricardo is usually approached in modern literature from two angles. One, oriented towards monetary policy and banking, is the "Bullion Controversy" of 1809–1811 on the depreciation of the pound sterling, where Ricardo affirmed a central proposition that he would maintain until the end of his life, namely that the depreciation of paper money may only be caused by an excess in its quantity. The other angle, oriented towards macroeconomic theory, is Say's Law, endorsed by Ricardo in *Principles* and implying that the level of aggregate output is only determined on the side of production – in which money is supposed to have no part – with aggregate demand being passive. These two angles are usually simply juxtaposed, the emphasis being put either on one or the other aspect, with the supposition that they complement each other under the loose acceptance that the Quantity Theory of Money – the alleged rational foundation of Ricardo's central monetary proposition – implies Say's Law and vice-versa.

The first angle leads to observe that, antedating Ricardo's theory of value and distribution established in *Principles*, his theory of money – if it is to be found in the Bullion Essays of 1809–1811 – was in no way affected by this other theory. There is only one step to infer that this was the reason why Ricardo's views on money did not change from 1809 to 1823. Reciprocally, the second angle leads to emphasise the neutrality of money – except temporarily – in respect to the real level of aggregate output. This neutrality results from the two assumptions that aggregate output is only constrained by the availability of capital, and that money has no permanent effect on the determinants of this availability (in particular the rate of interest). There is only one step to infer that there is no relation whatsoever between real magnitudes and money, which belong to completely separated spheres of Ricardo's political economy.

One of the objects of the present book is to show that these two steps are unwarranted. In other words, it aims at challenging the conventional approach to Ricardo on money and at establishing how Ricardo integrates money in his theory of value and distribution. I will contend that this theory gave to Ricardo's views on money a theoretical foundation that was lacking in the Bullion Essays. There was consequently an evolution in Ricardo's theory of money from the Bullion Essays of 1809–1811 to *Proposals* (1816) and *Principles* (1817–1821), an evolution that explains why, in his various interventions from 1819 to 1823, he consistently emphasised the distinction between a depreciation of money and a fall in its value – a distinction which did not exist in the Bullion Essays.

It is generally acknowledged that, leaving aside the first round (1797–1803) of the Bullionist Controversy in which Ricardo took no part, his main influence in the monetary debates of his time manifested itself during the third round (1816–1821) – where the issue was the conditions under which the convertibility of the Bank of England note should be resumed – rather than in its second round (1809–1811) – where the issue was the effect of the inconvertibility of the Bank of England note. As Laidler put it, "Ricardo dominated the later stages of the bullionist controversy, as Thornton had dominated its earlier stages" (Laidler 1987: 293). However, it is also generally assumed that Ricardo's views on money did not change significantly from the Bullion Essays of the second round (*Price of Gold, High Price, Reply to Bosanquet*) to his publications during the third (*Proposals, Principles, Plan for a National Bank*): there were indeed improvements in the applied plans of monetary reform advocated by Ricardo (the Ingot Plan; the plan for a public bank of issue), but they are supposed to be based on unchanged theoretical foundations – namely a quantity theory of money in its most simplistic form, leading to the extreme bullionist proposition that the depreciation of paper money may only be caused by an excess in its quantity.

This conventional appraisal of Ricardo on money raises two doubts. First, the distinction between the second and third rounds of the Bullionist Controversy justly emphasises the difference between the issues at stake: the working of a monetary system with inconvertible (second round) or convertible (third round) paper money. Indeed the debate on the inconvertibility of the Bank of England note – around the question of whether it was the main (if not the sole) cause of the depreciation of the pound sterling, by allowing the Bank of England to issue notes in excess – implied the understanding of how convertibility worked before its suspension in 1797. But the originality of Ricardo's position during the third round of the Bullionist Controversy was precisely that England should not simply revert to the pre-1797 monetary system but base the resumption of convertibility of the note on a radical change: convertibility into bullion instead of coin (in the

Ingot Plan defended by Ricardo in Parliament in 1819), or transfer of note issuing from the Bank of England to a public bank (in the *Plan for the Establishment of a National Bank* drafted in 1823 and published posthumously in 1824). This originality makes it legitimate to inquire whether there was not something new in Ricardo's mature views on money as compared with the Bullion Essays, something not only to be found in the major writings but also in Ricardo's expression in Parliament and in correspondence.

The second doubt raised by the common belief that there was no substantial evolution of Ricardo on money after the Bullion Essays concerns the theoretical foundations of his views. In the Bullion Essays, the main charge made by Ricardo against inconvertibility was that it deprived the note of being regulated by a standard. This was reaffirmed in *Proposals*:

> Without a standard it [the currency] would be exposed to all the fluctuations to which the ignorance or the interests of the issuers might subject it.
>
> (*Proposals*; IV: 59)

For Ricardo, this standard of money was bullion, that is, a commodity chosen as standard because its value was assumed to be less variable than that of all other commodities, although it could not be absolutely invariable. This is why Ricardo could not have in 1809–1811 a solid theoretical foundation for an analysis of a monetary system endowed with a standard – to be opposed to the then ruling system deprived of such standard: he did not have yet a theory of the value of commodities of his own and he consequently was not equipped to discuss the question of the invariability of the standard. As is well-known, this question preoccupied Ricardo in the successive editions of *Principles* (1817, 1819, 1821), and until his last manuscript on "Absolute value and exchangeable value" in 1823.

In contrast with the conventional statement according to which Ricardo's views on money did not change substantially from 1809 to 1823, the present book aims at establishing that: (a) there has been a substantial evolution from the Bullion Essays of 1809–1811 to the papers of 1819–1823; (b) this evolution is of a theoretical nature and concerns the relation between money and the standard; (c) Ricardo's mature theory of money is rooted in his theory of value and distribution; and (d) it provides a foundation to his applied plans of monetary reform.

Ricardo's mature theory of money in brief

Starting with *Proposals* (1816) and culminating with the 1819–1823 papers, Ricardo's mature monetary writings contain an original theory of a monetary system endowed with convertibility both ways between money and the standard – a theory of money consistent with the theory of value and distribution developed in *Principles* (1817–1821).

In this theory, a discretionary change in the quantity of money does not affect its value directly (as in the Quantity Theory of Money) but indirectly, through a change in the market price of the standard. The value of money consequently varies under two influences: a change in the *value* of the standard (with a positive sign), and (with a negative sign) a change in its market *price* which departs from the legal price when the quantity of money is inadequate for the needs of circulation. Since the value of the standard is regulated by its cost of production with the portion of capital paying no rent, every permanent change in its difficulty of production affects permanently the value of money in the same direction. Since the market price of the standard adjusts itself to the level of the legal price by arbitrage, an inadequate quantity of money – whether in excess or deficient – relatively to "the wants of commerce" only affects the value of money temporarily and is endogenously adjusted. In contrast with inconvertibility where an excess quantity of bank notes is eliminated by the export of bullion, the regulation of the convertible-note issue operates thanks to domestic arbitrage on bullion, which constrains the behaviour of the issuing bank. Ricardo's analysis then provides the theoretical foundation of his plan of reform of the currency (the Ingot Plan), based on two pillars: convertibility of notes into bullion – which rules out the use of gold in circulation and thus eliminates the monetary instability generated by this use – and the management of the note issue by watching the market price of the standard – which reinforces the domestic adjustment of the quantity of money by substituting central banking for private arbitrage.

3. The content of the book: history, theory, policy

Part I. History

The first part of the book is devoted to the history of Ricardo's monetary writings, which resulted from his participation in the Bullionist Controversy from 1809 to 1823.

Chapter 1 studies the historical context in which Ricardo contributed to the monetary debates with his writings and interventions. The chapter describes the English monetary system (currency and banking) at the time of Ricardo, and the international monetary relations in Europe, characterised by three interconnected monetary zones, centred respectively on London, Paris, and Hamburg, with two standards (gold and silver) operating side by side, and one superior bank in each zone: the Bank of England, the Bank of France, and the Bank of Hamburg. Then it evokes the main questions raised by the Bullionist Controversy (1797–1821) and focuses on the pivotal one: the responsibility of note-issuing in monetary disorder. Finally it analyses the first round of the Bullionist Controversy (1797–1803), marked by the search for analytical foundations and the influence of Henry Thornton's *Paper Credit of Great Britain* (1802).

Chapter 2 studies Ricardo's battles on currency and banks during the second and third rounds of the Bullionist Controversy in which he took part: the debates around the *Bullion Report* (1809–1811) and the debates around the resumption of the convertibility of the Bank of England note (1816–1821, continued until Ricardo's death in 1823). For each one, I consider the historical context and the questions raised in the debates, before analysing Ricardo's positions. In 1809–1811, he rejected the explanation of the high price of gold bullion and of the low exchange of the pound by an adverse foreign balance and contended that they resulted from the depreciation of the inconvertible paper money. In 1816–1823, in the perspective of the resumption of the convertibility of the Bank of England note, he designed successively two plans for reforming the monetary system with a gold standard. The Ingot Plan (1816) substituted convertibility of the note into bullion for convertibility into coin and introduced a management of the issue by watching the market price of gold bullion. The Plan for a national bank (1823) granted an independent public bank the monopoly of the note issue and introduced open-market operations on government securities.

Part II. Theory

The second and central part of the book is devoted to theory, around the main issue of the value of money. First some ambiguity in modern literature obliges to clarify how Ricardo defined the value of money: as its purchasing power over all commodities or only over the standard of money (gold bullion). In Chapter 3 textual evidence and analytical reasoning show that for Ricardo the value of money was its purchasing power over all commodities *except* the standard of money. This means that for Ricardo a change in the value of money in a certain direction was the only cause of – in fact was identical with – a homothetic change in all money prices (except that of the standard of money) in the opposite direction. The singularity of the standard was that "in a sound state of the currency" a change in its market *price* was constrained between narrow limits and temporary – it was self-adjusting – although its *value* could vary significantly and permanently. Since a change in the value of the standard caused the same change in the value of money, the question of the invariable standard became an integral part not only of Ricardo's theory of value and distribution but also of his theory of money. This led Ricardo to face a dilemma between stabilising the value of the standard of money and stabilising its price, that is, between two conditions for "a perfect currency": the invariability of the standard in value and the conformity of the currency to this standard.

Chapter 4 studies the determinants of a change in the value of money in a system endowed with a standard. It first considers the direction of the causality between the quantity and the value of money, about which Ricardo has been often accused of inconsistency or contradiction. It then emphasises an important distinction made by Ricardo in his papers from 1819 to 1823, between a fall in the value of money and a depreciation of money. This distinction leads to what I call the Money–Standard Equation, which combines two channels of change in the value of money. According to this equation, the value of money varies positively with the value of the standard and inversely with its price, as testified by a factual illustration given by Ricardo in a speech in Parliament in 1823. This conclusion calls for the analysis of the respective determinants of a change in the *value* and in the *price* of the standard: this is the subject of the three subsequent chapters.

Chapter 5 studies the first cause of change in the value of money: a change in the *value* of the standard. I first discuss the famous "analogy" made by Ricardo in the Bullion Essays between an increase in the quantity of money caused by the discovery of a new gold mine and one caused by an additional discretionary issue of inconvertible notes. Next I consider how Ricardo extended his theory of rent from land to mines, while acknowledging a specificity of gold bullion in respect to corn, which affected the adjustment process of the natural price of bullion after the discovery of a new gold mine. This adjustment is analysed in two steps: in the gold-producing country which exported bullion and in the gold-importing country where bullion was coined. A symmetrical case was the adjustment to an increased demand for gold bullion, which caused an increase in its value and thereby in the value of money. This occurred between 1819 and 1821 when the Bank of England purchased gold to prepare for the resumption of the convertibility of its note into coin – a behaviour much criticised by Ricardo.

Chapter 6 considers the case of a rise in the *price* of the standard – hence of a depreciation of money – caused by the debasement of a metallic currency. I first show how convertibility both ways between bullion and coin determined the boundaries that constrained the variations in the market price of gold bullion. Next it is necessary to clarify how a change in the market price of the standard affected the prices of all other commodities via the depreciation of the currency. It is then possible to analyse how the debasement of the coins, by triggering a rise in the market price of gold bullion, resulted in a price increase for all other commodities. This was for Ricardo an illustration of "the principle of limitation of quantity" of money – the same principle which applied to bank notes. Another cause of the variability in the value of a metallic currency existed when it was on a double standard (gold and silver). When he considered a mixed system of coins and notes, the critique of the double standard of money was for Ricardo the occasion of warning against the power of the Bank of England to change the value of the currency at will – a recurrent complaint by him.

Chapter 7 studies the regulation of the quantity of convertible notes by the standard, in a mixed monetary system of undebased coins and Bank of England notes convertible into coin – like that ruling in England before 1797 and from 1821 onwards. I analyse how, according to Ricardo, the value of money adjusted to a change in the quantity of notes issued, first by departing from the value of the standard (depreciation or appreciation), then by being brought back to it. This requires introducing the quantity of money into the Money–Standard Equation formulated in Chapter 4. Two cases of self-adjusting process are studied, in response to an increase in the "wants of commerce" or in the discretionary note issue. An important consequence ensues: contrary to what is generally said in the literature, Ricardo's monetary theory was *not* a quantity theory of money. Next I ask whether this theory applies to a money without a standard (in the case of inconvertibility), before concluding on the specificity of the market for gold bullion.

Part III. Policy

The last part of the book considers the consequences of Ricardo's theory of money for monetary policy. It may be surprising to find Chapter 8 in Part III of the book, since it deals with the international adjustment to a monetary shock. This adjustment is indeed an element of any monetary theory applying to an open economy and it could have been analysed in Part II of the book. However, the conclusion of this chapter is that for Ricardo an active management of the domestic quantity of money should substitute for international flows of bullion and of commodities to produce this adjustment, which became thus the outcome of monetary policy. I first show that Ricardo used notions widely accepted at the time – such as the real par of exchange and the bullion export and import points. He used them to explain how international adjustment operated in two successive steps, implying gold bullion and other commodities. The much-criticised proposition according to which a fall in the exchange rate could only be explained by a redundancy of currency appears then, with appropriate qualification, as a necessary outcome of his monetary theory. In Ricardo's view, international adjustment was not produced by the effect of hydraulics of money on the balance of trade – the so-called price-specie flow mechanism – but by the corrective properties of international bullion flows. The same correction could be obtained more quickly and safely from an active management of the quantity of money. This analysis fits Ricardo's general approach to money, as it is illustrated by the Ingot Plan, and includes the foreign balance in the policy rule to be applied to the monetary system – what will later be called the gold-exchange standard.

Chapter 9 studies the question of central banking and how its treatment by Ricardo led to what Bonar (1923) called "the euthanasia of metal currency". Rather than relying on a quantity theory of money and a price-specie flow mechanism, Ricardo's positions on central banking stemmed from the theory of money exposed in Chapters 3 to 7 and of its consequences for international adjustment as analysed in Chapter 8. The starting point was Ricardo's conception of the public nature of paper money, which was embodied in the two plans he designed for the monetary system, the Ingot Plan (1816) and the Plan for a national bank (1823). There was continuity between these plans on the two underlying principles of "a perfect currency" managed by a central bank: the ingot principle – convertibility of the note into bullion for foreign payments – and the management principle – varying the note issue inversely with the spread between the market price and the legal price of the standard. The plans not only aimed at stabilising the market price of the standard – hence eliminating the monetary cause of variation in the value of money – but also at increasing the security of the monetary system, by preventing an internal or external drain of the metallic reserve of the central bank. They were an application of Ricardo's theory of money.

The afterword sums up the main results obtained in the book, before evoking the legacy of Ricardo's theory of money for today.

As much as I felt necessary, I have quoted Ricardo extensively to substantiate my arguments and invite the reader to follow his way of thinking. I also tried, when it appeared possible and in the limited range of my capacity, to formalise in equations Ricardo's analysis of the determination of the value of money. The purpose was only to help formulating his views with rigour, a task emphasised by Ricardo in a letter to James Mill on 1 January 1821:

> Political Economy he [Malthus] says is not a strict science like the mathematics, and therefore he thinks he may use words in a vague way, sometimes attaching one meaning to them, sometimes another and quite different. No proposition can surely be more absurd.
>
> (VIII: 331)

Each chapter is accompanied with an appendix, which provides additional material on its subject or deals with a particular question in relation with it. Appendix 10, following the afterword, gathers the main equations constituting Ricardo's monetary model.

4. Two hundred years after

This book is the result of a 25-year companionship with Ricardo on money. On the basis of a former interest for his theory of value and distribution in the line of Piero Sraffa, I started dealing with this subject in the early 1990s, through the conjunction of a research on international monetary relations in the sixteenth century (Boyer-Xambeu, Deleplace and Gillard 1986, 1994a) and of the discovery of the book *Ricardo and the Gold Standard* (Marcuzzo and Rosselli 1991). Following the publication of a collection of essays by various contributors on money and the standard in Ricardo (Deleplace 1994), this subject has accompanied my studies on the nature of a monetary economy (Deleplace and Nell 1996a, 1996b), the logic of the history of economic thought (Deleplace 1999), the history and theory of international bimetallism in the nineteenth century (Boyer-Xambeu, Deleplace and Gillard 1994b, 1997, 2010a, 2013). Ricardo even became a member of my family thanks to the co-authorship with my wife of an article (which took 15 years to be written and published) confronting him with Bentham on money (Deleplace and Sigot 2012). He also became a target in letter-hunting (Deleplace, Depoortère and Rieucau 2013).

Greater familiarity with Ricardo's works and life aroused my growing admiration for "the little plain man with the acute features and the keen eye",[2] as he appears in the miniature by Thomas Heaphy (reproduced in Vol. VIII of *Works*). At the end of the day, two hundred years after the publication of *Proposals for an Economical and Secure Currency* (1816) and the first edition (1817) of *On the Principles of Political Economy, and Taxation*, my aim has been at showing that Ricardo was not only a giant on value, distribution, and accumulation, but on money too.

Notes

1 All quotations from Ricardo refer to the Sraffa edition of *The Works and Correspondence of David Ricardo* (Ricardo 1951–1973). When the extract is from a book, a pamphlet, or a manuscript written for publication, its title is indicated in abbreviation, with the volume (in Roman numeral) and pagination (in Arabic numeral) in *Works*. When it is from a speech, evidence, or correspondence, only the volume and pagination are indicated.
2 Obituary by Daniel Whittle Harvey in 1823, quoted in Weatherall (1976: 189).

Part I

History

1 The historical context

> *It is also forgotten, that from 1797 to 1819 we had no standard whatever, by which to regulate the quantity or value of our money.* [...] *Accordingly, we find that the currency varied in value considerably during the period of 22 years, when there was no other rule for regulating its quantity and value but the will of the Bank.*
>
> (*On Protection to Agriculture*; IV: 222–3)

When Ricardo made his first appearance in print in August 1809, England had been for twelve years in a monetary situation unprecedented in history. The bank note issued by the pivotal institution in the banking system – the Bank of England[1] – was no longer convertible into coin since 1797, and in the second half of the first decade of the century the gold and silver coins had progressively been melted and exported. Apart from small copper coinage, the circulating medium was thus composed almost exclusively of inconvertible paper-money, including newly issued low-denomination Bank of England notes (£5 and under). This situation changed dramatically the English monetary system inherited from the eighteenth century (Section 1.1), while the international monetary relations with Continental Europe were disturbed by the Napoleonic wars (Section 1.2). As may be expected, this unprecedented situation that was marked by a fall in the internal and external value of the pound sterling gave rise to intense debates known in the literature as the "Bullionist Controversy" (Section 1.3). Three successive rounds may be distinguished in this controversy, the first one (1797–1803) being without Ricardo (Section 1.4).[2]

1.1 The English monetary system at the time of Ricardo

Currency

The recoinage of silver coins in 1695–1699 and the monetary reform of 1717, inspired by Isaac Newton then Master of the Mint, had firmly established the English monetary system on a bimetallic foundation: the monetary unit (the pound sterling, divided in 20 shillings of 12 pence each) was defined on the basis of an ounce of silver 222/240 (that is, 0.925) fine valued 62 pence and coined in "crowns", while an ounce of gold 22/24 (that is, 0.91667) fine valued £3. 17 shillings 10½ pence was coined in "guineas" (of 21 shillings each). However, the monetary ratio resulting from this legal valuation – that is, the relative price of gold to silver in coin – equal to 15.21, was higher than on the Continent where it was at or below 15 (for details, see Shaw 1895). The consequence was that, in spite of the prohibition of exporting and melting the coin, the comparatively undervalued metal (silver) was exported and the comparatively overvalued one (gold) was imported. In the middle of the eighteenth century, silver was less and less brought to the Mint to be coined and England shifted progressively to a *de facto* gold standard.

The state of the gold coinage – the fact that guineas were worn or clipped – was all the more scrutinised since some authors (such as James Steuart) had shown that the "debasement" of the coin (their actual weight in gold being lower than their legal one) was responsible for the market price of an ounce of gold bullion being higher than the legal price of an ounce of gold in coin, so that the current value of the currency in terms of gold was below its official one. This situation became particularly acute in the 1770s when the alteration of the gold coinage was added to the already deteriorated state of the silver one. Inspired by Lord Liverpool, an Act of 1774 ordered the recoinage of the golden guineas. As for the silver coins, they were not recoined but became legal tender up to £25 only; above this sum, they were to be taken by weight and not by tale. Both measures reinforced the *de facto* gold standard.[3] As we will see below, however, the question of whether the standard of money in England was actually silver or gold was still hotly debated in 1810 when the causes of the depreciation of the pound were discussed. The drying-up of the circulation of guineas *and* of silver coins in England – most of them having been fraudulently exported – raised in 1810 the question of the consequences of a circulating medium that was composed almost exclusively of Bank of England notes made inconvertible since 1797 and extended to low-denomination ones. This was the start of the Bullion Controversy (see below).

After the end of the Napoleonic wars in 1815, the stabilisation of the currency was looked for in the reform of 1816 that established the gold standard *de jure*, making silver coinage a token currency: the mint was closed for silver to the public and the Bank of England, only the government having access to it; silver coins became legal tender up to £2 only; and their current legal value (66 pence per standard ounce) was made higher than their mint price (62 pence) by a 6.45 per cent seignorage. Ricardo entirely approved this currency reform, as he declared in a speech before the House of Commons on 24 May 1819:

> He thought it right here to pay the tribute of his approbation to the late excellent regulations of the mint. He entirely approved of making gold the standard, and of keeping silver as a token currency. It appeared to him to be a solid improvement in the system of our coinage.
>
> (V: 16)

A new gold coin, the "sovereign" of £1, was issued on the basis of the legal price of £3. 17s. 10½d. per ounce standard, the "mint price" that was unchanged since

1717. As before it was coined without seignorage, but the mint continued keeping the metal during two months before delivering the coins, and this amounted practically to a coining charge of a little less than 1 per cent at the ruling interest rate.

Banking

In 1694 the Bank of England had been created as a device to salvage public finance: being a joint-stock company, it allowed raising funds to be lent to the Crown, which was no longer able to do so. The first role of the Bank was thus to manage the public debt, and it derived large profits from this activity – a question that would become controversial in the 1810s. Its secondary role was to become important: for the first time in the history of banking, it could issue bank notes not only against bullion (as the Bank of Amsterdam already did; see Gillard 2004) but also by discounting commercial bills; these notes were convertible into full-bodied (that is, undebased) coins. This innovation, coupled with the monopoly of note issue in a 60-mile radius around the City of London and the prohibition of any other joint-stock banking in England, made the Bank of England acquire a prominent position in the English monetary system in the second half of the eighteenth century (see Clapham 1944).

The banking system was three-tiered. Country banks issued notes outside the London area, by receiving gold or discounting bills. To guarantee the convertibility of their notes, they kept gold reserves deposited (at interest) in London banks or in the Bank of England vaults; they also kept a reserve of Bank of England notes, since their only legal obligation was to give Bank of England notes for their own notes on demand. According to Ricardo, the quantity of country-bank notes was consequently regulated by the quantity of Bank of England notes:

> As the country banks are obliged to give Bank of England notes for their own when demanded [...] the Bank of England is the great regulator of the country paper. When they increase or decrease the amount of their notes, the country banks do the same; and in no case can country banks add to the general circulation, unless the Bank of England shall have previously increased the amount of their notes.
>
> (*High Price*; III: 87–8)

In 1797, the suspension of the convertibility of notes into coin only applied to the Bank of England but the effect was the same for country-bank notes, since they remained convertible in Bank of England notes that were no longer convertible into coin.

The second tier of the banking system was composed of London banks, whose business was to receive deposits, operate transfers, and discount bills for coins or Bank of England notes – but not for notes of their own, because of the monopoly of the Bank of England on note-issuing in the London area. Like the Bank of England and the country banks, the lending activity of the London banks was subject to a maximum rate of interest of 5 per cent, a limitation imposed by the

Usury Laws; in practice, however, this limitation was easily evaded, as testified by Ricardo when he was examined by the Select Committee on the Usury Laws on 30 April 1818:

> It appears to me, from the experience which I have had on the Stock Exchange, that, upon almost all occasions they [the Usury Laws] are evaded, and that they are disadvantageous to those only who conscientiously adhere to them. […]
>
> Question: In what manner evaded?
>
> In the particular market with which I am acquainted, namely, the Stock Market, they are evaded by means of the difference between the money price and the time price of stock, which enables a person to borrow at a higher rate of interest than 5 per cent, if possessed of stock, or to lend at a higher rate, if the difference between the money price and the time price, affords a higher rate.
>
> Question: Has that been acted upon extensively?
>
> Very extensively; it is the usual and constant practice.
>
> (V: 337–8)

The gold reserves required by the activity of the London banks were kept at the Bank of England, which was the third tier of the system. Two consequences resulted from this institutional network. First, since London was the centre for foreign payments, any demand for bullion generated by them (in case of a negative foreign balance) was translated into an "external drain" of Bank of England metallic reserves, when it became more beneficial to obtain gold from the Bank of England through conversion of its notes than in the bullion market. Only "sworn-off gold" could be legally exported, that is, gold declared as previously imported. In fact, the prohibition of melting and exporting the coin was easily evaded, and it was not therefore an obstacle to an external drain. Second, any demand for gold coins originating at any level of the domestic monetary system ended up in an "internal drain" of Bank of England metallic reserves, because the vaults at Threadneedle Street were *de facto* the central safe of the system. Not only was the Bank of England supposed to provide on demand the metallic currency for which its notes were considered as substitutes (they were not legal tender until 1833): in times of emergency, it was also supposed to provide, thanks to an enlarged note-issuing, the liquidity that was urgently needed. The Bank of England had become the *dernier resort* (lender of last resort), as Sir Francis Baring would call it in 1797, when this need became crucial.

The problem was that this increasingly pivotal role of the Bank of England was not accompanied by a corresponding consciousness of that role by its governors and directors, who were more interested in the security of their own establishment than in the needs of the monetary and financial system as a whole, and consequently reacted to a gold drain and/or a financial panic by contracting instead of enlarging their issues. This counterproductive behaviour was observed during the crisis of 1793, when, although the exchanges were favourable – preventing any "external drain" – the outbreak of the war with France led to a financial panic which degenerated into a high demand of guineas and Bank of England notes.

Forced by the legal convertibility of its notes to cash them, the Bank of England reacted by refusing to discount even good paper further, intensifying the panic that was only overcome by the Government announcing a massive issuing of Exchequer bills to relieve the liquidity pressure.

A new alarm occurred in 1795, when, after two war years, an explosive cocktail of financial transfers to the Continent, bad harvests in England, and expanded Government borrowing from the Bank of England led again to a drain of the latter's metallic reserves. This combination of external circumstances and of domestic expansion of credit would pave the way for the later controversy between those who would explain the monetary crisis by external factors and those who would blame an overissue of notes. The Bank of England responded again to the pressure on its reserves by a proportional rationing of its discounts, and again this behaviour started a wave of bank and commercial failures over the country. In February 1797, rumours of a French invasion provoked a panic which led to a run on some country banks. Because of the structure of the banking system outlined above, the Bank of England experienced a heavy drain of its reserves, which was felt as threatening the existence of that central institution. On 26 February, a Council convened by Prime Minister William Pitt ordered the Bank of England to suspend cash payments of its notes until Parliament had deliberated on the subject; this order was confirmed by the "Bank Restriction Act" passed on 3 May and was to remain in force till 24 June. Extended by further Acts of Parliament, this unprecedented inconvertibility situation would in fact last until 1819 (and 1821 for the return to the pre-war parity of the Bank of England note and the coin), that is, way after the troubled times – the Revolutionary and later Napoleonic wars with France – which were directly or indirectly held responsible for it.

1.2 International monetary relations in Europe: London, Paris, Hamburg

As early as the sixteenth century there existed a monetary integration of Western Europe, thanks to the organisation by Italian merchant-bankers of a network of fairs on which foreign bills of exchange were actively traded (see Boyer-Xambeu, Deleplace and Gillard 1986, 1994a). This network evolved in the seventeenth and eighteenth century through the shift of power among bankers' communities and financial centres (see Braudel 1981–1984; McCusker 1978; Boyer-Xambeu, Deleplace and Gillard 1995). At the beginning of the nineteenth century, Europe provided the only example of an international system composed of three interconnected monetary zones, with two standards operating side by side in the system, and one superior bank[4] in each zone: the Bank of England in a gold-standard zone (restricted to England), the Bank of France in a double-standard one (extending to southern Europe), and the Bank of Hamburg in a silver-standard one (extending to northern and eastern Europe).

Apart from special circumstances, international arbitrage on gold and silver did not operate through the barter of one metal for the other; bullion traders usually considered arbitrage between the market of one metal and the foreign exchange market. For example, the export of gold from London to Paris was financed by the sale of a bill in francs in London or followed by the remittance of a bill in pounds purchased in Paris. Thus, the working of the international monetary system under two standards depended on the relationship between the exchange rate for each pair of currencies and the corresponding commercial par of exchange for each metal (that is, the ratio of the market prices of that metal in the two countries). Although the working of this international bimetallism was jeopardized by the suspension of the convertibility of the Bank of England note and by the Napoleonic wars, it was never interrupted. It may thus be useful to give some indications about the foreign exchange and bullion trades between London, Paris, and Hamburg, since their characteristics appear in Ricardo, who was particularly aware of them (see Appendix 1).

In London, the operating mode of the bullion market and of the foreign exchange market had not changed much since the eighteenth century. The price of standard gold (916.66/1000 fine) and standard silver (925/1000 fine) bars was quoted and published on the metal markets every Tuesday and Friday. The course of the exchange was quoted the same days, for short and two-month bills with Paris and only two-month bills with Hamburg. By "short" exchange one meant the equivalent of today's spot exchange, with a delivery in a few days. By "long" exchange (two or three months), one did *not* mean today's forward exchange but the immediate payment of the bill purchased in one currency for the future delivery of the other currency. Such "long" foreign bill could be either kept in portfolio as any commercial paper or discounted in the foreign discount market when cash was needed there. In spite of the war, the exchange with Paris and Hamburg was quoted without interruption, but the range of variation of the exchange rate, constrained by the cost of sending gold or silver rather than a bill of exchange, was abnormally high during the war, because of the cost of smuggling the metal in breach of the blockade decreed by Napoleon (see Appendix 1). On the metal markets, silver was always quoted but the official quotation of gold was irregular until 1810.

The French monetary system was on a double standard and the *franc* was since 1803 defined on the basis of 3444.44 F per kilogram of pure gold and 222.22 F per kilogram of pure silver, giving the well-known monetary ratio of 15.50 (see Thuillier 1983). The alloy used to mint the actual coins being 900/1000 fine, they were legal tender for respectively 3100 F per kilogram of gold 900/1000 fine and 200 F per kilogram of silver 900/1000 fine. The public paid the cost of minting coins (a seignorage of 0.29 per cent on gold and 1.50 per cent on silver), so that the legal price of coined metal was higher than the legal price of bullion purchased by the mint (respectively 3434.44 F for pure gold and 218.89 F for pure silver). After the experiments of the *Caisse d'Escompte* (1776–1791) and of the *assignats* during the Revolutionary period, the *Banque de France* was founded in 1800 and granted the monopoly of note-issuing in Paris in 1803 (see Plessis 1982–1985; Leclercq 2010). It issued notes by discounting commercial paper already countersigned by other bankers. The discount rate was constrained by the legal maximum of 6 per cent, but the Bank of France invariably applied a uniform rate of 4 per cent.

Its notes were convertible at par on demand into gold or silver coins, at its choice; it could also agree to cash its notes with a premium in coins of the metal chosen by the holder. In the Paris metal markets, the relative deviation (*prime*) was quoted and published daily per kilogram 1000/1000 fine of gold and silver by reference to a given rate (*tarif du commerce*) equal to the legal price of bullion purchased by the mint. The course of the exchange with London and Hamburg was quoted daily for one-month and three-month bills. The exchange with London was interrupted between 1806 and 1814 (but bills on Paris were quoted in London) and the exchange with Hamburg was always quoted. In the metal markets the regular quotation of gold and silver suffered only a few exceptions.

Unlike London and Paris, Hamburg was not the monetary and financial capital of an integrated State. Its importance in these two domains was due to the fact that it was a relay centre for payments between Western Europe and the partitioned Germanic territories, as well as Northern and Eastern Europe, especially Sweden and Russia (see Achterberg and Lanz 1957–1958). The creation of *Die Hamburger Bank* in 1619, seventy-five years before the Bank of England, was an early manifestation of this relay role. Modelled after the Bank of Amsterdam, the Bank of Hamburg was a municipal deposit and transfer bank, which in addition had a monopoly on all foreign exchange transactions. All the drafts drawn and remittances made in Hamburg had to be accompanied with a book entry in the Bank of Hamburg. This institution did not practice discounting, nor did it issue bank notes and deal with public finance. Its operations were written in a special unit of account, the *Mark banco*, divided into 16 *Schillinge* containing 12 *Pfennige* each. This *Mark banco* was different from the current *Mark*, which had no role in the domestic or international wholesale trade: all the quotations at the Hamburg Exchange were made in *Mark banco*, except those for cereals and alcohol. Beginning in 1725, there was an official par value of 123⅓ current *Mark* for 100 *Mark banco*, but the premium between these two types of *Mark* was quoted daily for each of the principal coins (local or foreign) circulating in Hamburg. The existence of the Bank of Hamburg thus introduced a separation between silver by weight (whose accounting representation, the *Mark banco*, was used by big business through book transfers) and silver in coin (used in retail domestic transactions).

The *Mark banco* was defined as a silver weight. Starting in 1770, the Cologne *marco* of pure silver (233.855 grams today) was quoted at 27 *Mark* 10 *Schillinge banco*. The Bank of Hamburg received silver bullion at this price, and it gave back this metal at 27 *Mark* 12 *Schillinge banco*, thus making a profit of 0.45 per cent. Gold was quoted every Tuesday and Friday for a limited number of coins. The silver market reflected the rules applied by the Bank of Hamburg: bars of different degrees of fineness were quoted every Tuesday and Friday, with the differences in the quotations corresponding exactly to variations in fineness. Thus, there was a single market price for pure silver bullion, equal to 27 *Mark* 10 *Schillinge banco* (the price at which the Bank of Hamburg received deposits in bullion). Short and two-and-a-half month bills on London and two-month bills on Paris were quoted daily.

1.3 From Hume to the Bullionist Controversy

David Hume and James Steuart

What monetary theory were observers equipped with when convertibility of the Bank of England note into coin was suspended in 1797? Breaking with the mercantilist tradition, it was mainly inherited from David Hume's vision of an automatic adjustment mechanism of the aggregate quantity of money, which ensured the stability of its value. The following excerpt from Hume's essay *Of the Balance of Trade* (1752) sums up the adjustment mechanism which ensures internal and external monetary stability:

> Suppose four-fifths of all the money in Great Britain to be annihilated in one night, and the nation reduced to the same condition, with regard to specie, as in the reigns of the Harrys and Edwards, what would be the consequence? Must not the price of all labour and commodities sink in proportion, and every thing be sold as cheap as they were in those ages? What nation could then dispute with us in any foreign market, or pretend to navigate or to sell manufactures at the same price, which to us would afford sufficient profit? In how little time, therefore, must this bring back the money which we had lost, and raise us to the level of all the neighbouring nations? Where, after we have arrived, we immediately lose the advantage of the cheapness of labour and commodities; and the farther flowing in of money is stopped by our fulness and repletion. [...] Now, it is evident, that the same causes, which would correct these exorbitant inequalities, were they to happen miraculously, must prevent their happening in the common course of nature, and must for ever, in all neighbouring nations, preserve money nearly proportionable to the art and industry of each nation. All water, wherever it communicates, remains always at a level.
>
> (Hume 1752: 311–2)

Applied to the symmetrical case of an increase in the quantity of money – the case that would be discussed during the Bullionist Controversy – this so-called price-specie flow mechanism worked for a pure metallic monetary system in the following way. Suppose that for any reason the quantity of money increases in a greater proportion than output. The Quantity Theory of Money predicts that the value of money will fall, and this will be reflected in increased money prices of all commodities produced nationally. At the ruling exchange rate, these commodities will become dearer than foreign ones, and the balance of trade will sooner or later become negative, depressing the exchange rate until it reaches the bullion export point. Then gold and silver coins will be exported or melted into bullion for export, and this will decrease the domestic quantity of money, reversing the movements of prices and consequently the balance of trade, until the initial situation is restored: "All water, wherever it communicates, remains always at a level." This hydraulic conception introduced interdependence between the domestic value of money (inversely related to its quantity) and its external one (determined by the balance of trade). Because of this interdependence, the same stabilising mechanism, which relied on a quantity adjustment of domestic monetary circulation and a price adjustment of exports and imports, operated in any circumstance, whether exorbitant or common, and for whatever cause of disequilibrium, domestic (for example, an abnormal increase or decline in the quantity of money) or external (for example, a sudden negative or positive foreign balance).

This was not the opinion of James Steuart in *An Inquiry into the Principles of Political Economy*, published in 1767. Against Hume who praised the metallic basis of money because international flows of metal automatically eliminated any positive or negative foreign balance, Steuart explained the absence of self-adjustment by the inconveniences attached to metallic money. International transfers of precious metals, supposed to adjust the balance of trade, depended on the market prices of bullion in the various trading nations, which were affected by monetary factors such as the debasement of the coins by wear and tear and the existence of a seignorage on coining. A country could thus experience an outflow of bullion while the quantity of money was not in excess and the balance of trade not against her. Even worse, such outflow had a negative impact on the domestic market for credit: in a country like England where gold to be exported was obtained at the Bank of England against convertible notes, the fall in its metallic reserve led the Bank to reduce its discounts, and this resulted in a shrinkage of overall credit that hurt the economy. Rather than relying on a self-adjusting mechanism that was in fact prevented from operating by these malfunctions of metallic money, it was the task of the State to intervene actively so as to prevent outflows of bullion, by adapting the domestic monetary system (recoinage, imposition of a seignorage when there existed one in the other trading nations) and by paying the interest on the money to be borrowed by the Bank of England in Amsterdam in case of a temporary adverse shock on the foreign balance (for more details, see Deleplace 2015d):

> If this be a fair state of the case, I think we may determine that such balances ought to be paid by the assistance and intervention of a statesman's administration.
>
> The object is not so great as at first sight it may appear. We do not propose that the value of this balance should be advanced by the state: by no means. They who owe the balance must, as at present, find a value for the bills they demand. Neither would I propose such a plan for any nation who had, upon the average of their trade, a balance against them; but if, on the whole, the balance be favourable, I would not, for the sake of saving a little trouble and expence, suffer the alternate vibrations of exchange to disturb the uniformity of profits, which uniformity tends so much to encourage every branch of commerce.
>
> We have abundantly explained the fatal effects of a wrong balance to banks which circulate paper; and we have shewn how necessary it is that they

> should perform what we here recommend. There is therefore nothing new in this proposal: it is merely carrying the consequences of the same principle one step farther, by pointing out as a branch of policy, how government should be assisting to trade in the payment of balances, where credit abroad is required; and this assistance should be given out of the public money.
>
> (Steuart 1767, II: 346; III: 370–1)[5]

Steuart's anti-Humean approach[6] contrasted with that of Adam Smith in *An Inquiry into the Nature and Causes of the Wealth of Nations*, published in 1776. The question is debated in the literature about whether Smith actually used Hume's price-specie flow mechanism. It is, however, easy to see that Steuart's emphasis on the fact that gold to be exported was obtained at the Bank of England could be introduced in the analysis of a mixed monetary system (of metallic specie and convertible bank notes) so as to preserve Hume's conclusions. An abnormally great quantity of money could result from banks issuing an excess quantity of notes (overissue), but, if the notes were convertible, bullion exports would again correct the excess; these exports would now be fuelled by converting notes at the banks of issue rather than by gathering coins in domestic circulation. If the banks were sound – that is, if they kept enough metallic reserves – the adjustment mechanism operated as in Hume, the only change being that the aggregate quantity of money was reduced in its note component.

The 1797 crisis showed that, even if the banks of issue were sound, the adjustment mechanism could be at fault and require a radical and undesired change in the monetary system: the suspension of convertibility, which degenerated into an enduring fall in the value of the currency. This was a denial of the Humean approach and pressed for new debates.

The Bullionist Controversy

The name "Bullionist Controversy" was coined (at an unspecified date) after the *Bullion Report* issued in 1810 by the House of Commons' Select Committee "appointed to enquire into the Cause of the High Price of Gold Bullion, and to take into consideration the State of the Circulating Medium and of the Exchanges between Great Britain and Foreign Parts" (Cannan 1919: 3). The *Bullion Report* gave rise to a flurry of pamphlets and published letters,[7] and, in accordance with the name given later to the controversy, their authors were categorised as "Bullionists" – those in favour of the report – and "Anti-Bullionists" – those against it.[8] The questions raised by the report originated in the suspension of the convertibility of Bank of England notes in 1797 and had been already discussed as early as 1800. They would remain on the agenda until convertibility at pre-1797 parity was resumed in 1821. Therefore the "Bullionist Controversy" is usually considered as covering the whole period from 1797 to 1821.[9] Following the editor of Ricardo's *Works and Correspondence*, Piero Sraffa, I will also use the other name "Bullion Controversy" to describe the debates having occurred immediately around the *Bullion Report*, that is, from 1809 to 1811.[10] Ricardo himself used the expression in a letter of 26 January 1818 to Hutches Trower:

> Every thing that has since occurred has stimulated me to give a great deal of attention to such subjects: first, the Bullion controversy, and then my intimacy with Mill and Malthus, which was the consequence of the part I took in that question.
>
> (VII: 246)

The Bullionist Controversy has been for many commentators the most important debate in the history of monetary thought of all time. For Viner (1937: 120), "The germs at least of most of the current monetary theories are to be found in it", and for Hayek (1939: 37), it "may still be regarded as the greatest of all monetary debates". Comparing two periods separated by more than one century, Schumpeter (1954: 692) notes:

> The report of the Cunliffe Committee that recommended England's return to gold at pre-war parity in 1918 displayed little, if any, knowledge of monetary problems that was not possessed by the men who drafted the Bullion Report.

Summing up the controversy, Laidler (1987: 293) concludes that "it is hard to think of any other episode in the history of monetary economics when so much was accomplished in so short a period".

Bullionists versus Anti-Bullionists on two practical problems

If the questions debated during the Bullionist Controversy and the answers given to them had a long-lasting importance, the opposition between Bullionists and Anti-Bullionists was nevertheless framed in terms of the practical problems of the time. Two of them were central in the controversy. First there was the question of prolonging the suspension of convertibility or not. During the first and second rounds of the controversy – in 1800–1804 and 1809–1811 respectively – this question traced a dividing line between the two camps: the Bullionists answered in the negative and the Anti-Bullionists in the positive. During the third round – in 1819–1821 – that question lost its importance, the great majority of the participants to the controversy favouring the resumption of convertibility; the dividing line then shifted to the question of the conditions in which this resumption should occur. The second practical problem central to the controversy also boiled down to a question: should the Bank of England be blamed for the bad state of the currency? Again during the first and second rounds the dividing line was clear-cut: the Bullionists answered in the positive and the Anti-Bullionists in the negative. This opposition remained during the third round, the only difference being that the context of the first two was inflationist, while that of the third was deflationist.

The positions held on these two practical problems – the advisability or not of the suspension of convertibility; the defence or critique of the Bank of England – give thus an indication on the camp to which a particular author belongs. The changing conditions from one round of the controversy to another and the fact that these problems interrelated with other practical ones and several theoretical issues make however the cartography of the Bullionist Controversy more complex. A sentence introduced by Ricardo in the second edition of his *Principles of Political Economy, and Taxation* sums up the central issue of the Bullionist Controversy:

> It will scarcely be believed fifty years hence, that Bank [of England] directors and ministers gravely contended in our times, both in parliament, and before committees of parliament, that the issues of notes by the Bank of England, unchecked by any power in the holders of such notes, to demand in exchange either specie, or bullion, had not, nor could have any effect on the prices of commodities, bullion, or foreign exchanges.
>
> (*Principles*; I: 353–4)

The Bank of England and the uncompromising Anti-Bullionists maintained that the high price of bullion and the low exchange of the pound could *never* be produced by Bank of England notes being in excess. Ricardo and the uncompromising Bullionists maintained that they were *always* produced by such an overissue. The Bullionist Controversy was then bounded by these two extreme positions, most of the participants staying in the middle and arguing that, *in principle*, the high price of bullion and the low exchange of the pound could be explained by an excess note issue *and* other causes as well; they bended to a bullionist position when they considered that, *in the circumstances of the time*, the former factor was mainly operative, and to an anti-bullionist position when they denied that and stressed other causes.

The Bullionist Controversy was not then a steady and recurrent fight between two organised and permanent camps, because the emergence of its central issue implied relations with other secondary questions to be settled, and this left ample room for various, if not shifting or contradictory, opinions. However, on two particular occasions, when it was necessary to legislate on the monetary system, this variety of opinions did not preclude a clear-cut outcome. In 1811, the House of Commons rejected the report prepared by its Bullion Committee, which made a diagnosis and proposed remedies focusing on the necessity to regulate the note issue in view of resuming convertibility. That rejection was clearly a victory for the Anti-Bullionists. In 1821, Parliament decided on the restoration of the pre-1797 monetary system, including note convertibility into specie at the old parity and absence of any note-issuing rule. The Bullionists-versus-Anti-Bullionists reading key, manufactured under inconvertibility, no longer applied to the outcome of this debate on a regime with convertibility, although it still did in its uncompromising variant, which referred to both convertibility and inconvertibility: in 1821 as in 1811, the Bank of England won the field over Ricardo.

A central question: the role of note-issuing in monetary disorder

If the complexity of the interrelations between the central question of the Bullionist Controversy – the role of note-issuing in monetary disorder – and other questions somewhat obscures the historical account of the debates, it also explains the lasting theoretical influence of that controversy, because its analysis framed later monetary theory and policy. Before going through the successive rounds of the controversy, it may therefore be useful to delineate the interrelations between the various questions then debated.

The first question raised during the debates around the *Bullion Report* was: what was the exact state of the currency? Three tests were available: the rise in commodity prices, the high price of gold bullion, the low exchange rate of the pound. Each one raised specific difficulties. Assessing the rise in commodity prices implied first to distinguish between factors operating on all commodities and others specific to particular industries, and second to distinguish among the general factors between the real and monetary causes of variation. Bullionists usually maintained that the rise in prices was mostly general and had a monetary origin, while Anti-Bullionists insisted more on real factors, general (for example, war conditions) or specific (for example, agricultural conditions).

The high price of gold bullion was considered by Bullionists as signalling a depreciation of the currency, since gold was the *de facto* monetary standard. By "high" they meant a market price of bullion above the mint price of coined gold (£3. 17s. 10½d. per ounce of standard gold). The Anti-Bullionists objected that, convertibility having been suspended, gold was no longer the monetary standard, so that its price was not an indicator of the state of the currency. Bullion was then for them a commodity like any other, and its high price could be explained by real factors affecting the supply of and the demand for it, such as changes in the world production of the metal, demand on the Continent, domestic demand for hoarding purposes or for export (in the latter case, one had to look at the state of the foreign balance).

The low exchange of the pound raised first a difficulty of measurement. By "low" everybody meant: below the metallic par of exchange with the foreign currency considered. In contrast with the price of coined gold which was legally fixed – and could be used as the reference to ascertain the "high" price of gold bullion – there was no legal par of exchange and the benchmark against which to compare the observed exchange rate had to be computed on the basis of the metal weight contained in domestic and foreign coins. Technical difficulties then appeared: foreign coins might be debased, bear a seignorage, or have a fluctuating relation with the foreign money quoted on the exchange market (such as the *Mark banco* of Hamburg); moreover, the metal used as monetary standard might be different (London was on a *de facto* gold standard, Hamburg on a silver standard, Paris on a gold and silver one). A significant part of the literature during the Bullion Controversy was devoted to sort out whether and by how much the exchange was "low". This was not only important to assessing the state of the foreign balance but also to explaining it. For Bullionists, a high price of bullion and a low exchange were two sides of the same coin, which reflected a depreciation of the currency; the divergence with a normal situation was then expected to be of the same order of magnitude with both indicators. For Anti-Bullionists, the two indicators had to be treated separately, since each one reflected the operation of specific factors; a significant difference between the measures of bullion being high and the exchange being low strengthened their position.

When, leaving aside commodity prices, attention could be concentrated on the high price of gold bullion considered as a monetary indicator and on the appropriately measured low exchange, some further steps were still needed to approach the central issue of the controversy. If the high price of bullion reflected the degraded state of the currency, then which currency? The Bullionists insisted that the depreciation concerned Bank of England notes, and they disqualified any influence of other circulating mediums: specie (which was not degraded, and would soon completely disappear from domestic circulation), country bank notes (whose quantity was ultimately regulated by Bank of England issues), credit instruments (which were not part of the currency). These disqualified elements were of course debated. As for the low exchange, its monetary interpretation by the Bullionists gave rise to the Anti-Bullionist objection that real factors provided the explanation, such as bad harvests in Britain (leading to abnormal food imports) and/or war transfers.

Finally, one could get to the central issue. If note-issuing by the Bank of England was suspected of being responsible for the depreciation of the currency, how did this occur? The Bullionists put forward two complementary elements. On the one hand, the check on overissue imposed by convertibility – notes issued in excess would return back to the Bank of England and drain its reserves, forcing it to contract the issues – had disappeared in 1797, freeing the Bank of England from any constraint. On the other hand, the Bank of England had not adopted the only note-issuing rule which could have prevented an overissue under inconvertibility, that is, watching the price of bullion and the exchange rate. The answer of the Bank of England and of the Anti-Bullionists who supported it was also twofold. On the one hand, there were plenty of examples, before and since 1797, of an expansion of the note issue being concomitant to a decline in the price of bullion and/or an improvement of the exchange, or the symmetrical situation, so that the alleged monetary indicators had to be explained by other factors, mainly the foreign balance. On the other hand, an overissue was impossible, as long as – which was the practice claimed by the Bank of England – notes were issued by discounting good commercial paper generated by actual activity – what would be later called the Real Bills Doctrine. If too many notes had been issued, it could then only be at the request of the government, for which the Bank of England was not to blame.

Not many participants in the Bullionist Controversy were able to grasp the interrelations between all these questions and to weave them into a consistent whole. Two figures emerge from that difficult exercise: Henry Thornton and David Ricardo.

Considering the novelty of inconvertibility in England and the negative evaluation of previous foreign experiments of the kind – such as the system of *assignats* in Revolutionary France – one would have expected the Bank Restriction Act of 3 May 1797 to generate immediate debates, but Sir Francis Baring's *Observations* in favour of the suspension (see below) had no opponents. The main reason was that at first there were no adverse consequences of suspension. It was only in 1800 that the general price increase and the decline of the exchange rate of the pound led to the expression of diverging opinions. This was the first round of the Bullionist Controversy, which, considered from the point of view of analytical achievement, culminated with the publication in 1802 of Henry Thornton's *Paper Credit of Great Britain.*

1.4 The first round of the Bullionist Controversy (1797–1803)

The search for analytical foundations

In 1797 Sir Francis Baring, founder of the merchant bank wearing his name, published two pamphlets, *Observations on the Establishment of the Bank of England and on the Paper Circulation of the Country*, followed in the same year by *Further Observations*. He stressed the pivotal role of the Bank of England in the English banking system, especially when a run on country banks became contagious and jeopardised the system as a whole – the very situation which had led to the suspension of convertibility of Bank of England notes. In such a case, the responsibility of the Bank of England was to be the "*dernier resort*" in the money market – an expression borrowed from juridical French and which would later flourish in the literature under the phrasing "lender of last resort". Baring was confident in the directors of the Bank of England for having performed that role in an appropriate way during the crisis of 1793–1797. He nevertheless considered that the suspension of convertibility – which he found justified – called for improvements in the monetary system, such as the Bank of England notes becoming legal tender[11] and their issuing being regulated. Baring's positions in 1797 were thus a mix of what would later be anti-bullionist – the defence of the suspension and of the Bank of England – and bullionist – the necessity for guidelines for Bank directors' behaviour. This ambivalence was an illustration of the absence of controversy at the time.

The beginning of the Bullionist Controversy is generally associated with the writing in November 1800 of Walter Boyd's *Letter to the Right Honourable William Pitt on the Influence of the Stoppage of Issues in Specie at the Bank of England, on the Prices of Provisions and Other Commodities*; the letter was published in February 1801. William Pitt was then Prime Minister, and Boyd wrote to him to present his views about the inconvertible monetary system which was in force since 1797. According to Boyd, the crucial point was that, having been released from the obligation to reimburse its notes in specie, the Bank of England in its search for profits had increased the circulation of its notes by 30 per cent, hence the amount of the circulating medium since country banks' issues and London banks' deposits were limited by the availability of Bank of England notes. This overissue was responsible for the depreciation of the currency, which manifested itself in the general increase in prices. Although the exchanges resulted from various causes, it was likely that they had turned against the pound because of this excess circulation. The reason was that, while under convertibility the Bank of England was compelled to restrict its issues when it suffered an external drain, under inconvertibility it did not face such a drain and continued increasing its issues, fuelling the domestic depreciation and the deterioration of the exchanges. The solution to the bad state of the currency was thus to dispense with the forced paper-money which had been implemented since 1797 and to return to the discipline in the note-issuing behaviour of the Bank of England that had prevailed under convertibility.

In response, Sir Francis Baring published in early 1801 *Observations on the Publication of Walter Boyd.*[12] He blamed Boyd for unduly weakening confidence in the Bank of England note. He recognised that the circulation of Bank of England notes had increased by 30 per cent in four years, but maintained that this by itself could not have produced the observed general price increase and unfavourable exchanges, which were the consequences of the war, not of Bank of England notes being issued in excess. He availed himself of the authority of Adam Smith and affirmed that notes issued by discounting bills on good security could not be in excess. The fact that Smith had considered a competitive banking system (like the Scottish one) under convertibility should have raised doubts about the relevance of the Real Bills Doctrine in a centralised system (like the English one) under inconvertibility, but this was nevertheless a widespread opinion – including among Bank of England directors and government officials – that would be long-lived, as testified by Ricardo's later ironical remark in the quotation from *Principles* given above.

This opposition of views between Boyd and Baring thus reflected what would later be the dividing line between Bullionists and Anti-Bullionists. In these pamphlets, as in Boyd's second edition of the *Letter to Pitt* in 1801 (which answered to Baring's pamphlet), the controversy was, however, limited to the evaluation of the consequences of the increased circulation of Bank of England notes and to diverging opinions about the confidence which could be put in the directors of the Bank of England. The analytical foundations of the controversy were lacking. In particular, no test of the excess note issue, if any, was provided. Both Boyd and Baring contented themselves with the amount of the general price increase as being or not being a sign of that excess and with the observed absence of difference between prices of commodities quoted in coins and in Bank of England notes as being the proof that confidence in the notes had not declined.

This important analytical point of the test of an excess note issue was emphasised by Peter King, who published *Thoughts on the Restriction of Payments in Specie at the Banks of England and Ireland* in 1803.[13] He stated that the depreciation of the currency should not be judged by the general increase in prices but by two "tests": the increase in the market price of bullion and the decline in the exchange rate of the pound:

> All commercial writers have therefore agreed in considering the market price of gold and silver as the most accurate tests of a pure or depreciated currency.

> [...] Another test of a pure or depreciated currency of great importance, though in some respects less accurate than the former, is the state of foreign exchanges.
>
> (King 1803: 26–7)

The true test of the depreciation of the currency was thus the positive difference between the market price of the standard in bullion and its legal price in coin, and it was valid under both convertibility and inconvertibility. Ricardo would later praise this position in a pamphlet whose title expressed the same idea: *The High Price of Bullion, a Proof of the Depreciation of Bank Notes* (III: 51).

Another author contributed to the first round of the Bullionist Controversy on the bullionist side by introducing a statement which would have a great importance at the beginning of the second round, especially in Ricardo's writings. In his *Remarks on Currency and Commerce* published also in 1803, John Wheatley stated that the unfavourable exchanges could have only one cause – excess of notes – contrary to common opinion that recognised the possibility of other causes besides this one. Following Viner (1937: 106), commentators thus usually label Wheatley an "extreme Bullionist" – a qualifier also given to Ricardo for the same reason.

Both King and Wheatley wrote their pamphlets as a critique of a book published in 1802, whose author – Henry Thornton – outstripped all participants to the first round of the Bullionist Controversy.

Thornton's Paper Credit of Great Britain

The publication in 1802 of Henry Thornton's *An Enquiry into the Nature and Effects of the Paper Credit of Great Britain* marked a breakthrough on the questions raised since the beginning of the Bullionist Controversy.[14] In contrast with Hume's vision that was the reference of the previous participants to the debates, according to which the same adjustment mechanism applied in any circumstance, a first contribution of Thornton was to make a distinction between various cases, which required different analyses. One should avoid confusing an external shock, which disturbed foreign economic relations, and a domestic one, due to a defect in the working of the monetary system. Moreover, one should separate normal times, in which the adjustments operated mechanically, and special circumstances, which might justify active interventions.

Two main sources of monetary instability may be distinguished in Thornton, and each one required an appropriate treatment. One was an *exogenous* disequilibrium, originating domestically (for example, a bad harvest), in foreign relations (for example, a war), or at either level (for example, a panic, provoked by a mistrust in a local bank or a fear of invasion). The problem was then to avoid a cumulative instability, and to minimise the effects of the shock until new exogenous circumstances made it disappear. Active interventions were then required: "To understand how to provide against this pressure, and how to encounter it, is a great part of the wisdom of a commercial state" (Thornton 1802: 143). Two elements pointed to the right direction, one internal and the other external. First, a contraction of the domestic circulation should be avoided, because it would impair the capacity of the exporting industries to restore the balance of trade when better times returned. As a consequence, "the bank ought to avoid too contracted an issue of bank notes" (ibid: 153), even though its gold reserves were diminishing because of the distress, and precisely to compensate the shortage of liquidity induced by the export of the metallic currency. Here lay the foundation of lending of last resort, which would be advocated by Walter Bagehot seventy years later:

> For this reason, it may be the true policy and duty of the bank [of England] to permit, for a time, and to a certain extent, the continuance of that unfavourable exchange, which causes gold to leave the country, and to be drawn out of its own coffers: and it must, in that case, necessarily encrease its loans to the same extent to which its gold is diminished.
>
> (ibid: 152)

Second, the depressive impact on the exchange of a trade deficit or of transfers abroad might be counteracted by capital inflows generated by foreign speculators who anticipated the return of the pound to its previous parity and wanted to acquire positions in that currency while it was temporarily weak:

> The exchange is, in some degree, sustained for a time, which is thought likely to be short, through the readiness of foreigners to speculate in it; but protracted speculations of this sort do not equally answer, unless the fluctuation in the exchange is very considerable. If, for example, a foreigner remits money to London, at a period when the exchange has become unfavourable to England to the extent of three per cent., places it at interest in the hands of a British merchant, and draws for it in six months afterwards, the exchange having by that time returned to its usual level, he gains two and a half per cent. for half a year's interest on his money, and also three per cent. by the course of the exchange, which is five and a half per cent. in half a year, or eleven per cent. per annum. But if the same foreigner remits money to England when the exchange has, in like manner, varied three per cent., and draws for it not in six months but in two years, the exchange having returned to its usual level only at the end of that long period, the foreigner then gains ten per cent. interest on his money, and three per cent. by the exchange, or thirteen per cent. in two years: that is to say, he gains in this case six and a half per cent. per annum, but in the other eleven per cent. per annum. If a variation of three per cent. is supposed necessary to induce foreigners to speculate for a period which is expected to end in six months, a variation of no less than twelve per cent. would be necessary to induce them to speculate for a period which is expected to end in two years. The improvement of our exchange with Europe having been delayed through a second bad harvest, it is not surprising that the expectation of its recovery within a short time should have been weakened in the mind of foreigners.
>
> (ibid: 157)

In the first case considered by Thornton, capital inflows started when the exchange rate had fallen by 3 per cent: with the expectation of a 3 per cent gain when the exchange would return to parity six months later, added to 2.5 per cent interest on the investment in English short-term bills at 5 per cent yearly interest, the expected return was equal to 11 per cent per annum, enough to induce capital inflows (this was supposing that the interest rate abroad was below 11 per cent). In the second case, however, if the return to parity was expected only after two years, the expected return was only 6.5 per cent per annum, insufficient to trigger capital inflows. In such a situation, 12 per cent expected gain in the exchange were required, added to 10 per cent interest at a yearly rate of 5 per cent, to produce the same return of 11 per cent per annum as in the first case. This meant that the exchange rate could fall by 12 per cent before capital inflows were triggered and stopped this fall. The only way to limit the fall in the exchange rate to 3 per cent, as in the first case, was then to raise the yearly interest rate in England to 9.5 per cent. But this was impossible with the Usury Laws, which imposed a maximum interest rate of 5 per cent per annum. When two successive bad harvests delayed the return to parity during two years, the repeal of the Usury Laws would allow raising the discount rate of the Bank of England so as to attract foreign capital before the exchange rate fell too much. The importance of speculation – hence of the brake it put on the decline of the exchange and the export of gold – depended on two factors: the interest-rate differential between England and abroad (which was affected by the legislation on the maximum rate of interest), and the length of the period anticipated by foreigners for the return to parity. Here lay the foundation of uncovered interest parity (see Boyer-Xambeu 1994), which is part of modern common knowledge in international finance.

A completely different situation arose when the disequilibrium was *endogenous* to the domestic monetary system, for example in the case of an excess supply of bank notes. Now the threat to monetary stability was no longer an exogenous shock beyond the control of a "commercial state", whose "wisdom" might only help to *react* to it. The aim was at improving the monetary system, in order to *prevent* the endogenous depreciation from appearing. The solution had then to be found elsewhere, and again two elements might help, one internal, the other external. First, in a system where the volume of bank notes issued was endogenously driven by the demand for them, which depended itself on the difference between the expected return on investment and the interest rate at which one could borrow from the bank, overissue might be avoided if the Bank of England was allowed to increase its discount rate as much as necessary (which required repealing the Usury Laws), and was strongly induced to do so (which justified a controlled monopoly of issue). Second, the external constraint imposed by gold bullion being "the larger article serving for the commerce of the world" provided a criterion to judge whether bank notes were or were not in excess. In a domestic monetary system where convertibility ensured that gold coins and bank notes were "interchangeable", any excess supply of bank notes which depressed their value in terms of goods also depressed the value of the coin. If the purchasing power of bullion abroad remained unchanged – hence its purchasing power in England, which could not depart from its world purchasing power, because of international arbitrage – the double value of gold (lower in coin than in bullion) was reflected in its double money price in pounds (the market price of bullion being higher than the mint price).

By reducing the metallic circulation, this export of gold compensated the excess quantity of bank notes; hence it was a factor of monetary stabilisation (at the domestic level it depressed the market price of bullion and at the foreign one it rectified the exchange), *unless* the Bank increased its issues at the same time. Although the *absolute level* of these issues was impossible to determine, the excess of the market price of bullion over the mint price then provided a criterion for their required *variation*: they should be reduced whenever this divergence became abnormal.

An analytical conclusion emerged from the distinction between exogenous and endogenous sources of monetary instability. If both cases called for the repeal of the legislation imposing a maximum interest rate, they differed diametrically about the expected behaviour of the Bank of England: an exogenous shock might require expanding the issue (lending of last resort), while an endogenous fall in the value of money imposed contracting it.

This sophisticated analysis would allow Thornton to adapt his diagnosis and remedies to changing circumstances, without facing contradiction. In 1802, his analysis of the crisis of 1797 insisted on exogenous causes (bad harvests, war transfers), which had generated an adverse foreign balance: the causality ran from an external fall in the value of money (a decline in the exchange rate) to a domestic one (the increase in the market price of gold bullion). Instead of having contracted its note issue – precipitating the crisis[15] – the Bank of England should have increased it and raised its discount rate to attract foreign capital, until unfavourable circumstances had disappeared. By contrast, as a co-author of the *Bullion Report* in 1810, Thornton would blame the Bank of England for having overissued in times of inconvertibility: the causality now ran from a domestic fall in the value of money to an external one, and the remedy was a contraction of the note issue and the resumption of convertibility (see below Chapter 2).

Thanks to its theoretical foundations, Thornton's *Paper Credit* made thus bullionist and anti-bullionist arguments coexist. In contrast with the Bullionists Boyd, King, and Wheatley, Thornton did not blame in 1802 the Bank of England for having taken advantage of inconvertibility and issued in excess; he explained the bad state of the currency by external factors having generated an adverse foreign balance. His analysis of the effects of "a comparison of the rate of interest taken at the bank with the current rate of mercantile profit" (ibid: 254) nevertheless contained a powerful critique of what would long be a distinctive mark of Anti-Bullionism: the Real Bills Doctrine, according to which notes could never be in excess as long as they were issued by discounting bills generated by current production. Thornton pointed out that the supply of bills – hence the demand for notes – was not driven by the volume of goods under production but by the difference between the expected rate of return on the money borrowed and the actual discount rate at which the Bank of England monetised the bills – a point that would be emphasised by Wicksell nearly a century later when dealing with the relation between the natural rate of interest and the money rate of interest (see Wicksell 1934–1935 [1901–1906]). If this difference was large – a circumstance fostered by the legal maximum of 5 per cent imposed on the discount rate – the fact that the Bank of England only lent on good quality bills could not prevent the issuing of notes from being in excess, by comparison with what was required by the level of current production. This excess then pushed the market price of bullion upwards. Under convertibility, arbitrage triggered by the positive difference between the market price of gold bullion and the legal price at which the Bank of England was compelled to give specie for its notes led to a drain of its metallic reserves that forced the Bank of England to reduce its issues, thus correcting the excess. But this check on overissue disappeared under inconvertibility, and the depreciation of the currency then had no limit. This argument was consistent with a bullionist approach.

This ambivalence of Thornton's *Paper Credit* contrasts with the tradition started by Hayek (1939) that considered that his later co-authorship of the *Bullion Report* marked an evolution towards a growing concern for "the dangers of a paper currency" (Hayek 1939: 56) and the necessity of a return to convertibility.[16] The theoretical possibility of overissue was already present in *Paper Credit*, and Thornton would have no difficulty later basing on it his understanding of the situation discussed during the second round of the Bullionist Controversy. There is one Thornton indeed and it is all based on *Paper Credit*, but this book provides a unified theoretical foundation for both the defence of lending of last resort and the restriction of the note issue, under both convertibility and inconvertibility. The two speeches delivered by Thornton in 1811 before the House of Commons, where he defended the *Bullion Report*, are an illustration of that consistency. Thornton thus provides a link between the first and second rounds of the Bullionist Controversy. In this second round David Ricardo appeared.

Appendix 1: Ricardo on the bullion and foreign exchange markets

Ricardo was professionally involved neither in the bullion nor in the foreign exchange markets. However, his knowledge of their operations was sufficiently good to be used by him to invalidate the diagnoses made by his opponents and refute the arguments they derived from them. The following two examples are taken from the Bullion Controversy, one against Bosanquet, the other against Vansittart.

1. Ricardo contradicts Bosanquet on the rise of gold on the Continent

As illustrated by the title of his pamphlet *The High Price of Bullion, a Proof of the Depreciation of Bank Notes*, published in January 1810, Ricardo contended that the premium on gold bullion in the London market, as compared with the legal price of gold in coin, reflected entirely the depreciation of the Bank of England note (see below Chapter 2). After the publication of the *Bullion Report* in August 1810, which endorsed this view, Charles Bosanquet published in November of the same year *Practical Observations on the Report of the Bullion Committee*, in which he argued that the premium on gold bullion was not linked to the state of paper circulation in England, since the market price of gold bullion had risen on the Continent even more. The question of fact was thus whether this was true. In *Reply to Mr. Bosanquet's Practical Observations on the Report of the Bullion Committee*, published in January 1811, Ricardo denied this alleged fact:

> But the price of gold, we are told, has risen on the continent even more than it has here, because when it was 4*l*. 12*s*. in this country [England], 4*l*. 17*s*. might be procured for it at Hamburgh, a difference of 5½ per cent. This is so often repeated, and is so wholly fallacious, that it may be proper to give it particular consideration.
>
> (*Reply to Bosanquet*; III: 195)

Ricardo did not deny that the price in English money of an ounce of standard gold was then in Hamburg £4. 17s. The practice in Hamburg was to quote gold in *schillingen Vlams banco* ("Flemish schillings" in Ricardo's text; Fs. hereafter), each of them being divided in 12 *groten* and with 2⅔ *schillingen Vlams banco* being equal to one *Mark banco* of the Bank of Hamburg. £4. 17s. was thus the arbitrated price of an ounce of standard gold in Hamburg, that is, its price in Flemish schillings converted into English pound sterling at the ruling exchange rate applied to a bill drawn in Hamburg on London. This calculation was always made by the London bullion trader to determine the profit he could make

> by sending an ounce of bullion to Hamburgh, and having the produce remitted by bill payable in London in bank-notes.
>
> (ibid: 194)

The elements of the calculation were given by Ricardo:

> This ounce of gold, which we are told we sell at Hamburgh for 4*l*. 17*s*., actually produces no more than 140 schillings 8 grotes, an advance only of 3 per cent. [...] the currency of England [...] being estimated on the Hamburgh exchange 28 or 29 Flemish schillings.
>
> (ibid: 196)

One checks that the price of 140 Fs. 8 gr. (140.66 in decimals) is the equivalent of £4. 17s. (£4.85 in decimals) at the exchange rate of 29 Fs. per pound $(140.66/29 = 4.85)$. To sum up: an ounce of standard gold was sold for 140 Fs. 8 gr. in Hamburg, the proceeds being "remitted by a bill payable in London" at the rate of 29 Fs. per pound, thus giving £4. 17s. This was a fact; how could it be explained? For Bosanquet, the explanation was to be found in the high level of the market price of gold bullion in Hamburg, not in London. For Ricardo the explanation was to be found in the low level of the exchange rate – a consequence of the depreciation of the Bank of England note in which a bill of exchange drawn in Hamburg was paid in London ("a bill payable in London in bank-notes"). His argument was as follows.

If the exchange had been at par (on this notion, see below the case against Vansittart), an ounce of gold bullion at the legal price in London of an ounce of gold in coin (£3. 17s. 10½d.) and exported to Hamburg would have been sold there for 136 Fs. 7 gr:

> When an ounce of gold was to be bought in this country at 3*l.* 17*s.* 10½*d.*, and the relative value of gold was to silver as 15.07 to 1, it would have sold on the continent for nearly the same as here, or 3*l.* 17*s.* 10½*d.* in silver coin. In Hamburgh, for example, we should have received in payment of an ounce of gold 136 Flemish schillings and 7 grotes, that quantity of silver containing an equal quantity of pure metal, as 3*l.* 17*s.* 10½*d.* in our standard silver coin.
>
> (ibid: 195–6)

The calculation is thus: at a mint ratio of 15.07, an ounce of standard gold is legally equivalent to 15.07 ounces of standard silver, which in Hamburg have a price of 136 Fs. 7 gr. Since, as observed above, the same ounce of standard gold was now valued at 140 Fs. 8 gr., this meant that the rise in the price of gold bullion in Hamburg had been 3 per cent ("an advance of only 3 per cent."), much less than the rise of 18 per cent in London (£4. 12s. as compared with £3. 17s. 10½d.).[17] Not only was Bosanquet wrong in his diagnosis – gold bullion had risen much more in London than in Hamburg – but the explanation of the acknowledged £4. 17s. price of gold bullion in Hamburg was to be found in the fall of the exchange rate: it now cost 24.5 per cent more (£4. 17s. as compared with £3. 17s. 10½d.) to remit the proceeds of the export and sale in Hamburg of an ounce of gold bullion than it would have if the Bank of England note in which the bill was paid in London had not been depreciated relatively to gold:

> The currency of England being now depreciated, and being estimated on the Hamburgh exchange at 28 or 29 Flemish schillings, instead of 37, the true value of a pound sterling, 140 schillings 8 grotes, or 3 per cent. more than 136*s.* 7*g.* will now purchase a bill payable in London in Bank notes for 4*l.* 17*s.*; so that gold has not risen more than 3 per cent. in Hamburgh, but the currency of England, on a comparison with the currency of Hamburgh, has fallen 23½ per cent.
>
> (ibid: 196)[18]

Ricardo concluded that, against Bosanquet, he had thus established:

> The truth of my assertion, that it is not gold which has risen 16 or 18 per cent. in the general market of the world, but that it is the paper currency in which the price of gold is estimated in England, which alone has fallen.
>
> (ibid)

Ricardo did not say where the figure of 136 Fs. 7 gr. on which his calculation rested came from. The only indication he gave in the quotation above obscures the matter. One could believe that the exchange rate of 37 Fs. per pound, "the true value of a pound sterling", is the par of exchange, that is, the rate that would apply in the situation where an ounce of gold bullion exported to Hamburg would exchange there for 136 Fs. 7 gr. But if £3. 17s. 10½d. exchange for 136 Fs. 7 gr., the rate of the pound is 35 Fs. 1 gr., not 37. That this rate of 35 Fs. 1 gr. was the par of exchange was confirmed by Ricardo himself in one of the observations he made on Vansittart's propositions during the Bullion debate in May 1811 (see below):

> The real par of exchange between England and Hamburgh when the relative market value of gold and silver, agrees with the relative mint value viz as 1 to 15.07, is 35/1.
>
> (III: 417)

Checking the figures used by Ricardo requires a little calculation. First, one needs to correct a slight error made by Ricardo about the mint ratio (as shown in this quotation, he made the same mistake in his case against Vansittart). As mentioned in the text of Chapter 1 above, the mint ratio in England was 15.21 and not 15.07. The figure of 15.07 was obtained by dividing the legal price of an ounce of standard gold in coin (£3. 17s. 10½d.) by the legal price of an ounce of standard silver in coin (62d.). But one neglected thus that the fineness of standard gold (22/24, that is, 916.667/1000) was below that of standard silver (222/240, that is, 925/1000). Taking this difference into account gave a mint ratio of 15.21 instead of 15.07. One ounce of standard gold bullion was thus legally equivalent to 15.21 ounces of standard silver bullion, which contained 14.06925 ounces of pure silver, or, with one ounce = 31.1035 today's grams, 437.6029 grams of pure silver. A Cologne *marco* (the unit of weight used in Hamburg) being equal to 233.855 grams, this gave 1.8713 *marco*, hence, with one *marco* of pure silver being valued 27 *Mark* 10 *Schillinge banco* by the Bank of Hamburg, 51.6935 *Mark banco*. On the basis of the equivalence between one *Mark banco* and 2⅔ *schillingen Vlams banco* ("Flemish schillings"), this gave 137.8665 Fs., that is, 137 Fs. 10 gr., instead of 136 Fs. 7 gr. as indicated by Ricardo. The difference is small (0.9 per cent) and may be explained by slightly different definitions of the measures of weight, the English ounce and the Cologne *marco*. This calculation thus confirms Ricardo's knowledge of the practice of the time and still strengthens his conclusions: according to it, the rise in the price of gold bullion in Hamburg was actually 2 per cent (140 Fs. 8 gr. as compared with 137 Fs. 10 gr.), still lower than the 3 per cent acknowledged by him (140 Fs. 8 gr. as compared with 136 Fs. 7 gr.).

Another phrase by Ricardo shows that he was not only aware of the intricacies of the international bullion market but also of those of the foreign exchange market.[19] One of the much-debated questions during the Bullion Controversy was the explanation of the acknowledged fact that the export of gold had accelerated during the past few years. The answer by Bosanquet was simple: since the price of bullion was 5½ per cent higher in Hamburg than in London, it was profitable to export it. Again, the monetary situation in England was not to blame, but the high price of gold on the Continent. This Ricardo denied, first because the cost of exporting gold in these troubled times was higher than the expected gain in price, and second because this expected gain was actually smaller than the percentage difference between the prices of gold bullion in Hamburg and London:

> The exporter of an ounce of gold purchased here at 4*l.* 12*s.* would at least have had to wait three months before he could have received the 4*l.* 17*s.* because after the gold is sold at Hamburgh the remittance is made by a bill at 2½ usances; so that allowing for interest for this period he would actually have obtained a profit of 4¼ per cent. only; but as the expence of sending gold to Hamburgh is stated in evidence to be 7 per cent., a bill would at this time have been a cheaper remittance by 2¾ per cent.
>
> (*Reply to Bosanquet*; III: 198)

In Hamburg, the bills on London were "long", meaning that they were paid in London after a period of two and a half months. The exporter of gold bullion had thus either to wait until the bill came due before obtaining the sum remitted from Hamburg, or to have the bill discounted in London if he preferred to get the money immediately after reception of the bill. In both cases, he faced a cost of interest equal to 1¼ per cent (5 per cent yearly interest during two and a half months plus a few days for intermediation). The expected profit was thus 4¼ per cent instead of 5½, still lower than the 7 per cent cost in transport and insurance of the metal. An export of gold by arbitrage was thus not profitable. A corollary was that any debt contracted in London for payment in Hamburg could be advantageously discharged by selling in Hamburg a bill on London at a 4¼ per cent discount, rather than by exporting gold at a cost of 7 per cent.

2. Ricardo contradicts Vansittart on the state of the exchange with Hamburg in 1760

The issue was here whether the greatly unfavourable exchange at the time of the Bullion Controversy was an unprecedented phenomenon – to be related to the inconvertibility of the Bank of England note, as contended by Ricardo – or had been observed in the past, under convertibility. During the debate in Parliament in May 1811, Nicholas Vansittart moved seventeen counter-resolutions challenging the *Bullion Report* (see below Chapter 2). The fifth one read:

> That such unfavourable exchanges, and rise in the price of Bullion, occurred to a greater or less degree during the wars carried on by King William the 3d. and Queen Ann; and also during part of the Seven years war, and of the American war.
>
> (III: 416)

In his manuscript "Observations on Vansittart's Propositions respecting Money, Bullion and Exchanges", Ricardo commented on that proposition:

> During the seven years war the gold coin then the principal measure of value had become debased which will account for the price of gold having occasionally been as high as £4. 1. 6. The exchange was, though as low as 31.10 in 1760, never below the real par. The relative value of gold and silver was in the market at this time as 14 to 1. Gold was a legal tender in England and a pound sterling in gold was probably of less value in the market than the silver in 31/10 of Hamburgh. The real par of exchange between England and Hamburgh when the relative market value of gold and silver, agrees with the relative mint value viz as 1 to 15.07, is 35/1, – consequently when the relative value is as 1 to 14 the real par is 32/7. Now if we take into our consideration the debased state of the English coin in the year 1760 it is probable that the exchange when at 31/10 was really favourable to England.
>
> (ibid: 417)

Since the state of the exchange was determined by comparing the observed exchange rate with the par of exchange, the diagnosis depended on the appropriate calculation of the par (see Chapter 8 below). Between London and Hamburg, the exchange rate was the quantity of Flemish schillings that exchanged for one pound sterling and the par of exchange was accordingly the level R of the exchange rate that equalised the quantity of the standard contained in one pound sterling in gold or silver coin and in R Flemish schillings in gold coin or silver bullion. With gold as common standard, $\overline{P_{GC}^{\pounds}}$ the legal price in £ of an ounce of gold in coin in London, and $\overline{P_{GC}^{Fs}}$ the legal price in Fs. of an ounce of gold in coin in Hamburg, the par of exchange $\overline{R_G}$ computed on gold was given by $(1/\overline{P_{GC}^{\pounds}}) = \overline{R_G}\,(1/\overline{P_{GC}^{Fs}})$, hence:

$$\overline{R_G} = \frac{\overline{P_{GC}^{Fs}}}{\overline{P_{GC}^{\pounds}}} \tag{1.1}$$

However, this formula could not apply: although the old gold ducat introduced by the emperor Charles V was still coined in Hamburg for the international trade, it was quoted there as merchandise, having only a variable market price, not a legal one;[20] it could thus not be used to calculate the par. Ricardo was aware of the inaccuracy of a par of exchange computed on the basis of coins whose market valuation depended on their local use, as he wrote in a letter to Leonard Horner on 6 December 1812:

> Mr. Mushet's tables may be considered as an approximation to truth but by no means as critically correct. In making his calculations on the exchange he has been sometimes obliged to estimate the proportional value of silver to gold by

> comparing the price of *dollar* silver to the price of standard gold, – sometimes to the price of Portugal gold coin, or to the price of doubloons. At other times he has compared the price of *standard* silver with one or other of the above description of gold. He has indeed by calculation reduced them all to our standard, but it is obvious that each of the above species of gold & silver is liable to its peculiar variation in the general market on account of local demand, not deviating much from a common standard but still enough to prevent any thing like great accuracy in calculations on the exchange.
>
> (in Depoortère 2015: 344–5; Ricardo's emphasis)

Silver was a better candidate, because its legal price in Hamburg did not require resorting to any coin: there was a legal price quoted in *Mark banco* of the Bank of Hamburg for pure silver bullion, and the exchange was quoted in *schillingen Vlams banco* which were in a fixed relation with the *Mark banco*. Since in 1760 England was officially on a dual standard (gold and silver), one could extend formula (1.1) to silver. With $\overline{P_{SC}}^{£}$ the legal price in pound of an ounce of silver in coin in London, and $\overline{P_S}^{Fs}$ the legal price in Flemish schillings of an ounce of silver bullion in Hamburg, the par of exchange $\overline{R_S}$ computed on silver was given by:

$$\overline{R_S} = \frac{\overline{P_S}^{Fs}}{\overline{P_{SC}}^{£}} \tag{1.2}$$

But there was a difficulty: since the monetary reform of 1717, the English mint ratio $\overline{P_{GC}}^{£} / \overline{P_{SC}}^{£}$ was the highest in Europe and the undervalued silver left England rather than being carried to the mint to be coined. Although officially dual, the acknowledged standard in England was in 1760 already gold. As a consequence, the apparent par given by (1.2) did not reflect the actual arbitrage on precious metals between London and Hamburg. The par of exchange could thus be computed neither on gold alone nor on silver alone: one should take into account the difference in standard, by correcting the formula with the relative market price P_{GS} of gold bullion in silver bullion. As Ricardo wrote to Francis Horner on 6 February 1810:

> As gold is the standard of currency in England, and silver in all other countries, there can be no fixed par of exchange between England and those countries, it being subject to all the variations which may take place in the relative value of gold and silver.
>
> (VI: 8)

Taking P_{GS} computed in the London market as a proxy of its level in the Hamburg market (because of arbitrage in the international bullion market), one could substitute in (1.1) $P_{GS}\overline{P_S}^{Fs}$ for the lacking $\overline{P_{GC}}^{Fs}$; this gave the "real par of exchange" R_{GS}:

$$R_{GS} = P_{GS} \frac{\overline{P_S}^{Fs}}{\overline{P_{GC}}^{£}} \tag{1.3}$$

For given legal prices of gold in London and silver in Hamburg, the real par of exchange depended thus on the relative market price of gold in silver: the higher the latter, the higher was the par of the gold-backed pound in terms of the silver-backed schilling. Now suppose that the market ratio P_{GS} is equal to the mint ratio $\overline{P_{GC}}^{£} / \overline{P_{SC}}^{£}$. Rearranging (1.3) gives:

$$R_{GS} = \frac{\overline{P_{GC}}^{£}}{\overline{P_{SC}}^{£}} \frac{\overline{P_S}^{Fs}}{\overline{P_{GC}}^{£}} = \frac{\overline{P_S}^{Fs}}{\overline{P_{SC}}^{£}} = \overline{R_S}$$

The real par is in this particular case by definition equal to the silver par. With $\overline{P_{GC}}^{£} / \overline{P_{SC}}^{£} = 15.07$, the real par – hence the silver par – given in Ricardo's quotation was 35 Fs. 1 gr. (35.083 Fs. in decimals). It is likely that this silver par was used by Vansittart to infer the state of the exchange: at 31 Fs. 10 gr. (31.833 Fs. in decimals) the exchange rate was in 1760 9.3 per cent below the silver par – hence greatly unfavourable to England. Ricardo objected that the market ratio was then far below the mint ratio: 14 instead of 15.07. According to him, if for a market ratio equal to 15.07 the real par was 35 Fs. 1 gr., it was proportionally 32 Fs. 7 gr. only (32.583 Fs. in decimals) with a market ratio equal to 14. In other words, the real par was 7.1 per cent below the apparent silver par. In consequence, an exchange rate at 31 Fs. 10 gr. was *really* only 2.3 per cent below the par, four times less than when it was compared with the apparent silver par. In his comment on Vansittart Ricardo added that, considering the debasement of the English gold coin at the time, "it is probable that the exchange when at 31/10 was really favourable to England". This was overcharging the argument: as illustrated in the first sentence of this comment, the debasement of the gold coin was reflected in a high market price of gold bullion that was already taken into account in the computation of the market ratio, which was nevertheless low because the silver bullion was rated even higher in the market, as a consequence of the debasement and the scarcity of the silver coin. By definition, the market ratio of 14 reflected all the existing characteristics of the gold and silver coinage.

One may wish to check the relevance of the figures used by Ricardo. First, the market ratio of 14 in 1760 is confirmed by the available data: the actual quotations of gold and silver bars twice a week in London gave a market ratio varying in that year between 13.83 and 14.40 (see Boyer-Xambeu, Deleplace and Gillard 1995: 180). Second, the calculation of the mint ratio and of the par of exchange was as follows (see Boyer-Xambeu, Deleplace and Gillard 2010a, 2010b, 2013, for definitions and data). In England, the legal price of £3. 17s. 10½d. (£3. 89375 in decimals) per Troy ounce (of 31.1035 today's grams) of coined gold 22/24 fine was equivalent to £136.5675 per kilogram 1000/1000 fine; the legal price of 62d. (£0.2583) per Troy ounce of coined silver 222/240 fine was equivalent to £8.9790 per kilogram 1000/1000 fine: the two gave a legal mint ratio of 15.21 (instead of 15.07 as indicated by Ricardo). In Hamburg, the legal price of 27 *Mark* 10 *Schillinge Lübs* (27.625 in decimals, the *Mark* being divided in 16 *Schillinge*) per Cologne *marco* (of 233.855 today's grams) of silver bullion 1000/1000 fine was equivalent to 118.129 *Mark Lübs* per kilogram 1000/1000 fine. With 1 *Mark Lübs* = 2⅔ *schillingen Vlams* (of 12 *groten* each), this gave 315.095 *schillingen Vlams* per kilogram 1000/1000 fine. The silver par R_S given by (1.2) was thus $315.095 / 8.9790 = 35.09\,\text{Fs. per } \pounds = 35\text{ Fs. } 1\text{ gr}$. When the market ratio was equal to the mint ratio, the silver par R_S was by definition equal to the real par R_{GS} given by (1.3): $15.21 \times 315.095/136.5675 = 35.09\,\text{Fs. per } \pounds = 35\text{ Fs. } 1\text{ gr}$. as indicated by Ricardo (in spite of the slight error made by him on the mint ratio). With a market ratio equal to 14, the real par R_{GS} given by (1.3) was equal to $14 \times 315.095/136.5675 = 32.30\,\text{Fs. per } \pounds = 32$ Fs. 4 gr., close to the 32 Fs. 7 gr. as indicated by Ricardo. An exchange rate of 31 Fs. 10 gr. was 1.4 per cent only below the real par 32 Fs. 4 gr., as compared with 9.3 per cent below the apparent silver par 35 Fs. 1 gr.: Ricardo's conclusion is strengthened.[21]

Contrary to what was affirmed by Vansittart, the exchange in 1760 – under convertibility – was *not* unfavourable in a degree comparable to that of 1810 – under inconvertibility: the situation at the time of the Bullion Controversy was unprecedented and pointed to inconvertibility as the circumstance having made a greatly unfavourable exchange possible. Besides, the case of 1760 was for Ricardo no proof of an unfavourable exchange caused by a foreign balance against England – the explanation advocated by Vansittart and the Anti-Bullionists for the situation in 1810 (see below Chapter 2) – since the comparison between the exchange rate and the real par showed that the balance in 1760 was nearly even.

Notes

1 It should be recollected that at the time of Ricardo the Bank of England was always referred to in the plural. I have adopted here the present convention of referring to it in the singular neutral.
2 This chapter develops Deleplace (2015a).
3 Ricardo dated the adoption of the gold standard "some time between 1796 and 1798", although he acknowledged that "gold had, in fact become the standard" long before. In a speech before Parliament on 9 April 1821 he declared:

> The hon. member for Taunton [Alexander Baring] had entered into a speculation on the subject, as if a gold standard had been an innovation of 1819. But that standard had been adopted some time between 1796 and 1798. Up to that period, gold and silver had been the standard. The chancellor of the exchequer had labored under a mistake when he had said that silver had been a legal tender only to the amount of 25*l*. It was true that that had been the utmost amount in the degraded currency of the country; but a man might have gone to the mint with his silver, and 100,000*l*. might be paid in silver of standard value. This, however, had never been any man's interest. But gold had been carried to the Mint, and gold had, in fact become the standard. The change in the relative value of the metals had taken place in the period he had mentioned between 1796 and 1798; and large quantities

> of silver had been carried to the Mint, in order to profit by the state of the law, and the relative value of silver and gold. If government had not interfered, a guinea would not have been found in the country, and silver would have been the standard. The government, aware that there would be a silver currency of degraded value, and another of standard value, had by an act of parliament, he believed, shut the Mint against silver; and he [Ricardo] asked whether gold had not then become the standard?
>
> (V: 105–6)

In his calculation of the par of exchange between London and Hamburg for the year 1760, Ricardo considered that the pound sterling was already *de facto* on a gold standard at that time; see Appendix 1 above.

4 The expression "superior bank" is used here rather than "central bank", which would be anachronistic. In the nineteenth century, the Bank of France referred to itself as "the private superior bank" (see Leclercq 2010).

5 The first reference is to the 2015 edition of the original of Steuart (1767); the second reference is to the 1805 edition, reprinted in 1998. In both cases the roman figure indicates the volume in the edition.

6 For the links between Steuart, Thornton, Tooke, and Keynes in an unorthodox approach to the relation between the markets for foreign exchange and credit, see Deleplace (2014b).

7 After the House of Commons had rejected the *Bullion Report*, an anonymous publication of the Resolutions submitted to the vote included in 1811 a list of the publications occasioned by the report, with their publishers and prices; it contained no less than 73 entries (Cannan 1919, Second Part: 21–4).

8 The classic studies on the Bullionist Controversy are in Viner (1937) and Fetter (1965); also useful are Sraffa (1951c, 1952b), Laidler (1987), Arnon (2011), and for factual information Feaveryear (1931) and Clapham (1944).

9 Viner (1937) extends the "Bullionist Controversies" until 1825 and distinguishes "the inflation phase" (from 1797 till the end of the Napoleonic wars) and the "deflation phase" (from 1815 to the 1825 crisis).

10 The expression "Bullion controversy" is also used by Cannan (1919: xxvii). The use of one or the other expression was the subject of an undated foolscap sheet found in the *Sraffa Papers* (D3/11/65[30]) and containing questions addressed by Keynes to Sraffa on the "Bullion Pamphlets" to be published in Volume III of Ricardo's *Works*: "You speak of Bullion Controversy. Is not Bullionist Controversy more usual? I feel as though I was accustomed to speak of 'Bullion Committee', but 'Bullionist Controversy'." No answer by Sraffa is extant but he kept the expression "Bullion Controversy" in the "Prefatory Note to Volumes III and IV":

> These two volumes under the general title of 'Pamphlets and Papers' contain Ricardo's shorter writings. The division between the two volumes is chronological. Volume III has a greater unity in that it consists entirely of writings on monetary subjects of the period of the Bullion Controversy, while Volume IV is composed of miscellaneous pieces which extend over the later years of Ricardo's life.
>
> (Sraffa 1951b: vii)

The writings contained in Volume III cover the period from 1809 to 1811.

11 In the pre-1797 system as since the suspension, Bank of England notes were not legal tender: a creditor could refuse to be reimbursed in them and insist on being paid in specie. They would be made legal tender only in 1833.

12 For a detailed analysis of the controversy between Walter Boyd and Sir Francis Baring, see Arnon (2011), Chapter 6.

13 For an analysis of King's positions in respect to Smith and Thornton, see Rosier (1994).
14 The analysis of Thornton's *Paper Credit* draws on Deleplace (2004).
15 It might be found ironical that, ten years after Thornton's death, the bank in which he had been the main partner failed during the crisis of 1825, which was brought about by a contraction of the issues of the Bank of England – the same behaviour Thornton had criticised when discussing in *Paper Credit* the crisis of 1793. See Thomas Joplin quoted in Hayek (1939: 36, note *).
16 Referring to Thornton's first speech in Parliament in defence of the *Bullion Report*, Hayek wrote:

> By this time, although he had not altered his theoretical position in any essential respect, Thornton had become thoroughly convinced of the mismanagement of the note issue and the overwhelming danger of an excessive circulation in general, and was no longer afraid to apply the remedy of a severe contraction.
>
> (Hayek 1939: 56)

He then added that "his speech [...] is really a lecture on the dangers of a paper currency".
17 "In further proof", Ricardo reproduced a table "furnished to the Bullion Committee by Mr. Grefulhe" (III: 196–7) and showing that the difference between the highest price of gold bullion (in 1810) and its lowest price (in 1804) was 3¾ per cent in Hamburg and 3⅝ in Amsterdam, as compared with 16 per cent in England.
18 Ricardo obtains 23.5 per cent by adding the 18 per cent rise in the market price of gold bullion in London as compared with the legal price of gold in coin and the 5.5 per cent excess of the market price in pounds of gold bullion in Hamburg above its market price in London. This is an approximation: the actual rise in the market price in pounds of gold bullion in Hamburg, as compared with the legal price of gold in coin in London, is 24.5 per cent.
19 See the letter to Malthus of 30 December 1813: "I have been amusing myself for one or two evenings in calculating the exchanges, price of gold, &c, – at Amsterdam, and I enclose the result of my labours" (VI: 97–9), and the letter to Malthus of 1 January 1814 on the same with Hamburg (VI: 100–1). See also the letter to Horner of 6 February 1810 on the calculation of the par of exchange with Hamburg (VI: 8–10) and the letter to McCulloch of 22 June 1819 where on the latter's request Ricardo explained how the bills of exchange were quoted (VIII: 39–40).
20 See Achterberg and Lanz (1957: 126). This contradicts Marcuzzo and Rosselli who, besides a silver par of 35 Fs. 1 gr. per pound, calculate a gold par of 34 Fs. 3½ gr. on the basis of "the official price of gold in Hamburg" (Marcuzzo and Rosselli 1991: 115–16). Ricardo never mentioned such price.
21 Incidentally, the same calculation suggests an explanation for the figure of 37 Fs. per pound mentioned by Ricardo in the case against Bosanquet (see above). It gives a real par of 36 Fs. 11 gr. (one grote only below 37 Fs.) when the market ratio is equal to 16, that is, taking into account "the rise in the relative value of gold to silver, which from 15.07 to 1 is now about 16 to 1" (*Reply to Bosanquet*; III: 196).

2 Ricardo's battles on currency and banks

> *I expect to be the object of much personal attack next session* [of The House of Commons] *but I comfort myself with the reflection that truth will prevail at last, and justice will in the end be done to my motives and opinions.*
>
> (Letter from Paris to Osman and Harriet Ricardo, 23 November 1822; X: 349)

Not only was money what made Ricardo become an economist, but it shaped him as an economist committed to the debates of the time. As Piero Sraffa wrote in 1951 in his "Note on the Bullion Essays":

> Ricardo's first appearance in print marked the beginning of what came to be known as the Bullion Controversy. It took the shape of an anonymous article on The Price of Gold published in the *Morning Chronicle* of 29 August 1809.
>
> (Sraffa 1951c: 3)

This sentence emphasises two striking aspects of Ricardo's first monetary writing. On the one hand, it was the first time Ricardo expressed himself publicly (albeit anonymously), although he was at the time already aged 37 and had engaged for long in extensive business transactions as a jobber and a loan contractor, that is, a financial intermediary specialised in government funds. On the other hand, this article, together with two further published letters and Ricardo's 1810 pamphlet *The High Price of Bullion, a Proof of the Depreciation of Bank Notes* launched the so-called Bullion Controversy which culminated with the report of the Bullion Committee, appointed in 1810 by the House of Commons. Thus Ricardo's first publications on money gained him immediate recognition as a major figure in the economic debates of the time.

What Sraffa calls "the Bullion Essays" of 1809–1811 would remain the only works by Ricardo during four more years, until he published in 1815 *An Essay on the Influence of a Low Price of Corn on the Profits of Stock*. Again, during the interval that separated this essay from his 1817 masterpiece *On the Principles of Political Economy, and Taxation*, Ricardo published (in 1816) a new monetary pamphlet, *Proposals for an Economical and Secure Currency*, where he suggested a plan which he would later defend in Parliament. His last pamphlet, *Plan for the Establishment of a National Bank*, published posthumously in 1824, was also a monetary one. All in all, around one half of Ricardo's published writings are on money, and they all aimed at influencing, in a controversial but also constructive tone, the debates of his time. Not only was Ricardo a great monetary economist but he battled a lot to criticise others' views on currency and banks and to persuade his contemporaries of the beneficial practical consequences of his own views. He himself used the term "battle" and the war rhetoric in a letter to Hutches Trower on 28 May 1819 after his Ingot Plan had been adopted by the House of Commons:

> The feeble resistance, in point of argument, of the Bank Directors, was easily overcome. I had the courage to set myself foremost in the battle, and was amply rewarded by the support of the House, which enabled me to get to the end of my speech without any great degree of fear or trepidation. I hope that during the next fortnight we shall give the death blow to the theory of an abstract pound sterling.
>
> (VIII: 31–2)

During the 14 years when Ricardo wrote on money, two main periods may be distinguished. The first one covers "the Bullion Essays" of 1809–1811. The issue was then first to understand an unprecedented situation in which metallic currency had nearly disappeared, the only circulating medium being the Bank of England note that was inconvertible since 1797, and second to explain why this had resulted in a fall in the value of the pound sterling. Ricardo's tone was mainly critical (particularly of the Bank of England), although the last writing of that period contained a scheme for a new monetary system. The second period runs from 1816 to Ricardo's death in 1823. The end of the Napoleonic Wars opened up the possibility of a return to a normal (that is, with convertibility of the Bank of England note) monetary system, and Ricardo's aim was at showing that one should not just revert to the pre-1797 situation, but change it substantially. He successively advocated two plans, one in 1816 that was based on the convertibility of the Bank of England note into bullion (the Ingot Plan) and one in 1823 that was based on the substitution of a public bank for the Bank of England as sole issuer of bank notes (the Plan for a national bank). Although Ricardo won in 1819 the approval of Parliament for his first plan, the return to convertibility at pre-war parity actually took place in 1821 along the pre-1797 lines, and this led Ricardo to develop his second plan, which remained unsuccessful because of his death in 1823.

The present chapter deals successively with these two periods and exposes in each Ricardo's positions in the context of the controversy in which he took part.[1]

2.1 Ricardo and the Bullion Controversy (1809–1811)

The second round of the Bullionist Controversy

After a five-year remission, the fall in the value of the pound resumed in 1809, to reach 20 per cent in March 1810 (the market price of gold being £4. 13s. 7d., as compared with the legal mint price of £3. 17s. 10½d.). This was the time of the "Bullion Controversy", launched by Ricardo and marked by the *Bullion Report* laid before the House of Commons on 8 June 1810. This report explained the fall in the value of the pound by the excess issue of Bank of England notes and suggested contraction of the issue and return to convertibility as remedies. This suggestion was turned down by Parliament, and the matter remained unsettled, although the fall in the value of the pound was aggravated (with a maximum of 50 per cent in November 1813).

The Bullion Report

As mentioned above, the Bullion Controversy – the second round that marked the climax of the Bullionist Controversy – started with the publication of Ricardo's letter in the *Morning Chronicle* of 29 August 1809 (reproduced in Ricardo 1809). The responsibility of Ricardo in the launching of this controversy has been acknowledged not only by Sraffa: it was recognised by major participants in the debate. Francis Horner, who would be the chairman of the Bullion Committee, wrote on 16 July 1810 a letter to the editor of the *Edinburgh Review* which read:

> I will do a short article for you this time, to do justice to Mr Ricardo and Mr Mushet, who called the public attention to this very important subject at the end of last year.
>
> (quoted in Sraffa 1951c: 9–10)

Charles Bosanquet, whose pamphlet "was regarded at the time as the most effective of the criticisms published on the Bullion Report" (ibid: 10), attacked

> Mr Ricardo's work, not only as having been the immediate cause of the inquiry which has since taken place, under the authority of the house of commons, but as a syllabus of the Report which has been presented by the Committee.
>
> (ibid)

After two more letters to the *Morning Chronicle*, Ricardo expanded his views in his first book, published on 3 January 1810. The title of this pamphlet – *The High Price of Bullion, a Proof of the Depreciation of Bank Notes* – summed-up Ricardo's main argument: the Bank of England note was depreciated, as proved by the high price of gold bullion and the low exchange of the pound, and this depreciation was entirely due to its excess issue. On 1 February, Francis Horner delivered before the House of Commons a speech calling attention to the necessity of inquiring about these phenomena. On 19 February a committee composed of 22 members of the House of Commons was appointed, and until May it took evidence from numerous specialists. Its report was co-authored by Francis Horner, William Huskisson, and Henry Thornton; it stressed the excess note issue by the Bank of England and recommended the resumption of note convertibility within two years. The *Bullion Report* was laid before the House of Commons on 8 June

1810 and described in a private letter by the chairman of the committee, Francis Horner, as follows:

> The Report is in truth very clumsily and prolixly drawn; stating nothing but very old doctrines on the subject it treats of, and stating them in a more imperfect form than they have frequently appeared in before. It is a motley composition by Huskisson, Thornton, and myself; each having written parts which are tacked together without any care to give them an uniform style or a very exact connection. One great merit the Report, however, possesses; that it declares, in very plain and pointed terms, both the true doctrine and the existence of a great evil growing out of the neglect of that doctrine. By keeping up the discussion, which I mean to do, and by forcing it on the attention of Parliament, we shall in time (I trust) effect the restoration of the old and only safe system.
>
> (quoted in Cannan 1919: xxii)

The publication of the *Bullion Report* on 13 August 1810 initiated three favourable new letters of Ricardo to the *Morning Chronicle*, and many pamphlets, either supporting the report – such as William Huskisson's *The Question Concerning the Depreciation of our Currency Stated and Examined* – or attacking it – such as Charles Bosanquet's *Practical Observations on the Report of the Bullion Committee*, criticised by Ricardo in his *Reply to Mr. Bosanquet's Practical Observations on the Bullion Report*. In February 1811 Robert Malthus published in the *Edinburgh Review* an article discussing six of these pamphlets, including those of Huskisson, Bosanquet, and Ricardo; he defended a moderate bullionist position (Malthus 1811). In April a fourth edition of Ricardo's *High Price* was published, with an "Appendix" containing observations on Malthus's article and an outline of a plan for note convertibility into bullion instead of specie (to be later developed in his *Proposals for an Economical and Secure Currency* of 1816).

After the *Bullion Report* had been laid before the House of Commons, it took Francis Horner nearly one year to obtain a debate on it in a plenary session of the House. The resolutions discussed from 6 to 15 May 1811 summed-up the bullionist and anti-bullionist positions. Horner moved sixteen resolutions embodying the conclusions of the report; two of them were particularly important. The 14th stated a note-issuing rule to be applied as long as inconvertibility was maintained:

> During the continuance of the suspension of Cash Payments, it is the duty of the Directors of the Bank of England to advert to the state of the Foreign Exchanges, as well as to the price of Bullion, with a view to regulate the amount of their Issues.
>
> (Cannan 1919, Second Part: 9)

Horner's 16th resolution read as follows:

> In order to revert gradually to this Security [provided by convertibility] and to enforce meanwhile a due Limitation of the Paper of the Bank of England as

> well as of all the other Bank Paper of the Country, it is expedient to amend the Act which suspends the Cash Payments of the Bank, by altering the time, till which the Suspension shall continue, from Six Months after the Ratification of a Definitive Treaty of Peace, to that of Two Years from the present Time.
>
> (ibid: 10)

This was a complete change of view from what had been repeated by the successive Restriction Acts, because the resumption of convertibility would now occur whether after two years the war was at an end or not.

Another Member of Parliament, Nicholas Vansittart,[2] moved seventeen counter-resolutions. The third read as follows:

> The Promissory Notes of the said Company [the Bank of England] have hitherto been, and are at this time, held in public estimation to be equivalent to the legal Coin of the Realm, and generally accepted as such in all pecuniary transactions to which such Coin is lawfully applicable.
>
> (ibid: 11–12)

This amounted to rejecting the idea that the Bank of England note was depreciated.[3] Consequently, the high price of bullion and the low exchange of the pound were entirely to be explained by the adverse foreign balance, as stated by the 15th counter-resolution:

> The situation of this Kingdom, in respect of its political and commercial relations with foreign Countries, as above stated, is sufficient, without any change in the internal value of its Currency, to account for the unfavourable state of the foreign Exchanges, and for the high price of Bullion.
>
> (ibid: 19)

Vansittart's 17th counter-resolution repeated the term fixed by the last Restriction Act for the resumption of convertibility, that is, "six months after the conclusion of a Definitive Treaty of Peace" (ibid).

Although only one dissenting voice was heard among the 22 members of the Bullion Committee during the plenary debate in the House of Commons, Horner's 15 first resolutions were rejected by the 226 Members of the House by a majority of two-thirds, the last one (on the resumption of convertibility) by a majority of four-fifths. This negative vote was confirmed by the adoption of Vansittart's counter-resolutions by a majority of two-thirds. This was a defeat for the Bullionists, both on the diagnosis – the depreciation of the Bank of England note due to its overissue – and the remedies – the note-issuing rule and the resumption of convertibility. Eight more years would be needed to resurrect the debate in Parliament.

Before moving to that third round of the Bullionist Controversy, we should pay attention to the arguments of the two major authoritative figures supporting the *Bullion Report*, Henry Thornton and David Ricardo. In spite of their defeat in 1811, they would have a lasting influence on monetary theory and policy.

Another Thornton?

Thornton delivered two speeches during the 1811 debate in Parliament, one supporting Horner's resolutions, the other criticising Vansittart's counter-resolutions. At the beginning of the first, Thornton emphasised that "the main point at this moment in issue" was not the resumption of cash payments but the note-issuing rule to be adopted by the Bank of England:

> That main point was, not whether the Bank should open at any particular time, or any change be made as to the law in this respect, which would be a second consideration; but whether with a view to facilitate such opening if it should be prescribed, or with a view to secure the due maintenance of our standard during the long continuance of the restriction of cash payments, if the continuance should be deemed advisable, it was or was not expedient that the Bank should regulate the issues of its paper with a reference to the price of Bullion, and the state of the Exchanges. The Bank and the Bullion Committee were at variance on this leading and essential point.
>
> (Thornton 1811: 327)

As testified by this quotation, the note-issuing rule advocated by Thornton should apply in convertibility and inconvertibility as well, and in both cases implied the rejection of discretionary monetary policies.

In his second speech, Thornton refuted the interpretation of Locke given by the Governor of the Bank of England, according to which the export of bullion was *always* a consequence of an adverse balance of trade, a circumstance on which the Bank of England could have no influence. Thornton underlined that "Mr. Locke, therefore, refers to either of two causes the disappearance of coin" (ibid: 352), the other cause being that "two kinds of circulating medium, if of different value, cannot long continue to pass interchangeably" (ibid), a principle that also applied to the coexistence of specie and depreciated bank notes and pointed to the responsibility of the Bank of England – whose excess issue was the cause of that depreciation – in the export of bullion. And Thornton added:

> Still, however, the language of Mr. Locke was certainly inaccurate, when he said, that the 'coming and going of our treasure depends wholly on the balance of our trade,' and served to countenance that dangerous doctrine which now prevailed. According to this doctrine, the fact of the disappearance of our guineas attended with the highest imaginable price of gold, was no indication of an excess of paper or of a depreciation of it, but was simply an evidence of an unfavourable balance of trade; and the only remedy was generally to promote national industry and oeconomy. It might, indeed, be imagined by some, that according to this view of the subject, even additional issues of paper would operate as a remedy; for it might be said that an increased emission of it tended to encourage manufactures, an augmented

> quantity of manufactures supplied the means of enlarging our exports, and more extended exports improved the balance of trade; and thus an increased issue of paper might be assumed to be the means of rectifying the exchange, instead of prejudicing it. [...] It was an error to which he himself [Thornton] had once inclined, but he had stood corrected after a fuller consideration of the subject. [...] The utmost admission which he was disposed to make was, that in proceeding to limit our paper with a view to the improvement of the exchange, we ought to avoid that severity of pressure by which manufacturing industry might be seriously interrupted.
>
> (ibid: 352–3)

The contraction of the note issue was then (in 1811) the appropriate remedy, as it should already have been in 1802, contrary to what Thornton maintained at the time – "an error to which he himself had once inclined":

> Our coin had for the most part left us in 1801. The state of our trade and foreign expenditure seemed not likely to improve materially. The exchange could not be corrected, as heretofore, by the transmission of specie. The cautious limitation of our paper was, therefore, a principle to which every consideration of prudence should lead us to resort.
>
> (ibid: 354)

This "error" – having overlooked in 1802 the consequences of the fact that coins were no longer present in domestic circulation – was thus *not* to have rejected the bullionist argument that the exportation of gold (when possible) was the solution to a disequilibrium – instead of its cause – *but* to have believed that, in the circumstances of the time (the want of specie in domestic circulation), this solution could still work. It was not a theoretical error – *Paper Credit* explicitly mentioned in 1802 that a contraction of the note issue was necessary when the disequilibrium was caused by its excess – but a factual one.

To conclude on Thornton, the nature of the monetary system – convertibility or inconvertibility – does not seem to be the right key to evaluate the consistency of his positions in 1802 and 1811. In the first as in the second rounds of the Bullionist controversy, the question of the return to convertibility was for Thornton of secondary importance. Central in his positions was his analysis of the causes of and remedies to monetary disequilibrium. As to the former, Thornton affirmed that they might be two, exogenous or endogenous to the monetary system, and as to the latter he advocated discretion or the note-issuing rule, according to the particular cause of disequilibrium.

David Ricardo opposed the first statement: for him there could be only one cause of monetary disequilibrium, an excess issue of notes. For general reasons, he thus defended the same note-issuing rule as that advocated by Thornton in the circumstances of the time: a contraction motivated by the high price of bullion and the low exchange of the pound. Hence both authors converged in the defence of the *Bullion Report*.

Ricardo's positions

The main writing by Ricardo during that period was *The High Price of Bullion, a Proof of the Depreciation of Bank Notes*, published in early January 1810 and republished three times, the fourth edition of April 1811 being complemented with an *Appendix*. Together with three letters previously published in the *Morning Chronicle* in 1809, this pamphlet launched the debate that led to the *Bullion Report*. Three other letters published in the same newspaper in 1810, and the pamphlet *Reply to Mr. Bosanquet's Practical Observations on the Report of the Bullion Committee*, of January 1811, were a defence of that report.[4]

The focus of the Bullion Controversy was on the causes of the fall in the value of the pound. The starting point of Ricardo was the established fact of a high price of gold bullion in pound sterling, that is, a market price above the legal price of gold in coin (£3. 17s. 10½d. an ounce of standard gold). In other words, the current value of the pound in terms of gold taken as the standard was below its legal one. What did that fact reflect? In Ricardo's terms, of what was it "a proof"? The market price of bullion being a money price, its high level could mean that gold was "high" or that money was "low". In the first case, it was a proof of something happening on the side of gold and affecting the relation between the supply of and the demand for gold in the market, independently of money. In the second case, it was a proof of something happening on the side of money: its depreciation, measured by the spread between the market price of gold bullion and the legal price of gold in coin. Then the first task of Ricardo was to distinguish between these two cases. According to Ricardo, the distinction between them was usually obscured by confusion between the value and the price of gold:

> The error of this [Thornton's] reasoning proceeds from not distinguishing between an increase in the value of gold, and an increase in its money price.
> (*High Price*; III: 60)

This confusion would always be a matter of recurrent complaint by Ricardo, together with the related confusion between a fall in the value of money and its depreciation, and he tried to dispel both in his later writings (see Chapter 4 below).

The distinction between two possible causes of the high price of gold bullion was at the heart of the Bullion Controversy and of Ricardo's contributions to it. First Ricardo rejected the explanation by an adverse foreign balance; second he explained the high price of bullion by the depreciation of the inconvertible bank notes. He finally suggested remedies.

Ricardo's rejection of the explanation by an adverse foreign balance

In the case of a diagnosis that gold was "high", one had to look for the (real) factors affecting the relation between the supply of and the demand for it. Here another established fact should be considered: the fall in the exchange rate of the pound. A great part of the *Reply to Bosanquet* was devoted to a discussion of the amount of this fall. In contrast with the internal depreciation of the currency, which might be precisely measured by the spread between two observable magnitudes (the market price of gold bullion and the legal price of gold in coin), the external depreciation (the amount by which the exchange was "against" England) was harder to compute, because it was measured by the spread between an observed magnitude (the quoted exchange rate of the pound in terms of a chosen foreign currency) and a computed one (the par of exchange on the coins). In the case of the exchange with Hamburg – the other important centre in Europe, in addition to Paris – the computation of the par was all the more complicated since the pound was on a *de facto* gold standard and the *Mark banco* was on a *de jure* silver standard (see Appendix 1 above).

The fall in the exchange rate of the pound disqualified any factor operating at the world level (for example, a decline in gold production), since in that case the exchange rate would have been left unchanged. In the absence of an observed increase in the domestic demand for gold, there remained one candidate only: the demand for export, generated by an adverse foreign balance of England. This had been well-known for long: in such a case (whatever the reason of the adverse balance), the demand for bills of exchange denominated in foreign currencies was higher than the demand for bills denominated in pounds, and the exchange rate of the pound declined. When it reached the export bullion point, gold was demanded in London for export and its price moved upward.

The first question raised by Ricardo was thus: did the adverse foreign balance, independently of any monetary disorder, account for the high price of bullion? Thornton in his 1802 book had recognised this possibility, which, according to him, explained the crisis of 1793–1797 and the fall of the exchange in 1800–1802. Was it happening again? The answer by Ricardo, as early as his first 1809 article and in all his subsequent writings, was that not only did this *not* happen in the circumstances of the time, but it could *never* happen. An adverse foreign balance was *necessarily* a *consequence* of the depreciation of the currency, *never* its *cause*.[5]

The reason for that was the following. In normal conditions (that is, a monetary system with metallic coins and convertible bank notes, as before 1797), the fall of the exchange rate would stop at the export bullion point, computed on the basis of the legal price of gold (obtained from the Bank of England against notes) and the cost of its transportation abroad – this was the so-called "gold-points mechanism". The export of gold would then correct the balance, since gold was a commodity like any other, and its export would continue until it stopped the fall of the exchange rate.[6] But, in the conditions of the time, when bank notes had ceased to be convertible and consequently gold could not be obtained from the Bank of England at the legal price, exportable gold was only to be found in the market, and the cost of its export now also included the spread between the market price of gold bullion and the legal price of gold in coin, that is, the depreciation of the currency. The gold-points mechanism still operated (as in normal conditions), but the depreciation of the currency opened a greater margin of fall of the exchange rate:

> While the circulating medium consists, therefore, of coin undebased, or of paper-money immediately exchangeable for undebased coin, the exchange can

> never be more above, or more below, par, than the expenses attending the transportation of the precious metals. But when it consists of a depreciated paper-money, it necessarily will fall according to the degree of the depreciation.
> (ibid: 72)

The conclusion was clear-cut: the fall in the exchange rate of the pound was the *consequence* of the high price of gold bullion, not its *cause*. This disqualified the explanation of the fall in the value of the pound by autonomous real factors causing an adverse foreign balance; on the contrary the balance (gold excluded) was against England because her currency was depreciated. The explanation had to be found on the side of money.

Ricardo's explanation by the depreciation of inconvertible paper money

Turning to money, a second question arose: which money was responsible for the high price of gold bullion? It could be metallic money (specie) or paper money (bank notes). In the first case, the state of the gold and/or silver coinage was at fault. Such a possibility had been debated at the end of the seventeenth century (at the time of the 1696 silver recoinage) and again in the 1760s (leading to the gold recoinage of 1774). Was it happening again? In the second case, bank notes were depreciated, and their excess issue was at fault. The suspension of convertibility and the behaviour of the issuing banks (the Bank of England and country banks) were then placed centre stage.

On this question Ricardo's answer was again clear-cut: although he admitted that the state of the coinage could in general be responsible for the depreciation of the currency (this was the reason why Ricardo would advocate the complete substitution of bank notes for metallic coins), he denied it was the case in the conditions of the time. The general case was the following:

> An excess in the market above the mint price of gold or silver bullion, may, whilst the coins of both metals are legal tender, and there is no prohibition against the coinage of either metal, be caused by a variation in the relative value of those metals; but an excess of the market above the mint price proceeding from this cause will be at once perceived by its affecting only the price of one of the metals. Thus gold would be at or below, while silver was above, its mint price, or silver at or below its mint price, whilst gold was above.
> (ibid: 77)

This general possibility of the market price of one metal being above its legal one (signalling a depreciation of the currency in terms of that metal) explained why Ricardo was against bimetallism (ibid: 65–6). But, as shown in the quotation, it required specific conditions to be verified. Two possible situations consistent with a high price of gold bullion might be considered. The first one, with coins of both metals being undebased (that is, their actual intrinsic content in each precious metal being the legal one), happened when, for whatever reason, the market ratio between the price of gold and the price of silver rose above the legal ratio. Nobody would then bring gold to the mint to be coined, because it was more advantageous to sell it in the market; as a consequence silver became the *de facto* standard. This situation, however, was contradicted by the conditions of the time, where the mint was closed to private agents for silver and the observed market price was above the legal one for both metals (and not only gold). This latter observation was consistent with a second situation, in which coins of one metal (or both) were debased;[7] but this possibility was contradicted by the fact that debased coins were then restricted legal tender (up to £25). In the end, the depreciation of the currency could not be explained by the state of the coinage.

Therefore, as stated in the title of Ricardo's 1810 pamphlet, "the high price of bullion" was *entirely* "a proof of the depreciation of bank notes". More precisely, the Bank of England, no longer constrained by the convertibility of its notes, had overissued. It alone was at fault, because the circulation of its notes regulated that of the country banks:

> The writer [Ricardo] proposes, from the admitted principles of political economy, to advance reasons, which, in his opinion, prove, that the paper-currency of this country has long been, and now is, at a considerable discount, proceeding from a superabundance in its quantity, and not from any want of confidence in the Bank of England, or from any doubts of their ability to fulfil their engagements.
>
> (ibid: 51)

One should observe that, according to Ricardo, the ultimate cause of the observed monetary disorders was not the loss of confidence in the Bank of England note (a subjective element), but the excess of its quantity issued (an objective one). In the absence of convertibility, the issuing of notes could not be regulated; there was still a standard of the currency (gold) but it could not play its role of regulator of the quantity of money – hence of its value. This statement would be central in Ricardo's later monetary theory.

Ricardo's remedies

Having diagnosed that the disease of the pound was a monetary one, caused by an excess issue of Bank of England notes permitted by inconvertibility, Ricardo deduced the appropriate remedy: an immediate contraction of the note issue by the Bank of England:

> The remedy which I propose for all the evils in our currency, is that the Bank [of England] should gradually decrease the amount of their notes in circulation until they shall have rendered the remainder of equal value with the coins which they represent, or, in other words, till the prices of gold and silver bullion shall be brought down to their mint price.
>
> (ibid: 94)

This reduction in the market price of bullion would then allow resuming convertibility, without jeopardising the security of the Bank of England. The argument put forward by the opponents to such resumption, namely that it should be delayed until the foreign balance ceased to be against England, was then put upside down. As Ricardo had already written ironically in one of his 1809 letters:

> What becomes then of the argument which has so often been urged in Parliament, that whilst the rate of exchange continued against us, it would not be safe for the Bank to pay in specie; when it is evident that their not paying in specie is the cause of the present low exchange.
>
> (III: 20–1)

These conclusions were in agreement with the *Bullion Report*. But Ricardo went further: the return to convertibility should not be done along pre-1797 lines; the monetary system had to be adapted to increase its security against future disorders. This was the aim of a plan sketched out as early as 1811 (in the *Appendix* to the fourth edition of *High Price*) and which would be at the heart of all his later monetary proposals.

2.2 Ricardo and the resumption of convertibility (1816–1823)

The third round of the Bullionist Controversy

After the end of the war in 1815, a monetary reform took place in England in 1816 with the legal adoption of the gold standard. Until then England was legally on a bimetallic standard (gold and silver), although the golden guinea had been *de facto* the reference in domestic payments since the 1717 reform. The 1816 reform introduced a new golden coin (the sovereign) and made silver coins a token currency.

The return to convertibility seemed, however, still hazardous. In *Proposals for an Economical and Secure Currency*, Ricardo nevertheless published the same year a plan for a new monetary system, along the lines sketched in 1811. This Ingot Plan had two main aspects: on the one hand Bank of England notes were to be convertible into bullion and no longer into specie; on the other hand, the note issue should be regulated by the Bank of England according to the observed market price of bullion, the quantity of notes being expanded when this price was below the legal price at which notes could be obtained from the Bank against bullion, and contracted when this price was above the legal price at which bullion could be obtained from the Bank against notes.

The debates on the monetary system resumed in early 1819, two secret committees, one in the House of Commons and one in the House of Lords, being appointed "to consider the State of the Bank of England, with reference to the Expediency of the Resumption of Cash Payments at the period fixed by law, and into such other matters as are connected therewith" (quoted in Sraffa 1952b: 350). The committees took evidence from 24 witnesses between 8 February and

1 May; they issued their final reports on 6 and 7 May. On 26 May 1819, the House of Commons adopted the nine resolutions embodied in the report of its committee.

Four main questions

Four main interrelated questions were raised during these debates. First, should bank notes be made convertible again or should inconvertibility be prolonged? Second, if the resumption of note convertibility was decided, should it be into gold only or into gold and silver? Third, at which level should the legal price of the standard be fixed, the pre-1797 one or a higher one, to account for the past depreciation of the pound? And fourth, should notes be made convertible again into specie, or, according to Ricardo's Ingot Plan, into bullion?

Only a small minority defended the maintenance of inconvertibility. As seen above, the debate between Bullionists and Anti-Bullionists at the time of the *Bullion Report* had been about the timing of the resumption, not its desirability. For example, Nicholas Vansittart, who in 1811 had defended the maintenance of the suspension until six months after the end of the war, was now, as Chancellor of the Exchequer, in favour of the resumption, more than three years having elapsed since Waterloo. The main impetus for advocating the maintenance of inconvertibility came from the disruptions provoked by the return to a peacetime economy. The two main sectors that suffered from this movement were those that had benefited from the war: agriculture, where high prices of the products had been sustained by the reduction of imports generated by the impediments to transportation by sea, and metalworking industries, which had boomed with the needs of the war. Since these post-war adjustments occurred simultaneously with the general deflation and the consequent contraction of the note issue, the blame was put on money by interests vested in these sectors. The Birmingham School, so designated after the city that was the centre of metalworking industries, was mainly represented by Thomas Attwood, who would develop until the 1840s a doctrine favourable to the management of an inconvertible currency (see Diatkine 1994), and his brother Matthias Attwood, who opposed the resumption in Parliament. The question of whether Thomas Attwood anticipated modern analysis of inconvertible money or was simply a crude inflationist has been much debated in the literature (see Fetter 1965).

On the question of the standard, the majority was also in favour of a single one, most of the discussion being on whether it should be gold *or* silver. For example, Ricardo had favoured silver in his 1816 *Proposals* because of its use as standard by most foreign countries, but he changed his view in favour of gold in 1819, because of the effects of machinery on the production of silver, hence on its value. The double standard (gold *and* silver) was, however, supported by one of the most powerful financiers in Europe, Alexander Baring.[8] Before both committees he defended resumption at pre-war parity and Ricardo's convertibility into bullion, but he dissented on the standard, arguing that:

> Great Advantages would result to Commerce, and great general Facility in procuring a sufficient Abundance of the precious Metals, by not excluding

> either, and more especially not that Metal which forms the Standard of Value in almost every other Part of the World [silver].
>
> (House of Lords 1819: 132)

Baring's suggestion had, however, no echo in the final reports of the committees. With the general deflation spreading, Baring put it again forward on 8 February 1821 in the House of Commons when a petition of the citizens of Birmingham was discussed. Having observed that "A very considerable part of the distress, he was convinced, arose from the nature of the currency" (Hansard 1820–1830, series 2, IV: 532), he asked for a committee to investigate the question and suggested:

> The expediency of giving to the Bank the option of paying either in gold or silver, that the value of the two precious metals might be rendered more equal, and the present pound sterling, which was somewhat too high, relaxed. He wished to relax a cord which was at present stretched somewhat too tightly.
>
> (ibid: 535)

This quotation shows that Baring had by then changed his mind about the advisability of the return to pre-war parity for the pound, and he now linked his double-standard proposal with an argument in favour of devaluation. But again he did not succeed: on 9 April 1821, his proposition to appoint a Select Committee to reconsider the 1819 Resumption of Cash Payments was defeated 141 to 27.[9]

Deflation versus devaluation

As was already clear in the discussions about the maintenance of inconvertibility or the question of the double standard, what was mainly at stake in the debate on the parity between the pound and gold was the alternative between deflation and devaluation. Advocates of deflation wished to re-establish the monetary system as it was before 1797, the only difference being the substitution of a *de jure* to a *de facto* gold standard. But in their eyes this implied the fulfilment of two conditions: a contraction of note circulation, in order to lower the market price of gold bullion to the pre-war mint price of £3. 17s. 10½d. per ounce standard; and the reconstitution of the gold reserves of the Bank of England, to respond to any possible drain on them. Both conditions were liable to increase the difficulties of a return to a peacetime economy, the former by creating liquidity crunches, the latter by exerting an upward pressure on the value of gold in terms of commodities (because of the demand by the Bank of England), hence aggravating deflation. The option of devaluation was symmetrical with that of deflation: by acknowledging that the twenty-year period of inconvertibility had produced consequences which could not easily be dispensed of, it made the resumption of convertibility easier. A mint price above £3. 17s. 10½d. implied less contraction of the note circulation and lower reserves of the Bank of England, but it hurt the interests of the creditors by diminishing the value of debts in terms of gold.

Ricardo had for long warned against the evils of depreciation and complained that they were underestimated:

> No relief is ever afforded to those who suffer from a fall in the value of money, but every heart sympathizes with those who are losers by its rise.
>
> (Letter to McCulloch, 9 June 1816; VII: 38)

One of these evils was a distributional effect, which favoured accumulation at the expense of the largest part of the population:

> Depreciation of money may be beneficial because it generally favours that class who are disposed to accumulate,– but I should say that it augmented riches by diminishing happiness, that it was advantageous only by occasioning a great pressure on the labouring classes and on those who lived on fixed incomes.
>
> (Letter to Malthus, 27 June 1815; VI: 233)

During the debates around the resumption of convertibility, the discussion crystallised on the advantages derived by "the public creditor" (the holders of public debt) from the stabilisation of the pound at the pre-war parity. Ricardo maintained that his present gain was not greater than the loss he had suffered when the currency was depreciated. He declared before the House of Commons on 26 February 1823:

> It would be found that the stockholder had had nothing more than was just; and that if the interest which he had been paid in depreciated currency, upon capital which when lent had not been depreciated, were to be set against the interest which he was receiving in undepreciated currency now, upon capital which when lent had been depreciated, then, not only would the loss in the one case compensate all that had been hitherto paid in the other, but would actually be equal to a perpetual annuity to that annual amount, which he was at present receiving.
>
> (V: 252)

Among the creditors was the Bank of England; as Ricardo put it before the House of Commons on 24 May 1819:

> They [the Bank of England] had no real interest in the depreciation of the currency; it would be rather their interest to raise it, even to double the value. They were in the situation of creditors, not of debtors; their whole capital being in money or other securities representing money.
>
> (V: 13)

As always with the alternative between deflation and devaluation, the outcome depended on the balance of power between creditors and debtors. This conflict of interest was, however, softened by the fact that, although this was not the result of a deliberate policy of the Bank of England, the post-war stagnation in trade and the consequent general fall of prices had reduced the demand for Bank of England notes hence their quantity in circulation. The amount of further deflation needed to resume convertibility at pre-war parity was consequently smaller and made acceptable. The position held by Ricardo on this question was an illustration of the pragmatism with which he approached it. Being heard by the Commons' Committee on 4 March 1819, he declared that the currency would have to be raised 5 or 6 per cent in value; this figure became 4 per cent on 24 March before the Lords' Committee, and finally 3 per cent on 24 May in his speech in the plenary session of the House of Commons. There was no fickleness in these changes: they simply reflected the fall in the market price of gold bullion,[10] hence the size of the remaining adjustment necessary to make it conform to the pre-war mint price. Ricardo insisted that he only recommended such adjustment because it was actually small. Had the required deflation been greater he would have favoured devaluation. On 8 February 1821 he declared in the House of Commons:

> The question, then [in 1819], before the House was, whether it was advisable to return to the old standard, or to take the existing market rate, which was then about 4 per cent above that standard as the measure of value in future. But his hon. friend had argued on this subject as if bullion had been at that time, as it formerly was, at 5*l.* or 5*l.* 10*s.*, an ounce. If, instead of being at 4*l.* 1*s.* bullion had been much higher, he should not have proposed a recurrence to the mint standard. What he was anxious about, was not to restore the old, but to establish a fixed standard; for, however desirable it might be to a body of merchants or bankers to possess the power of raising or lowering a fourth or fifth the value of the currency, and to make 3*l.* 17*s.* 10½*d.* at one time, equivalent to 5*l.* at another, it was a power destructive of every engagement, and finally ruinous to every interest. He was not anxious to restore the old standard; but the market price of bullion being then only 4*l.* 1*s.*, he did not think it necessary to deviate from the ancient standard.
>
> (V: 73)[11]

Convertibility into bullion versus convertibility into specie

Ricardo was all the more inclined to neglect the deflationary consequences of resumption at pre-war parity since he himself advocated a plan that would allow dispensing with an increase in the gold reserves held by the Bank of England, hence with the upward pressure on the relative value of gold. This plan raised the last question debated, that of the kind of note convertibility, into specie (as before 1797) or into bullion (as in Ricardo's Ingot Plan). The House of Commons adopted a resolution compelling the Bank of England to deliver standard bullion for its notes:

> The Bank [of England] shall be liable to deliver, on demand, Gold of standard fineness, having been assayed and stamped at His Majesty's mint, a quantity

> of not less than sixty ounces being required in exchange for such an amount of Notes of the Bank as shall be equal to the value of the Gold so required. (V: 7–8)

A calendar was set to implement a gradual return to note convertibility at decreasing rates – it started on 1 February 1820 to end up on 1 May 1821 at the pre-1797 rate of £3. 17s. 10½d. per ounce of standard gold. In spite of the Bank's objection that this resolution "would have the effect of fettering the Bank so as to cause an inconvenient reduction of the currency" (V: 8), and although the return to convertibility *into coin* was announced for 1 May 1823, this three-year implementation of convertibility into bullion – with the prospect that, if it worked, it could be made permanent – was a success for Ricardo, which he described in a letter to Trower of 8 July 1819 as "the triumph of science and truth in the great councils of the Nation" (VIII: 44). Before starting his speech on the day of the general debate in the House of Commons (24 May 1819), "Mr. Ricardo rose, amidst loud invitations" (V: 9n), and at the end "The hon. member sat down amidst loud and general cheering from all sides of the House" (ibid: 17). Sraffa quotes McCulloch who also wrote that "he [Ricardo] did not rise until he was loudly called upon from all sides of the House" (Sraffa 1952a: xx). In his diary John Mallet wrote after the debate that "the phenomena of that night was Ricardo" and reported that in a private party a few days afterwards, the Duke of Wellington had "remained in conversation with him [Ricardo] for 20 minutes" (quoted by Sraffa; V: 17n). Ricardo became famous: *The New Times* of 15 May 1819 wrote that "the proposed Ingots have already obtained a name. They are called *Ricardoes* from their inventor, as the gold Napoleons were named from Bonaparte" (quoted in Sraffa 1952b: 368), and on 15 June 1819 the same newspaper observed that "Mr Ricardo's *ingots* were the fashionable novelties of the day, like the automaton chess player, or the fair Circassian" (ibid). Fashionable but not always understood: commenting on the reactions to the adoption of bullion convertibility, Bonar (1923: 292) writes: "Sheffield hears that there is a general bewilderment, especially in the West of England; for himself he thinks that not one person in ten thousand will comprehend the new measure."[12]

Unfortunately, this "triumph" did not last. During the 1819 legislative process an amendment had been introduced according to which, starting on 1 May 1822, the Bank of England would have the choice to pay its notes in coin or bullion (V: 8 n1). Knowing the hostility of the Bank of England to note convertibility into bullion, this implied to shorten the Ingot Plan experiment by one year. When the date of the return to pre-war parity (1 May 1821) came, a new act decided to anticipate this possibility of choice. Finally, Ricardo's plan was legal only from 1 February 1820 until 1 May 1821; this was purely formal, since during that period the market price of gold was below the legal price, so that only 13 "Ricardoes" were demanded as collectors' pieces out of the 2028 delivered in 1820 by the mint to the Bank of England (Sraffa 1952b: 368–70).

After the resumption of cash payments there were still debates about the responsibility of Ricardo's plan in the deflation observed in the following years, but the monetary system retained the main characteristics of the pre-1797 system: on the one hand a mixed circulation of coins issued by the mint and notes issued by the Bank of England (in the London area) and convertible into gold coins or issued by country banks (outside the London area) and convertible into Bank of England notes; on the other hand a pivotal position of the Bank of England in the system, although not associated with any explicit rule or doctrine related to its note-issuing behaviour. The 1825 monetary crisis shook confidence into that system but nearly 20 more years would elapse before another monetary controversy, this time between the Currency School and the Banking School, led to the Bank Charter Act of 1844, which settled an institutional framework for the gold-standard monetary system and associated central-banking rules that would remain operative in Britain until World War I.

Ricardo's two plans

The debates around the return to convertibility led Ricardo to design two plans, contained in two pamphlets written in 1816 and 1823 respectively (the latter being published posthumously in 1824). The link between these two writings is chapter XXVII, "On Currency and Banks" of *On the Principles of Political Economy, and Taxation*, which, in its second (1819) and third (1821) editions, quoted extensively the 1816 essay (*Proposals*), and, as early as the first edition (1817), put forward the idea, mentioned in *Proposals* and developed in the 1823 essay, of an independent public bank.[13]

The Ingot Plan (1816)

The pamphlet *Proposals for an Economical and Secure Currency* was published in 1816; it contains what is known in the literature as the Ingot Plan. It introduced two main novelties for Bank of England notes: they were to be convertible into bullion (stamped ingots valued at the legal price of gold but deprived of legal tender in domestic circulation, hence the name Ingot Plan) instead of specie (as before 1797), and their quantity issued was to vary inversely with the sign of the spread between the market price of gold bullion and the legal price at which it could be obtained (against notes) from the Bank of England. As for the notes issued by country banks, Ricardo suggested to make them convertible either into bullion or into Bank of England notes that would be legal tender.

The note-issuing rule constituted a radical change with the liberty left until then to the Bank of England directors to decide at will upon an expansion or a contraction in the note circulation. This liberty was unrestrained since the suspension of convertibility, but, according to Ricardo, it was already dangerous when (before 1797) they knew that notes issued in excess could be returned to them. The reason was that, as for any banker, they were only interested in the quality of the bills they discounted, but, disregarding the market price of gold or the exchange rate, they were not in a position to vary the overall note circulation in an appropriate way:

> Though I am fully assured, that it is both against the interest and the wish of the Bank [of England] to exercise this power to the detriment of the public, yet, when I contemplate the evil consequences which might ensue from a sudden and great reduction of the circulation, as well as from a great addition to it, I cannot but deprecate the facility with which the State has armed the Bank with so formidable a prerogative.
>
> (*Proposals*; IV: 69; *Principles*; I: 359–60)

The management principle of the note issue suggested by Ricardo was to eliminate these "evil consequences". As for the first provision of the plan – the ingot principle, that is, note convertibility into bullion – it introduced a revolutionary change in the monetary system: the circulation would be composed of bank notes *only*, and the elimination of metallic coins amounted to demonetise gold as domestic means of payment. Gold remained solely the standard regulating the value of money in a more economical but above all more secure way:

> To secure the public against any other variations in the value of the currency than those to which the standard itself is subject, and, at the same time, to carry on the circulation with a medium the least expensive, is to attain the most perfect state to which a currency can be brought.
>
> (*Proposals*; IV: 66; *Principles*; I: 356–7)

That the object of the plan was to substitute (convertible) paper money for specie was stated by Ricardo in the sentence following immediately the four pages of *Proposals* inserted in *Principles*:

> A currency is in its most perfect state when it consists wholly of paper money, but of paper money of an equal value with the gold which it professes to represent.
>
> (*Principles*; I: 361)

When the debates on the return to convertibility resumed in 1819, Ricardo defended his Ingot Plan successfully in the House of Commons (where he had been elected), which adopted it as the basis of the return to convertibility. As seen above, this plan was finally abandoned when convertibility at pre-war parity was resumed on 1 May 1821. In spite of his plan having been dropped, Ricardo was accused, inside and outside Parliament, of being responsible for the deflation which followed the resumption of cash payments. In a controversy with Charles Western which covered two Parliamentary sessions (it started on 12 June 1822 and ended up on 11 June 1823), Ricardo maintained that the resumption of cash payments could only explain an increase in the value of money up to 10 per cent, one half as a consequence of the return to the pre-1797 mint price of gold, the other half as a consequence of an increase in the world value of gold, provoked by the purchases of the Bank of England in the perspective of a return to convertibility *into coin*. In Ricardo's view, his Ingot Plan could not be held responsible for that outcome, since, by economising on the gold reserves of the Bank of England, convertibility *into bullion*, if prolonged indefinitely, would have avoided half of the deflation having a monetary origin.

There was more: Ricardo was convinced that his plan had been torpedoed by the Bank of England, which, from the very beginning, had opposed it. Another plan was found in his papers after his death on 11 September 1823; it developed an idea already present in *Proposals* and in *Principles*: the transfer of the note issue from the Bank of England to an independent public bank (for a comparison between the two plans, see below Chapter 9).

The Plan for a national bank (1823)

Besides the Ingot Plan, a large part of the 1816 pamphlet had been devoted to a critique of the excessive profits made by the Bank of England in its lending activity to the Government (an activity which had been the initial reason of its establishment in 1694). This cost incurred by the management of the National Debt was an inconvenience that added up to the incompetence of the Bank of England in the management of the note issue. Both defects could be eradicated if the monopoly of the note issue were transferred from the Bank of England to a public bank, whose independent commissioners would also manage the National Debt.

This idea appeared in a letter to Malthus of 10 September 1815:

> I cannot help considering the issuing of paper money as a privilege which belongs exclusively to the state. – I regard it as a sort of seignorage, and I am convinced, if the principles of currency were rightly understood, that Commissioners might be appointed independent of all ministerial controul who should be the sole issuers of paper money.
>
> (VI: 268)

It was introduced publicly in *Proposals* and in the first edition of *Principles* (1817), and preserved for the two later editions in addition to the Ingot Plan. It was only when it became clear in 1821 that the Bank of England had torpedoed the Ingot Plan that Ricardo developed his other idea in a proper plan.

The *Plan for the Establishment of a National Bank* was written by Ricardo in July and August 1823, shortly before his death, and was published by his brother Moses Ricardo in February 1824. It had been anticipated in Chapter XXVII of *Principles*, where the proposal of an independent public bank included the ingot and management principles, which in this case were transferred from the existing Bank of England note to a new public note. Its advantage was to do away with the interest paid by the State on the money borrowed from the Bank of England, and consequently to save individuals the taxes necessary to pay for that charge of interest. Ricardo discarded two objections which could be raised to that proposal.

The first objection was that a public note issue would soon become beyond control. Ricardo responded as follows:

> Under an arbitrary Government, this objection would have great force; but, in a free country, with an enlightened legislature, the power of issuing paper money, under the requisite checks of convertibility at the will of the holder, might be safely lodged in the hands of commissioners appointed for that special purpose, and they might be made totally independent of the control of ministers.
>
> (*Principles*; I: 362)

The second objection was that, by removing the possibility of issuing notes through the discounting of bills, the proposal would reduce the availability of borrowed funds to merchants and slow down their activity. Ricardo was here straightforward: referring to his theory of value and rent, he maintained that the rate of interest at which the Bank of England lent to some of the merchants had no influence on the overall accumulation of capital, which would remain the same under the proposed banking system:

> In another part of this work, I have endeavoured to shew, that the real value of a commodity is regulated, not by the accidental advantages which may be enjoyed by some of its producers, but by the real difficulties encountered by that producer who is least favoured. It is so with respect to the interest for money; it is not regulated by the rate at which the Bank will lend, whether it be 5, 4, or 3 per cent, but by the rate of profits which can be made by the employment of capital, and which is totally independent of the quantity, or of the value of money.
>
> (ibid: 363)

In his 1823 plan, Ricardo again advocated that the issuing of notes and discount lending, linked in the Bank of England, could and should be separated. He stated that:

> Five Commissioners shall be appointed, in whom the full power of issuing all the paper money of the country shall be exclusively vested.
>
> (*Plan for a National Bank*; IV: 285)

This had three consequences. First, the Bank of England would remain solely a discount bank, like any other. Second, since the new bank got the monopoly of the note issue for the whole country – and not only for the London area, as was the case previously for the Bank of England – country banks were also deprived of their issuing power. Third, after his Ingot Plan had been abandoned in 1821, Ricardo stepped back to a mixed monetary system (coins and notes) and to note convertibility into specie; he nevertheless suggested obliging the new bank to sell gold bullion at a fixed price, which amounted to separate convertibility for domestic and foreign payments. Moreover, Ricardo stood firmly on the management principle of varying the note issue with the observed market price of gold bullion ("Regulating their issues by the price of gold, the commissioners could never err"; ibid: 293). This variation would be obtained through purchases or sales by the bank, either on the gold-bullion market or on the Government-securities market.[14] The bank was, however, forbidden to lend directly to the State:

> I propose also to prevent all intercourse between these Commissioners and ministers, by forbidding every species of money transaction between them. The Commissioners should never, on any pretence, lend money to Government, nor be in the slightest degree under its control or influence.
>
> (ibid: 282)

Published by his brother Moses five months after Ricardo's death, the plan did not arouse much attention, then or in 1838 when another of his brothers, Samson, republished it as an appendix to a pamphlet.

2.3 Conclusion: the legacy of Ricardo's monetary battles

The usual – albeit incorrect – assimilation of Ricardo with monetary orthodoxy manifests itself by an overemphasis, in much of the literature since, on what that doctrine inherited from him. One may here mention the supposed link with the *Currency School*, through which Ricardo's orthodoxy is usually acknowledged. Although this current of thought used the posthumous patronage of Ricardo, the orthodox model of central banking it implemented was in fact at odds with his explicit principles, and Ricardo's most important monetary proposals – note convertibility into bullion, management and public monopoly of the note issue – did not find their way until the twentieth century.

The division of the Bank of England in an Issue department and a Banking department, which was embodied in the Bank Charter Act of 1844, is often presented as deriving from Ricardo's conception of central banking. This is misleading for two reasons. First, this division maintained the note issue in the hands of (to use Ricardo's words) "a company of merchants" (the Bank of England), instead of nationalising it. Second, it did put an end to the liberty of the Bank's directors to vary the issue at will, but replaced it by a rule that linked the change in the quantity of notes issued to the variation of the metallic reserves of the Issue department. This was at odds with Ricardo's statement that the note issue should be *managed*,[15] irrespective of the amount of the metallic reserves of the issuer and of the absolute volume of the existing circulation, but solely in reference to the market price of the standard.[16]

This discrepancy between Ricardo's proposed regulation of the note issue and the "Currency Principle" was not just the outcome of circumstances. It was rooted in different conceptions of the monetary system. The Currency School maintained a mixed monetary system (where domestic circulation was composed of full-bodied gold coins, bank notes convertible into gold coins, and token silver currency) that contrasted with Ricardo's proposal of an exclusive circulation of paper convertible into gold bullion. It also applied the two main aspects of Hume's price-specie flow mechanism: its automaticity and the interdependence between domestic circulation and international payments. The metallic reserve of the Bank of England which constrained the note issue varied with the foreign balance, which in turn depended on the volume of domestic circulation; this automatic adjustment – which was unable to prevent the crises of 1847, 1857, and 1866, when the Bank Charter Act had to be suspended – contrasted with Ricardo's attempt, thanks to convertibility into bullion, to separate domestic note circulation and international bullion payments (see Chapter 8 below).

Ricardo's concept of convertibility *de facto* restricted to foreign payments, as it was embodied in the ingot principle, was his belated but lasting legacy. Later known as the gold-exchange standard, it was resurrected as a practical device by Alfred Marshall in 1887 and by Alexander Lindsay in 1892, with explicit reference in both cases to Ricardo. Marshall (1887: 204) stressed that "the currency scheme which I wish to submit for consideration differs from his [Ricardo's 1816 *Proposals*] only by being bimetallic instead of monometallic" (for a comparison between Ricardo's Ingot Plan and Marshall's bimetallic scheme, see Deleplace 2013b). As for the pamphlet published by Lindsay in 1892, it was entitled *Ricardo's Exchange Remedy* (see Chapter 8 below). In 1913 Keynes observed approvingly that "in the last ten years the gold-exchange standard has become the prevailing monetary system of Asia" (Keynes 1913: 25). As is well known, this system was extended to other countries in interwar years, and later institutionalised, with qualifications, at Bretton Woods.

Appendix 2 offers a sample of the attacks mounted at Ricardo during his battles on currency and banks, and lists the weapons he used: his monetary works, whether published, written for publication, left as notes, sent in correspondence, or reported as speeches. These writings constitute the basis on which Part II of the present book proposes a reconstruction of Ricardo's theory of money.

Appendix 2: Attacks and weapons

During the debates in which he took part Ricardo aroused contrasted opinions. Everyone praised the clearness of his mind and his gentle manners; his death was lamented in the *Morning Chronicle* as "a great national calamity" (Gilbert 1987: 22). However, he was often criticised for being too much of "a philosopher" and attacked as "an oracle". To illustrate the battles he fought on currency and banks, a selection of opinions expressed by his contemporaries is given below, with some of the answers he gave to them. For another example of the attacks made upon him, see below Appendix 4. Biographical information may be found in Moses Ricardo (1824), Sraffa (1952a, 1955a, 1955b), Weatherall (1976), Henderson (1997). Since Ricardo considered himself as a feeble orator, he mostly relied on writing to defend himself. A list of his contributions on money is also given below; with the exception of five letters, they are published in the Sraffa edition of *The Works and Correspondence of David Ricardo.*

1. Attacks: critical opinions on Ricardo

The basic critique addressed to Ricardo in his lifetime was to be a "theorist", as Mallet's diary on 7 May 1821 reported him having said about the members of the Agricultural Committee:

> Ricardo says that they look upon him as a mere Theorist, but that they are very civil and allow him to take his own course with a view of establishing his principles by evidence.
>
> (quoted in Sraffa 1952a: xxv)

This mixture of critique and respect is illustrated by the following excerpt of the same diary on 14 January 1820:

> It is impossible to be in company with Ricardo and not to admire his placid temper, the candour of his disposition, his patience and attention, and the clearness of his mind; but he is as the French would express it "*herissé de principes*" he meets you upon every subject that he has studied *with a mind made up,* and opinions in the nature of mathematical truths. He spoke of Parliamentary reform and vote by Ballot as a man who would bring such things about, and destroy the existing system tomorrow, if it were in his power, and without the slightest doubt as to the result. And yet there was not one person at Table, several of them Individuals whose opinion he highly valued, who would have agreed with him. It is this very quality of the man's mind; his entire disregard of experience and practice, which makes me doubtful of his opinions on political oeconomy.
>
> (quoted by Sraffa, VIII: 152n)

One of Ricardo's opponents in Parliament, Lord Brougham – the man who dubbed him "an oracle" (see below) – expressed the same sentiment in a speech of 30 May 1820 with the following image:

> His hon. friend, the member for Portarlington [Ricardo], had argued as if he had dropped from another planet.
>
> (V: 56)

And in a sketch of Ricardo in Parliament written sixteen years after his death he observed:

> His views were often, indeed, abundantly theoretical, sometimes too refined for his audience, occasionally extravagant from his propensity to follow a

> right principle into all its consequences, without duly taking into account in practice the condition of things to which he was applying it.
>
> (quoted in Sraffa 1952a: xxxiii)

In a speech of 8 February 1821, another Member of Parliament, Alexander Baring, criticised Ricardo's monetary views "although the establishment of such a standard might be more agreeable to the views of the Royal Society, or other abstract philosophers, who would regulate weights and measures by the vibrations of the pendulum" (V: 77) and on 7 May 1822 Sir T. Lethbridge trusted the House would not be led away by "the abominable theories of political economists" (ibid: 169). In a letter to Thomas Smith, John Wishaw summed-up how Ricardo was received in the House of Commons: "I think, indeed, that, considering the audience whom he addressed, he spoke too much as a theorist, and in a manner likely to be misrepresented" (V: 128 n1).

Although he was a shy person – "I do not know whether you know it, but I am very shy, which I, sometimes, perhaps generally, hide under as bold an exterior as I can assume" (Letter to Maria Edgeworth, 13 December 1822; IX: 235) – Ricardo nevertheless maintained firmly that his approach to the problems was appropriate. Answering Baring he declared before the House on 9 April 1821:

> His hon. friend's theories thus changed very often; his own were unchanged, though he had been represented as moving with the vibrations of a pendulum, and entertaining views of placing the currency in a degree of perfection not suited to our situation.
>
> (V: 106–7)

His belief in theory was not different in public from what he boldly affirmed in his correspondence with his friend Malthus, as in a letter of 7 October 1815:

> I should be more pleased that we did not so materially differ. If I am too theoretical which I really believe is the case, – you I think are too practical. There are so many combinations, – so many operating causes in Political Economy, that there is great danger in appealing to experience in favor of a particular doctrine, unless we are sure that all the causes of variation are seen and their effects duly estimated.
>
> (VI: 295)

Beyond his personal case, what was in dispute with his opponents in Parliament was what Ricardo called "the science of political economy", as in several speeches in 1823:

> Mr. Ricardo said, he remembered, that at the termination of the last session, he had frequently to repel the attacks which were made upon the science of political economy.
>
> (21 February 1823; V: 248)

> The hon. member for Weymouth had observed, that the petitioners knew nothing about political economy, the principles of which seemed to change every two or three years. Now, the principles of true political economy never changed; and those who did not understand that science had better say nothing about it.
>
> (21 May 1823; V: 296)

> An hon. member for Bristol had talked about political economy; but the words 'political economy' had, of late, become terms of ridicule and reproach. They were used as a substitute for an argument.
>
> (9 June 1823; V: 307)

This general atmosphere against Political Economy concentrated on Ricardo, as it appeared when after his death some friends raised funds for projected lectures on political economy in his honour. In a letter of 10 January 1824 to McCulloch – who would deliver the lectures – James Mill told the story:

> You can have little notion of the dread of publicity which hangs over many of us: and of the aversion to Political Economy which yet is here almost universal. Take this as an example: When Hume who has a project of his own for a bust and tablet to Ricardo in West. Abbey, asked subscription from Hudson Gurney M.P., he said he would give £50 if needed to the bust, but not one farthing to the lectures. Think of the *terrae filius*! And Huskisson, when applied to, in like manner, by Hume, slunk away, saying, he was by no means convinced of the utility of such lectures; and besides, in his public situation, he was not yet prepared to like having his name published, as that of a Political Economist. Oh, you coward! said Hume to him. And he replied I must confess it is the right name.
>
> (quoted in Porta (ed.) 1992b: 58; Joseph Hume, Hudson Gurney, and William Huskisson were Members of Parliament)

In addition to the general critique of being a "theorist", Ricardo was also attacked on particular subjects on which he stood at odds with most of his fellow MPs. In a letter to McCulloch of 13 June 1820 he confessed about his position in favour of free trade:

> I am treated as an ultra reformer and a visionary on commercial subjects by both Agriculturists and Manufacturers.
>
> (VIII: 197)

He also felt isolated on his proposal of repaying the National Debt by a once-for-all tax on property, as he told Trower in a letter of 28 December 1819:

> There must be I think an end of loans; we cannot go on adding to a debt of 800 millions. A great deal more has been said than I intended there should be of an incidental observation of mine respecting the payment of the debt, as it usually happens I am attacked by the most opposite parties.
>
> (ibid: 147)

This iconoclast proposal raised a condescending reaction by two MPs used to criticise Ricardo's theoretical inclination:

> There was however one point on which he had wished so great an oracle, as he must ever consider him on such subjects, had not pronounced the decided opinion he had.
>
> (Lord Brougham, 24 December 1819; V: 40)

> To begin with the plan of paying off a part of the debt, by a new disposition of the property of the country, he [Baring] must be allowed to say, that it was the plan of a man who might calculate well and read deeply, but who had not studied mankind. It was ingenious in theory, and obvious enough; but not very sound for practice. He did not pretend to any thing like the reach of intellect possessed by his hon. friend, but he thought his hon. friend sometimes over-reached himself, and lost sight of man, and of all practical conclusions.
>
> (Alexander Baring, 6 March 1823; V: 270)

It was of course on money that the most violent attacks occurred, all the more so since Ricardo's Ingot Plan had provided the basis of Peel's bill of 1819. In his 1839 sketch of Ricardo in Parliament, Lord Brougham recollected:

> He always greatly undervalued the amount of the depreciation in the currency upon prices generally, estimating it solely by the difference between the Mint price and the Market price of gold; and so confidently did he believe in his speculative estimate, that his practical plan for restoring the currency was grounded upon it. But while such were his errors, and those of a kind to excite very strong feelings in certain large and important classes in the House of Commons, he was uniformly and universally respected for the sterling qualities of his capacity and his character, which were acknowledged by all.
>
> (quoted in Sraffa 1952a: xxxiii)

Another MP, Edmond Wodehouse complained on 12 June 1823 that Ministers:

> [W]ere too ready to listen to the suggestions of the hon. member for Portarlington (Mr. Ricardo), whose conclusions on this head [the currency] appeared to him to be utterly incomprehensible. [...] To believe that he had a clear perception on the subject of money, was utterly impossible.
>
> (V: 321–2)

Ricardo suffered from these attacks, especially when he felt that his views were misrepresented. He nevertheless believed that finally justice would be done to him, as shown by the following letter of 16 December 1822 to Malthus:

> I am sorry to find the agricultural distress continue – I was in hopes that it would have subsided before this time. I suppose we shall hear much on this

> subject next session of Parliament and that I shall be a mark for all the country gentlemen. There is not an opinion I have given on this subject which I desire to recall – I only regret that my adversaries do not do me justice, and that they put sentiments in my mouth which I never uttered. Dr. Copplestone in his article in the Quarterly Review charges me with maintaining the absurd doctrine that the price of gold bullion is a sure test of the value of bullion and currency. A Mr. Paget has addressed a (printed) letter to me in which I am accused of holding the same opinion, and every body knows how pertinaciously Cobbet persists in saying that I have always done so. I must fight my cause as well as I can, I know it is an honest one (in spite of Mr. Western's insinuations) and if it be also founded in truth, and on correct views, justice will be finally done to me.
>
> (IX: 249–50)

2. Weapons: Ricardo's contributions on money (with the volume and pagination in Works*)*

The Bullion Essays (1809–1811)

The Price of Gold. Three contributions to the *Morning Chronicle*, 1809 (III: 13–46)
The High Price of Bullion, a Proof of the Depreciation of Bank Notes, 1810–1811 (III: 47–127)
Three letters to the *Morning Chronicle* on the *Bullion Report*, 1810 (III: 129–53)
Reply to Mr. Bosanquet's 'Practical Observations on the Report of the Bullion Committee', 1811 (III: 155–256)

Notes from manuscripts of 1810–1811

Notes on Bentham's 'Sur les Prix', 1810–1811 (III: 267–341)
Notes on the *Bullion Report* and Evidence, 1810 (III: 347–78)
Notes on Trotter's *Principles of Currency and Exchanges*, 1810 (III: 381–403)
Observations on Trower's notes on Trotter, 1811 (III: 407–9)
Observations on Vansittart's propositions respecting money, bullion and exchanges, 1811 (III: 415–23)

Proposals for an Economical and Secure Currency, 1816 (IV: 49–141)

On the Principles of Political Economy, and Taxation, 1817–1821 (I: 1–442)

The 1819–1823 papers

This corpus is composed of (a) parts of pamphlets and papers written by Ricardo for publication, whether they were actually published – such as *On Protection to Agriculture* (1822) or some speeches in Parliament – or not – such as a draft of a letter to a newspaper; (b) manuscript notes; (c) reports of speeches in Parliament and of evidence before committees of Parliament.

Papers written by Ricardo for publication:

On Protection to Agriculture, April 1822, Section V "On the Effects produced on the Price of Corn by Mr. Peel's Bill for restoring the Ancient Standard" (IV: 222–35) and "Conclusion" (ibid: 261–6)
Draft of a letter to a newspaper on the effects of Peel's bill, December 1821 (V: 515–21)
Speech in Parliament on Bank of England – Resumption of Cash Payments, 24 May 1819; transcript for *Hansard* prepared by Ricardo (V: 9–17)[17]
Speech in Parliament on Mr. Western's motion respecting the altered state of the currency, 10 July 1822; original transcript in Ricardo's handwriting (V: 231–45)[18]
Speech in Parliament on Mr. Western's motion concerning the resumption of cash payments, 11 June 1823; transcript for *Hansard* prepared by Ricardo (V: 309–21)[19]
Plan for the Establishment of a National Bank, July–August 1823, published posthumously in February 1824 (IV: 275–300)

Manuscript notes:

Notes on Blake's *Observations on the Effects Produced by the Expenditure of Government during the Restriction of Cash Payments*, March 1823 (IV: 327–56)
"Absolute Value and Exchangeable Value", August–September 1823 (IV: 361–412)

Reports of Ricardo's declarations:

Major speeches in Parliament on the subject (other than the three mentioned above):

Petition of the Merchants of London Respecting Commercial Distress, 24 December 1819 (V: 37–41)
Commercial Restrictions – Petition of the Merchants of London, 8 May 1820 (V: 42–6)
Loan – Ways and Means, 9 June 1820 (V: 58–62)
Supply – Bank of Ireland, 2 February 1821 (V: 70)
Trade of Birmingham – Petition of the Merchants, 8 February 1821 (V: 71–8)
Bank Cash Payments Bill, 9 April 1821 (V: 105–8)
Motion for a committee on the agricultural distress, 18 February 1822 (V: 129–38)
Banks of England, and of Ireland, 8 March 1822 (V: 143–4)
Agricultural distress and the financial and other measures for its relief, 29 April 1822 (V: 155–9)
Agricultural Distress Report, 7 May 1822 (V: 162–76)
Absentees, 16 May 1822 (V: 186–8)
Mr. Western's motion concerning the resumption of cash payments, 12 June 1822 (V: 198–218)
The budget, 1 July 1822 (V: 220–3)
Agricultural distress – Surrey petition, 26 February 1823 (V: 251–5)

Evidence before committees of Parliament:

Minutes of evidence taken before the Select Committee on the Usury Laws, 30 April 1818 (V: 337–47)
Minutes of evidence taken before the Secret Committee on the Expediency of the Bank resuming Cash Payments – House of Commons, 4, 19 March 1819 (V: 371–415)
Minutes of evidence taken before the Lords Committees appointed a Secret Committee to enquire into the State of the Bank of England, with Reference to the Expediency of the Resumption of Cash Payments at the Period now fixed by Law, 24, 26 March 1819 (V: 416–57)

Speech outside Parliament:

Meeting at Hereford in Honour of Joseph Hume, 7 December 1821 (V: 471–4)

Letters, 1810–1823 (with reference to subjects in relation to money)

To Francis Horner, 5 February 1810 (VI: 1–7) (On the causes of depreciation)
To Horner, 6 February 1810 (VI: 8–10) (On the par with Hamburg)
To Sir Philip Francis, 24 April 1810 (VI: 10–13) (On Country Banks' notes)
To James Mill, 1 January 1811 (VI: 14–18) (On Bentham's "Sur les prix" about the limit to circulation)
To Thomas Robert Malthus, 18 June 1811 (VI: 23–8) (On the absence of difference between bullion and other commodities, and on the significance of redundancy)
To Malthus, 17 July 1811 (VI: 35–40) (On redundancy and international adjustment)
To Spencer Perceval, 27 July 1811 (VI: 43–5) (On the Ingot Plan)
To Mill, 26 September 1811 (VI: 51–6) (On the necessity of a standard)
To Malthus, 22 October 1811 (VI: 63–5) (On excess of currency and its exportation)
To George Tierney, 11 December 1811 (VI: 67–71) (On arresting depreciation and returning to the standard with a decreasing scale)
To Malthus, 22 December 1811 (VI: 72–6) (On redundancy and international adjustment)
To Horner, 4 January 1812 (VI: 78–81) (On the determination of exchange)
To Malthus, 17 December 1812 (VI: 87–8) (idem)
To Leonard Horner, 6 December 1812 (Depoortère 2015) (depreciation of the coin as distinct from its deterioration; difficulty of calculating the par of exchange; necessity to discard small notes when calculating the increase in circulation)
To Malthus, 25 February 1813 (VI: 88–9) (On the determination of exchange)
To Malthus, 22 March 1813 (VI: 90–1) (On bullion merchants)
To Malthus, 30 December 1813 (VI: 97–9) (On the calculation of the pars of exchange with Amsterdam and Hamburg)
To Malthus, 1 January 1814 (VI: 100–1) (idem)

To Malthus, 26 June 1814 (VI: 107–9) (Demand only limited by production; international trade is barter)
To Jean-Baptiste Say, 24 December 1814 (VI: 165–6) (On the Ingot Plan and the theory of money)
To Malthus, 13 January 1815 (VI: 169–71) (On the level of prices of the mass of commodities)
To Malthus, 27 March 1815 (VI: 202–6) (On money as a commodity)
To Malthus, 4 April 1815 (VI: 209–11) (idem)
To Malthus, 21 April 1815 (VI: 219–21) (On adjustment in the production of corn)
To Malthus, 27 June 1815 (VI: 232–4) (On two causes of rise in money prices)
To Say, 18 August 1815 (VI: 246–9) (Money not a good measure of value)
To Malthus, 10 September 1815 (VI: 267–9) (On a public bank)
From Malthus to Ricardo, 1 October 1815 (VI: 288–92) (On disagreement with *Proposals*, because of the instability of an exclusive paper circulation)
To Malthus, 7 October 1815 (VI: 292–5) (On the aim of *Proposals*)
From Malthus to Ricardo, 15 October 1815 (VI: 298–9) (On disagreement with *Proposals*, because of the instability of an exclusive paper circulation)
To Malthus, 17 October 1815 (VI: 300–2) (Answer to Malthus's critique of *Proposals*)
To Mill, 24 October 1815 (VI: 310–4) (On the topics covered by *Proposals*)
From Hutches Trower to Ricardo, 26 November 1815 (VI: 325–8) (On the cause of the fall in the price of bullion)
To Trower, 25 December 1815 (VI: 343–5) (On MS of *Proposals*)
To Mill, 30 December 1815 (VI: 347–9) (On the projected *Principles*)
From Malthus to Ricardo, 9 February 1816 (VII: 20–1) (On the variability induced by convertibility into bullion)
To Malthus, 23 February 1816 (VII: 23–5) (The most important topic of Political Economy; the sale of *Proposals*; Bank of England profits)
To John Ramsey McCulloch, 9 June 1816 (VII: 37–8) (On the fall in precious metals and the rise in paper)
To John Broadley, 14 June 1816 (VII: 41–4) (A lecture on money and exchange)
To Mill, 8 September 1816 (VII: 65–7) (On slow adjustment in prices when there is a big change in the structure of demand)
To Malthus, 24 January 1817 (VII: 119–21) (On "permanent" vs "temporary")
To John Sinclair, 4 May 1817 (VII: 151) (On paper circulation)
To Pascoe Grenfell, 27 August 1817 (Heertje 1991: 520–2) (On the rate of interest)
To Malthus, 21 October 1817 (VII: 199–203) (idem)
To Malthus, 30 January 1818 (VII: 250–2) (On the influence of supply and demand on prices)
To Trower, 18 September 1818 (VII: 296–300) (On the difference between value and price)
To Mill, 22 December 1818 (VII: 371–3) (On the last portion of capital)
To Mill, 28 December 1818 (VII: 376–83) (On the causes of exchange value in Smith)
To McCulloch, 3 January 1819 (VIII: 1–4) (On metal to choose as standard; on the last portion of capital)
To McCulloch, 7 April 1819 (VIII: 20–3) (On the alarm of Bank directors)

To Thomas Smith, 27 April 1819 (Heertje and Weatherall 1978: 569–71) (On the distress of the economy)
To McCulloch, 8 May 1819 (VIII: 26–8) (On Ingot Plan)
To Trower, 28 May 1819 (VIII: 31–3) (On victory for the Ingot Plan)
To Trower, 1 June 1819 (VIII: 33–5) (Specie payments restrain the circulation)
From McCulloch to Ricardo, 30 May 1819 (VIII: 35–8) (On victory for the Ingot Plan)
To McCulloch, 22 June 1819 (VIII: 38–41) (On Ingot Plan made permanent; on bills of exchange)
To Trower, 8 July 1819 (VIII: 44–7) (On the triumph of science)
To Malthus, 21 September 1819 (VIII: 72–5) (Money a variable commodity)
To Trower, 25 September 1819 (VIII: 77–81) (On victory for the Ingot Plan)
To McCulloch, 2 October 1819 (VIII: 85–94) (On the exchange rate)
To James Brown, 13 October 1819 (VIII: 100–4) (On money as an equivalent)
To McCulloch, 18 December 1819 (VIII: 140–3) (On the par of exchange and gold points; on value)
To Trower, 28 January 1820 (VIII: 152–6) (On the effect of taxation on prices)
To McCulloch 2 May 1820 (VIII: 178–83) (On the invariable standard; two causes of value)
To John Sinclair, 11 May 1820 (VIII: 186–7) (On paper money only)
To McCulloch, 13 June 1820 (VIII: 191–7) (On standard as medium between extremes; two causes of value; last portion of capital)
To Malthus, 9 October 1820 (VIII: 276–80) (On value fixed by sellers; object of political economy; two causes of value)
To Mill, 16 November 1820 (VIII: 294–7) (Critique of Bentham's annuity notes)
To McCulloch, 25 January 1821 (VIII: 342–5) (On the standard as a means between extremes)
To Trower, 2 March 1821 (VIII: 348–51) (Discussions with Malthus; no rise in the value of money higher than 10 per cent)
To McCulloch, 30 June 1821 (VIII: 396–400) (On the temptation of altering the standard; on the effects of depreciation; movements of capital when profit rates diverge)
To Malthus, 9 July 1821 (IX: 14–18) (Giving up the Ingot Plan)
To John Wheatley, 18 September 1821 (IX: 71–4) (On the effects of resumption; devaluation)
To Malthus, 28 September 1821 (IX: 80–6) (On the level of prices; differences in the rates of profit across countries)
To Trower, 11 December 1821 (IX: 120–4) (On Peel's bill; "oracle")
To Mill, 18 December 1821 (IX: 125–33) (On the behaviour of the Bank of England; gold points)
To McCulloch, 3 January 1822 (IX: 138–42) (On purchases of gold by the Bank of England; Ingot Plan a permanent system)
To Trower, 25 January 1822 (IX: 151–5) (On the cause of low price of corn)
To McCulloch, 8 February 1822 (IX: 156–9) (On the cause of agricultural distress)
To Trower, 20 February 1822 (IX: 165–7) (idem)

To Trower, 5 March 1822 (IX: 174–7) (Ricardo not understood; "Ingot plan of payment")
To McCulloch, 19 March 1822 (IX: 177–9) (On value not entirely explained by labour)
To Trower, 9 June 1822 (IX: 201–2) (On the amount of circulation)
To Maria Edgeworh, 13 December 1822 (IX: 233–40) (On greatest happiness; price)
To Malthus, 16 December 1822 (IX: 247–51) (On attacks at Ricardo on the price of bullion)
To Grenfell, 19 January 1823 (Deleplace, Depoortère and Rieucau 2013: 4–7) (Critique of the double standard)
To Trower, 30 January 1823 (IX: 266–70) (Ricardo a reformer; double standard)
To Francis Finch, 24 February 1823 (Heertje, Weatherall and Polak 1985: 1091–2) (On the exportation of capital)
To McCulloch, 25 March 1823 (IX: 275–7) (On the definition of depreciation and actual depreciation)
To Malthus, 29 April 1823 (IX: 280–4) (On different rates of profit across countries)
To McCulloch, 3 May 1823 (IX: 284–7) (On movements of gold)
To Malthus, 28 May 1823 (IX: 297–300) (On the definition of absolute value, in particular conditions)
To Malthus, 13 July 1823 (IX: 303–6) (On the measure of value)
To Trower, 24 July 1823 (IX: 311–5) (idem)
To Trower, 24 July 1823 (IX: 318–9) (idem)
To Malthus, 3 August 1823 (IX: 320–6) (On the measure of value; Plan for a National Bank)
To Mill, 7 August 1823 (IX: 326–30) (idem)
To McCulloch 8 August 1823 (IX: 330–1) (idem)
To Malthus, 15 August 1823 (IX: 345–52) (On the measure of value; method of critique; labour value; international trade)
To McCulloch, 15 August 1823 (IX: 353–7) (On the measure of value)
To McCulloch, 21 August 1823 (IX: 358–62) (On the measure of value; causes of value)
To Malthus, 31 August 1823 (IX: 380–2) (On the measure of value)
To Mill, 5 September 1823 (IX: 385–8) (idem)

Notes

1 This chapter develops Deleplace (2015a and 2015b). On the historical context of Ricardo's contributions to the monetary debates, see Sraffa (1951c, 1951e, 1952a, 1952b) and Davis (2005). Although Ricardo himself used the word "battle", I have borrowed the title of the chapter from the far-reaching book by the late Gilles Dostaler *Kcynes and his Battles* (Dostaler 2007).
2 He would be later Chancellor of the Exchequer from 1812 to 1822.
3 Volume III of Ricardo's *Works* (pp. 415–23) contains observations in manuscript form on Vansittart's ten first Resolutions. On the third Ricardo wrote:

> The Promissory Notes of the Bank of England cannot justly be said to be at 'this time held to be equivalent to the legal coin of the Realm' when the coin is bought at a premium of 6 and 7 pc^t, – and when it is prevented from openly rising to 15 or 18 pc^t (its real and intrinsic value above paper) by the terror of the law which deters

all men of character from engaging in a traffic which is disreputable and illegal. Whilst the law can be enforced the currency may be depreciated 50 pc[t], and yet the coin and paper may preserve the same value as currency.

(III: 415–16)

4 Vol. III of *Works* also contains notes from Ricardo's manuscripts of 1810–1811, mainly on the *Bullion Report* and contributors to the controversy, except for a manuscript in French by Jeremy Bentham, *Sur les prix* (on Ricardo's critique of this manuscript see Deleplace and Sigot 2012).

5 Referring to Thornton (1802), Malthus criticised this statement in his review of *High Price* for the *Edinburgh Review*, to which Ricardo answered in the *Appendix* to the fourth edition. Paradoxically, this marked the beginning of their acquaintance and friendship; see Sraffa (1951c: 11–12).

6 Ricardo emphasised that it was inappropriate in that case to speak of an "adverse" balance of trade, since the export of gold paid for the import of foreign commodities which were useful to the country:

> In return for the gold exported, commodities would be imported; and though what is usually termed the balance of trade would be against the country exporting money or bullion, it would be evident that she was carrying on a most advantageous trade, exporting that which was no way useful to her, for commodities which might be employed in the extension of her manufactures, and the increase of her wealth.
>
> (*High Price*; III: 54)

7 The role of debased silver coins was highlighted by a reply to Ricardo's 1809 unsigned article in the *Morning Chronicle*. This reply was signed "A Friend to Bank Notes, but no Bank Director", who happened to be one of Ricardo's friends, Hutches Trower; see Sraffa (1951c: 4).

8 Alexander Baring was the second son of Sir Francis Baring (see Chapter 1 above) and a partner in the merchant bank Baring Brothers & Co.

9 The proposal of a double standard resurfaced in 1823, again without any success. Ricardo was also involved in the opposition to it. See Chapter 6 below.

10 The actual figures given by *The Course of the Exchange* for these dates were respectively £4. 1s. 6d. (4.7 per cent above the legal price of gold in coin), £4. 1s. (4 per cent), and £4. 0s. 6d. (3.4 per cent). See Boyer-Xambeu, Deleplace and Gillard (2010a, 2010b).

11 See also on 8 May 1820:

> [In the first instance] he certainly would rather have been inclined to have altered the standard than to have recurred to the old standard. But while the committee [on the resumption of cash payments] was sitting, a reduction took place in the price of gold, which fell to 4*l*. 2*s*. and it then became a question whether we should sacrifice a great principle in establishing a new standard, or incur a small degree of embarrassment and difficulty in recurring to the old.
>
> (V: 43)

> He [Ricardo] had never imagined that the currency had never been depreciated more than 4 per cent. He had merely contended, that at the time when the subject was taken up by parliament in the last year, there was only that depreciation; which was too small to warrant an alteration of the ancient standard. He was well aware that during some of the latter years of the war, the depreciation had been as great as 25 per cent.
>
> (ibid: 46)

A market price of bullion 25 per cent above the mint price was rated at £4. 17s. 4d.; the quotation was occasionally above this level beginning on 12 February 1811 and permanently from 26 May 1812 to 7 June 1814 (Napoleon abdicated for the first time on 6 April 1814 and left Fontainebleau for the Elba island on 20 April) and again from 28 March (Napoleon had returned to Paris on 20 March) to 30 June 1815 (after Waterloo on 18 June, Napoleon abdicated a second time on 22 June). The highest peak was £5. 16s. 8d. from 29 October to 12 November 1813 – as much as 50 per cent above the mint price.

12 On the discussions in 1819 about the Ingot Plan, see Bonar (1923), Sraffa (1952b) and Weatherall (1976).

13 Both pamphlets are published in vol. IV of Sraffa's edition of *Works*, *Principles* being the object of vol. I. There is no other writing in vol. IV (published or in manuscript form) directly devoted to money (*On Protection to Agriculture*, published in 1822, contains one section on this question; see below Appendix 4). Of course, vol. V of *Speeches and Evidence* and vols VI to IX of *Letters* contain numerous mentions of monetary subjects. An important letter written by Ricardo in January 1823 on the question of the double standard came to light recently (see Deleplace, Depoortère and Rieucau 2013).

14 The initial transition from the existing system to the new one would be carried out by £15 million being issued to reimburse the capital of the Bank of England (thus extinguishing the interest-bearing public debt) and £10 million to buy from it an appropriate amount of gold reserve and exchequer bills.

15 Keynes perceived rightly that Ricardo's views about note-issuing were not followed: "If Ricardo had had his way with his ingot proposals, commodity money would never have been restored, and a pure managed money would have come into force in England in 1819" (Keynes 1930: 14). The management of the currency by the Bank of England would start on a regular basis in the 1850s, after the Bank Charter Act proved inefficient to prevent the crises of 1847 and 1857; but it did not follow Ricardo's lines and was mainly inspired by the "Banking Principle" of adjusting the discount rate, in the limits imposed by the "Currency Principle".

16 The "open-market" policy – the purchase or sale of government securities in the market – was introduced by the Bank of England after the Bank Charter Act of 1844, but it was constrained by the legal link between the variation of the note issue and the variation of the metallic reserve.

17 "The transcript of this speech prepared for *Hansard* by Ricardo partly with cuttings from the *Morning Chronicle*'s report, is reproduced in the plate facing p. 332 below" (Note by Sraffa; V: 9).

18

> There is, however, one speech of which we are now able to read Ricardo's own report, undoubtedly written within a day after the debate; that is the speech on Mr Western's Motion of 10 July 1822. The original transcript, hitherto unpublished, was found in the Mill-Ricardo papers and is given in the present volume instead of *Hansard's* version, of which it is four times as extensive. This report, having been written by Ricardo himself so soon after delivering it, has an authority unequalled by any others, even by those of which we know, or can guess from their quality, that they were revised by him, since this revision would normally be carried out months later, owing to the delays in the preparation of *Hansard*. One can therefore take the report of the speech of 10 July 1822 as a standard by which to judge the quality of the others.
>
> (Sraffa, 1952a: xxxi)

19 *Hansard*'s note reads: "This speech was written out by Mr. Ricardo for this work, and sent to the Editor a few days before his death" (V: 309) that is, at the end of August or the beginning of September 1823. It may thus be considered as the last paper on money written by Ricardo for publication.

Part II

Theory

3 Money and the invariable standard

In a sound state of the currency the value of gold may vary, but its price cannot.

(Evidence before the Commons' Committee on Resumption, 4 March 1819; V: 392)

First it may be useful to give in Section 3.1 some definitions of the main notions used by Ricardo in his theory of money (additional ones will be introduced in subsequent chapters). They are deliberately borrowed from *Principles* or later papers. Two issues are raised in Sections 3.2 and 3.3 respectively: the relation between the value of money, the price of gold bullion, and the general price level, and the relation between the standard of money and the standard of value. Section 3.4 concludes on the contribution of Ricardo's theory of value and distribution to his understanding of both relations, hence to his theory of money.

3.1 Some definitions

Commodities: exchangeable value, money price, absolute value

The commodities considered by Ricardo in *Principles* are exclusively those which are produced in competitive conditions:

> In speaking then of commodities, of their exchangeable value, and of the laws which regulate their relative prices, we mean always such commodities only as can be increased in quantity by the exertion of human industry, and on the production of which competition operates without restraint.
>
> (*Principles*; I: 12)

Ricardo distinguished between the *value* of such a commodity and its *price* (*Principles*, Chapter I). The value of a commodity is expressed in terms of another commodity; Ricardo indifferently used to designate it the terms "exchangeable value", "relative value", "proportional value", or simply "value". The price of a commodity is expressed in terms of money. It can thus change either because of a change on the side of the commodity – affecting its value – or of a change on the side of money – that is, a variation in the value of money:

> In stating the principles which regulate exchangeable value and price, we should carefully distinguish between those variations which belong to the commodity itself, and those which are occasioned by a variation in the medium in which value is estimated, or price expressed.
>
> (ibid: 48)

These two kinds of variations combine to affect the price of a commodity; in other words, the money price of a commodity is equal to the ratio of the value of the commodity to the value of money, as illustrated by the following quotation (in which the "real value" is understood by Ricardo as the quantity of labour supposed to determine the value of shoes as well as of gold-money):

> The word *price* I think should be confined wholly to the value of commodities estimated in *money,* and money only. If so confined, a commodity may rise in *real value* without rising in *price*. If more labour should be required than before to work the mines, and to manufacture shoes, it is possible that shoes may continue unaltered in *price*, but both the shoes, and gold (or money) will have *risen in value*.
>
> (Letter to Trower, 18 September 1818; VII: 297, Ricardo's emphasis)

When all competitively produced commodities sell for money at their "natural price", all portions of capital advanced in their production earn the same rate of profit. A synonym of natural price is "cost of production", expressed in money and including the same rate of profit on all portions of capital: "In cost of production I always include profits at their current rate" (*Notes on Malthus*; II: 369). By "market price" of a commodity Ricardo meant the price as it results from the interplay of the supply of and the demand for the commodity (the same distinction occasionally applied to "natural value" – corresponding to the permanent state of the economy – and "market value" – reflecting temporary market forces). In the case of competitively produced commodities, the market price of a commodity may deviate from the natural price, but this creates differences in the rate of profit that generate movements of capital from one employment to the other. Consequently the rate of profit tends to equalise for all portions of capital (*Principles*, Chapter IV), and "cost of production [is] the pivot about which all market price moves" (*Notes on Malthus*; II: 25). Commodities that are monopolised – and to which Ricardo devoted interest insofar as they contrasted with competitively produced ones – have only a market price, since their quantity cannot be increased by the competition of other portions of capital than those applied to them:

> Commodities which are monopolized, either by an individual, or by a company, vary according to the law which Lord Lauderdale has laid down: they fall in proportion as the sellers augment their quantity, and rise in proportion to the eagerness of the buyers to purchase them; their price has no necessary

> connexion with their natural value: but the prices of commodities, which are subject to competition, and whose quantity may be increased in any moderate degree, will ultimately depend, not on the state of demand and supply, but on the increased or diminished cost of their production.
>
> (*Principles*; I: 385)

In contrast with the "nominal value" of a commodity ("either in coats, hats, money, or corn", ibid: 50) – that is, its exchangeable value in any commodity or its money price – Ricardo called "absolute value" of a commodity its value in terms of an "invariable measure of value" or invariable "standard of value" (see below Section 3.3).

Money: measure of price, circulating medium, standard of money

The two aspects of money are mentioned in the summary heading, introduced for the second edition of 1819 and kept in the third, of Chapter I Section VII of *Principles*:

> Different effects from the alteration in the value of money, the medium in which *PRICE* is always expressed, or from the alteration in the value of commodities which money purchases.
>
> (ibid: 47; Ricardo's emphasis)

As "the medium in which price is always expressed", money is itself measured in a unit (in England the pound sterling, divided in 20 shillings of 12 pence each). In a system endowed with a metallic standard of money, this monetary unit is legally defined as a given weight of standard metal, gold or silver in bullion. This amounts to proclaiming that one unit of weight of the standard metal in coin is legal tender for a given amount of the monetary unit. In England, the unit of weight of standard gold and silver was the ounce, divided in 20 dwts. (pennyweights) of 24 grains each. After the *de jure* adoption of the gold standard in 1816, the pound sterling was legally defined as 5 dwts. 3.274 grains (or 123.274 grains) of standard gold 22/24 fine,[1] making 3 pounds 17 shillings 10½ pence the legal price of an ounce of standard gold – the "mint price" already adopted since 1717 for the coining of gold.

As the medium of exchange (between "commodities which money purchases"), money appears in Ricardo under two names: "currency" and "circulating medium". By currency he meant money being legal tender, that is, in the circumstances of the time, coin: even when in 1821 the Bank of England note was again made convertible into gold coin, it was not legal tender (it would only become so in 1833). By circulating medium Ricardo meant the currency plus the bank notes "representing" the currency, that is, the Bank of England note and the Country Banks notes (which were convertible into Bank of England notes). He did *not* include in the circulating medium the various instruments of credit, the use of which, however, affected the quantity of money required to circulate commodities (see Chapter 9 below).

The "value of money" in circulation is defined by Ricardo as its purchasing power in the market for all commodities taken together except the standard of money, to be distinguished from the purchasing power of money over the standard itself – the reciprocal of the market price of bullion (see Section 3.2 below). Accordingly, a fall (or a rise) in the value of money meant a proportional rise (respectively a fall) in all money prices except that of bullion, while a depreciation (or appreciation) of money was measured by a rise (respectively a fall) in the market price of bullion.

Two functions of the standard of money corresponded to the two aspects of money – measure of price and circulating medium. On the one hand, with gold bullion the standard of money, a given weight of gold defined the monetary unit (the pound sterling) and the unit of currency (from 1816 on, the coin called sovereign). On the other hand, convertibility of gold bullion into money and of money into gold bullion regulated the quantity of money (see below Chapter 7). Although he clearly made the distinction between the notions of standard of value and of standard of money, Ricardo assumed that gold bullion could be both (see below Section 3.3).

The condition of coherence of the price system

Let me express in modern parlance how the question of the integration of money in the theory of value is raised in Ricardo. In a market economy, the condition of coherence of any system of relative prices V_{ij} (what Ricardo called exchangeable values, relative values, or simply values) between commodities $1, \ldots, i, j, \ldots, n$, reads:

$$V_{ij} = V_{in} V_{nj} \tag{3.1}$$

with V_{ij} the relative price of i in terms of j.

Stating that a monetary economy is a market economy in which transactions operate through a means of exchange M amounts to replacing j in (3.1) by M. The condition of coherence of the price system becomes:

$$V_{iM} = V_{in} V_{nM} \tag{3.2}$$

Since V_{iM} is the money price of i and V_{nM} the reciprocal of the value of money in terms of commodity n, (3.2) makes sense of the above quotation from the letter to Trower of 18 September 1818: "shoes [i] may continue unaltered in *price* [V_{iM}], but both shoes, and gold (or money [M]) will have *risen in value* [in terms of n, that is, respectively V_{in} and $1/V_{nM}$]".

Calling P_i and P_n the (money) prices V_{iM} and V_{nM} of respectively i and n in (3.2), one obtains another expression of the condition of coherence of the price system:

$$V_{in} = \frac{P_i}{P_n} \tag{3.3}$$

In a monetary economy, the value of commodity *i* in terms of commodity *n* (the relative price of *i* in terms of *n*) is equal to the ratio of the (money) price of *i* to the (money) price of *n*.

In Ricardo's approach, the theory of value determines the relative prices of commodities independently of money – V_{in} is "real" and money is neutral in respect to relative prices – while the theory of money determines the value of money. To integrate money in the theory of value is to determine the value of money in a way consistent with the theory of relative prices of commodities – that is, allowing the money prices P_i and P_n to fulfil the condition (3.3) of coherence of the price system. However, nothing in this condition specifies what money is, and how its value is determined. To do this one needs first clarifying what is meant by value of money in Ricardo, all the more so since there are some ambiguities on this point in modern literature.

3.2 Value of money, price of gold bullion, and the general price level

The legal and the current value of money

By fixing a given weight of the standard metal (say, gold) as the legal definition of the monetary unit (say, the pound sterling), the State not only fixes the legal value of money in terms of gold. By declaring legal tender this weight in coin (say, the sovereign), it also fixes the legal purchasing power of the currency in terms of all other commodities, for given prices of them denominated in pounds. However, this is only the legal side of the story. It had been recognised for long that, in actual circulation, the current value of the currency could depart from its legal one. In the sixteenth century "voluntary values" of coins were distinguished from their "legal values", meaning that a given coin would actually pass for a higher amount of the monetary unit than the one decreed by the State (see Boyer-Xambeu, Deleplace and Gillard 1994a). Although this practice had since disappeared, thanks mostly to the prohibition of foreign coins in circulation, the question of the actual current value of the currency remained, as shown by the debates raised in England by the debasement of the coin, in the 1690s for the silver one and in the 1770s for the gold one. The Bullion Controversy of 1809–1811 also raised this issue, this time for the inconvertible Bank of England note. An aspect of these repeated debates was the question of how this current value of the currency should be ascertained. Steuart (1767) had established that the debasement of the coin by wear and tear or clipping led to a rise in the market price of the standard metal in bullion over and above its legal price in full-bodied coin (see Deleplace 2015d). The spread between these two prices was consequently an index of the difference between the legal and the current value of the currency.

This was not the only manifestation of a change in the value of the currency. In the market for all other commodities than bullion, money prices also experienced variations, and if they all changed in the same direction and the same proportion, this signalled an opposite change in the current value of money in terms of commodities. The question was thus: which expression of the current value of money was appropriate, its purchasing power in terms of bullion or in terms of all other commodities?

A related question was how much of the rise in the money prices of commodities in general was reflected in the rise in the money price of bullion. This was a distinct question. One thing is to ask whether the agreed fact of a rise in the money price of gold bullion above the legal price of gold in coin should be explained by a monetary cause – such as the debasement of the coin or the excess issue of notes – or by other independent causes – such as a deficit of the foreign balance. This was the main issue debated during the Bullion Controversy in 1809–1811. Another thing is to ask whether the change in the money price of gold bullion accurately reflected the change in prices of other commodities. This would be the main issue debated around the resumption of convertibility in 1819–1823, this time in the context of falling prices, and not of rising prices as in 1809–1811. Ricardo contended in 1819–1823 that the appreciation of the Bank of England note only accounted for half of the rise in the value of money, which itself accounted for only a small part of the fall in the money prices of some commodities, such as agricultural products. This suggests that the definition of the value of money in Ricardo is something to be clarified, all the more so since the literature provides conflicting views on this question.

The purchasing power of money over all commodities except gold or over gold alone

Ambiguities in modern literature

In spite of a shift of emphasis on the questions raised by Ricardo, his definition of the value of money remained the same from the Bullion Essays until the end. However, there are in the literature some ambiguities on this definition, which concern the relation between money prices of commodities in general – in modern terms the general price level – and the money price of the particular commodity acting as the standard of money, gold bullion. Some modern commentators of Ricardo contend that, in the absence of the concept of general price level, Ricardo used the money price of gold bullion as a proxy of it. The following examples illustrate this interpretation, without being exhaustive:

> To some extent Ricardo and his contemporaries focused in their formal discussions on the price of bullion and the foreign exchanges rather than the general price level because, while they knew *something* was happening to prices, there existed no consensus regarding the method of index numbers whereby the behavior of groups of commodities might be evaluated; at best only intelligent guesses could be made regarding general prices.
>
> (Hollander 1979: 416; Hollander's emphasis)

> [In *High Price*, Ricardo] concentrated on giving an exceptionally clear statement of the nature of the long run equilibrium relationship that rules between

> the quantity of paper money, the exchange rate and the price of specie (which, as Hollander (1979) persuasively argues, is to be understood in this context as standing as a proxy for what we would now term the general price level).
>
> (Laidler 1987: 291)

> Ricardo led the Bullionists with the argument that the Bank [of England] had overissued and that this was the cause of inflation or, to use the language of the day, the cause of 'the depreciation of bank notes'. In the absence of any confidence in the then little-used tool of an index-number of prices, the first problem was to prove that British prices had risen relative to other trading countries. Ricardo's test was the premium actually quoted on bullion.
>
> (Blaug 1996: 128)

In contrast, other commentators rightly emphasise the existence of a conceptual distinction in Ricardo between the general price level and the price of gold bullion, but insist that Ricardo deliberately defined the value of money as its purchasing power over gold bullion, *not* over all commodities taken together. The following example illustrates this position:

> Ricardo distinguished between variations in the value of money and variations in money prices, emphasising that the value of money was measured by the purchasing power of the currency over the commodity which acted as a standard, and not by its purchasing power over all commodities. Thus the depreciation of currency was proved by an increase in the price of the standard, rather than by an increase in money prices.
>
> (Marcuzzo and Rosselli 1991: 41)[2]

Another example is to be found in Takenaga (2013), where the distinction between two definitions of the value of money is rooted in another distinction between the nature of money – gold as a commodity, which has a value in terms of all other commodities – and institutional forms of money representing gold (coin, convertible note, inconvertible note), the value of which is their purchasing power in terms of the "true" money, gold. According to Takenaga, as long as the value of gold as a commodity was supposed to vary little, the stability of the value of a given form of money in terms of gold – the reciprocal of the money price of gold bullion – was the same as the stability of the value of money in terms of commodities, and the former stood practically for the latter.

Ricardo's definition

Whether the price of gold bullion is a proxy by default of the general price level or fits the analytical requirements of an adequate expression of the value of money, both interpretations thus consider that for Ricardo a fall in the value of money was *not* expressed by a rise in the general price level *but* by a rise in the sole money price of gold bullion. This apparently accords with the title of Ricardo's celebrated pamphlet of 1810–1811 – *The High Price of Bullion, a Proof of the Depreciation of Bank Notes* – but is contradicted by Ricardo's repeated distinction, during the debates in Parliament in 1819–1823, between a fall in the value of money and a depreciation of money, as in the following extract of a speech on 12 June 1822:

> The great mistake committed on this subject was in confounding the words "depreciation" and "diminution in value." With reference to the currency, he [Ricardo] had said, and he now repeated it, that the price of gold was the index of the depreciation of the currency, not the index of the value of the currency, and it was in this that he had been misunderstood.
>
> (V: 203–4)[3]

In a letter to Malthus of 16 December 1822 Ricardo was also clear:

> Dr. Copplestone in his article in the Quarterly Review charges me with maintaining the absurd doctrine that the price of gold bullion is a sure test of the value of bullion and currency.
>
> (IX: 249)

And in a speech of 7 May 1822 he emphasised that there could be depreciation while the value of money was actually *rising* (more on this below in Chapter 4):

> It might so happen that a currency might be depreciated, when it had actually risen, as compared with commodities, because the standard might have risen in value in a still greater proportion.
>
> (V: 166)

A further example of the equivalence between an increase in the value of money and a general fall in prices is to be found in a letter to Malthus of 28 September 1821, where Ricardo discussed the case of a country where corn is supposedly produced with half the labour required in all others, which consequently import the corn and pay it in money:

> As part of their exports in return for corn must in the first instance be money – the general level of currency will be reduced and commodities generally will fall, not because they can be produced cheaper, but because they are measured by a more valuable money.
>
> (IX: 81)

One should note that the expression "level of money" or "level of the currency" (used several times in the letter) does *not* mean here the general price level *but* the aggregate quantity of money, which decreases in the countries importing corn because the latter is paid in money. The consequence is "a more valuable money", hence a general fall in prices ("commodities generally will fall").[4]

Indeed, that the value of money had to be ascertained by the price of all commodities taken together was already stated in *High Price*, and it was repeated in *Principles*:

> Commodities measure the value of money in the same manner as money measures the value of commodities.
>
> (*High Price*; III: 104)

> The advance in the value of money is the same thing as the decline in the price of commodities.
>
> (*Principles*; I: 342)

> To say that commodities are raised in price, is the same thing as to say that money is lowered in relative value; for it is by commodities that the relative value of gold is estimated.
>
> (ibid: 105)

The latter extract is part of Ricardo's discussion of the possibility – rejected by him – of a general rise in prices as a consequence of a rise in wages, and he here assumed that the value of money was equal to the value of gold bullion – a situation corresponding to an absence of depreciation or appreciation of the currency. It was then equivalent to say that "commodities are raised in price", "money is lowered in relative value", and "the relative value of gold" declined. A logical consequence ensued: not only the price of gold bullion was "not the index of the value of the currency" as stated above, but *it should not be included among the prices of commodities in general constituting such index*. The value of money was thus defined as its purchasing power over all commodities except the standard.

A further indication that this was Ricardo's definition of the value of money is to be found in his repeated contention that the value of money ought to conform to the value of bullion – a condition which would not make sense if the value of money were defined as its purchasing power over bullion since it would always be equal to unity. This condition of conformity, which appeared in *Proposals*, played a central role in Ricardo's mature theory of money.

The condition of conformity of money to the standard

This condition was one of the three characteristics of "a perfect currency" as they were mentioned in *Proposals*:

> A currency may be considered as perfect, of which the standard is invariable, which always conforms to that standard, and in the use of which the utmost economy is practised.
>
> (*Proposals*; IV: 55)

With gold or silver as the standard, the conformity of money to the standard meant for Ricardo that a given weight of the metal in money (whether coin or convertible note) was of equal value with the same weight of the metal in bullion, both values being in terms of all commodities except the standard. A corollary was that the market price of bullion should be equal to the legal price of the metal in coin (the mint price). If it was higher, money was less valuable than bullion:

> While these metals [gold and silver] are the standard, the currency should conform in value to them, and, whenever it does not, and the market price of bullion is above the mint price, the currency is depreciated. This proposition is unanswered, and is unanswerable.
>
> (ibid: 62–3)

And symmetrically:

> To say that money is more valuable than bullion or the standard, is to say that bullion is selling in the market under the mint price.
>
> (ibid: 57)

That the inequality between the value of money and the value of the standard could be expressed by an inequality of opposite direction between the market price of gold bullion and the legal price of gold in coin was repeated by Ricardo when he was examined on 4 March 1819 by the Commons' Secret Committee on the Expediency of the Bank resuming Cash Payments. Being asked "Do you consider the high price of gold to be a certain sign of the depreciation of bank notes?", he answered:

> I consider it to be a certain sign of the depreciation of bank notes, because I consider the standard of the currency to be bullion, and whether that bullion be more or less valuable, the paper ought to conform to that value, and would, under the system that we pursued previously to 1797.
>
> (V: 373)

This correspondence between a comparison in value and a comparison in price to establish the conformity of money to the standard may be demonstrated by using the formalisation presented in Section 3.1 above.

Let me call R a composite commodity, each unit of it being constituted of all transacted commodities (except gold bullion) in the proportions in which they appear in transactions. In the condition (3.2) of coherence of the price system, replacing i by R and n by gold bullion G gives:

$$V_{RM} = V_{RG} V_{GM} \tag{3.4}$$

In this equation, V_{RM} is the reciprocal of V_{MR}, the value of money defined as the purchasing power of a unit of money over all commodities except the standard (gold bullion), V_{RG} is the reciprocal of V_{GR}, the value of gold bullion in terms of all other commodities, and V_{GM} is the value of gold bullion in terms of money, that is its money price. (3.4) may thus be turned into:

$$V_{MR} = \frac{V_{GR}}{V_{GM}} \tag{3.5}$$

As mentioned above, (3.5) only expresses that the prices at which the composite commodity *R* and gold bullion *G* exchange for money are coherent with the (real) relative price V_{GR} of gold bullion in terms of commodity *R*, as it is determined by the theory of value. However, nothing in (3.5) specifies what money is, apart from the fact that it is the medium of exchange. In order to build a monetary theory, one should now add that money is also "the medium in which price is always expressed", as quoted above from *Principles*, that is, the unit of account legally fixed. As mentioned in Section 3.1 above, this unit of account (say, the pound) was defined through the legal proclamation of a fixed price of the standard (say, gold bullion) in the form of money (say, a given coin, such as the sovereign). Money is thus specified by its relation to the standard, that is, the legal price of the standard in money.[5] Let me call $\overline{P_{GC}}$ this legal price in pounds of an ounce of gold in coin. The legal value V_{MG} of money in terms of gold may thus be defined as:

$$\overline{V_{MG}} = \frac{1}{\overline{P_{GC}}} \tag{3.6}$$

In other words, gold bullion, which in Ricardo's terms is in (3.4) the standard of value – in which all (real) relative prices are expressed – becomes in (3.6) the standard of money – in which the monetary unit is expressed.

Ricardo's condition of conformity may consequently be interpreted as follows: money conforms to the standard when its value V_{MR} as medium of exchange – that is, its circulating value in terms of all commodities except the standard – is consistent with its value V_{MG} as unit of account – that is, its legal value in terms of the standard. This condition is fulfilled when $1/V_{GM}$ in (3.5) is equal to $\overline{V_{MG}}$. Let me call $V_{MR}{}^*$ the value of money in terms of *R* for which this equality applies. One obtains:

$$V_{MR}{}^* = \overline{V_{MG}}\, V_{GR} \tag{3.7}$$

Replacing $\overline{V_{MG}}$ by its definition in (3.6) gives:

$$V_{MR}{}^* = \frac{1}{\overline{P_{GC}}} V_{GR} \tag{3.8}$$

Equation (3.8) expresses the condition of conformity of money to the standard as an equality between the value of money in circulation and the value of the standard (both in terms of all commodities except the standard), given the legal price of the standard. As it is, (3.8) embodies the second condition for what Ricardo called "a perfect currency" in the above quotation from *Proposals*, but it is hardly useful to determine whether an actual currency conforms to the standard because it requires the knowledge of two magnitudes measured in terms of *R*.[6] This difficulty, called later in the literature the index-number problem, was not addressed by Ricardo: the modern expression of the general price level – as a weighted average of the money prices of individual commodities – is not to be found in his writings (as shown below in Section 3.3, Ricardo's search for an invariable standard answered to another question), although he used the expressions of "the general price of goods" (I: 169) or of "the mass of prices" (III: 299). And Ricardo had good reasons not to look for an index-number: he could leave this difficulty aside, because there was another expression of the condition of conformity. Since this condition is fulfilled when $1/V_{GM}$ in (3.5) is equal to $\overline{V_{MG}}$ – in other words when $V_{MR} = V_{MR}{}^*$ – and since V_{GM} is the market price P_G of gold bullion, one obtains:

$$P_G = \overline{P_{GC}} \tag{3.9}$$

This was Ricardo's first tour de force in his monetary theory: the condition of conformity of money to the standard was to be expressed as an equality between two observable magnitudes, the market price of gold bullion and the legal price of gold in coin. Ricardo's concern with the stabilisation of the market price of gold bullion had thus nothing to do with the stabilisation of a proxy of the general price level: the market price of gold was to be stabilised at its legal level because this meant that money was actually conforming to its legal standard.

In what follows, I will assume that the reader is aware of the fact that the value of money and the value of the standard (gold bullion) are both defined in terms of all commodities except the standard, and I will simplify $V_{MR}, V_{MR}{}^*$, and V_{GR} into respectively $V_M, V_M{}^*$, and V_G. Substituting P_G for V_{GM} as the market price of gold bullion and recalling that $\overline{P_{GC}}$ is the legal price of gold in coin, the main relations analysed above read:

Condition of coherence of the price system:

$$V_M = \frac{V_G}{P_G} \tag{3.5}$$

Condition of conformity of money to the standard:

$$V_M{}^* = \frac{1}{\overline{P_{GC}}} V_G \tag{3.8}$$

that is,

$$P_G = \overline{P_{GC}} \tag{3.9}$$

We will see in Chapter 7 below that, thanks to convertibility of bullion into money and of money into bullion (money being whether coin or note), arbitrage ensures the fulfilment of (3.9), taking into account the costs incurred by convertibility both ways. In such "sound state of the currency" money conformed to the standard. According to Ricardo, money was depreciated if $V_M < V_M^*$ and appreciated if $V_M > V_M^*$ (see Chapter 4 below). This was equivalent respectively to $P_G > \overline{P_{GC}}$ and $P_G < \overline{P_{GC}}$.

Although the modern expression of the general price level did not appear in Ricardo, the notion was present when he referred to causes having "a general effect on price", in contrast with causes affecting some commodities only or all commodities in a non-homothetic way, and thus responsible for a change in relative prices:

> A rise in wages, from an alteration in the value of money, produces *a general effect on price*, and for that reason it produces no real effect whatever on profits. On the contrary, a rise of wages, from the circumstance of the labourer being more liberally rewarded, or from a difficulty of procuring the necessaries on which wages are expended, does not, except in some instances, produce the effect of raising price, but has a great effect in lowering profits. In the one case, no greater proportion of the annual labour of the country is devoted to the support of the labourers; in the other case, a larger proportion is so devoted.
>
> (*Principles*, I: 48–9; my emphasis)

This distinction between the general effect on "the mass of prices" of a change in the value of money and a particular effect on some prices due to other causes was already made by Ricardo at the time of the Bullion Essays, as when he discussed Bentham's explanation of "the causes influencing the rise in prices":

> This is true taking all commodities together, – but fashion or other causes may create an increased demand for one article and consequently the demand for some one or more of others must diminish. Will not this operate on prices? The author [Bentham] evidently means *all commodities together or the mass of prices*.
>
> (III: 298–9; my emphasis)

Two remarks should be made before going further. The first is that a distinction is to be made between the definition of the value of money – as may now be clear, in terms of all commodities taken together except the standard of money – and the choice of the standard of money – for which Ricardo rejected this "mass of commodities" (*Proposals*; IV: 59; see below Section 3.3). The second remark is that, for reasons analysed at length below, Ricardo always stressed that, except in a situation like the one observed in 1810 – characterised by the inconvertibility of the Bank of England note *and* the quasi-disappearance of gold coins in domestic circulation – a change in the market *price* of gold bullion was constrained between narrow limits and temporary (it was self-adjusting), although the *value* of gold bullion could vary significantly and permanently. This was summarised in a compact form during his evidence of 4 March 1819 as follows:

> In a sound state of the currency the value of gold may vary, but its price cannot.
>
> (V: 392)

This meant that the value of money could change with the value of gold bullion, while the market price of gold bullion – the reciprocal of the value of money in terms of gold bullion – remained stationary. This should be remembered when discussing changes in the value of money (see Chapter 4 below).

A non-monetary cause of rise in the general price level? The question of taxation

We may now go back to the above-mentioned use by some commentators of the conceptual distinction between the general price level and the price of gold bullion to define the value of money in reference to the latter rather than the former. A reason advanced for this use is to account for Ricardo's contention that, indeed, an excess quantity of paper money did generate a rise in the money prices of all commodities, but this was not the only possible cause of such rise. This contention is obviously at odds with that of modern advocates of the Quantity Theory of Money for whom inflation may only be caused by money being in excess, and, as we will see, it plays an important role in Ricardo's theory of money. However, it does not require rejecting the definition of the value of money by its purchasing power over all commodities except the standard of money.

At the time of the Bullion Essays, Ricardo already distinguished what in the rise of prices could be ascribed to the depreciation of paper money – which he explained by its excess quantity – and to other causes – of a non-monetary character:

> Eighteen per cent. is, therefore, equal to the rise in the price of commodities, occasioned by the depreciation of paper. All above such rise may be either traced to the effects of taxation, to the increased scarcity of the commodity, or to any other cause which may appear satisfactory to those who take pleasure in such enquiries.
>
> (*Reply to Bosanquet*; III: 239)

One should remark that Ricardo speaks here of depreciation – *not* of a fall in the value of money – and that it is unclear whether the other causes of "the rise in the price of commodities" apply to some commodities or to all: "the increased scarcity" is that of "the commodity" (in the singular) and taxation may be general or particular. At that time, Ricardo was not yet equipped with the appropriate tools to deal with this kind of problem. Things changed with *Principles*. On the one hand, the contention that aggregate demand was regulated by aggregate supply – labelled Say's Law in the literature – excluded a general rise or fall in prices caused by, respectively, a deficiency or a glut of *all* commodities.[7] On the other hand, Ricardo could now analyse "the effects of taxation", thanks to a proper theory of value and distribution. It is necessary here to say a few words on this theory, since it will have consequences at various levels for the theory of money.

As is well-known, the titles of Section IV and V of Chapter I "On value" of *Principles* are explicit as to the "modification" of the law that determines the exchange value of commodities by the relative quantity of labour necessary to their production:

> The principle that the quantity of labour bestowed on the production of commodities regulates their relative value, [is] considerably modified by the employment of machinery and other fixed and durable capital.
>
> (*Principles*; I: 30)

> The principle that value does not vary with the rise or fall of wages, [is] modified also by the unequal durability of capital, and by the unequal rapidity with which it is returned to its employer.
>
> (ibid: 38)

As mentioned by Sraffa quoting a letter from Ricardo to McCulloch of 13 June 1820:

> Ricardo had suggested that 'all the exceptions to the general rule' could be reduced to 'one of time': *i.e.* all those deriving from different proportions of fixed and circulating capitals, different durabilities of fixed capital, or differences in the 'time it takes to market' (or durability of circulating capital) could be reduced to terms of labour employed for a longer or a shorter time.
>
> (Sraffa 1951a: xlv)

Before analysing the consequences of the taxation of profits, Ricardo summed-up this effect on relative prices created by the unequal length with which capital is advanced to produce commodities and bring them to market:

> In a former part of this work, we discussed the effects of the division of capital into fixed and circulating, or rather into durable and perishable capital, on the prices of commodities. We shewed that two manufacturers might employ precisely the same amount of capital, and might derive from it precisely the same amount of profits, but that they would sell their commodities for very

> different sums of money, according as the capitals they employed were rapidly, or slowly, consumed and reproduced.
>
> (*Principles*; I: 207)

It is not the place here to discuss the implications of such "modification" of the labour theory of value; there is an extended literature on this question. All we need is to emphasise the uncontroversial result that a change in the rate of profit or in the wage rate – these two distributive variables being inversely related – affects relative prices because of differences between commodities as to the durability of capital advanced in their production. This is enough to derive the effects of taxation, and consequently to inquire whether it can be another cause of change in the general price level, independent of the effect of a change in the value of money.

Leaving aside taxation levied on particular activities or commodities – which obviously alters relative prices – there are two kinds of taxation that may be levied at a uniform rate on all activities or commodities, and hence be eligible as cause of change in the general price level: taxes on incomes, and taxes on the production or on the sale of commodities. Taxes on profits and on wages (analysed respectively in Chapters XV and XVI of *Principles*) both affect the level of these distributive variables[8] and trigger the above-mentioned "modification" of the law of value – namely a change in relative prices:[9]

> A tax upon income, whilst money continued unaltered in value, would alter the relative prices and value of commodities. This would be true also, if the tax instead of being laid on the profits, were laid on the commodities themselves: provided they were taxed in proportion to the value of the capital employed on their production, they would rise equally, whatever might be their value, and therefore they would not preserve the same proportion as before.
>
> (ibid: 208)[10]

Taxes on the production or on the sale of commodities ("a tax on the produce when obtained;" ibid: 156) are analysed in Chapter IX "Taxes on raw produce" and Chapter XVII "Taxes on other commodities than raw produce" of *Principles*. They amount to increasing the cost of production of commodities and as such affect all prices inasmuch as these commodities enter directly or indirectly in the production of all of them – in Sraffa's terms these commodities are "basic products" (Sraffa 1960: 8) – but they alter the methods of production and consequently affect relative prices. In all cases, the theory of value and distribution developed in *Principles* leads to the conclusion that taxation, even at the same rate in all industries, generates a change in the relative prices of commodities:

> Taxation can never be so equally applied, as to operate in the same proportion on the value of all commodities, and still to preserve them at the same relative value.
>
> (*Principles*; I: 239)

Before concluding on this point, one may mention a curiosity concerning the relation between taxation and the value of money. Not only did Ricardo rightly contend that taxation altered relative prices, but he went as far as suggesting that, because of this effect, a change in the value of money *also* altered relative prices, in a country where profits were taxed. In Chapter XV "Taxes on profits" of *Principles*, Ricardo focused on "the understanding of a very important principle, which, I believe, has never been adverted to" (ibid: 208). This principle was that, in contrast with "a country where no taxation subsists", "in a country where prices are artificially raised by taxation [of profits]" a change in the value of money "will not operate in the same proportion on the prices of all commodities" (ibid: 209). This "very important principle" – the discovery of which Ricardo attributed to himself – raises two questions, one analytical, the other historical. From an analytical point of view, the question is that of the effect of a change in the value of money on relative prices: in modern parlance, Ricardo unexpectedly contended that a taxation of the profits of capital turned the neutrality of money in respect to relative prices into non-neutrality. From a historical point of view, Ricardo suggested that this "very important principle" not only applied to a hypothetical case but might explain what materially happened when money was depreciated during the period of inconvertibility of the Bank of England note. However, the study of the numerical example used by Ricardo to establish this point does not validate the conclusion he drew from it. This may thus be considered as an aborted attempt at the non-neutrality of money in respect to relative prices (see Appendix 3).

I may now conclude on the question of the definition of the value of money. Ricardo's analysis in *Principles* shows that taxation, which alters relative prices, cannot be considered as a cause of change in the general price level, defined as an equiproportional change in all money prices. It is not even possible to say that taxation generates a *rise* in all money prices, although in different proportions, since the prices of some commodities may actually *fall*, as a consequence of the effect produced by the difference between durabilities of capital in the production of these commodities and of the standard of money (see below Section 3.3). In other words, taxation does not call for a distinction between a change in the value of money and a change in the general price level in the opposite direction: they are one and the same thing, provided the price of the standard of money is excluded from the general price level. Now, does this conclusion contradict Ricardo's contention that an excess quantity of paper money generates a rise in the money prices of all commodities, but that this is not the only possible cause of such rise? Not at all, provided we keep in mind the above-mentioned distinction, emphasised by Ricardo in his papers of 1819–1823, between a depreciation of money and a fall in the value of money.

Depreciation, consequent upon the quantity of money being in excess, was indeed one cause of a fall in the value of money, defined as an equiproportional rise in money prices of all commodities except the standard of money. Symmetrically, an appreciation of money, consequent upon the quantity of money being deficient, was one cause of a rise in the value of money, defined as an equiproportional fall in money prices of all commodities except the standard of money. However, there was another possible cause of a change in the value of money so defined: not taxation – which altered relative prices – but a change in the value of the standard itself. Ricardo's contention remains perfectly valid: *not* every rise in the general price level should be attributed to an excess of paper money; but there is only one other cause of such rise and it is a fall in the value of the standard, gold bullion. In both cases it is equivalent to say that the prices of all commodities (except the standard) rise in the same proportion and that the value of money falls by this proportion. But in one case (depreciation) the cause is an excess quantity of money while in the other the cause is real: a fall in the value of the commodity acting as the standard of money.

The notion of standard appears then central in Ricardo's theory of money, and in *Principles* Ricardo developed a theory of value and distribution that allowed him to analyse its properties, as the next section will show.

3.3 The standard of money and the standard of value

It is widely recognised that the question of the invariable standard is an integral part of Ricardo's theory of value and distribution. I will contend that it is also an integral part of his theory of money. On this question, the evolution of the former had indeed a disappointing effect on the latter: the more Ricardo dug into the invariable standard of value, the more the possibility of an invariable standard of money moved away. However, here also, the theory of value and distribution contained in *Principles* contributed to the clarification of the question of the value of money.

The word "standard" appears in Ricardo with two different meanings: standard of money (or of currency) and standard of value. The former pervades all monetary writings, from the Bullion Essays to *Plan for a National Bank*, while the latter emerged with Ricardo's interest for the issue of value and distribution and was the object of the last manuscript interrupted by his death in 1823. The link between these two meanings is provided by the fact that money is the measure of price and by their having both something to do with the question of invariability. They are consequently often confused by Ricardo under the name of "gold", although he carefully made the distinction between them. An indication of this distinction is to be found in Sraffa's *Index* of *Works* (Vol. XI). The only specific entry for the word "standard" is "standard of currency", which is half a column long (mainly overlapping with "standard of" in the entry "money"). However, in the entry "value", two full columns are devoted to "measure or standard of". This disproportion might reflect Sraffa's own interest for this question, but it should be noted that, while the entry "standard of currency" contains references to writings of all periods, the longer sub-entry "Value: measure or standard of" has only two references prior to the publication of *Principles*.[11]

The invariable standard of value: "a mean between the extremes"

Invariable standard and absolute values

The search for an invariable standard of value was for Ricardo an integral part of his theory of value and distribution. As Sraffa put it, this search aimed at "finding the conditions which a commodity would have to satisfy in order to be invariable in value – and this came close to identifying the problem of a measure with that of the law of value" (Sraffa, 1951a: xli), since "the idea of an 'invariable measure' has for Ricardo its necessary complement in that of 'absolute value'" (ibid: xlvi). This question is well-documented in the literature (see for example Sraffa 1951a; Kurz and Salvadori 2015a, and on the controversy between Malthus and Ricardo on the measure of value, Porta 1992a) and it is consequently not necessary here to deal with it in detail.

A special Section VI, entitled "On an invariable measure of value" was introduced in Chapter I "On value" of *Principles* for the third edition of 1821, and Ricardo's last manuscript, interrupted by his death on 11 September 1823, was devoted to the analysis of this invariable standard of value; it was entitled "Absolute Value and Exchangeable Value". The absolute value of a commodity was defined by Ricardo as its exchangeable value in terms of an invariable standard of value. The need for and at the same time the impossibility of such standard was explained by Ricardo in *Principles* as follows:

> When commodities varied in relative value, it would be desirable to have the means of ascertaining which of them fell and which rose in real value, and this could be effected only by comparing them one after another with some invariable standard measure of value, which should itself be subject to none of the fluctuations to which other commodities are exposed. Of such a measure it is impossible to be possessed, because there is no commodity which is not itself exposed to the same variations as the things, the value of which is to be ascertained.
>
> (*Principles*; I: 43–4)

This contradiction between the necessity of having an invariable standard of value and the impossibility of finding one would again obsess Ricardo after *Principles*, as testified by the manuscript "Absolute Value and Exchangeable Value":

> It can not be too often repeated that nothing can be a measure of value which is not itself invariable.
>
> (IV: 394; see also, ibid: 401)

> It must then be confessed that there is no such thing in nature as a perfect measure of value.
>
> (ibid: 404)

In the absence of a perfect standard of value, it would nevertheless be desirable if an agreement could be made on the least imperfect one:

> What are we to do in this difficulty, are we to leave every one to chuse his own measure of value or should we agree to take some one commodity and provided it were always produced under the same circumstances constitute that as a general measure to which we should all refer that we may at least understand each other when we are talking of the rise or fall in the value of things.
>
> (ibid: 371–2)

> The difficulty being stated, the question is how it shall be best overcome, and if we cannot have an absolutely uniform measure of value what would be the best approximation to it?
>
> (ibid: 381)

As the first quotation makes clear, Ricardo started by raising this question of invariability in respect to time ("provided it were always produced under the same circumstances"), that is, "at distant periods":

> It is a great desideratum in Polit. Econ. to have a perfect measure of absolute value in order to be able to ascertain what relation commodities bear to each other at distant periods. Any thing having value is a good measure of the comparative value of all other commodities at the same time and place, but will be of no use in indicating the variations in their absolute value at distant times and in distant places.
>
> (ibid: 396)

One should thus lean on the permanent causes that rendered commodities variable in value, so as to choose the commodity that was the least affected by them.[12] As analysed in Chapter I of *Principles* there were two such causes: a change in the quantity of labour necessary for their production and a change in the distribution between wages and profits (which were inversely related). The second cause "modified" the effect of the first and, as mentioned above in Section 3.2, it operated because of the unequal durability of the capital advanced in the production of the various commodities. However, Ricardo observed that:

> This cause of the variation of commodities is comparatively slight in its effects, [which] could not exceed 6 or 7 per cent.; for profits could not, probably, under any circumstances, admit of a greater general and permanent depression than to that amount.
>
> (*Principles*; I: 36; see also "a minor variation", ibid: 42)

Consequently, the constancy in the quantity of labour required in the production was the main criterion for the choice of the standard:

> I have already remarked, that the effect on the relative prices of things, from a variation in profits, is comparatively slight; that by far the most important effects are produced by the varying quantities of labour required for production; and therefore, if we suppose this important cause of variation removed from the production of gold, we shall probably possess as near an approximation to a standard measure of value as can be theoretically conceived.
>
> (ibid: 45)

As is well-known, this concession made by Ricardo on the effect of a change in wages on relative prices – an effect he emphatically rejected in the generality of cases – has given birth to the ironical label of a "93% Labour Theory of Value" (Stigler 1958). But it should be remarked that this argument of "slight effect", however feeble it may look, does not play *any* role in Ricardo's analysis of the criterions of choice of the standard. The previous quotation goes on as follows:

> May not gold be considered as a commodity produced with such proportions of the two kinds of capital as approach nearest to the average quantity employed in the production of most commodities? May not these proportions be so nearly equally distant from the two extremes, the one where little fixed capital is used, the other where little labour is employed, as to form a just mean between them?
> (*Principles*; I: 45–6)

The argument here is no longer that we may neglect the effect of a change in distribution on relative prices because the observed small variations in the rate of profit made it "slight", but that, *whatever these variations*, they would be of *no* consequence on the capacity of the standard to measure adequately the absolute values of commodities, provided it were "a just mean" between these commodities. The reason is that, although relative prices of commodities vary with distribution, as a consequence of the unequal durability of capital advanced in their production, this effect is eliminated for commodities produced with the same durability of capital. The second cause of variability of a standard thus disappears whenever this standard is used to measure the value of the commodities produced with the same durability of capital:

> It would be a perfect measure of value for all things produced under the same circumstances precisely as itself, but for no others.
> (ibid: 45; see also "Absolute Value"; IV: 386–7)

This argument reflects a shift of emphasis in the question of the variability of the standard, from changes occurring "at distant periods" – that is, through time (in dynamics) – to variations in the levels of the distributive variables at a point in time (in comparative statics).

A shift of emphasis

To understand this shift, one needs to go back to Ricardo's theory of the rate of profit. In *An Essay on the Influence of a low Price of Corn on the Profits of Stock* (generally referred to as the *Essay on Profits*), published in 1815, Ricardo suggested that the level of the rate of profit depended on the ratio of the quantity of corn produced in the economy to the quantity of corn consumed in this production. This "corn-ratio theory of profits", as it was called by Sraffa (1951a: xlix), provided the cornerstone of the relationship between the rate of profit, wages, and the price of wage-goods, developed two years later in *Principles*. As Sraffa put it:

> [I]t was now labour, instead of corn, that appeared on both sides of the account – in modern terms, both as input and output: as a result, the rate of profits was

> no longer determined by the ratio of corn produced to the corn used up in production, but, instead, by the ratio of the total labour of the country to the labour required to produce the necessaries for that labour.
>
> (ibid: xxxii)

There was, however, a difficulty: the differences between commodities as to the durability of the capital advanced in their production made exchangeable values depend on the rate of profit, generating a circular reasoning: the distribution of the aggregate surplus, measured in value, affected the size of the surplus to be distributed. Hence there was a need for a measure of the value of commodities that would be invariable in respect to variations in distribution and would turn exchangeable values measured in a variable standard into absolute values measured in an invariable one. As Sraffa put it:

> [T]hus the problem of value which interested Ricardo was how to find a measure of value which would be invariant to changes in the division of the product; for, if a rise or fall of wages by itself brought about a change in the magnitude of the social product, it would be hard to determine accurately the effect on profits. (This was, of course, the same problem as has been mentioned earlier in connection with Ricardo's corn-ratio theory of profits.)
>
> (ibid: xlviii–xlix)

This use of the standard of value to analyse the relationship between wages and the rate of profit is summed-up in *Principles* for a particular case as follows:

> If we had an invariable standard by which to measure the value of this produce, we should find that a less value had fallen to the class of labourers and landlords, and a greater to the class of capitalists, than had been given before.
>
> (*Principles*; I: 49)

The selection of the appropriate standard for that use was thus subject to two criteria: (a) it should always require the same quantity of labour for its production – a correction being applied in case this quantity changed; and (b) the durability of the capital advanced in its production should be a "mean between the extremes" of the commodities composing the aggregate product to be distributed – this mean being supposed to be one year:

> To me it appears most clear that we should chuse a measure produced by labour employed for a certain period, and which always supposes an advance of capital, because 1st. it is a perfect measure for all commodities produced under the same circumstances of time as the measure itself – 2dly. By far the greatest number of commodities which are the objects of exchange are produced by the union of capital and labour, that is to say of labour employed for a certain time. 3dly. That a commodity produced by labour employed for a year is a mean between the extremes of commodities produced on one side by labour and advances for much more than a year, and on the other by

> labour employed for a day only without any advances, and the mean will in most cases give a much less deviation from truth than if either of the extremes were used as a measure.
>
> ("Absolute Value"; IV: 405)

There was a fourth characteristic that would make the chosen standard suitable: this "mean between the extremes" would be "a perfect measure" for wage-goods produced by agriculture – that is, most of the goods consumed by workers – supposing that they were *also* produced with capital advanced during one year. The quotation went on as follows:

> Let us suppose money to be produced in precisely the same time as corn is produced, that would be the measure proposed by me, provided it always required the same uniform quantity of labour to produce it, and if it did not provided an allowance were made for the alteration in the value of the measure itself in consequence of its requiring more or less labour to obtain it. The circumstance of this measure being produced in the same length of time as corn and most other vegetable food which forms by far the most valuable article of daily consumption would decide me in giving it a preference.
>
> (ibid: 405–6)

This "preference" was consistent with Ricardo's theory of the rate of profit as being inversely related to the prices of wage-goods. Since the chosen standard (here called "money" for reasons that will be explained below) is supposed to be produced with the same durability of capital as most of the wage-goods, it may be used to measure the changes in their prices independently of the rate of profit – hence the change in wages and the consequent change in the rate of profit itself.

In spite of these precisions contained in the manuscript "Absolute Value" as compared with *Principles*, Ricardo was disappointed by the outcome of his enquiry into that issue. His last letter of 5 September 1823 – the day, as Sraffa put it, when he "was struck with his fatal illness" – and addressed to James Mill ended as follows:

> I have been thinking a good deal on this subject lately but without much improvement – I see the same difficulties as before and am more confirmed than ever that strictly speaking there is not in nature any correct measure of value nor can any ingenuity suggest one, for what constitutes a correct measure for some things is a reason why it cannot be a correct one for others.
>
> (IX: 387)[13]

What was the reason of this disappointment? The writing of the manuscript "Absolute Value" having been interrupted by Ricardo's death, one may only conjecture about it. One reason may be the intuitive consciousness of a difficulty that only became apparent with Sraffa's development of Ricardo's search for an invariable standard in his book *Production of Commodities by Means of Commodities* (1960). As is well-known, Sraffa's standard commodity is a composite one, constructed on the basis of the given methods of production of actual "basic commodities" combined in adequate proportions. Kurz and Salvadori (2015a) observe that Ricardo "did not take the composite commodity 'social product', or, in his terms, the 'mass of commodities', as the standard of value", because "in the context of a discussion of the impact of distribution on relative value, given the technical conditions of production, [...] it does not meet with the criterion of technological invariability", since many commodities composing the product experienced technological change (Kurz and Salvadori 2015a: 210). It may be added that, even if a single commodity were adopted as the invariable standard in respect to distribution because it was at one time "a mean between the extremes" computed on the basis of given techniques of production (durability of capital), it could hardly be used also to measure variations in the absolute values of the commodities through time, hence with heterogeneous changes in the techniques of production that implied a change in the "mean" itself.

Another reason – more relevant for the present book – of Ricardo's disappointment may be suggested. It was the link between the standard of value and the standard of money.

The link with the standard of money

In Ricardo's view, the standard of value was indeed an instrument in the hands of the "Political Economist" ("Absolute Value"; IV: 404) to make real changes in absolute values visible under the apparent changes in exchangeable values (see above "It is a great desideratum in Polit. Econ. to have a perfect measure of absolute value", ibid: 396; and also: "in Political Economy we want something more", ibid: 375). But, as developed below, it was also to be an instrument to dissipate another source of variability in prices than changes in conditions of production and distribution: changes in the value of money. To do that, the standard of value should also be the standard of money.

This is a direction to which Sraffa himself pointed in *Production of Commodities*, where Appendix D "References to the literature" reads as follows: "The conception of a standard measure of value as a medium between two extremes (§ 17 ff.) also belongs to Ricardo[1] and [...] the Standard commodity [...] has been evolved from it" (Sraffa 1960: 94). Footnote 1 attached to "Ricardo" directs the reader to Sraffa's own introduction to his edition of *Principles*, where he wrote: "In edition 3 [of *Principles*], therefore, the standard adopted was money 'produced with such proportions of the two kinds of capital as approach nearest to the average quantity employed in the production of most commodities'" (Sraffa 1951a: xliv). This excerpt from Ricardo's third edition of *Principles* (I: 45) was in fact attached to "gold considered as a commodity", and not to money as Sraffa writes, but this matters little since Ricardo himself ended up his argument saying:

> To facilitate, then, the object of this enquiry, although I fully allow that *money made of gold* is subject to most of the variations of other things, I shall suppose it to be invariable, and therefore all alterations in price to be

> occasioned by some alteration in the value of the commodity of which I may be speaking.
>
> (*Principles*; I: 46; my emphasis)

Under the assumption that gold bullion was both the standard of value and the standard of money, "price and value would be synonymous" for any commodity ("Absolute Value"; IV: 373), a statement to be understood as follows. Calling *s* the commodity selected as the invariable standard of value, the absolute value V_i of commodity *i* is defined by:

$$V_i = V_{is} \tag{3.10}$$

Gold bullion being the standard of money, gold has two prices, a price P_G in the market for bullion and a legal price $\overline{P_{GC}}$ when coined. As seen above in equation (3.9), for Ricardo the value of money conformed to the value of the standard when these two prices were equal $(P_G = \overline{P_{GC}})$. Replacing commodity *n* in (3.3) by gold bullion and assuming that this condition of conformity is fulfilled gives:

$$V_{iG} = \frac{P_i}{\overline{P_{GC}}} \tag{3.11}$$

Gold bullion being also by assumption the invariable standard of value, the absolute value of any commodity *i* is, according to (3.10):

$$V_i = V_{iG} \tag{3.12}$$

Hence:

$$V_i = \frac{P_i}{\overline{P_{GC}}} \tag{3.13}$$

Since $(1/\overline{P_{GC}})$ is the definition of the monetary unit (the pound) in terms of gold, the absolute value of any commodity – that is, its exchangeable value in terms of gold bullion – is equal to its gold-price: "price and value [are] synonymous". The relation between the standard of value and the standard of money should now be analysed in detail.

The standard of money

The notion of invariable measure of value first appeared in *High Price*, in a note on a paragraph where Ricardo criticised the double standard of money:

> No permanent* measure of value can be said to exist in any nation while the circulating medium consists of two metals, because they are constantly subject to vary in value with respect to each other.

> *Strictly speaking, there can be no permanent measure of value. A measure of value should itself be invariable; but this is not the case with either gold or silver, they being subject to fluctuations as well as other commodities. Experience has indeed taught us, that though the variations in the *value* of gold or silver may be considerable, on a comparison of distant periods, yet for short spaces of time their value is tolerably fixed. It is this property, among their other excellencies, which fits them better than any other commodity for the uses of money. Either gold or silver may therefore, in the point of view in which we are considering them, be called a measure of value.
>
> (*High Price*; III: 65; Ricardo's emphasis)

Ricardo then felt content with the value of gold or silver being "tolerably fixed" in the short run, although it might change a lot in the long run. This was enough in his perspective at the time, which was to show that the recent fall in the value of money was to be ascribed to an excess quantity of inconvertible notes issued, not to a fall in the value of the precious metals. This was not a sign of short-sightedness. Another factor might explain this neglect for the possible effect of a change in the value of the standard on the value of money: Ricardo considered that, because the Bank of England note was inconvertible and gold coins had disappeared from circulation, the value of money (whether the note or the coin) was then no longer regulated by a standard:

> That gold is no longer in practice the standard by which our currency is regulated is a truth. It is the ground of the complaint of the [Bullion] Committee (and of all who have written on the same side) against the present system.
>
> (*Reply to Bosanquet*; III: 255; see also V: 519: it was then "a currency regulated by no standard")

In other words, what happened to the value of the standard of money was then beyond the point. What had to be explained was the rise in the money *price* of gold bullion, which should be carefully distinguished from its *value*. Ricardo considered that failing to recognise this distinction was the source of much "error", particularly by Henry Thornton:

> The error of this [Thornton's] reasoning proceeds from not distinguishing between an increase in the value of gold, and an increase in its money price.
>
> (*High Price*, III: 60)

The rise in the price of gold was to be related to the excess issue of inconvertible notes, and the question of the possibility of a change in the value of gold could be left aside:

> In saying however that gold is at a high price, we are mistaken; it is not gold, it is paper which has changed its value.
>
> (ibid: 80)

This is the reason why, in the Bullion Essays, there is not more than a handful of references to a change in the value of gold – the most notable being to what happens when a new productive gold mine is discovered (see below Chapter 5).

Things changed in 1815. First, with the end of the Napoleonic wars the historical perspective was now the resumption of the convertibility of the Bank of England note and the question was henceforth how to ensure a "secure currency", *even in the long run.* Second, from an analytical point of view, Ricardo had since August 1813 (according to Sraffa, 1951d: 3) broadened his interest in political economy to the question of the rate of profit, which was the subject of the *Essay on Profits*, published in February 1815. This essay and the monetary pamphlet *Proposals for an Economical and Secure Currency*, published in February 1816, testify to the two lines of enquiry developed by Ricardo at the time and may be considered as blueprints of *On the Principles of Political Economy, and Taxation*, published in April 1817. It is not surprising that these two lines merged in Ricardo's mind, as shown in the following letter of 30 December 1815, sent to James Mill who had invited him to put his thoughts on paper on what would later become *Principles*:

> I know I shall be soon stopped by the word price, and then I must apply to you for advice and assistance. Before my readers can understand the proof I mean to offer, they must understand the theory of currency and of price. They must know that the prices of commodities are affected two ways one by the alteration in the relative value of money, which affects all commodities nearly at the same time, – the other by an alteration in the value of the particular commodity, and which affects the value of no other thing, excepting it enter into its composition. – This invariability of the value of the precious metals, but from particular causes relating to themselves only, such as supply and demand, is the sheet anchor on which all my propositions are built; for those who maintain that an alteration in the value of corn will alter the value of all other things, independently of its effects on the value of the raw material of which they are made, do in fact deny this doctrine of the cause of the variation in the value of gold and silver.
>
> (VI: 348–9)[14]

One should note that Ricardo evoked the difficulty raised by the word "price", *not* the word "value". The price of a commodity being measured in money – in contrast with its exchangeable value that was measured in any other commodity – a change in this price could as well reflect a change on the side of money – "the alteration of the relative value of money" – and on the side of the commodity – "an alteration in the value of the particular commodity". The difficulty mentioned here was thus *not* that considered above of a circular determination of exchangeable values and the rate of profit, a difficulty that occurred on the side of commodities. It concerned the possibility of disentangling these "two ways" through which "the prices of commodities may be affected". In order to isolate what was to be studied by the theory of value and distribution, Ricardo neutralised the operation of the monetary way by assuming the absence of any "alteration of the relative value of money". This method, which was "the sheet anchor on which all my propositions are built", would be subject to several emphatic warnings in all three successive editions of *Principles*, such as those quoted above (on pp. 108–9 and 86 respectively) from I: 46 and 48 and the following:

> I have already in a former part of this work considered gold as endowed with this uniformity [of value], and in the following chapter I shall continue the supposition. In speaking therefore of varying price, the variation will be always considered as being in the commodity, and never in the medium in which it is estimated.
>
> (*Principles*; I: 87)

> The reader is desired to bear in mind, that for the purpose of making the subject more clear, I consider money to be invariable in value, and therefore every variation of price to be referable to an alteration in the value of the commodity.
>
> (ibid: 110)

In contrast with what in modern theory is called the neutrality of money in respect to relative prices – namely that a *change* in the value of money in terms of commodities does not alter their relative prices – Ricardo discarded this question by making "the supposition" that there was *no* change in the value of money. And this he did (as quoted above from the letter to Mill of 30 December 1815) by assuming "this invariability of the value of the precious metals, but from particular causes relating to themselves only".[15] The invariability of the standard was consequently not only required to study the distribution of aggregate income or variations in the exchangeable values of commodities relatively to each other (as acknowledged by the modern literature), but also to allow interpreting a change in the money price of a commodity as reflecting the same change in the real value of that commodity – what Ricardo would call in his last manuscript its absolute value.

One may, however, notice a short cut in Ricardo's letter to Mill, which calls for an explanation. What is required to make visible a change in the value of a commodity under the variation in its price is the assumption of the invariability in the value of *money*. And this is considered by Ricardo as equivalent to the assumption of the invariability in the value of *gold*. This equivalence could be guaranteed if money and gold were one and the same thing, as suggested by Sraffa in his comment on the letter to Mill:

> The distinction between the two types of influences upon value (on the side of money and on the side of commodities) is made possible by Ricardo's treatment of money as a commodity like any other. Thus a change in wages could not alter the prices of commodities, since (if the gold mine from which money was obtained were in the same country) a rise of wages would affect the owner of the gold mine as much as the other industries. Hence it was the relative conditions of production of gold and of other commodities that determined prices, and not the remuneration of labour.
>
> (Sraffa 1951a: xxxiv–xxxv)

It is my contention throughout the present book that, in spite of numerous examples where Ricardo used one word for the other, he did *not* confuse gold and money, the standard and the currency. This means that, in order to consider the two assumptions on invariability as equivalent, Ricardo needed a theory of money establishing that the conditions under which the value of the standard was invariable would *also* ensure the invariability in the value of the currency. This is what he announced to Mill in his letter above: "Before my readers can understand the proof I mean to offer [on value and distribution], they must understand the theory of currency and of price." More precisely, what was needed was a theory of the value of money conforming to the value of the standard, so that the invariability of the latter ensured the invariability of the former. This was a shift away from the Bullion Essays where Ricardo had focused on the *difference* produced by inconvertibility between the value of paper money and the value of gold. Now, the object of the enquiry was the conditions under which the value of convertible paper money would *conform* to the value of gold.

At the time of the above letter to Mill, Ricardo was corresponding with him on the revised MS of *Proposals* (see Sraffa 1951e: 46–7), which contained the basic elements of this theory of money, as they were exposed at the beginning of the pamphlet:

> All writers on the subject of money have agreed that uniformity in the value of the circulating medium is an object greatly to be desired. Every improvement therefore which can promote an approximation to that object, by diminishing the causes of variation, should be adopted. No plan can possibly be devised which will maintain money at an absolutely uniform value, because it will always be subject to those variations to which the commodity itself is subject, which has been fixed upon as the standard. While the precious metals continue to be the standard of our currency, money must necessarily undergo the same variations in value as those metals. It was the comparative steadiness in the value of the precious metals, for periods of some duration, which probably was the cause of the preference given to them in all countries, as a standard by which to measure the value of other things. *A currency may be considered as perfect, of which the standard is invariable, which always conforms to that standard,* and in the use of which the utmost economy is practised.
>
> (*Proposals*; IV: 54–5; my emphasis)

Leaving aside the "economical" aspect, two conditions were thus required to obtain "a currency [that] may be considered as perfect": (a) the invariability of its standard; (b) its conformity to that standard. Gold being the standard of money, the first condition concerned the value of bullion and the second its price:

> While a standard is used, we are subject to only such a variation in the value of money, as the *standard* itself is subject to; but against such variation there is no possible remedy, and late events have proved that, during periods of war, when gold and silver are used for the payment of large armies, distant

> from home, those variations are much more considerable than has been generally allowed. This admission only proves that gold and silver are not so good a standard as they have been hitherto supposed; that they are themselves subject to greater variations than it is desirable a standard should be subject to. They are, however, the best with which we are acquainted. If any other commodity, less variable, could be found, it might very properly be adopted as the future standard of our money, provided it had all the other qualities which fitted it for that purpose; but, while these metals are the standard, the currency should conform in value to them, and whenever it does not, and the market price of bullion is above the mint price, the currency is depreciated. – This proposition is unanswered, and is unanswerable.
>
> (ibid: 62–3; Ricardo's emphasis)

The currency thus does not "conform in value" to its standard when "the market price of bullion is above the mint price" – a situation that, as in *High Price* for the case of inconvertibility, Ricardo described as a depreciation of the currency. While there was "no possible remedy" against a defect in the first condition (of invariability in the value of the standard), the second condition (of conformity of money to the standard) was fulfilled thanks to the existence of the standard itself. It was no longer its invariability in value that was operative but its capacity of "regulating" the quantity of the currency (more on this below in Chapter 4):

> The only use of a standard is to regulate the quantity, and by the quantity the value of a currency.
>
> (ibid: 59)

At the time of *Proposals*, Ricardo mostly focused on the condition of conformity: the Ingot Plan contained in this pamphlet was designed to ensure its fulfilment in the most "economical and secure" way. The difficulty raised by the condition of invariability was simply assumed away by contending that it was of no consequence for the working of the monetary system. To John Broadley who criticised him for considering bullion as standard, because "as the price of Bullion does and ever will *vary* it cannot deserve the denomination of *Standard*" (VII: 40; emphasis in the original) Ricardo answered on 14 June 1816:

> With respect to a standard measure of value, strictly so called, neither gold nor any other commodity can be such, for what is itself variable can never be an invariable measure of other things. But though it can not be an invariable measure of other things, it may be a variable measure of them, – and as we are possessed of none other than variable measures, this particular one has been by law constituted the general measure of value. It is not so variable as other things, and was therefore probably chosen; but if it were 20 times more so, – if from year to year it varied 30–40 or 50 pct., however inconvenient it might be; however desirable to alter the law; and change the commodity by which to estimate the value of other things; there would be no physical impossibility, as you seem to intimate, against making our paper money conform to this

> varying commodity. Suppose that the influence of the atmosphere were such on our measures of length, the yard for example, that it varied one fourth, being sometimes longer and sometimes shorter, than a given portion of the arc of the meridian which is supposed invariable. We might still use the yard measure and might justly call it (by law) our standard measure.
>
> (VII: 42–3)

This reference to a varying standard "constituted by law" to which paper money could conform is to be found also in *Principles*, at the last page of Chapter VII "On foreign trade":

> The nations of the world must have been early convinced, that there was no standard of value in nature, to which they might unerringly refer, and therefore chose a medium, which on the whole appeared to them less variable than any other commodity. To this standard we must conform till the law is changed, and till some other commodity is discovered, by the use of which we shall obtain a more perfect standard, than that which we have established.
>
> (*Principles*; I: 149)

As in the Bullion Essays, Ricardo's disregard of the variability in the value of the standard – in contrast with his interest for the invariability of its price – was based on the common argument that, although it might be great, it was probably lower than that of every other commodity, as testified by the fact that it had been chosen as standard by "the nations of the world".[16] This was a first reason for rejecting a standard of money composed of all the commodities: its average value would by definition be more variable than that of the least variable of them. There was, however, another reason, more practical:

> It has indeed been said that we might judge of its value by its relation, not to one, but to the mass of commodities. If it should be conceded, which it cannot be, that the issuers of paper money would be willing to regulate the amount of their circulation by such a test, they would have no means of so doing; for when we consider that commodities are continually varying in value, as compared with each other; and that when such variation takes place, it is impossible to ascertain which commodity has increased, which diminished in value, it must be allowed that such a test would be of no use whatever.
>
> (*Proposals*; IV: 59)

As noted earlier, what is here at stake is not the definition of the value of money but the impossibility of measuring it. One thing was to define the value of money as its purchasing power upon "the mass of commodities" (see Section 3.2 above), another thing to design a "test" by which "the issuers of paper money would be willing to regulate the amount of their circulation".[17] The argument was that a test based on this mass could not target a change in the value of money – which affected all prices of commodities proportionally – since this change would be mixed with changes in relative prices that happened all the time, independently of the value of money. Here also, the interpretation of the price of bullion as being in Ricardo a proxy of the general price level is not only contrary to textual evidence but also to theory: Ricardo was no forerunner of inflation targeting. The only price that for him could be targeted unambiguously was the *price* of the standard, knowing that this did not guarantee the stability of the value of money, liable to change with the *value* of the standard. Against such change, as quoted above, "there is no possible remedy"; the only mitigation of this accepted drawback was to choose as the standard of money the commodity believed to be the least variable in value. With the theory of value adopted in *Principles*, it would be the commodity whose conditions of production were the least liable to change: this was the criterion used by Ricardo to favour gold rather than silver (see V: 390–1; 427).

A dilemma

Up to this point, Ricardo's analysis of the standard of money was in line with his analysis of the standard of value: as long as law validates as the standard of money the commodity (gold bullion) believed to be the least variable in value through time, that is, produced with quantities of labour varying little, the aim of the most perfect monetary system was to stabilise the market price of this standard at the level of its legal price. However, digging into the analysis of the standard of value for the third edition of *Principles* and the manuscript "Absolute Value" showed that the assumed invariability of the cost of production of gold bullion through time was a necessary but not a sufficient condition for adopting it as standard. It should also be, as far as the durability of capital was concerned, "a mean between the extremes" ("Absolute Value"; IV: 405). And this led to a dilemma. *Either*, the standard of money was the actual gold bullion and there was no reason why it would be produced in such average conditions; consequently, it varied in *value* even if it remained produced with the same quantity of labour through time, since its exchangeable value was affected by any change in the distribution between wages and profits. *Or*, since no commodity produced in average conditions could be found in nature, one should adopt as the standard of money a composite commodity constructed in appropriate proportions.

Both options were unsatisfactory. The variability in the value of the standard of money destroyed "the sheet anchor on which all my propositions [on value and distribution] are built", as Ricardo wrote in his letter to Mill of 30 December 1815. In "Absolute Value", Ricardo repeated that the adoption as the standard of money of his "mean between the extremes" – supposing it produced in unchanged conditions through time – was necessary to render the values of commodities visible under their money prices:

> In Mr. Ricardo's measure [...] price and value would be synonymous while gold the standard of money cost the same expenditure of capital and labour to produce it.
>
> ("Absolute Value"; IV: 373)

But at the same time he did not envisage the option of replacing actual gold bullion by a constructed composite standard of money. One may explain this unwillingness by the existence of an important difference between the use of a standard of value by "the Political Economist" and the use of a standard of money by individuals in a monetary economy. This difference was law, which had two consequences that emphasised the social character of the standard of value conceived by Ricardo as the standard of money – a social character consistent with his repeated assertion that no such standard could be found in nature.[18] The first consequence was that the commodity chosen as the standard of money had not only a market price but also a legal one, and decisions of the issuer of money as to its quantity should aim at making the market price of the standard conform to its legal level. This interference with the private activity of the producers of the "standard commodity" (*Proposals*; IV: 58) was welcome since it prevented money from being depreciated (or appreciated). However, the adoption of a composite "standard commodity" constructed with actual commodities combined in appropriate proportions would extend such interference to the private activity of the producers of all these selected commodities, even if only a weighted average of their market prices was legally fixed – a provision at odds with Ricardo's general conception of society. Moreover the interference with the activity of the private producers of the standard commodity was all the more acceptable in the case of gold bullion since it was a commodity produced abroad; this would no longer be the case if the individual commodities entering the composition of the standard were produced nationally. Such a composite standard of money was consequently undesirable.

It was also impossible because of a second consequence of law applied to money. In contrast with a measure of length, law did not only enforce the use of a unit of measure, however variable. It enforced it in a particular way, by opening the possibility of arbitrages, permitted by the necessary complement to the legal definition of the monetary unit: convertibility of the standard into the currency and of the currency into the standard. According to Ricardo, these arbitrages had a stabilising effect (see below in Chapter 7), except in the case of a double standard of money (gold *and* silver) and this was the reason why he opposed it. One may think that, in Ricardo's view, such destabilising effect of a double standard would be magnified with a composite standard, even if his plan of a circulation exclusively composed of notes convertible into the standard (instead of coins) were adopted. In the 1880s, Alfred Marshall tried to marry Ricardo's proposal of note convertibility into bullion with bimetallism (conceived by him as a scale model of a "tabular standard" composed of many commodities combined in certain proportions so as to reduce its variations in value), recommending the adoption of note convertibility into a bimetallic bullion standard as a way to reduce the variability of the *value* of the standard of money (Marshall 1887). But it may be shown that Ricardo's intuition proved well-founded: this reduction had a counterpart in the impossibility of stabilising the *price* of the standard of money (see Deleplace 2013b).

The conclusion is that the above-quoted requirement formulated in *Proposals* ("A currency may be considered as perfect, of which the standard is invariable, which always conforms to that standard"; IV: 55) could not be met: what made the standard "invariable" (being "a mean between the extremes") prevented money from "conforming" to it, and what allowed money conforming to the standard (the selection by law of an actual commodity) prevented the standard from being invariable in value.

To overcome this dilemma, Ricardo assumed in the third edition of *Principles* that gold was *actually* "a mean between the extremes". As already quoted above:

> May not gold be considered as a commodity produced with such proportions of the two kinds of capital as approach nearest to the average quantity employed in the production of most commodities? May not these proportions be so nearly equally distant from the two extremes, the one where little fixed capital is used, the other where little labour is employed, as to form a just mean between them?
>
> (*Principles*; I: 45–6)

This solution presented in an interrogative form was evidently a *petitio principii*, as acknowledged in Ricardo's answer to Malthus's critique addressed to his "invariable measure of value":

> It was never contended that gold under the present circumstances was a good measure of value, it was only hypothetically, and for the purpose of illustrating a principle, supposed that all the known causes of the variability of gold, were removed.
>
> (*Notes on Malthus*; II: 82–3)[19]

The disillusion expressed in Ricardo's last letter of 5 September 1823 quoted above was thus probably caused by the understanding that, even if the invariable standard of value could be conceived by "the Political Economist", it could not act as the standard of money in the actual working of a monetary economy.[20]

3.4 Conclusion

The theory of value and distribution contained in *Principles* dissipated some ambiguities that weakened the Bullion Essays: the demonstration that a change in the rate of profit or in the wage rate – these two distributive variables being inversely related – affected relative prices because of differences between commodities as to the durability of capital advanced in their production allowed Ricardo to exclude taxation as a possible cause of equiproportional change in all money prices and to define rigorously the value of money as its purchasing power over all commodities except the standard (gold bullion).

However, this theory had another consequence: the demonstration that the value of any standard could only be invariable in terms of those commodities being produced with the same durability of capital forced Ricardo to face a dilemma between stabilising the value of the standard of money and stabilising its price. This meant that two of the conditions for a perfect currency, the invariability in value of the standard of money and the conformity of the currency to that standard, could not both be fulfilled. This resulted in the admission that changes in the value of the standard were actually responsible for changes in the value of money more than was usually believed.

The theory of value and distribution adopted in *Principles* thus paved the way to Ricardo's mature theory of money, in which changes in the value of money were caused directly by changes in the value of the standard and indirectly (through the price of the standard) by variations in the quantity of money. This is what the next chapter will show.

Appendix 3: An aborted attempt at the non-neutrality of money in respect to relative prices

In Chapter XV "Taxes on profits" of *Principles*, Ricardo emphasised that, if profits are taxed, a fall in the value of money alters relative prices, an effect that would not occur in the absence of such taxation:

> If a country were not taxed, and money should fall in value, its abundance in every market would produce similar effects in each. If meat rose 20 per cent., bread, beer, shoes, labour, and every commodity, would also rise 20 per cent.; it is necessary they should do so, to secure to each trade the same rate of profits. But this is no longer true when any of these commodities is taxed; if in that case they should all rise in proportion to the fall in the value of money, profits would be rendered unequal [...] and capital would be removed from one employment to another, till an equilibrium of profits was restored, which could only be, after the relative prices were altered.
>
> (*Principles*; I: 209)

This non-neutrality of money in the case of taxation on profits is the consequence of the unequal effect of such taxation on the prices of commodities, because, as mentioned above in the text of Chapter 3, commodities differ as to the durability of capital advanced to produce and bring them to market. Ricardo even suggests that this "very important principle" might explain what happened when money was depreciated during the period of inconvertibility. The quotation continues:

> Will not this principle account for the different effects, which it was remarked were produced on the prices of commodities, from the altered value of money during the Bank-restriction? It was objected to those who contended that the currency was at that period depreciated, from the too great abundance of the paper circulation, that, if that were the fact, all commodities ought to have risen in the same proportion; but it was found that many had varied considerably more than others, and thence it was inferred that the rise of prices was owing to something affecting the value of commodities, and not to any alteration in the value of the currency. It appears, however, as we have just seen, that in a country where commodities are taxed, they will not all vary in

> price in the same proportion, either in consequence of a rise or of a fall in the value of currency.
>
> (ibid: 209–10)

As is well-known, the question of how much of a change in money prices should be ascribed to a change in the value of money and to other causes was much debated at Ricardo's time, in the context of first rising and later falling prices, and it is curious that such a striking argument was not used by Ricardo in these debates. Since the disturbing influence on prices of differences between commodities in the durability of capital was only discovered by Ricardo in *Principles*, one could not expect this argument to have been used in the Bullion Essays. When the debate on money and prices was again aroused in 1819–1823, the aim of Ricardo was now at minimising the general effect of the rise of the pound to pre-war parity and at explaining accordingly the huge fall in agricultural prices by specific non-monetary phenomena; the effect of a change in the value of money on relative prices may have been considered by Ricardo as a counterproductive complexity in public discussion.

As far as I know, the only other mention by Ricardo of taxation making money non-neutral in respect to relative prices is the one referred to by Sraffa in a footnote of the same chapter of *Principles*: "this subject is further discussed in a letter to Trower of 28 Jan. 1820" (I: 210 n). In this letter, Ricardo answered to questions raised by his correspondent presumably about this chapter (the letter from Trower is not extant):

> I have looked to the passages in my book to which you refer. [...] I have supposed a case of our having the mines which supplied our standard, in this country, and that the profits of the miner were not taxed, then commodities would rise in price to the amount of the tax, or the miners business would be more profitable than any other, and consequently would draw capital to that concern. If then all commodities rose in price what would they rise? not in proportion to their value, but in proportion to the capitals employed in their production.
>
> (VIII: 153)

Although both this hypothetical case and the historical one mentioned above concern the effect of a *fall* in the value of money when commodities are taxed, the statement that they "will not all vary in price in the same proportion" applies "either in consequence of a rise or of a fall in the value of currency" (I: 210). In fact, the numerical example used by Ricardo in the chapter and commented on in the letter to Trower concerns the effect of a *rise* in the value of money. The quotation given above in the text of Chapter 3 and mentioning "two manufacturers [who] might employ precisely the same amount of capital" continues:

> The one might sell his goods for 4000*l.*, the other for 10,000*l.*, and they might both employ 10,000*l.* of capital, and obtain 20 per cent. profit or 2000*l.* The capital of one might consist, for example, of 2000*l.* circulating capital, to

> be reproduced, and 8000*l.* fixed, in buildings and machinery; the capital of the other, on the contrary, might consist of 8000*l.* of circulating, and of only 2000*l.* fixed capital in machinery and buildings. Now, if each of these persons were to be taxed ten per cent. on his income, or 200*l.*, the one, to make his business yield him the general rate of profit, must raise his goods from 10,000*l.* to 10,200*l.*; the other would also be obliged to raise the price of his goods from 4000*l.* to 4200*l.* Before the tax, the goods sold by one of these manufacturers were 2½ times more valuable than the goods of the other; after the tax they will be 2.42 times more valuable: the one kind will have risen two per cent.; the other five per cent.: consequently a tax upon income, whilst money continued unaltered in value, would alter the relative prices and value of commodities. [...] If under these circumstances, money rose in value, from whatever cause it might proceed, it would not affect the prices of commodities in the same proportion. The same cause which would lower the price of one from 10,200*l.* to 10,000*l.* or less than two per cent. would lower the price of the other from 4200*l.* to 4000*l.* or 4¾ per cent. If they fell in any different proportion, profits would not be equal; for to make them equal, when the price of the first commodity was 10,000*l.*, the price of the second should be 4000*l.*; and when the price of the first was 10,200*l.*, the price of the other should be 4200*l.*
>
> (*Principles*; I: 207–8)

Ricardo's assumption was therefore that the (unequal) effect on prices of the rise in the value of money exactly counteracted the (unequal) effect on prices of the imposition of a tax on profits. This assumption is repeated four times in the same chapter. First Ricardo analyses the consequence for the farmer of a taxation of all trades except his, in the case where "an alteration in the value of money might sink all the taxed commodities to their former price" (ibid: 210). He then supposes that the profits of the farmer are also taxed and analyses the situation of his landlord "if in consequence of a rise in the value of money, commodities sold at their former price" (ibid: 211) and again "if money should rise in value, and all things should, after a tax on the profits of stock, fall to their former prices" (ibid: 212). Finally he considers how taxation affects the stock-holder "if, from the alteration in the value of money, all commodities were to sink to their former price" (ibid: 213).

Besides these consequences of a tax on profits combined with a rise in the value of money for the respective situations of various income-earners, the main conclusion drawn by Ricardo from his numerical example was the symmetrical effect on prices of both phenomena: since the taxation of profits affected prices in unequal proportions, the counteracting effect of a rise in the value of money also affected them in the same unequal proportions and made the price of each commodity revert to its initial level before taxation.

In his letter to Trower, Ricardo repeated his example of two commodities produced with a capital of £10000 each, and also his conclusion that, after their prices have been increased by taxation, they revert to their original levels if the value of money rises. An addition to the example was, however, made by Ricardo, with the above quotation from the letter continuing as follows:

> [A]nd therefore as commodities selling for £4000 may be the result of the employment of the same amount of capital as commodities which sell for £10000, these commodities would not rise in proportion to their prices but if one rose £200 – the other would also rise £200. Now in this situation of things suppose money to rise in value and the goods which sell for £10200 to fall to £10000 the other goods which sell for £4200 will fall to £4000, but if money should continue to rise in value and consequently the goods which sold for £10000 should fall to £5000, then those which sold for £4000 would fall to £2000. Up to [a] certain point then they fall in proportion to the capitals employed in their production, but subsequently in proportion to the value of the goods themselves. This is the opinion which I wished to express, whether it be a correct one is another question. On the hasty consideration which I can now give it I see no reason to doubt it.
>
> (VIII: 153–4)

This "opinion" here subject to "hasty consideration" concerned a curious situation: starting from the level of prices obtained after imposition of the tax, a rise in the value of money lowered prices in *unequal* proportions until they reached their levels before tax, after which it lowered them in *equal* proportions, as would occur had there been no tax. Such situation requires digging a little further into the numerical example.

Before doing it, one may inquire whether this is worthwhile, that is, whether the particular case considered by Ricardo is general enough to support the analytical conclusion and the historical inference drawn from it. In his letter to Trower, Ricardo recalled that he assumed in his book that gold-money was produced domestically and not taxed – a hypothetical case allowing to consider a situation where all prices except that of gold should rise after taxation in order to maintain the uniformity of the rate of profit on all capitals, including the one advanced in the production of gold. This hypothetical case of course did not apply to England who had no gold mines, and one might wonder whether it was relevant to analyse the case of a country that imported gold – in other words, whether it was relevant in general. Three reasons suggest that for Ricardo it was so. First the production of gold abroad was by definition exempt from taxation on profits in England, and this corresponded to the hypothetical case in which the price of gold was unaffected by the tax, while all domestically produced goods bore it. Second, as quoted above, relative prices were affected by a rise in the value of money "from whatever cause it might proceed" (*Principles*; I: 208), that is, whether it was caused by a greater difficulty of production which increased the value of gold bullion or by a reduction in the quantity of money which made it appreciate – a situation that could occur in all countries. Third, the allusion made by Ricardo to the restriction period in England was precisely an example of the effect on relative prices produced by "the altered value of money" when this alteration was a depreciation of money and not a fall in the value of gold bullion wherever it was produced.

Another peculiarity of the numerical example given by Ricardo is in the round figures chosen by him. They suggest that he adopted the simplifying assumption that the durability of fixed capital was infinite, while only circulating capital was "to be reproduced" (ibid: 207) in one year. If commodity *i*, the production of which requires a capital of £10000 divided into £2000 of circulating capital and £8000 of fixed capital, is sold at a price of £4000, the reproduction of circulating capital in one year absorbs £2000 and nothing is left after payment of the £2000 profit. Similarly, if commodity *j*, the production of which requires a capital of £10000 divided into £8000 of circulating capital and £2000 of fixed capital, is sold at a price of £10000, the reproduction of circulating capital absorbs £8000 and nothing is left after payment of the £2000 profit. This simplifying assumption is, however, in no way necessary: as observed by Sraffa (1951a: xlii), beginning with the second edition of *Principles* Ricardo introduced differences between commodities in the durability of circulating capital because of unequal times it took to bring them to market, and various examples may be given allowing the durability of circulating *and* fixed capital being consistent with the figures chosen by Ricardo.[21]

We may now return to Ricardo's numerical example of two commodities produced with the same amount of capital but different proportions of circulating and fixed capital – that is, a different length with which the same amount of capital is advanced to produce each commodity and bring it to market. Table 3.1 illustrates the different situations involved in this example. Let $\Delta V_M / V_M$ be the rate at which the value of money increases, P_i and P_j the respective money prices of commodities *i* and *j*, C_i and C_j the circulating capital to be reproduced, T_i and T_j the amount of the tax on profits at the rate of 10 per cent, π_i and π_j the profits, K_i and K_j the capitals advanced, and r_i and r_j the rates of profit.

As mentioned in the quotation, Ricardo's first statement was that the imposition of a tax on profits, while the value of money remained unchanged, raised both prices in unequal proportions. A 10 per cent tax turned initial situation A into B, with the price of *i* rising from £4000 to £4200 and the price of *j* from £10000 to £10200. The rise in price was 5 per cent for *i* and 2 per cent for *j*, higher for the commodity the production of which required the £10000 capital being advanced for the longer time. The relative price of *j* in terms of *i* was thus lowered from 2.5 to 2.42 (2.4286 exactly), as a consequence of the tax. Ricardo's second statement was that, after prices had been raised by taxation, a rise in the value of money: (a) should lower them in different proportions if the rate of profit was to remain equal in both industries; (b) might lower them to their respective levels before taxation. Both propositions are, however, unwarranted, as it may be shown on the basis of the numerical example.

On the one hand, a proportional fall, applied to both prices and to their component parts, keeps the rate of profit uniform, whatever the magnitude of the rise in the value of money. For example, a rise of "less than 2 per cent" (1.96 per cent exactly) turns situation B into C: P_j reverts to its initial level of £10000 and r_j = £1961 / £9804 = 20 per cent, P_i being lowered to £4118 and $r_i = r_j$. Alternatively, a rise in the value of money of "4¾ per cent" (4.76 per cent exactly) turns situation B into D : P_i reverts to its initial level of

Table 3.1 Various situations involved in Ricardo's numerical example in Chapter XV "Taxes on profits" of *Principles*

Situation	$\Delta V_M / V_M$ in per cent	P_i in £	C_i in £	T_i in £	π_i in £	K_i in £	r_i in per cent	P_j in £	C_j in £	T_j in £	π_j in £	K_j in £	r_j in per cent
A	0	4000	2000	0	2000	10000	20	10000	8000	0	2000	10000	20
B	0	4200	2000	200	2000	10000	20	10200	8000	200	2000	10000	20
C	1.96	4118	1961	196	1961	9804	20	10000	7843	196	1961	9804	20
D	4.76	4000	1905	190	1905	9524	20	9714	7619	190	1905	9524	20
E	1.96	4000	1961	185	1854	9804	18.9	10000	7843	196	1961	9804	20
F	4.76	4000	1905	190	1905	9524	20	10000	7619	216	2165	9524	22.7
G	?	4000	1905	190	1905	9524	20	10000	7843	196	1961	9804	20

£4000 and $r_i =$ £1905 / £9524 = 20 per cent, P_j sinking to £9714 and $r_j = r_i$. A fall of both prices in the same proportion, whatever it is, thus preserves the uniformity (and the level) of the rate of profit, contrary to Ricardo's affirmation that it cannot.

On the other hand, after a rise in the value of money, the return of both prices to their respective levels before taxation is not consistent with a uniform rate of profit. As seen above, with a "less than 2 per cent" rise in the value of money bringing P_j back to £10000 and allowing the capital advanced in the production of *j* earning a 20 per cent rate of profit, P_i should be equal to £4118 to allow the same capital earning the same rate of profit. If situation B is turned into E and *i* sells for £4000 (its initial price before taxation), capital advanced in its production earns a rate of profit r_i of 18.9 per cent only. Alternatively, with a "4¾ per cent" rise in the value of money bringing P_i back to £4000 and allowing the capital advanced in the production of *i* earning a 20 per cent rate of profit, P_j should be equal to £9714 to allow the same capital earning the same rate of profit. If situation B is turned into F and *j* sells for £10000 (its initial price before taxation), capital advanced in its production earns a higher rate of profit r_j of 22.7 per cent. In both cases, the rate of profit in the production of *j* is higher than in the production of *i*; capital then moves from *i* to *j* and consequently P_i increases above £4000 and P_j falls below £10000, until the rate of profit is again uniform. This testifies to the fact that a combination of $P_i =$ £4000 and $P_j =$ £10000 is not consistent with a tax on profits and a uniform rate of profit, contrary to Ricardo's affirmation that it is.

When thus Ricardo wrote in the above quotation from *Principles* that "to make them [profits] equal, when the price of the first commodity was 10,000*l.*, the price of the second should be 4000*l.*; and when the price of the first was 10,200*l.*, the price of the other should be 4200*l.*" he overlooked that in the first case profits were not taxed, while in the second they were. Prices could not revert to their initial levels unless profits ceased to be taxed. But this reversal was then not due to the fact that the rise in the value of money exactly counteracted the effect of the tax but to the removal of the tax itself. This is implied in the curious addition to the example in the letter to Trower: "Up to certain point then they [prices] fall in proportion to the capitals employed in their production, but subsequently in proportion to the value of the goods themselves." Starting from levels reverted to after removal of the tax, the second fall in proportion to prices (from £4000 to £2000 for P_i and £10000 to £5000 for P_j) was consequent upon the rise in the value of money, but the first fall in proportion to capitals (from £4200 to £4000 for P_i and £10200 to £10000 for P_j) was due to that removal, not to the rise in the value of money, as asserted by Ricardo.

There is, however, one special case in which the reversal to the initial prices preserves the existence of the tax and the uniformity of the rate of profit: it is when each commodity only requires itself to be produced. In this case of self-reproducing commodities situation B is turned into G: if P_i and its component parts fall by 4.76 per cent, and P_j and its component parts by 1.96 per cent, both commodities sell at their initial prices and the rate of profit remains at 20 per cent on both capitals. Not only Ricardo's result is restricted to this special case, but the notion of change in the value of money seems then to be deprived of any definite meaning, since the magnitude of this change is different in each self-reproducing industry, with the consequence that capitals advanced now differ in price.

The conclusion is that Ricardo's unexpected attempt at the non-neutrality of money in respect to relative prices when commodities are taxed on profits cannot rely on his numerical example. On the contrary, this example shows that money should be neutral – that is, a change in the value of money should affect prices proportionately in the opposite direction – if that kind of tax based on capital is to affect prices in a non-proportional way when commodities differ in the durability of capital advanced in their production.[22]

Notes

1 The reference to standard metal implied stating its fineness; see above Chapter 1.

2 Marcuzzo and Rosselli's last sentence is valid as far as *depreciation* is concerned, but does not apply to *a fall in the value of money*, which is essentially distinct from depreciation – see the next quotation from Ricardo in the text – and is identical with a general rise in money prices, except that of bullion.

3 This statement was already contained in *Principles*:

> Some indeed more reasonably maintained, that 130*l.* in paper was not of equal value with 130 *l.* in metallic money; but they said that it was the metallic money which had changed its value, and not the paper money. They wished to confine the meaning of the word depreciation to an actual fall of value, and not to a comparative difference between the value of money, and the standard by which by law it is regulated.
>
> (I: 149)

4 This letter is, according to Viner, one of the illustrations of the fact that "Ricardo, in his published writings, seems to have avoided the use of the term 'level' for the

general state of prices, although he used it in this sense freely in his private correspondence"(Viner 1937: 313; the other examples given by Viner are, in the later Sraffa edition, VI: 40, 108–9, 170). Contrary to Viner's observation, the word 'level' is not used here by Ricardo to designate "the general state of prices", but the result is the same, provided a change in the aggregate level of the quantity of money generates a proportional change in the general price level in the same direction.

5 Equation (3.5) is formally the same as the equation in Marcuzzo and Rosselli (1994b: 1254): "It follows that the value of money affects the determination of commodity prices through the money/gold ratio, not the gold/commodities ratio, as can be seen in the following equation: $P_{\text{money/commodities}} = P_{\text{money/gold}} \cdot P_{\text{gold/commodities}}$". As mentioned above, Marcuzzo and Rosselli define the value of money as V_{MG} ("$P_{\text{money/gold}}$") and not V_{MR} like here. However, defining the current value of money by its purchasing power over gold bullion in its market is not enough to specify money by its relation to the standard: the existence of a legal price of gold in the form of money is required. In modern parlance, gold in (3.5) as in Marcuzzo and Rosselli's equation is only a numéraire, not the standard of money.

6 Incidentally, the definition by Ricardo of the condition of conformity as an equality between the value of money and the value of gold bullion should dispel any doubt about the definition of the value of money as its purchasing power over all commodities except gold bullion: since V_{GR} is measured in terms of *R*, it must also be the case of V_{MR}.

7 Taxation itself did not change aggregate demand:

> If a tax, however burdensome it may be, falls on revenue, and not on capital, it does not diminish demand, it only alters the nature of it. It enables Government to consume as much of the produce of the land and labour of the country, as was before consumed by the individuals who contribute to the tax, an evil sufficiently great without overcharging it.
>
> (*Principles*; I: 237)

If the tax diminished capital, it reduced the aggregate supply of commodities, hence the aggregate demand. What Ricardo contended was that no taxation, of whichever kind and with whichever consequence, could reduce the aggregate demand independently of the aggregate supply, hence resulted in a general glut.

8

> This principle of the division of the produce of labour and capital between wages and profits, which I have attempted to establish, appears to me so certain, that excepting in the immediate effects, I should think it of little importance whether the profits of stock, or the wages of labour, were taxed.
>
> (*Principles*; I: 226)

9 A tax on capital lowers the rate of profit and has the same effect as a tax on profits. A tax on rent has no effect on prices since rent is not a component of price; such tax falls entirely on the landlord (see I: 173, 181, 257).

10 Ricardo here assumes that all commodities are taxed on profits, except money ("whilst money continued unaltered in value").

11 We will see below that these two references in fact concern the standard of value in the course of a discussion by Ricardo of the standard of the currency.

12 On this notion of permanent causes in Ricardo, as opposed to temporary ones, see Depoortère (2008, 2013) and Marcuzzo (2014).

13 These were probably the last written words by Ricardo. In note 1 of IX: 385, attached to the title: "552. Ricardo to Mill", Sraffa writes: "On the same day (5 September) Ricardo was struck with his fatal illness (see the following letters)." The first "following letter"

is dated 6 September 1823 and was sent by Anthony Austin (Ricardo's son-in-law) to Hutches Trower. It reads: "I am grieved to tell you that Mr. Ricardo is at this moment confined to his bed by an Illness originating from cold in the ear. The Ladies have been in constant attendance at his bedside for the last 2 days it has therefore devolved on me to write to you" (IX: 388). Ricardo died on 11 September at about noon.

14 The first two sentences are quoted by Sraffa in his "Introduction" to *Principles* (Sraffa 1951a: xiv). He further commented on the rest of the quotation:

> This is the first time that he [Ricardo] faces the necessity for a general solution of the problem, instead of being content with dealing with the difficulties of price piece-meal as they arise in particular problems [in the *Essay on Profits*]. At once a proper understanding of the matter appears to him as involving: (a) the distinction between causes which affect the value of money and causes which affect the value of commodities; (b) the supposition of the invariability of the precious metals as a standard of value; (c) the opposition to the view that the price of corn regulates the prices of all other commodities. These three things, which are so closely connected in his mind as to be almost identified, are what he calls 'the sheet anchor on which all my propositions are built'.
>
> (ibid: xxxiv)

15 It will be noticed that at the end of 1815 Ricardo still emphasised "supply and demand" among the "particular causes" of variation in "the value of the precious metals", as he had done in 1810 – the theory of value based on the cost of production would have to wait one more year.

16 Discussing "the effect on the natural price of the precious metals" produced by "the discovery of America and the rich mines in which it abounds" and by "improvements in working the mines" (*Principles*; I: 86), Ricardo observed:

> From whatever cause it may have proceeded, the effect has been so slow and gradual, that little practical inconvenience has been felt from gold and silver being the general medium in which the value of all other things is estimated. Though undoubtedly a variable measure of value, there is probably no commodity subject to fewer variations. This and the other advantages which these metals possess, such as their hardness, their malleability, their divisibility, and many more, have justly secured the preference every where given to them, as a standard for the money of civilized countries.
>
> (ibid: 86–7)

17 This quotation was used by Viner as an illustration of the fact that "Even after 1798, the leading economists until the time of Jevons either revealed no acquaintance with the notion of representing, by means of statistical averages, either a level of prices, or changes in such level, or found it inacceptable for various reasons, good or bad" (Viner 1937: 312–13). What according to Viner was "inacceptable" by Ricardo was the use of "statistical averages", not the notion of general price level, which, as mentioned above in Section 3.2, was acknowledged by Viner. Although mentioning Viner, however, Schumpeter considered the same extract of *Proposals* as a "categorical statement" on the general price level, which would prove that Ricardo "definitely rejected it" (Schumpeter 1954: 701 and n.7). This wrong inference may be Schumpeter's only respectful – albeit indirect – opinion on Ricardo's theory of money:

> The refusal to recognize the price level as a meaningful, or measurable, concept is, however, a point against Ricardo only from the standpoint of modern economists,

> who handle it as a matter of course. From the standpoint of the small but distinguished group who believe neither in price index numbers nor in the price-level concept itself (like Professor von Mises, von Hayek, and, with some qualifications, also von Haberler) it is, of course, a point in his favor and proof of sound insight.
>
> (ibid)

18 See for example the above quotations from *Principles*, I: 149, "Absolute Value", IV: 404, and IX: 387. This social character casts a doubt on the suggestion by Kurz and Salvadori that, referring to the durability of capital applied to the production of commodities, "the reduction of all differences to one of time complies with Ricardo's pre-conception that the standard of value should ultimately be referred back to some 'object in nature'" (Kurz and Salvadori 2015a: 210). This cannot apply to a standard of value used as the standard of money.

19 Sinha (2010a) uses this sentence to prove that for Ricardo the invariable standard was only an abstraction, unrelated to the standard of money at the time: "Of course, Ricardo's choice of gold as his measure of value was not made on any empirical consideration but was simply a theoretical abstraction" (Sinha 2010a: 124; for Sinha's interpretation of Ricardo's invariable measure of value, see Sinha 2010b). Ricardo's quotation continues as follows:

> I said 'suppose all variations in the value of gold to cease, it would then be a good measure of value. I know they cannot cease – I know it is a metal liable to the same variations as other things and therefore not a good measure of value, but *I beg you to suppose all causes of variation removed, that we may speak about the variations of other things in an unvarying measure without confusion.*' Am I answered by being told that gold is variable, and that I have omitted to mention some of the causes of its variation?
>
> (II: 83; my emphasis)

This method was indeed meant to abstract from the "causes of variation" in the exchange values of commodities, but also to remove the causes of variations in prices originating on the side of money, in line with the above-quoted letter to Mill. And to do that one should assume an invariable standard *of money*. The fact that gold the standard of money was not *actually* invariable in value was precisely the source of Ricardo's dilemma.

20 For another discussion of the relation between the standard of value and the standard of money, see Marcuzzo and Rosselli (1994a) and Cartelier (1994). Mason (1963) studies in depth the genealogy of the notion of monetary standard.

21 The constraint for commodity i is $2000\,c_i + 8000\,f_i = 4000 - 2000$ with c_i and f_i the ratio of the annual amortization to the value of the circulating or fixed capital (the reciprocal of their durability in years). With $c_i = 1$, $f_i = 0$, but, for example, with $c_i = 0.8$ (the durability of circulating capital being 1.25 year), $f_i = 0.05$ (the durability of fixed capital being 20 years). Similarly, the constraint for commodity j is $8000\,c_j + 2000\,f_j = 10000 - 2000$. With $c_j = 1$, $f_j = 0$, but, for example, with $c_j = 0.95$ (the durability of circulating capital being 1.05 year), $f_i = 0.2$ (the durability of fixed capital being 5 years).

22 In their study of the same question, Carr and Ahiakpor (1982) also observe that, contrary to Ricardo's affirmation, a proportional fall in price of the two commodities consequent upon a rise in the value of money preserves the equality of profits, so that "the source of the non-neutrality is something of a mystery" (Carr and Ahiakpor 1982: 149). They try to rescue Ricardo's conclusion by assuming that the historical type of tax that

Ricardo had in mind was subject to an effective rate that changed as a consequence of the change in the value of money:

> We have now seen that the structure of commodity taxes and profit taxes that existed in England just prior to the writing of the *Principles* made real effective tax rates a function of the [general] level of prices. Under these circumstances, a change in the money supply would lead to a change in the level of prices and this would lead to a change in effective tax rates and, as a result, change relative prices. We would like to advance the hypothesis that this is the mechanism that was in the background of Ricardo's analysis when he stated the principle that in a world of taxes a change in the money supply would lead to a change in relative prices. This interpretation of the Ricardian non-neutrality principle – that it arises from the dependence of real effective tax rates on the price level, for commodity and/or profit taxes – [...] explains why in a world of taxes, money will have non-neutral effects.
>
> (ibid: 163)

Apart from the fact that neither in Chapter XV of *Principles* nor in the letter to Trower, Ricardo was making such supposition, it would be no proof of the non-neutrality of money in a world of taxes but simply reiterates the statement – disputed by no one – that a change in the rate of this kind of tax alters relative prices.

4 The two causes of change in the value of money

> *A currency might be depreciated, without falling in value; it might fall in value, without being depreciated, because depreciation is estimated only by reference to a standard.*
>
> (Speech in the House of Commons, 11 June 1823; V: 311)

Being defined in terms of all commodities except the standard, the value of money expressed the purchasing power of the people over goods. A change in this value consequently affected their real wealth (for the part of it composed of assets denominated in money) and their relative position as income-earners. It impacted debt contracts, such as land leases and loans to the State: as seen in Chapter 2 above, the question of whether the return to the pre-war parity of the pound compensated or not the loss suffered by the "public creditor" during the period of depreciation was hotly debated when resumption of convertibility was discussed. A rise in the value of money increased the real burden of taxation, and the general fall in money prices was held by the land interest as responsible for the post-war distress in agriculture. Public opinion was concerned about changes in the value of money; as Ricardo wrote to McCulloch on 9 June 1816:

> No relief is ever afforded to those who suffer from a fall in the value of money, but every heart sympathizes with those who are losers by its rise.
>
> (VII: 38)

The question of the causes of a change in the value of money and of the means to prevent them from operating was thus given much attention. In the continuity of his distinction in the Bullion Essays between the value of gold and its price, Ricardo emphasised in *Proposals* and beyond the distinction between two causes of variation in the value of money: a change in the value of the standard and a spread between the market price of bullion and the legal price of the metal in coin:

> When a standard is used, we are subject only to such a variation in the value of money as the *standard* itself is subject to; but against such variation there is no possible remedy. [...] While these metals [gold and silver] are the

> standard, the currency should conform in value to them, and, whenever it does not, and the market price of bullion is above the Mint price, the currency is depreciated.
>
> (*Proposals*; IV: 62–3; Ricardo's emphasis)

One should notice that Ricardo spoke here of a monetary system endowed with a standard.[1] This contrasts with a frequent misunderstanding in the literature which leads to consider that for Ricardo, either the Bank of England note was not convertible into the standard and it was depreciated because of an excess quantity, or it was convertible and depreciation was made impossible, so that the value of money was exclusively determined by the value of the standard. The difference between the two regimes was *not* for Ricardo that the price of bullion was variable in the former and fixed in the latter (depreciation being thus excluded), *but* that it varied without or within limits. His theory of money aimed at determining these limits, and his Ingot Plan at reducing them to the minimum.

Misunderstanding has nourished a recurrent accusation made against Ricardo of having two contradictory theories of the value of money, one based on its quantity and one based on the value of gold. Section 4.1 intends to refute this accusation by analysing the direction of the causality between the quantity and the value of money. Section 4.2 exposes next the crucial distinction between "a fall in the value of money" and "a depreciation of money". This leads in Section 4.3 to Ricardo's idiosyncratic theory of the value of money, formalised in what I call the Money–Standard Equation. Section 4.4 concludes on the two causes of change in the value of money.

4.1 The direction of the causality between the quantity and the value of money

An alleged inconsistency or contradiction

On this question the modern literature often points to an inconsistency or a contradiction in Ricardo between the defence of a commodity-theory of money – which implies that the causality runs from the value to the quantity of money – and the adherence to the Quantity Theory of Money – which implies that the causality runs the other way round.

As recalled by De Vivo (1987), this accusation is already to be found in Marx:

> The contradiction between a quantity and a labour (or a cost of production) theory of the value of money is obvious, and has often been discussed, as for instance by Marx, who deals with it in his critique of Ricardo's monetary theory in *A Contribution to the Critique of Political Economy* (Marx however overlooks the presence in the Ricardo of the early 1810s of a scarcity conception of value). As Marx writes, 'if the value of gold is given [by the labour embodied in it], the amount of money in circulation is determined by the prices of commodities' (1859, p. 171), and not the other way

> round. […] There is no explicit attempt at reconciling the two conflicting views in Ricardo.
>
> (De Vivo 1987: 195)

An example of how Marx's influence in academic circles contributed to the propagation of this critique of inconsistency is given by the reception of Ricardo in Japan during the interwar period, as documented by Takenaga (2016: 16): "As for the theory of money and finance, the almost exclusive aim of a small number of research works was, after Marx, to highlight the inconsistency and contradiction between Ricardo's theory of money and his theory of value in *High Price*."

Schumpeter, however, did not see the coexistence of cost-of-production and quantity elements in the value of money as a contradiction and criticised Marx for having failed to see that the latter adjusted to the former:

> It seems that he [Marx] took this position under the impression that the quantity theory of the value of money and the cost of production theory of money are alternatives between which the analyst has to choose. This is not so: the value of money as 'determined' by quantity and the value of money as determined by cost of production must, in the long run, necessarily coincide.
>
> (Schumpeter 1954: 703n)[2]

Schumpeter thus considered this coexistence as a mere extension of the "Classical" theory of value:

> The leading 'classics' solved the problem of this rather dubious value of money simply by extending to it their general theory of value. Accordingly, they distinguished a natural or long-run normal value of money and a short-run equilibrium value. The former or, as they also said – misleadingly – the 'permanent' value was determined by the cost of producing (or obtaining) the precious metals, the latter by supply and demand. […] Even Ricardo, in spite of his bent for long-run analysis, reasoned about money chiefly in terms of the [short-run equilibrium], that is, in terms of supply and demand. […] [He] tried to *deduce* the quantity theorem from the 'law' of supply and demand.
>
> (ibid: 701–3; Schumpeter's emphasis)

Further authors accordingly questioned Ricardo's incapacity for linking short term and long term in a consistent way – a recurrent complaint about him. Some of them considered that the two levels were simply juxtaposed and applied to different cases; see for example Laidler (1975: 217):

> Ricardo's work contains two different but not incompatible theories of the price level. In his policy writings during the period of the bank restriction he relied on the quantity theory of money as a short-run theory of prices, but in the *Principles* the price level was viewed as being determined in the long run by the cost of production of gold relative to the cost of production of other goods.

Others were more critical, such as Blaug:

> Ricardo continued to expound a labour theory of value of the monetary metal while at the same time espousing a hard-line version of the quantity theory. He might have reconciled the two by reserving the quantity theory for short-run problems and for inconvertible paper, while maintaining the cost-of production theory for the long run and for specie money and convertible paper only. In fact, however, he left the two doctrines standing in an unresolved relationship to each other.
>
> (Blaug 1995: 31; see also Blaug 1996: 127)

This was the old suspicion of contradiction in new dresses. In modern literature, the contention that Ricardo had two theories of money is also to be found in Arnon (2011), Green (1992), and King (2013).

The culprit of this alleged contradiction is the labour (or cost-of-production) theory of value, as stressed by De Vivo (1987: 195):

> It is also to be remembered that the contradiction is only to be found in the *Principles*, and not in Ricardo's earlier works on monetary theory, where he does not yet have a labour theory of value (this is the case also for *Economical and Secure Currency*).

According to De Vivo, these "earlier works" would more easily bend to the quantity theory of money because of a scarcity approach to value:

> Ricardo's early idea that scarcity is a regulator of prices alongside cost of production, is (partly also thanks to its vagueness) much more in accordance with a quantity theory of money than his later labour theory of value, whose consistency with his monetary theory is problematic. These problems of consistency Ricardo failed to solve, and to a large extent even to consider.
>
> (ibid: 186)

On the contrary, I will argue that not only did this scarcity approach to value vitiate Ricardo's position on money in the Bullion Essays, but an essential aspect of the theory of value advocated in *Principles* allows discarding the suspicion of contradiction: the determination of the value of competitively produced commodities by the cost of production with the portion of capital that pays no rent.

The "analogy" with a gold mine

In the Bullion Essays, scarcity was among the various factors that determined the value of every commodity, including precious metals:

> Gold and silver, like other commodities, have an intrinsic value, which is not arbitrary, but is dependent on their scarcity, the quantity of labour bestowed

in procuring them, and the value of the capital employed in the mines which produce them.

(*High Price*; III: 52)

The role of scarcity in the determination of the value of gold was instrumental in the famous comparison made by Ricardo between the effects of the discovery of a gold mine and those of an additional issue of Bank of England notes, a comparison still made more dramatic by his supposition, in *Reply to Bosanquet*, that a gold mine was discovered on the premises of the Bank of England.[3] This supposition allowed Ricardo to make an "analogy" between an increase in the quantity of money caused by an increased production of bullion and one by a discretionary issuing of inconvertible notes by the Bank of England:

> Commerce is insatiable in its demands [for currency], and the same portions of it may employ 10 millions or 100 millions of circulating medium; the quantity depends wholly on its value. If the mines had been ten times more productive, ten times more money would the same commerce employ. This Mr. Bosanquet admits, but denies the analogy between the issues of the Bank and the produce of a new gold mine. [...] Now supposing the gold mine to be actually the property of the Bank, even to be situated on their own premises, and that they procured the gold which it produced to be coined into guineas, and in lieu of issuing their notes when they discounted bills or lent money to Government that they issued nothing but guineas; could there be any other limit to their issues but the want of the further productiveness in their mine? [...] Now if the mine should double the quantity of money, it would depress its value in the same proportion, and there would be double the demand for it. [...] The analogy seems to me to be complete, and not to admit of dispute. The issues of paper not convertible are guided by the same principle, and will be attended with the same effect as if the Bank were the proprietor of the mine, and issued nothing but gold.
>
> (*Reply to Bosanquet*; III: 215–7)

Elsewhere in the Bullion Essays, Ricardo also drew a parallel between a gold mine and the Bank of England to emphasise that the fall in the value of money – that is, the general rise in money prices – was to be ascribed to the increase in the quantity of money, whether specie or paper:

> If instead of a mine being discovered in any country, a bank were established, such as the Bank of England, with the power of issuing its notes for a circulating medium; after a large amount had been issued either by way of loan to merchants, or by advances to government, thereby adding considerably to the sum of the currency, the same effect would follow as in the case of the mine. The circulating medium would be lowered in value, and goods would experience a proportionate rise.
>
> (*High Price*; III: 54–5)

Given the conception of value held by Ricardo at the time, the cases of the mine and of the bank had in common that the fall in value resulted from a diminished scarcity. The explanation of the variations in the value of money did not differ from that of the variations in the value of gold: when a new mine was discovered, the supply of gold bullion increased and its value in terms of all other commodities declined, as the value of notes in terms of commodities declined when they were issued in a greater quantity (in both cases, unless for any reason the demand itself increased). Both for gold bullion and money, an increase in the quantity lowered the value, so that the effect of the discovery of a new gold mine descended directly to the fall in the value of money: an increased quantity of bullion sunk its value in terms of all other commodities and generated an increased quantity of money which also sunk its value. The "analogy" with an increased issue of inconvertible Bank of England notes was complete.[4]

Things changed with *Principles*. Applied to gold bullion, the adoption of a theory of the value of commodities based on their cost of production with the portion of capital that pays no rent paved the way to the rejection of an explanation of the permanent fall in the value of gold-money by the increase in the *quantity* of bullion, in favour of an explanation stressing the fall in its *value*. This was now in sharp contrast with the explanation of the effect of an increase in the note issue: here, the *quantity* of notes caused their depreciation, which, as the title of Ricardo's 1810 pamphlet made explicit, was "proved" by a high *price* of gold bullion. A value effect – that of the discovery of a new gold mine – could now be clearly distinguished from a quantity effect – that of an increase in the note issue.

Paradoxically, the theory of value and distribution contained in *Principles* stressed the importance of a distinction already made by Ricardo in the Bullion Essays but obscured by the scarcity approach to value that he then adopted. This distinction was between the value and the price of gold, and he considered that failing to recognise it was the source of much "error" (see Chapter 3 above).[5]

The theory of value and distribution contained in *Principles* thus allowed understanding that the value of money might be affected either by a cause of change in the *value* of gold bullion – such as a change in its cost of production following the discovery of a new mine – or by a cause of change in the *price* of gold bullion – that is, a variation in the quantity of money issued. These two causes of change in the value of money being complementary and additive, the contradiction between his alleged commodity-theory of money and his alleged quantity theory of money vanishes.[6] Still more important, we will see in Section 4.2 below that this distinction provides a key to a coherent theory of the value of money.

Incidentally, it seems that, in spite of this theoretical achievement, the "analogy" between a gold mine and the Bank of England survived in *Principles*:

> If by the discovery of a new mine, by the abuses of banking, or by any other cause, the quantity of money be greatly increased, its ultimate effect is to raise the prices of commodities in proportion to the increased quantity of

> money; but there is probably always an interval, during which some effect is produced on the rate of interest.
>
> (*Principles*; I: 298)

This quotation from Chapter XXI "Effects of accumulation on profits and interest" is part of Ricardo's contention that the quantity of money had no permanent effect on the rate of interest, only a temporary one. It is the reason why he mentioned various causes which might generate an increase in the quantity of money, and he then recalled that, in such cases, the money prices of commodities increased proportionately – that is, the value of money declined. But this does not imply that the *modus operandi* of this decline was the same: as shown by Ricardo's distinction (analysed below) between "a fall in the value of money" and "a depreciation of money", "the discovery of a new mine" sunk the value of money through a *fall* in the *value* of gold, while "the abuses of banking" sunk it through a *rise* in the *price* of gold. One should of course be explicit about what this *modus operandi* is in both cases: this will be done below in Chapter 5 (where the "analogy" is further discussed) and Chapter 7 respectively.

The effect of a monopoly in issuing money

The understanding of these two separate and additive effects on the value of money also allows clarifying the first pages of Chapter XXVII "On currency and banks" of *Principles*, which might again be used as an illustration of the contradiction discussed above. This chapter opens with a paragraph that seems to fit perfectly a commodity-theory of money:

> Gold and silver, like all other commodities, are valuable only in proportion to the quantity of labour necessary to produce them, and bring them to market. Gold is about fifteen times dearer than silver [...] solely because fifteen times the quantity of labour is necessary to procure a given quantity of it. The quantity of money that can be employed in a country must depend on its value: if gold alone were employed for the circulation of commodities, a quantity would be required, one fifteenth only of what would be necessary, if silver were made use of for the same purpose. A circulation can never be so abundant as to overflow; for by diminishing its value, in the same proportion you will increase its quantity, and by increasing its value, diminish its quantity.
>
> (*Principles*; I: 352)

The causal relation is here from the value of money to its quantity, so that "a circulation can never be so abundant as to overflow". The reason is simple: the circulating medium is here a commodity (gold or silver) produced in competitive conditions, as testified by the fact that the labour-theory of value applies to it, in the same way as it applies to all other competitively produced commodities. In the next paragraph, Ricardo considers what happens "while the State coins money" (ibid: 353): the (say, gold) coin will now have the same value as any piece of the same weight in gold whenever the State does not charge a seignorage for coinage, and a higher value if the seignorage reflects the labour cost of fabricating the coin. The causal relation from value to quantity remains the same, since the role of the State is restricted to fabricate the coin and put a stamp on it: coins simply replace bullion as means of circulation, without altering the competitive determination of their value.

Things change with metallic coinage being subject to a monopoly:

> While the State alone coins, there can be no limit to this charge of seignorage; for by limiting the quantity of coin, it can be raised to any conceivable value.
> (ibid)

The causal relation is here reversed: if the State monopolist of coined money restricts its quantity, it may increase its value above the value of gold it contains, without limit. The three successive steps mentioned by Ricardo are not meant to provide a history of metallic money: there is no indication, here or elsewhere, that Ricardo had historical situations in mind. They only illustrate the two channels by which the value of metallic money may change: either because the value of the standard (gold), produced in competitive conditions, varies, or because the quantity of coined money issued, subject to a monopoly, itself varies. We will see below in Section 4.3 how these two causes of change in the value of money add up.

Once this is understood for metallic money, one further step is to extend this approach to paper money:

> It is on this principle that paper money circulates: the whole charge for paper money may be considered as seignorage. Though it has no intrinsic value, yet, by limiting its quantity, its value in exchange is as great as an equal denomination of coin, or of bullion in that coin. [...] There is no point more important in issuing paper money, than to be fully impressed with the effects which follow from the principle of limitation of quantity.
> (ibid)

This does not mean that the value of paper money, when it is issued by a monopoly – such as the one enjoyed by the Bank of England in the London area – only obeys "the principle of limitation of quantity". This would be the case if the note were deprived of any link with a standard – that is, if it were inconvertible, like the Bank of England note after 1797. Provided the working of the monetary system equalises the value of paper money with the value of "an equal denomination of coin, or of bullion in that coin", this value also varies with changes in the value of the standard, as metallic money does.

A conclusion emerges: the value of money (whether coin or paper) is determined neither like that of competitively produced commodities nor like that of monopolised commodities. It obeys a determination *sui generis*, as the next sections will show.

4.2 Ricardo's distinction between "a fall in the value of money" and "a depreciation of money"

From the Bullion Essays to Proposals *and beyond*

As already mentioned above in Chapter 3, the knotty point in the understanding of the value of money in Ricardo is the distinction between "a fall in the value of money" and "a depreciation of money". We will see below that this distinction is consistent with a theory of money that separates the two channels through which the causes of a change in the value of money are transmitted: the *value* of the standard and the *price* of the standard. It is consequently worthwhile to ask whether the distinction between a fall in the value of money and a depreciation of money was already implied by the distinction made in the Bullion Essays between the value of gold and the price of gold. The answer to this question is not straightforward. As testified by the title of the 1810 pamphlet, *The High Price of Bullion, a Proof of the Depreciation of Bank Notes*, Ricardo then already emphasised the link between "depreciation" and the "price of bullion". The ambiguity concerns the other channel of transmission, from a fall in the value of bullion to a fall in the value of money. In the papers of 1819–1823 both channels would be clearly distinguished, but there are still until 1816 mixed signals on this point. The denunciation of Thornton's "error" that "proceeds from not distinguishing between an increase in the value of gold, and an increase in its money price" (III: 60) indeed led Ricardo to separate what happened on the side of gold – which was reflected in a change in the value of bullion, *not* in its price – from what happened on the side of money – which was reflected in a change in the price of bullion, *not* in its value:

> That the scarcity of gold should increase its value cannot be doubted; [...] but no scarcity, however great, can raise the market price much above the mint price, unless it be measured by a depreciated currency.
>
> (*The Price of Gold*; III: 22)

> In saying however that gold is at a high price, we are mistaken; it is not gold, it is paper which has changed its value.
>
> (*High Price*; III: 80)

In the last quotation, Ricardo speaks of a change in the "value" of paper, which, because it is associated with "a high price" of gold, is confused with its depreciation. In a letter to Francis Horner of 5 February 1810 (discussed below in Chapter 6), Ricardo mentioned four possible causes of "the excess of the market above the mint price of gold bullion" (VI: 1–2), that is, of a depreciation of money: the debasement of the coins, a market ratio of the price of gold to silver higher than the legal one, "a superabundance of paper circulation" (ibid: 2), and "the severity of the law against the exportation of gold coins" (ibid). A lower scarcity of gold bullion was *not* mentioned here, and this might infer that it was not for Ricardo a cause of the depreciation of money but of a fall in its value. However, still in the *Essay on Profits* of February 1815, Ricardo, while criticising an observation by Malthus on the beneficial effect of a rise in prices, listed a fall in the value of bullion among the various causes of a depreciation of money:

> A rise of prices [of commodities] has been stated [by Malthus] to be one of the advantages, to counterbalance the many evils attendant on a depreciation of money, from a real fall in the value of the precious metals, from raising the denomination of the coin, or from the overissue of paper money.
>
> (*Essay on Profits*; IV: 36)

Such ambiguity disappeared in *Principles*. In Chapter VII "On Foreign Trade", after having discussed the notion of par of exchange (see Chapter 8 below) Ricardo concluded:

> Some indeed more reasonably maintained, that 130*l.* in paper was not of equal value with 130*l.* in metallic money; but they said that it was the metallic money which had changed its value, and not the paper money. They wished to confine the meaning of the word depreciation to an actual fall of value, and not to a comparative difference between the value of money, and the standard by which by law it is regulated.
>
> (*Principles*; I: 149)

This was also clear in the papers of 1819–1823, as testified by the extract of a speech on 12 June 1822 given above in Chapter 3. This extract continues as follows, with Ricardo stressing the difference between the respective effects on prices of a depreciation of money and of a change in the value of bullion, and emphasising the continuity with what he had written six years before in *Proposals*:

> If, for instance, the standard of the currency remained at the same fixed value, and the coin were depreciated by clipping, or the paper money by the increase of its quantity, five per cent, a fall to that amount and no more, would take place in the price of commodities, as affected by the value of money.[7] If the metal gold (the standard) continued of the same precise value, and it was required to restore the currency thus depreciated five per cent, to par, it would be necessary only to raise its value five per cent, and no greater than that proportionate fall could take place in the price of commodities. In these cases he had supposed gold always to remain at the same fixed value; but had he ever said that there were not many causes which might operate on the value of gold as on the value of all other commodities? No, he had not, but just the contrary. No country that used the precious metals as a standard, were exempted from variations in the prices of commodities, occasioned by a variation in the value of their standard. To such variations we had been subject before 1797, and must be subject to again, now that we have reverted to a metallic standard. [...] It had been imputed to him that he entertained the extravagant idea, that if a metallic standard was adopted, from that moment commodities were never to vary more than 5 per cent. A proposition so absurd he had

> never maintained – his opinion on that subject had never changed, and, if not intruding too much on the time of the House, he would quote a passage from a pamphlet he had published in 1816, on the subject of his plan of bullion payments, to show the House what that opinion had then been:
>
> 'When a standard is used, we are subject only to such a variation in the value of money as the standard itself is subject to; but against such variation there is no possible remedy; and late events have proved that, during periods of war, when gold and silver are used for the payment of large armies, distant from home, those variations are much more considerable than has been generally allowed. This admission only proves that gold and silver are not so good a standard as they have been hitherto supposed; that they are themselves subject to greater variations than it is desirable a standard should be subject to. They are, however, the best with which we are acquainted. If any other commodity less variable could be found, it might very properly be adopted as the future standard of our money, provided it had all the other qualities which fitted it for that purpose; but while these metals are the standard, the currency should conform in value to them, and, whenever it does not, and the market price of bullion is above the Mint price, the currency is depreciated.'
>
> (V: 204–6; the quotation of *Proposals* by Ricardo is in IV: 62–3)

The distinction between a fall in the value of money and its depreciation was then rooted in the idea that each term should be expressed in reference to something different: a fall in the value of money in reference to all commodities except the standard, and depreciation in reference to the standard itself. As a consequence, depreciation might infer a fall in the value of money, but since the value of money also changed with any change in the value of the standard in terms of all other commodities, this inference was not systematic: it could happen that the two causes of a change in the value of money operated in opposite directions, so that the value of money actually rose while money at the same time depreciated:

> The term 'depreciation,' I conceive, does not mean a mere diminution in value, but it means a diminished relative value, on a comparison with something which is a standard; and therefore I think it quite possible that a bank note may be depreciated, although it should rise in value, if it did not rise in value in a degree equal to the standard, by which only its depreciation is measured.
>
> (Evidence of 4 March 1819; V: 393–4)

This possibility would be reaffirmed by Ricardo before Parliament in his speeches of 7 May 1822 and 11 June 1823 (see below) and mentioned in a letter to McCulloch of 25 March 1823:

> Depreciation as applied to money must be understood to mean relative lowness as compared with the standard, and nothing else, and therefore money may be depreciated although it should rise in absolute value.
>
> (IX: 276)

The evolution from the Bullion Essays to the 1819–1823 papers, permitted by the writing of *Principles*, was from the critique of an "error" – "the error of this reasoning proceeds from not distinguishing between an increase in the value of gold, and an increase in its money price" (*High Price*; III: 60) – to that of a "mistake" – "the great mistake committed on this subject was in confounding the words 'depreciation' and 'diminution in value'" (speech of 12 June 1822; V: 203), that is, confounding the value of money in terms of the standard and the value of money in terms of all other commodities. In order to formalise the relation between a depreciation of money and a fall in the value of money, it is first necessary to explicit what the definition and the measure of depreciation were for Ricardo.

The definition and measure of depreciation

Money was for Ricardo depreciated when its value V_M was below the value V_G of the standard of money, both values being expressed in terms of all commodities except this standard:

> Depreciation meant a lowering of the value of the currency, as compared with the standard by which it was professedly regulated.
>
> (Speech of 7 May 1822; V: 166)

How "the value of the currency" should be "compared" had been made explicit in *Principles*:

> While gold is exclusively the standard in this country, money will be depreciated, when a pound sterling is not of equal value with 5 dwts. and 3 grs. of standard gold, and that, whether gold rises or falls in general value.
>
> (*Principles*; I: 149)

The pound sterling was *depreciated* when its value in terms of goods was below that of the quantity (5 pennyweights and 3 grains) of standard gold corresponding to its legal definition. This depreciation was distinct from what happened to the *value* of gold ("whether gold rises or falls in general value") and it was reflected in the spread between the market *price* in pounds of 5 dwts. and 3 grs. of standard gold and its legal level (one pound). The following extract of the speech of 12 June 1822 already quoted above illustrates how Ricardo exactly measured such depreciation:

> His hon. friend (Mr. Bennet) had stated, that the depreciation in the value of the currency was in 1813 about 42 per cent. He thought his hon. friend had much overstated the amount of depreciation. The highest price to which gold had ever risen, and that only for a short time, was 5l. 10s. per ounce. Even then the Bank-note was depreciated only 29 per cent, because 5l. 10s. in Bank-notes could purchase the same quantity of goods as the gold in 3l. 17s. $10^{1/2}$d. of coin. If, then, 5l. 10s. in Bank-notes was worth 3l. 17s. 10½d. in gold, 100 l. was worth 71l., and one pound about fourteen shillings, which is a depreciation

> of 29 per cent, and not 42 per cent, as stated by his hon. friend. Another way of stating this proposition might make it appear that money had risen 42 per cent; for if 14s. of the money of 1813 were now worth 20s., 100l. was now worth 142l.; but as he had already observed, nothing was more difficult than to ascertain the variations in the value of money – to do so with any accuracy, we should have an invariable measure of value; but such a measure we never had, nor ever could have. In the present case, gold might have fallen in value, at the same time that paper-money had been rising; and therefore, when they met, and were at par with each other, the rise in paper-money might not have been equal to the whole of the former difference. To speak with precision, therefore, of the value of money at any particular period, was what no man could do; but when we spoke of depreciation, there was always a standard by which that might be estimated.
>
> (V: 216–7)

The situation discussed by Ricardo was such that the highest level reached by the market price P_G of an ounce of gold bullion during the period of inconvertibility had been £5. 10s. in 1813, above the legal price $\overline{P_{GC}}$ of an ounce of gold in coin, equal to £3. 17s. 10½d. At the moment when Ricardo spoke (in 1822), P_G had for one year returned to the same level of $\overline{P_{GC}}$. Two conclusions could be drawn from these figures: one – rigorously established – was that in 1813 the Bank of England note was depreciated 29 per cent; the other – which, according to Ricardo, lacked precision – was that the Bank of England note had increased in value by 42 per cent between 1813 and 1822. The second part of the quotation explains why the latter inference should be discarded. On the one hand, measuring precisely the change in the value of money through time required expressing this value in terms of "an invariable measure of value" – something that could not be had (see Chapter 3 above). On the other hand, a change in the value of money between two moments in time "might not have been equal" to the difference in the price of bullion between them, for a reason that will appear clearly below: part of this change might be ascribed to a change in the value of bullion, not in its price. In contrast, depreciation was assessed at a given moment in time and in reference to an observable and unambiguous magnitude: the mint price.

The first part of the quotation mentions a disagreement about the measure of depreciation in 1813: 42 per cent ([£5. 10s. – £3. 17s. 10½d.] / £3. 17s. 10½d.) or 29 per cent ([£5. 10s. – £3. 17s. 10½d.] / £5. 10s.). Ricardo's choice of the latter might seem arbitrary and only dictated by the wish not to "overstate" the maximum amount of depreciation observed during the inconvertibility period. There is nevertheless a rationale for this choice, consequent upon his definition of depreciation, as it is illustrated by the sentence: "the Bank-note was depreciated only 29 per cent, because 5l. 10s. in Bank-notes could purchase the same quantity of goods as the gold in 3l. 17s. $10^{1/2}$d. of coin". The "quantity of goods" purchased by "5l. 10s. in Bank-notes" is by definition the value (in goods) of the quantity of notes that purchases an ounce of gold bullion in the market, because £5. 10s. was in this case (in 1813) the market price of an ounce of gold bullion when paid in notes. As for the "quantity of goods" purchased by "gold [bullion contained] in 3l. 17s. $10^{1/2}$d. of coin", it is by definition the value (in the same goods) of an ounce of gold bullion, since £3. 17s. 10½d. was the legal price of an ounce of gold bullion when coined. This equality in value thus reads $P_G V_M = V_G$, which is the condition (3.5) of coherence of the price system in Chapter 3 ($V_M = V_G / P_G$).

For Ricardo money was in this case depreciated by 29 per cent. Following the definition given above, money is depreciated when the current value V_M of one pound is below V_M*, the value of the quantity of gold bullion legally coined in one pound, that is, according to the condition of conformity (3.8), $V_M^* = (1/\overline{P_{GC}})V_G$. The measure d of depreciation, in percentage of this value, is consequently given by:

$$d = \frac{V_M^* - V_M}{V_M^*} \tag{4.1}$$

By definition, $d = 0$ when the condition of conformity of money to the standard applies $(V_M = V_M^*)$. Replacing in (4.1) V_M^* by its value in (3.8) and V_M by its value in (3.5) gives:

$$d = \frac{P_G - \overline{P_{GC}}}{P_G} \tag{4.2}$$

When money is depreciated, it is the same to say that its value is below that of the standard or to say that the market price of gold bullion is above the mint price. After conversion of £5. 10s. and £3. 17s. 10½d. in pence for the sake of calculation, d in 1813 was equal to (1320 – 934.5) / 1320 = 0.29, as announced by Ricardo.

In the symmetrical case of an appreciation of money relatively to the standard, $d < 0$, that is, $P_G < \overline{P_{GC}}$:

> To say that money is more valuable than bullion or the standard, is to say that bullion is selling in the market under the mint price.
>
> (*Proposals*; IV: 57)

One may now determine accordingly the rate of change in the value of money.

4.3 The Money–Standard Equation

Two channels of change in the value of money

Let me consider a period of a given length, starting in [1] and ending in [2], and the following notations:

$\Delta V_M / V_M = (V_{M[2]} - V_{M[1]}) / V_{M[1]}$: rate of change in the value of one unit of money (the £) in terms of all commodities except gold bullion.

$\Delta V_G / V_G = (V_{G[2]} - V_{G[1]}) / V_{G[1]}$: rate of change in the value of an ounce of gold bullion in terms of all other commodities.

$\Delta P_G / P_G = (P_{G[2]} - P_{G[1]}) / P_{G[1]}$: rate of change in the market price of an ounce of gold bullion.

$d_{[1]}$, $d_{[2]}$: depreciation of the £ in [1] or [2], in percentage ($d > 0$: depreciation; $d < 0$: appreciation).

Equality (4.1) defining d may be rewritten as follows:

$$V_M = V_M{}^*(1 - d) \tag{4.3}$$

Applying (4.3) to [1] and [2] gives, according to the definition of $\Delta V_M / V_M$:

$$1 + \frac{\Delta V_M}{V_M} = \frac{\dfrac{V_{M[2]}{}^*}{V_{M[1]}{}^*}}{\dfrac{1 - d_{[2]}}{1 - d_{[1]}}} \tag{4.4}$$

According to the definition of $V_M{}^*$ given by (3.8), $V_{M[2]}{}^*/V_{M[1]}{}^* = V_{G[2]}/V_{G[1]} = 1 + \Delta V_G / V_G$. Equation (4.4) thus becomes:

$$\frac{\Delta V_M}{V_M} = \frac{\Delta V_G}{V_G}\frac{1 - d_{[2]}}{1 - d_{[1]}} + \frac{d_{[1]} - d_{[2]}}{1 - d_{[1]}} \tag{4.5}$$

The rate of change in the value of money during the period is positively related to the rate of change in the value of the standard, this relation depending on the percentage of depreciation at the beginning and at the end of the period.

"In a sound state of the currency" – that is, for Ricardo, with convertibility of the standard into money and of money into the standard – d is constrained within narrow limits (see Chapter 6 below) so that the factors $[(1 - d_{[2]})/(1 - d_{[1]})]$ and $[1/(1 - d_{[1]})]$ may be neglected. Relation (4.5) may thus be rewritten as:

$$\frac{\Delta V_M}{V_M} = \frac{\Delta V_G}{V_G} + d_{[1]} - d_{[2]} \tag{4.6}$$

This relation states that the rate of change in the value of money during the period is equal to the rate of change in the value of the standard plus the difference between the percentage depreciation of money at the beginning and at the end of the period.

Replacing $d_{[1]}$ and $d_{[2]}$ in (4.5) by their values according to (4.2) gives:

$$\frac{\Delta V_M}{V_M} = \frac{\frac{\Delta V_G}{V_G} - \frac{\Delta P_G}{P_G}}{1 + \frac{\Delta P_G}{P_G}} \quad (4.7)$$

Here also, "in a sound state of the currency" $\Delta P_G / P_G$ is constrained within narrow limits so that the factor $[1/(1+\Delta P_G / P_G)]$ may be neglected. Relation (4.7) may thus be rewritten as:

$$\frac{\Delta V_M}{V_M} = \frac{\Delta V_G}{V_G} - \frac{\Delta P_G}{P_G} \quad (4.8)$$

I will call (4.7) the **Money–Standard Equation** (in short MSE), with (4.8) its simplified form. It states that the rate of change in the value of money during the period is determined by the rate of change in the value of the standard minus the rate of change in the price of the standard.[8] The MSE thus formalises the conjunction of two additive channels through which the value of money may vary: a change in the value of the standard and a change in its price. In particular, money could rise in value while being depreciated – as testified by a rise in the price of bullion – because the value of bullion had risen more than its price:

> Depreciation meant a lowering of the value of the currency, as compared with the standard by which it was professedly regulated. When he used the word, he used it in this obvious and proper sense. The standard itself might be altered, as compared with other things; and it might so happen that a currency might be depreciated, when it had actually risen, as compared with commodities, because the standard might have risen in value in a still greater proportion.
>
> (Speech of 7 May 1822; V: 166)[9]

The MSE thus accounts for any combination of change in the value of gold bullion and of change in its price, the resultant being a rise, a fall, or constancy in the value of money:

> A currency might be depreciated, without falling in value; it might fall in value, without being depreciated, because depreciation is estimated only by reference to a standard.
>
> (Speech of 11 June 1823; V: 311)

The Money–Standard Equation embodies Ricardo's particular theory of the value of money. The approximation used in (4.6) and (4.8) should not obscure the fact that (4.5) is rigorously deduced from the definition of depreciation (4.1), hence from the condition of conformity (3.8), and that (4.7) is rigorously deduced from (4.5): the determination of the rate of change in the value of money by the MSE is a consequence of its being a function of the rate of change in the value of bullion and of the difference between the depreciation at the beginning and at the end of the period. There is a particular case that shows even more clearly the link between the two expressions of the rate of change in the value of money: this is when $d_{[2]} = 0$. In this case, (4.5) simplifies in:

$$\frac{\Delta V_M}{V_M} = \frac{\frac{\Delta V_G}{V_G} + d_{[1]}}{1 - d_{[1]}} \tag{4.9}$$

Neglecting $[1/(1-d_{[1]})]$ gives the simplified relation:

$$\frac{\Delta V_M}{V_M} = \frac{\Delta V_G}{V_G} + d_{[1]} \tag{4.10}$$

Since in this case $P_{G[2]} = \overline{P_{GC}}$, one has $\Delta P_G / P_G = (\overline{P_{GC}} - P_{G[1]}) / P_{G[1]} = -d_{[1]}$ as given by the relation of definition (4.2): the simplified relation (4.10) between the rate of change in the value of money and depreciation is *ipso facto* the MSE in its simplified form (4.8).

The significance of this particular case is the following. When during the period money returns from a depreciated state $(d_{[1]} > 0)$ to a state of conformity to the standard $(d_{[2]} = 0)$ the rate of change in the value of money is approximately equal to the rate of change in the value of bullion plus the initial depreciation. This was the case repeatedly discussed by Ricardo in 1819–1823: although the lack of an invariable measure of value resulted in that "nothing was more difficult than to ascertain the variations in the value of money" (see above the quotation from the speech of 12 June 1822), Ricardo found it worthwhile to try and he had in mind a formula to evaluate these variations – the Money–Standard Equation. And we will see below that with the figures he used in his calculation the MSE in its simplified form (4.8) was not far from the exact relation (4.7): such approximation implied $\Delta V_M / V_M$ being underestimated by 0.5 per cent only.

Ricardo's factual illustration

As exposed in Chapter 2 above, Parliament adopted in 1819 Ricardo's Ingot Plan as the basis for the resumption of the convertibility of the Bank of England note, which consequently would be into bullion instead of coins as before 1797. In addition, a decreasing scale was decided for the legal price of gold (the *de jure* standard of money since 1816), which was intended to lower the market price of bullion – thanks to an appropriate contraction of the Bank of England note issue – so as to bring it in 1821 to the pre-war parity of £3. 17s. 10½d. Knowing the hostility of the Bank of England to a plan that compelled it to supply the circulation with small notes (£5 and under) instead of coins, Ricardo had opposed during the debates a proposition that offered the Bank of England the choice of paying its notes in bullion or in coin. His argument was that the necessity of purchasing large amounts of bullion to have it coined would increase the demand for it in the world market and trigger an increase in its *value*. The consequent rise in the value of money would add up to the effect of the anticipated fall in the market *price* of bullion – in accordance with the MSE – and generate an unnecessary general deflation of money prices:

> By withdrawing paper, so as to restore the note to its bullion value (an alteration, by the bye, only of 3 per cent.), the House would have done all that was required. But if the House adopted the proposition of the hon. Gentleman (Mr. Ellice), another variation in the value of the currency would take place, which it was his (Mr. R.'s) wish to guard against. If that amendment were agreed to, an extraordinary demand would take place for gold, for the purpose of coinage which would enhance the value of the currency 3 or 4 per cent in addition to the first enhancement.
>
> (Speech in the House of Commons of 24 May 1819; V: 11)

Although the proposition opposed by Ricardo was rejected, it was only for him a half-victory, since Peel's bill stipulated that convertibility *into coin* would be resumed in 1823, treating thus the Ingot Plan as a temporary device, aimed only at facilitating the return to the pre-1797 situation. Confident in the advantages of his plan, Ricardo nevertheless believed that after having been tried during three years it would be made permanent when the legislature would consider again in 1822 the return to convertibility into coin scheduled for 1823. Unfortunately, things did not go that way; on the contrary, when the return to the pre-war parity in 1821 approached, Parliament decided to anticipate the resumption of convertibility into coin, and Ricardo's Ingot Plan was dropped two years in advance. Lobbying by the Bank of England was not the only reason for this move; the acceleration of the fall in agricultural prices – which had started at the end of the war in 1815 – played its part in a Parliament dominated by the land interest, because it was attributed by those who suffered from it to the Ingot Plan itself.

The debates on this point continued after 1821 and Ricardo had to defend himself against the repeated accusation of being responsible for the general deflation. His defence was along two lines. First, relying on estimates made by Thomas Tooke, he argued that the fall in agricultural prices was not representative of the general deflation but could be explained by a specific factor: the excess of the supply of over the demand for agricultural products. Second, the Ingot Plan implemented between 1819 and 1821 was in no way responsible for the general deflation, estimated by Ricardo at 10 per cent. Half of it was the rightly anticipated consequence of the fall in the market price of bullion that had been managed in order to return to prewar parity – an aspect that was distinct from the plan itself. The other half was the consequence of what he had warned against in 1819: sabotaging the plan, the Bank of England had immediately started to make heavy purchases of bullion to have it coined, and when its vaults were full of coins it had pressed Parliament to resume convertibility into specie so as to release them through the exchange of its small notes (more on this behaviour of the Bank of England below in Chapter 5). The estimated five per cent increase in the value of bullion triggered by the purchases of the Bank had doubled the resulting general deflation – a fact that could not be imputed to the Ingot Plan since it was precisely the outcome of the sabotage of it:

> He [Ricardo] had undoubtedly given an opinion in 1819, that, by the measure then proposed, the prices of commodities would not be altered more than 5 per cent; but, let it be explained under what circumstances that opinion had been given. The difference in 1819, between paper and gold, was 5 per cent, and the paper being brought, by the bill of 1819, up to the gold standard, he had considered that, as the value of the currency was only altered 5 per cent, there could be no greater variation than 5 per cent, in the result as to prices. But this calculation had always been subject to a supposition, that no change was to take place in the value of gold. Mr. Peel's bill, as originally constituted, led the way to no such change. [...] The charge against him [Ricardo] was, that he had not foreseen the alteration in the value of the standard, to which, by the bill, the paper money was required to conform. No doubt, gold had altered in value, and why? Why, because the Bank [of England], from the moment of the passing of the bill in 1819, set their faces against the due execution of it. [...] By their measures they [the Bank] occasioned a demand for gold, which was, in no way, necessarily consequent upon the bill of 1819; and so raising the value of gold in the general market of the world, they changed the value of the standard with reference to which our currency had been calculated, in a manner which had not been presumed upon.
>
> This, then, was the error which he (Mr. Ricardo) had been guilty of: he had not foreseen these unnecessary, and, as he must add, mischievous operations of the Bank. Fully allowing, as he did, for the effect thus produced on the value of gold, it remained to consider what that effect really had been. The hon. member for Essex estimated it at 30 per cent; he (Mr. Ricardo) calculated it at 5 per cent; and he was therefore now ready to admit, that Mr. Peel's bill had raised the value of the currency 10 per cent. By increasing the value of gold 5 per cent, it had become necessary to raise the value of paper 10 per cent, instead of 5 per cent, to make it conform to the enhanced value of gold.
>
> (Speech of 11 June 1823; V: 311–2)

As in 1819, Ricardo's argument in 1822–1823, which combined a 5 per cent increase in the value of bullion and a 5 per cent fall in its price to produce a 10 per cent rise in the value of money, is thus an illustration of the MSE:

$$\frac{\Delta V_M}{V_M} = \frac{\Delta V_G}{V_G} - \frac{\Delta P_G}{P_G} \tag{4.8}$$

In this particular case: $0.10 = 0.05 - (-0.05)$ With these figures, the use of the simplified form (4.8) of the MSE instead of the exact form (4.7) leads to underestimate the rise in the value of money by 0.5 per cent only (for additional textual evidence on the MSE see below Appendix 4).

As far as I know, the only author having noticed Ricardo's numerical example in his 1822–1823 speeches is Richard Sayers:

> Ricardo estimated the damage done by the Bank's action as a 5 per cent appreciation in gold against commodities which, added to the 5 per cent appreciation in paper against gold as forecast in 1819, made it 'necessary to raise the value of paper 10 per cent, instead of 5 per cent'.
>
> (Sayers 1953: 42)

But Sayers did not interpret this numerical example as an illustration of a general relation providing a foundation of Ricardo's monetary theory. Referring to this episode, Peach mentions that Ricardo:

> [D]id not foresee the events that were to follow [Peel's Bill] which led, in his 1822 estimation, to a ten per cent depreciation of paper [after] the Bank of England had (in his opinion) needlessly purchased large quantities of gold in anticipation of resumption, thus raising its market price *independently* of note issues.
>
> (Peach 2008: 12; his emphasis)

As seen above, this was neither Ricardo's observation nor his argument: according to him, the purchases of the Bank of England had led to a rise in the *value* of gold bullion (while its *market price* was in fact *decreasing* as a consequence of a contraction of note issues), resulting in a ten per cent *rise in the value of money*, of which five per cent were the consequence of its *appreciation*.

4.4 Conclusion

The theory of value and distribution contained in *Principles* allowed combining the distinction – already emphasised in the Bullion Essays – between the value of gold and the price of gold with the other distinction – which would be emphasised by Ricardo during the debates of 1819–1823 – between the value of gold and the value of money. In addition to the two aspects analysed in Chapter 3 above – the conclusion that a general rise (fall) in money prices and a fall (rise) in the value of money were one and the same thing and the dilemma between stabilising the value of the standard of money and stabilising its price – the determination of relative prices by the comparative cost of production of commodities with the portion of capital that pays no rent allowed Ricardo understanding that, in a monetary system regulated by a standard, it was not by its quantity that the standard affected the value of money (as he believed in the Bullion Essays) but by its cost of production.

In various papers of 1819–1823, Ricardo developed what had been germinating since *Proposals* (1816) and benefited from the theory of value and distribution contained in *Principles* (1817): an idiosyncratic theory of the value of money. At the same time he deepened his inquiry into an invariable standard of value, which, as shown in Chapter 3 above, led him to the conclusion that, although they were central in the analysis of the value of money, changes in the value of the standard of money – gold bullion – could not be ascertained with precision. Only a depreciation (or appreciation) of money could be measured unambiguously, since it was the difference between two observable magnitudes: the market price of gold bullion and the legal price of gold in coin – a claim he had repeated since the Bullion Essays of 1809–1811. Nevertheless, the difficulty of measuring the effect of a change in the value of the standard on the value of money did not prevent Ricardo from theorising it.

Three conclusions may be derived from this analysis. First, a change in the value of money during a period results from the combination of a change in the value of the standard during that period and the difference in depreciation between the beginning and the end (equation (4.6)). Second, because depreciation is measured by the spread between the market price of gold bullion and the legal price of gold in coin – as advocated by Ricardo since the Bullion Essays – one may deduce the Money–Standard Equation (MSE): the rate of change in the value of money during a period is equal to the difference between the rate of change in the value of the standard and the rate of change in its price (equation (4.8)). Third, the MSE leads to conjecture how a change in the quantity of money may affect its value: through a change in the price of the standard. Not only does the MSE provide a key to the integration of money in Ricardo's theory of value and distribution, but it also allows refuting the often-alleged contradiction between a supposed commodity-theory of money and a supposed quantity-theory of money: as will be shown in the next three chapters, a change in the cost of production of the standard (gold bullion) causes a change in the value of money in the same direction, while a change in the quantity of money causes a change in the market price of the standard in the same direction, hence a change in the value of money in the opposite direction. In other words, the quantity of money affects its value *indirectly*, through the market price of the standard – and not directly as in the Quantity Theory of Money – and this quantity effect adds up to the value effect generated by the conditions of production of the standard.

A striking consequence emerges: in a monetary system with convertibility of bullion into money (whether coin or note) and of money into bullion, the value of money is not determined by the ratio of the aggregate value of commodities to the exogenous quantity of money (its velocity of circulation being given). The quantity of money endogenously adjusts to the level that equalises the value of money with the value of the standard. And it does so through arbitrage that equalises the (variable) market price of the standard with its (fixed) legal price. Of course, this theory of money only applies to a monetary system with convertibility.

Ricardo obviously did not formalise the Money–Standard Equation. But he gave a numerical illustration of it, based on what actually happened between 1819 and 1821. He showed that the value of money had increased by 10 per cent during this period, as a consequence of the combination of a rise of 5 per cent in the value of gold bullion and of a fall of 5 per cent in its price – in conformity with what would be expected from the MSE. The rise in the *value* of bullion had then resulted from the unanticipated (by Ricardo) increase in the demand on the world market consequent upon the purchases by the Bank of England to replenish its reserve in coin. As for the fall in the market *price* of bullion, it had resulted from the deliberate contraction of the note issue aimed at making this price conform in 1821 to the pre-war legal price of gold in coin.

It remains now to explain how the value of money adjusts in response to a change either in the value of the standard – in relation with the difficulty of production of gold bullion – or in the market price of the standard – associated with a change in the quantity of money. This will be done in Chapter 5 for the former and in Chapters 6 and 7 for the latter.

Appendix 4: Evidence on the Money–Standard Equation: the "Draft on Peel" (1821)

As shown above in Chapter 4, the Money–Standard Equation (MSE) encapsulates Ricardo's theory of the value of money when it is regulated by a standard. The MSE states that the rate of change in the value of money during a given period is equal to the rate of change in the value of the standard in terms of all other commodities minus the rate of change in the market price of the standard in terms of money. Since the rate of change in the value of money is by definition equal to (with an opposite sign) the homothetic rate of change in the money prices of all commodities except the standard (see Chapter 3 above), the MSE also determines what in modern terms is called the rate of change in the general price level so defined.

Chapter 4 has provided many textual proofs of the MSE that may be found in Ricardo's speeches and evidence in Parliament between 1819 and 1823 (speeches in the House of Commons on 24 May 1819, 18 February, 3 April, 7 May, 12 June, 10 July 1822, 26 February, 11 June 1823, and evidence before the Committee on Resumption on 4 and 24 March 1819). Three texts, all of them written between December 1821 and April 1822, also illustrate the MSE. The most explicit is the draft of a letter that Ricardo envisaged to send to a newspaper to defend himself against the accusations made by William Cobbett and his followers. This "Draft on Peel" summarised Ricardo's arguments on the rise in the value of money that had occurred since the adoption of Peel's bill in 1819. Sraffa mentions in the presentation of the draft (V: 515) that the same arguments appeared in a letter to McCulloch, dated 3 January 1822; this is the second text quoted and commented on here. The third one is the section devoted to this question in Ricardo's last pamphlet published in his lifetime, *On Protection to Agriculture* (April 1822).

After having described the context in which these three texts were written, I will comment on them in order to account for Ricardo's arguments in terms of the MSE.

1. The context

The context of the extracts reproduced below was that of recurrent attacks on Ricardo in public opinion, which he summed-up in a letter of 11 December 1821 to Trower as follows:

> In the country I find much error prevailing on the subject of the currency, every ill which befals the country is by some ascribed to Peel's bill, and Peel's bill is as invariably ascribed to me.
>
> (IX: 122)

There was first the campaign launched against him by "the man who over the years was to write more about David Ricardo than any other among his contemporaries, William Cobbett" (Weatherall 1976: 55). Cobbett had created the *Weekly Political Register*, in which:

> [H]is prejudices were very strong. They were never stronger than when he came to write about stockbrokers or Jews: stockbrokers were always Muckworms, metaphorically, in the *Weekly Political Register*; while Jews strained the resources of a remarkable vocabulary of abuse. To him, of course, impatient of fact, David Ricardo was always both a Muckworm and a Jew.
>
> (ibid: 58)[10]

Cobbett had mocked Ricardo's *Principles* in the *Register* of 20 May 1820:

> [I]t has taken but a few months to shew that '*a Ricardo*' is a heap of senseless, Change-Alley jargon, put upon paper and bound up into book; that the measure [the Ingot Plan], founded upon it, must be abandoned, or will cause millions to be starved.
>
> (quoted in V: 41n; Cobbett's emphasis)

Since Henry Brougham had in Parliament called Ricardo "so great an oracle" on 24 December 1819, Cobbett ironically dubbed him "the Oracle" and even "the Oracle by excellence", as in his article of 20 October 1821 on the Agricultural Report and Evidence:

> To refer to the *market price of gold as a standard* is exactly what the Oracle did; the Oracle of the '*Collective Wisdom.*' Gold, says he, being the *standard of all things in the world*; every price *depending on that of gold*; and gold now being within *four and a half per cent.* of its lowest possible price, the prices of *other things* cannot, by this measure, be brought down more than four and a half per cent. [...] This was the ground *upon which Peel's Bill was passed!* This queer, this 'Change-Alley, this Jew-like notion of the price of gold being the standard. However, this was no *new* notion; it had been harped on by

> *Oracle Horner* and his Bullion Committee; by *Lord King;* and by a great many others, long before *the Oracle by excellence* spouted it forth.
>
> (quoted in IX: 123n; Cobbett's emphasis)

Cobbett's attack on this question of gold as the standard was echoed in Ricardo's above-quoted letter to Trower of 11 December 1821:

> I proposed a scheme by the adoption of which there would not have been a demand for one ounce of gold, either on the part of the Bank, or of any one else, and another is adopted by which both the Bank and individuals are obliged to demand a great quantity of gold and I am held responsible for the consequences. If I had been a bank director, and had had the management of this currency question, I maintain that I could have reverted to a metallic standard by raising money (only) 5 pc., I do not say that having a metallic standard I could protect it from the usual fluctuations to which standards have at all times been subject. Cobbett says I am little better than a fool in speaking of gold as a standard, that the only fair standard is corn. He shews his ignorance in saying so, but supposing it true, can he tell me what is to secure us from variations in his standard, – it would perhaps be more variable than any other.
>
> (IX: 123)

Ricardo's particular irritation at the end of 1821 was consequent upon a meeting in honour of his friend in Parliament, Joseph Hume, held in Hereford on 7 December. Ricardo spoke there briefly to recall his proposal of extinguishing the national debt with "a general and fair contribution of a portion of every man's property; not, as had been said, of the property of the landowner only, but of that of the merchant, the manufacturer, and the fundholder" (V: 472). He also advocated a reform of Parliament extending the right of vote to any householder, increasing the frequency of elections, and introducing "election by ballot", that is, secrecy of suffrage (ibid: 473–4). In this speech he did not touch the question of money and falling prices, but three days later, in a meeting in Monmouth again in honour of Joseph Hume to which Ricardo was not present, he was attacked on this subject by two speakers, Mr. Moggridge and Mr. Palmer. This led Ricardo to draft a six-page letter supposedly to be sent to a newspaper by someone defending him, as testified by the expressions "I regret that Mr. Ricardo was not present to answer for himself …" (ibid: 516), "To this Mr. Ricardo would probably answer that …" (ibid: 518), or "I am of opinion with Mr. Ricardo that …" (ibid: 519). This MS was discovered by Sraffa among the Mill–Ricardo papers and published by him under the name "Draft of a letter to a newspaper on the effects of Peel's bill". Sraffa mentioned that "the following draft letter was intended for an unidentified newspaper which had reported those speeches [by Mr. Moggridge and Mr. Palmer]: there is no evidence of its having been published or even sent" (V: 515).

In this draft, Ricardo referred directly to both speakers and settled the question of the change in money prices in terms of the relation between the change in the value of gold and the contraction in the quantity of notes:

> What is the cause of this difference [in the price of wheat since 1819], – it is owing entirely to the alteration in the value of gold say Mr. Moggridge and Mr. Palmer. I want to know to what cause they ascribe this alteration in the value of gold and on this subject they are silent, they give us no satisfaction whatever. If the question had been asked them at the Meeting when they delivered their opinions they would probably have said it is owing to the contracted quantity of paper currency, – but this would have been far from a satisfactory answer, for they were bound to shew how the contraction of a paper currency acted on the value of gold.
>
> ("Draft on Peel"; V: 516)

Meanwhile, Cobbett had taken advantage of what had happened during the meetings at Hereford and Monmouth and published in the issue of the *Register* dated 29 December 1821 a new vitriolic attack at Ricardo, under the title "MESSRS HUME AND RICARDO":

> That the former was invited to a dinner in *Herefordshire* I heard and was glad of; but, what the devil did the *latter* do there? What merits had *he*, except those of having asserted, that it was the *easiest thing in the world to carry Peel's Bill into effect*, and that the fall in prices *could* be only *four and a half per cent.?* He is, to be sure, the *Oracle* in a certain place; but, what could the *Herefordshire farmers* see in him, or have to do with him? Faith! the Radical shoe-makers and carpenters and smiths and labourers know a little better than this. Their *Oracles* are a little more correct in their predictions. At *Monmouth*, to which place Mr Hume went, there was a little of good sense in the proceedings. There the Oracle got some decent raps on the fingers; but, there he was not.
>
> (quoted in IX: 141n; Cobbett's emphasis)

A few days later, on 3 January 1822, Ricardo wrote to McCulloch and complained about these attacks. After having presented in a compact form the arguments contained in the "Draft on Peel" he concluded:

> Some of Mr. Cobbett's admirers spoke of my false predictions at Monmouth – the same men were at Hereford, where I had an opportunity of speaking for myself, for I was present, and then they said nothing.
>
> (ibid: 141)

Ricardo's irritation against Cobbett did not weaken. In a letter to Trower of 20 February 1822, the same man in whom Mallet in his diary admired "his placid temper, the candour of his disposition, his patience and attention" (quoted in VIII: 152) called his opponent "a mischievous scoundrel":

> Cobbett is a mischievous scoundrel; he ascribes the evils under which the country is laboring to the altered value of money, and yet recommends the people to hoard gold, which he knows will increase the value of money still more. It is confusion he wants, and he cares not what means he takes to produce it. But in spite of him the country will get over its difficulties, and when it is again prosperous he will have the insolence to say that he foretold it.
>
> (IX: 167)

This may be the reason why Ricardo felt it necessary to introduce in April 1822 in his pamphlet *On Protection to Agriculture* a whole section devoted to the demonstration that Peel's bill could not be responsible for more than a ten per cent general fall in prices, of which half was to be attributed to an unnecessary and harmful behaviour of the Bank of England and nothing to his Ingot Plan.

2. Ricardo's "Draft of a letter to a newspaper on the effects of Peel's bill", December 1821

Ricardo started to recall the existence of the Ingot Plan which he had exposed in *Proposals*:

> It will be recollected that Mr. Ricardo wrote a pamphlet to shew that a currency might be regulated by a metallic standard without the use of any other metal as money but silver and copper the latter for payments under a shilling the former for payments under a pound. For this purpose Mr. Ricardo proposed that the Bank should be obliged to give gold in bullion in exchange for their notes if of a certain amount on the demand of the holder of them.
>
> (V: 516–7)

The quotation given below goes uninterrupted on pp. 517–21 of Vol. V of *Works*. I have cut it here so as to comment on it in the light of the MSE.

In *Proposals* Ricardo had acknowledged that, if the Ingot Plan were adopted, it would *not* prevent future variations in the value of gold bullion, hence in the value of money. All currencies regulated by a standard were liable to the inconvenience of varying in value with the value of this standard. What he had contended was that the adoption of a currency so regulated by the standard would *not in itself* require a demand for bullion by the Bank of England to replenish its metallic reserve and thus would *not in itself* raise the value of gold bullion, hence the value of money. The only rise in the value of money to be expected was consequent upon the increase in the value of the Bank of England note so as to make it conform to the value of gold bullion – that is, according to the MSE, with a zero change generated by the Ingot Plan in the value of the standard the rise in the value of money would be equal to the 5 per cent fall in the market price of gold bullion necessary to make it agree with the pre-war mint price:

> Did Mr. Ricardo mean by this that gold itself could not thereafter vary, and that if it did the currency which was to be regulated by the value of gold would not vary with it? Quite the contrary, it is evident from the whole of the reasoning of the pamphlet in question that he considered gold as a variable commodity, as well as corn or any other merchandize, but his argument was, 'adopt my system which will render all demand for gold unnecessary, and will therefore probably be unattended with any variation in the value of that metal, and then the whole variation in the value of money will be only equal to the difference between the value of paper and the value of gold or 5pc^t^. You can now buy a quarter of corn with as much gold as is coined into £ [blank] for the same quantity of corn you are obliged to give £ [blank] in bank notes. Diminish the quantity of bank notes and you will raise them 5pc. in value and when this is effected you will obtain a quarter of corn for £ [blank] in paper as well as in gold – the price of corn in gold will not be altered, its price in paper will fall 5 pc^t^.' it is for Mr. Palmer to shew what is defective in this reasoning. Mr. Ricardo could not mean to say that no variation should thereafter take place in the value of gold, he must have known full well that the currency of every country regulated by a metallic standard was liable to all the variations of that standard. In Mr. Ricardo's speeches on Mr. Peel's bill, to which reference has been made, he said that we should be still liable to have our currency vary in proportion as the metal varied which was the standard, but that this was an inconvenience to which all metallic currencies were exposed – it was one to which France, Holland, Hamburgh and all those countries whose currencies were on the most solid system were exposed, and no case could even be imagined to exempt a currency from such variations.
>
> (ibid: 517–18)

Contrary to the Ingot Plan, Peel's bill of 1819 opened the possibility of a belated rise in the value of the standard, when convertibility into coin would be reverted to four years later and the Bank of England would purchase bullion to have it coined. Ricardo was well aware of that when the bill was adopted and thus he should not have maintained that the rise in the value of money would be limited to five per cent after the resumption of cash payments. However, according to him, such resumption might have proved unnecessary, if the advantages of the Ingot Plan had been fairly tested. This is why in 1819 Ricardo had advised the Bank of England to sell gold rather than to buy it:

> It may be said that this is a good defence for Mr. Ricardo's evidence before the committee, when he had reason to think that his plan was the one contemplated respecting the operation of which only he was examined, but it is not equally good for the opinion which he afterwards expressed in his speech

> when he had seen Mr. Peel's bill and which was essentially different from his proposed plan as it provided for payments in coin in 1823 and therefore made a demand for gold obviously necessary and the rise of its value certain. To this Mr. Ricardo would probably answer that he saw no such obvious necessity for the demand for gold – that as he understood the bill no specie would be necessary till May 1823 four years distant from the time of discussion and he might confidently rely that if for 3 out of these 4 years his plan had a fair trial it would be found so efficient for all the objects of the most improved currency that the legislature would have altered the law and dispensed with specie payments altogether: In the speech to which allusion has been made I recollect he advised the Bank to sell gold instead of buying it so little did he think the quantity actually in the possession of the Bank inadequate for all the purposes of bullion payments.
>
> (ibid: 518)

Ricardo's expectations had been deceived because of the behaviour of the Bank of England, which immediately after Peel's bill purchased bullion to have it coined in anticipation of the resumption of cash payments. This demand for gold by the Bank of England was implemented through a greater contraction of its issue than what would have been necessary to make the price of bullion fall by five per cent and be thus brought to the pre-war parity. The price of foreign bills consequently fell and this made the import of gold bullion in England advantageous (when the exchange rate of the pound rose to the import gold point; see Chapter 8 below). The Bank of England then purchased this additional bullion in the London market and had it coined by the Mint. When its vaults were filled with gold coins, the Bank of England applied to Parliament for having the right to release them against its small notes as early as 1821 – a request agreed by Parliament when it decided to resume at that date convertibility of the Bank of England note into coin. This demand for gold by the Bank of England, and the consequent rise in the value of gold, provoked a rise in the value of money (in addition to the one provoked by the fall in the market price of gold bullion) which could not fairly be imputed to Ricardo:

> Mr. Ricardo cannot fairly be held responsible for the narrow views, and obstinate prejudices of the Bank of England. He could not contemplate that the Bank would so narrow the circulation of paper as to occasion such a rise in its comparative value to gold and the currencies of other countries as to make the influx of gold into this unexampled in amount. He could not foresee that they would immediately provide themselves with so large a quantity of gold coin as to make it incumbent on them to apply to the legislature to permit them to withdraw all their small notes and fill the circulation with gold coin even so early as the middle of 1821 – this is what Mr. Ricardo could not anticipate – he relied on there being no demand for gold and the Bank by their injudicious measures occasioned a demand for many millions. He supposed that the reverting from a currency regulated by no standard, to one regulated

> by a fixed one, the greatest care would be taken to make the transition as little burthensome as possible, but the fact is that if the object had been to make the alteration from the one system to the other as distressing to the country as possible no measures could have been taken by the Bank of England so well calculated to produce that effect as those which they actually adopted.
>
> (ibid: 518–19)

Taking into account the additional rise in the value of money caused by the behaviour of the Bank of England did not, however, lead to explain the whole of the fall in prices mentioned by Ricardo's opponents to the rise in the value of money. Only a fall by 10 per cent was general and could be explained by it; 5 per cent due to the rise in the value of the standard consequent upon the demand for gold by the Bank of England (as evaluated by Thomas Tooke), plus 5 per cent due to the fall in the market price of the standard necessary to raise the value of the Bank of England note to the value of bullion (that is, to lower the market price of gold to its pre-war legal level). Ascribing to the rise in the value of money the 50 per cent fall in the prices of commodities, as Ricardo's opponents did, could be proven absurd. Because the effect of the rise in the value of the Bank of England note as compared to gold on the rise in the value of money since 1819 was recognized as being 5 per cent – the difference between the market price of gold in 1819 and that in 1821 (equal to the mint price) – saying that the value of money had risen by 50 per cent amounted (according to the MSE) to saying that the value of gold bullion in terms of all other commodities had risen by 45 per cent. The value of gold bullion being established at the world level, such an enormous change in the gold-price of all commodities would have been observed everywhere in Europe. It was not so and this proved that contending that the value of money rose in England by 50 per cent was absurd:

> In saying this it must not be supposed that I agree with Mr. Moggridge and Mr. Palmer that any thing like the effect which they compute has been produced on the value of the currency by reverting to specie payments. I am of opinion with Mr. Ricardo that if the Bank had followed the obvious course of policy which they ought to have pursued this great measure might have been accomplished with no other alteration in the value of money but 5pc^{t}, but by the course which they did adopt and the demand which they in consequence occasioned for gold bullion they have raised the value of that metal about 5pc^{t} more and consequently that the whole alteration in the value of the currency since 1819 has been about 10 pc^{t}. My reason for thinking that the demand for gold has caused a rise of 5pc. in that metal is nearly the same as that expressed by Mr. Tooke in his evidence before the Agricultural committee. This rise in the value of gold it must always be remembered is not confined to this country, it is common to all, and if the standard of all were gold and not silver, the money of all would have varied 5 pc^{t}. What cannot be too often insisted on is that that paper money has only increased in value 5 pc. more than gold – it could not have increased more because it is now on a par with gold and

> in 1819 and for 4 years before 1819 had not been depressed more than 5 pc. below gold. When Mr. Palmer says therefore that money has altered 50 pc[t] in value in consequence of Mr. Peel's bill he must mean that Paper money has risen 50 pc[t] and gold bullion 45 pc[t]. If this be true all commodities in this country as well as in every other ought to have varied 45 pc. as compared with gold – Does he or any other man believe this to be the fact? Are the people of France, Germany, Italy, Spain, Holland and Hamburgh obliged to give nearly double the quantity of commodities for the purchase of a given weight of gold. Can the Stock holder with the same money dividend procure double the quantity of all commodities he desires – it is notoriously otherwise and how men with such good understandings as Mr. Moggridge and Mr. Palmer can be made the dupes of such an absurd theory I am at loss to conceive.
>
> (ibid: 519–20)

Hence, if it was contended that the price of corn and other raw produce had fallen by 50 per cent, only 10 per cent could be ascribed to the rise in the value of money. The other 40 per cent were to be explained by causes specific to these commodities:

> That raw produce is frightfully depressed no one can deny but that this depression is either wholly or in any very great part occasioned by the rise in the value of money is not made out by any plausible arguments. Corn and raw produce are not exempted from a fall of value more than other commodities and if it be true that they have fallen 50 pc[t] 40 of that 50pc[t] fall is entirely owing to causes which have operated on their value. Such variations are by no means uncommon. In 1792 wheat was at 39/- in 1800 134/- 1804 52/- 1808 81/- 1812 140/- 1814 67/- 1816 53/- 1817 109/- and it cannot be pretended that these variations were occasioned by the altered value of money. That some part of these variations may be imputed to variations in the value of money is not disputed, but while money varied 10 pc. corn varied 100 pc. and why may not the same have occurred now. Those who deny this are bound to give some reason for their opinion – hitherto they have given none.
>
> (ibid: 520–1)

3. Ricardo's letter to McCulloch of 3 January 1822

The quotation given below goes uninterrupted on pp. 140–1 of Vol. IX of *Works*. Here also, my comments aim at accounting for Ricardo's arguments in terms of the MSE.

The forecast made by Ricardo in 1819 was that the Ingot Plan would require no additional demand for gold, so that its value would remain unaltered. The only expected change in the value of money was thus consequent upon the fall in the market price of an ounce of gold bullion from £4. 2s. to £3. 17s. 10½d., required to make the value of the Bank of England note conform to the value of bullion – that is, £3. 17s. 10½d. in notes (and no longer £4. 2s.) having henceforth the same value as an ounce of gold bullion (the legal price of which as anticipated by Peel's bill for 1821 was £3. 17s. 10½d.). This expected 5 per cent fall in the market price of bullion – in Ricardo's terms its appreciation – would raise the value of paper money by 5 per cent:

> Cobbett and his followers keep up incessant attacks upon me, for having said in my evidence before the Bank Committee, that the restoring the currency to the ancient standard, would only alter its value 5pc^{t}. He forgets that I was speaking of the plan recommended by me for restoring it, which would not have called for the use of any gold, and which would therefore not have occasioned any demand for that metal; and then, I ask, what there was in reverting to a bullion standard to make prices alter more than 5 pct.? Suppose that in 1819, when gold was at £4. 2 – pr. oz, we had had two prices, a paper price and a bullion price; £4. 2 –, in paper, would have purchased no more than £3. 17. 10½ in gold. By raising the value of paper 5 p^{t}. would not £3. 17. 10½ in paper purchase the same, as the like sum in gold?
>
> (IX: 140)

All that the Bank of England had to do, according to the Ingot Plan implemented by Peel's bill, was to reduce its issues so as to bring back the market price of an ounce of gold bullion from £4. 2s. to £3. 17s. 10½d. But at the same time the Bank of England purchased gold in anticipation of the return to convertibility of its notes in specie, which had been stipulated in Peel's bill as scheduled for 1823. So doing, it provoked an increase in the value of bullion, hence in the value of paper money, at a moment when the latter was already raised – through the above-mentioned fall in the market price of bullion – to make its value in commodities conform to that of bullion. The result was harmful to the country:

> If indeed during the operation of limiting the amount of paper, I make immense purchases of gold, and lock it up in a chest, or devote it to uses to which it had not before been applied, I raise the value of gold, and thereby lower the prices of goods, both in gold and in paper, which latter must conform to the value of gold; and this is precisely what the Bank have done. They have, from ignorance, made the reverting to a fixed currency as difficult a task to the country as possible.
>
> (ibid)

Such behaviour of the Bank of England was wholly unnecessary. Surely, the resumption of convertibility into specie required additional metallic reserves. But the adoption of the Ingot Plan – that is, convertibility into bullion – from 1819 to 1823, as decided in Peel's bill, was intended to prevent such immediate additional demand for gold, with its harmful consequences. One could even hope that the success of the plan would postpone the resumption of specie payments indefinitely, and with it the additional deflation imposed on the country.

The abrupt move by the Bank of England had unfortunately the opposite result: it accelerated the resumption of convertibility into specie as early as 1821 and consequently the substitution of coins for small notes – the very object of the Bank of England:

> Cobbett forgets too that Peel's bill absolutely prohibited the Bank from paying in specie till 1823. All the friends of that bill had a right to expect that the Bank would make no preparation for specie payments till 1822, one year before the period fixed, and I for one flattered myself that if from 1819 to 1822 it were found that the system of bullion payments was a safe and easy one, specie payments would be still further deferred, but the Bank had strong prejudices against the plan and immediately commenced purchasing bullion and coining money, and were absolutely forced to come to the legislature for permission, last year, to pay in specie, as they had accumulated a large quantity of coin. After they had been foolish enough to do so, it became a matter of indifference whether parliament agreed to their request or refused it – indeed it was more desirable to comply with it: – the evil had already been done by the purchase and accumulation of gold, and no further mischief could arise from the substitution of the coins (in circulation) for the paper which they were desirous of withdrawing.
>
> (ibid: 140–1)

4. The pamphlet **On Protection to Agriculture,** *April 1822*

In Section V of this pamphlet, entitled "On the Effects produced on the Price of Corn by Mr. Peel's Bill for restoring the Ancient Standard" (IV: 222–35) and in the "Conclusion" to it (ibid: 261–6), Ricardo used the same arguments as in the two preceding texts:

> There was nothing in the plan [the Ingot Plan] which could cause a rise in the value of gold, for no additional quantity of gold would have been required, and therefore 5 per cent. would have been the full extent of the rise in the value of money.
>
> (IV: 224)

> Their [the Bank of England] issues were so regulated, that the exchange became extremely favourable to this country, gold flowed into it in a continued stream, and all that came the Bank eagerly purchased at 3l. 17s. 10½d. per ounce. Such a demand for gold could not fail to elevate its value, compared with the value of all commodities. Not only, then, had we to elevate the value of our currency 5 per cent., the amount of the difference between the value of paper and of gold before these operations commenced, but we had still further to elevate it to the new value to which gold itself was raised, by the injudicious purchases which the Bank made of that metal.
>
> (ibid: 225)

> Mr. Tooke [...] came to the conclusion that the eager demand for gold made by the bank in order to substitute coin for their small notes, had raised the value of currency about five per cent. In this conclusion, I quite concur with Mr. Tooke. If it be well founded, the whole increased value of our currency since the passing of Mr. Peel's bill in 1819, may be estimated at about ten per cent. To that amount, taxation has been increased by the measure for restoring specie payment; to that amount the fall of grain, and with it of all other commodities has taken place as far as this cause alone has operated on them; but all above that amount, all the further depression which the price of corn has sustained, must be accounted for by the supply having exceeded the demand; a depression, which would have equally occurred, if no alteration whatever had been made in the value of the currency.
>
> (ibid: 228)

> The cause of the present low price of agricultural produce is partly the alteration in the value of the currency, and mainly an excess of supply above the demand. To Mr. Peel's bill, even in conjunction with the operation of the Bank, no greater effect on the price of corn can, with any fairness, be attributed than 10 per cent., and to that amount the far greatest part of the taxation of the country has been increased: but this increased taxation does not fall on the landed interest only; it falls equally on the funded interest, and every other interest in the country.
>
> (ibid: 262)

Notes

1 At the time of the publication of *Proposals* (February 1816) gold had not yet been legally declared as the sole standard. It is the reason why the quotation refers to metals (in the plural).

2 For another refutation of Marx's critique, see Marcuzzo and Rosselli (1991: 56):

> Marx's interpretation loses the distinction between the fall in the value of gold and the depreciation of money. In Ricardo's view, a variation in the quantity of money with respect to its natural level would provoke a change in the value of money, defined as the purchasing power of the currency over the standard; but it would not change the value of the standard, which depended on the specific conditions prevailing on the gold market.

This argument is, however, weakened by the adoption of a definition of the value of money by its purchasing power over the standard.

3 The same supposition is already to be found in one of the three letters on the *Bullion Report* published by Ricardo in the *Morning Chronicle*, that of 24 September 1810 (III: 150).

4 According to Schumpeter (1954: 704 n13), "His [Ricardo's] famous analogy between the Bank's power under the Restriction Act and the discovery of a gold mine in the Bank's courtyard was not only telling but, so far as it went, also correct."

5 The denunciation of this "error" would be repeated by Ricardo each time it led to a wrong diagnosis, such as the one made by the Directors of the Bank of England in 1819: "They still maintain that the high price of bullion in their depreciated medium,

means the same thing as a high exchangeable value of bullion in all other things" (Letter to McCulloch, 7 April 1819; VIII: 21).

6 For another refutation, based on the notion of "natural quantity of money", of this alleged contradiction, see Marcuzzo and Rosselli (2015: 373–4).

7 One should understand that such a fall would occur if depreciation were to be eliminated, as it is stated in the following sentence. Depreciation *raised* prices by five per cent, and consequently prices would *fall* by five per cent if "it was required to restore the currency thus depreciated five per cent, to par".

8 In previous publications where the Money–Standard Equation appeared I presented it in continuous time (see Deleplace, 2008: 26; 2013a: 119; 2013b: 984; 2015c: 348). Its presentation in discrete time seems closer to what Ricardo had in mind, as in the factual illustration above.

9 The sentence about a currency being depreciated while it rises in value was quoted in substance in Blake (1823) on which Ricardo's notes have been published in *Works*: "And in another part of his evidence he [Mr. Ricardo] says, 'I think it quite possible that a bank note may be depreciated, although it should rise in value, if it did not rise in value in a degree equal to the standard'", a sentence that gave rise to Ricardo's modest comment: "I believe all the other witnesses agreed with Mr. Ricardo in this explanation of the meaning of the word depreciation" (IV: 330). He had, however, many occasions to complain of it not being the case, as in his speech in the House of Commons of 10 July 1822: this meaning was "a doctrine which I have always maintained but which is now very often in this house and out of it called in question" (V: 236)

10 Cobbett's animus survived Ricardo's death, as testified by his observations on Gatcombe (then owned by Ricardo's second son David) and Bromesberrow Place (owned by Ricardo's elder son Osman) during his tours of England in 1825 (see Weatherall 1976: 99, 131).

5 The adjustment to a change in the value of the standard

No country that used the precious metals as a standard, were exempted from variations in the prices of commodities, occasioned by a variation in the value of their standard.

(Speech in the House of Commons, 12 June 1822; V: 204)

In Chapter 4 above I already discussed the "analogy" made by Ricardo in the Bullion Essays between an increase in the quantity of money caused by the discovery of a new gold mine and one caused by an additional discretionary issue of inconvertible notes. I contended that the adoption in *Principles* of a theory of the value of commodities based on their cost of production with the portion of capital that pays no rent allowed Ricardo to understand that, in a monetary system regulated by a standard, it is not by its quantity that the standard affected permanently the value of money (as he believed in the Bullion Essays) but by its cost of production. However, Ricardo maintained that, as in the case of an excess issue of bank notes, the discovery of a new mine caused a fall in the value of money through an increased quantity of money:

> If by the discovery of a new mine, by the abuses of banking, or by any other cause, the quantity of money be greatly increased, its ultimate effect is to raise the prices of commodities in proportion to the increased quantity of money.

(*Principles*; I: 298)

In the case of notes, an excess issue of them (consequent upon "abuses of banking") caused a general rise in money prices because it induced a depreciation of money, that is, a market price of gold bullion paid for in notes above the legal price of gold in coin. The question should thus be raised: Did the discovery of a new gold mine also cause an excess quantity of money and thereby its depreciation? I will contend that while in 1810 Ricardo remained rather ambiguous about an interpretation of the effect of a newly discovered gold mine in terms of depreciation of money, his later insistence on the distinction between a depreciation of money caused by its excess quantity and a fall in the value of money caused by a fall in the value of gold bullion implied that the effect of the discovery of a new gold mine belonged to the latter case, *not* to the former. Paradoxically, this became clear when, during the debates in 1819–1823 around the resumption of convertibility, Ricardo discussed another aspect of the behaviour of the Bank of England than its note issuing: the faulty management of its gold reserve that caused an increase in the value of bullion and thereby in the value of money. This effect was symmetrical, *not* about the depreciation of the currency caused by an excess issue of notes, *but* about the fall in the value of money caused by a fall in the value of bullion after the discovery of a new gold mine.

In the Bullion Essays Ricardo contended that the discovery of a new mine more productive than at least some of those previously worked led to a permanent fall in the value of gold-money:

> If a mine of gold were discovered in either of these countries, the currency of that country would be lowered in value in consequence of the increased quantity of the precious metals brought into circulation.
>
> (*High Price*; III: 54)

Here, the effect of the discovery of a new gold mine on the value of money was ascribed to an increase in the quantity of gold produced, which generated an increase in the quantity of coins ("in consequence of the increased quantity of the precious metals brought into circulation"). There was one step then to consider this quantity of money as being in excess, and one step more to conclude that money was not only "lowered in value" but in fact depreciated. Did Ricardo make these steps? As shown below, there is some ambiguity in his writings of that period. However, after he adopted a few years later a theory of value based on the concept of difficulty of production, this ambiguity disappeared: the discovery of a new mine did lower the value of money and hence raised the money prices of commodities, but the channel of transmission was *not* an excess quantity and a depreciation of money. A reduction in the cost of production of gold – consequent upon the discovery of a new highly productive mine or the introduction of a new cost-reducing technique – was henceforth translated into a fall in the value of money through a fall in the value of bullion in terms of all other commodities, and not through a depreciation of money caused by an excess quantity (Section 5.1). This explanation of the effect of a newly discovered gold mine on the value of money was permitted by the extension of Ricardo's theory of rent from land to mines (Section 5.2). There was, however, a specificity of gold bullion in respect to corn, which affected the adjustment process of the natural price to the discovery of a new gold mine (Section 5.3). This adjustment may be analysed in two steps: in the gold-producing country (Section 5.4) and in the gold-importing country where bullion was coined (Section 5.5). A symmetrical case was the adjustment to an increased demand for gold bullion, as that implemented by the Bank of England in the perspective of the resumption of the convertibility of its note into coin (Section 5.6). Both cases illustrate the relevance of the Money–Standard Equation (Section 5.7).

5.1 From an ambiguity in the Bullion Essays to a clarification in *Principles*

Criticising Bentham on the cause of the general rise in prices

At the time of the Bullion Essays, Ricardo sometimes interpreted the discovery of a new gold mine as causing a depreciation of money. This was implied in *Reply to Bosanquet* by the "analogy" between the discovery of a new gold mine and the additional discretionary issuing of inconvertible notes, and illustrated by his manuscript comments on the minutes of evidence before the Bullion Committee in 1810. On someone being asked about "an excessive currency, though not forced", and answering "I do not conceive the thing possible", Ricardo commented:

> This seems to be the source of all the errors of these practical men. A paper currency cannot be excessive, according to them, if no one is obliged to take it against his will. They must be of opinion that a given quantity of currency can be employed by a given quantity of commerce and payments, and no more, – not reflecting that by depreciating its value the same commerce will employ an additional quantity. Did not the discovery of the American mines depreciate the value of money, and has not the consequences been an increased use of it. By constantly depreciating its value there is no quantity of money which the same state of commerce may not absorb.
>
> (III: 362)

And contradicting a Director of the Bank of England:

> The bank during the suspension of Cash payments, with its present excessive issues produces the same effect as the discovery of a new mine of gold which should materially depreciate the value of money.
>
> (ibid: 376–7)

Speaking of the relative redundancy of money in two countries, Ricardo wrote in a letter to Malthus of 18 June 1811:

> This relative redundancy may be produced as well by a diminution of goods as by an actual increase of money, (or which is the same thing by an increased economy in the use of it) in one country; or by an increased quantity of goods, or by a diminished amount of money in another. In either of these cases a redundancy of money is produced as effectually as if the mines had become more productive.
>
> (VI: 26)

Elsewhere at the same time, however, Ricardo seemed to discard such interpretation in terms of depreciation, as in his manuscript "Notes on Bentham's 'Sur les prix'", written at the very end of 1810 (for the history of these notes on Bentham's manuscript "Sur les prix" and a comparison between the two writings see Deleplace and Sigot 2012). Although Ricardo acknowledged that an increase in the quantity of coins and an increase in the quantity of notes would both cause a general rise in prices, he noticed a difference between the two cases:

> The argument in this chapter [by Bentham] is that an increase of paper money has the same effects in increasing prices as an increase in metallic money. This is no doubt true, but we should recollect that paper money cannot be increased without causing a depreciation of such money as compared with the precious metals.
>
> (III: 269)

The depreciation of the notes being "as compared with the precious metals", it was reflected in a rise of the market price of bullion paid for in notes. An increase in the quantity of notes thus caused a rise in all prices of commodities paid for in notes, including that of gold bullion. In contrast, an increase in the quantity of coins, although it also raised the prices of all other commodities paid for in coins, did *not* raise the price of gold bullion (provided the coins were full-bodied) since an ounce of gold bullion always exchanged for an ounce of gold in coin (see Chapter 6 below). This excerpt shows that, at the time of the Bullion Essays, Ricardo already made a distinction between a general rise in prices (*including* that of bullion), caused by a depreciation of money, and a general rise in prices (*excluding* that of bullion), caused by a fall in the value of gold. This distinction was, however, obscured by the fact that, *at that time*, Ricardo understood this fall in the value of gold as being caused by an increase in its quantity produced, so that, as in the case of notes, the rise in price of all other commodities was explained by an increase in quantity – of gold as of notes. This explanation allowed Ricardo to express his agreement with Bentham on the general rise in price of commodities having been caused by an increase in the quantity of money, and his disagreement with him on the kind of money that was responsible for that rise. On Bentham saying: "The value of money is at present [in 1801] only half of what it was forty years ago: in forty years it will only be half of what it is at present"[1] Ricardo commented with a phrase preceding the previous excerpt:

> As I attribute the fall in the value of money during the last 40 years to the increase of the metals from which money is made, I cannot anticipate a similar fall in the next 40 years unless we should discover new and abundant mines of the precious metals.
>
> (ibid)

By "increase of the metals" Ricardo meant an increase in the quantity produced of them. He had in view the long-term phenomenon ("40 years") of "the fall in the value of money", which he explained by the discovery of "new and abundant mines" that had increased the quantity produced of precious metals, hence reduced their value in terms of all other commodities. It was this fall in the value of gold which had provoked a fall in the value of money made of gold, and consequently a general rise in prices. On the contrary, Bentham attributed this rise to an overissue of notes. For Ricardo, such overissue did explain the depreciation of money – also responsible for a general rise in prices – although not at the period considered by Bentham (the 40 years before 1801) but more recently, after the suspension of convertibility in 1797 had produced its effects.

This critique addressed by Ricardo to Bentham anticipated the distinction made by him later (see Chapter 4 above) between a general increase in prices due to a *fall* in the *value* of gold in terms of all other commodities, and one due to a depreciation of money, measured by a *rise* in the *price* of gold in terms of money (that is, a fall in the value of money in terms of gold). The discovery of gold mines provoked a general rise in prices through the first channel and exclusively through it. The overissue of paper provoked a general rise in prices through the second channel and exclusively through it. However, when, in the above quotation from *Principles*, Ricardo mentioned "the discovery of a new mine" and "the abuses of banking", he stressed that in both cases the prices of commodities were raised while the quantity of money increased, but he abstracted from the difference between coins and notes as to the transmission channel associated with an increase in the quantity of money. This point should, however, be clarified.

From the mine to the mint

When in *Reply to Bosanquet* Ricardo made his "analogy" between an increased quantity of money caused by the discovery of a new gold mine "on the own premises" of the Bank of England and one caused by an additional discretionary issue of inconvertible notes, he supposed that gold was immediately coined by the Bank of England itself:

> Now supposing the gold mine to be actually the property of the Bank, even to be situated on their own premises, and that they procured the gold which it produced to be coined into guineas, and in lieu of issuing their notes when they discounted bills or lent money to Government that they issued nothing but guineas; could there be any other limit to their issues but the want of the further productiveness in their mine? In what would the circumstances differ if the mine were the property of the king, of a company of merchants, or of a single individual? In that case Mr. Bosanquet admits that the value of money would fall, and I suppose he would also admit that it would fall in exact proportion to its increase.
>
> (*Reply to Bosanquet*; III: 216–17)

If the Bank of England itself issued coins, there would indeed be no difference with its issuing of notes: the exogenous increase in the quantity of gold bullion would immediately mean an increase in the quantity of money, as when the Bank of England discretionarily issued an additional quantity of notes. But would it be so "if the mine were the property of the king, of a company of merchants, or of a single individual"? It would for the king, who enjoyed the privilege of issuing coins. But it would not in the case "of a company of merchants, or of a single individual", who needed to carry the gold bullion to the mint to have it coined. And so was it actually for that particular "company of merchants" called the Bank of England. However, all these private owners of the gold bullion produced by a new mine had also the possibility of selling it in the market against existing coins or notes, rather than carry it to the mint to get new coins. As already noted in Chapter 3 above, Ricardo was well aware that gold bullion could only be converted into money if its market price was below the legal price of gold in coin, which was the same as saying that the value of money was above the value of bullion. As he would write five years later in *Proposals*:

> It is the rise in the value of money above the value of bullion which is always, in a sound state of the currency, the cause of its increase in quantity; for it is at these times that either an opening is made for the issue of more paper money, which is always attended with profit to the issuers; or that a profit is made by carrying bullion to the mint to be coined. To say that money is more valuable than bullion or the standard, is to say that bullion is selling in the market under the mint price.
>
> (*Proposals*; IV: 56–7)

Two inferences might be drawn from this necessary condition for an increased quantity of money to follow on an increased quantity of bullion. First, any interpretation of such situation in terms of depreciation caused by money being in excess should be discarded, in contrast with what happened in the case of an additional discretionary issuing of notes. The increase in the quantity of money after the discovery of a new gold mine was the *consequence* of a *fall* in the market price of bullion *below* the legal price of gold in coin; the increase in the quantity of money discretionarily decided by an issuing bank was the *cause* of a *rise* in the market price of bullion *above* the legal price of gold in coin. We will see that, "in a sound state of the currency", the final outcome of the adjustment was in both cases the return of the market price of gold bullion to the level of the legal price of gold in coin, but in the case of the mine it was *from below* (through coining) while in the case of the bank it was *from above* (through melting).

The second inference is that, to explain how the quantity of money increased after the discovery of a new gold mine, one should understand what happened to the market price of gold bullion. Why did Ricardo in his "analogy" make the simplifying assumption that the Bank of England itself issued coins, thus bypassing the adjustment in the bullion market? One may suggest two reasons, one on the side of money the other on the side of gold bullion as commodity.

On the side of money, the "analogy" was at the time of the Bullion Essays explicitly made by Ricardo with the discretionary issuing of *inconvertible* bank notes. Ricardo considered that, in a situation where Bank of England notes had been made inconvertible and gold and silver coins had disappeared from circulation, money was no longer regulated by the standard:

> That gold is no longer in practice the standard by which our currency is regulated is a truth. It is the ground of the complaint of the [Bullion] Committee (and of all who have written on the same side) against the present system.
>
> (*Reply to Bosanquet*; III: 255)

In his writings of 1819–1823 Ricardo would again emphasise this absence of regulation of the note issue by the standard during the period of inconvertibility:

> It is also forgotten, that from 1797 to 1819 we had no standard whatever, by which to regulate the quantity or value of our money. Its quantity and its value depended entirely on the Bank of England, the directors of which establishment, however desirous they might have been to act with fairness and justice to the public, avowed that they were guided in their issues by principles which, it is no longer disputed, exposed the country to the greatest embarrassment. Accordingly, we find that the currency varied in value considerably during the period of 22 years, when there was no other rule for regulating its quantity and value but the will of the Bank.
>
> (*Protection to Agriculture*; IV: 222–3)

The value of money not being regulated by the standard meant that it was detached from the value of the latter. What happened to the market price of bullion only indicated by how much money departed from a situation in which it would be so regulated: this price was only "a proof of the depreciation of bank notes". When in 1816 Ricardo developed in *Proposals* the plan of note convertibility into bullion outlined in 1811 in the Appendix to the fourth edition of *High Price*, he explicitly considered "a sound state of the currency", that is, "the reverting from a currency regulated by no standard, to one regulated by a fixed one" as he would say in the "Draft on Peel" of 1821 (V: 519). Abstracting from the bullion market was thus no longer possible since its working was at the heart of this regulation, hence a central piece of the theory of money.

On the side of gold bullion as commodity, in the Bullion Essays its market price reflected its scarcity, like that of any commodity (see Chapter 4 above). The increased quantity of bullion produced after the discovery of a new mine was the only element to be taken into account in the adjustment of the quantity and the value of money, whether the owner of the new mine carried himself its production to the mint or sold it in the market, thus depressing the price of bullion so that its buyers carried it to the mint. Things changed when in *Principles* Ricardo adopted the view according to which "it is not quantity that regulates price, but facility or difficulty of production" (Letter to Maria Edgeworth of 13 December 1822; IX: 239). A corollary was that the market price of any competitively produced commodity varied temporarily with the quantity supplied but was ultimately regulated by the natural price, determined by the cost of production. Of course the increased quantity of bullion consequent upon the discovery of a new mine immediately depressed its market price, but since it was produced in competitive conditions one should inquire about what happened to its natural price before drawing a conclusion on the permanent change in the value of money. The adjustment in the market for gold bullion had henceforth to be made explicit: the simplifying assumption that the owner of the new mine bypassed the market was no longer acceptable – and neither was the "analogy". The production of gold bullion was now to be compared with the production of corn, *not* with the issuing of inconvertible bank notes. A preliminary step was to extend the theory of rent from land to mines.

5.2 The extension of the theory of rent from land to mines

As with every commodity produced with capital in competitive conditions, gold had a natural price allowing any portion of capital advanced in its production to earn the same general rate of profit as in any other employment. Being produced in mines of different qualities, its natural price was determined by the cost of production with that portion of capital which was the least productive and paid no rent. According to Ricardo, the theory of differential rent applied to mines: after having exposed it for land in Chapter II of *Principles* "On rent", Ricardo extended it in Chapter III "On the rent of mines":

> Mines, as well as land, generally pay a rent to their owner; and this rent, as well as the rent of land, is the effect, and never the cause of the high value of their produce.
>
> If there were abundance of equally fertile mines, which any one might appropriate, they could yield no rent; the value of their produce would depend on the quantity of labour necessary to extract the metal from the mine and bring it to market.
>
> But there are mines of various qualities, affording very different results, with equal quantities of labour. The metal produced from the poorest mine that is worked, must at least have an exchangeable value, not only sufficient to procure all the clothes, food, and other necessaries consumed by those employed in working it, and bringing the produce to market, but also to afford the common and ordinary profits to him who advances the stock necessary to carry on the undertaking. The return for capital from the poorest mine paying no rent, would regulate the rent of all the other more productive mines. This mine is supposed to yield the usual profits of stock. All that the other mines produce more than this, will necessarily be paid to the owners for rent. Since this principle is precisely the same as that which we have already laid down respecting land, it will not be necessary further to enlarge on it.
>
> (*Principles*; I: 85)

As for land, the theory of rent applied to mines raises two distinct questions: first the effects of a change in the demand for the commodity produced in the mines; second, the effects of a change in the supply of that commodity, whether it be a consequence of the discovery of new mines or of the introduction of new production techniques. It seems that Ricardo himself and the subsequent Ricardian theory of the rent of land have mostly concentrated on the effect of changes on the side of demand, as part of a dynamic analysis of the interrelations between the determination of prices, the distribution of income, and the accumulation of capital. The cultivation of new lands and the introduction of new techniques are indeed considered, but as a response to a change in demand, not as an independent change on the supply side.[2] In contrast, since the analysis of the relation between the quantity and the value of money was approached by Ricardo from the point of view of an exogenous change in the quantity of money issued, he concentrated his attention on changes occurring on the supply side. Typically, Ricardo considered the effects of the discovery of a new mine, which illustrated the analytical case of an exogenous increase in the quantity of gold-money issued and the historical fact of the large inflow of precious metals in Europe having followed the conquest of America.

It should be emphasised that, as for the analysis of the rent on land, Ricardo's reasoning was in terms of portions of capital rather than in terms of mines or pieces of land. Capital is what should earn the general rate of profit in the natural state, and portions of capital are added or withdrawn according to whether more or less than the general rate of profit may be earned, no matter a new mine (piece of land) be opened (cultivated) or an old one be closed down (left fallow).[3] This point was stressed by Ricardo in *Principles* as an answer to Say and Malthus who contended, as a matter of fact, that every land paid a rent. In Chapter XXXII "Mr. Malthus's opinions on rent", Ricardo wrote:

> It is not necessary to state, on every occasion, but it must be always understood, that the same results will follow, as far as regards the price of raw produce and the rise of rents, whether an additional capital of a given amount, be employed on new land, for which no rent is paid, or on land already in cultivation, if the produce obtained from both be precisely the same in quantity. See p. 72. M. Say, in his notes to the French translation of this work, had endeavoured to shew that there is not at any time land in cultivation which does not pay a rent, and having satisfied himself on this point, he concludes that he has overturned all the conclusions which result from that doctrine. [...] But before M. Say can establish the correctness of this inference [on the effect of taxes on corn] he must also shew that there is not any capital employed on the land for which no rent is paid (see the beginning of this note, and pages 67 and 74 of the present work); now this he has not attempted to do. In no part of his notes has he refuted, or even noticed that important doctrine.
>
> (ibid: 412–13)[4]

On p. 72 of *Principles* to which Ricardo referred, a numerical example ends with: "In this case, as well as in the other, the capital last employed pays no rent." Leaving aside questions of facts, it might seem that Ricardo's assumption according to which the least productive land or mine pays no rent contradicts his repeated insistence that individuals are driven by interest alone: why would the owner of a land or a mine agree to lease it if it does not afford any rent? The other references made by Ricardo to pages of his Chapter II "On rent" suggest that reasoning in terms of portions of capital allowed answering this logical objection, as it did to Malthus's and Say's factual objection. The reference to p. 67 in the above quotation is to the definition of rent, based on the distinction between "that portion of the produce of the earth, which is paid to the landlord for the use of the original and indestructible powers of the soil", and what is paid "for the improved farm". Only the former is properly rent, "in the strict sense to which I am desirous of confining it", while the latter is in the nature of profit, even if it is like rent paid to the landlord (since it is not the farmer but the landlord who in the past advanced the capital responsible for the improvement of the land for which the lease is contracted). When a portion of capital is added to an existing land, it yields an additional profit – as every previous portion of capital that improved the land in the past – but no rent is paid since there is no change in "the original and indestructible powers of the soil". Rent consequently did not enter the determination of the cost of production with the last portion of capital, and this was of the utmost importance for Ricardo's theory of distribution:

> By getting rid of rent, which we may do on the corn produced with the capital last employed, and on all commodities produced by labour in manufactures, the distribution between capitalist and labourer becomes a much more simple consideration.
>
> (Letter to McCulloch, 13 June 1820; VIII: 194)

Reasoning in terms of last portion of capital invested and not in terms of last land cultivated was justified by Ricardo as follows, in a speech on Agricultural Distress Report in the House of Commons on 7 May 1822:

> It was not that cultivators were always driven by the increase of population to lands of inferior quality, but that from the additional demand for grain, they might be driven to employ on land previously cultivated a second portion of capital, which did not produce as much as the first. On a still farther demand a third portion might be employed, which did not produce so much as the second: it was manifestly by the return on the last portion of capital applied, that the cost of production was determined.
>
> (V: 167)

Keeping then in mind that Ricardo's proper reasoning was in terms of portion of capital and not in terms of land or of mine, I will nevertheless use these expressions indifferently as Ricardo often did himself:

> My argument respecting rent, profit and taxes, is founded on a supposition that there is land in every country which pays no rent, or that there is capital

> employed on land before in cultivation for which no rent is paid. You answer the first position, but you take no notice of the second. The admission of either will answer my purpose.
>
> (Letter to Say, 11 January 1820; VIII: 149–50)

The extension of the theory of rent from land to mines now raises the question of the comparison between Ricardo's treatment of corn and that of gold bullion.

5.3 The specificity of gold bullion in respect to corn

The adjustment to a new land growing corn with a higher productivity

The situation created by the discovery of a new gold mine may be compared with that of a new technique of production of corn which allows a land previously lying fallow to become cultivated with a higher productivity than at least the land of the lowest quality already cultivated ("If a large tract of rich land were added to the Island [England]", letter to Malthus, 21 April 1815, VI: 220; one may think of a new technique of draining a marsh, making it useful for cultivation with a high yield). In such a case, the increase in the total production of corn sinks its market price below the natural price determined by the cost of production on the previously cultivated land of the lowest quality, and the capital advanced on this land is withdrawn and transferred to another employment. This has two consequences: first, the production of corn is lowered by the amount produced previously on the land abandoned; second, the natural price declines because it is now determined by the cost of production on a land more productive than before. Capital goes on being withdrawn until the market price and the natural price of corn equalise, that is, until every portion of capital advanced on the still cultivated lands (including the one where the new technique has been applied) earns the general rate of profit. On the land which is henceforth of the lowest quality, no rent is paid, and differential rents are paid to the proprietors of the lands of better qualities, according to their respective productivity. In the final situation, the total quantity of corn produced is the same as in the initial situation, the quantity produced by the newly cultivated land having substituted for that produced by the abandoned ones. The total quantity of corn in the final situation is again equal to the natural demand, and it is produced at a lower natural price than in the initial situation.

This adjustment process has an important effect, which is the reverse of the well-known increase in natural wages consequent upon the new cultivation of *less* productive lands. Here, since the natural price of corn declines when less productive lands are abandoned, natural wages are lowered and the natural rate of profit increases accordingly. Answering a question by Malthus on this point, Ricardo quoted literally his friend's supposition of his view of the subject:

> You have correctly anticipated my answer: 'Capital will' I think 'be withdrawn from the land, till the last capital yields the profit obtained (by the fall

of wages) in manufactures, on the supposition of the price of such manufactures remaining stationary'.

(Letter from Ricardo to Malthus, 9 November 1819; VIII: 130; the quotation is from a letter from Malthus to Ricardo, 14 October 1819; ibid: 108)

This "supposition" was, however, contradicted by the effect of a change in distribution on relative prices (see Chapter 3 above) and, as shown in Sraffa (1960), the ranking of the lands was also altered by this change in distribution, creating a major difficulty for the theory of rent.

In *Principles*, Ricardo gave two examples of such an adjustment process "in consequence of permanent abundance" of corn (*Principles*; I: 268). In Chapter II "On rent", an improvement in cultivation techniques does not lead to the withdrawal of the whole capital advanced on the least productive land but only to the transfer of the least productive portion of capital advanced on that land. In the initial situation, four "successive portions of capital" (ibid: 81) yield respectively 100, 90, 80, and 70 quarters of corn, so that the whole rent is equal to 60 quarters out of a total production of 340. After an improvement in cultivation applied equally to each portion of capital, these respective yields become 125, 115, 105, and 95, so that total production on the land mounts to 440 quarters:

> But with such an increase of produce, without an increase in demand, there could be no motive for employing so much capital on the land; one portion would be withdrawn, and consequently the last portion of capital would yield 105 instead of 95, and rent would fall to 30, [...] the demand being only for 340 quarters.
>
> (ibid: 81–2)

The increased production of corn consequent upon the improvement in cultivation faces an unchanged demand for the reproduction of the population,[5] so that the market price falls below the natural price determined by the least productive portion of capital which becomes unprofitable (at the general rate of profit) and is withdrawn from the production of corn. The total production on the land is brought back approximately to its initial level (345 quarters instead of 340), in line with the unchanged natural demand for corn.

In Chapter XIX "On sudden changes in the channels of trade", Ricardo considered "a revulsion of trade" (ibid: 265) such as a war which interrupts the importation of corn. The diminution of the quantity supplied, while the demand remains unaltered, pushes the market price of corn upwards, so that the cultivation of less fertile lands becomes profitable.The balance between the supply and the demand is then re-established, although at a higher natural price than before the war. When the war terminates and importation of corn resumes, the opposite movement occurs: the excess quantity of corn available sinks its market price, and the less fertile lands cannot be profitably cultivated any longer:

> In examining the question of rent, we found, that with every increase in the supply of corn, capital would be withdrawn from the poorer land; and land

> of a better description, which would then pay no rent, would become the standard by which the natural price of corn would be regulated. At 4*l*. per quarter, land of inferior quality, which may be designated by No. 6, might be cultivated; at 3*l*. 10*s*. No. 5; at 3*l*. No. 4, and so on. If corn, in consequence of permanent abundance, fell to 3*l*. 10*s*., the capital employed in No. 6 would cease to be employed; for it was only when corn was at 4*l*. that it could obtain the general profits, even without paying rent: it would, therefore, be withdrawn to manufacture those commodities with which all the corn grown on No. 6 would be purchased and imported.
>
> (ibid: 268)

In this example, the fall in the market price of corn, due to its "permanent abundance", makes capital advanced on land No. 6 unprofitable (at the general rate of profit) so that it is withdrawn from the production of corn and transferred to an employment in manufactures. The total quantity of corn supplied is again equal to the unchanged natural demand, since the production of the land abandoned is replaced by imported corn produced at a cost consistent with the diminished market price. This foreign corn is itself purchased by the export of the commodities now produced by the capital transferred from the abandoned land.

In both examples, when corn becomes permanently abundant for an exogenous reason (an improvement in cultivation, the resumption of importation at the end of a war), the adjustment process occurs solely on the side of the quantity supplied, not on the side of demand, because there is a natural demand which must be satisfied, neither less nor more:

> If the natural price of bread should fall 50 per cent. from some great discovery in the science of agriculture, the demand would not greatly increase, for no man would desire more than would satisfy his wants, and as the demand would not increase, neither would the supply; for a commodity is not supplied merely because it can be produced, but because there is a demand for it. Here, then, we have a case where the supply and demand have scarcely varied, or if they have increased, they have increased in the same proportion; and yet the price of bread will have fallen 50 per cent. at a time, too, when the value of money had continued invariable.
>
> (ibid: 385)[6]

When it is in excess, the quantity of corn produced is adjusted to the natural demand through the successive withdrawal of the less productive portions of capital (on the same land or on different lands), until the balance between supply and demand is re-established through the equalisation of the market price with the natural price. It should be observed that in both examples, the withdrawal of capital is just enough to ensure this equalisation and thus to bring the supply of corn in line with the natural demand. Although there are discontinuities in production – "successive portions of capital" provide successive yields – its reduction through the withdrawal of one or more of these portions does not overshoot the excess, so that the market price never becomes higher than the natural price. Two reasons may explain this assumption. First, the successive withdrawal of portions of capital is nothing else as the reverse of their previous successive application to the production of corn when it was in short supply; if this process had been implemented smoothly[7] – as Ricardo himself assumes by stating that the increase in production may not necessarily require the cultivation of new lands but only the inflow of new portions of capital applied to the same lands – its reverse may follow the same route. Second, corn is produced in competitive conditions, and if for any reason the production of corn were cut by more than what is required to match the natural demand, the market price would rise above the natural price, and abnormal profits would induce an inflow of capital into the production of corn until they disappear. This adjustment is the one which occurs when, because of a domestic increase in population or a higher foreign demand, an increase in the demand for corn raises its market price above its natural price.[8]

Two differences between gold bullion and corn

In Chapter XIII of *Principles* "Taxes on gold", Ricardo emphasises two differences between corn and gold bullion, one on the supply side the other on the demand side. They both affect the adjustment process triggered by an increase in the quantity of the commodity produced.

On the supply side, the speed at which the market price adjusts is greater for corn than for gold, due to a difference in durability:

> The agreement of the market and natural prices of all commodities depends at all times on the facility with which the supply can be increased or diminished. In the case of gold, houses, and labour, as well as many other things, this effect cannot, under some circumstances, be speedily produced. But it is different with those commodities which are consumed and reproduced from year to year, such as hats, shoes, corn, and cloth; they may be reduced, if necessary, and the interval cannot be long before the supply is contracted in proportion to the increased charge of producing them.
>
> (ibid: 196)

The difference in durability manifests itself in a high or low ratio of the flow of new production to the existing stock. In the case of corn, the annual production is totally consumed in the period as wage-good or seeds, and no stock is carried from one period to the other. In the case of "gold, houses, and labour", the stock is large in comparison with annual production, so that a change in the latter affects only slowly the market price (on the importance of the durability of gold in Ricardo's theory of the value of money, see Takenaga 2013). This is particularly the case with gold used as money:

> The metal gold, like all other commodities, has its value in the market ultimately regulated by the comparative facility or difficulty of producing it;

> and although from its durable nature, and from the difficulty of reducing its quantity, it does not readily bend to variations in its market value, yet that difficulty is much increased from the circumstance of its being used as money. If the quantity of gold in the market for the purpose of commerce only, were 10,000 ounces, and the consumption in our manufactures were 2000 ounces annually, it might be raised one fourth, or 25 per cent. in its value, in one year, by withholding the annual supply; but if in consequence of its being used as money, the quantity employed were 100,000 ounces, it would not be raised one fourth in value in less than ten years.
>
> (*Principles*; I: 193–4)[9]

Nevertheless, in the numerical example which illustrates the effects of taxes on gold, Ricardo supposes that the market price of gold-money increases in the same proportion as its quantity produced decreases (see Appendix 5 below); this amounts to neglecting the difference in durability between corn and gold bullion and considering only the initial and the final situations. As will be seen below, this does *not* mean, as Ricardo is often blamed for in the literature, that he gives no indication about the forces at work during the adjustment process. This simply means that this difference in durability, while affecting the speed of adjustment, does not affect its *modus operandi*.

On the demand side, the difference between gold and corn is that, in contrast with necessaries which must be consumed if the population is to be reproduced, there is no natural quantity of money made of gold:

> The demand for money is not for a definite quantity, as is the demand for clothes, or for food. The demand for money is regulated entirely by its value and its value by its quantity. If gold were of double the value, half the quantity would perform the same functions in circulation, and if it were of half the value, double the quantity would be required. If the market value of corn be increased one tenth by taxation, or by difficulty of production, it is doubtful whether any effect whatever would be produced on the quantity consumed, because every man's want is for a definite quantity, and, therefore, if he has the means of purchasing, he will continue to consume as before: but for money, the demand is exactly proportioned to its value. No man could consume twice the quantity of corn, which is usually necessary for his support, but every man purchasing and selling only the same quantity of goods, may be obliged to employ twice, thrice, or any number of times the same quantity of money.
>
> (ibid: 193)

The aggregate value of the commodities to be circulated being given, any quantity of money will do.[10] A small quantity of money performs the same circulating office as a large one: the commodities "would be circulated with a less quantity, because a more valuable money" (ibid: 196). Already in his "Notes on Bentham's 'Sur les prix'" in 1810, Ricardo had observed that the specificity of the demand for gold used as money prevented a gold-importing country from being benefited by an improvement in its production abroad, in contrast with any other commodity:

> If in a foreign country new means of improving the production of commodities be discovered it will be attended with real advantage to all countries which consume that commodity. – If the article were french cambrics for example England would import the quantity of cambrics she required at a less sacrifice of the produce of her own industry: – but when gold and silver are the commodities that become cheap in consequence of improved means of working the mine or the discovery of new mines no such advantage will accrue to England because the quantity of money she requires is not a fixed quantity but depends altogether on its value.
>
> (III: 305–6)

One may now examine the consequences of the specificity of gold bullion for the adjustment process triggered by the discovery of a new mine. For the time being I will leave aside the question of whether gold bullion is produced in the country that transforms it into money or in a foreign country before it is imported and coined. This amounts to considering that the adjustment is triggered by an increase in the supply of gold bullion that lowers its market price, whether this increased supply is consequent upon the discovery of a new mine or upon importation. The justification for this assumption is that, contrary to what is usually said of the price of internationally traded commodities being determined in Ricardo by supply and demand, the price of imported goods is regulated by their cost of production in the exporting country. This was repeated by Ricardo in *Principles* and elsewhere:[11]

> All that I contend for is, that it is the natural price of commodities in the exporting country, which ultimately regulates the prices at which they shall be sold, if they are not the objects of monopoly in the importing country.
>
> (*Principles*; I: 375)

The difference between domestically produced and imported bullion is thus here only in the intervention of the exchange rate (see below Section 5.5). However, we will see in the conclusive section of Chapter 7 that the specificity of the market for bullion in the country where it is the standard of money logically implies that it should be produced abroad. This is what happened in the circumstances of the time: gold was produced outside England in competitive conditions. It was then exported as bullion (no matter whether in the form of merchandise or of coins taken by weight) to England, where it was coined at the mint, with the monopoly power of issuing coins belonging to the State. When a new mine was discovered, more productive than some or all previous ones, the adjustment process thus operated successively in the gold-producing country and in the gold-importing one.

5.4 The adjustment in the gold-producing country: a new "distribution of capital"

A fall in the value of gold bullion

As mentioned above, in the case of the discovery of a new mine, a fall in the value of money occurred because of a fall in the value of gold bullion in terms of all other commodities, *not* of a depreciation of money in terms of gold bullion. The question is now: how did this transmission channel work? The answer required a condition that Ricardo had not yet mastered at the time of the Bullion Essays: the appropriate link between the discovery of a new mine and the fall in the value of gold bullion in terms of all other commodities. In 1810, Ricardo understood this link through the scarcity principle: the discovery of a new mine increased the total quantity of gold bullion produced and an increased supply lowered its value. This led to an adjustment described in the sequel of the quotation from *High Price* given above:

> If a mine of gold were discovered in either of these countries, the currency of that country would be lowered in value in consequence of the increased quantity of the precious metals brought into circulation, and would therefore no longer be of the same value as that of other countries. Gold and silver, whether in coin or in bullion, obeying the law which regulates all other commodities, would immediately become articles of exportation; they would leave the country where they were cheap, for those countries where they were dear, and would continue to do so, as long as the mine should prove productive, and till the proportion existing between capital and money in each country before the discovery of the mine, were again established, and gold and silver restored every where to one value.
>
> (*High Price*; III: 54)

Here Ricardo explained that the immediate consequence of the discovery of a new mine would be a fall in the value of gold in the producing country, lowering it below its value in the other countries and leading to its exportation. The final outcome was to be a new equalisation of this value across all countries, presumably at a lower level than the initial one, because of the increased quantity of bullion. But Ricardo would soon feel dissatisfied by this scarcity approach to the value of commodities. As he would write to Mill on 30 December 1815: "I know I shall be soon stopped by the word price" (VI: 348). On 5 October 1816 he would confess to Malthus: "I have been very much impeded by the question of price and value, my former ideas on those points not being correct" (VII: 71).[12] This difficulty was to be overcome with the theory of value contained in *Principles*, which determined the relative value of competitively produced commodities by their cost of production with the portion of capital that pays no rent.

In contrast with corn for which, as seen above, Ricardo explained how the adjustment operated, he did not do the same for gold bullion and contented himself with observing that the discovery of a new rich mine or an improvement in the technique of production caused a fall in the value of gold bullion:

> By the discovery of America and the rich mines in which it abounds, a very great effect was produced on the natural price of the precious metals. This effect is by many supposed not yet to have terminated. It is probable, however, that all the effects on the value of the metals, resulting from the discovery of America, have long ceased; and if any fall has of late years taken place in their value, it is to be attributed to improvements in the mode of working the mines.
> (*Principles*; I: 86)

The discovery of a new mine of a better quality than all or some of the mines previously worked increased the quantity produced of bullion, so that its market price fell below its natural price. What happened to the value of gold bullion thus depended on the adjustment process triggered by this gap.

The closure of existing mines as a consequence of the discovery of a new one

To capture how Ricardo understood the adjustment to the new value of gold bullion, one may consider his treatment of another issue that raised the same question of the market price of gold being lower than its natural price because of an exogenous change on the supply side, although another kind of change: the imposition of a tax levied on the production of gold, the effects of which were analysed in Chapter XIII "Taxes on gold" of *Principles*. When each existing mine was taxed a uniform quantity of gold, the cost of production in each mine increased – and so did the natural price of bullion, determined in the least productive one – while the market price remained the same. The market price of bullion being below the natural price, some mines were forced to close down because the capital invested in them no longer earned the general rate of profit. The same situation occurs in the case of the discovery of a new mine, although for different reasons: the market price of gold falls below the natural price, and here also this gap forces some mines to close down. One can thus transpose Ricardo's argument about the adjustment process triggered by such a gap from the effect of taxes on gold to the effect of the discovery of a new mine (for a detailed analysis of Ricardo's argument on the effects of taxes on gold, see Appendix 5 below).

Such transposition leads to the following adjustment. In the initial situation, the market price of gold bullion produced in competitive conditions by mines differing in the quantity produced with the same capital is equal to the natural price, determined by the cost of production with the least productive portion of capital that pays no rent. Suppose now that a new mine is discovered, which is at least more productive than the least productive one previously worked. Since that discovery increases the total quantity of gold bullion brought to market, the new market price falls below the initial natural level. Consequently the portion of capital that initially determined this level no longer earns the general rate of profit and is withdrawn, with two consequences: the cost of production with the least productive portion of capital (the initial next-to-last one) decreases, and the quantity of gold brought to market diminishes, making its market price rise. This process goes on until the rising market price and the falling natural price of gold bullion equalise again at a level that is necessarily lower than the one before the discovery of the new mine. In other words, the value of gold bullion in terms of all other commodities falls because of this discovery.

On the supply side, this adjustment is the same as that for corn, since both commodities are produced in competitive conditions, so that the driving force in the adjustment is the equalisation of the rate of profit earned on each portion of capital invested in the production of bullion at the general rate of profit. The difference is on the demand side: while in the final position the total quantity of corn produced is the same as the initial one – equal to the natural quantity required to reproduce the population – there is no such constraint for gold. The demand for bullion to be transformed into money is not for a definite total *quantity* but, with a given aggregate value of the commodities to be circulated, for an aggregate *value*. To any fall in the value of gold bullion consequent upon the discovery of a new mine corresponds a proportionate increase in the total quantity demanded because, as quoted above, "for money, the demand is exactly proportioned to its value" (ibid: 193). When gold bullion is imported to be coined as money, the quantity demanded also adjusts to its value (see below Section 5.6):

> While money is the general medium of exchange, the demand for it is never a matter of choice, but always of necessity: you must take it in exchange for your goods, and, therefore, there are no limits to the quantity which may be forced on you by foreign trade, if it fall in value; and no reduction to which you must not submit, if it rise.
>
> (ibid: 194–5)

The adjustment described by Ricardo after the imposition of taxes on gold is also instructive about how a new "distribution of capital" (ibid: 198) among the mines and between the production of gold and other employments of capital is implemented. Since after the discovery of a new mine the market price of gold bullion falls in the first place, it may only increase later to agree with the natural price if the total quantity of gold brought to market is reduced. Ricardo's reasoning is that this reduction is obtained by the closure of one or more of the previously existing mines. This assumption is consistent with an analysis of production in which, when the market price of gold is equal to the natural price, portions of capital advanced in mines of different qualities earn the same general rate of profit, the one advanced in the mine of the lowest quality paying no rent. When the market price falls, this particular portion of capital ceases to be profitable (at the general rate of profit) and is withdrawn from that mine, which closes down. The only mines remaining in operation are those where the capital advanced may still earn the general rate of profit, by cutting part – or all, in the case of the mine becoming of the lowest quality in the final situation – of the rent it paid previously.

Ricardo's description of the adjustment process is such that the reduction of the quantity of gold produced occurs successively, one mine closing down after the other in the order given by the comparative cost of production, until the portions of capital advanced in the remaining mines earn the general rate of profit. Because gold is not a wage-good, a change in its natural price does not modify the level of the general rate of profit. The ranking of the mines by their physical productivity is thus exempt from the effect of a change in the distribution of income (in contrast with corn-producing lands), and the order in which they should close down successively is hence unaffected by the adjustment consequent upon the discovery of a new mine.[13]

Moreover, assuming that the total quantity of gold produced is *not* reduced because each mine lowers its production *but* because some mines completely close down while others keep their initial level of production implies that no assumption about constant returns is necessary: each mine eligible to go on being worked produces the same quantity of gold with the same capital as before, hence at the same cost. As is well known, the question of whether it is necessary to assume constant returns is a sensitive one in classical economics. According to Piero Sraffa:

> [T]his standpoint, which is that of the old classical economists from Adam Smith to Ricardo, [is such] that no question arises as to the variation or constancy of returns. The investigation is concerned exclusively with such properties of an economic system as do not depend on changes in the scale of production or in the proportion of 'factors'.
>
> (Sraffa, 1960: v)

The adjustment process thus conforms to this "classical standpoint". It may now be formalised as follows.

A formalisation of the adjustment

Let me call:

$P_{nG}{}^{\mathrm{p}}$: Natural price of one ounce of gold bullion, in pesos;

$P_G{}^{\mathrm{p}}$: Market price of one ounce of gold bullion, in pesos;

$c_{G(h)}{}^{\mathrm{p}}$: Cost of production (in pesos) of one ounce of gold bullion in mine h, including profit at the general rate, with $h = 1, 2, \ldots, k$, ranked according to their decreasing productivity;

$q_{G(h)}$: Quantity of gold bullion produced by capital advanced in mine h, in ounces.

Supposing that the same amount of capital is advanced in each mine where it produces a different quantity of gold bullion, the cost of production of one ounce of gold in mine h is given by:

$$c_{G(h)}{}^{\mathrm{p}} = c_{G(k)}{}^{\mathrm{p}} \frac{q_{G(k)}}{q_{G(h)}} \tag{5.1}$$

The initial natural situation 0 is such that, with all k mines being worked, the market price of gold bullion is equal to its natural price, determined by the cost of production in mine k:

$$P_G{}^{\mathrm{p}0} = P_{nG}{}^{\mathrm{p}0} = c_{G(k)}{}^{\mathrm{p}} \tag{5.2}$$

Since the totality of gold produced is sold at its natural price, the demand D_G, expressed in money price, is given by:

$$D_G{}^{p} = c_{G(k)}{}^{p} \sum_{h=1}^{h=k} q_{G(h)} \tag{5.3}$$

Let me now suppose that a new mine *z* is discovered, the productivity of which is higher than that of at least mine *k*: with a capital equal to the one advanced in each of the previous mines, it produces $q_{G(z)} > q_{G(k)}$. To simplify, I will also assume that the productivity of mine *z* is higher than that of any mine previously worked, so that $q_{G(z)} > q_{G(h)}$ for all *h*[14] Equations (5.2) and (5.3) state that, in the initial natural situation, the total quantity of gold produced by the existing mines allowed its market price being just equal to the cost of production in mine *k*, and that made this mine profitable (at the general rate of profit). Now, with an unchanged effective demand for gold bullion, expressed in money – as implied by the specificity of gold bullion noted above – the addition of $q_{G(z)}$ sinks the market price below its initial level. Calling $P_G{}^{p1}$ this new market price, equal to the ratio of $D_G{}^{p}$ to the new quantity of bullion, one gets:

$$P_G{}^{p1} = c_{G(k)}{}^{p} \frac{\sum_{h=1}^{h=k} q_{G(h)}}{\sum_{h=1}^{h=k} q_{G(h)} + q_{G(z)}} < c_{G(k)}{}^{p} \tag{5.4}$$

The capital invested in mine *k* having ceased to be profitable (at the general rate of profit), it is withdrawn. Depending on the level of $c_{G(k-1)}{}^{p}$, $c_{G(k-2)}{}^{p}$, and so on, other portions of capital may also become unprofitable at *this* market price $P_G{}^{p1}$ and become eligible to be withdrawn. However, the closure of mine *k* makes the total production of gold decrease, and its market price consequently rise, so that a given portion of capital may be unprofitable *before* mine *k* closes down and become again profitable *after* its closure. The actual path of adjustment thus depends on the assumption made on the conditions under which the portions of capital are withdrawn. Ricardo's assumption is that the withdrawal occurs *successively*, one portion after the other, that is, after the total production of gold has adjusted to the withdrawal of the last portion.[15]

The final new natural position is such that, with *b* of the previous mines closing down ($b \leq k$), the new final market price $P_G{}^{p2}$ is equal to the new natural price $P_{nG}{}^{p2}$, equal to the cost of production in mine $h = k - b$. It is thus given by:

$$P_G{}^{p2} = c_{G(k)}{}^{p} \frac{\sum_{h=1}^{h=k} q_{G(h)}}{\sum_{h=1}^{h=k-b} q_{G(h)} + q_{G(z)}} \tag{5.5}$$

As in the initial situation (equation (5.2)), the condition of the existence of a new permanent natural position is the equality of the market price and the natural price of gold bullion, the latter being determined by the least productive portion of capital that pays no rent:

$$P_G{}^{p2} = P_{nG}{}^{p2} = c_{G(k-b)}{}^{p} \tag{5.6}$$

Competition ensures that the market price of gold bullion equalises with the natural price, and each portion of capital advanced in its production except the least productive one pays a differential rent, after as before the discovery of the new mine.

Combining (5.1), (5.5), and (5.6), the condition of the existence of a new permanent natural position reads:

$$\frac{\sum_{h=1}^{h=k} q_{G(h)}}{\sum_{h=1}^{h=k-b} q_{G(h)} + q_{G(z)}} = \frac{q_{G(k)}}{q_{G(k-b)}} \tag{5.7}$$

Since by construction the productivity of the least productive mine in the new permanent natural position is higher than that in the initial situation ($q_{G(k-b)} > q_{G(k)}$), condition (5.7) means that the total production of gold bullion is now permanently greater than before the discovery of the new mine, that is, the production of the newly discovered mine is greater than the combined previous production of the abandoned mines. Condition (5.7) is necessarily fulfilled because the demand for gold bullion (expressed in money) has remained unchanged. Since the new natural price (determined in mine $k - b$) is lower than the initial one (determined in mine k which has been abandoned), the total quantity produced at the new natural price and facing this unchanged money demand is necessarily higher. As emphasised in the above comparison between corn and gold, this greater quantity will be absorbed in the circulation of the gold-importing country at a lower value to circulate the unchanged aggregate value of commodities. Before examining how this occurs, it may be useful to illustrate the consequences of the discovery of a new mine with a numerical example derived from that used by Ricardo when he analysed the effect of taxes on gold.

A numerical example

Let me assume an initial situation in which three mines 1, 2, 3 are worked ($k = 3$), where the same capital invested in each produces respectively $q_{G(1)}, q_{G(2)}$, and $q_{G(3)}$, with $q_{G(1)} > q_{G(2)} > q_{G(3)}$. A new mine z is then discovered, which by assumption produces $q_{G(z)} > q_{G(1)}$. The question is asked of the conditions under which a new permanent natural position may exist such that, with mine 3 being closed, mines 1 and 2 plus mine z produce together a quantity of gold which sells at a market price equal to the new natural price, equal to the cost of production in mine 2. This new natural position exists if the quantity produced by the newly discovered mine z is such that, in application of equation (5.7):

$$q_{G(z)} = \frac{q_{G(2)}\left(q_{G(1)} + q_{G(2)}\right)}{q_{G(3)}} - q_{G(1)}$$

The quantity of gold being measured in ounces, suppose that $q_{G(1)} = 100$, $q_{G(2)} = 80$, and $q_{G(3)} = 70$. In the initial natural position, the total production of gold is 250, and $P_{nG}^{p0} = P_G^{p0} = c_{G(3)}^{p}$ in pesos, the cost of production of one ounce of gold in the least productive mine (including a profit at the general rate). The demand for gold, expressed in price, is consequently equal to 250 $c_{G(3)}^{p}$, and the cost of production in the two other mines is (70/80) $c_{G(3)}^{p} = 0.875\ c_{G(3)}^{p}$ in mine 2 and (70/100) $c_{G(3)}^{p} = 0.7\ c_{G(3)}^{p}$ in mine 1. A new mine z is then discovered, which, with the same capital as that advanced in each of the previous mines, produces $q_{G(z)} = 105.7$, hence at a cost of production of (70/105.7) $c_{G(3)}^{p} = 0.662\ c_{G(3)}^{p}$. Tables 5.1 and 5.2 sum up the natural positions before and after the discovery of the new mine.

After the discovery of mine z, the four mines produce together 355.7 ounces, and the market price of gold falls consequently to $P_G^{p1} = (250/355.7)\ c_{G(3)}^{p} = 0.7\, c_{G(3)}^{p}$. Capital invested in mine 3 at a cost $c_{G(3)}^{p}$ ceases to be profitable and is withdrawn. One observes that capital invested in mine 2 is also unprofitable at this level of the market price, since it produces at a cost equal to $0.875\ c_{G(3)}^{p}$, higher than the market price $0.7\ c_{G(3)}^{p}$. However, assuming the successive withdrawal rule, mine 2 remains worked if, *after the closure of mine 3*, capital invested in it is still

Table 5.1 Natural position before the discovery of a new gold mine

	Mine 1	*Mine 2*	*Mine 3*	*Together*
Production of gold (in ounces)	100	80	70	250
Cost of production per ounce (in pesos)	$0.7\ c_{G(3)}^{p}$	$0.875\ c_{G(3)}^{p}$	$c_{G(3)}^{p}$	
Market and natural price per ounce (in pesos)				$c_{G(3)}^{p}$

Table 5.2 Natural position after the discovery of a new gold mine

	Mine 1	*Mine 2*	*Mine z*	*Together*
Production	100	80	105.7	285.7
Cost	$0.7\ c_{G(3)}^{p}$	$0.875\ c_{G(3)}^{p}$	$0.662\ c_{G(3)}^{p}$	
Price				$0.875\ c_{G(3)}^{p}$

profitable.After the closure of mine 3, the total production falls to 285.7 and the market price rises again at $P_G^{p2} = (250/285.7)c_{G(3)}^{p} = 0.875c_{G(3)}^{p}$, equal to the cost of production in mine 2, which consequently sets the new level of the natural price of gold. By comparison with the initial natural position, the total production of gold has increased from 250 to 285.7 ounces and the natural price has fallen from $c_{G(3)}^{p}$ to 0.875 $c_{G(3)}^{p}$.

5.5 The adjustment in the gold-importing country: minting

From the foreign mine to importation

Importing goods produced abroad is an activity in which, as in any other, capital invested requires the natural rate of profit. This means that it may only be implemented permanently if the commodity imported is sold at a market price equal to its cost, including a rate of profit at the general level. In the gold-producing country, this condition is fulfilled if bullion sells at a natural price equal to the cost of production with the portion of capital that pays no rent. In the gold-importing country, the condition is that bullion sells at a natural price equal to the cost of importing it, including the rate of profit at the natural level in this country.

Let me call:

P_{nG}^{p}: Natural price of an ounce of bullion in the gold-producing country, in pesos;
P_G^{p}: Market price of an ounce of bullion in the gold-producing country, in pesos;
$P_{nG}^{£}$: Natural price of an ounce of bullion in the gold-importing country, in pounds;
$P_G^{£}$: Market price of an ounce of bullion in the gold-importing country, in pounds;
$P_{GC}^{£}$: Legal price of an ounce of gold in coin in the gold-importing country, in pounds;
e: exchange rate of £1 against pesos;
r: Natural rate of profit in the gold-importing country during the time capital is invested in the importation and sale of bullion, in percentage;
c_{GM}: parametric cost of transfer of bullion from the gold-producing to the gold-importing country, in percentage.

The condition for gold bullion to be imported in England is that the cost of its purchase in Spanish America and of its transfer to England (including the natural rate of profit in England) should be inferior or equal to the price at which it is sold in the London market:

$$\frac{1}{e} P_G^{p}\ (1+c_{GM})(1+r) \leq P_G^{£} \tag{5.8}$$

As seen above, in the gold-producing country the natural position (in which every portion of capital earns the natural rate of profit in this country) is characterised by the equality between the natural price and the market price of gold bullion:

$$P_G^{\text{p}} = P_{nG}^{\text{p}} \tag{5.2}$$

Similarly, the existence of a natural position in the gold-importing country is characterised by such equality:

$$\frac{1}{e} P_{nG}^{\text{p}} (1 + c_{GM})(1 + r) = P_G^{£} \tag{5.9}$$

To simplify, let me suppose that the only currency circulating in the gold-importing country is composed of full-bodied gold coins minted without seignorage and being legal tender for $\overline{P_{GC}}^{£}$ per ounce of gold in coin.[16] The condition of conformity of money to the standard (gold bullion) has been defined in Chapter 3 above as:

$$P_G^{£} = \overline{P_{GC}}^{£} \tag{3.9}$$

"In a sound state of the currency" condition (5.9) may thus be rewritten as:

$$\frac{1}{e} P_{nG}^{\text{p}} (1 + c_{GM})(1 + r) = \overline{P_{GC}}^{£} \tag{5.10}$$

Let me suppose that, before the discovery of a new mine in Spanish America, condition (5.10) is *not* fulfilled, so that gold bullion is *not* imported in England. This means that, given the natural price of bullion in Spanish America, the monetary conditions and/or the cost of transfer to England do not allow bullion to be profitably exported to this country (while it may be to others). The natural situation in time 0 is thus such that:

$$\frac{1}{e^0} P_{nG}^{\text{p}0} (1 + c_{GM})(1 + r) > \overline{P_{GC}}^{£} \tag{5.11}$$

The question is now: do things change after a new highly productive gold mine has been discovered in time 1? As indicated above, the increase in the total production of bullion sinks its market price $P_G^{\text{p}1}$ and I will assume that at this level the cost of imported bullion falls below its price in the London market, so that importation begins:

$$\frac{1}{e^0} P_G^{\text{p}1} (1 + c_{GM})(1 + r) < P_G^{£0} \tag{5.12}$$

However, this importation will only become permanent if, after the adjustment has been completed in Spanish America (through the closure of some mines) and in England (as a consequence of the import), it is consistent with the new natural position in both countries. As noted above, since gold bullion is not directly or indirectly a wage-good, the natural rate of profit r in England is not affected. The import in England has only two effects: in the gold market the price $P_G^{£}$ is lowered, and in the foreign exchange market the demand for pesos against pounds by the importers to finance their purchases of bullion or by the exporters to return the proceeds of their sales lowers the exchange rate e of the pound in pesos. This double adjustment is all the more active since with inequality (5.12) capital invested in the importation of gold earns extra profits and additional capital is diverted to it from other employments. This adjustment at both ends stops when (5.9) applies to the new natural price in Spanish America, given by (5.6) above:

$$\frac{1}{e^2} P_{nG}^{\text{p}2}(1+c_{GM})(1+r) = P_G^{£2} \tag{5.13}$$

In this new natural position, gold bullion is permanently imported in England from Spanish America, as would any foreign commodity experiencing a reduction in its cost of production after the introduction of a new technique. Equation (5.13) simply applies Ricardo's already mentioned contention that the price of a commodity in an importing country is regulated by its natural price in the exporting country.

However, gold was not *any* commodity.

From importation to the mint

Being the standard of money in England, gold was there the only commodity which besides its market price in bullion had also a legal price in coin. In contrast with any other commodity, equation (5.13) generated by the international adjustment is not the end of the story, as long as the resulting market price $P_G^{£2}$ is below the legal price $\overline{P_{GC}}^{£}$. Another arbitrage then exists for the owners of imported bullion, between the market and the mint: finding that it is profitable to have it coined, they carry it to the mint, and the reduction of the supply in the bullion market raises its price until it equalises with $\overline{P_{GC}}^{£}$ and accordingly fulfils the condition of conformity (3.9). Practically, both arbitrages occurred simultaneously, the importers of bullion having the choice of selling it in the market or to the mint. The outcome of the complete adjustment was that the whole quantity of bullion imported nourished an increased quantity of money, because coining only stopped when the difference between $\overline{P_{GC}}^{£}$ and $P_G^{£}$ was eliminated.

The new natural position corresponding to a permanent import of bullion converted into money is thus given by:

$$\frac{1}{e^2} P_{nG}^{\text{p}2}(1+c_{GM})(1+r) = \overline{P_{GC}}^{£} \tag{5.14}$$

Comparing (5.14) with (5.11) shows that, after the discovery of a new highly productive mine in Spanish America, the natural price of gold bullion there has declined ($P_{nG}{}^{p2} < P_{nG}{}^{p0}$) and the exchange rate of the pound in pesos has proportionately fallen ($e^2 < e^0$) while the quantity of money in England has increased. One should note that the fall in the exchange rate of the pound is *not* a consequence of the increase in the quantity of money: both are effects of the import of gold bullion in England. In fact, the fall in the exchange rate *e* in the final position as compared with the initial one is what in (5.14) reconciles the fixed legal price of gold $\overline{P_{GC}{}^{£}}$ in the gold-importing country (England) with the fall in its natural price $P_{nG}{}^{p}$ in the foreign gold-producing country (the Spanish colonies).

There remains an apparent difficulty. In (5.14) as in (5.11), the left-hand side of the equation is the natural price of gold bullion *in England*, which is consequently at the same level (equal to the legal price of gold in coin) before and after the discovery of the new mine in Spanish America. This raises two riddles. First, one should expect that this discovery would lower the *value* of gold bullion in terms of all other commodities, not only in the gold-producing country but in the gold-importing country too. Since, speaking of gold bullion, Ricardo contended that "its market value in Europe is ultimately regulated by its natural value in Spanish America" (ibid: 195), the fall in the latter should give rise to a fall in the former. This is how international trade was usually described by Ricardo: a fall in the value of any commodity in a country below its level in other countries made it profitable to export this commodity to them, before its value in these importing countries was lowered to its level in the exporting one. Second, the question arises of what becomes of the increased quantity of money consequent upon the coining of the imported bullion. Given the unchanged circulation of commodities in England, it may only enter this circulation if the value of coined money has itself fallen. One is thus led to look at the fall in the value of money as being what reconciles the fall in the *value* of gold bullion in England after a new mine has been discovered abroad with the constancy of its natural *price* in pounds.

This is precisely what is stated by the Money–Standard Equation exposed above in Chapter 4: the fall in the value of the standard (gold bullion) in terms of all other commodities causes a proportionate fall in the value of money in terms of all commodities except the standard, while the market price of the standard remains unaltered. A constancy of the natural (and market) price of gold bullion – at the level of the legal price of gold in coin – is thus consistent with a fall in its natural (and market) value because it goes with a fall in the value of coined money, that is, a proportional rise in money prices of all commodities except gold bullion. A change in the world value of the standard of money was thus reflected in an opposite and proportional change in the domestic prices of all other commodities:

> The value of gold as a commodity must be regulated by the quantity of goods which must be given to foreigners in exchange for it. When gold is cheap, commodities are dear; and when gold is dear, commodities are cheap, and fall in price.
>
> (*Principles*; I: 169)

When a new highly productive mine was discovered, the foreign value of bullion fell ("gold is cheap") and domestic prices rose ("commodities are dear"). When mines were being exhausted, the foreign value of bullion rose ("gold is dear") and domestic prices fell ("commodities are cheap, and fall in price"). The only commodity that did not change in price although its value might change was the standard of money. As Ricardo summed-up in a compact form before the Commons' Committee on Resumption on 4 March 1819:

> In a sound state of the currency the value of gold may vary, but its price cannot.
> (V: 392)

This provided a rational foundation to what Ricardo only hinted at in 1810 in his "Notes on Trotter":

> The discovery of the American mines though they had quadrupled the amount of gold would not have sunk its price, whilst the mint price has not altered, and whilst it was measured by gold coin.
> (III: 391)

Among the "many causes which might operate on the value of gold" (V: 204), the discovery of a new mine or of a new technique of producing gold was on the supply side, but there might also be causes on the demand side, particularly in relation to the behaviour of the note-issuing bank.

5.6 The effect of an increased demand for bullion by the issuing bank

The case of the Bank of England from 1819 to 1821

As mentioned in Chapter 2 above, the Bank of England started to enlarge its metallic reserve through purchases of gold bullion immediately after Peel's bill was adopted in 1819. Although the resumption of the convertibility of Bank of England notes into coin was only scheduled for 1823 by the bill, the Bank wished to speed up such resumption in order to discontinue the circulation of its small notes (£5 and under), which could thus be replaced by specie. The official reason was that these small notes were easily forged, but the real motive was the conception held by the Bank of England of its role as an issuing bank for the circle of traders and not for people at large. It should be noted that the increased demand for bullion by the Bank of England had nothing to do with its management of the note issue. At a time when this issue was to be contracted, so as to lower the market price of gold bullion in 1819 (£4. 2s.; see the letter to McCulloch of 3 January 1822 in Appendix 4 above) to the pre-war level of the legal price of gold in coin (£3.17s. 10½d) there was no reason to enlarge the metallic reserve to back the issue. Such enlargement was decided by the Bank of England in relation to a shift from a monetary regime in which inconvertible Bank of England notes (including small ones) had totally substituted for specie to the pre-war mixed regime of coins and high-denomination notes, disregarding the regime of exclusive circulation of notes convertible into bullion which was planned by Peel's bill until 1823.

Designed to prepare for a change in monetary regime, this demand for bullion by the Bank of England was consequently once and for all. In contrast with the discovery of a new highly productive mine which had the permanent effect of increasing the total production of bullion, such demand had a temporary effect: after it had been satisfied, the world demand for gold bullion was to return to its previous level. There would only be an increase in the value of bullion until the metallic reserve of the Bank of England reached the desired level. Nevertheless, even temporary, the consequent rise in the value of money – that is, a general fall in money prices – was to be badly felt: taxation increased in real terms and the depressive situation of many sectors (particularly agriculture) deepened. This was the critique addressed by Ricardo to the Bank of England: its demand for gold could have been wholly dispensed with, had convertibility into bullion fairly been tried. As he wrote to McCulloch on 3 January 1822:

> They [the Bank of England] have, from ignorance, made the reverting to a fixed currency as difficult a task to the country as possible.
>
> (IX: 140)

The increased demand for bullion by the Bank of England raised the value of bullion and hence the value of money, that is, lowered money prices. As Ricardo exposed before Parliament on 12 June 1822:

> It was undeniable, that the manner in which the Bank had gone on purchasing gold to provide for a metallic currency, had materially affected the public interests. It was impossible to ascertain what was the amount of the effect of that mistake on the part of the Bank, or to what precise extent their bullion purchases affected the value of gold; but, whatever the extent was, so far exactly had the value of the currency been increased, and the prices of commodities been lowered.
>
> (V: 199)

The Bank had done exactly the opposite of what Ricardo had recommended during the discussion of Peel's bill: it had purchased gold bullion instead of selling it. During his speech of 24 May 1819 before the House of Commons, in which he supported Peel's bill that embodied his Ingot Plan, Ricardo had declared:

> If he might give them [the Bank] advice, he should recommend to them not to buy bullion, but even though they had but a few millions [of gold in reserve], if he had the management of their concerns, he should boldly sell.
>
> (V: 13)

Selling gold would have depressed the value of bullion, hence of money, at a time when the programmed return to the pre-war parity of the pound and the transition from a war to a peace economy had deflationary effects. On the contrary, the purchases of gold by the Bank raised the value of money and accelerated deflation. Two years later, during the debate in the House which would bury the experiment of the Ingot Plan, Ricardo recalled on 9 April 1821 his former advice and again blamed the Bank:

> He [Ricardo] was not answerable, he said, for the effect which the present measure [the resumption of convertibility into coin at pre-war parity] might have upon particular classes; but he contended that if the advice which he had given long ago had been adopted – if the Bank, instead of buying, had sold gold, as he recommended – the effect would have been very different from what it was at present. [...] If the Bank had not bought gold, contrary to his opinion and recommendation, gold would not have risen.
>
> (ibid: 105–6)

Although temporary, the demand for bullion by the Bank of England operated on the value of money as the discovery of a new gold mine did: through a change in the value of bullion. In the speech of 12 June 1822 Ricardo declared:

> He fully agreed with the hon. member for Essex that there were various causes operating, also, on the value of gold, some of which were of a permanent, and others of a temporary nature. The more or less productiveness of the mines were among the permanent causes; the demands for currency, or for plate, in consequence of increased wealth and population, were temporary causes, though probably of some considerable duration. A demand for hats or for cloth would elevate the value of those commodities, but as soon as the requisite quantity of capital was employed in producing the increased quantity required, their value would fall to the former level. The same was true of gold: an increased demand would raise its value, and would ultimately lead to an increased supply, when it would fall to its original level, if the cost of production had not also been increased. No principle was more true than that the cost of production was the regulator of value, and that demand only produced temporary effects.
>
> (ibid: 212)

This argument should be qualified. According to Ricardo, an increased "demand for hats or for cloth" had only temporary effects on the value of these commodities, because he assumed (as often in *Principles*) that manufactured goods were produced with constant returns. On the basis of his own analysis, this would not be the case for goods produced with land (such as corn) or in mines (such as bullion), since "an increased supply" required the employment of less productive portions of capital. In these cases, the value of the commodity would permanently increase as a consequence of a permanent increase in demand. This is accounted for in the above quotation by the phrase "[its value] would fall to its original level, if the cost of production had not also been increased". In the case of the Bank of England after 1819, what made the rise in the value of bullion temporary was something else: the increased demand for bullion was itself temporary, until all small notes had been exchanged for coins at the Bank.

As in the case of the discovery of a mine, one should now analyse the adjustment in response to this increase in the demand for bullion by the Bank of England. It was in two ways symmetrical about that described above. First, the initial shock was no longer abroad – the discovery of a new gold mine – but domestic – a once-for-all demand for gold by the Bank of England. Second, its outcome was no longer a fall in the value of gold bullion accompanied with a fall in the value of money but a rise in the former accompanied with a rise in the latter.

The adjustment

In England, for reasons which will be detailed below in Chapter 7, this adjustment could not operate through a demand by the Bank of England in the London market without it being preceded by a corresponding import of bullion. When Bank of England notes were convertible (as was the case after Peel's bill of 1819), the rise in the market price $P_G^{£}$ that followed an increased demand immediately triggered an arbitrage between the market for bullion and the Bank of England: coins obtained at $\overline{P_{GC}}^{£}$ at the Bank of England against notes were melted and the bullion sold back to the Bank of England in the market at $P_G^{£} > \overline{P_{GC}}^{£}$. The metallic reserve of the Bank of England could not increase because it was depleted as quickly as bullion was purchased at a loss by the Bank. The only way for the Bank to stop these losses was to contract its issues: as will be explained in Chapter 7, the reduction in the quantity of money lowered the market price of bullion and accordingly raised the value of money (in application of the Money–Standard Equation; see Chapter 4 above). The exchange rate e of the pound rose while at the same time $P_G^{£}$ was raised again to the level of $\overline{P_{GC}}^{£}$ through coining. When $e\,P_G^{£} > P_G^{p}$ by a difference equal to c_{MG}, imports of gold bullion began (see below Chapter 8). The increased supply in the London market matched the demand by the Bank of England at a market price equal to $\overline{P_{GC}}^{£}$ and filled its metallic reserve. The return of $P_G^{£}$ to its level before the demand by the Bank illustrated what Ricardo contended in the Bullion Essays to disqualify Thornton's explanation of a high price of bullion by another cause of demand – to pay for an adverse foreign balance (see Chapter 8 below):

> No demand for gold bullion, arising from this or any other cause, can raise the money price of that commodity.
>
> (*High Price*; III: 60)

By symmetry with the case of the mine, the increase in the value of gold bullion in terms of all other commodities was made consistent with the constancy of its market price in terms of money through a fall in the money prices of all commodities except gold bullion – that is, an increase in the value of money.

In Spanish America, the higher demand for bullion raised the market price P_G^{p} above the natural price P_{nG}^{p}, making less productive mines profitable; the cost of production in the mine paying no rent rose and so did P_{nG}^{p}. The "world value" of gold bullion was consequently increased, in line with its increased value in England: in contrast with what happened in the case of a newly discovered mine, the change in the value of bullion in the gold-producing country was here the consequence – and not the cause – of its change in the gold-importing one.

This adjustment was illustrated for its domestic part by what Ricardo wrote in 1821 in the "Draft on Peel" (for details see Appendix 4 above), keeping in mind that "a rise of paper in its comparative value to gold" is the same as a fall in the market price of gold bullion paid for in notes below the legal price of gold in coin (see Chapter 3 above about the condition of conformity):

> He [Ricardo] could not contemplate [in 1819] that the Bank would so narrow the circulation of paper as to occasion such a rise in its comparative value to gold and the currencies of other countries as to make the influx of gold into this unexampled in amount.
>
> (V: 519)

This argument was used in April 1822 in the pamphlet *On Protection to Agriculture*:

> Their [the Bank of England] issues were so regulated, that the exchange became extremely favourable to this country, gold flowed into it in a continued stream, and all that came the Bank eagerly purchased at 3*l.* 17*s.* 10½*d.* per ounce. Such a demand for gold could not fail to elevate its value, compared with the value of all commodities. Not only, then, had we to elevate the value of our currency 5 per cent., the amount of the difference between the value of paper and of gold before these operations commenced, but we had still further to elevate it to the new value to which gold itself was raised, by the injudicious purchases which the Bank made of that metal.
>
> (IV: 225)

This quotation emphasises the distinction between two contractions in the note issue. The contraction required by the increase in the metallic reserve of the Bank of England raised the value of money by lowering the market price of bullion below the legal price of gold in coin ($P_G^{£} < \overline{P_{GC}^{£}}$). It added to that intended by Peel's bill to lower the market price of bullion from its level at that time to the legal price (from $P_G^{£} > \overline{P_{GC}^{£}}$ to $P_G^{£} = \overline{P_{GC}^{£}}$). This was Ricardo's critique to the Bank of England: it had contracted its issues more than was required by the stabilisation of the market price of bullion at the pre-war level of the legal price of gold in coin (£3. 17s. 10½d.) because, refusing convertibility into bullion advocated by Ricardo, it had favoured convertibility into coin, which called for a bigger metallic reserve. Ricardo clearly distinguished between the welcome contraction of the issue to eliminate the 5 per cent depreciation of paper that still existed in 1819 (the difference between £4. 2s. and £3. 17s. 10½ d. per ounce standard) and the unnecessary contraction of the issue aiming at enlarging the metallic reserve.

The charge against the Bank of England of having contracted its issues too much was not contradictory with the contention by the Bank of having increased them. The point was not the absolute level of the issues but the level that would have ensured the conformity of the value of money with the value of gold bullion. As argued by Ricardo in the same pamphlet:

> At a late Court of Proprietors of Bank Stock, the Directors said that, so far from having reduced the amount of the circulation since 1819, they had considerably increased it. [...] If the Directors were quite correct in this statement, it is no answer to the charge of their having kept the circulation too low, and thereby caused the great influx of gold. My question to them is, 'Was your circulation so high as to keep the exchange at par?' To this they must answer in the negative; and therefore I say, that if in consequence of the importation of gold, that metal is enhanced in value, and the pressure on the country is thereby increased, it is because the Bank did not issue a sufficient quantity of notes to keep the exchange at par. This charge is of the same force whether the amount of banknotes has, in point of fact, been stationary, increasing, or diminishing.
>
> (ibid: 231–2)[17]

The same argument is to be found in the letter to McCulloch of 3 January 1822:

> If indeed during the operation of limiting the amount of paper, I make immense purchases of gold, and lock it up in a chest, or devote it to uses to which it had not before been applied, I raise the value of gold, and thereby lower the prices of goods, both in gold and in paper, which latter must conform to the value of gold; and this is precisely what the Bank have done.
>
> (IX: 140)

As for the foreign part of the adjustment – the increase in the world value of gold as a consequence of its increased value in England – it was difficult to quantify it precisely. Echoing with his inquiry at the time into an invariable standard, Ricardo was very cautious in doing that and relied on estimates made by Thomas Tooke:

> It is a question exceedingly difficult to determine what the effect has been on the value of gold, and consequently on the value of money produced by

the purchases of bullion made by the Bank. When two commodities vary, it is impossible to be certain whether one has risen, or the other fallen. There are no means of even approximating to the knowledge of this fact, but by a careful comparison of the value of the two commodities, during the period of their variation, with the value of many other commodities.

Even this comparison does not afford a certain test, because one half of the commodities to which they are compared may have varied in one direction, while the other half may have varied in another: by which half shall the variation of gold be tried? If by one it appears to have risen, if by the other to have fallen. From observations, however, on the price of silver, and of various other commodities, making due allowance for the particular causes which may have specially operated on the value of each, Mr. Tooke, one of the most intelligent witnesses examined by the Agricultural Committee, came to the conclusion that the eager demand for gold made by the Bank in order to substitute coin for their small notes, had raised the value of currency about five per cent. In this conclusion, I quite concur with Mr. Tooke. If it be well founded, the whole increased value of our currency since the passing of Mr. Peel's bill in 1819, may be estimated at about ten per cent.

(*Protection to Agriculture*; IV: 227–8)[18]

Ricardo had used the same argument before Parliament on 18 February 1822:

If the affairs of the Bank had been conducted with skill, the directors, instead of forcing so great an importation of gold, should have kept the exchange as nearly as possible at par. He [Ricardo] repeated then, that the consequence of the law [Peel's bill], if skilfully acted upon, was only to cause a rise of 5 per cent. But the Bank had acted very differently, and had imported a great quantity of gold; as much perhaps as twenty millions. This, of course, had created a change in the price of commodities, in addition to the apparent difference between paper and gold. The buying up of this quantity of gold must have affected a change in the value of it (as compared with other commodities) throughout Europe. What the amount of this change was, it was impossible to say – it was mere matter of conjecture. But when they took the quantity of gold in circulation in Europe into the calculation, and all the paper also, for that too must be reckoned, he did not conceive that it could be great, and he should imagine that 5 per cent would be an ample allowance for the effect.

(V: 135–6)

And again on 12 June 1822:

Remarks had frequently been made upon an opinion which he (Mr. Ricardo) had given of the effect which had been produced on the value of gold, and therefore on the value of money, by the purchases made by the Bank, which

> he had computed at five per cent, making the whole rise in the value of money ten per cent. He confessed that he had very little ground for forming any correct opinion on this subject. By comparing money with its standard, we had certain means of judging of its depreciation, but he knew of none by which we were able to ascertain with certainty alterations in real or absolute value. His opinion of the standard itself having been raised five per cent in value, by the purchases of the bank, was principally founded on the effect which he should expect to follow, from a demand from the general stock of the world of from fifteen to twenty millions worth of coined money. If, as he believed, there was in the world twenty times as much gold and silver as England had lately required to establish her standard on its ancient footing, he should say that the effect of that measure could not have exceeded five per cent.
>
> (ibid: 209–10)

5.7 Conclusion: the Money–Standard Equation and a real shock on the value of money

A change in the value of money, but no depreciation or appreciation

When a new mine was discovered in a gold-producing country, the final position in England was that described by Ricardo in the quotation from *Principles* given at the beginning: the quantity of money increased, and its value fell with the value of gold bullion. But the increase in the quantity of money was *not* the cause of the fall in its value: both were the effects of the discovery of the mine and it was the fall in the value of the standard that caused the fall in the value of money *and* the increase in its quantity. In other words *the currency fell in value but did not depreciate.* Another striking conclusion emerges from this analysis: there could never be an excess of coins – hence their depreciation – following an increase in the quantity produced of gold bullion, simply because coining required the market price of gold bullion to be *below* the legal price of gold in coin, while an excess of the currency and its corresponding depreciation only occurred when the market price of gold bullion was *above* the legal price of gold in coin. Coining thus did start when the increase in the quantity of bullion lowered its market price, but it stopped when the latter again equalised with the legal price of gold in coin, preventing any excess from occurring. The increase in the quantity of money simply went with the fall in its value, but did not imply any excess.

The conclusion of this analysis is that, after the discovery of a new mine in the gold-producing country, the fall in the *value* of gold bullion in terms of all other commodities caused in the gold-importing country a fall in the *value* of money but had no permanent effect on the *market price* of gold bullion. Ricardo would often repeat that a change in the value of bullion affected the value of money in the same direction but had no influence on the price of bullion. The same reasoning applied when an increased demand for bullion by the issuing bank to enlarge its metallic reserve raised the value of gold bullion and hence the value of money, while arbitrage ensured the equality between the market price of gold bullion and the fixed legal price of gold in coin (money was *not* appreciated). As explained by the Money–Standard Equation, any change in the value V_G of gold bullion in terms of all other commodities was combined with a constancy of its market price P_G in any country where gold bullion was the standard of money. The addition of these two aspects resulted in a proportional change in the value of money V_M in the same direction as V_G – that is, a proportional change in the money prices of all commodities except the standard in the opposite direction.

The timing of the adjustment

The effect of a real shock on the value of money was the outcome of several adjustments implying different markets, each one having its own duration. In the case of the discovery of a new gold mine, the fall in the market price in the gold-producing country after the total quantity produced had increased might occur rapidly, while the subsequent equalisation of this market price with the new natural price only occurred after enough time had elapsed to close down the mines becoming unprofitable. In the world market for bullion, the speed at which a fall in the market price in the gold-producing country was translated into a fall in the market price in the gold-importing ones depended on the ratio of the flow of new production of gold to the existing stock of the metal in whatever form – an element emphasised by Ricardo to explain the slowness of the adjustment for commodities like houses, labour, and precious metals. In contrast, the domestic adjustment triggered by such a fall in the market price of bullion was quick, since arbitrage between the market and the mint was immediate and at a trifling cost. Finally, the fall in the value of money – hence the proportional rise in the money prices of all commodities except bullion – which reconciled a fall in the value of gold bullion with a constancy of its price took the time required by the adjustment in the markets for all commodities, thanks to the mobility of capital that ensured the uniformity of the rate of profit at higher money prices.

In the case of the demand for gold bullion by the Bank to enlarge its metallic reserve, the timing of the adjustment depended in the first place on the time it took for the Bank to understand that it could not achieve this goal without reducing its issues. Then there was the time necessary to trigger the import of bullion to satisfy the demand by the Bank at a market price equal to the legal price of gold in coin; this time might be expected to be short since it only required arbitrage between the market for bullion, the foreign-exchange market, and the mint. Finally, there was the time of the adjustment of the rising price of bullion in the world market and the time of the adjustment of its rising natural price (through the employment of capital in less productive mines) in the gold-producing country.

Although a precise pattern of adjustment durations in the case of a real shock on the value of money would probably imply arbitrary assumptions, one may nevertheless contrast, on the one hand, the short duration of the adjustment triggered by domestic arbitrage between the market for bullion and the mint or international arbitrage between the market for bullion and the foreign-exchange market, with on the other hand the longer duration of the respective adjustments in the production of bullion, in the world market for bullion, and in the domestic markets for all other commodities.

Symmetrical real shock versus asymmetrical monetary shock

A real shock on the value of money was produced either by a permanent change on the supply side of the market of the standard – the discovery of a new gold mine – or by a temporary change on the demand side of this market – a once-for-all demand by the issuing bank to accommodate a change in the monetary regime. In both cases, this real shock affected the value of money through a change in the value of the standard. The discovery of a new highly productive gold mine lowered permanently the value of bullion, hence the value of money. A new demand for gold by the issuing bank – namely the Bank of England in 1819–1821 to enlarge its metallic reserve raised temporarily the value of bullion, hence the value of money. Although in the second case the issuing bank was involved, it was nevertheless a real shock, not a monetary one: the new demand for metallic reserve was *not* motivated by an increase in the quantity of notes issued. On the contrary, it went along with a *reduction* in the new issues and was motivated by the wish of the Bank to substitute gold coins for the stock of small notes in circulation – a change in the working of the domestic payments system.

Affecting the value of money through the channel of the value of the standard, such a real shock was symmetrical: it concerned all the currencies having gold as standard and consequently left the exchange rates between these currencies unaltered. The variation in the value of a particular currency was an inconvenience in itself, but it did not change the respective positions of this currency in respect to the others. Examined on 26 March 1819 by a Secret Committee of the House of Commons, Ricardo answered to questions on this subject as follows, keeping in mind that "a sound state of the currency" is that of convertibility of the bank note into the standard:

Question: Do you recollect whether within these last eight years we have not frequently seen the circulating medium of the country undergo much more formidable changes with respect to value than 4 per cent., within a shorter period than six months, judging of the value of the circulating medium by the price of gold?

Answer: In my opinion it has undergone much greater variations than 4 per cent.; and in the soundest state of our currency, it would be liable to such variations.

Question: From what causes could it undergo variations, exceeding that amount, if the currency were restored to its soundest possible state?

Answer: It would not undergo any variation, as compared with the standard; but I mean, that the standard itself might undergo variations exceeding that amount; the whole currency is of course subject to all the variations of the standard.

Question: In that case, would not the currency of other countries, in an equally sound state, undergo similar variations?

Answer: Certainly; the inconvenience, as far as regarded England, would not be less on that account; I consider any variation in the value of the currency as an evil, from producing a variation in the prices of all articles.

(V: 441–2)

According to Ricardo, the inconvenience of subjecting the value of money to any change in the value of the standard was the unavoidable counterpart of the self-regulating adjustment of the quantity of money permitted by the existence of a standard of money, which prevented any permanent variation in the value of money produced by a monetary shock. Such a monetary shock took the form of an exogenous change in the quantity of money, whether produced by the debasement of the circulating coin or a discretionary change in the note issue. The monetary shock was asymmetrical: it was restricted to the currency of the country where it occurred. The channel of transmission to the value of money was now a change in the *price* of the standard – instead of its *value* when the shock was real. The object of the next two chapters is to analyse the self-adjustment of the value of money generated by the standard in the case of a monetary shock.

Appendix 5: Taxes on gold

The case examined by Ricardo in Chapter XIII of *Principles* analytically differs from that considered above in Chapter 5 in two respects. First, instead of being only lowered in the newly discovered mine, the cost of production of gold bullion is increased in all mines by the imposition of a tax at a uniform rate. Second, instead of being produced in competitive conditions, so that the market price cannot be raised permanently above the natural price, gold bullion is considered by Ricardo as "a monopolised commodity" (*Principles*; I: 197), because the King of Spain is supposed "to be in exclusive possession of the mines" (ibid: 195). However, in both cases all portions of capital invested in the mines of different quality require the same rate of profit, and they are withdrawn from the production of gold bullion when they fail to do so. This is what matters to allow transposing Ricardo's analysis from the effect of taxation to the effect of the discovery of a new gold mine on the value of gold bullion.

1. The case examined by Ricardo

In Ricardo's analysis of the effects of taxes on gold, the adjustment process starts when a negative gap between the market price and the natural price of gold – provoked by an increase in the cost of production due to taxation, while the market price remains unchanged – forces one or more existing mines to close down. The final outcome is a sharp decline in production, without any harmful consequence for the users of gold-money because, as noted in Chapter 5 above, any quantity produced in the Spanish colonies may satisfy the European circulation. After the adjustment, the market price of gold not only rises to the level of the natural price determined by the cost of production in the least productive mine still worked, but *above* that level. It is so because, in Ricardo's example, the only mine still worked in the final situation produces a lower quantity of gold than what would be required to prevent the market price from overshooting the natural price. The absence of a smooth adjustment of supply allows the excess of the market price remaining permanent and the proprietor of that mine earning a rent. This, according to Ricardo, is due to the assumption that gold is "a monopolised commodity":

> Its [market] value might be higher, but it could not be lower [than its natural value], or even this mine would cease to be worked. Being a monopolised commodity, it could exceed its natural value, and then it would pay a rent equal to that excess; but no funds would be employed in the mine, if it were below this value.
>
> (ibid: 197–8)

The situation considered by Ricardo is as follows:

> If then the King of Spain, supposing him to be in exclusive possession of the mines, and gold alone to be used for money, were to lay a considerable tax on gold, he would very much raise its natural value; and as its market value in Europe is ultimately regulated by its natural value in Spanish America, more commodities would be given by Europe for a given quantity of gold. But the same quantity of gold would not be produced in America, as its value would only be increased in proportion to the diminution of quantity consequent on its increased cost of production. No more goods then would be obtained in America, in exchange for all their gold exported, than before; and it may be asked, where then would be the benefit to Spain and her Colonies? The benefit would be this, that if less gold were produced, less capital would be employed in producing it; the same value of goods from Europe would be imported by the employment of the smaller capital, that was before obtained by the employment of the larger; and, therefore, all the productions obtained by the employment of the capital withdrawn from the mines, would be a benefit which Spain would derive from the imposition of the tax, and which she could not obtain in such abundance, or with such certainty, by possessing the monopoly of any other commodity whatever. From such a tax, as far as money was concerned, the nations of Europe would suffer no injury whatever; they would have the same quantity of goods, and consequently the same means of enjoyment as before, but these goods would be circulated with a less quantity, because a more valuable money.
>
> (ibid: 195–6)

This case is characterised by two aspects. First, gold is produced only in the Spanish American colonies, so that the King of Spain may impose a tax, however great, on the production of gold, without having to fear the competition of gold produced elsewhere. This assumption does *not* mean that the gold mines are publicly owned: capital is advanced in the privately owned mines and must earn the general rate of profit. Second, gold is the only money used in Europe, which has to import it against commodities exported to the Spanish kingdom. In application of Ricardo's theory of international prices, the exchange rate of Spanish gold against European commodities is regulated by the natural price of each, so that the imposition of a tax on Spanish gold increasing its natural price, this exchange rate itself increases: "more commodities would be given by Europe for a given quantity of gold". This however does *not* mean that more European commodities will be obtained by Spain *against gold*, since the quantity of gold produced and exported will be lower, as a consequence of some mines closing down because the cost of production of gold has been increased by taxation. An additional quantity of European commodities is therefore obtained by Spain, not against gold, but against the commodities produced by the capital withdrawn from the closed-down mines. This benefit derived by Spain from the imposition of the tax has no counterpart in a diminution of the value obtained by Europe from her trade with Spain: she obtains a smaller quantity of gold but of the same total value as before, and the value of the additional commodities she exports to Spain is balanced by the value of the additional Spanish commodities imported besides gold. The reduction in the quantity of gold imported in Europe has no harmful consequence whatsoever, since this reduced quantity has the same aggregate value – hence circulates the same value of domestic commodities – as the higher quantity before: "these goods would be circulated with a less quantity, because a more valuable money".

2. Ricardo's numerical example

Ricardo illustrates these conclusions with a numerical example. The initial situation is such that three mines 1, 2, 3 are worked and produce a total quantity of 250 pounds (of weight) of gold; the same capital is advanced in each mine, but the quality being different from one mine to the other, it produces respectively 100, 80, and 70 pounds of gold. According to the general law of value, the natural price of gold is determined in such a way that each capital earns the general rate of profit, hence by the cost (profit included) of gold produced with the capital advanced in mine 3 and paying no rent. The capital advanced in mines 1 and 2 consequently pays to their proprietors a rent equal to 30 and 10 pounds of gold respectively. The whole production of gold is exported and exchanged for (by supposition) 10,000 yards of European cloth. A new situation occurs when the King of Spain imposes a uniform tax of 70 pounds of gold on each mine. The comparison between the initial and the final situations is made by Ricardo as follows:

The account of Spain would stand thus:

Formerly produced:	
Gold 250 pounds, of the value of (suppose)	10,000 yards of cloth.
Now produced:	
By the two capitalists who quitted the mines, the same value as 140 pounds formerly exchanged for; equal to	5,600 yards of cloth.
By the capitalist who works the mine, No. 1, thirty pounds of gold, increased in value, as 1 to 2½ and therefore now of the value of	3,000 yards of cloth.
Tax to the King seventy pounds, increased also in value as 1 to 2½ and therefore now of the value of	7,000 yards of cloth.
	15,600

(ibid: 198)

3. Three questions

This numerical example raises three questions: (1) Why has gold "increased in value, as 1 to 2½"? (2) How does Spain obtain more cloth from Europe after taxation? and (3) Who pays the tax?

The first question concerns the determination of the value of gold after taxation. The "market value in Europe" of gold-money before taxation was such that the quantity of gold imported from the Spanish colonies circulated the aggregate market value of commodities in Europe. Since the latter remains unchanged, the market value of gold-money after taxation depends on the new quantity of gold imported, that is, produced by the mines remaining in operation.[19] This in turn depends on the cost of production of each mine after taxation. Now mine 3 ceases obviously to be worked, since its whole production of 70 pounds of gold would be taken away by the tax, and the capital advanced in it could no longer earn the general rate of profit. Ricardo assumes that mine 2 also closes down, although it produces more than the tax.[20] Only mine 1 remains operated, and the total quantity of gold produced in the Spanish colonies and imported in Europe is now equal to the production of this mine: 100 pounds. The quantity of gold-money circulating the unchanged value of commodities in Europe having fallen from 250 to 100 pounds, it is there "increased in value, as 1 to 2½". This increase is that of the market value of gold in Europe, *not* of the "natural value" in the Spanish colonies. Ricardo analyses the increase in the natural value as follows:

> The value, then, of what remains to the capitalist of the mine No. 1, must be the same as before, or he would not obtain the common profits of stock; and, consequently, after paying seventy out of his 100 pounds for tax, the value

> of the remaining thirty must be as great as the value of seventy was before, and therefore the value of the whole hundred as great as 233 pounds before.
>
> (ibid: 197)

Before the imposition of the tax, the natural value of gold was determined by the cost of production in mine 3, including profit at the general rate. Now that mines 2 and 3 have closed down, it is determined in mine 1, and it is affected by two factors. First, mine 1 being of a better quality than mine 3, the cost of production per unit of gold produced (tax excluded) should decrease; second it increases after taxation since the tax is added to the previous costs. The new level of the natural value should be such that it still allows the unchanged capital advanced in mine 1 to obtain the unchanged general rate of profit. Before taxation, it was so when the capitalist exploiting mine 1 sold 70 pounds of gold (the production of 100 pounds minus 30 pounds paid to the owner of the mine as rent) at the natural value (determined by the cost of production in mine 3). After taxation, the natural value is determined in the only mine still exploited, mine 1, and *if gold is sold at its natural value*, so that no rent is paid any more to the owner of the mine since this is the mine in which this value is henceforth determined, the same capitalist now sells 30 pounds of gold (the unchanged production of 100 pounds minus 70 pounds paid to the King of Spain as tax). The natural value has thus been multiplied by $70/30 = 2.33$.

As seen above, however, after taxation gold is sold at a market value multiplied by 2.5 (as compared with the situation before taxation) *and not* at its initial natural value multiplied by 2.33. To be sold at a market value equal to its natural value, gold should be produced by mine 1 in a quantity equal to $250/2.33 = 107.3$ pounds. But this mine only produced 100 pounds of gold in the initial situation, and *its production – henceforth the total production of gold – is supposed by Ricardo to remain at this level.* The rationing of the quantity of gold brought to market allows the market value of gold after taxation remaining permanently above its natural value. The capitalist exploiting mine 1 does not however benefit from the excess of the market on the natural value of gold, because he has to transfer it to the owner of the mine as rent. Using the same reasoning as Ricardo in the last quotation, one can calculate the level R of that rent: $30 - R$ pounds of gold sold at a market value multiplied by 2.5 should bring to the capitalist exploiting mine 1 the same profit at the general rate than 70 pounds before taxation, so that $R = 2$ pounds of gold.

The second question raised by Ricardo's numerical example is: How does Spain obtain more cloth from Europe after taxation? By supposition, 10,000 yards of European cloth were previously exchanged against 250 pounds of Spanish gold, the exchange rate being thus 40 yards of cloth per pound of gold. After taxation, the market value of gold is multiplied by 2.5 and so does its exchange rate, which is raised to 100 yards of cloth per pound of gold. The 100 pounds of gold exported exchange for the same 10000 yards of European cloth as the 250 did before. As mentioned by Ricardo in his numerical table, 3000 out of these 10000 yards exchange for the 30 pounds of gold kept by the capitalist operating mine *n*°1 after payment of the tax (but it should be noticed that 200 out of these 3000 exchange for the 2 pounds of gold paid to the owner of the land as rent, so that the capitalist actually obtains 2800 yards of cloth for his gold), and 7000 exchange for the 70 pounds of gold levied by the King of Spain as tax.

Tables 5.3 and 5.4 sum up the situations before and after taxation.

Table 5.3 Initial situation (before taxation) in Ricardo's numerical example in Chapter XIII "Taxes on gold" of *Principles*

	Mine 1	*Mine 2*	*Mine 3*	*Total*
Production of gold (in pounds of weight)	100	80	70	250
Quantity of gold earned by the capitalist	70	70	70	210
Rent in gold	30	10	0	40
Quantity of foreign cloth exchanged against gold (in yards)				10000
Ditto: by the capitalist	2800	2800	2800	8400
Ditto: by the owner of the mine	1200	400	0	1600

Table 5.4 Final situation (after taxation) in Ricardo's numerical example in Chapter XIII "Taxes on gold" of *Principles*

	Capital invested in mine 1	*Capital withdrawn from mine 2*	*Capital withdrawn from mine 3*	*Total*
Production of gold (in pounds of weight)	100	0	0	100
Quantity of gold earned by the capitalist	28	0	0	28
Rent in gold	2	0	0	2
Tax in gold	70	0	0	70
Quantity of foreign cloth exchanged against gold and commodities newly produced (in yards)				15600
Ditto: by the capitalist	2800	2800	2800	8400
Ditto: by the owner of the mine	200	0	0	200
Ditto: by the sovereign				7000

After taxation, the capitalist of mine 1 obtains a smaller quantity of gold (28 instead of 70 pounds), but since the market price of gold has been multiplied by 2.5, his returns in value remain the same as his returns measured in foreign cloth. As for the capital withdrawn from mines 2 and 3, it has moved to other employments. Before taxation, it exchanged 140 pounds of gold – the 150 pounds produced minus the 10 pounds paid as rent to the proprietor of mine 2 – for 5600 yards of foreign cloth, at the ruling exchange rate of 40 yards of cloth per pound of gold. To earn the unchanged general rate of profit it should now sell whichever commodities it produces for the same value as before, that is, the equivalent of the same 5600 yards of cloth. After as before taxation, each equal capital formerly advanced in one of the three mines exchanges what it keeps of the value of its production against the same 2800 yards of European cloth.

The capitalists together obtain 8400 yards – the same as before taxation – the proprietors of the mines 200 yards – instead of 1600 –and the King of Spain exchanges the proceeds of the tax against 7000 yards. On the whole, the same capital as that previously invested in gold mines allows Spain receiving now 15600 yards of European cloth instead of 10000.

The third and last question is: Who pays the tax? In the Spanish colonies, the burden of the tax falls entirely on the proprietors of the mines who lose most of their rents (divided by 20 in terms of gold and by 8 in value or in foreign cloth), no change occurring for the profits on capital. This loss represents however only a part of the tax, a small one if measured in foreign cloth (1400 out of 7000 yards); most of it is "pure gain". Ricardo comments on his numerical table as follows:

> In return for one third of the labour and capital employed in the mines, Spain would obtain as much gold as would exchange for the same, or very nearly the same quantity of commodities as before. She would be richer by the produce of the two thirds liberated from the mines. If the value of the 100 pounds of gold should be equal to that of the 250 pounds extracted before; the King of Spain's portion, his seventy pounds, would be equal to 175 at the former value: a small part of the King's tax only would fall on his own subjects, the greater part being obtained by the better distribution of capital. [...] Of the 7000 [yards of foreign cloth] received by the King, the people of Spain would contribute only 1400, and 5600 would be pure gain, effected by the liberated capital.
>
> (ibid: 198–9)

What is the nature of this "pure gain" of 5600 yards of cloth? It is indisputably wealth: the quantity of use-values obtained by Spain through foreign trade is greater than before taxation. Is it a creation of additional value? The same quantity of labour is embodied in the commodities now produced with the capital withdrawn from mines 2 and 3 than in the gold produced previously in these two mines; as for mine 1, it produces the same quantity of gold with the same labour as before. No creation of value has therefore occurred in the Spanish colonies, only a transfer of value from the proprietors of the mines to the King of Spain. It is true however that the same aggregate value created by labour in the Spanish colonies now exchanges for more value created by labour in Europe (embodied in 15600 yards of cloth instead of 10000, while no change occurred in its conditions of production); but this results simply from the fact that the relative price of gold in cloth has been multiplied by 2.5, because taxation has increased the cost of production of gold and monopoly sustains its market price above its natural price.[21]

In terms of wealth (use-values), Ricardo may rightly speak of "pure gain", since the gain of the Spanish colonies (5600 yards of European cloth) is *not* associated with a loss for Europe – the 100 pounds of gold imported are as useful to circulate commodities in Europe than the 250 pounds were before, and the additional 5600 yards of cloth are exchanged against additional Spanish commodities. This "pure gain" is thus entirely to be explained by "the better distribution of capital" in the Spanish colonies, resulting from the imposition of the tax: a smaller capital – that advanced in the only still-operated mine 1 – produces the smaller quantity of gold required as money, and "the liberated capital" may be invested in the production of other commodities:

> A part of the tax would be paid by the people of the Spanish colonies, and the other part would be a new creation of produce, by increasing the power of the instrument used as a medium of exchange.
>
> (ibid: 199)

The value of a pound of gold – its "power" – has been multiplied by 2.5, and the quantity of it used "as a medium of exchange" has been accordingly divided in the same proportion, allowing "a new creation of produce" by the capital transferred to other employments.

Nevertheless, *in terms of value*, the origin of the gain is crystal-clear: by imposing a tax on gold, Spain is in a position to exchange the same aggregate quantity of her labour for a greater aggregate quantity of European labour than before. This explains why, out of the 7000 yards of imported cloth which will be used to dress soldiers of the King of Spain, 1400 yards only are diverted from dressing servants of the Spanish proprietors of mines, and the greater part is obtained for free from European labour. The following sentence should be read in this light:

> *If gold were the produce of one country only, and it were used universally for money*, a very considerable tax might be imposed on it, which would not fall on any country, except in proportion as they used it in manufactures, and for utensils; upon that portion which was used for money, though a large tax might be received, *nobody would pay it.*
>
> (ibid: 194; emphasis added)

Not only – as acknowledged by Ricardo – the Spanish proprietors of mines would indeed pay part of the tax, but Europe also would greatly contribute to paying it. This in no way violates the principles which determine international prices, since it is merely the consequence of the increase in the Spanish price of gold consequent upon taxation. Europe cannot however avoid submitting to the rise in the relative price of gold in order to obtain her circulating medium because of the monopolistic character of gold-money: it may not be replaced by something else – "it [is] used universally for money" – and the Spanish colonies monopolise its production – "gold [is] the produce of one country only".

Ricardo's general favour for taxation (rather than public debt) to finance the unavoidable government expenses is here all the more justified since the burden of most of the tax falls on foreign countries. This practical conclusion is however of no use in the case of Britain, because it only applies to countries enjoying a monopoly in the production of gold-money. Although the argument does not seem to have been used by Ricardo, this analysis provides a further reason for adopting a gold-economising monetary system such as Ricardo's Ingot Plan, which would prevent Britain from being subject to the obligation of increasing the part of her labour and her capital devoted to the purchase of foreign gold when the countries enjoying the monopoly of its production decide to impose a tax on it.

4. A generalisation

In order to generalise Ricardo's analysis of the effect of taxation on the value of gold, his numerical example may be formalised as follows. Let me call:

$P_{nG}{}^{\mathrm{p}}$: Natural price of one ounce of gold bullion, in pesos;

$P_G{}^{\mathrm{p}}$: Market price of one ounce of gold bullion, in pesos;

$c_{G(h)}{}^{\mathrm{p}}$: Cost of production (in pesos) of one ounce of gold bullion in mine h, including profit at the general rate and excluding the tax, with $h = 1, 2, \ldots, k$, ranked according to their decreasing productivity;

$q_{G(h)}$: Quantity of gold bullion produced by capital advanced in mine h, in ounces;

T: Uniform tax imposed on each mine operated, in ounces of gold.

The initial natural situation 0 has been described in Chapter 5 above and is summed-up by:

$$c_{G(h)}{}^{\mathrm{p}0} = c_{G(k)}{}^{\mathrm{p}0} \frac{q_{G(k)}}{q_{G(h)}} \tag{5.1}$$

$$P_G{}^{\mathrm{p}0} = P_{nG}{}^{\mathrm{p}0} = c_{G(k)}{}^{\mathrm{p}0} \tag{5.2}$$

$$D_G{}^{\mathrm{p}} = c_{G(k)}{}^{\mathrm{p}0} \sum_{h=1}^{h=k} q_{G(h)} \tag{5.3}$$

In time 1, taxation is introduced in the form of a given quantity T of gold to be paid by each mine, whatever its cost of production. This tax increases the cost of production in each mine by the value of the tax levied on every ounce of gold produced by that mine. With $P_G{}^{\mathrm{p}1}$ the market price of gold after taxation, this tax in money terms is thus equal to $T\ P_G{}^{\mathrm{p}1}$ and with an unchanged quantity $q_{G(h)}$ produced in mine h it increases the cost of production per ounce by $T\ P_G{}^{\mathrm{p}1} / q_{G(h)}$:

$$c_{G(h)}{}^{\mathrm{p}1} = c_{G(h)}{}^{\mathrm{p}0} + \frac{TP_G{}^{\mathrm{p}1}}{q_{G(h)}} \tag{5.15}$$

According to (5.1), $c_{G(h)}{}^{\mathrm{p}1}$ may be rewritten as:

$$c_{G(h)}{}^{\mathrm{p}1} = \frac{1}{q_{G(h)}}\left(c_{G(k)}{}^{\mathrm{p}0}\, q_{G(k)} + TP_G{}^{\mathrm{p}1}\right) \tag{5.16}$$

If after taxation b mines cease to be profitable at the general rate of profit (with $0 \leq b < k$), so that $k - b$ of them remain worked, $P_G{}^{\mathrm{p}1}$ is equal to the ratio of the unchanged demand $D_G{}^{\mathrm{p}}$ given by (5.3) to the new total quantity of gold produced:

$$P_G{}^{\mathrm{p}1} = c_{G(k)}{}^{\mathrm{p}0} \frac{\sum_{h=1}^{h=k} q_{G(h)}}{\sum_{h=1}^{h=k-b} q_{G(h)}} \tag{5.17}$$

The condition for mine h to remain profitable after taxation is that $P_G{}^{\mathrm{p}1}$ at least covers the cost of production $c_{G(h)}{}^{\mathrm{p}1}$. According to (5.16) and (5.17) this condition is thus:

$$T \leq q_{G(h)} - q_{G(k)} \frac{\sum_{h=1}^{h=k-b} q_{G(h)}}{\sum_{h=1}^{h=k} q_{G(h)}} \tag{5.18}$$

For any combination of the parameters transforming (5.18) into a strict equality, $P_G{}^{\mathrm{p}1} = P_{nG}{}^{\mathrm{p}1} = c_{G(h)}{}^{\mathrm{p}1}$: the market price of gold is equal to its natural price determined by the cost of production in mine h, and all rent disappears. This may however only happen by chance; in the general case the market price of gold is higher than its natural price, and this excess generates an absolute rent.

The example given by Ricardo is: $k = 3$; $q_{G(1)}$=100; $q_{G(2)}$= 80; $q_{G(3)}$= 70; T = 70. If the three mines which were profitable before taxation are to remain so after, condition (5.18) is $T \leq 30$ for mine 1, $T \leq 10$ for mine 2, and $T \leq 0$ for mine 3; with $T = 70$, this condition is fulfilled for none of them. As explained in Chapter 5 above, Ricardo assumes that, instead of the three mines closing down altogether, the mine of the lowest quality closes down first, and so on until the reduction in the quantity produced allows at least one mine to be profitable. Mine 3 is thus the first to close down, so that the total quantity of gold produced decreases from 250 to 180 and the market price of gold increases accordingly in the proportion of 1 to 1.39. Condition (5.18) becomes $T \leq 49.6$ for mine 1 and $T \leq 29.6$ for mine 2; with $T = 70$, this condition is not yet fulfilled for any of the two remaining mines. Mine 2 then closes down, and condition (5.18) becomes $T \leq 72$ for mine 1; now this mine may be worked with profit at the general rate.

If gold were sold at its natural price, so that $P_G{}^{\mathrm{p1}} = c_{G(1)}{}^{\mathrm{p1}}$, (5.16) would give $P_{nG}{}^{\mathrm{p1}} = c_{G(1)}{}^{\mathrm{p1}} = 2.33\, c_{G(3)}{}^{\mathrm{p0}}$; the natural price would be increased by taxation in the proportion of 1 to 2.33 mentioned by Ricardo in the above quotation (ibid: 197). But since the total quantity of gold produced is not enough to ensure the equality between the market and natural prices, (5.17) gives $P_G{}^{\mathrm{p1}} = 2.50\, c_{G(3)}{}^{\mathrm{p0}}$ (gold is "increased in [market] value, as 1 to 2½"), and (5.16) gives $P_{nG}{}^{\mathrm{p1}} = c_{G(1)}{}^{\mathrm{p1}} = 2.45\, c_{G(3)}{}^{\mathrm{p0}}$ (the natural price is increased in the proportion of 1 to 2.45 and not 1 to 2.33, as would be the case if the market and natural prices of gold were equal, because the tax is now paid at a market price higher than the natural one). Consequently the capital advanced in mine 1 earns an extra-profit of $0.05\, c_{G(3)}{}^{\mathrm{p0}}$ per ounce of gold which is paid as rent to the owner of the mine, who gets $0.05\, c_{G(3)}{}^{\mathrm{p0}} / 2.50\, c_{G(3)}{}^{\mathrm{p0}} = 0.02$ ounce of gold per ounce of gold produced. On the 100 ounces of gold produced by the only mine still worked, 70 go to the King of Spain as tax, 2 to the owner of the mine as absolute rent, and 28 are kept by the capitalist as profit at the general rate. The tax could be increased to 72 ounces of gold – making the market price of gold be equal to its natural price and all rent disappear – but not more, otherwise mine 1 would close down and any production of gold would vanish.

Notes

1 Bentham's manuscript is in French and reads as follows: "La valeur de l'argent n'est à présent que la moitié de ce qu'elle étoit il y a 40 ans; elle ne sera dans 40 ans que la moitié de ce qu'elle est à présent" (III: 269).

2 See Bidard (2014) for an evaluation of this "dynamic approach which consists in following the transformations of a long-term equilibrium when demand increases" (Bidard 2014: 3).

3 In Chapter II "On rent" of *Principles*, Ricardo gives a numerical example of the withdrawal of a portion of capital from a land, which ends as follows:

> But with such an increase of produce, without an increase in demand, there could be no motive for employing so much capital on the land; one portion would be withdrawn, and consequently the last portion of capital would yield 105 instead of 95, and rent would fall to 30. (I: 81–2)

4 Say was mentioned in a chapter of *Principles* devoted to "Mr. Malthus's opinions on rent" because, in Ricardo's opinion, Malthus was guilty of the same error as him. Ricardo pointed out in a letter to James Mill on 22 December 1818:

> He [Malthus] read to me some more of his intended publication [*Principles of Political Economy*, 1820]. He has altered his opinion you know about there being land in every country which pays no rent, and appears like M Say to think that when that is proved, my doctrine of rent not entering into price is overthrown – they neither of them advert to the other principle which cannot be touched, of capital being employed on land, already in cultivation, which pays no rent. I have entered my protest against his omitting the consideration of this important fact. (VII: 372)

For Ricardo's critique of Say, see also the letter to McCulloch of 3 January 1819:

> He [Say] attempts to shew that there is no land which does not pay rent, and then thinks that I am confuted – never noticing the other point on which I lay most stress, that there is in every country a portion of capital employed on land already in cultivation for which no rent is paid, or rather that no additional rent is paid in consequence of the employment of such additional capital. (VIII: 4)

5 "The demands for the produce of agriculture are uniform, they are not under the influence of fashion, prejudice or caprice. To sustain life, food is necessary, and the demand for food must continue in all ages, and in all countries" (*Principles*; I: 263).

6 This quotation is from Chapter XXX "On the influence of demand and supply on prices", where Ricardo criticises:

> [T]he opinion that the price of commodities depends solely on the proportion of supply to demand, or demand to supply, [an opinion which] has become almost an axiom in political economy, and has been the source of much error in that science. (ibid: 382)

In the new final position, the supply has "scarcely varied" as compared with the initial one, since the increase in the supply of corn resulting from "some great discovery in the science of agriculture" has been followed by its nearly equal reduction when the less productive lands have been abandoned. The fall in the price of bread, consequent upon the fall in the price of corn, is thus entirely due to the fall in its money cost of production, which is itself the consequence of a diminution in its difficulty of production since by assumption the value of money has not changed.

7 Analysing the case of the supply being adjusted to a change in demand, Bidard emphasises that "the smooth adaptation of activity levels is a universal property which reduces the core of the dynamics to the identification of the outgoing marginal method and the incoming marginal method at critical moments; we call that phenomenon the law of succession of methods" (Bidard 2014: 5–6). According to him, "Ricardo's views [...] assumed a smooth physical transition at breaking points and the progressive introduction of one new method" (ibid: 12).

8 "This is in fact the mode in which the cultivation of corn is always extended, and the increased wants of the market supplied" (*Principles*; I: 306; see also 301–2, 312).

9 This inconvenience could be eliminated with paper money, even if convertible into gold. The quotation goes on:

> As money made of paper may be readily reduced in quantity, its value, though its standard were gold, would be increased as rapidly as that of the metal itself would

be increased, if the metal, by forming a very small part of the circulation, had a very slight connexion with money. (ibid: 194).

10 Another question is what happens when there is a change in the aggregate value of the commodities to be circulated; see below Chapter 7.

11 See also in *Principles*:

> It may, however, be again remarked, that unless the monopoly of the foreign market be in the hands of an exclusive company, no more will be paid for commodities by foreign purchasers than by home purchasers; the price which they both will pay will not differ greatly from their natural price in the country where they are produced. England, for example, will, under ordinary circumstances, always be able to buy French goods, at the natural price of those goods in France, and France would have an equal privilege of buying English goods at their natural price in England. (ibid: 340–1)

This was repeated in Ricardo's speech in Parliament on 22 May 1823 about East and West India Sugars:

> In the speech [of Mr. K. Douglas], however, it was stated, that the price of any commodity did not depend on the cost of cultivation, but on the relation of the supply to the demand. Now, nothing was more unsound. In all cases, the cost of cultivation was sure to regulate the price which any commodity must bear in the markets of the world. As, therefore, the cost of production was acknowledged to be less in the East Indies in the production of sugar, the price of that article in the markets of the world must in the long run be regulated by that cost. (V: 300)

The same applied to gold bullion: "its market value in Europe is ultimately regulated by its natural value in Spanish America" where it is produced (*Principles*; I: 195).

12 See also: "I have been beyond measure puzzled to find out the law of price. I found on a reference to figures that my former opinion could not be correct and I was full a fortnight pondering on my difficulty before I knew how to solve it" (Letter to James Mill, 14 October 1816; VII: 83–4). The solution was "the curious effect which the rise of wages produces on the prices of those commodities which are chiefly obtained by the aid of machinery and fixed capital" (ibid: 82). Ricardo's correction of "former ideas not being correct" is echoed in a letter by Hutches Trower of 19 November 1816, answering to a wanting letter by Ricardo:

> The detection of error is as important as the discovery of truth; and therefore I cannot allow, that those two months were useless to you, by the labors of which you were enabled to ascertain the fallacy of the theory you were endeavouring to establish. (VII: 95)

13 The adoption in a Sraffian framework of Ricardo's assumption about the closure of mines would consequently require gold bullion to be a non-basic good. See also the conclusive section of Chapter 7 below.

14 The argument is the same if the productivity of mine z is lower than that of some of the previous mines, the formalisation being only more complex, since it is then possible that the new natural price is determined by the cost of production in mine z, and not in one of the previous mines.

15 A more complex assumption would be that all portions of capital that become unprofitable after the discovery of the new mine are withdrawn *at once*. The fall in the total production would push the market price upwards, making it overshoot the cost of

production with the least productive portion of capital still earning the general rate of profit. An extra profit would occur, which would induce portions of capital that had been withdrawn to be invested again in the production of gold, till the new natural position is established. The production of gold being competitive, there is no obstacle to capital flowing in after having flown out: provided the adjustment is strictly reversible, the final new natural position would be the same.

16 At the time of Ricardo, the Bank of England was not compelled to buy gold bullion at a fixed price against its notes and only purchased it in the market to replenish the metallic reserve. In his Ingot Plan, Ricardo recommended introducing such legal obligation (see Chapter 9 below) but he was not followed on this point when convertibility into bullion was adopted in 1819. Starting in 1828 the Bank of England committed itself to buy any bullion at the price of £3. 17s. 9d., that is, 0.16 per cent below the legal price of gold in coin. This was later officially introduced in the Bank Charter Act of 1844.

17 Ricardo also objected that the absolute increase had been in fact lower than claimed by the directors of the Bank of England (IV: 232–3).

18 Quoting the "Minutes of Evidence" before the Agricultural Committee of 1821, Sraffa observes in a footnote that "Tooke actually said 'About six per cent'" (IV: 228n).

19 As mentioned in Chapter 5 above, Ricardo emphasised that, by contrast with corn which is totally consumed during the circulation period, gold may be used as money during a long time, so that the adjustment process of its market value is slower. He assumed here by simplicity that the total quantity of gold used as money had again to be produced (in the Spanish colonies) and imported (in Europe) after the imposition of the tax.

20 See the model below for the reason why Ricardo is right in supposing that mine 2 must also close down.

21 Dome (2004) interprets the consequences of a tax on gold in the usual terms of the price-specie flow mechanism: "The money supply would diminish, and the general price level would fall. The balance of trade would become favourable to this country. However, such a trade surplus would disappear in the long run because of the specie-flow price mechanism" (Dome, 2004: 125). As the numerical example given by Ricardo makes clear, the adjustment to the tax entirely takes place in the domestic gold industry and in no way implies any other international change than an increase in the real price of gold in cloth. The "pure gain" consequent upon this change is permanent.

6 The depreciation of metallic money

> *We all know that it is the melting pot only which keeps all currency in a wholesome state.*
>
> (Letter to Pascoe Grenfell, 19 January 1823; in Deleplace, Depoortère and Rieucau 2013: 4)

The starting point of the present chapter and of the next one is a consequence of the Money–Standard Equation analysed in Chapter 4 above: a monetary shock was transmitted *indirectly* to the prices of all commodities, through a change in the market price of the standard (gold bullion). Discussing in *High Price* the possibility "to carry the law against melting or exporting of coin into strict execution" (see below), Ricardo mentioned the case of:

> [A] real depreciation of our currency, raising the prices of all other commodities in the same proportion as it increased that of gold bullion.
>
> (*High Price*, III: 56)

This sentence may be interpreted in two ways. The usual one, inspired by the Quantity Theory of Money, is to consider that, when the currency was depreciated, the prices of all commodities increased *directly* "in the same proportion", *including* "that of gold bullion". In contrast I will contend that Ricardo maintained that depreciation increased the price of gold bullion and *through this channel* raised "the prices of all other commodities in the same proportion". The first task is thus to study what happened when, whatever the monetary shock, the market price of gold bullion departed from the legal price of gold in coin, and how this difference was transmitted to the prices of all other commodities. This will be done below in Section 6.1 and Section 6.2 respectively. After having thus clarified how a change in the market price of the standard affected the prices of all other commodities via a change in the value of money, it will be possible to analyse which kind of monetary shock affected the market price of the standard itself.

A monetary shock was an excess or deficiency in the aggregate quantity of money, which became inconsistent with the conformity of money to the standard – that is, with the equality between the market price of bullion and the legal price of the metal in coin. In a letter to Francis Horner of 5 February 1810 Ricardo listed four causes that might explain a situation in which the former was above the latter:

> It appears then to me, that no point can be more satisfactorily established, than that the excess of the market above the mint price of gold bullion, is, at present, wholly, and solely, owing to the too abundant quantity of paper circulation. There are in my opinion but three causes which can, at any time, produce an excess of price such as we are now speaking of.
>
> First, The debasement of the coins, or rather of that coin which is the principal measure of value.
>
> Secondly, A proportion in the relative value of gold to silver in the market, greater than in their relative value in the coins.
>
> Thirdly, A superabundance of paper circulation. By superabundance I mean that quantity of paper money which could not by any means be kept in circulation if it were immediately exchangeable for specie on demand.
>
> I might add here a fourth cause. The severity of the law against the exportation of gold coins, but from experience we know that this law is so easily evaded, that it is considered by all writers on political economy, as operating in a very small degree on the price of gold bullion.
>
> (VI: 1–2)

The fourth cause – the legal prohibition of melting and exporting the domestic coin – will be considered below in Section 6.1 because it affects the working of the market for bullion. Among the three main causes of "the excess of the market above the mint price of gold bullion", the first two might look like historical curiosities, even at the time of Ricardo. Since the gold recoinage of 1774 (see Chapter 1 above), gold coins were considered as undebased. The recoinage of silver coins went back to 1695–1699, and some Anti-Bullionists contended that their debasement was responsible for the monetary disorder; but Ricardo emphasised that the gold coin, not the silver one, was "the principal measure of value". In other words, gold was the actual standard of money, in spite of the legal double standard at the time of the *Bullion Report* – so that debasement was then irrelevant (see Chapter 2 above). As for the effect of "the relative value of gold to silver in the market", it could be neglected (except in international relations, foreign countries being on a silver or a double standard) because of the *de facto* gold standard and the disposition of the Act of 1774 making silver coins legal tender up to £25 only (they were taken by weight above this sum). The currency reform of 1816 would reinforce this historical tendency, by establishing a *de jure* gold standard and making silver coins a token money, although the return to a legal double standard was again debated in the context of the resumption of convertibility in 1819–1823 (see Chapter 2 above).

Nevertheless, it is worthwhile to analyse Ricardo's treatment of the depreciation of a metallic money before concentrating on the question of the excess issue of notes in the next chapter, for two reasons. First, as the first pages of Chapter XXVII of *Principles* make clear, Ricardo considered that the debasement of coins and the excess issue of notes had the same effect on the depreciation of money and that debased coins and notes issued in excess were both subject to "the principle of limitation of quantity" (I: 353). This will be shown in Section 6.3 below. Second, the discussion of the double standard led Ricardo to warn against the power of the Bank of England to change the value of the currency at will – a recurrent complaint by him. This will be the object of Section 6.4.

6.1 Convertibility and adjustment in the market for bullion

In a mixed monetary system like that ruling before 1797 and after 1821, gold coins – supposedly full-bodied (undebased) – circulated side by side with Bank of England notes convertible into coin (I leave aside notes issued by country banks which were convertible into Bank of England notes; see Chapter 1 above). Two kinds of convertibility had then to be considered.

There was first convertibility both ways between metallic money (the gold coin) and its standard (gold bullion). The market price of bullion fluctuated with supply and demand between two fixed limits because two symmetrical operations ensured the convertibility of bullion into coin and of coin into bullion, as Ricardo called them in his "Notes on Trotter" in 1810:

> Who has asserted that gold is an unvarying standard of value? There is no unvarying standard in existence. Gold is however unvarying with regard to that money which is made of gold, and this proceeds from it being at all times convertible without expence into such money, and also from money being again convertible into gold bullion.
>
> (III: 391)

One operation was legal and public: the minting of bullion into coins at a fixed legal price. Although no seignorage was charged by the Royal Mint, which had the monopoly of coining, there was a small cost (around 0.5 per cent) borne by this operation, because the metal had to be assayed and the mint delivered the coins only after some time (usually two months), during which interest had to be paid on the funds borrowed to purchase the metal in the market. The second operation was illegal and private: the melting of coins, which was prohibited because it facilitated the export of gold – an operation also illegal, unless it concerned foreign coins or "sworn-off" gold, that is, bullion whose owner swore that it had been imported before. Every observer testified that this legislation was easily evaded:

> But these gentlemen do not dispute the fact of the convertibility of coin into bullion, in spite of the law to prevent it. Does it not follow, therefore, that the value of gold in coin, and the value of gold in bullion, would speedily approach a perfect equality?
>
> (*Reply to Bosanquet*; III: 211)

Recalling that the equality between the value of money (here gold in coin) and the value of its standard (gold bullion) was obtained when the market price of gold bullion was equal to the legal price of gold in coin (the condition of conformity established in Chapter 3 above), convertibility both ways between coin and bullion ensured that the market price of gold bullion was constrained between narrow limits around the legal price of gold in coin. The owner of an ounce of standard gold bullion had the choice between selling it in the market against coins at a price P_G and carrying it to the mint to obtain $\overline{P_{GC}}$ in coins at a percentage cost s_G equal to the rate of interest until the mint delivered the coins. This arbitrage permitted by the convertibility of bullion into coin determined a lower limit to the variation of P_G, equal to $\overline{P_{GC}}\ (1 - s_G)$: if P_G fell below this limit, owners of bullion stopped offering it in the market and carried it to the mint; the reduction in the supply raised the price to $\overline{P_{GC}}\ (1 - s_G)$. The demander for gold bullion had the choice between buying it with coins in the market at P_G and having his coins melted into bullion at a percentage cost m_G. This cost included that of the operation of the melting pot, the rate of interest until the bullion was delivered, and since melting was prohibited, the compensation for the risk of infringing the law, which depended on the severity of its enforcement. This arbitrage permitted by the convertibility of coin into bullion determined an upper limit to the variation of P_G, equal to $\overline{P_{GC}}\left(1 + m_G\right)$: if P_G rose above his limit, the owners of coins had them melted and offered the bullion in the market; the increased supply lowered the price to $\overline{P_{GC}}\left(1 + m_G\right)$. Convertibility both ways between coin and bullion thus ensured that:

$$\overline{P_{GC}}\ (1 + m_G) \geq P_G \geq \overline{P_{GC}}\ (1 - s_G) \tag{6.1}$$

Inequalities (6.1) applied if circulating coins were full-bodied. If they were debased, an additional cost had to be borne when they were converted into bullion, reflecting the rate of debasement (see Section 6.3 below). This raised *pro tanto* the upper limit of variation of P_G

The second convertibility was between the Bank of England note and the coin, and after 1821 as before 1797 it was only one-way. The Bank was compelled by law to deliver on demand and at no cost full-bodied coins against an equal quantity of its notes. But it was *not* compelled to issue notes against coins or bullion brought to it. When the Bank judged necessary to enlarge its reserve in coins, it purchased bullion at the market price and had it coined by the mint. In other words, notes could be converted at a fixed price into bullion, through exchanging them at no cost at the Bank against coins and melting the coins at the cost m_G. Bullion could not be converted into notes at a fixed price but only into coins at the mint. Convertibility of the Bank of England note into coin consequently played no role for the lower limit of variation in the market price of gold bullion but only for its upper limit. And it did so also through the melting pot, into which coins obtained from the Bank against notes were poured.

Inequalities (6.1) consequently determined the range of variation of the market price of gold bullion provided coins were convertible into bullion through the melting pot and bullion was convertible into coin through the mint, whether the Bank of England note was itself convertible into coin or not. However, the level of the parameters involved $\left(m_G \text{ and } s_G\right)$ depended on the monetary regime, and hence also the variability of the market price of gold bullion at both ends of inequalities (6.1).

The effect of the melting pot on the upper limit of variation in the market price of bullion

As Ricardo put it in a letter to Grenfell of 19 January 1823 where he discussed the prospect of depreciation if the double standard were adopted in a system having resumed convertibility of the Bank of England note:

> We all know that it is the melting pot only which keeps all currency in a wholesome state.
>
> (Deleplace, Depoortère and Rieucau 2013: 4)

Were the note inconvertible, as was the case between 1797 and 1819, the melting pot would still play a role to convert notes issued in excess into bullion, as long as there were still coins in circulation purchased with notes with a view to melting them. An additional cost had to be borne to purchase the coins with depreciated notes from money-changers. The situation was the same as that of a pure metallic circulation when the coin was debased: the upper limit of variation of P_G was raised *pro tanto*.

When convertible notes circulated side by side with coins, P_G rated in notes could not differ from P_G rated in coins, since notes might always be exchanged at par for undebased coins at the Bank. If an increase in the quantity of notes issued pushed P_G to $\overline{P_{GC}}\left(1 + m_G\right)$ – notes were depreciated – the buyer of bullion could not insist on paying a lower price in coins, because the only alternative he had to obtain bullion was to have his coins melted at the same price $\overline{P_{GC}}\left(1 + m_G\right)$. The market price of gold bullion was thus the same whether the transaction was paid for in convertible notes or in coins. Neglecting the costs of minting and of melting, one ounce of gold bullion consequently exchanged for one ounce of gold in coin or the quantity of convertible notes representing one ounce of gold in coin. In the case of an excess quantity of notes issued, the adjustment process did not eliminate the excess in totality because melting had a cost and it stopped when P_G was equalised by arbitrage with $\overline{P_{GC}}\left(1 + m_G\right)$, not with $\overline{P_{GC}}$. As mentioned by Ricardo in his letter to Horner of 5 February 1810 quoted at the beginning, the legal prohibition of melting and exporting the coin could thus be responsible for a depreciation of money.

For the sake of argument, Ricardo sometimes assumed that the law was strictly enforced, so that the market price of gold bullion, paid for in coins, might be as high as twice the legal price of gold in coin:

> Were it possible to carry the law against melting or exporting of coin into strict execution, at the same time that the exportation of bullion was freely

> allowed, no advantage could accrue from it, but great injury must arise to those who might have to pay, possibly, two ounces or more of coined gold for one of uncoined gold. This would be a real depreciation of our currency, raising the prices of all other commodities in the same proportion as it increased that of gold bullion. The owner of money would in this case suffer an injury equal to what a proprietor of corn would suffer, were a law to be passed prohibiting him from selling his corn for more than half its market value. The law against the exportation of the coin has this tendency, but it is so easily evaded, that gold in bullion has always been nearly of the same value as gold in coin.
>
> (*High Price*, III: 56)

Were the law strictly enforced, it could possibly double the market price of gold bullion purchased with gold coins, because, bullion being freely exportable, those who would like to obtain it with a view to exportation would have to pay a high premium to compensate for the risk of fraud. This hypothetical case materially applied to inconvertible bank notes, which could be neither converted into bullion nor exported:

> Now a paper circulation, not convertible into specie, differs in its effects in no respect from a metallic currency, with the law against exportation strictly executed.
>
> (*Reply to Bosanquet*; III: 194)

Even with convertible notes, the legal prohibition of melting and exporting the coin opened a small margin of depreciation of money and this was the reason why Ricardo consistently advocated the repeal of this legislation. In his Ingot Plan, convertibility of notes into bullion completely eliminated m_G and prevented the market price of the standard from rising above its legal price (see Chapter 9 below).

The effect of seignorage on the lower limit of variation in the market price of bullion

At the other end of inequalities (6.1), the existence of a minting cost s_G opened a margin of appreciation of money, hence of a general fall in prices. Although Ricardo generally advocated the equality of the market price of the standard with its legal price – the condition of conformity mentioned in Chapter 3 above – he was in favour of such seignorage, provided it was small. As he wrote in *Principles*:

> To a moderate seignorage on the coinage of money there cannot be much objection.
>
> (I: 371)

Being examined by the Secret Committee on Resumption on 4 March 1819, he had first recommended the possibility to obtain immediately the gold coin against bullion at the mint (V: 380, 387), instead of the then delivery at two months' notice which because of the loss of interest implied what "may strictly be called a small seignorage" (ibid: 402). In an unusual manner, he asked to be again examined on 19 March and, probably to be correctly understood, he delivered a written paper. He stood to his former answer "as far as regards our circulation" (ibid: 401), but he wanted "to amend" it by stressing an inconvenience linked to the absence of seignorage: "a great inducement offered to all exporters of gold, to exchange their bullion for coin previously to its exportation" (ibid), since the advantages of the coins (certified fineness, divisibility) would no longer be compensated by the cost of obtaining them. Ricardo's proposal was the following:

> If it be decided, that under all circumstances, a currency, partly made up of gold coin, is desirable, the most perfect footing on which it could be put, would be to charge a moderate seignorage on the gold coin, giving at the same time the privilege to the holder of bank notes, to demand of the bank, either gold coin or gold bullion at the mint price, as he should think best.
>
> (ibid: 402)

This was the proposal made in *Principles* (see I: 372 and also V: 429, 431) However, even "moderate", a seignorage on a coin "has also its inconveniences" (V: 402), as shown by (6.1): it opened a margin of fall in the market price of bullion – hence also in all other prices – when the Bank of England contracted its issues. Ricardo's conclusion was straightforward:

> I am still of opinion, that we should have all its advantages [of a seignorage], with the additional one of economy, by adopting the plan, which I had the honour of laying before the Committee when I was last before them.
>
> (ibid: 403)

This was of course the Ingot Plan, in which the currency (bank notes exclusively) was to be obtained from the Bank against standard bullion at £3. 17s. 6d. per ounce, 0.5 per cent below the price at which it was legal tender – a difference sufficient to cover the cost of management of the currency while maintaining at a trifling level the margin of fall in the market price of bullion (see Chapter 9 below).

6.2 Price adjustment in the markets for other commodities than bullion

The effect of a change in the value of money on the competition of capitals

The question of price adjustment has already been evoked in Chapter 3 above, when I discussed the relation between the standard of money and the standard of value in Ricardo. We saw that around 1815 Ricardo became conscious that the understanding of commodity price required the coordination between two theories: a theory of value and distribution – which he started to envisage in his *Essay on Profits*, published in February 1815 – and a theory of money – the foundations of which he gave in *Proposals for an Economical and Secure Currency*, published in February 1816. This requirement was expressed in the letter to Malthus of 27 June 1815:

> It appears to me that there are two causes which may cause a rise of prices, – one the depreciation of money, the other the difficulty of producing.
>
> (VI: 233)

Six months later, Ricardo emphasised the difficulty of the task of writing what would become *Principles*, in the letter to Mill of 30 December 1815 discussed in Chapter 3:

> I know I shall be soon stopped by the word price, and then I must apply to you for advice and assistance. Before my readers can understand the proof I mean to offer, they must understand the theory of currency and of price.
>
> (VI: 348)

It should be recalled that the "two causes" of price mentioned in the letter to Malthus – which became in the letter to Mill the "two ways" the prices of commodities were affected – are *not* to be confused with the "two causes" of "relative value" ("the relative quantity of labour" and "the rate of profit"), mentioned by Ricardo in a well-known letter to McCulloch of 13 June 1820, which concerned the determination of the exchangeable value, that is, the second cause of price in the letter to Malthus ("the difficulty of producing").[1]

The distinction between the respective effects on the price of any commodity of its exchangeable value and of the value of money was central for Ricardo's analysis of the distribution of income, when this distinction was applied to the price of wage-goods. If the price of corn increased as a consequence of a fall in the value of money, the rate of profit remained undisturbed, since only money wages rose, not real wages. On the contrary, if the price of corn increased as a consequence of a rise in its exchangeable value, the rate of profit declined, real wages having increased.[2] This was a central proposition of *Principles*:

> It has been my endeavour carefully to distinguish between a low value of money, and a high value of corn, or any other commodity with which money may be compared. These have been generally considered as meaning the same thing; but it is evident, that when corn rises from five to ten shillings a bushel, it may be owing either to a fall in the value of money, or to a rise in the value of corn. Thus we have seen, that from the necessity of having recourse successively to land of a worse and worse quality, in order to feed an increasing population, corn must rise in relative value to other things. If therefore money continue permanently of the same value, corn will exchange for more of such money, that is to say, it will rise in price. The same rise in the price of corn will be produced by such improvement of machinery in manufactures, as shall enable us to manufacture commodities with peculiar

> advantages: for the influx of money will be the consequence; it will fall in value, and therefore exchange for less corn. But the effects resulting from a high price of corn when produced by the rise in the value of corn, and when caused by a fall in the value of money, are totally different. In both cases the money price of wages will rise, but if it be in consequence of the fall in the value of money, not only wages and corn, but all other commodities will rise. If the manufacturer has more to pay for wages, he will receive more for his manufactured goods, and the rate of profits will remain unaffected. But when the rise in the price of corn is the effect of the difficulty of production, profits will fall; for the manufacturer will be obliged to pay more wages, and will not be enabled to remunerate himself by raising the price of his manufactured commodity.
>
> (*Principles*; I: 145–6)[3]

The distinction between the two ways the price of any commodity could vary had an important consequence: a change in the "difficulty of producing" a commodity affected its price and only it, while a change in the value of money affected all prices:

> This, I apprehend, is the correct account of all permanent variations in price, whether of corn or of any other commodity. A commodity can only permanently rise in price, either because a greater quantity of capital and labour must be employed to produce it, or because money has fallen in value; and, on the contrary, it can only fall in price, either because a less quantity of capital and labour may be employed to produce it, or because money has risen in value. A variation arising from the latter of these alternatives, an altered value of money, is common at once to all commodities; but a variation arising from the former cause, is confined to the particular commodity requiring more or less labour in its production.
>
> (ibid: 417)

A change in the value of money not only affected all prices, but it did so in the same proportion:

> If a country were not taxed, and money should fall in value, its abundance in every market would produce similar effects in each. If meat rose 20 per cent., bread, beer, shoes, labour, and every commodity, would also rise 20 per cent.; it is necessary they should do so, to secure to each trade the same rate of profits.
>
> (ibid: 209)[4]

The role of what Ricardo called "the competition of capitals" in the fact that a change in the value of money induced an opposite and proportional change in all prices focused on the behaviour of the sellers in the fixation of prices, because it was on this side that capital moved from one employment to another. In a letter to Malthus of 9 October 1820, Ricardo criticised Say for contending that buyers "regulated the value of commodities":

> He [Say] certainly has not a correct notion of what is meant by value, when he contends that a commodity is valuable in proportion to its utility. This would be true if buyers only regulated the value of commodities; then indeed we might expect that all men would be willing to give a price for things in proportion to the estimation in which they held them, but the fact appears to me to be that the buyers have the least in the world to do in regulating price – it is all done by the competition of the sellers, and however the buyers might be really willing to give more for iron, than for gold, they could not, because the supply would be regulated by the cost of production, and therefore gold would inevitably be in the proportion which it now is to iron, altho' it probably is by all mankind considered as the less useful metal.
>
> (VIII: 276–7)

From the market price of bullion to the market prices of commodities

Since gold bullion was the standard of money, the seller of any commodity *i* sold it for a quantity of pounds – the price P_i – equivalent to a certain quantity of gold bullion. The exchangeable value of commodity *i* in gold bullion was translated into its price P_i in pounds thanks to the legal definition of the pound as a quantity of gold. In circulation commodity *i* exchanged at price P_i for the required quantity of gold in full-bodied coins or in notes convertible into full-bodied coins. If circulating coins were debased or convertible notes were in excess, this was reflected in a market price of gold bullion above the legal price of gold in coin (the circulating medium was depreciated), and the sellers raised their prices by the amount of this spread. If the market price of gold bullion fell below the legal price of gold in coin (the circulating medium was appreciated) competition forced the sellers to lower their prices. The market for gold bullion thus triggered a change in prices generated by a change in the value of money, and, because of the competition of capitals for the general rate of profit, all sellers of commodities passed the change in the value of money on to their prices in the same proportion, leaving relative prices unaltered.

This price adjustment occurred whatever the circumstances leading to such change in the value of money. It also applied when the circulating medium was composed of inconvertible notes, and it is how it was described by Ricardo in the Bullion Essays:

> The effect produced on prices by the depreciation has been most accurately defined [by the Bullion Committee], and amounts to the difference between the market and the mint price of gold. An ounce of gold coin cannot be of less value, the Committee say, than an ounce of gold bullion of the same standard; a purchaser of corn therefore is entitled to as much of that commodity for an ounce of gold coin, or 3*l*. 17s. 10½d., as can be obtained for an ounce of

> gold bullion. Now, as 4*l*.12s. of paper currency is of no more value than an ounce of gold bullion, prices are actually raised to the purchaser 18 per cent., in consequence of his purchase being made with paper instead of coin of its bullion value. Eighteen per cent. is, therefore, equal to the rise in the price of commodities, occasioned by the depreciation of paper. All above such rise may be either traced to the effects of taxation, to the increased scarcity of the commodity, or to any other cause which may appear satisfactory to those who take pleasure in such enquiries.
>
> (*Reply to Bosanquet*; III: 239)

If the notes were not depreciated – that is, if the market price of an ounce of gold bullion paid for in notes were equal to the legal price of an ounce of gold in coin (£3. 17s. 10½d.) – a given quantity of corn having a relative value of an ounce of gold bullion would exchange for £3. 17s. 10½d. in notes. But the actual situation was such that notes were depreciated by 18 per cent, as testified by the fact that an ounce of gold bullion was paid for in notes at a price of £4. 12s. The relative value of the given quantity of corn in terms of gold bullion remained an ounce if it now exchanged for £4. 12s. in depreciated notes. The 18 per cent increase in the market price of gold bullion (as compared with a situation of no-depreciation) was thus translated into an 18 per cent increase in the market price of corn. The same applied to any other commodity – "Eighteen per cent. is, therefore, equal to the rise in the price of commodities, occasioned by the depreciation of paper" – so as to preserve the uniformity of the rate of profit on all portions of capital.

One should observe that this price increase occurred whether the commodity was paid for in notes or in undebased coins, because the whole money was depreciated: the coin partook in the depreciation of the note issued in excess. As explained by Ricardo:

> If an addition be made to a currency consisting partly of gold and partly of paper, by an increase of paper currency the value of the whole currency would be diminished, or, in other words, the prices of commodities would rise, estimated either in gold coin or in paper currency. The same commodity would purchase, after the increase of paper, a greater number of ounces of gold coin, because it would exchange for a greater quantity of money.
>
> (ibid: 210–11)

After as before depreciation there was one price only for each commodity, whether the circulating medium used to pay for it was paper or metallic money. Since, according to (6.1), the upper limit of the market price of gold bullion, paid for in depreciated notes, was the legal price of gold in coin plus the melting cost, it was indifferent to the seller of gold to be paid £4. 12s. in notes, with which he could purchase an ounce of gold bullion in the market, or £4. 12s. in undebased coins, which he could melt at 18 per cent cost to obtain the same ounce of gold bullion.

A bullion-price channel of transmission of a monetary shock

The same adjustment of the market prices of commodities to changes in the market price of gold bullion was mentioned in the papers of 1819–1823, as in the speech in Parliament of 12 June 1822 already quoted in Chapter 4 above, which considered what happened when, after the note had been depreciated (and prices had risen accordingly), the market price of gold bullion fell back to the unchanged level of the legal price of gold in coin:

> If, for instance, the standard of the currency remained at the same fixed value, and the coin were depreciated by clipping, or the paper money by the increase of its quantity, five per cent, a fall to that amount and no more, would take place in the price of commodities, as affected by the value of money. If the metal gold (the standard) continued of the same precise value, and it was required to restore the currency thus depreciated five per cent, to par, it would be necessary only to raise its value five per cent, and no greater than that proportionate fall could take place in the price of commodities.
>
> (V: 204)

It was the business of bullion traders to be at all times informed about the market price P_G of gold bullion – all the more so since in London it was fixed every Tuesday and Friday by the main houses in this trade, such as Mocatta and Goldsmid – and arbitrage with the legal price of gold in coin $\overline{P_{GC}}$ was thus immediate. One may think that this deviation of P_G from $\overline{P_{GC}}$ had to continue for some time before the sellers of all other commodities understood that the currency for which they traded them was depreciated (or appreciated) and adjusted their prices accordingly. However, Ricardo maintained that this lag was not great. Being examined by the House of Lords Committee on Resumption on 26 March 1819, he answered to questions on this point as follows:

> Question: Do the prices of commodities conform to the fluctuations in the market price of gold, or does not a length of time elapse before such conformity takes place?
>
> Answer: They do not immediately conform, but I do not think it very long before they do.
>
> Question: If the prices of commodities have not already fallen to a level with the present market price of gold, is it certain there will not be a greater reduction in their prices than 4 per cent., on the market price of gold falling to the mint price?
>
> Answer: I think the prices of commodities fall from a reduction of the paper circulation quite as soon as gold falls.
>
> (V: 452)

Let me now sum up the question of price adjustments as it may be understood up to this point in Ricardo. In the market for gold bullion, convertibility both ways between this standard of money and metallic money (the coin) and convertibility one-way between paper money (the Bank of England note) and metallic money generated a specific adjustment of the market price to the legal price of gold in coin which constrained the former in a given margin around the latter (inequalities (6.1) above). In the markets for all other commodities, prices responded in the same proportion to any deviation of the market price of gold bullion from the legal price of gold in coin. Since, as will be analysed in Chapter 7 below, an excess or a deficiency in the note issue was the primary cause of such (respectively positive or negative) deviation, a monetary shock was transmitted to the prices of all commodities through a change in the market price of gold bullion: an excess in the note issue caused a proportional rise in all prices and a deficiency a proportional fall. This bullion-price channel of transmission of a monetary shock to the value of money hence to commodity prices contrasts other transmission channels attributed to Ricardo in modern literature, based on the real-balance effect or the rate of interest. This point will be discussed in Appendix 7 below.

Before analysing in the next chapter the adjustment to an excess note issue, I will consider the two other monetary shocks mentioned by Ricardo: the debasement of the coin and a change in the relative price of gold to silver in a double-standard system.

6.3 Debasement of the coin and depreciation of money

The effect of debasement on the market price of gold bullion

In Chapter 5 above I showed that a theory of a monetary system endowed with a standard, as it was developed by Ricardo from *Proposals for an Economical and Secure Currency* onwards, implied discarding the "analogy" (made by Ricardo in the Bullion Essays) between the discovery of a new gold mine and a discretionary increase in the note issue. Another analogy was more appropriate, between debased coins and Bank of England notes issued in excess. That both circumstances had the same effect was contended by Ricardo in his speech of 12 June 1822 quoted in Chapter 4 and again above in Section 6.2: "If, for instance, the standard of the currency remained at the same fixed value, and the coin were depreciated by clipping, or the paper money by the increase of its quantity, five per cent [...]" (V: 204). Such analogy did not point to a circumstance affecting the standard of money – such as the discovery of a new gold mine – but to one affecting metallic money itself: its debasement.

The interpretation by Ricardo of the debasement of the coins in terms of depreciation of the currency was already to be found in the Bullion Essays:

> The public has sustained, at different times, very serious loss from the depreciation of the circulating medium, arising from the unlawful practice of clipping the coins.
>
> (*High Price*; III: 69)

The same statement was repeated in the mature monetary writings, as in a letter to McCulloch dated 2 October 1819: "The depreciation of the currency is inferred as a necessary consequence of a clipped coin" (VIII: 90). More details were given in the speech of 12 June 1822, where Ricardo criticised the opinion of one of his colleagues in Parliament:

> Suppose the only currency in the country was a metallic one, and that, by clipping, it had lost 10 per cent of its weight; suppose, for instance, that the sovereign only retained 9-10ths of the metal which by law it should contain, and that, in consequence, gold bullion, in such a medium, should rise above its mint price, would not the money of the country be depreciated? He was quite sure the hon. alderman would admit the truth of this inference.
>
> (V: 203)

One of the reasons of Ricardo's constancy on this question is that it was disputed by nobody, as suggested by the end of the quotation. The causal relation between the debasement of the coins and a high market price of gold bullion was generally admitted at the time of Ricardo and had been established with great clarity by James Steuart more than forty years before in his *Principles of Political Economy* of 1767.[5] It was precisely this relation which led some Anti-Bullionists to deny an excess issue of Bank of England notes any responsibility in the high price of bullion and to explain it by the debasement of the coins. As seen in Chapter 2 above, Ricardo opposed them not on the general effect of debasement on the market price of bullion but on its relevance in the circumstances of the time, the divergence being about "that coin which is the principal measure of value" (VI: 2) – the gold or the silver one – Ricardo arguing that it was the gold one and that it was not debased.

The relation between debasement and depreciation may be formalised as follows. Supposing gold is the standard, let $\overline{q_{GC}}$ be the intrinsic weight of the standard coin "fresh from the mint" (undebased), that is, the quantity of gold (measured in ounces) legally contained in it, and q_{GC} the quantity of gold contained in the average circulating coin of the same denomination, with $q_{GC} \leq \overline{q_{GC}}$. One may define the rate of debasement D as the percentage difference between the legal gold weight of the undebased coin and the actual average gold weight of the debased one:

$$D = \frac{\overline{q_{GC}} - q_{GC}}{\overline{q_{GC}}} \tag{6.2}$$

Neglecting for the moment the coining and melting costs, let me suppose, as in the above quotation, that the average circulating coin is debased by $D = 10$ per cent, but the law is such that it passes indifferently with an undebased one. If the seller of an ounce of gold bullion is paid £3. 17s. 10½d. in such debased coins – that is, at a market price equal to the legal price of an ounce of gold in undebased coin – he really exchanges one ounce of gold bullion for 0.9 ounce of gold in coin. He may alternatively bring his bullion to the mint to have it coined in £3. 17s. 10½d. in undebased coins. The diminished supply of bullion in the market raises its price, until one ounce of gold bullion exchanges at this higher price for one ounce of gold in debased coins. This occurs when the market price of gold bullion is 10 per cent above the legal price of gold in coin. If this premium overtakes 10 per cent, the owner of debased coins, rather than buying bullion at that price, prefers to melt them to sell the bullion thus obtained. The increased supply of bullion in the market sinks its price, until the premium falls back to 10 per cent. Arbitrage thus sustains the market price of gold bullion above the legal price of gold in undebased coin, by a margin determined by the rate of debasement. In other words, £3. 17s. 10½d. in debased coin buy in the market 10 per cent less in gold bullion than it should according to the legal definition of the pound: measured in gold bullion, the debased currency is depreciated by 10 per cent and this depreciation continues as long as the average circulating coin remains debased by 10 per cent.

The relation between the rate of debasement and the rate of depreciation is as follows. By definition one ounce of gold contains $1/\overline{q_{GC}}$ undebased coins, each one declared to be legal tender for £1, so that the legal price $\overline{P_{GC}}$ in pounds of one ounce of gold in undebased coins is given by:

$$\overline{P_{GC}} = \frac{1}{\overline{q_{GC}}} \tag{6.3}$$

In circulation, one ounce of gold contains $1/q_{GC}$ debased coins, each one being also legal tender for £1. The no-arbitrage condition in the market for gold bullion states that one ounce of gold bullion exchanges for one ounce of gold in debased coins, so that, with P_G the market price in pounds of one ounce of gold bullion:

$$P_G = \frac{1}{q_{GC}} \tag{6.4}$$

As seen in Chapter 4 above, the rate of depreciation d of money is equal to:

$$d = \frac{P_G - \overline{P_{GC}}}{P_G} \tag{4.2}$$

Combining (6.2), (6.3), (6.4) and (4.2) gives:

$$d = D \tag{6.5}$$

As stated by Ricardo in the above quotation, the higher the rate of debasement of the coin, the higher the rate of depreciation of money. It should be noticed that the level of depreciation of the currency entirely results from the no-arbitrage condition in the market for gold bullion. It does *not* depend on any relation between the quantity of money, its value, and the aggregate money price of all circulated commodities. This is consistent with the logic of the Money–Standard Equation analysed in Chapter 4 above, according to which the causal relation between the quantity of money and its value results – for a given value of the standard – from the causal relation between the quantity of money and the price of gold bullion.

In practice convertibility of bullion into coin (minting) and of coin into bullion (melting) was costly: the delay to obtain the coin at the mint exposed the owner of bullion to a loss of interest; the legal prohibition of melting and exporting the coin exposed its owner to a melting cost that included the compensation paid to the intermediary for the risk of fraud. As seen in Section 6.1 above, the market price of gold bullion P_G could thus vary around the legal price $\overline{P_{GC}}$ of gold in undebased coin between narrow limits corresponding to s_G the minting cost and m_G the melting cost (both in percentage of the price):

$$\overline{P_{GC}}\left(1+m_G\right)\geq P_G\geq\overline{P_{GC}}\ (1-s_G) \tag{6.1}$$

When the circulating coins were debased, the upper limit of the market price of gold bullion was augmented by the rate of debasement D:

$$\overline{P_{GC}}\ (1+D)(1+m_G)\geq P_G\geq\overline{P_{GC}}\ (1-s_G) \tag{6.6}$$

The rate of depreciation could now be greater than the rate of debasement, by a margin equal to the melting cost. When the circulation was composed of debased coins, they were all the more depreciated since their melting and exporting was legally prohibited.

Debasement and "the principle of limitation of quantity"

As noted earlier, there was no novelty in Ricardo's statement of the causal relation between the debasement of the coins and a high price of gold bullion: such relation was currently recognised at the time. The singularity of Ricardo, however, is to be found in his interpretation of this relation as a particular case of application of "the principle of limitation of quantity" of money. This interpretation clearly shows up in *Principles*, in connection with the application of this principle to an excess issue of notes. According to Ricardo, when the circulation was composed of debased coins, the quantity of currency was also in excess. After having mentioned that an excess of paper money would generate an unfavourable exchange exactly proportional to that excess, he added:

> To produce this effect it is not, however, necessary that paper money should be employed: any cause which retains in circulation a greater quantity of pounds

> than would have circulated, if commerce had been free, and the precious metals of a known weight and fineness had been used, either for money, or for the standard of money, would exactly produce the same effects. *Suppose that by clipping the money, each pound did not contain the quantity of gold or silver which by law it should contain, a greater number of such pounds might be employed in the circulation, than if they were not clipped.* If from each pound one tenth were taken away, 11 millions of such pounds might be used instead of 10; if two tenths were taken away, 12 millions might be employed; and if one half were taken away, 20 millions might not be found superfluous. If the latter sum were used instead of 10 millions, *every commodity in England would be raised to double its former price*, and the exchange would be 50 per cent. against England.
>
> (*Principles*; I: 230–1; my emphasis)

According to Ricardo, if debased coins were allowed to pass as undebased ones, this meant that the aggregate value in pounds borne by these coins was in excess as compared with what it would have been had the coins been undebased: a debasement of the coin was identical with an excess in the aggregate quantity of money. Consequently, diminishing the depreciation of the currency might be obtained by reducing the quantity of coins in circulation. The rationing of new (undebased) coins by the mint could not do, since, with a market price of bullion above the mint price, nobody brought bullion to the mint anyway. The reduction had to concern the debased coins, the circulation of which was in fact heterogeneous: some coins of old coinages were debased by wear and tear, as compared with more recent ones; some coins of a given coinage might have been clipped and weighed less than other coins of the same coinage. The State could then decide a partial recoinage, that is, to cry down the coins with a weight inferior to a certain limit: they stopped being legal tender and were received at the mint at their actual weight as bullion to be recoined. Rather than bringing them to the mint, their owners might prefer to melt them fraudulently and sell the bullion in the market at the higher price. The increase in the supply of bullion then made its market price fall. Thanks to the melting of the coins – although it was legally prohibited – the State had thus a tool to diminish the depreciation of the metallic currency. In equation (6.6), the reduction of the quantity of circulating coins by crying down the most debased ones amounted to diminish the *average* rate of debasement D and consequently the maximum rate of depreciation.

The parallelism between debased coins and notes issued in excess is explicitly made in Chapter XXVII of *Principles*, with the consequence that in both cases a limitation of the quantity of the currency may sustain its value:

> While the State alone coins, there can be no limit to this charge of seignorage; for by limiting the quantity of coin, it can be raised to any conceivable value.
>
> It is on this principle that paper money circulates: the whole charge for paper money may be considered as seignorage. Though it has no intrinsic value, yet, by limiting its quantity, its value in exchange is as great as an

> equal denomination of coin, or of bullion in that coin. On the same principle, too, namely, by a limitation of its quantity, a debased coin would circulate at the value it should bear, if it were of the legal weight and fineness, and not at the value of the quantity of metal which it actually contained. In the history of the British coinage, we find, accordingly, that the currency was never depreciated in the same proportion that it was debased; the reason of which was, that it never was increased in quantity, in proportion to its diminished intrinsic value.
>
> (*Principles*; I: 353)

According to Ricardo, the limitation of the quantity of debased coins allowed to circulate (that is, as mentioned above, their partial recoinage) had historically maintained the actual depreciation of the metallic currency below its maximum rate equal to the sum of the debasement rate and of the melting cost. Nevertheless, even so contained, depreciation consequent upon debasement was harmful to a mixed monetary system of coins and convertible notes such as the one in England before 1797, for two reasons. First, as for the other causes of depreciation, an excess of the market price of gold bullion above the legal price of gold in coin made it possible to gain by arbitrage by melting the coins (although fraudulently) and exporting the bullion. Second, since the Bank of England was legally compelled to exchange its notes at par for undebased coins, it was not necessary for the arbitrager to gather in circulation the debased coins to be melted: he discounted bills for Bank notes, exchanged them at the gold window of the Bank for guineas "fresh from the mint", had them melted, sold the bullion in the market and pocketed the difference. When the Bank had to purchase bullion at a high price in the market to have it coined at the mint and replenish its reserve, it bore the loss that was the counterpart of the arbitrager's profit. The Bank then reacted by contracting its issues, with negative effects on the loan market and thus on economic activity in general. Both inconveniences – the export of bullion which dried up domestic circulation and the contraction of discounts by the Bank which disturbed the credit market – were also to be found when the depreciation of money was the outcome of an excess issue of notes and I will analyse them when discussing this question in the next chapter. When they were the consequences of debasement, the only permanent solution was its eradication through a general recoinage, with or without devaluation. There was, however, a more radical solution which was advocated by Ricardo as early as 1811, in the Appendix to the fourth edition of *High Price*: note convertibility into bullion rather than into specie, which amounted to eliminate the use of coins in circulation, and consequently their debasement. This solution will be studied in detail in Chapter 9 below.

6.4 The instability of the double standard

Ricardo constantly opposed the double standard from the Bullion Essays till his last writings. This opposition is to be found in *High Price*, in Chapter XXVII of *Principles*, and in an important letter of 19 January 1823 to Pascoe Grenfell recently discovered (see Appendix 6); it relied on two arguments. One was general and applied to any standard-based monetary system: the variability of the relative market price of gold in silver prevented a double standard from actually working and condemned the monetary system to the inconveniences of an alternating standard. The other argument was more specific to a monetary system in which part of the circulation was composed of Bank of England notes: the behaviour of the Bank could have the aggravating effect of triggering a fall in the value of money.

The variability of the relative market price of gold in silver and the alternating standard

In *High Price* Ricardo already opposed the double standard, on the ground of the unavoidable change in the effective standard that it would entail:

> No permanent*[6] measure of value can be said to exist in any nation while the circulating medium consists of two metals, because they are constantly subject to vary in value with respect to each other.
>
> (*High Price*; III: 65)

It was so because the market ratio of the price of gold to that of silver was subject to changes, as for every commodity, whereas the relative value of gold and silver in the coins was legally fixed. Whenever the market ratio fell below the legal ratio, no one would bring silver to the mint to be coined, because it was more advantageous to sell it in the market for gold coins; gold became the "*practical standard*" (as it is labelled in the letter of 19 January 1823, in Deleplace, Depoortère and Rieucau 2013: 4). The opposite occurred when the market ratio rose above the legal ratio:

> Not only would not gold be carried to the mint to be coined, but the illicit trader would melt the gold coin, and sell it as bullion for more than its nominal value in the silver coin. Thus then gold would disappear from circulation, and silver coin become the standard measure of value.
>
> (*High Price*; III: 68)

Examined by a Lords committee on 24 March 1819, Ricardo produced figures, extracted from Mushet's Tables, showing that in the 1770s and 1780s the market ratio had varied up to 15 per cent in the space of two or three years, and he concluded: "The greatest inconvenience would result in raising or lowering suddenly the value of the currency to so great an extent" (V: 427).

Therefore, although it was legally proclaimed, there could never be practically a double standard, except by chance when the market ratio happened to coincide with the legal ratio. One corollary was that, in such a monetary system, only one metal at a time could have a market price above its mint price. For example, if the market ratio was below the legal one, gold was the standard and consequently at or below its mint price, while silver was above it:

> An excess in the market above the mint price of gold or silver bullion, may, whilst the coins of both metals are legal tender, and there is no prohibition against the coinage of either metal, be caused by a variation in the relative value of those metals; but an excess of the market above the mint price proceeding from this cause will be at once perceived by its affecting only the price of one of the metals. Thus gold would be at or below, while silver was above, its mint price, or silver at or below its mint price, whilst gold was above.
>
> (*High Price*; III: 77)

According to Ricardo, this situation of a legal double standard working practically as an alternate single one operated until 1797.[7] Although the relative value of gold in silver was such that gold was *de facto* the standard, an increase in this relative value could have promoted silver as the sole standard, and this possibility of change in the standard was enough for Ricardo to reject the legal double standard. One should observe that, according to him, silver could have become the standard, in spite of the fact that it was legal tender only up to £25. As explained in *Principles*:

> [Before 1797] gold was in practice the real standard of currency. That it was so, is no where denied; but it has been contended, that it was made so by the law, which declared that silver should not be a legal tender for any debt exceeding 25*l*., unless by weight, according to the Mint standard. But this law did not prevent any debtor from paying his debt, however large its amount, in silver currency fresh from the Mint; that the debtor did not pay in this metal, was not a matter of chance, nor a matter of compulsion, but wholly the effect of choice; it did not suit him to take silver to the Mint, it did suit him to take gold thither.
>
> (*Principles*; I: 368)

In fact, silver was not prevented by its restricted legal tender from being the standard because this restriction only applied to the debased coin; since the law authorized to pay any amount "by weight, according to the Mint standard", that meant that full-bodied silver coins ("fresh from the Mint") were full legal tender in the same way as were gold coins.[8] Consequently, for silver becoming the standard, the important points were the legal possibility of paying by standard weight and the free access to the mint to obtain new silver coins, not the restricted legal tender of debased coins.

These two crucial provisions, which existed before 1797, disappeared in 1817. First "it was enacted that gold only should be a legal tender for any sum exceeding forty shillings" (ibid: 369), that is, silver was no longer legal tender above this sum, *even by standard weight*. Second, for contingent reasons (the market price of silver was then below the mint price of 5s. 2d., and the mint would have been flooded with silver bullion brought in for coinage), the royal proclamation implementing free access to the mint for silver was not issued (see Fetter 1965: 67). Both provisions reflected the secondary role devoted to silver in the monetary system: silver coins were *de facto* reduced to token currency.

After the resumption of Bank of England note convertibility into coin and at pre-war parity in 1821, this evolution was called into question by some influential persons – such as the financier Alexander Baring – who advocated a return to the double standard as a way to alleviate the deflation then experienced in England. But if the double standard was to be reintroduced, silver currency had to be again put on the same footing as the gold one. In the above-mentioned letter of 19 January 1823, Ricardo insisted on the fact that one could not avoid in that case granting again free access to the mint:

> In the present state of the law the public cannot take silver to the mint to be coined, a very proper regulation while silver performs only the office of counters or tokens, but once make it the standard metal, & the mint must be open to the Bank, & the public.
>
> (in Deleplace, Depoortère and Rieucau 2013: 4)

This reintroduction also implied the possibility of paying any sum in full-bodied silver coins to be enacted again (unrestricted legal tender). It seemed therefore that, if the legal double standard was to be reintroduced, the British monetary system would be put again in the state ruling before 1797, with the same inconveniences, namely the practical possibility of a change of standard in the course of time. According to Ricardo, however, the situation could be even worse, because of the issuing behaviour of the Bank of England.

The behaviour of the Bank of England and the prospective fall in the value of money

As mentioned in Chapter 2 above, the question of the double standard was raised in Parliament in 1819 during the debates on the resumption of convertibility of the Bank of England note. It was suggested to couple Ricardo's proposal for convertibility into bullion with a double standard.[9] Being examined on 24 March 1819 by a Lords' committee, Ricardo was asked to give his opinion about the Bank of England having the choice of paying its notes either in gold bullion or in silver bullion, at a fixed ratio between them. He answered:

> The greatest inconvenience would result from such a provision. I consider it a great improvement having established one of the metals as the standard for money. The Bank and all other debtors would naturally pay their debts in the metal which could at the time be most cheaply purchased, and at certain fixed periods the currency might be suddenly increased or lowered in value, in proportion to the variation in the relative value of the two metals from one of these periods to the other.
>
> (V: 426)

Ricardo thus worried about the Bank having the power of changing the standard at will. The double-standard proposal resurfaced in 1821 when convertibility of the Bank of England note into coin and at pre-war parity was resumed, and Ricardo opposed it again publicly in a speech in Parliament on 19 March 1821:

> The attempt to procure the best possible standard had been characterized by his hon. friend [Baring] as a piece of coxcombry to which he attached no value; but, in a question of finance, if we could get a better system than our neighbours, we were surely justified in adopting it. He [Ricardo] undoubtedly did wish for a better system, and it was for that reason that he wished to see one metal adopted as a standard of currency, and the system of two metals rejected.
>
> (V: 95–6)

When in 1823 the causes of the economic depression were again hotly debated, Ricardo deepened his argument against the double standard in a letter to Pascoe Grenfell (for more details, see Deleplace, Depoortère and Rieucau 2013). This time Ricardo worried about the Bank having the power of degrading the value of money at will, because of a recent new provision of the currency system: the seignorage on the silver coin.

After the Silver coinage Act adopted by Parliament in 1816 and proclaimed in 1817, the legal double-standard system, if again implemented, would not work in the same way as the pre-1797 one did. Indeed it would retain from the latter its general inconveniences but it would add a specific difficulty:

> Since the new act for regulating the silver coinage, the execution of the plan will not be found so easy as the friends to it suppose. Formerly, when we had the two standards we were liable to the inconveniences of changing from one to the other, accordingly as one or the other of the metals became the cheapest medium whereby to discharge a debt, but whichever metal was for the time the practical standard that metal could not be under the mint price, whilst the other was always above it.– Now, however, with a seignorage on the silver currency, nothing is to prevent the price of silver from rising to 5/6 an ounce whilst it is the standard metal.
>
> (in Deleplace, Depoortère and Rieucau 2013: 4)

As seen above, in the pre-1797 legal double-standard system (that is *without* seignorage), one metal only (whichever it was, gold or silver) could have a market price above its mint price: the one which was *not* the "*practical standard*" at the time. This had not more monetary consequence than for any ordinary commodity, since the currency was then attached to *the other* metal, which was at its mint price. With seignorage, one metal could have a market price above its mint price *and remain the practical standard*; therefore this rise did have a monetary consequence: a fall in the value of money. In the present circumstances that metal was silver, because since 1817 the silver coin bore a seignorage. There laid, according to Ricardo, the novelty of the new project of legal double-standard. The following question thus arises: Why did the existence of a seignorage on the silver coin – which Ricardo considered as a favourable provision in itself (see Section 6.1 above) – add a new inconvenience – no less than a 10 per cent fall in the value of the pound – to an already objectionable double-standard system? In other words, with a seignorage on the silver coin, why might the market price of silver rise up to 5s. 6d., signalling a fall of 10 per cent in the value of the pound, measured in this restored standard?

The answer is not straightforward. When Ricardo's correspondent, Pascoe Grenfell, transmitted his letter to Lord Grenville, he wrote:

> Ricardo seems to me to assume, that if that alteration [the double standard] takes place, the *Mint* price of Silver will be at the present *current* value of the Tokens – viz 66 – I take it for granted, however, that if we are to be implicated with this alteration, the Mint price – as standard will not exceed its old rate of 62.
>
> (ibid: 22; Grenfell's emphasis)

Obviously, Grenfell did not understand Ricardo's argument: it is the *market* price of silver – not its mint price – which Ricardo assumed to rise up to 66 pence (5s. 6d.), that is, the appropriate measure of the *current* value of the pound – not its legal one – expressed in this standard. But why such a rise? It is interesting to notice that, in his speech of 8 February 1821 when he already opposed Baring's double-standard proposal, Ricardo himself had mentioned 62 pence (5s. 2d.) as the market price of silver which would result from that proposal:

> With respect to his hon. friend's [Baring] recommendation of a double tender, it was obvious, that if that recommendation were adopted, the Bank [of England], although it seldom saw its own interest, would be likely to realise a considerable sum by the purchase of silver at its present reduced price of 4*s*. 11*d*. an ounce. But as this purchase would serve to raise silver to the Mint price of 5*s*. 2*d*. and comparatively to advance the price of gold, the consequence of which would be to drive gold out of the country, this was, among other reasons, an argument with him for resisting his hon. friend's doctrine.
>
> (V: 77–8)

Two years later, in his letter to Grenfell of 19 January 1823, Ricardo mentioned 5s. 6d. – instead of 5s. 2d. – as the prospective market price of silver resulting from the introduction of a double standard. This new figure strengthened his argument against the proposal, since the corresponding fall in the value of the pound would be 10 per cent instead of 5 per cent. How can this change be explained? The answer was in the letter itself:

> It is true that no one would carry silver to be coined when its price rose to 5/2, and therefore if the mint were the only channel by which additions could be

> made to the circulation the price of silver would probably seldom be above 5/2, (unless there were to be a great fall in the relative value of gold), but as these additions can be made by the Bank of England's increasing the paper circulation, it is quite possible that if the new project be adopted the value of new money may fall in the proportion of 5/6 to 4/11½, or 10 pc.[t].
>
> (in Deleplace, Depoortère and Rieucau 2013: 4–5)

Let me present the argument in detail. One should look at this question from the point of view of interest. As long as the market price of an ounce of standard silver bullion was below 5s. 2d. (the mint price), it was in the interest of its owner to bring it to the mint to have it coined, rather than to sell it in the market. But this stopped when a rising market price of silver reached the mint price. In a system of pure metallic circulation ("if the mint were the only channel by which additions could be made to the circulation"), this would put a check on any additional amount of silver coins, and consequently, according to Ricardo's doctrine linking the value of the currency to its quantity, would prevent any further increase in the market price of silver: "the price of silver would probably seldom be above 5/2". In this hypothetical case there was however a restriction: "(unless there were to be a great fall in the relative value of gold)". It was the consequence of the general inconvenience of a double standard: a sharp decline in the relative value of gold in terms of silver would bring it below the ratio of their mint prices; silver would cease being a standard, gold alone playing that role, and, as seen above, the market price of silver could rise above its mint price. But silver being no longer a standard, this rise did not mean a depreciation of the currency: no such depreciation could therefore occur in a hypothetical pure metallic circulation.[10]

Now, what about the case of a mixed circulation of coins of both metals and of notes convertible in specie ("as these additions can be made by the Bank of England's increasing the paper circulation")? There the seignorage came into play: as long as the market price of an ounce of standard silver had not reached 5s. 6d. (the current legal value of the silver coin), the Bank of England could not lose in paying its notes in silver specie, as it was its interest to do so (like any debtor) whenever silver was the "practical standard". As a consequence, the Bank could expand its issues (and would do it because issuing notes by discounting bills was its way of earning profit) until that expansion depreciated the currency and raised the market price of silver to 5s. 6d. And this would occur "whilst it [silver] is the standard metal" by which the value of the currency was reckoned. At a time when silver was rated 4s. 11½d. in the market,[11] this rise in price up to 5s. 6d. implied a fall in the value of the currency by 10 per cent: "it is quite possible that if the new project be adopted the value of new money may fall in the proportion of 5/6 to 4/11½, or 10 pc.[t]".

Could the market price of silver rise higher than 5s. 6d.? Nothing could prevent the Bank from increasing further its issues. But it would be at its own expense: above that level, it was the interest of any arbitrager to cash notes for silver coins at the Bank at 5s. 6d., to melt them down and to sell the bullion back to the Bank (obliged to buy it in order to replenish its cash reserves) at a higher market price.

These losses would soon lead the Bank to reduce its issues, and that prevented the market price from rising above 5s. 6d.:

> Till it rises above 5/6, it will not be advantageous to melt the coin, and we all know that it is the melting pot only which keeps all currency in a wholesome state.
>
> (ibid: 4)

The argument contained in the letter of 19 January 1823 was complex (so complex that his correspondent Grenfell did not catch it). In his 1821 speech against Baring's double-standard proposal, Ricardo had explained the rise in price up to 5s. 2d. by the *arbitrage* behaviour of the Bank of England: its purchases of silver for profit pushed the market price of that metal up to the mint price. Now in the letter Ricardo explained the rise in price up to 5s. 6d. by the *issuing* behaviour of the Bank of England: its increased note issue would push the market price of silver as standard up to the current legal price of silver in coin.

Such a pernicious influence of the Bank on the value of the currency, in relation to the existence of a seignorage on the silver coin, had already been mentioned by Ricardo when he had been examined on 19 March 1819 by the committee on the resumption of cash payments. The double standard was not then the question but the seignorage itself, and I mentioned earlier that Ricardo was favourable to it. He nevertheless observed that "a coin with a seignorage has also its inconveniences" (V: 402): it gave the opportunity to the Bank of England of changing the value of the currency,[12] a recurrent complaint by him.[13] In the letter to Grenfell Ricardo was more specific: the combination of a bad monetary system (the double-standard one), of a good provision (the seignorage on the silver coin), and of the power given to the Bank to increase at will the circulation, might lead to a fall in the value of the currency.

As seen above, Ricardo had frequently mentioned the variability in the value of money due to the double standard as a consequence of a change in the relative value of gold to silver in the market, not of the issuing behaviour of the Bank of England. He did publicly mention this behaviour as a source of instability in his defence of the seignorage on the silver coin, not his critique of the double standard per se. He also mentioned publicly that the double standard would lead to a rise in the market price of silver in relation to an arbitrage behaviour of the Bank of England, not its issuing one. Here, in an argument on the variability of the value of money, Ricardo linked the double standard, the seignorage on the silver coin, and the issuing behaviour of the Bank of England.

In 1823 Ricardo's critique of the double standard in relation with the behaviour of the Bank of England had also political implications, as testified by the end of the letter to Grenfell:

> The projected change [in favour of the double standard] is neither more nor less as Lord Grenville has justly stated it, but to do indirectly what Parliament, tho so much urged, has refused to do directly.
>
> (in Deleplace, Depoortère and Rieucau 2013: 5)

What had Parliament "*refused to do*"? By imposing the return to the pre-1797 price of £3. 17s. 10½d. for an ounce of standard gold, Parliament had refused in 1819 to devaluate the sterling. If Ricardo's forecast was right, the "*projected change*" would be nothing else but a disguised way of having the currency fall in value. For him, such a change was not the right answer to the problems of the time: as witnessed by his interventions in Parliament in 1822–1823, he argued that the distress of the country had its origin neither in the existence of a gold standard nor in the level of the legal price of gold. As a consequence he could not accept an alleged remedy which would have been the reintroduction of a double standard and the falling value of the currency.

Ricardo's discussion of the double standard is only one of the many examples of his recurrent critique of the Bank's pernicious influence on the value of money. From the Bullion Essays in 1809–1811 to the *Plan for a National Bank* in 1823, he regularly complained about "the facility with which the state has armed the Bank with so formidable a prerogative" (*Proposals*, IV: 69; *Principles*, I: 360). In the above-quoted letter to Horner of 5 February 1810 the third and main cause of depreciation of money was "A superabundance of paper circulation." At that time Ricardo was concerned with the excess of inconvertible Bank of England notes. This did not mean that depreciation was impossible when notes were convertible; it was, however, constrained between narrow limits, while depreciation under inconvertibility had no limit. The regulation of the quantity of convertible notes by the standard is the object of the next chapter.

Appendix 6: A letter on the double standard of money

This letter was discovered in 2010 by Christophe Depoortère and myself amongst Lord Grenville's papers deposited at the British Library. It was published for the first time in 2013 (for its description, historical context and analytical content, see Deleplace, Depoortère and Rieucau 2013). It had been written by Ricardo on 19 January 1823 to his friend and Member of Parliament Pascoe Grenfell (1761–1838), at a time when there were rumours of restoring the double standard (gold and silver), legally abandoned since 1816. These rumours were mentioned by Ricardo in a subsequent letter to Hutches Trower of 30 January 1823:

> There has been a talk, I believe nothing more, amongst ministers about restoring the two standards, but I am assured all thoughts of it are relinquished.
>
> (IX: 270)

The letter to Grenfell not only restates Ricardo's arguments against the double standard but also deals with the more general question of the variability of the value of money, as it is affected by the existence of seignorage and by the issuing behaviour of the Bank of England. The complex links between these various monetary aspects are here analysed by Ricardo in a compact form that may not be found elsewhere in his writings.

The transcript in full of the letter reads as follows:

Widcomb, Bath,
19 Jan.[y] 1823

My Dear Grenfell

If I knew how to write like Lord Grenville I should express myself just as he has done on the proposed plan of again introducing the two standards. – I agree with every word that Lord Grenville has written on this subject. Since the new act for regulating the silver coinage, the execution of the plan will not be found so easy as the friends to it suppose. Formerly, when we had the two standards we were liable to the inconveniences of changing from one to the other, accordingly as one or the other of the metals became the cheapest medium whereby to discharge a debt, but whichever metal was for the time the practical standard that metal could not be under the mint price, whilst the other was always above it. – Now, however, with a seignorage on the silver currency, nothing is to prevent the price of silver from rising to 5s. 6d. an ounce whilst it is the standard metal. Till it rises above 5s. 6d., it will not be advantageous to melt the coin, and we all know that it is the melting pot only which keeps all currency in a wholesome state. In the present state of the law the public cannot take silver to the mint to be coined, a very proper regulation while silver performs only the office of counters or tokens, but once make it the standard metal, & the mint must be open to the Bank, & the public.

It is true that no one would carry silver to be coined when its price rose to 5s. 2d., and therefore if the mint were the only channel by which additions could be made to the circulation the price of silver would probably seldom be above 5s. 2d., (unless there were to be a great fall in the relative value of gold), but as these additions can be made by the Bank of England's increasing the paper circulation, it is quite possible that if the new project be adopted the value of new money may fall in the proportion of 5s. 6d. to 4s.11½d., or 10 pc.[t].

I believe that we now possess the best system of currency that has ever been established in any country, & I shall very much regret its being interfered with. It would under our present circumstances be wrong I think to make any alteration in our system even if it could be shewn to be one strictly accordant to sound principles, because after what has occurred all changes are apt to weaken our reliance on the fixedness of the currency, without which it must be in an unsatisfactory state: How much stronger is this objection against the projected change, which is neither more nor less as Lord Grenville has justly stated it, but to do indirectly what Parliament, tho so much urged, has refused to do directly. – I shall be sorry if Huskisson lends himself to such a scheme – if he does, he will lose a little of that respect which his conduct on the subject of the currency has hitherto entitled him to.

I know of no book to which Lord Grenville could refer for the information he wants.

I am passing a fortnight with my daughter M[rs]. Clutterbuck & her husband, at Widcomb. I have visited successively, for the same period, my son, & my daughter, M[rs]. Austin. My reception from them all has been such as to make me think these 6 weeks the happiest period of my life – there has not been the least alloy to my satisfaction at witnessing their happiness and amiable qualities.

M[rs]. Ricardo & my daughters are thankful to you & your daughters for your kind remembrance, they beg you all to accept their best wishes.

Ever my dear Grenfell –

Y[rs]. truly
David Ricardo

I shall be in London on the 1st of feb.[ry]. I agree with you in your opinion of the situation of the country.

Notes

1 In this letter to McCulloch, the "two causes" of "the relative value of commodities" — in contrast with the "two causes" of their (money) "prices" mentioned in the letter to Malthus — were pointed out by Ricardo as follows:

> I sometimes think that if I were to write the chapter on value again which is in my book, I should acknowledge that the relative value of commodities was regulated by two causes instead of by one, namely, by the relative quantity of labour necessary to produce the commodities in question, and by the rate of profit for the time that the capital remained dormant, and until the commodities were brought to market. (VIII: 194)

2 See the quotation from *Principles* (I: 48–9) given in Chapter 3 above. See also in the pamphlet *Funding System*, published in 1820: "A real rise of wages is necessarily followed by a real fall of profits" (IV: 179).

3 It may be observed that in this quotation "the improvement of machinery in manufactures" affected the price of corn indirectly, through the fall in the value of money consequent upon "the influx of money". This raises the question of the monetary consequences of an increase in the export of manufactured goods. See Chapter 8 below.

4 For the effect of taxation, see Appendix 3 above.

5 One of the few quotations from Steuart to be found in Ricardo's writings immediately follows the latter's statement that "the exchange will, therefore, be a tolerably accurate criterion by which we may judge of the debasement of the currency, proceeding either from a clipped coinage, or a depreciated paper-money" (*High Price*; III: 72). Ricardo then quoted Steuart on the exchange rate which allowed discovering the variations in the value of the pound sterling. On Steuart's monetary analysis, see Cartelier (2015) and Deleplace (2015d), and on his political economy Longhitano (2015).

6 The asterisk refers to a footnote by Ricardo which begins so: "Strictly speaking, there can be no permanent measure of value. A measure of value should itself be invariable; but this is not the case with either gold or silver, they being subject to fluctuations as well as other commodities" (III: 65). Ricardo had here in mind the theoretical problem of the invariable measure of value, which would upset him until the end of his life (see Chapter 3 above).

7 The legal double standard continued after 1797, but the suspension of cash payments of notes changed completely the working of the monetary system. As mentioned by Ricardo in 1809 "when the prices of both the metals are above the mint prices it is proof

conclusive of bank notes being at a discount" (III: 43), in contrast with the pre-1797 situation when the market price of only one metal could be above the mint price.

8 That restriction did not prevent the double standard from having legally existed before 1797; see *Reply to Bosanquet* (III: 177), and Ricardo's speech in Parliament of 9 April 1821 (V: 106).

9 Such a proposal would again be made by Alfred Marshall in 1887; see Deleplace (2013b).

10 Unless the circulating coins were debased. But this is not the point here: only full-bodied coins are considered.

11 According to *The Course of Exchange*, the market price of silver bullion was quoted continuously at this rate from 19 November 1822 till 7 January 1823, after which date it was quoted at 4s. 11¼d.; see Boyer-Xambeu, Deleplace and Gillard (1995: 272–3).

12 Ricardo then declared:

> The bank have the undisputed power of increasing the quantity of currency, and thereby of diminishing its value to its intrinsic worth. If silver, for example, were now the standard of our currency, and therefore a legal tender to any amount, the bank might issue their paper till they raised the price of silver bullion to 5s 6d per ounce, (the current value of the silver coin) without inconvenience to themselves; they might then reduce their issues, till silver fell to 5s 2d; and thus they might alternately raise and lower the price of silver, between the limits of 5s 6d and 5s 2d as often as to them it might appear expedient. If there were no seignorage on the silver coin, and it were immediately exchangeable for silver bullion on the demand of the holder of bullion, it is evident that the price of silver would not rise above, nor fall below 5s 2d the mint price.
>
> (V: 402)

13 In *Principles* Ricardo developed the same argument:

> It must, however, be remarked, that in a country where a paper currency is established, although the issuers of such paper should be liable to pay it in specie on the demand of the holder, still, both their notes and the coin might be depreciated to the full amount of the seignorage on that coin, which is alone the legal tender, before the check [melting], which limits the circulation of paper, would operate.
>
> (I: 372)

7 The regulation of the quantity of convertible notes by the standard

The only use of a standard is to regulate the quantity, and by the quantity the value of a currency.

(*Proposals*; IV: 59)

According to Ricardo in his letter to Francis Horner of 5 February 1810, the third cause of depreciation of money was "a superabundance of paper circulation" (VI: 2). By "superabundance" Ricardo meant "that quantity of paper money which could not by any means be kept in circulation if it were immediately exchangeable for specie on demand", as was expected in a discussion of the consequences of inconvertibility. This implied that under convertibility paper money could not be permanently in excess. The reason for that would be a matter of debates, not only during the Bullion Controversy but also long after the resumption of convertibility, including during the controversy in the 1840s between the Currency School and the Banking School. Some authors contended that an excess issue of notes was absorbed in circulation, but this absorption triggered a corrective process that eliminated the excess. Others contended that, if notes were issued through the discounting of "real bills", an excess could not even occur.

Ricardo maintained that, however cautious the Bank of England could be in discounting bills for *bona fide* transactions, this did not prevent the aggregate quantity of money from being in excess, under inconvertibility and convertibility as well. Contrary to what happened under inconvertibility, however, depreciation was only temporary when notes were convertible into the standard (gold bullion), even if convertibility was indirect – notes being converted into coin with a view to melting the coin into bullion. During the transition, the economy suffered inconveniences and Ricardo proposed the Ingot Plan as a way to get rid of them.

The present chapter analyses how, according to Ricardo, the value of money adjusts to a change in the quantity issued of convertible notes, first by departing from the value of the standard (depreciation or appreciation), then by being brought back to it. This requires introducing the quantity of money into the Money–Standard Equation formulated in Chapter 4 above (Section 7.1). Two cases of self-adjusting process are then studied, in response to an increase in the "wants of commerce" (Section 7.2) or in the discretionary note issue (Section 7.3). An important consequence ensues: contrary to what is generally found in the literature, Ricardo's monetary theory was *not* a quantity theory of money (Section 7.4). I will then ask whether this theory applies to money without a standard (Section 7.5), before concluding on the specificity of the market for gold bullion (Section 7.6).

With the exception of Section 7.5, this chapter considers a mixed monetary system of undebased coins and Bank of England notes convertible into coin – like that ruling in England before 1797 and from 1821 onwards – leaving to Chapter 9 below the analysis of Ricardo's proposals for a circulation exclusively composed of notes convertible into bullion (the Ingot Plan) and for a mixed monetary system of undebased coins and notes convertible into coin but issued by a public bank (the Plan for a national bank).

7.1 The Money–Standard Equation and the quantity of money

As emphasised in Chapter 3 above, the condition of conformity of money to the standard is expressed by the equality between the value of money and the value of the standard (both in terms of all commodities except the standard), given the legal price of the standard:

$$V_M{}^* = \frac{1}{\overline{P_{GC}}} V_G \tag{3.8}$$

with $V_M{}^*$ the value of money conforming to the standard, V_G the value of gold bullion (the standard of money), and $\overline{P_{GC}}$ the legal price of gold in coin.

Let me call M^* the conformable quantity of money (measured in pounds) – that is, the quantity consistent with the condition of conformity (3.8) – and M the actual quantity of money, each unit of M circulating at a value V_M to which the condition (3.5) of coherence of the price system applies:

$$V_M = \frac{V_G}{P_G} \tag{3.5}$$

with P_G the market price of gold bullion. Since M circulates the same aggregate value of commodities as M^*, the following equality applies:

$$M^* V_M^* = M\ V_M \tag{7.1}$$

Replacing $V_M{}^*$ and V_M in (7.1) by their respective values in (3.8) and (3.5) gives:

$$\frac{M}{M^*} = \frac{P_G}{\overline{P_{GC}}} \tag{7.2}$$

When the actual quantity of money is in excess (deficient) relative to the quantity that fulfils the condition of conformity of money to the standard, money is depreciated (appreciated) in proportion to the excess (deficiency), as testified by the market price of gold bullion being above (below) the legal price of gold in coin. It should be observed that equation (7.2) is a direct consequence of: (a) the normative condition (3.8) of conformity of money to the standard; (b) the normative condition (3.5) of coherence of the price system; and (c) Ricardo's contention (7.1) that whatever the quantity of money issued it was absorbed in circulation ("a circulation can never be so abundant as to overflow"; *Principles*; I: 352). Equation (7.2) does *not* result from a description of the working of the market for the standard (gold bullion) in the case of convertible notes (more on this point in the Afterword of the present book).

With $\overline{P_{GC}}$ remaining unchanged, one derives from (7.2) the following relation:

$$\frac{\Delta P_G}{P_G} = \frac{\Delta M}{M} - \frac{\Delta M^*}{M^*} \tag{7.3}$$

with $\Delta P_G / P_G$ the rate of change of the market price of gold bullion, $\Delta M / M$ and $\Delta M^* / M^*$ the rates of change of respectively the actual and the conformable quantities of money.

Let me recall the Money–Standard Equation in simplified form analysed in Chapter 4:

$$\frac{\Delta V_M}{V_M} = \frac{\Delta V_G}{V_G} - \frac{\Delta P_G}{P_G} \tag{4.8}$$

From (7.3) and (4.8) one obtains:

$$\frac{\Delta V_M}{V_M} = \frac{\Delta V_G}{V_G} - \left[\frac{\Delta M}{M} - \frac{\Delta M^*}{M^*}\right] \tag{7.4}$$

Equation (7.4) reformulates the Money–Standard Equation to take into account how a change in the aggregate quantity of money affects the market price of gold bullion. The two causes of change in the value of money (a change in the value of the standard and a change in its market price), distinguished in Chapter 4 above, now become a change in the value of the standard (with a positive sign) and the difference between the rates of change in the actual and the conformable quantities of money (with a negative sign). In Chapter 5, I analysed how an exogenous change in the value of gold bullion V_G – such as the discovery of a new mine in a foreign gold-producing country or an unusual demand from the bank of issue in the domestic gold-importing country – caused a change in the domestic value of money. As for the second cause of change in the value of money, namely the difference between the rates of change in the actual and the conformable quantities of money, Ricardo exposed it in *Proposals*:

> The value of money then does not wholly depend upon its absolute quantity, but on its quantity relatively to the payments which it has to accomplish; and the same effects would follow from either of two causes – from increasing the uses for money one tenth – or from diminishing its quantity one tenth; for, in either case, its value would rise one tenth.
>
> (*Proposals*; IV: 56)

In this example, $\Delta V_M / V_M = + 0.1$ because either $\Delta M^* / M^* = + 0.1$ or $\Delta M / M = -0.1$.

I will now examine how, according to Ricardo, the value of money adjusts to a change either in the conformable quantity of money M^*, following a change in the "wants of commerce", or in its actual quantity M, consequent upon a discretionary change in the note issue. In what follows, I will consequently assume that no exogenous variation in the value of gold bullion occurs.

7.2 The adjustment of the value of money to an increase in the "wants of commerce"

The notion of wants of commerce

The expression "wants of commerce" was used in the Appendix to the fourth edition of *High Price* where Ricardo outlined his Ingot Plan:

> On just principles [of Ricardo's plan] we should possess the most economical and the most invariable currency in the world. [...] The amount of the circulation would be adjusted to the wants of commerce with the greatest precision.
>
> (*High Price*; III: 127)

Developing this plan in *Proposals*, Ricardo again argued that the quantity of notes could be endogenously adjusted to the needs of the circulation in a more secure and cheaper way than with coins:

> Amongst the advantages of a paper over a metallic circulation, may be reckoned, as not the least, the facility with which it may be altered in quantity, as the wants of commerce and temporary circumstances may require: enabling the desirable object of keeping money at an uniform value to be, as far as it is otherwise practicable, securely and cheaply attained.
>
> (*Proposals*; IV: 55)

The same expression had been introduced by Ricardo in *Reply to Bosanquet* when he criticised the view (later called the Real Bills doctrine in the literature) according to which notes could not be issued in excess as long as they were put into circulation by discounting bills generated in actual transactions:

> The refusal to discount any bills but those for *bona fide* transactions would be as little effectual in limiting the circulation; because, though the directors should have the means of distinguishing such bills, which can by no means be allowed, a greater portion of paper currency might be called into circulation, not than the wants of commerce could employ, but greater than what could remain in the channel of currency without depreciation.
>
> (*Reply to Bosanquet*; III: 219)

Ricardo quoted Bosanquet who supposed that the Bullion Report had used "the term excess of currency [...] in the sense in which it is used by Dr. Smith, as denoting a quantity greater than the circulation of the country can easily absorb or employ" (ibid: 228), and he objected:

> This is not the sense in which I consider the Committee to use the word *excess*. In that sense there can be no excess whilst the Bank does not pay in specie, because the commerce of the country can easily employ and absorb any sum which the Bank may send into circulation. It is from so understanding the word excess that Mr. Bosanquet thinks the circulation cannot be excessive, because the commerce of the country could not easily employ it. In proportion as the pound sterling becomes depreciated will the want of the nominal amount of pounds increase, and no part of the larger sum will be excessive, more than the smaller sum was before. By excess, then, the Committee must mean the difference in amount of circulation between the sum actually employed, and that sum which would be employed if the pound sterling were to regain its bullion value. This is a distinction of more consequence than at first sight appears, and Mr. Bosanquet was well aware that it was in this sense that it was used by me.
>
> (ibid: 228–9; Ricardo's emphasis)

The wants of commerce consequently not only depended on the aggregate value of the commodities to be circulated but also on the value of the currency which circulated it. As Ricardo declared when on 4 March 1819 he was examined by the Commons' Committee on the Resumption of Cash Payments:

> I consider, in all cases, that the quantity of circulation must depend upon its value, and the quantity of business which it has to perform.
>
> (V: 372–3)

Such contention was consistent with what he had written in *Principles*:

> A circulation can never be so abundant as to overflow; for by diminishing its value, in the same proportion you will increase its quantity, and by increasing its value, diminish its quantity.
>
> (I: 352)

If the currency was depreciated, "the want of the nominal amount of pounds increase[d]", and all the notes issued were absorbed by circulation:

> If money be but depreciated sufficiently, there is no amount which may not be absorbed.
>
> (*Reply to Bosanquet*; III: 217)

In other words, notes could be in excess while being wanted by commerce and absorbed by circulation, because "commerce is insatiable in its demands" for currency (ibid: 215) when the latter is depreciated:

> When we speak, therefore, of an excess of bank-notes, we mean that portion of the amount of the issues of the Bank, which can now circulate, but could not, if the currency were of its bullion value.
>
> (ibid: 230)

The quantity of money which would circulate "if the currency were of its bullion value" is what I have called the conformable quantity of money (M^*) – that is, the quantity consistent with the condition (3.8) of conformity of money to the standard. In what follows, an increase in the "wants of commerce" will be understood as requiring a positive $\Delta M^*/M^*$ consistent with the maintenance of the equality between the value of money and the value of bullion (in other words the absence of depreciation or appreciation).

It should be observed that for Ricardo, even supposing its value unchanged, the quantity of money required to circulate a given aggregate value of commodities did not remain constant, since it depended on the "state of credit". Being examined on 24 March 1819 by a Lords' Committee, he observed:

> One of the causes which operate on the value and the quantity of currency, I have omitted to mention, namely, the varying state of credit, which considerably affects the quantity necessary to perform the same business.
>
> (V: 419)

To the question "Do you conceive that the amount of trade, capital, and revenue, and the amount of currency required, must necessarily bear any fixed ratio or proportion to each other?", Ricardo answered:

> Certainly not; I think the proportion must depend on the economy in the use of money, which again must depend on the state of credit at the time.
>
> (ibid: 420)

Already in *High Price*, Ricardo had observed that this "proportion" varied across countries, and in the same country according to "the degree of confidence":

> The value of the circulating medium of every country bears some proportion to the value of the commodities which it circulates. In some countries this proportion is much greater than in others, and varies, on some occasions,

> in the same country. It depends upon the rapidity of circulation, upon the degree of confidence and credit existing between traders, and above all, on the judicious operations of banking. In England so many means of economizing the use of circulating medium have been adopted, that its value, compared with the value of the commodities which it circulates, is probably (during a period of confidence*) reduced to as small a proportion as is practicable. (*High Price*; III: 90) [The footnote* reads: "In the following observations, I wish it to be understood, as supposing always the same degree of confidence and credit to exist."]

Ricardo thus abstracted from these variations in order to determine the quantity of money required by the wants of commerce. Let me call k this supposedly constant "proportion" which "the value of the circulating medium [...] bears [...] to the value of the commodities which it circulates", and Y the latter aggregate value, as given by the "real" system of exchangeable values and natural quantities. By definition, the conformable state is such that:

$$M^* V_M{}^* = kY \tag{7.5}$$

In Chapter 3 above, the condition of conformity of money to the standard read:

$$V_M{}^* = \frac{1}{\overline{P_{GC}}} V_G \tag{3.8}$$

In other words, the value of money in the conformable state is independent of its quantity: given the definition of the monetary unit in terms of the standard – hence fixing $\overline{P_{GC}}$ – it only depends on the value of the standard. Combining (7.5) with (3.8) gives the level of the conformable quantity of money M^*, that is, the quantity of money consistent with the condition of conformity:

$$M^* = k\,\overline{P_{GC}}\,\frac{Y}{V_G} \tag{7.6}$$

The conformable quantity of money M^* is thus endogenously determined: it is an increasing function of the aggregate value Y of the commodities to be circulated and a decreasing function of the value V_G of the standard. When the conformable state is maintained through time, one derives from (3.8) that the value of money only varies positively with the value of the standard:

$$\frac{\Delta V_{M^*}}{V_{M^*}} = \frac{\Delta V_G}{V_G} \tag{7.7}$$

Since by definition the maintenance of the conformable state implies $\Delta M / M = \Delta M^* / M^*$, one checks that this result is also obtained by making $[\Delta M / M - \Delta M^* / M^*] = 0$ in (7.4). As for the conformable quantity of money, one derives from (7.6) that it varies positively with the aggregate value of commodities and inversely with the value of the standard:

$$\frac{\Delta M^*}{M^*} = \frac{\Delta Y}{Y} - \frac{\Delta V_G}{V_G} \tag{7.8}$$

Let me now consider the following case: starting from a situation in which money conformed to the standard, the wants of commerce increased, while the actual quantity of money remained the same ($\Delta M^* / M^* > 0$; $\Delta M / M = 0$, so that according to (7.3) $\Delta P_G / P_G < 0$). The symmetrical case of a reduction in the wants of commerce implied an excess quantity of money, if the note issue was not contracted in proportion ($\Delta M^* / M^* < 0$; $\Delta M / M = 0$, so that $\Delta P_G / P_G > 0$). The adjustment was thus the same as in the case of a discretionary increase in the note issue, while the wants of commerce remained unaltered ($\Delta M^* / M^* = 0$; $\Delta M / M > 0$, so that $\Delta P_G / P_G > 0$), and it will be analysed in Section 7.3 below.

An endogenous adjustment

I recall that the adjustment is analysed under the assumption that no exogenous variation in the value V_G of gold bullion occurs. As a consequence, (7.7) gives $\Delta V_M^* / V_M^* = 0$ and (7.8) $\Delta M^* / M^* = \Delta Y / Y$: the conformable quantity of money rises at the same rate as the aggregate value of commodities. In the absence of any change in the actual quantity of money ($\Delta M / M = 0$), equations (7.4) and (7.8) give:

$$\frac{\Delta V_M}{V_M} = \frac{\Delta M^*}{M^*} = \frac{\Delta Y}{Y} \tag{7.9}$$

The unchanged actual quantity of money M circulates a greater aggregate value of commodities Y because the actual value V_M of each unit of money increases in the same proportion. This case was described by Ricardo in *Proposals* as follows:

> When the number of transactions increase in any country from its increasing opulence and industry – bullion remaining at the same value, and the economy in the use of money also continuing unaltered – the value of money will rise on account of the increased use which will be made of it, and will continue permanently above the value of bullion, unless the quantity be increased, either by the addition of paper, or by procuring bullion to be coined into money. There will be more commodities bought and sold, but at lower

prices; so that the same money will still be adequate to the increased number of transactions, by passing in each transaction at a higher value.

(*Proposals*; IV: 56)

Since $\Delta V_M^* / V_M^* = 0$, the actual value of money V_M rose above its conformable level V_M^* in the same proportion as the wants of commerce increased. It has been shown in Chapter 3 that for Ricardo the condition of conformity of money to the standard could be written in value (equation (3.8)) or in price (equation (3.9) so that $V_M > V_M^*$ is identical with $P_G < \overline{P_{GC}}$: the market price of gold bullion is below the legal price of gold in coin. The sequence of events was thus as follows. The increase in the aggregate value of commodities Y required an increase in the conformable quantity of money M^* which was not immediately met by an increase in the actual quantity of money M. According to (7.3) the market price of gold bullion P_G fell below the legal price of gold in coin $\overline{P_{GC}}$ and, according indifferently to (4.8) or (7.4), this raised the actual value of money V_M above its conformable level V_M^*. In other words, all prices $P_{i \neq G}$ fell in the same proportion as P_G.

The next step was described by Ricardo supposing that "the increase in the circulation were supplied by means of coins" (ibid: 57). With P_G below $\overline{P_{GC}}$, a profit by arbitrage could be made by purchasing gold bullion in the market and having it coined at the mint:

> To say that money is more valuable than bullion or the standard, is to say that bullion is selling in the market under the mint price. It can therefore be purchased, coined, and issued as money, with a profit equal to the difference between the market and mint prices. The mint price of gold is 3*l.* 17*s.* 10½*d.* If, from increasing opulence, more commodities came to be bought and sold, the first effect would be that the value of money would rise. Instead of 3*l.* 17*s.* 10½*d.* of coined money being equal in value to an ounce of gold, 3*l.* 15*s.* 0*d.* might be equal to that value; and therefore a profit of 2*s.* 10½*d.* might be made on every ounce of gold that was carried to the mint to be coined.
>
> (ibid)

An endogenous increase in the quantity of money ended thus the first stage of the adjustment. The quotation goes on:

> This profit, however, could not long continue; for the quantity of money which, by these means, would be added to the circulation, would sink its value, whilst the diminishing quantity of bullion in the market would also tend to raise the value of bullion to that of coin: from one or both these causes a perfect equality in their value could not fail to be soon restored.
>
> (ibid)

The increase in the quantity of money in circulation ($\Delta M / M > 0$) raised the market price of gold bullion ($\Delta P_G / P_G > 0$), hence according to (4.8) or (7.4) it lowered the value of money ($\Delta V_M / V_M < 0$). This fall in the value of money now caused a rise in all prices $P_{i \neq G}$ in the same proportion as the rise in P_G. To this general effect of monetary origin was added a specific effect in the sole market for bullion: since part of the quantity available had been coined, the supply was reduced and consequently the market price of bullion increased more than all other commodity prices which were not subject to this market effect. In other words, the relative value of gold bullion in terms of all other commodities rose. It should be observed that such rise was of another nature than a rise occurring when the difficulty of producing gold increased for exogenous reasons: here the rise was endogenous to the adjustment process. In equation (7.4) this endogenous rise in the value of gold ($\Delta V_G / V_G > 0$) mitigates the fall in the value of money consequent upon the increase in its quantity. As emphasised by Ricardo, at the end of the second stage of the adjustment the equality between the value of money and the value of gold bullion was restored but at a higher level than the initial one (before the increase in the wants of commerce):

> It appears then, that, if the increase in the circulation were supplied by means of coin, the value both of bullion and money would, for a time at least, even after they had found their level, be higher than before; a circumstance which though often unavoidable, is inconvenient, as it affects all former contracts.
> (ibid)

In *Proposals*, Ricardo emphasised this inconvenience to advocate the substitution of notes for coins. This did not mean, however, that with a metallic circulation no return to the initial value of money was possible: as observed above by Ricardo, it remained at a higher level "for a time at least". A third stage of the adjustment completed it, which was the consequence of the rise in the domestic value of bullion. If in the initial situation the value of bullion in terms of all other commodities was the same in the country and abroad, so that there was no inflow or outflow of it, the domestic increase in this value – supposing that the foreign value of gold remained unaltered – made it profitable to import it, as soon as the difference was greater than the cost of importation (see Chapter 8 below). This international adjustment had been described by Ricardo in 1810 in one of his three letters to the *Morning Chronicle* on the Bullion Report:

> Before 1797, when the Bank paid in specie, increased commerce, and increased taxation might have required, precisely as they do now, an addition to the circulating medium, which the Bank might have supplied with their notes without causing any depreciation in their value as compared with gold; but if they had refused or neglected to do so, the increased demand for money would have raised the foreign exchange above par, and the mint price of gold above the market price; or in more popular language, the market price of gold would have fallen below the mint price, and would have so continued till the Bullion Merchants had availed themselves of the advantage attending the

> importation of gold at the favourable exchange, and the subsequent coining of it into money, and thereby supplied the demand for currency. The exchange would then have been at or about par, and the market and mint prices of gold at the usual level.
>
> (III: 140)

Since at the end of the second stage the value of money was equal to the domestic value of bullion (at a higher level than initially and abroad), the market price of gold bullion was again equal to the legal price of gold in coin. The import of bullion sunk its market price below the legal price, and, as in the first stage, imported gold was coined until both prices were again equalised. The value of money consequently fell and equalised with the domestic value of bullion at the initial (and foreign) level.

The superiority of paper money over coins

With a metallic circulation, the adjustment to an increase in the wants of commerce thus finally occurred: the higher required quantity of money was coined and the value of money returned to its initial level.[1] But this took time and in the interval the rise in the value of money raised the value of previous debt contracts and was accompanied with a deflation of prices that hurt activity in general.[2] However, there was another way of accommodating an increase in the wants of commerce: the issuing of paper money. As Ricardo observed before starting to describe the adjustment of a metallic circulation:

> It is the rise in the value of money above the value of bullion which is always, in a sound state of the currency, the cause of its increase in quantity; for it is at these times that either an opening is made for the issue of more paper money, which is always attended with profit to the issuers; or that a profit is made by carrying bullion to the mint to be coined.
>
> (*Proposals*; IV: 56–7)

The increase in the wants of commerce $(\Delta M^* / M^* > 0)$ led owners of commercial bills to apply for notes at the discount window of the Bank of England, and this demand was "attended with profit" to the Bank. The actual quantity of money immediately increased accordingly $(\Delta M / M > 0)$, and the inconvenience consequent upon the adjustment of a metallic circulation was avoided:

> This inconvenience [a rise in the value of money] is wholly got rid of, by the issue of paper money; for, in that case, there will be no additional demand for bullion; consequently its value will continue unaltered; and the new paper money, as well as the old, will conform to that value. Besides, then, all the other advantages attending the use of paper money; by the judicious management of the quantity, a degree of uniformity, which is by no other means

attainable, is secured to the value of the circulating medium in which all payments are made.

(ibid: 57–8)

One should observe that for Ricardo the increase in the note issue did not require an additional quantity of coin or bullion in the reserve of the Bank to back it. There was no threat of conversion of these notes: the paper was not in excess since its increase responded to the wants of commerce. Whether with a metallic or a paper circulation, the quantity of money adjusted endogenously. With paper money it did so quicker and safer than with specie.

7.3 The adjustment to a discretionary increase in the convertible-note issue

"Forcing" Bank of England notes into circulation

I will here consider the following case: starting from a situation in which money conformed to the standard, the bank discretionarily increased its issues of convertible notes, while the wants of commerce remained unaltered ($\Delta M^*/M^* = 0$; $\Delta M / M > 0$, so that according to (7.3) $\Delta P_G / P_G > 0$). The notes became consequently in excess, in the sense defined above when discussing the notion of "wants of commerce": the actual quantity of money (*M*) became greater than its conformable one (M^*). The symmetrical case of a discretionary contraction of the note issue implied a deficiency in the quantity of money, if the wants of commerce were unaltered ($\Delta M^*/M^* = 0$; $\Delta M / M < 0$, so that $\Delta P_G / P_G < 0$). The adjustment was thus the same as in the case of an increase in the wants of commerce, while the quantity of money remained the same ($\Delta M^*/M^* > 0$; $\Delta M / M = 0$, so that $\Delta P_G / P_G < 0$), and it has been analysed above.[3]

A discretionary increase in the convertible-note issue could occur when the Bank made advances to government but also when it "forced" its notes into circulation by lowering its discount rate below the rate in the money market (see Chapter 9 below). In a speech in Parliament on 1 July 1822, Ricardo emphasised that the only way the Bank could increase the demand for its notes and put them into circulation was to lower its discount rate:

> He [Ricardo] was glad that the Bank had determined to reduce its rate of interest to four per cent.; indeed, they would have done wrong in declining to do so, as by that means only could they bring their notes into circulation. If the Bank had not reduced its interest to four per cent. the country must necessarily resort to a metallic currency, or else notes must be issued from some other quarter, as it would be impossible for the Bank of England to put a single pound note into circulation.
>
> (V: 223 n1)

In contrast with the case of the adjustment in the value of money to an increase in the wants of commerce, there is no description in *Proposals* or later writings of the adjustment to a discretionary increase in the convertible-note issue. Two reasons may be conjectured for this absence. First, Ricardo had already given such a description in *High Price*, both for the part of the adjustment which was common to inconvertibility and convertibility and for that part which was specific to convertibility. We will see below that when notes were convertible, the adjustment of their value was the outcome of the adjustment of the market price of gold bullion to the legal price of gold in coin, and this adjustment was not affected by the theory of value of commodities developed in *Principles* because, in the country where gold bullion was the standard of money, it was *not* subject to the general adjustment process (gravitation) that applied to any competitively produced commodity. It was thus unnecessary for Ricardo to repeat himself on something which remained valid under his general theory of value. The second reason for the absence of a detailed analysis of the adjustment in the value of money to a discretionary increase in the convertible-note issue may be that, from *Proposals* onwards, Ricardo repeatedly advocated a monetary plan which, although embodying the convertibility of the note, substituted a policy rule – the regulation of the quantity of money by a central bank – for private arbitrage on the standard (see Chapter 9 below). His aim was consequently to show that such a plan could implement a nearly "perfect" currency, rather than to analyse how private arbitrage actually taking advantage of convertibility did the job in an imperfect way.

The analysis of the adjustment to a discretionary increase in the convertible-note issue raises two questions: (1) In a mixed system of coins and convertible notes, which part of the adjustment fell on the circulation of coins? And (2) Which part of the adjustment depended on the behaviour of the bank of issue (the Bank of England)? Let me consider these two questions successively.

The melting of circulating coins

The part of the adjustment which fell on the circulation of coins was common to both a convertibility and an inconvertibility regime and it is why it could be described by Ricardo when in *High Price* he considered the case of a mixed system of coins and *inconvertible* notes. The adjustment is exactly symmetrical with that of an increase in the wants of commerce in a purely metallic circulation: we have seen above that when the wants of commerce exogenously increased $\left(\Delta M^* / M^* > 0\right)$, the circulation of coins increased through the coining of bullion; now that the quantity of money exogenously increased ($\Delta M / M > 0$), the circulation of coins was contracted through their melting into bullion. In other words, this part of the adjustment relied on the convertibility of coin into bullion, as the adjustment to the wants of commerce in a pure metallic circulation relied on the convertibility of bullion into coin.

In *High Price*, this part of the adjustment was described as follows:

> It has been observed [by Francis Horner[4]] that an increase in the paper currency will only occasion a rise in the *paper* or *currency* price of commodities,

> but will not cause an increase in their bullion price. This would be true at a time when the currency consisted wholly of paper not convertible into specie, but not while specie formed any part of the circulation. In the latter case the effect of an increased issue of paper would be to throw out of circulation an equal amount of specie; but this could not be done without adding to the quantity of bullion in the market, and thereby lowering its value, or in other words, *increasing the bullion price of commodities*. It is only in consequence of this fall in the value of the metallic currency, and of bullion, that the temptation to export them arises; and the penalties on melting the coin is the sole cause of a small difference between the value of the coin and of bullion, or a small excess of the market above the mint price.
>
> (*High Price*, III: 64; note; Ricardo's emphasis)

There were three successive stages in the adjustment of the metallic circulation. Consider an initial situation in which money conformed to the standard, so that $P_G = \overline{P_{GC}}$ and $M = M^*$. The Bank then discretionarily increased its note issue, so that the aggregate quantity of money increased at a rate $\Delta M / M$, while the legal price $\overline{P_{GC}}$ of gold in coin and the quantity of money M^* required by the wants of commerce remained unchanged $\left(\Delta M^* / M^* = 0\right)$. During the first stage of the adjustment, the excess of $\Delta M / M$ over $\Delta M^* / M^*$ resulted in a rise of the market price of gold bullion $\left(\Delta P_G / P_G > 0\right)$. According indifferently to equation (4.8) or (7.4), and supposing no exogenous change in the value of gold bullion $\left(\Delta V_G / V_G = 0\right)$, the value of money fell $\left(\Delta V_M / V_M < 0\right)$ and all prices $P_{i \neq G}$ rose in the same proportion as P_G, that is, at the same rate $\Delta M / M$ as the aggregate quantity of money. Now, with P_G above $\overline{P_{GC}}$ (money was depreciated), a profit by arbitrage could be made by collecting gold coins in circulation at $\overline{P_{GC}}$, melting them, and selling bullion in the market at the higher P_G. Arbitrage was implemented as soon as the difference between P_G and $\overline{P_{GC}}$ was greater than the melting cost m_G, which may here be neglected, as Ricardo did. An endogenous contraction in the quantity of money, equal to the quantity of coins removed from circulation, ended thus the first stage of the adjustment: "the effect of an increased issue of paper would be to throw out of circulation an equal amount of specie".

In the second stage, this contraction in the quantity of money in circulation $\left(\Delta M / M < 0\right)$ sunk the market price of gold bullion $\left(\Delta P_G / P_G < 0\right)$, hence according to (4.8) or (7.4) it increased the value of money $\left(\Delta V_M / V_M > 0\right)$. This rise in the value of money now caused a fall in all prices $P_{i \neq G}$ in the same proportion as the fall in P_G. To this general effect of monetary origin was added a specific effect in the sole market for bullion: because of the increased supply consequent upon the melting of coins the market price of bullion fell more than all other commodity prices (which were not subject to this market effect). In other words, the relative value of gold bullion in terms of all other commodities fell. The quotation goes on: "but this could not be done without adding to the quantity of bullion in the market, and thereby lowering its value". This fall was endogenous to the adjustment process and should be distinguished from an exogenous fall consequent upon the discovery of a new productive mine. In equation (7.4) this endogenous fall in the value of gold $(\Delta V_G / V_G < 0)$ mitigated the rise in the value of money consequent upon the contraction in its quantity. At the end of the second stage of the adjustment the equality between the value of money and the value of gold bullion was restored but at a lower level than the initial one (before the monetary shock).

The third stage of the adjustment started, which was the consequence of the fall in the domestic value of bullion. If in the initial situation the value of bullion in terms of all other commodities was the same in the country and abroad, so that there was no inflow or outflow of it, the domestic fall in this value – supposing that the foreign value of gold remained unaltered – made it profitable to export it, as soon as the difference was greater than the cost of exportation (see Chapter 8 below). The quotation goes on: "It is only in consequence of this fall in the value of the metallic currency, and of bullion, that the temptation to export them arises." Since at the end of the second stage the value of money was equal to the domestic value of bullion (at a lower level than initially and abroad), the market price of gold bullion was again equal to the legal price of gold in coin (or slightly above the latter, by the "small difference" due to the melting cost). The export of bullion reduced its supply in the domestic market, so that its market price rose above the legal price, and, as in the first stage, coins were removed from circulation, melted, and the bullion sold in the market for profit, until both prices were again equalised. The value of money consequently rose and equalised with the domestic value of bullion at the initial (and foreign) level.[5]

Now the distinction between the cases of convertibility or inconvertibility of the Bank of England note entered the picture for the second question raised above: Which part of the adjustment depended on the behaviour of the Bank? Under inconvertibility, the adjustment through the melting of coins gathered in circulation and the exporting of the bullion thus obtained restored the initial situation – the increased issue of notes simply substituting for the coins melted and exported – but nothing could prevent the Bank from increasing again its issue. The outcome of the repeated adjustment process was the complete elimination of coins from domestic circulation, which became exclusively filled with inconvertible notes. This was the situation actually achieved in England in 1810. The lack of circulating coins obviated the operation of the adjustment process and the depreciation of money increased without limit (for a discussion of this case, see Section 7.5 below).

Such a fatal outcome could not happen under convertibility. It happened under inconvertibility when the reservoir of gold provided by the domestic circulation of coins was exhausted. Such exhaustion was excluded under convertibility for a simple reason: coins to be melted with a view to exporting the bullion were not gathered in circulation (at a cost equal to the commission of money-changers) but obtained by arbitragers from the Bank of England at no cost, when they returned to the Bank the notes issued by it. This difference apparently did not affect the adjustment process based on melting the coin and exporting the bullion:

> While their notes were payable in specie on demand, [the Bank] could never issue more notes than the value of the coin which would have circulated had

> there been no bank. If they attempted to exceed this amount, the excess would be immediately returned to them for specie; because our currency, being thereby diminished in value, could be advantageously exported, and could not be retained in our circulation.
>
> (*High Price*; III: 57)

At the end of the first stage of the adjustment process, the quantity of money was now reduced in its note component (because notes were returned by arbitragers to the Bank for coins) instead of its metallic component, but in the second stage the general effect on all prices and the specific market effect on the price of bullion operated as above, with the same consequences for the value of bullion and its exportation. However, the final outcome of the adjustment process now depended on the reaction of the Bank of England to the conversion of its notes consequent upon its discretionary increased issuing.

The Penelope effect

At the time of the Bullion Essays, Ricardo already contended that, if the note was convertible into coin, a fall in the value of money would only be temporary:

> Whilst Banks pay in specie there can be no additions to the circulation which can permanently lower the value of money, – because they cannot permanently lower the value of gold and silver. Those metals would not have been of greater value now if no bank had ever been heard of.
>
> ("Notes on Bentham's 'Sur les prix'"; III: 278)

According to Ricardo, the only permanent cause of a fall in the value of money, when the note was convertible, was a fall in the value of the standard, and such fall could only temporarily be caused by an excess issue (in contrast with an exogenous fall consequent upon the discovery of a new mine). This endogenous fall only occurred in the interval between the moment arbitrage between the Bank and the bullion market started and the moment when it stopped. However, if the Bank re-issued the notes returned to it, the adjustment process was again set into motion and with it the fall in the value of the standard. This is why the export of bullion – permitted by the fall in its value – could not by itself correct the excess issue and eliminate depreciation, as long as the Bank re-issued the notes in excess. The excess of notes generating their depreciation could only be eliminated if something prevented the Bank from renewing its increased issues, and this is precisely what convertibility did. It prevented the Bank from issuing in excess during a prolonged period of time, because of an effect borrowed by Ricardo from Smith and Thornton:

> In this manner if the Bank persisted in returning their notes into circulation, every guinea might be drawn out of their coffers. If to supply the deficiency of their stock of gold they were to purchase gold bullion at the advanced

> price, and have it coined into guineas, this would not remedy the evil, guineas would still be demanded, but instead of being exported would be melted and sold to the Bank as bullion at the advanced price. 'The operations of the bank,' observed Dr. Smith, alluding to an analogous case, 'were upon this account somewhat like the web of Penelope, the work that was done in the day was undone in the night.' The same sentiment is expressed by Mr. Thornton:– 'Finding the guineas in their coffers to lessen every day, they must naturally be supposed to be desirous of replacing them by all effectual and not extravagantly expensive means. They will be disposed, to a certain degree, to buy gold, though at a losing price, and to coin it into new guineas; but they will have to do this at the very moment when many are privately melting what is coined. The one party will be melting and selling while the other is buying and coining. And each of these two contending businesses will now be carried on, not on account of an actual exportation of each melted guinea to Hamburgh, but the operation or at least a great part of it will be confined to London; the coiners and the melters living on the same spot, and giving constant employment to each other.
>
> 'The Bank,' continues Mr. Thornton, 'if we suppose it, as we now do, to carry on this sort of contest with the melters, is obviously waging a very unequal war; and even though it should not be tired early, it will be likely to be tired sooner than its adversaries.'
>
> The Bank would be obliged therefore ultimately to adopt the only remedy in their power to put a stop to the demand for guineas. They would withdraw part of their notes from circulation, till they should have increased the value of the remainder to that of gold bullion, and consequently to the value of the currencies of other countries. All advantage from the exportation of gold bullion would then cease, and there would be no temptation to exchange bank-notes for guineas.
>
> (*High Price*; III: 58–9)[6]

What I will henceforth call the Penelope effect operated in two steps. First, the reserve in coins at the Bank shrank with the conversion of the notes and after a certain time the Bank had to purchase bullion in the market, in order to have it coined at the mint and replenish its reserve. The export of bullion consequently stopped – "guineas would still be demanded, but instead of being exported would be melted and sold to the Bank as bullion at the advanced price" – because the sale of bullion to the Bank in the London market did not expose its owner to the cost of transporting it to a foreign market. The demand for bullion by the Bank replaced the demand for exportation and sustained its market price above the legal price of gold in coin, "the coiners [the Bank] and the melters [the arbitragers] living on the same spot, and giving constant employment to each other", as Thornton wrote. But this was for the Bank a loss-making activity, since it purchased bullion in the market above the price at which it was legally compelled to give coins against its notes. Then the second step of the Penelope effect started: after a certain time, "the Bank would be obliged therefore ultimately to adopt the only remedy in their power to put a stop to the demand for guineas. They would withdraw part of their notes from circulation." The Bank did that, not because it finally understood that the high price of bullion was caused by the excess issue – Ricardo repeatedly complained that Bank directors were notoriously ignorant of this relation – but simply in the hope that, issuing fewer notes through discounting, fewer notes would be returned to be converted into coin. This reduction took place until arbitragers ceased to return notes to the Bank, that is, until the spread between the market price of gold bullion and the legal price of gold in coin fell below the melting cost (so that "there would be no temptation to exchange bank-notes for guineas") – in other words, "till they [the Bank] should have increased the value of the remainder [of notes] to that of gold bullion".

The same adjustment was mentioned in Chapter XXVII of *Principles* when Ricardo discussed the positions of Smith and of the editor of the *Wealth of Nations*, Buchanan, on the respective effects of the debasement of the coin and of an excess issue of notes on the Bank experiencing a loss when it was obliged to purchase bullion at a high price and to have it coined at the legal price. Ricardo's object was then to defend "the principle of limitation of quantity" (I: 353) according to which a reduction in the quantity of money, whether debased coins or notes issued in excess, could elevate its value to that of the full-bodied coin, stopping the Penelope effect:

> On the principle above stated, it appears to me most clear, that by not re-issuing the paper thus brought in, the value of the whole currency, of the degraded as well as the new gold coin, would have been raised, when all demands on the Bank would have ceased.
>
> (*Principles*; I: 355)

And again in a letter to Mill of 18 December 1821 where he commented on pages of the latter's *Elements of Political Economy*, Ricardo evoked the losing business of the Bank:

> 119 "But in these circumstances" &ca. The latter part of this paragraph is not clear. Why would the bank pay for their notes when they came back £4? Answer. Their stock of gold would inevitably be soon exhausted and they would be obliged to buy in the market at £4–what they sold at £3. 17. 10½ in order to replace that stock.
>
> (IX: 128)

In conclusion on the adjustment to a discretionary increase in the convertible-note issue, one can make four remarks. First, in contrast with the case of inconvertibility, there could not be a permanent excess of convertible notes. Second, contrary to what is usually ascribed to Ricardo, the exportation of bullion, which under inconvertibility adjusted the aggregate quantity of money when it was in excess, only played a role at the beginning of the adjustment process under convertibility. As soon as the Bank purchased bullion to replenish its metallic reserve, the exportation of bullion was replaced by a domestic adjustment: the reduction of the Bank issue under the pressure of the Penelope effect.[7] Third, such adjustment explains how the rise in the market price of gold bullion above the legal price of gold in coin eventually led to a contraction in the note component of the aggregate quantity of money which restored their equality. Fourth, although arbitrage was quickly triggered by such spread, the adjustment through the Penelope effect might take quite a long time, depending on the lag with which the Bank first purchased bullion to replenish its reserve, and second contracted the issue to stop its losses. During this interval, the market price of gold bullion remained above the legal price of gold in coin: money was depreciated. According to Ricardo, this was one of the reasons why the monetary system should be improved, instead of simply restoring the pre-1797 convertibility of the Bank of England note into coin (see Chapter 9 below).

7.4 A non-quantitative approach

Two conclusions may be drawn from equations (7.2) to (7.4) above. The first derives from (7.2): the introduction by Ricardo in 1816 (in *Proposals*) of the condition of conformity of money to the standard gave a theoretical foundation to the proposition that, not only the high price of bullion was "a proof" of the depreciation of bank notes (as stated in 1810 in the title of *High Price*), but it also indicated that the actual aggregate quantity of money M was in excess of its conformable level M^*. Ricardo's tour de force was thus to provide a simple test – the comparison of the two observable magnitudes P_G and P_{GC} – of whether the actual aggregate quantity of money was or not in excess (or deficient), without having to know what this level and the required (conformable) level were.

A second conclusion derives from (7.4), which reformulates the Money–Standard Equation: Ricardo's mature theory of money, consistent with *Principles* and contained in the 1819–1823 papers, is *not* a quantity theory of money. Of course, the quantity of money mattered, as emphasised in *Principles*:

> There is no point more important in issuing paper money, than to be fully impressed with the effects which follow from the principle of limitation of quantity.
>
> (I: 353)

The above analysis of how the value of money adjusts to an increase in the wants of commerce or in the discretionary issuing of convertible notes shows that the understanding of the link between the quantity and the value of money requires putting the standard of money centre-stage, as emphasised by the sentence in *Proposals* which is the epigraph of the present chapter:

> The only use of a standard is to regulate the quantity, and by the quantity the value of a currency.
>
> (IV: 59)

One should refrain from jumping on the second part of the sentence to conclude that Ricardo advocated a quantity theory of money. As appears in the first part of the sentence, the quantity of a currency only "regulates" its value since it is itself regulated by the standard. The above analysis of this regulation allows clarifying the difference between Ricardo's theory of money and the so-called Quantity Theory of Money.

The Quantity Theory of Money is traditionally presented in the form of the Cambridge equation $M = KPT$ (with M the supply of money, K the proportion of the real volume of their planned transactions T which individuals wish to hold as real balances, and P the price level of the commodities transacted, so that KPT is the demand for money) or in the form of the equation of exchange $Mv = PT$, in which the velocity of circulation v replaces its reciprocal K (see Patinkin 1956: 97). The value of money V_M being defined as the reciprocal of the general price level P, both expressions lead to the following relation, with K (respectively v) supposed to be a given parameter reflecting the organisation of monetary transactions:

$$\frac{\Delta V_M}{V_M} = \frac{\Delta T}{T} - \frac{\Delta M}{M} \tag{i}$$

Equation (i) leads to the well-known conclusion that the value of money V_M falls (the general price level P rises) if the exogenous supply of money M increases faster than the volume of transactions T determined independently (money being neutral in respect to aggregate output).

Ricardo's analysis of the relation between a change in the value of money and a change in its quantity is summed-up by equation (7.4):

$$\frac{\Delta V_M}{V_M} = \frac{\Delta V_G}{V_G} - \left[\frac{\Delta M}{M} - \frac{\Delta M^*}{M^*}\right] \tag{7.4}$$

As already emphasised in Chapters 3 and 4 above, it is necessary to distinguish between what I will call the conformable state of the monetary system – in which "money conforms to the standard", that is $V_M = V_M^*$ and $M = M^*$ – and situations in which these equalities are not fulfilled; these situations may thus be conveniently called monetary disequilibrium (this term being only used here because it speaks for itself in the literature, without implying that the conformable state is an equilibrium state).

In the conformable state the value of money V_M^* is independent of its quantity and only depends on the value of the standard V_G and on its legal price $\overline{P_{GC}}$ when coined into money (equation (3.8)). If this state is maintained through time, (7.4) simplifies in:

$$\frac{\Delta V_{M^*}}{V_{M^*}} = \frac{\Delta V_G}{V_G} \tag{7.7}$$

The conformable value of money varies with the value of the standard and only with it. As for the conformable quantity of money M^*, it is a function of its value $V_M{}^*$ – hence of the value of the standard V_G – and of the aggregate value Y of the commodities which it circulates (equation (7.6)). It is thus endogenously determined. In the conformable state, there is no equilibrium value of money determined by the equality between an exogenously given supply of money and a demand for real balances, in contrast with the Quantity Theory of Money. In Ricardo, M^* varies positively with the aggregate value of commodities to be circulated and inversely with the value of the standard:

$$\frac{\Delta M^*}{M^*} = \frac{\Delta Y}{Y} - \frac{\Delta V_G}{V_G} \tag{7.8}$$

Disequilibrium occurs when the monetary system departs from its conformable state because $\Delta M / M \neq \Delta M^* / M^*$. The rate of change in the value of money $\Delta V_M / V_M$, as given by (7.4), is now affected by the rate of change in the actual quantity of money $\Delta M / M$. Combining (7.8) with (7.4) gives:

$$\frac{\Delta V_M}{V_M} = \frac{\Delta Y}{Y} - \frac{\Delta M}{M} \tag{7.10}$$

Formally, this equation is analogous to equation (i) of the Quantity Theory of Money. However, it should be noted that, while (i) is an equilibrium relation, (7.10) is only valid in disequilibrium: the value of money varies inversely with its quantity only in disequilibrium. Moreover, as shown in Sections 7.2 and 7.3 above, such disequilibrium triggers an endogenous adjustment of the actual to the conformable quantity of money, what Ricardo calls in *Principles* "the principle of limitation of quantity" (I: 353). If $\Delta M / M < \Delta M^* / M^*$ (the actual quantity of money is deficient), this adjustment operates through new coining and / or discounting of bills for notes. If $\Delta M / M > \Delta M^* / M^*$ (the actual quantity of money is in excess), it operates through melting and forced reduction in the note issue, under the pressure of the Penelope effect. Finally, Ricardo's theory of money is specific because of the channel of transmission of a change in the quantity to the value of money. This is concealed in equation (7.4) where, thanks to (7.3), $[\Delta M / M - \Delta M^* / M^*]$ substitutes for $\Delta P_G / P_G$ in the Money–Standard Equation (4.8). In disequilibrium, a change in the quantity of money affects its value indirectly, through a change in the market price of the standard. This contrasts with the Quantity Theory of Money in which a change in the quantity of money affects its value directly thanks to real-balance effects on the demand for money.

To sum up, Ricardo's integration of money in his theory of value and the Quantity Theory of Money have in common that they assume the neutrality of money in respect to the relative prices of commodities (for a justification of this assumption see Section 6.2 of Chapter 6, and see Appendix 3 for Ricardo's aborted attempt at non-neutrality when commodities were taxed on profits). A monetary disequilibrium (that is, an inequality between the actual quantity of money and its conformable level) has no real effects on the markets for commodities, which are supposed to remain in their natural state (a corollary is the specificity of the market for gold bullion as compared with the market for any other commodity; see Section 7.6 below). However, Ricardo's theory of money is *not* a quantity theory of money for three reasons: (a) In the conformable state, the causal relation between the quantity and the value of money is turned upside down; (b) "the principle of limitation of quantity" only operates in disequilibrium, provided there is convertibility; and (c) it operates on the value of money through a change in the market price of the standard. A practical consequence ensues: the bank of issue should not target the rate of change in the absolute quantity of money but the rate of change that preserves the equalisation of the value of money with its conformable level, that is, the equalisation of the market price of the standard with the legal price at which the note is convertible into it (see Chapter 9 below):

> The issuers of paper money should regulate their issues solely by the price of bullion, and never by the quantity of their paper in circulation. The quantity can never be too great nor too little, while it preserves the same value as the standard.
>
> (*Proposals*; IV: 64)

In contrast with the Quantity Theory of Money, an exogenously given supply of money does *not* confront an independently given demand for real balances, but the actual quantity of money M endogenously adjusts to the quantity M^* required by the wants of commerce. When the Bank discretionarily increases its note issue, commodity prices do *not* rise because there is a stable demand function for money, but do so thanks to a sequence of effects in which an excess of the actual quantity of money over its conformable level raises the market price of the standard, hence lowers the value of money, hence raises all prices (except the market price of the standard which is brought back to its legal convertibility level). There is indeed a self-adjusting process (the Penelope effect) which eliminates the excess issue of notes and restores the conformity of money to the standard, but it is *not* the adjustment to an equilibrium value of money determined by a supply-and-demand mechanism.[8] Finally, one does *not* need to measure the variation in the money supply (with the related problems of choosing the appropriate monetary aggregate) to explain the variation in its value; it is enough to compare the market price of gold bullion with the legal price of gold in coin to conclude whether money conforms to the standard or not.

To conclude on this point, although changes in the aggregate quantity of money affect its value in disequilibrium, Ricardo's mature theory of money, as it is embodied in the Money–Standard Equation, is *not* a quantity theory of money. Modern attempts at introducing real-balance effects, at linking the quantity of money and prices through the rate of interest, or at connecting Ricardo's alleged quantity theory of money with Say's Law are therefore irrelevant (see Appendix 7 below).

7.5 Money without a standard

It is striking that the sentence in *Proposals* which best sums up Ricardo's view of how the standard regulates the value of money is in a paragraph where he criticised a currency without a standard for its value being unstable. And it is noteworthy that this paragraph is one of the very few references to an author who was in the eighteenth century the most acute on this question of the standard of money: James Steuart (see Deleplace 2015d). Ricardo's judgement on Steuart was ambivalent, mixing a critique in the main text with a laudatory appreciation in a footnote, and it is to be regretted that he did not develop this point more:

> This idea of a currency without a specific standard was, I believe, first advanced by Sir James Steuart,* but no one has yet been able to offer any test by which we could ascertain the uniformity in the value of a money so constituted. Those who supported this opinion did not see, that such a currency, instead of being invariable, was subject to the greatest variations, – that the only use of a standard is to regulate the quantity, and by the quantity the value of the currency – and that without a standard it would be exposed to all the fluctuations to which the ignorance or the interests of the issuers might subject it.
>
> *The writings of Sir James Steuart on the subject of coin and money are full of instruction, and it appears surprising that he could have adopted the above opinion, which is so directly at variance with the general principles he endeavoured to establish.
>
> (*Proposals*; IV: 59)

Ricardo's contention that the value of a money without a standard could not be "regulated" originated in the Bullion Essays, where it was linked to the double inconvertibility which characterised the English currency at the time. However, the question should be raised of whether Ricardo's mature theory of money, from *Proposals* onwards, applies to such money.

A double inconvertibility

It was Ricardo's contention that from 1797 (when the convertibility of the Bank of England note was suspended) to 1819 (when it was resumed) money had no standard. As he wrote in 1822 in his pamphlet *On Protection to Agriculture*:

> It is also forgotten, that from 1797 to 1819 we had no standard whatever, by which to regulate the quantity or value of our money. Its quantity and its value depended entirely on the Bank of England, the directors of which establishment, however desirous they might have been to act with fairness and justice to the public, avowed that they were guided in their issues by principles which, it is no longer disputed, exposed the country to the greatest embarrassment. Accordingly, we find that the currency varied in value considerably

> during the period of 22 years, when there was no other rule for regulating its quantity and value but the will of the Bank.
>
> (IV: 222–3)

This was not only a retrospective statement:[9] at the time of the *Bullion Report*, when the question of the consequences of inconvertibility was hotly debated, Ricardo had already affirmed:

> That gold is no longer in practice the standard by which our currency is regulated is a truth. It is the ground of the complaint of the [Bullion] Committee (and of all who have written on the same side) against the present system.
>
> (*Reply to Bosanquet*; III: 255)

Indeed, there was still a legal price of gold in coin, and the difference between the market price of gold bullion and this legal price was for Ricardo "a proof" of the depreciation of bank notes, as he wrote in the title of *High Price*. Formally gold was still the standard of money, but it no longer actually "regulated" its quantity, hence its value, because paper money was no longer convertible into this standard. The above analysis allows understanding why it was so. With the suspension in 1797 of the convertibility of the Bank of England note into coin, the Penelope effect had disappeared, and the quantity of notes issued faced henceforth no other limit than "the will of the Bank". Some kind of "regulation", however, still survived because of the other (illegal but usual) convertibility, from coin into bullion (the melting pot). The more the Bank issued notes, the more coins were displaced from domestic circulation to be melted with a view to exporting the bullion. But this "regulation" only operated during the first ten years of suspension, until nearly all coins had disappeared. With the growing shortage of coins to be obtained from money-changers against notes, the cost of gathering them increased and the melting cost increased with it, pushing the market price ever and ever upwards, without limit. This was the situation in 1809–1810 which motivated Ricardo's first writings and the appointment of the Bullion Committee:

> The same cause which has produced a difference of from fifteen to twenty per cent. in bank-notes when compared with gold bullion, may increase it to fifty per cent. There can be no limit to the depreciation which may arise from a constantly increasing quantity of paper. The stimulus which a redundant currency gives to the exportation of the coin has acquired new force, but cannot, as formerly, relieve itself.
>
> (*High Price*; III: 78)

The excess of money consequent upon an ever-increasing issue of Bank of England notes could no longer be corrected by the contraction of the metallic circulation, because there were no longer any coins to be melted with a view to exporting bullion. In the absence of the convertibility of the note into coin, the convertibility of the coin into bullion was condemned to disappear sooner or later. This double inconvertibility made the regulation of money by the standard impossible, in contrast with the double convertibility which ensured it before 1797.

This impossibility meant that not only was "gold no longer in practice the standard by which our currency is regulated", as quoted above, but also that gold had not been replaced by another standard, contrary to what Bosanquet contended. For the latter, the Bank of England note had become the standard because it was used in the relations between the State and the public. In the *Appendix* to his *Reply to Bosanquet*, Ricardo quoted him:

> Let us hear what he says: "If a pound note be the denomination, it will, of course, be asked what is the standard? The question is not easy of solution. But, considering the high proportion which the dealings between government and the public bear to the general circulation, it is probable the standard may be found in those transactions; and it seems not more difficult to imagine that the standard value of a one pound note may be the interest of 33*l*. 6*s*. 8*d*. – 3 per cent stock, than that such standard has reference to a metal, of which none remains in circulation".
>
> (III: 255–6)

As mentioned above, there remained one use of the standard under inconvertibility: measuring the depreciation of the bank note. But this disqualified the bank note as standard, because it could evidently not measure its own depreciation. For once, Ricardo's irony was ferocious:

> So then we *have* a standard for a pound Bank note, it is the interest of 33*l*. 6*s*. 8*d*. – 3 per cent stock. Now, in what medium is this interest paid? because *that* must be the standard. The holder of 33*l*. 6*s*. 8*d*. stock receives at the Bank a one pound note. Bank notes are, therefore, according to the theory of a *practical* man, the standard by which alone the depreciation of Bank notes can be estimated!
>
> A puncheon of rum has 16 per cent. of its contents taken out, and water poured in for it. What is the standard by which Mr. Bosanquet attempts to detect the adulteration? A sample of the adulterated liquor taken out of the same cask.
>
> (ibid: 256; Ricardo's emphasis)

The Money–Standard Equation and inconvertibility

The question is simple: does Ricardo's mature theory of money, as it is embodied in the Money–Standard Equation, apply to inconvertibility? Since this equation, whether in the form of (4.8) or (7.4), is derived from the condition (3.8) of conformity of money to the standard, this question may be reformulated as follows: what is the meaning, if any, of this condition of conformity in the inconvertibility case?

Under convertibility, this condition has both a normative and a positive meaning. It must be fulfilled if money is to be "perfect" – to use Ricardo's word – *and* it is fulfilled as the consequence of a self-adjusting process. Under inconvertibility, the normative meaning subsists but the positive one is ruled out. Although the melting of circulating coins and the exportation of the bullion thus obtained provide a corrective process to the excess issue of notes, their operation faces an obvious limit: the disappearance of all coins from domestic circulation. At this point, depreciation starts to increase without limit, and money can no longer conform to the standard. In this sense, there is no self-adjusting process under inconvertibility. The reason is obvious: the institutional set-up which guarantees its operation under convertibility does not exist under inconvertibility. Under the convertibility of the Bank of England note into coin, this set-up was made of three aspects: (a) a legal price of gold in coin; (b) convertibility both ways between bullion and the coin; and (c) convertibility one-way of the note into the coin. As it was practised after the suspension of 1797, inconvertibility preserved (a) but not (c): the Penelope effect, which constrained the issuing behaviour of the Bank of England, was discontinued. And this led after several years to the disappearance of (b): there were no longer circulating coins to be converted into bullion, hence no further correction of the excess issue of notes by the exportation of bullion.

The persistence of the normative meaning of the condition of conformity might nevertheless suggest another role for it than being the outcome of a self-adjusting process: to provide a target for a policy rule. In the absence of the full convertibility set-up, the bank of issue could mimic its working by varying the quantity of notes inversely with the sign of the difference between the market price of gold bullion and the legal price of gold in coin. Ricardo himself observed in *Proposals* (IV: 67) that this was "the criterion which I have so often mentioned", and this "judicious management of the quantity" of money (ibid: 57) was one of the two pillars of his Ingot Plan. As will be developed in Chapter 9 below, this policy rule substituted for actual convertibility by making it superfluous: an excess quantity of notes was immediately corrected by the central bank when it observed a rise of the market price of bullion, before arbitrage was triggered and notes returned to the bank. However, this does not mean that for Ricardo this policy rule could dispense from convertibility. When he wrote:

> On these principles, it will be seen that it is not necessary that paper money should be payable in specie to secure its value; it is only necessary that its quantity should be regulated according to the metal which is declared to be the standard.
>
> (*Principles*; I: 354)

he did not contend that convertibility was unnecessary but that convertibility *into coin* was unnecessary and should be replaced by convertibility *into bullion*. With the Ingot Plan the clerks at the gold window of the Bank of England would be condemned to idleness only if convertibility forced the Bank to apply the policy rule. Only its interest – provided it was correctly understood by the directors of the Bank – could induce it to do so, and its interest was to avoid being exposed to the Penelope effect. Even the independent commissioners of the public bank advocated by Ricardo as a substitute for the Bank of England (see Chapter 9 below) would implement the policy rule if they knew it was the only way to avoid the shrinking of a metallic reserve voluntarily maintained at a low level. The stabilisation of the market price of the standard at the level of its legal price could not simply be the target of a policy rule without convertibility forcing the implementation of this rule.

I may now conclude on the question raised above: does Ricardo's mature theory of money, as it is embodied in the Money–Standard Equation, apply to inconvertibility? The answer should be that it does not, whether as analysis of the self-adjusting property of the value of money – absent under inconvertibility – or as the theoretical foundation of a monetary policy rule – implausible under inconvertibility. The only use of Ricardo's mature theory of money for the analysis of inconvertibility is to show that the latter is neither self-adjusting nor practicable. Nothing can be said beyond that, something which is not to be regretted since for Ricardo a money without a standard was not viable.

7.6 Conclusion: the specificity of the market for gold bullion

According to Ricardo, in a mixed system of coins and notes convertible into coin, and in the absence of a policy rule applied to the issuing of notes – such as the one advocated by him in his two plans – the quantity of money adjusted thanks to private arbitrage between the market for gold bullion and the bank of issue, whether in the case of a change in the wants of commerce or in the discretionary issuing by the bank. It is thus useful to sum up the specificity of Ricardo's theory of money as regards the relation between the quantity and the value of money and the specificity of the market for gold bullion.

Ricardo's analysis, although it assumed the neutrality of money in respect to the relative prices of commodities, was *not* a quantity theory of money. The integration of the value of money in Ricardo's general theory of value relied on the distinction between a real cause of change – when the relative value of the standard in terms of all other commodities varied for exogenous reasons – and a monetary cause of change – when the actual quantity of money departed from its conformable level and affected the market price of the standard. Whatever the cause of change in the value of money a self-adjusting process was at work. If the cause was real (such as a change in the difficulty of production of gold bullion), the value of money settled permanently at a new level and the prices of all commodities except the standard adjusted accordingly in the same proportion. If the cause was monetary (such as a discretionary change in the note issue, not required by the wants of commerce), the value of money departed temporarily from its initial (conformable) level, before returning to it after the excess or deficiency in the quantity of money had been endogenously eliminated. This corrective process first gave rise to an exportation or importation of bullion but ended up with the Bank changing its issues appropriately for reasons of interest.

The self-adjusting process of the quantity, hence of the value, of money depended on the working of the market for gold bullion, but because gold bullion was the standard of money, its market was very peculiar. Arbitrage was practised on it as on every other market, but the conditions of this practice were unique, because arbitrage was not only with its foreign markets but also with domestic monetary institutions: the mint, where bullion was converted at a legal price into coin, and the Bank of England, where notes were converted at par into coins to be melted into bullion. The outcome of this domestic arbitrage was the equalisation of the market price of bullion with the fixed legal price at which bullion and money were convertible into each other (taking into account the costs of this convertibility). This meant that the market price of the standard was affected by the laws governing these monetary institutions and by their behaviour, independently of what happened to the market prices of all other commodities. In other words, as soon as gold bullion became the standard of money, its market price did *not* gravitate around its natural price – as was the case for all commodities to which the competition of capitals applied – but was stabilised thanks to an adjustment process *sui generis*. As quoted in the epigraph of Chapter 3 above, "In a sound state of the currency the value of gold may vary, but its price cannot" (V: 392).

From a theoretical point of view, the commodity acting as the standard of money thus resembles all other commodities in that it has two prices, one regulating (in Ricardo's parlance) the other. For any commodity produced in competitive conditions there exists a natural price which regulates its market price (according to the so-called Smithian "gravitation"). For the standard of money there exists a legal price, to which the market price adjusts. However, this resemblance conceals a crucial difference. The natural regulating price of any commodity can be determined independently of the market process, that is, independently of any theory of the market price. In the modern Classical theory of prices to be found in Sraffa (1960) and derived from Ricardo, the determination of the price system requires the knowledge of the technical methods of production and of one exogenous distribution variable, under the assumption of a uniform rate of profit, but no particular theory of the market prices: the only assumption is that the system of (natural) prices is "adopted by the market" (Sraffa 1960: 3), whatever the market process that makes it to be so. Nothing of the kind for the legal price of the standard of money: this institutional datum only acquires an economic meaning because of a specific process which adjusts the market price of the standard to it. Far from being of secondary importance, the adjustment process of the market price of gold bullion makes the legal price effective and therefore constitutes it as an economic magnitude: for want of such adjustment, this datum would simply remain outside of economic theory, and money with it.[10]

It is the reason why two symmetrical errors usually stand in the way of a proper understanding of Ricardo's monetary theory: either treating the standard of money (gold bullion) like any other commodity (its market price gravitating around its natural price) or assuming its market price as constant because it is imposed by law. Either way is equally irrelevant since it evacuates the singularity of the standard of money as commodity: the determination of its market price by two apparently contradictory adjustment processes. As a competitively produced commodity, gold bullion is subject to the competition of capitals and its market price is regulated by its cost of production in the least productive mine, which varies exogenously with the discovery of new mines and new mining techniques. The only particular assumption required by Ricardo's analysis of this adjustment is (in modern Sraffian parlance) that gold bullion should be a non-basic commodity so that it affects the rate of profit neither in the gold-producing nor in the gold-importing country (see Chapter 5 above).[11] As the standard of money, gold bullion is subject to arbitrage with domestic monetary institutions and its market price is regulated by the fixed legal price at which bullion is convertible into money and money is convertible into it, independently of its cost of production. A conclusion emerges: this double regulation of the market price of gold bullion may only be non-contradictory if one assumes that *gold bullion is produced outside of the country in which it is used as the standard of money*. The market price of gold bullion in the foreign producing-country (regulated by the cost of production) and its domestic market price (regulated by the legal price) are made coherent with each other through the exchange rate (equation (5.9) in Chapter 5 above).

Being produced abroad was thus for gold bullion *not* a point of fact, consequent upon the absence of mines in England, but a point of theory: the "sound state of a currency" – that is, the self-adjustment of a monetary system endowed with a standard – required this standard to be: (a) non-basic, and (b) produced abroad.[12] In other words, the commodity used as the standard of money in an economy should not be part of the system of production of commodities that determines the relative prices and the distribution of income in this economy.

The determination of the exchange rate which linked the domestic market price of gold bullion and its price in what Ricardo called its "world market" was consequently part of the theory of money. And appropriate monetary rules could stabilise the market price of the standard at the level of its legal price – thus ensuring the conformity of money to the standard – better than a mixed system of coins and notes convertible into coin. These questions will respectively be the objects of the next two chapters.

Appendix 7: The effects of a change in the money supply: real balances, the rate of interest, and Say's Law

Chapters 6 and 7 above have analysed the bullion-price channel of transmission of a monetary shock to the value of money hence to commodity prices, which contrasts with other transmission channels attributed to Ricardo in modern literature, based on the real-balance effect or the rate of interest. The rejection of an interpretation of Ricardo's monetary theory in terms of the Quantity Theory of Money also leads to consider the role of Say's Law in that theory as irrelevant.

1. The real-balance effect

The origin of the idea that in Ricardo a change in the money supply affected commodity prices thanks to a real-balance effect is to be found in Patinkin's discussion of "Neoclassical monetary theory", that is, "the once widely-accepted body of thought which organized monetary theory around a transactions or cash-balance type of equation, and which then used these equations to validate the classical theory of money" (Patinkin 1956: 96). In this context, the real-balance effect was defined by Patinkin as follows:

> The most persuasive formulations of this [classical quantity] theory were developments of the following tripartite thesis: an increase in the amount of money disturbs the optimum relation between the level of money balances and the individual's expenditures; this disturbance generates an increase in the planned volume of these expenditures (the real-balance effect); and this increase creates pressures on the price level which push it upwards until it has risen in the same proportion as the amount of money.
>
> (ibid: 97)

Although "only Wicksell and Fisher provided complete, systematic statements of this thesis" (ibid):

> [I]ndeed, the basic fact underlined by the foregoing thesis – that the causal relationship between money and prices is not at all a mechanical one, but is instead the economic consequence of the prior effect of changes in the amount of money on the demand for commodities – was already a commonplace of the classical quantity-theory tradition of Cantillon, Thornton, Ricardo, and Mill.
>
> (ibid: 98)

Patinkin, however, adds a restriction:

> It must be emphasised that, in contrast to the neoclassical ones, none of these earlier expositions of the quantity theory should be regarded as having recognized the real-balance effect in the fullest sense of the term; for none of them brought out the crucial intermediary stage of the foregoing thesis in which people increase their *flow* of expenditures because they feel that their *stock* of money is too large for their needs. Instead, in a Keynesian-like fashion, these expositions more or less directly connected the increased *outflow* of money expenditures with the increased *inflow* of money receipts.
>
> (ibid; Patinkin's emphasis)

In a note on "the mechanism of the quantity theory in the earlier literature", Patinkin repeats that

> [E]xamples of early expositions of the quantity theory which make it clear that an increase in the quantity of money raises prices through its prior effect in increasing demand are provided by Richard Cantillon, Henry Thornton, David Ricardo, and John Stuart Mill.
>
> (ibid: 375)

Concerning Ricardo, Patinkin refers to four instances in the Bullion Essays and adds: "As against the purely mechanical exposition of the quantity theory in his

Principles, we have the other passages already cited that show that he fully understood the effect of an increase in the quantity of money in increasing demand", the reference to *Principles* being to Chapter XXVII "On currency and banks" with the mention "see in particular" its first page. It may be useful to quote the four passages in the Bullion Essays where, according to Patinkin, "the quantity of money raises prices through its prior effect in increasing demand":

> I do not dispute, that if the Bank were to bring a large additional sum of notes into the market, and offer them on loan, but that they would for a time affect the rate of interest. The same effects would follow from the discovery of a hidden treasure of gold or silver coin. If the amount were large, the Bank, or the owner of the treasure, might not be able to lend the notes or the money at four, nor perhaps, above three per cent.; but having done so, neither the notes, nor the money, would be retained unemployed by the borrowers; they would be sent into every market, and would every where raise the prices of commodities, till they were absorbed in the general circulation. It is only during the interval of the issues of the Bank, and their effect on prices, that we should be sensible of an abundance of money; interest would, during that interval, be under its natural level; but as soon as the additional sum of notes or of money became absorbed in the general circulation, the rate of interest would be as high, and new loans would be demanded with as much eagerness as before the additional issues.
>
> (*High Price*, III: 91)

> What would be done with the gold by the owner of the mine? It must be either employed at interest by himself, or it would finally find its way into the hands of those who would so employ it. This is its natural destination; it may pass through the hands of 100, or 1000 persons, but it could be employed in no other manner at last. Now if the mine should double the quantity of money, it would depress its value in the same proportion, and there would be double the demand for it. A merchant who before required the loan of 10,000*l.* would now want 20,000*l.;* and it could be of little importance to him whether he continued to borrow 10,000*l.* of the Bank, and 10,000*l.* of those with whom the money finally rested, or whether he borrowed the whole 20,000*l.* of the Bank. The analogy seems to me to be complete, and not to admit of dispute. The issues of paper not convertible are guided by the same principle, and will be attended with the same effect as if the Bank were the proprietor of the mine, and issued nothing but gold. However much gold may be increased, borrowers will increase to the same amount, in consequence of its depreciation; and the same rule is equally true with respect to paper. If money be but depreciated sufficiently, there is no amount which may not be absorbed, and it would not make the slightest difference whether the Bank with their notes actually purchased the commodities themselves, or whether they discounted the bills of those who would so employ them.
>
> (*Reply to Bosanquet*, III: 217)

> Suppose the paper in circulation not convertible into specie to be 20 millions, and I have credit sufficient with the bank to get a bill discounted at the Bank for £1000 – wishing to extend my business to that amount. Suppose too that all the other trades possess equal facilities and that by these various bills being discounted a million is added to the circulation. Now the possessors of this additional million have not borrowed it to let it remain idle but for the purpose of extending their different trades. The distiller goes to the corn market with his portion; the cotton manufacturer, the sugar baker &c. with theirs; the quantity of corn, sugar, and cotton in the country remaining precisely the same as before. Will not the effect of this additional million be to raise the prices of all commodities 1/20 or 5 pct. that being the proportion in which the currency is increased. These borrowers of the Bank will succeed in their object of increasing their trade, but by rendering the 20 millions which was before in circulation less efficient there will be a corresponding loss in the trade of those who were before possessed of this sum. As no addition had been made to the quantity of the corn, the sugar or the cotton but only to the prices of those commodities there would be no increased trade but a different division of it. If another million were added to the circulation by new demands for discounts, the same effects would again follow. There can be no limits to the depreciation of money from such repeated additions.
>
> ("Notes on the Bullion Report", III: 362–3)

> The same cause, namely, an increase of money which will induce him [the merchant who buys to sell again] to give a higher price for goods, will secure him one proportionally higher when he sells again. A competition of capitalists keeps down prices, but money is not capital. An increase of capital is attended with all the benefits enumerated; an increase of money to be retained in circulation is unattended with any benefit whatever.
>
> ("Notes on Trotter", III: 390)

These quotations – all from the Bullion Essays – convey an impression of ambivalence. The first and the third seem to validate the real-balance effect interpretation: a given demand for real balances – dependent on the aggregate value of commodities to be circulated – faces an exogenous increase in the money supply, and the commodity prices adjust upwards, through the spending of undesired money balances. It is thus no surprise that, referring to Patinkin, Hollander (1979: 480–1) also used these quotations as proofs of "a clear account of the effect on commodity demand of increased money supplies" (ibid: 481n).

In the second quotation, however, the picture is different. Leaving aside the "analogy" between a mine and the Bank (see Chapter 4 above), commodity prices increase as a consequence of the fall in the value of money which is itself caused by an increase in its supply. The demand for money adjusts to commodity prices, not the other way round. As for the fourth quotation, it is unclear whether the merchant "give[s] a higher price for goods" because he agrees to do so (to deplete his undesired money balances) or is forced to do so (because the seller has passed the fall in the value of money on to price).

One should notice that no quotation consistent with the real-balance effect was found by Patinkin or others in writings beginning with *Proposals for an Economical and Secure Currency* (1816). On the contrary, there are in them numerous examples of statements along the line of the second quotation, as in *Principles*:

> The demand for money is not for a definite quantity, as is the demand for clothes, or for food. The demand for money is regulated entirely by its value, and its value by its quantity.
>
> (I: 193)

In addition, Ricardo's assumption in *Principles* that the system of relative prices of commodities is unaffected by changes in the value of money would require, if the real-balance effect were introduced, that the spending of undesired money balances left relative prices unaltered, an assumption difficult to admit. In contrast, as noted in Chapter 6 above, the competition of capitals for the general rate of profit forced all sellers of commodities to pass the fall in the value of money on to their prices in the same proportion, leaving relative prices unaltered.

In any case, the contention in the present book that Ricardo's mature theory of money was *not* a "quantity theory" – in Patinkin's sense – makes it irrelevant to search for a real-balance effect in it.[13]

2. The rate of interest and changes in commodity prices

The fact that in the instances above the quantity of money increases through discounts by the Bank of England has led some commentators to emphasise the role of the rate of interest in the transmission of a change in the money supply to commodity prices.

Inquiring about the relation between the rate of interest and the rate of profit in Ricardo, Panico (1988) emphasises the relation between the market for loans and the markets for commodities:

> As soon as the market interest rate is below that *natural* level 'solely' determined by the rate of profits (see Ricardo, III, pp. 143 and 376), the demand for loans increases. The opposite happens if the market rate is above the average rate. According to Ricardo, this mechanism enforces the gravitation of the market around the average rate. The increased (decreased) demand for loans will be attended by an increased (decreased) demand for commodities, which creates a rise (fall) in the price level. This process will go on up to when the market interest rate adjusts to the average interest rate.
>
> (Panico, 1988: 17; Panico's emphasis)

The above quotation from *High Price* is then used to show that "the length of the variation of the market interest rate around the average interest rate [...] depended upon the time required by the borrowers to spend in the commodity market the money obtained through new loans" (ibid: 18).

Davis (2005) leans on the same quotation to emphasise the role of the rate of interest in the rise of the price level:

> Ricardo envisioned the process as follows. An expansion of the money supply lowers the rate of interest. The fall of interest stimulates demand in all markets and thereby raises prices. As prices rise, the demand for loanable funds increases until such time as interest rates return to normal levels.
>
> (Davis 2005: 9)

As the quotation from Ricardo makes clear, the rise in prices was envisaged by him to contend that an increase in the amount of money did not permanently lower the rate of interest, which ultimately depended on the rate of profit – a statement repeated over and over again from the Bullion Essays to the 1819–1823 papers. Although Ricardo admitted that an increased note issue by the Bank of England temporarily depressed the rate of interest, it is doubtful that any functional relation according to which "the fall of interest stimulates demand in all markets" might be found in his writings. The fall in the rate of interest and the rise in prices were two parallel effects of the increase in the money supply, including when there was a speculative boom. Being examined on 26 March 1819 by the Lords' Committee on the Resumption of Cash Payments and asked "Has not the increase of prices during the progressive depreciation of paper a tendency to produce over-trading, and excessive speculation?" Ricardo answered:

> I think over-speculation has rather been encouraged by the facility with which speculators have been enabled to raise money upon discount, in consequence of the progressive increase of paper issues.
>
> (V: 446)

The question of the effect of a change in the quantity of money on general prices through a change in the rate of interest could be clarified by a comparison between Ricardo and Wicksell, who in his *Lectures on Political Economy* (originally published in 1901–1906 and translated into English in 1934–1935) elaborated his own theory by starting from a detailed and critical analysis of Ricardo's. The following aspects are only an indication of the direction that such a comparison could take. As mentioned in Chapters 5 and 7 above, Ricardo contended that any quantity of money could "perform the same functions in circulation" depending on its value, because "the demand for money is not for a definite quantity, as is the demand for clothes, or for food. The demand for money is regulated entirely by its value, and its value by its quantity" (*Principles*; I: 193). This idea was echoed in Wicksell:

> That a large and a small quantity of money *can* serve the same purposes of turnover if commodity prices rise or fall proportionately to the quantity is one

> thing. It is another thing to show why such a change of price must always follow a change in the quantity of money and to describe what happens.
>
> (Wicksell 1934–1935, Vol. II: 160; Wicksell's emphasis)

Ricardo's analysis and what Wicksell calls "the positive solution" to the problem of money (ibid: 190 sq.) have in common to consider an indirect link between the quantity of money and general prices, to describe the adjustment triggered by a monetary disequilibrium and restrict it to a system with convertibility (Ricardo excluding it under inconvertibility and Wicksell in "a pure credit economy"), and to suggest a policy rule that allows stabilising the value of money at the required level without having to know what this level is. However, they differ on the exact content of each of these aspects: the transmission channel of the quantity of money to prices is the market price of gold in Ricardo and the bank rate of interest in Wicksell; the adjustment to a discretionary increase in the quantity of money restores the initial level of prices in Ricardo and only stops their rise in Wicksell (prices remaining at the new equilibrium level); the policy rule enforces in Ricardo the fulfilment of the equality between the value of money and the (unknown) value of the standard and in Wicksell that of the equality between the bank rate of interest and the (unknown) natural rate. The general perspective is also different: while Wicksell wished to rescue the Quantity Theory of Money from its shortcomings, Ricardo's analysis, as shown in Chapter 7 above, was not a quantity theory of money.

3. Say's Law

The usual link between the role of Say's Law in Ricardo's macroeconomics and his alleged quantity theory of money wanders from the subject if, beginning with *Proposals on Economical and Secure Currency*, such theory is not to be found in Ricardo. The conventional view is, however, endorsed by King (2013: 120): "There is a very clear link between Ricardo's position on Say's Law and his approach to monetary theory, and here again there is strong support for the conventional interpretation", an interpretation which King summarises as follows:

> [Say's Law] induced Ricardo to deny the existence of 'general gluts', and with them any possibility that output might be constrained by deficient effective demand. This also led Ricardo to endorse a strict version of the Quantity Theory of Money and thereby also to accept the neutrality of money.
>
> (ibid: 112–13)

In his "Note on Say's Law", Patinkin had discussed "the question as to whether Say, Ricardo, Mill – both senior and junior – and other deniers of the possibility of a 'general glut' did or did not think in terms of this [Say's] identity" (Patinkin 1956: 472). For Patinkin, Keynes and Lange subscribed to the interpretation of the Classicals as advocates of Say's Law as an identity, while Becker, Baumol, and Schumpeter:

> [M]aintain that Say's Law was not intended as an identity; that classical economists had reference only to the long-run ability of the economy to absorb any increase in output; and that this is attested by their explicit recognition of the possibility of short-run oversupply in the market.
>
> (ibid: 474)

Concerning Ricardo, Patinkin mentioned several illustrations tending to give credit to the latter interpretation but nevertheless concluded: "Even if we accept this secular interpretation of Say's Law – and the evidence in favour of it is convincing – we must again emphasize that classical economists failed to specify the market mechanism which makes this law valid" (ibid: 475).

Taking up this question Hollander (1979) devoted a whole chapter to "The quantity theory and the law of markets", which concluded that:

> [M]y analysis of the quantity theory earlier in this chapter has demonstrated a conscious allowance on Ricardo's part for depressions generated by sudden contraction of the money supply, and a conscious treatment of the effects on prices generated by money supply increases in terms of an initial pressure on commodity demand in commodity markets.
>
> (Hollander 1979: 512)

According to Hollander, an illustration of the fact that "it is 'Say's Equality' to which Ricardo ascribed" (ibid) was provided by Ricardo's position in the post-war depression.

Following Hollander, there has been a vast literature which thus concerned both the analytics of Say's Law in Ricardo and its use in his understanding of facts. Peach (1993) and O'Brien (1995) converge in considering that Ricardo was guilty of Schumpeter's famous Ricardian-Vice accusation of applying "to the solution of practical problems" a method in which "the desired results emerged almost as tautologies" (Schumpeter 1954: 473). For Peach:

> [Say's Law] was also much more than a purely abstract doctrine. The 'law', which subsumed the principles of rationality and near-perfect market knowledge, was evidently thought to capture the *modus operandi* of the real economic system; and, contrary to S. Hollander's account, the nature of the doctrine and, more importantly, the manner in which it was applied by Ricardo, are alone sufficient to convict him on the charge of the 'Ricardian Vice'. This judgment stands regardless of his adherence to the 'equality' version of the doctrine (an interpretation which, I argue, is *weakly* preferable to the 'identity' alternative). For, although Ricardo did make limited allowance for temporary maladjustments, his emphasis always remained firmly, and

> characteristically, on 'equilibrium' tendencies. Moreover, when he was confronted by an external world which confounded his 'law'-based expectations, his response was to blame reality, not his model.
>
> (Peach 1993: 15, Peach's emphasis; see also: 140–1)

For O'Brien (1995: 52), Schumpeter's Ricardian Vice implied:

> [A]nother vice which may be called the 'Ricardian telescope' [...] Ricardo habitually concentrated on the long-run equilibrium position and ignored the process of adjustment. Economists who concentrate only upon the relationship between the long-run equilibrium values of macroeconomic variables are guilty of the vice of employing the Ricardian Telescope.

This evaluation was left unchanged twelve years later when this article was included as Chapter 5 of O'Brien (2007: 81–2).

Other authors, however, have introduced qualifications to such a charge. Before Hollander, Gootzeit had tried to show that "a more careful formulation of its basic elements would have saved the Ricardian system from one of its most fundamental weaknesses – the lack of integration between the monetary and real sectors of the economy" (Gootzeit 1975: ix). For him, it is true that in *Principles* Ricardo "did not think it necessary to include a carefully coordinated analysis of his monetary system, which was more descriptive than theoretical" (ibid: 9). However, "Ricardo's monetary writings [the Bullion Essays] exhibited a 'sophisticated' version of Say's Law because his analysis of the market clearing relationship in a growing inflationary economy concentrated on short run maladjustments generated from the money to the output market" (ibid: 19). It should be noted that this "integration" suggested by Gootzeit takes for granted that Ricardo advocated a quantity theory of money.

Ahiakpor (1985: 19–20) also emphasises that:

> [W]ith regard to the variations in the quantity of money and their possible effect on relative prices, Ricardo offered three reasons for the non-neutrality of money: [...] lagged adjustment [of nominal prices], income distributional effects, [...] and the role played by taxes on prices (or profits).

For Davis (2005: 185):

> Ricardo's preference for stable prices above all other monetary objectives does not imply that he was blind to the effects of money on output and employment. His ingot plan, his allowance for devaluation if the currency was highly depreciated, and his criticism of the Bank's return to gold all demonstrate that he recognized the nonneutrality of money.

Focusing on Ricardo as "an empirical economist", Davis maintains that "Ricardo's account of the postwar period relied on a distinction between temporary and permanent causes of distress" (ibid: 41) with monetary shocks being listed in the temporary causes, and that he "attributed postwar economic crises to a series of exogenous shocks [to which] Britain responded quickly", a diagnosis confirmed by historical facts (ibid: 37). Recognising the link in Ricardo between his quantity theory of money and short-run adjustment does not, however, necessarily lead to exonerate him from the toxic influence of Say's Law, as illustrated by Green:

> This group [the bullionists "led by Ricardo"] maintained that exogenous changes in the money supply would be reflected in corresponding variations in the price level, which followed from their assumption of a fixed level of output and monetary velocity. In other words, *their short-run quantity 'theory' of money was no theory at all but simply a logical outcome of assuming Say's Law*. The inflationary process was seen as the transitional mechanism by which monetary deviations were corrected: 'That commodities would rise or fall in price, in proportion to the increase or diminution of money, I assume as a fact which is incontrovertible' (Ricardo, *Works*, III, p. 193fn).
>
> (Green 1998: 137; my emphasis)

As shown by equation (7.4) in Chapter 7 above, Ricardo's "incontrovertible" conclusion neither requires a quantity theory of money nor does it derive from Say's Law.

There is no doubt that the existence of maladjustments in the employment of capital was considered by Ricardo as a possible cause of economic crisis. Sraffa quotes a witness of a discussion between Malthus and Ricardo in December 1820 writing in his diary:

> Mr Ricardo and Mr Malthus came and entertained us for two hours and upwards with an argument in defence of their respective theories on Political Economy. Mr Malthus contending that the present distress arose from unemployed capital and Ricardo from misemployed capital which would soon assume its proper channels.
>
> (quoted in VIII: 334n)

A little earlier, Ricardo had written to Malthus on 9 October 1820:

> With abundance of capital and a low price of labour there cannot fail to be some employments which would yield good profits, and if a superior genius had the arrangement of the capital of the country under his controul, he might, in a very little time, make trade as active as ever. Men err in their productions, there is no deficiency of demand.
>
> (VIII: 277)

However, as mentioned in Chapter 7 above, Ricardo's method was to analyse monetary disequilibrium – defined by the divergence between the actual and the conformable quantities of money – in reference to a real economy in its natural state. The study of maladjustments in the employment of capital appears thus separate from the study of monetary disequilibrium.[14]

In any case, despite contrasting views in modern literature about the link between Ricardo's alleged quantity theory of money and his use of Say's Law, this question loses a great part of its importance in the absence of such theory.

Notes

1 Unless the demand for import addressed to the world market for bullion induced the opening of less productive mines and consequently raised the value of bullion, hence the value of money. This might occur if the wants of commerce increased simultaneously in all countries, but was unlikely if it was the case in only one.

2 The "great distress" suffered by the economy in the interval before the coining of imported bullion was also emphasised by Ricardo in the analytically identical case of an import of bullion generated by a discretionary contraction in the note issue by the Bank of England. See the speech in Parliament on 12 June 1822 referred to in the following note.

3 In a speech in Parliament on 12 June 1822, Ricardo emphasised the hurtful consequences for the economy of a discretionary contraction in the note issue by the Bank of England, because there would be an interval of "great distress" before imported gold would be coined and fill the gap in the required quantity of money:

> His hon. friend had said, that whilst the Bank was obliged to pay its notes in gold, the public had no interest in interfering with the Bank respecting the amount of the paper circulation, for if it were too low, the deficiency would be supplied by the importation of gold, and if it were too high, it would be reduced by the exchange of paper for gold. In this opinion he did not entirely concur, because there might be an interval during which the country might sustain great inconvenience from an undue reduction of the Bank circulation. Let him put a case to elucidate his views on this subject. Suppose the Bank were to reduce the amount of their issues to five millions, what would be the consequence? The foreign exchanges would be turned in our favour, and large quantities of bullion would be imported. This bullion would be ultimately coined into money, and would replace the paper-money which had previously been withdrawn; but, before it was so coined, while all these operations were going on, the currency would be at a very low level, the prices of commodities would fall, and great distress would be suffered. Something of this kind had, in fact, happened.
>
> (V: 199–200)

4 In an article published in 1802 in the *Edinburgh Review* and commenting on Thornton's *Paper Credit* (see III: 64 n3). At that time there were still coins in circulation side by side with inconvertible Bank of England notes, and it is the reason why Ricardo discussed this case, although when he did so (in 1810) nearly all coins had disappeared.

5 The role of the specific effect in the market for bullion in lowering its value and prompting its exportation was *a contrario* emphasised by Ricardo when he described the actual case (in 1810): all coins having disappeared from domestic circulation, the supply of bullion in the market could no longer be increased by their melting, hence the value of bullion did *not* fall. The above-quoted note in *High Price* continues:

> When the circulation consists wholly of paper, any increase in its quantity will raise the *money* price of bullion without lowering its *value*, in the same manner, and in the same proportion, as it will raise the prices of other commodities, and for

the same reason will lower the foreign exchanges; but this will only be a *nominal*, not a *real* fall, and will not occasion the exportation of bullion, because the real value of bullion will not be diminished, as there will be no increase to the quantity in the market.

(*High Price*, III: 64; note; Ricardo's emphasis)

6 In the Appendix to the fourth edition of *High Price*, Ricardo used an expression very similar to the one he quoted from Thornton about "the coiners and melters": with his plan of convertibility of the Bank of England note into bullion, "there would be no temptation to melt the coin, and consequently the labour which has been so uselessly bestowed by one party in recoining what another party found it their interest to melt into bullion, would be effectually saved" (III: 127).

7 Comparing the inconvertibility case with two monetary systems, one with "*a mixed currency of coin and notes*, convertible into specie on demand, and freedom of metallic exportation" and one "*where (convertible) notes alone circulate*", Hollander (1979: 439–40) concludes:

> As far as concerns the mechanism of bullion movement, *the two cases of convertibility are analytically identical with the inconvertible case where a mixed currency circulates*, for in this case too an addition to the note issue will generate corrective outflows.
>
> (Hollander's emphasis)

It appears that for the "corrective outflows" of bullion convertibility and inconvertibility are *not* "analytically identical": under convertibility of the Bank of England note, the reduction of the note issue under the pressure of the Penelope effect sooner or later substitutes for the exportation of bullion as corrective process.

8 Marcuzzo and Rosselli also reject the traditional interpretation of Ricardo's monetary theory as a quantity theory of money, and they contrast the notion of "natural" quantity of money with the usual notion of "equilibrium" quantity of money: "It is our contention that the definition of the natural quantity of money in Ricardo is given by analogy with the definition of natural wages and natural prices" (Marcuzzo and Rosselli 2015: 374). This "analogy" is based on two common aspects: first, "the natural quantity of money, like other natural magnitudes, puts to rest the forces that determine its changes"; second, a distinction applies between variations which "may be permanent, that is, reflecting changes in the structure of the economy that require a different natural level for the quantity of money, or temporary" (ibid). These two aspects are obviously linked: the "temporary" deviations from the "permanent" level of "natural" magnitudes are corrected by a self-adjusting process, and the question is thus whether the analogy may hold for it. This seems dubious for two reasons. First, the quantity of money permanently required by the wants of commerce is endogenous, in contrast with natural quantities of commodities which are exogenous. Second, the adjustment process is specific to money: one thing is to say that the adjustment of the quantity of money is market-driven because it responds to profitability conditions in the bullion market; another thing is to draw an analogy with the adjustment in the markets for all other commodities. Arbitrage in the domestic market for gold bullion is permitted by the existence of an institutional set-up (convertibility at a legal price) which makes this particular commodity the standard of money and has no equivalent for any other commodity. On the specificity of this market, see Section 7.6 above.

9 See also in the manuscript "Draft on Peel" of December 1821:

> He supposed that the reverting from a currency regulated by no standard, to one regulated by a fixed one, the greatest care would be taken to make the transition as

> little burthensome as possible, but the fact is that if the object had been to make the alteration from the one system to the other as distressing to the country as possible no measures could have been taken by the Bank of England so well calculated to produce that effect as those which they actually adopted.
>
> (V: 519)

10 In modern parlance, one would say that for all other commodities produced in competitive conditions the question of the existence of the price system can be solved in the absence of a definite analysis of its stability – the price system analysed in Sraffa (1960) is an example of this method – while for the commodity acting as the standard of money, the existence of its legal price as an economic magnitude depends on a specific analysis of its stability. In other words, the Ricardo–Sraffa tradition on the price question leaves stability (the determination of price in disequilibrium) outside the theory, while Ricardo's theory of money puts it centre-stage: the legal price of the standard actually rules the roost insofar as its market price is subject to a definite adjustment process.

11 "The criterion is whether a commodity enters (no matter whether directly or indirectly) into the production of *all* commodities. Those that do we shall call *basic*, and those that do not, *non-basic* products" (Sraffa 1960: 8; Sraffa's emphasis). The consequences of this distinction are as follows:

> These [non-basic] products have no part in the determination of the system. Their role is purely passive. If an invention were to reduce by half the quantity of each of the means of production which are required to produce a unit of a 'luxury' commodity of this type, the commodity itself would be halved in price, but there would be no further consequences; the price-relations of the other products and the rate of profits would remain unaffected. But if such a change occurred in the production of the opposite [basic] type, which *does* enter the means of production, all prices would be affected and the rate of profits would be changed.
>
> (ibid: 7–8; Sraffa's emphasis)

12 In this sense, Ricardo's image of a gold mine being discovered on the premises of the Bank of England was not only inappropriate to the understanding of an increased note issue (see Chapter 4 above) but also unfortunate for the understanding of the nature of the standard. This may be the reason why Ricardo only used this image in the Bullion Essays, not in his mature theory of money, which put the standard centre-stage.

13 Discussing Ricardo's "failure to tease out the implications for the demand for money of a bad harvest or of foreign remittances", Glasner (2013: 20) remarks that:

> [T]he demand for money was not part of Ricardo's basic theoretical repertoire, although he was able to recognize cases in which there was an exceptional demand for money, e.g. during a financial crisis. The idea of a functional change in the demand for money was just slightly beyond the limits of his prodigious theoretical reach.

The absence of a "functional" demand for money was rather an advantage than a shortcoming in Ricardo's theory of money, and his analysis of a shock on the exchange rate could dispense with it (see Chapter 8 below).

14 For a different view see Martin (2008).

Part III

Policy

8 The international adjustment to a monetary shock

It appears to me, that the balance of payments is frequently the effect of the situation of our currency, and not the cause.

(Evidence before the Commons' Committee on the Resumption of Cash Payments, 4 March 1819; V: 395)

Among the many paradoxes that plague the evaluation of Ricardo in the literature, his treatment of international economics does not give rise to the least. On the one hand, modern economic textbooks frequently only mention Ricardo for his contribution to the analysis of international trade, the exchange of English cloth for Portuguese wine being one of the favourite landmarks in basic economic knowledge. On the other hand, his contention that an excess note issue was in all circumstances the sole cause of a fall in the exchange rate has nourished the recurrent accusation of theoretical extremism, in contrast with someone like Thornton who acknowledged that exogenous factors affecting the balance of payments could also be responsible for such unfavourable exchange. It is not difficult to explain why in the same field of economic analysis universal praise may coexist with utmost indignity. The fame of the Ricardian model of international specialisation owes much to its reformulation in neo-classical terms by the so-called Heckscher–Ohlin–Samuelson theorem, which abstracts from money. And the question of whether an excess quantity of money is a necessary and sufficient condition for a fall in the exchange rate is usually understood as a short-term macroeconomic problem, distinct from the long-term microeconomic selection (based on comparative costs) of the pattern of international trade. The supposed absence of linkage between the two questions makes it easy to applaud Ricardo for the one and blame him for the other.

Along the path opened by Viner (1937: 138–7, 295–6) and Rist (1940 [1938]: 159–70), modern literature has discussed the role of international adjustment in Ricardo's monetary theory, although with diverse and often conflicting interpretations (see, for example, Mason 1957, Grubel 1961, O'Brien 1975, Peake 1978, Hollander 1979, Chipman 1984, Perlman 1986, Marcuzzo and Rosselli 1987, 1991, Deleplace 2001, 2008, Davis 2005, de Boyer des Roches 2007, 2008, 2013, Rosselli 2008). Most – but not all – of this literature attributes to Ricardo a crude version of the price-specie flow mechanism, originating in Hume (1752) (see Chapter 1 above), which relies on changes both in the quantity of money and in the balance of trade. In this literature the story of the international adjustment in Ricardo usually goes like this. The only possible cause of a country's foreign deficit is the excess in the domestic quantity of money. Starting by assumption from an equilibrium situation, characterised by a given distribution of the precious metals amongst the nations of the world, an increase in the domestic quantity of money above the natural level corresponding to that distribution lowers the value of the currency in terms of commodities, a corollary being that the money prices of all commodities proportionally increase. Goods produced domestically become dearer in comparison with the same goods produced abroad; exports are reduced and imports increased, so that the balance of trade is against the country. By the same token, the depreciated domestic currency becomes cheaper in terms of the foreign ones. The coin and bullion are exported, paying for the trade deficit, and the quantity of money is consequently reduced. This process goes on as long as the currency remains in excess, and stops only when the natural level of the quantity of money is restored. Domestic prices regain their equilibrium level and so do exports and imports, bringing the trade balance back to even and the exchange rate at its equilibrium level.

Following the demonstration, made in Chapter 7 above, that the usual attribution to Ricardo of a quantity theory of money is erroneous, the object of the present chapter is to show that this usual story does not fit Ricardo's analysis of international adjustment to a monetary shock. So doing, it is in keeping with a trend of research opened by Marcuzzo and Rosselli (1991) and complementing the old question of real versus monetary causes of gold flows and of variation in the exchange rate with the new question of how these changes were implemented (for the most recent and compact exposition of this shift in perspective, see Rosselli 2008). The chapter is divided into five sections. First, I will show that Ricardo used notions widely accepted at the time – such as the real par of exchange and the bullion export and import points (Section 8.1). He used them to explain how international adjustment operated in two successive steps, implying gold bullion and other commodities (Section 8.2). The much-criticised proposition according to which a fall in the exchange rate could only be explained by a redundancy of currency appears then, with appropriate qualification, as a necessary outcome of his monetary theory (Section 8.3). In Ricardo's view, international adjustment was not to be expected from the effect of hydraulics of money on the balance of trade – the so-called price-specie flow mechanism – but from an active management of the quantity of money (Section 8.4). This analysis fits Ricardo's general approach to money, as it is illustrated by the Ingot Plan, and includes the foreign balance in the policy rule to be applied to the monetary system – what will later be called the gold-exchange standard (Section 8.5).

8.1 Real par of exchange and bullion points

The legal par of exchange

The notion of par of exchange is as old as the trade in foreign bills of exchange. In the sixteenth century, at the peak of the European network of exchange by bills centred on the fairs of Lyons, Italian merchant-bankers were accustomed to calculate the "*parità*" on the basis of the legal values of the coins accepted to discharge the balance after clearing of their credits and debts. Knowing the intrinsic weight of pure metal legally contained in the gold coins of the various countries between which they traded bills, and the values in each monetary unit at which these coins were legal tender, they could calculate for any pair of these monetary units the level of the exchange rate that equalised the quantities of gold contained in the corresponding coins. This benchmark – the par of exchange – could then be used by the merchant-bankers collectively – when the list of exchange rates ("*conto*") was voted at the end of each of the four yearly Lyons fairs – or individually – when a particular bill was negotiated – to determine the actual exchange rates written in the bills. Since at that time the best gold coins of the major continental coinages (France, Spain, Florence, Genoa, Venice) were legal tender in the countries linked by the network of bills of exchange, there was not one but several legal pars according to the coin on which they were calculated. The "art" – as it was then called – of merchant-banking was to take advantage of this variety for the calculation of the exchange rates written in the bills, so as both to generate profit and to comply with the legal values of the currencies fixed by the States (see Boyer-Xambeu, Deleplace and Gillard 1986, 1994a).

Things changed in the seventeenth century, for two reasons. First an institutional one: in most countries foreign coins were prohibited from circulating and had to be exchanged for domestic coins at the counters of money-changers. There existed now one single legal par of exchange for each pair of monetary units, equal to the ratio of the legal prices of a given weight of pure metal coined by each of the two mints. Secondly there was a theoretical reason: it was more and more recognised that the divergence between the actual exchange rate, quoted regularly in the foreign-exchange market, and the legal par of exchange, was an indicator of the state of the balance of trade between the two corresponding countries. When the aggregate value (measured in any of the two monetary units) of the exports from country A to country B was equal to the aggregate value (measured in the same unit) of the imports of A from B, bills issued in A on B to pay for the imports exactly balanced bills issued in B on A to pay for the exports. The foreign-exchange market cleared the payments between the two countries without any transfer of precious metal being necessary. Neither exporters nor importers were in a position to obtain in this market more of the foreign money than what was indicated by the par. In contrast, when the aggregate value of the exports from A to B was greater (lower) than the aggregate value of the imports of A from B, competition among exporters (importers) to sell (buy) the foreign money increased (decreased) the exchange rate of the domestic money above (below) the par. By comparing the actual exchange rate with the par it was thus possible to infer the state of the balance of trade between the two countries.

This was not just a matter of diagnosis; the cure of the illness was also involved. When the balance of trade of A with B was adverse, it had to be paid one way or another. If A had a positive balance with C, credits on C could be used to pay for the deficit with B. It was the job of traders in bills of exchange to implement such international arbitrage between foreign-exchange markets – with profit. But if the foreign balance of A – that is, the consolidated balance with all foreign countries – was adverse, precious metals (gold and silver) had to be transported abroad in order to pay for the deficit. Here also, this operation was implemented by private arbitragers, and, in addition to the foreign-exchange markets, it involved the markets for bullion. By bullion one meant exportable gold or silver, whether in the form of bars or coins taken by weight, since, because foreign coins were not legal tender, a debt could only be discharged abroad through the coining of the exported bullion at the local mint. This exportation of bullion consequent upon an adverse foreign balance was not only a source of profit for private arbitragers. From a mercantilist point of view, in which precious metals were considered as a privileged form of wealth, it meant that the country impoverished itself: it was an illness to be cured.

Again, both an institutional and a theoretical question were raised by international arbitrage on bullion. First, a market for bullion had to be organised in each main centre where bills of exchange were traded, with regular quotations advertised publicly. In London, John Castaing, "brooker at his office, Jonathans Coffee House", started in 1698 to publish every Tuesday and Friday (the days of quotation) *The Course of Exchange*, which contained quotations of the exchange rates of the pound against various foreign currencies, as well as the prices of gold and silver bars and of some foreign coins taken by weight. Second, the observed practice of arbitrage on foreign exchange and bullion raised the question of the conditions of arbitrage. When, because of an adverse balance of trade, the exchange rate of the pound against a given foreign currency (say, French *livres*) fell, there came a moment when traders in the London market for bullion discovered that a profit could be made with the following operations: they sold at a high price a bill of exchange in *livres* payable in Paris, purchased gold bullion with the proceeds in pounds, exported it to Paris where it was sold for *livres* used to pay the bill. Alternatively, they could advance their own money to purchase in London gold bullion to be sold in Paris, and reimburse themselves by buying in Paris at a low price a bill of exchange in pounds payable in London. In both cases, the profit by arbitrage was equal to the difference between the arbitrated price of bullion in Paris – that is, its market price in *livres* converted into pounds at the ruling exchange rate – and its price in the London market, taking into account the cost of transportation of gold bullion from London to Paris.

This international arbitrage on foreign exchange and bullion had an effect on the exchange rate of the pound against *livres*: since arbitragers sold in London a bill in *livres* payable in Paris or bought in Paris a bill in pounds payable in London, an upward pressure was triggered on the pound, which counteracted the downward pressure consequent upon the adverse balance of trade. If arbitrage was powerful enough – thanks to the organisation of the bullion markets – it stopped the fall of the pound. Arbitrage itself stopped when the rise of the pound triggered by it cancelled the profit made. The level at which the exchange rate then settled was the export bullion-point: exportation of bullion by arbitrage started when the falling exchange rate of the pound hit this point. Symmetrically, a rise in the exchange rate of the pound consequent upon a favourable balance of trade with France triggered an import of gold when it hit the import bullion-point, and this prevented the pound from rising further.

The main conclusion was that international arbitrage on bullion stabilised the exchange rate within limits which depended on the magnitudes entering the calculation of the arbitragers. These magnitudes were of two kinds: the various costs involved by the transfer of bullion from, say, London to Paris (at the export) and Paris to London (at the import) and the price of gold in each of the two financial centres. In the same manner as the deviation of the exchange rate from the legal par was an indicator of the state of the balance of payments between two countries, the addition (subtraction) of the parametric cost of transfer of bullion to (from) the legal par of exchange gave the import (export) bullion-point at which international arbitrage started and stopped the rise (fall) of the exchange rate. At the end of the seventeenth century, these notions of par of exchange and of bullion points were common knowledge among international arbitragers and authors discussing the state of the exchange.

The real par of exchange according to Steuart

The use of the legal par of exchange to infer whether the balance of payments with a given foreign country was favourable or adverse and to calculate the import and export bullion points by which the variations in the exchange rate were constrained was convenient because the legal price of gold in coin in each country was a given magnitude which was left unchanged by the State, except in extraordinary circumstances. But it nevertheless opened a margin of error, both for the diagnosis of the balance of payments and the calculation of the bullion points. The reason for this error was to be found in the inaccuracy of the circulating coins for calculating the par of exchange that equalised the quantities of gold contained in them. This was obvious when circulating coins were debased, that is, when wear and tear or clipping made them contain less pure gold than they legally should. The real par of exchange, as it was called – that is, the par that equalised the *actual* quantities of gold contained in the domestic and the foreign coins – then differed from the legal par of exchange – calculated on the basis of the *legal* quantities. More generally, international arbitragers on gold bullion purchased and sold it in its domestic and foreign markets, where the price – hence the conditions of arbitrage – could differ from the legal price of gold in coin. The diagnosis of the balance of payments and the understanding of the limits between which the exchange rate could vary required the analysis of the factors which could make the market price of gold bullion diverge from the legal price of gold in coin – hence the real par of exchange diverge from the legal par.

The author who in the second half of the eighteenth century most attracted attention on this question was Sir James Steuart, of whom Ricardo said that "[his] writings on the subject of coin and money are full of instruction" (*Proposals*, IV: 59). In his *Principles of Political Oeconomy* (1767), Steuart criticised Cantillon[1] for calculating "the par of exchange according to the common rule", that is, the legal par:

> Mr. Cantillon, in his *Analysis of Trade*, which I suppose he understood by practice as well as by theory, has the following passage in his 99th page: "The

> course of exchange between Paris and London since the year 1726, has been at a medium price of 32 pence sterling for the crown of three livres; that is to say, we pay for this French crown of three livres, 32 pence sterling, *when calculated on gold*, when in fact it is worth but thirty-pence and three farthings, which is giving four pounds in the hundred for this French money; and consequently, upon gold, the balance of trade is 4 *per cent.* against England in favour of France." In this place, Mr. Cantillon calculates the par of exchange according to the common rule, to wit, gold bullion against gold bullion in the coins of both nations, where both are supposed to be of legal weight; and he finds that there has been, these thirty-four years past, a balance of 4 *per cent.* against England. Now, according to my theory, it is exactly what the coinage in France ought to produce, supposing on an average that the trade had been at par.
>
> (Steuart 1767, II: 17; III: 35)[2]

What was Steuart's "theory", which attributed the alleged unfavourable exchange of 32 pence per French crown (above the legal par of 30.75) to the characteristics of coinage in France, and not to an adverse English balance with France as supposed by Cantillon? It was based on the notion of "real par of exchange":

> The general rule, therefore, I think, is, to settle the real par of different coins, not according to the *bullion* they contain, but according to the bullion they are worth in their own market at the time.
>
> (ibid, II: 23; III: 41; Steuart's emphasis)

One should thus determine the par by calculating, not the ratio of the respective quantities of gold legally contained in the full-bodied coins of both nations, but the ratio of the respective market prices of the same quantity of gold bullion. An analysis based on the legal par of exchange did not reflect the "complicated operations" of merchants and precluded the understanding of "the principles upon which they are founded":

> To calculate, as every body does, the par of the French crown, either by the gold or the silver in the English *standard* coin, when no such *standard* coin exists; and to state all that is given for the crown above 29½*d.*, if you reckon by the silver, or 30¾*d.* if you reckon by the gold, for the price of a wrong balance, is an error which may lead to the most fatal consequences.
>
> (ibid, II: 320; III: 344)

In contrast with the legal par of exchange which was fixed, the real par of exchange might take a maximum or a minimum value according to the possible deviation of the market price of gold bullion from the legal price of gold in coin in each country:

> But suppose two cases which may happen, viz. 1. That gold bullion at Paris should be at the price of coin, while at London it may be at mint price; or,

> 2. That at Paris it may be at mint price, when at London it is at 4*l*. 0*s*. 8*d*. what will then the real par of exchange be? I answer, that on the first supposition, it will be [...] the crown of 3 livres equal to 30.076 pence sterling. In the other, [it will be] for the crown of 3 livres 33.728. A difference of no less than 8.9 *per cent*. Is it not evident that these variations *must* occur in the exchange between London and Paris? And is it not also plain, that they proceed from the fluctuation of the price of bullion, not from exchange?
>
> (ibid, II: 319; III: 343)

In the first case, the market price of gold bullion was at its maximum in Paris (equal to "the price of coin") and at its minimum in London (equal to "mint price"); the real par of exchange of the French crown in English money – equal to the ratio of the market price of gold bullion in London to that in Paris[3] – was at its minimum, viz. 30.076 pence sterling per crown. In the second case, the market price of gold bullion was at its minimum in Paris (equal to "mint price") and at its maximum in London (equal to £4. 0s. 8d., giving a melting cost of 3.6 per cent);[4] the real par of exchange was at its maximum, viz. 33.728 pence sterling per crown. An observed exchange rate of 32 pence per crown, which, compared to the legal par of 30.75, seemed to indicate a balance with France of 4 per cent against England, really revealed a favourable balance for England when compared to a real par of 33.728 (for more details, see Deleplace 2015d).

The bullion points in Ricardo

At the time of Ricardo, all that was well-known, and the gold-points mechanism, as it would be called later in the literature, was disputed by no one. This of course included Ricardo.[5] The two factors constraining the variations in the exchange rate – the cost of transferring bullion from one country to the other, and the real par of exchange – were mentioned by him on various occasions, in the Bullion Essays or in later writings.

In addition to the profit at the general rate, the transfer cost included transportation and the interest rate during the length of the operation:

> Your remark that if no expences whatever attended the transmission of the metals from one country to another the exchange might nevertheless deviate from par on account of the time necessary to transmit them is quite correct, I consider the loss of interest for the time occupied in transmitting them as a part of the expence.
>
> (Letter to McCulloch, 18 December 1819; VIII: 141)

In peacetime, the cost of transferring bullion was low, viz. less than 1 per cent with Paris in 1822:

> Mr. Ricardo wished to set the hon. baronet right, as to the state of the exchange, which was now, he could assure him, very nearly at par; and it was impossible

> it could be far otherwise, because with a metallic circulation in this country and in France, the exchange could never vary more than from ½ to ¾ per cent.
>
> (Speech in Parliament on 16 May 1822; V: 186–7)

However, during the Napoleonic wars, this cost was equal to several percentage points (Ricardo mentioned 4 or 5 per cent between London and Hamburg in 1809 and 7 per cent in 1811; III: 24 and 198 respectively), especially after the Milan decrees implemented a blockade of all trade between Britain and the Continent:

> The exchange in my opinion is, even in these turbulent times, rarely operated upon but by two causes: one, and that by far the most common is an alteration, or an apprehended alteration, in the relative prices of commodities in the two countries between which the exchange is estimated, and is in most cases to be traced to some augmentation or diminution in the amount of the currency of one of them. The other is an increased or diminished difficulty and expence, (or the anticipation of such) attending the transmission of money. The exchange with the continent has, I believe, for a length of time, not only been unfavourable to this country to the amount of the depreciation of our currency but considerably more, as much more probably as to 10 to 15 pc[t]. This real difference in the *price* of money, (for the exchange expresses nothing more than the relative price, and not the relative value of money) as well as the real difference in the price of sugar or coffee, may be attributed to the difficulties which our enemy has interposed in the way of exportation. If then these difficulties should diminish, or should be expected to diminish, from the pacific disposition of one or more of the continental Powers the relative price of money as well as of all other commodities would be raised in England, – or in other words, the exchange would become less unfavourable to England by the whole amount of the diminished risk and expence attending the exportation of money.
>
> (Letter to Horner, 4 January 1812; VI: 79–80; Ricardo's emphasis)

When the domestic currency was neither depreciated nor appreciated, the market price of gold bullion was equal to the legal price of gold in coin and, supposing the same in the foreign country, the real par of exchange was consequently equal to the legal par. The exchange rate could then only diverge from the par in the limit set by the cost of transferring bullion:

> If the trade in the precious metals were perfectly free, and money could be exported without any expense whatever, the exchanges could be no otherwise in every country than at par. If the trade in the precious metals were perfectly free, if they were generally used in circulation, even with the expenses of transporting them, the exchange could never in any of them deviate more from par, than by these expenses. These principles, I believe, are now no where disputed.
>
> (*Principles*; I: 230)[6]

When the domestic currency was depreciated, the discount on the bank notes paying for the bills of exchange opened an additional margin of variation in the exchange rate:

> While the circulating medium consists, therefore, of coin undebased, or of paper-money immediately exchangeable for undebased coin, the exchange can never be more above, or more below, par, than the expences attending the transportation of the precious metals. But when it consists of a depreciated paper-money, it necessarily will fall according to the degree of the depreciation.
>
> (*High Price*; III: 72)

This meant that to determine the actual limits set to the variations of the exchange rate by the transfer costs one had to substitute the market price of gold bullion in each of the two countries for the legal price of gold in coin. Instead of calculating the bullion points by adding to (subtracting from) the legal par the cost of importation (exportation) of bullion, one should calculate them on the basis of the real par of exchange, that is, the ratio of the market prices of gold bullion. This is what Ricardo explained to McCulloch in a letter dated 2 October 1819:

> Double the quantity of currency in England and commodities will rise to double their former price in England, and twice the quantity of the money of England will be given for the former quantity of the currency of France. This is undoubtedly a mere nominal alteration, the real value both of commodities and bills will be the same as before. In fact the real par is altered, and nothing else. Instead of ascertaining the par by a consideration of what the pound sterling was formerly worth, it should be computed with reference to its present value, which is to be known by the value of the bullion which a pound can command. [...] The real par is justly estimated by the current value of the pound sterling – that current value is depreciated, hence a new real par is, or ought to be, established.
>
> (VIII: 87–8, 91)[7]

The associated notion of real exchange rate was also present in Ricardo, as in the same letter:

> If the exchange be 5pc[t] against Rio Janeiro and money therefore comes to England,[8] I agree with you that it is to that amount relatively depreciated in Rio Janeiro, 105 ounces of silver in one place is really paid to obtain 100 ounces in the other, but the exchange which is the consequence of this relative depreciation should I think be called real and not nominal.
>
> (ibid: 92–3)

Suppose that gold bullion may be transported from Rio to London at no cost. Because of arbitrage triggered by competition in the world market for bullion, 100 ounces of bullion purchased in Rio would exchange in London for 100 ounces of bullion, meaning that the price of 100 ounces in Brazilian money would be equal to the price of 100 ounces in English money, at the ruling exchange rate of the two currencies. If, however, the cost of transferring bullion from Rio to London is 5 per cent, 105 ounces of bullion purchased in Rio are necessary to exchange in London for 100 ounces of bullion, because 5 ounces cover the transfer cost. This circumstance is real – it applies to the market of any commodity, the level of the transfer cost depending on the characteristics of the commodity – and the 5 per cent unfavourable exchange of the Brazilian money may consequently be called real, in contrast with an unfavourable nominal exchange which would reflect a domestic depreciation of the currency due to its redundancy. The real exchange rate of the Brazilian money in terms of the English pound is here 0.95, that is, the quantity of gold bullion obtained in London against an ounce purchased in Rio.

The two notions of real par of exchange and of real exchange rate put the market for gold bullion centre-stage in international adjustment. This is at odds with the frequent contention in modern literature that the real par of exchange was only a proxy of the purchasing power parity over all commodities. This contention should be disclaimed, as was in Chapter 3 above the related statement that the market price of gold bullion was only a proxy of the general price level.

The real par computed on gold bullion, not *the purchasing power parity over commodities*

"I know I shall be soon stopped by the word price" (VI: 348): we saw in Chapter 3 above that in 1815 Ricardo became conscious of the necessity, when the money price of a commodity changed, to disentangle what was caused by a change on the side of money and by a change on the side of the commodity. This question was crucial for the theory of value and distribution developed two years later in *Principles*, as emphasised in Chapter VII "On foreign trade". In both cases the money price of the commodity would change, but a change in the value of money would not affect the general rate of profit, while a change in the difficulty of production of the commodity would affect it, if this commodity was a wage-good or used to produce a wage-good (see the long quotation from I: 145–6 in Chapter 6 above).

After having considered in the previous chapters the effect of the conditions of production of a commodity on its relative value and on the distribution of income, Ricardo concentrated in Chapter VII of *Principles* on their effect on the value of money, as might be expected in a chapter devoted to the analysis of foreign trade. The case was the following: a country (England) enjoying a particular advantage increased her exports of some commodities and, the exchange rate of her money having consequently risen to the bullion import point, it received bullion that was coined. This increase in the quantity of money acted as a monetary shock which ended up in a general rise in prices:

> When any particular country excels in manufactures, so as to occasion an influx of money towards it, the value of money will be lower, and the prices of corn and labour will be relatively higher in that country, than in any other.

This higher[9] value of money will not be indicated by the exchange; bills may continue to be negociated at par, although the prices of corn and labour should be 10, 20, or 30 per cent. higher in one country than another. Under the circumstances supposed, such a difference of prices is the natural order of things, and the exchange can only be at par, when a sufficient quantity of money is introduced into the country excelling in manufactures, so as to raise the price of its corn and labour. If foreign countries should prohibit the exportation of money, and could successfully enforce obedience to such a law, they might indeed prevent the rise in the prices of the corn and labour of the manufacturing country; for such a rise can only take place after the influx of the precious metals, supposing paper money not to be used; but they could not prevent the exchange from being very unfavourable to them. If England were the manufacturing country, and it were possible to prevent the importation of money, the exchange with France, Holland, and Spain, might be 5, 10, or 20 per cent. against those countries.

Whenever the current of money is forcibly stopped, and when money is prevented from settling at its just level, there are no limits to the possible variations of the exchange.

(*Principles*; I: 146–7)[10]

In this extract Ricardo distinguished between two cases. If there was no obstacle to the international transfer of gold bullion, prices in England rose and the exchange rate of the pound, which had previously risen with the additional exports, was lowered till it was brought back to par. The ensuing situation was thus characterised by the coexistence of higher prices in England and an exchange rate at par: this was "the natural order of things". If there were obstacles (for example, of a legal nature) to the international transfer of gold, which prevented it from being imported in England, prices did not rise and the exchange of the pound remained above par, that is, against the other countries ("France, Holland, and Spain") who imported the English commodities.

One observes that in "the natural order of things" – when there was no obstacle to the international transfer of gold bullion – the exchange was at par while the value of money (which, it should be recalled, was its purchasing power over all commodities except the standard; see Chapter 3 above) would differ in each country. In other words, money prices would differ, except for the standard:

When each country has precisely the quantity of money which it ought to have, money will not indeed be of the same value in each, for with respect to many commodities it may differ 5, 10, or even 20 per cent., but the exchange will be at par. One hundred pounds in England, or the silver which is in 100*l.* will purchase a bill of 100*l.*, or an equal quantity of silver in France, Spain, or Holland.

In speaking of the exchange and the comparative value of money in different countries, we must not in the least refer to the value of money estimated in commodities, in either country. The exchange is never ascertained by estimating the comparative value of money in corn, cloth, or any commodity

> whatever, but by estimating the value of the currency of one country, in the currency of the other.
>
> (ibid: 147)

When the exchange was at par (here computed on silver) between England and France, Spain, or Holland, £100 purchased in the London bullion market the same quantity of silver which exchanged in Paris, Madrid, or Amsterdam for a bill of £100 on London. In other words, the price of this quantity of silver was in England £100, and its price abroad was also £100, since it could exchange for a bill of £100 on London. This was the definition of the exchange of the pound against the French, Spanish, or Dutch currency being at (the real) par. But the price of a given quantity of any other commodity, which was in England £100, could be £80 or £120 abroad, meaning that it exchanged for a bill of £80 or £120 on London. One cannot be clearer: the exchange being at par – that is, the purchasing power of money over the standard being equalised across countries – did *not* imply that the value of money was the same in these countries – in other words that the purchasing power parity over commodities held.[11]

This analysis leads to an important conclusion: what in Chapter VII "On foreign trade" of *Principles* Ricardo called "the equilibrium of money"[12] was such that the value of money *in terms of the standard* was the same in all countries (the exchanges were at par), *not* that the value of money *in terms of all other commodities* was the same. His emphatic distinction between the real par of exchange (computed on gold bullion) and the ratio of the respective values of money in terms of all commodities except the standard was the direct consequence of his distinction between the depreciation of money and a fall in the value of money, a distinction in which his theory of money – as illustrated by the Money–Standard Equation – was grounded (see Chapter 4 above). It is noteworthy that this chapter was the first occasion when this distinction was introduced in Ricardo's writings, before it became so important in his papers of 1819–1823:

> Some indeed more reasonably maintained, that 130*l.* in paper was not of equal value with 130*l.* in metallic money; but they said that it was the metallic money which had changed its value, and not the paper money. They wished to confine the meaning of the word depreciation to an actual fall of value, and not to a comparative difference between the value of money, and the standard by which by law it is regulated.
>
> (ibid: 149)

The notion of par of exchange being now clarified,[13] the relations between the magnitudes involved in international adjustment may be formalised.

The limits to the variations of the exchange rate

Let me suppose that gold is the monetary standard in the two countries – for example England and France – for which the exchange is quoted. During the

Napoleonic wars, the exchange between London and Paris was quoted irregularly, and the examples given by Ricardo in the Bullion Essays concerned the exchange with Hamburg, more complicated since England was on a *de facto* gold standard while Hamburg was on a *de jure* silver standard (see Appendices 1 and 8). In his later writings Ricardo referred mostly to the exchange with Paris. The French monetary system was on a double standard, and the par of exchange could consequently be calculated on the basis of the common standard, gold. London (L) and Paris (P) thus quoted the nominal exchange rate e of the pound (£) in terms of French *francs* (F)[14] and the respective market prices $P_G^{£}$ and P_G^{F} of gold bullion. With $\overline{P_{GC}}^{£}$ and $\overline{P_{GC}}^{F}$ the respective legal prices of gold in coin, the legal par of exchange of the pound in *francs* was defined as the level $\overline{R_{GC}}$ of the exchange rate which equalised the quantity of coined gold legally contained in one pound and in $\overline{R_{GC}}$ *francs*:

$$\overline{R_{GC}} = \frac{\overline{P_{GC}}^{F}}{\overline{P_{GC}}^{£}} \tag{8.1}$$

The real par of exchange of the pound in *francs* was defined as the level R_G of the exchange rate which equalised the quantity of gold bullion purchased by one pound in the London market and by R_G *francs* in the Paris market:

$$R_G = \frac{P_G^{F}}{P_G^{£}} \tag{8.2}$$

The real exchange RE_G of the pound in terms of French *francs* was the quantity of gold bullion (in ounces) purchased in Paris exchanging at the ruling nominal exchange rate for an ounce purchased in London. If an ounce was purchased in London $P_G^{£}$, hence $e\ P_G^{£}$ in French *francs* at the ruling nominal exchange rate e of the pound in *francs*, it exchanged in Paris for $e\ (P_G^{£} / P_G^{F})$ ounces, with P_G^{F} the price of the ounce in Paris. In other words, the real exchange rate of the pound in terms of French *francs* was the price of bullion in London relative to its price in Paris, the numerator and the denominator being both expressed in *francs*:[15]

$$RE_G = e\frac{P_G^{£}}{P_G^{F}} \tag{8.3}$$

From (8.2) and (8.3) one derives the relation between the real exchange rate and the real par:

$$RE_G = \frac{e}{R_G} \tag{8.4}$$

It was thus equivalent to say that the exchange was favourable (unfavourable) to England when the nominal exchange rate of the pound was above (below) the real par or when the real exchange rate of the pound was above (below) one.

International arbitrage constrained the nominal exchange rate e between an upper limit at which importation of gold bullion started and a lower limit at which its exportation started. Gold bullion purchased in Paris at P_G^{F} was transferred to London at a percentage cost c_{GM} and sold in the London market at $P_G^{£}$; the import bullion point was thus the quantity of *francs* that should be given in Paris to obtain one pound in London by such operation. The same bullion purchased in London at $P_G^{£}$ was transferred to Paris at a percentage cost c_{GX} and sold in the Paris market at P_G^{F}; the export bullion point was thus the quantity of *francs* that could be obtained in Paris against one pound in London by such operation. The limits of variation of e thus depended on the real par of exchange R_G and the cost of transferring bullion both ways:

$$R_G(1+c_{GM}) \geq e \geq R_G(1-c_{GX}) \tag{8.5}$$

In Chapter 6 above, inequalities (6.1) expressed the limits between which the market price P_G of gold bullion could vary when bullion was converted into coin at the mint at a cost s_G and coin was converted into bullion in the melting pot at a cost m_G:

$$\overline{P_{GC}}\,(1+m_G) \geq P_G \geq \overline{P_{GC}}\,(1-s_G) \tag{6.1}$$

Applying (6.1) to England and France, one may use Steuart's method and calculate the maximum level of the real par R_G, which according to (8.2) obtained when P_G^{F} was at its upper limit and $P_G^{£}$ at its lower limit:

$$R_{GMAX} = \frac{\overline{P_{GC}}^{\text{F}}}{\overline{P_{GC}}^{£}} \frac{1+m_G{}^{P}}{1-s_G{}^{L}} \tag{8.6}$$

Hence, according to the definition of the legal par of exchange $\overline{R_{GC}}$ given by (8.1):

$$R_{GMAX} = \overline{R_{GC}}\,\frac{1+m_G{}^{P}}{1-s_G{}^{L}} \tag{8.7}$$

Symmetrically, the minimum level of the real par R_G obtained when P_G^{F} was at its lower limit and $P_G^{£}$ at its upper limit:

$$R_{GMIN} = \frac{\overline{P_{GC}}^{\text{F}}}{\overline{P_{GC}}^{£}} \frac{1-s_G{}^{P}}{1+m_G{}^{L}} \tag{8.8}$$

Hence:

$$R_{GMIN} = \overline{R_{GC}} \frac{1 - s_G^{\ P}}{1 + m_G^{\ L}} \tag{8.9}$$

From (8.5), (8.7), and (8.9) one may deduce the upper and lower limits of variation of the exchange rate e of the pound:

$$\overline{R_{GC}} \frac{1 + m_G^{\ P}}{1 - s_G^L} (1 + c_{GM}) \geq e \geq \overline{R_{GC}} \frac{1 - s_G^{\ P}}{1 + m_G^{\ L}} (1 - c_{GX}) \tag{8.10}$$

Another expression of the bullion points was given by the limits that constrained the real exchange rate RE_G. When $RE_G = 1$, the price of gold bullion in London, converted in francs at the ruling nominal exchange rate, was equal to the price in Paris: there was no incentive to move gold between the two centres either way. When $RE_G > 1$, an ounce of gold bullion was dearer in London than in Paris: it paid to import it in London from Paris, provided the percentage difference with 1 covered the percentage cost c_{GM} of this importation. When $RE_G < 1$, an ounce of gold bullion was cheaper in London than in Paris: it paid to export gold bullion from London to Paris, provided the percentage difference with 1 covered the percentage cost c_{GX} of this exportation. From (8.4) and (8.5), one may deduce:

$$1 + c_{GM} \geq RE_G \geq 1 - c_{GX} \tag{8.11}$$

As mentioned by Ricardo in the letter to McCulloch dated 2 October 1819:

> The expence of sending it [money] from one country to the other [...] is always the range within which the real exchange varies.
>
> (VIII: 93)

Ricardo could then use the notions of real par of exchange and of real exchange rate to explain how international adjustment operated through the transfer of gold bullion.

8.2 A two-stage international adjustment process

A double condition on the exchange rate

Whatever the commodity (including gold bullion) the profitability of exporting or importing it was computed by comparing its domestic and its foreign price. Since the latter was denominated in a foreign currency, it should be expressed in the domestic currency thanks to the exchange rate. As mentioned above, at the time of the Bullion Essays the exchange rate significant in expressing the foreign value of the pound was against the Flemish schilling, the monetary unit used to quote the exchange in Hamburg (see Appendix 1 above). The market price

$P_i^{£}$ of commodity *i* in London was thus to be compared with its arbitrated price $P_i^{Fs}(1/e)$ in Hamburg, with P_i^{Fs} the market price in Flemish schillings and *e* the exchange rate of the pound sterling in Flemish schillings. If the domestic price differed from the foreign arbitrated price by at least the cost of transferring *i* (including the ordinary profit) one direction or the other, it was profitable to export or import it, according to the sign of the difference.

One of the objects of Ricardo's inquiry in the Bullion Essays was to analyse the effect of a depreciation of the English currency – defined as the excess of the market price of gold bullion above the legal price of gold in coin – on the terms of such comparison, when it was made for gold bullion. In other words, the question was whether the observed exportation of gold bullion was caused by the domestic depreciation of the pound or by other (non-monetary) factors. Ricardo defended the former explanation – as it was also contended by the *Bullion Report*. It was thus necessary for him to demonstrate how the depreciation of the pound led to the exportation of gold bullion.

However, this was not enough. It was contended by some participants to the Bullion debates that the causality between the excess of the market price of gold bullion above the legal price of gold in coin and the exportation of bullion could be reversed: the deficit of the balance of payments – explained by non-monetary factors, such as abnormal imports of corn following a bad harvest, financial transfers caused by war, or impediments to exports – pulled the exchange rate of the pound downwards. When it reached the export bullion point, gold was exported to pay for the deficit, and in the London market the higher demand for bullion with a view to exportation pushed its market price above the legal price of gold in coin. With this reversed causality Ricardo consistently disagreed, in the Bullion Essays as in later writings:

> The fall in the exchange, or the unfavourable balance of trade, is stated to be the cause of the excess of the market above the mint price of gold, but to me it appears to be the effect of such excess.
>
> (*High Price*; III: 64)[16]

> Question: Assuming that the balance of payments should be against this country, must the payment not necessarily be made, either in specie or in bullion?
>
> Answer: It appears to me, that the balance of payments is frequently the effect of the situation of our currency, and not the cause.
>
> (Evidence before the Commons' Committee on Resumption of Cash Payments, 4 March 1819; V: 395)

It was thus necessary for Ricardo to show, not only that the depreciation of the English currency caused the exportation of gold bullion, but also that it was this exportation which triggered an additional importation of commodities, making the foreign balance apparently unfavourable, instead of the exportation of bullion paying for a pre-existing unfavourable foreign balance, as contended by some. The demonstration thus required a two-stage adjustment process.

Starting from an even trade balance – that is, a given pattern of exports and imports of commodities, excluding any transfer of gold either way – and for a given price of bullion in Hamburg P_G^{Fs}, an export of gold bullion was to be implemented according to the respective variations in $P_G^{£}$ and e. If $P_G^{£}$ increased and e declined by the same percentage, the terms of the comparison between the domestic price and the foreign arbitrated price of gold bullion were similarly affected, and, as in the initial situation, no profitable export of it from London to Hamburg occurred. In *Reply to Bosanquet*, this conclusion was borrowed by Ricardo from Blake – to criticise it:

> Many pages are employed [by Blake] in proving, that on every addition to the paper circulation, even when a great part of the currency consists of the precious metals, the price of bullion will be raised in the same proportion as other commodities; and as the foreign exchange will be nominally depressed in the same degree, no advantage will arise from the exportation of bullion.
>
> (*Reply to Bosanquet*; III: 209)

The condition for gold to be exported in response to the depreciation of the currency was therefore that the price of bullion increased *less* than the prices of all other commodities, including the prices of the bills of exchange denominated in foreign currencies – that is, less than the exchange rate of the pound declined – so that the foreign arbitrated price of gold exceeded the domestic price by a margin covering the cost of the export.

Symmetrically, the condition for commodity i to be imported in response to the depreciation of the currency was that the domestic price of i increased *more* than the exchange rate of the pound declined. If both moved in the same proportion (in opposite directions), the gain on the sale in London of the commodity imported from Hamburg would be exactly compensated by the loss on the bill of exchange, and this import would not be more profitable than in the initial situation.

It appears then that the decline in the relative price of gold bullion in terms of commodities in England was not a sufficient condition to trigger an export of gold and an additional import of commodities. Since international trade was no barter but an exchange implemented through bills of exchange, the condition on the exchange rate of the pound was that it should decline *more* than the domestic price of bullion increased but *less* than the domestic price of importable commodities increased. Since all market prices (including prices of gold bullion and of the bills of exchange denominated in foreign currencies) were affected in the same proportion by the depreciation of the currency, this double condition implied that something special occurred, either in the market for gold bullion or the market for bills of exchange or both. Let me examine successively each part of this condition on the exchange rate.

The first stage: the exportation of gold bullion

We saw in Chapter 6 that the immediate consequence of the depreciation of the currency was that the increase in the money price of bullion was channelled in the same proportion to all prices of commodities. The same phenomenon occurred in the market for bills of exchange: in Hamburg, a buyer of a bill in pounds on London offered fewer Flemish schillings than when the exchange was at the legal par, since he knew that the bill would be paid to him in London in depreciated Bank of England notes:

> When it is said that we may obtain 1*l*. 5*s*. for a guinea by sending it to Hamburg, what is meant but that we may get for it a bill on London for 1*l*. 5*s*. in bank-notes? Could this be the case if the bank paid in specie? Would any one be so blind to his interest as to offer me one guinea in specie and four shillings, for a guinea, when he might obtain the same at Hamburg at par, paying only the expenses of freight, &c.? It is only because he cannot get a guinea at the Bank for notes, that he consents to pay it with notes at the best price he can, or in other words he sells 1*l*. 5*s*. of his bank-notes for a guinea in specie.
>
> (*The Price of Gold*; III : 16–17)

Ricardo described the situation in 1809, under inconvertibility. An arbitrager exported a guinea (of 21s.) from London to Hamburg. There he sold it in the bullion market against Flemish schillings (see Appendix 1 above) with which he bought a bill of exchange drawn on London where it was paid 25s. in Bank of England notes (the equivalent of "one guinea in specie and four shillings"). The seller of the bill in Hamburg agreed to give 25s. payable in London because he had no other way of obtaining for them in Hamburg the quantity of Flemish schillings necessary to purchase the guinea. If the Bank of England note had been convertible into coin ("if the bank paid in specie"), he could have obtained the guinea from the Bank against 21s. in notes and would only have paid "the expenses of freight, &c" from London to Hamburg to get it there. Supposing that this transfer cost was 1s., the seller in Hamburg of a bill on London would have agreed to give 22s. to get the guinea, not 25s. If, under inconvertibility, he agreed to pay 25s., it was not because the transfer cost had suddenly jumped from 5 to 20 per cent, but because the Bank of England note in which the bill of exchange was paid in London was depreciated by 15 per cent, as compared with what it would have been worth under convertibility. Under convertibility as inconvertibility, the quantity of English money equivalent to the quantity of Flemish schillings paying for a guinea in Hamburg could depart from 21s. in the limit set by the transfer cost (1s.), but under inconvertibility 3s. more were added to compensate for the depreciation of the Bank of England note, that is, for the difference between the market price of gold bullion and the legal price of gold in coin in London. This is an illustration of the right-hand side of inequalities (8.10), with $m_G{}^L$ accounting for this difference of 15 per cent and c_{GX} for the transfer cost of 5 per cent. The same argument may be found in Chapter VII "On foreign trade" of *Principles* (see Appendix 8 below).

The depreciation of money – that is, the excess of the market price of gold bullion above the legal price of gold in coin – thus raised in the London market the price of bills of exchange denominated in foreign currencies – and hence lowered the exchange rate of the pound below the legal par. I may now recall what was said in Chapter 7 about the relation between the rise in the market price of gold bullion and the rise in price of all other commodities. A specific phenomenon occurred in the market for bullion – and in that market only: convertibility of coin into bullion through the melting pot increased the supply of bullion, so that its domestic price rose less than the prices of all other commodities. This applied equally to the price of bills of exchange: the domestic price of gold bullion increased less than the exchange rate of the pound declined. In *Reply to Bosanquet*, referring to the period "when an ounce of gold was to be bought in this country at 3*l.* 17*s.* 10½*d.* [the mint price]" (III: 195), Ricardo observed (for more details see Appendix 1 above):

> Gold has since that period risen in this country 18 per cent, and is now at 4*l.* 12*s.* per ounce, [...] but the currency of England, on a comparison with the currency of Hamburgh, has fallen 23½ per cent.
>
> (ibid: 196)

When this difference between the rise in the market price of gold bullion and the fall in the exchange rate of the pound reached the cost of transporting bullion abroad, its exportation began:

> It appears, therefore, evident, first, that by the addition of paper to a currency consisting partly of gold and partly of paper, gold bullion will not necessarily rise in the same degree as other commodities; and, secondly, that such addition will cause depression not in the nominal but in the real exchange, and therefore that gold will be exported.
>
> (ibid: 213)

In the expression of the real exchange rate given by (8.3) and now applied to London and Hamburg, $P_G^{£}$ increased less than e declined, and RE_G fell below 1. When it reached $1 - c_{GX}$ exportation of gold bullion began.

A contrario, in a monetary regime (such as in 1810) where inconvertible Bank of England notes had substituted for all circulating coins, the market price of gold bullion increased *in the same proportion* as all other commodities (including the price of bills of exchange), because no additional supply could make it increase less:

> When the circulation consists wholly of paper, any increase in its quantity will raise the *money* price of bullion without lowering its *value*, in the same manner, and in the same proportion, as it will raise the prices of other commodities, and for the same reason will lower the foreign exchanges; but this will only be a *nominal*, not a *real* fall, and will not occasion the exportation of bullion, because the real value of bullion will not be diminished, as there will be no increase to the quantity in the market.
>
> (*High Price*; III: 64; Ricardo's emphasis).

This analysis clarifies the meaning of gold being "the cheapest exportable commodity":

> If I owed a debt in Hamburgh of 100*l*. I should endeavour to find out the cheapest mode of paying it. If I send money, the expence attending its transportation being I suppose 5*l*. to discharge my debt will cost me 105*l*. If I purchase cloth here, which, with the expenses attending its exportation, will cost me 106*l*. and which will, in Hamburgh, sell for 100*l*. it is evidently more to my advantage to send the money. If the purchases and expences of sending hardware to pay my debt, will take 107*l*. I should prefer sending cloth to hardware, but I would send neither in preference to money, because money would be the cheapest exportable commodity in the London market.
>
> (ibid: 62; see also ibid: 57, 104–5)

Here Ricardo insisted on the fact that, for exogenous reasons such as its great value per unit of weight and the developed organisation of its market, gold bullion was charged a lower parametric cost of transfer than any other commodity. When the exchange rate of the pound fell, it was the first additional commodity which became profitable to be exported, because it was the cheapest to transfer. But under convertibility there was another reason why gold bullion was more eligible to international arbitrage in response to a depreciation of the currency: its market price increased less than the market price of all other commodities did and than the exchange rate declined. It was cheaper to export than any other commodity, not only because of a lower exogenous transfer cost, but because of a lower endogenous rise in its domestic market price. And this characteristic was entirely explained by the fact that gold was the monetary standard, hence had a fixed legal price in coin whose difference with its market price in bullion triggered domestic arbitrage.

The second stage: the additional importation of commodities

As mentioned earlier, the fact that the market price of gold bullion increased less than the market price of all other commodities – so that the relative price of gold in terms of all other commodities decreased – did not guarantee that the export of gold was accompanied with the import of another commodity i: the exchange rate of the pound should also decline less than the domestic price of i increased. This was the second part of the condition on the exchange rate. At first sight, the proportional price-change in all markets (including that for bills of exchange) consequent upon the depreciation of the currency – with the exception of the market for gold bullion – prevented this part of the condition from being fulfilled. However, as in the market for gold bullion, something special occurred in the market for bills of exchange, *as a consequence of the export of gold bullion itself.*

Arbitragers who exported bullion from London to Hamburg needed to repatriate the proceeds of their sales in Hamburg, and to do that they demanded in that centre a bill of exchange in pounds on London; alternatively, they might finance their export of bullion by selling in London a bill in Flemish schillings on Hamburg. This means that, as in the market for bullion, the variation in the exchange rate of the pound against Flemish schillings resulted from the conjunction of two factors: a monetary one – the domestic depreciation of the English currency – which pulled the exchange downwards in the same proportion as it pushed the domestic prices of all commodities upwards – and a market one – the increased demand (supply) by arbitragers for bills denominated in pounds (Flemish schillings) – which exercised an upward pressure on the exchange. These opposite forces made the exchange rate of the pound consequently decline less than the prices of domestic commodities increased, and the commodities for which the difference compensated the transportation cost (including the ordinary profit) started to be imported.

This may be formalised by using again the notion of real exchange rate, now computed on any commodity other than gold bullion, as given by:

$$RE_{i \neq G} = e \frac{P_{i \neq G}^{£}}{P_{i \neq G}^{\text{Fs}}} \quad (8.12)$$

In (8.12) e fell less than $P_{i \neq G}^{£}$ increased, and $RE_{i \neq G}$ rose above 1. When, with c_{iM} the percentage cost of importation of commodity i from Hamburg, $RE_{i \neq G}$ reached $1 + c_{iM}$, the importation of i began.

The upward pressure on the exchange rate of the pound consequent upon the exportation of gold bullion was of the same nature as what happened when any new commodity was exported, or when any previous importation of a commodity was discontinued, for reasons due to this or that commodity. This general effect was illustrated in Chapter VII "On foreign trade" of *Principles* by the famous example of the Portuguese wine and the English cloth. After having assumed that their respective cost of production made it profitable to import wine from Portugal to England and to export cloth from England to Portugal, Ricardo supposed that an improvement in making wine occurred in England and lowered its cost, so that the import of Portuguese wine ceased to be profitable and was discontinued. The export of English cloth to Portugal went on for a time, since "every transaction in commerce is an independent transaction" (*Principles*; I: 137). However, bills in pounds being no longer sold in Lisbon (or bills in Portuguese money being no longer bought in London) by importers of Portuguese wine, the exchange rate of the pound in Portuguese money rose. This premium on the pound reduced the profit of the importer of English cloth in Portugal, until this importation stopped. Describing how international trade was settled by bills of exchange, within the limits imposed by the bullion points, Ricardo compared the situation before and after the improvement in making English wine – hence before and after the importation of Portuguese wine was discontinued – as follows:

> If the markets be favourable for the exportation of wine from Portugal to England, the exporter of the wine will be a seller of the bill, which will be

> purchased either by the importer of the cloth, or by the person who sold him his bill; and thus without the necessity of money passing from either country, the exporters in each country will be paid for their goods. Without having any direct transaction with each other, the money paid in Portugal by the importer of cloth will be paid to the Portuguese exporter of wine; and in England by the negotiation of the same bill, the exporter of the cloth will be authorized to receive its value from the importer of wine.
>
> But if the prices of wine were such that no wine could be exported to England, the importer of cloth would equally purchase a bill; but the price of that bill would be higher, from the knowledge which the seller of it would possess, that there was no counter bill in the market by which he could ultimately settle the transactions between the two countries; he might know that the gold or silver money which he received in exchange for his bill, must be actually exported to his correspondent in England, to enable him to pay the demand which he had authorized to be made upon him, and he might therefore charge in the price of his bill all the expenses to be incurred, together with his fair and usual profit.
>
> If then this premium for a bill on England should be equal to the profit on importing cloth, the importation would of course cease.
>
> (*Principles*; I: 138–9)

In this example, the link between two successive events connected by the rise in the exchange rate of the pound operated symmetrically with the case discussed previously: instead of an exportation of gold bullion from London to Hamburg causing an importation of commodity *i* from Hamburg to London, the interruption of an importation of wine from Portugal to England caused the interruption of the exportation of cloth from England to Portugal.

"The natural trade of barter"

It appears thus possible to reconstruct Ricardo's analysis of the international adjustment to a monetary shock.[17] Two conclusions emerge from this analysis. On the one hand, this adjustment required both markets for gold bullion and bills of exchange being subject to the *combination* of two factors of price variation, a monetary one (the effect of the depreciation of the currency) and a market one (an increase in the supply or in the demand, respectively). On the other hand, this combination of factors operated *successively* in the two markets, first in the market for bullion, and second, as a consequence, in the market for bills of exchange. This two-stage international adjustment process – the additional import of commodities occurring *after* the export of gold bullion – was the consequence of the fact that international trade was no barter but an exchange implemented through bills of exchange.

This conclusion may seem at odds with many instances where Ricardo literally wrote that trade in general, and international trade in particular, *is* barter, such as:

> If any cause should raise the price of a few manufactured commodities, it would prevent or check their exportation; but if the same cause operated

> generally on all, the effect would be merely nominal, and would neither interfere with their relative value, nor in any degree diminish the stimulus to a trade of barter, which all commerce, both foreign and domestic, really is.
>
> (ibid: 228)

> All trade is in fact a trade of barter, and if money can by any laws be so distributed or accumulated as to raise the price of exportable commodities, it will also raise the price of imported commodities; so that whether money be of a high or of a low value, it will not affect foreign trade; for a given quantity of a home commodity in either case will be bartered for a given quantity of a foreign commodity.
>
> (*Notes on Malthus*; II: 146–7)[18]

> All foreign trade finally resolves itself into an interchange of commodities; money is but the measure by which the respective quantities are ascertained.
>
> (*On Protection to Agriculture*; IV: 214)

Referring to barter in international trade, Ricardo did not mean, as is often supposed in the literature, that commodities directly exchanged for one another or for gold bullion, but that transactions were settled exclusively through a multilateral clearing of bills of exchange, in contrast with a situation in which, in addition to bills of exchange, precious metals were also transferred. This "natural trade of barter" was "the equilibrium of money" discussed in Section 8.1 above:

> Beside the improvements in arts and machinery, there are various other causes which are constantly operating on the natural course of trade, and which interfere with the equilibrium, and the relative value of money. Bounties on exportation or importation, new taxes on commodities, sometimes by their direct, and at other times by their indirect operation, *disturb the natural trade of barter, and produce a consequent necessity of importing or exporting money*, in order that prices may be accommodated to the natural course of commerce; and this effect is produced not only in the country where the disturbing cause takes place, but, in a greater or less degree, in every country of the commercial world.
>
> (*Principles*; I: 141–2; emphasis added)

This interpretation is consistent with Ricardo's repeated statement that precious metals were distributed amongst the different countries in the proportions required by the domestic circulation in each of them, so that, once this distribution was implemented, international payments did not require any transfer of them and were exclusively settled through bills of exchange, as in "purely a trade of barter":

> Gold and silver having been chosen for the general medium of circulation, they are, by the competition of commerce, distributed in such proportions amongst the different countries of the world, as to accommodate themselves to the natural traffic which would take place if no such metals existed, and the trade between countries were purely a trade of barter.
>
> (ibid: 137)[19]

Ricardo was aware of the theoretical and practical implications of the two-stage international adjustment process. On the level of theory, in contrast with the price-specie flow mechanism, the adjustment in international trade was not the engine of the restoration of the exchange but the *consequence* of arbitrage between the market for gold bullion and the market for bills of exchange.[20] This explains Ricardo's often misunderstood claim that the export of gold did not pay for a previously existing foreign balance against England – explained by exogenous causes such as a bad harvest or war transfers – but was the condition – itself explained by the depreciation of the currency – for imports of other commodities being greater than their exports. Consequently, the issue was not whether the foreign balance was for or against England:

> The fact of the balance of payments being for or against this country could be of little consequence, in my estimation, to the proof of the theory which I maintain.
>
> (*Reply to Bosanquet*; III: 213)

On the level of practice, Ricardo's awareness of the organisation of the market for bills of exchange led him to consider that the import of commodities being triggered by the export of gold bullion was a fact, not a doctrinal prejudice. In the example of the trade between London and Hamburg, the import of commodities in London was financed in Hamburg by the sale of long bills on London to exporters of gold bullion from England, and when, two and a half months later, these bills came due in London, the importers were in a position to pay for them with the proceeds of the sale of the imported commodities having occurred in the meantime in the English markets. The international adjustment process triggered by a domestic depreciation of the pound thus relied on three kinds of economic agents: arbitragers who exported gold bullion and repatriated the proceeds by purchasing long bills, merchants who financed the import of goods in England by the sale of these bills, and London banks who discounted the long bills supplied by the arbitragers.

A corollary of Ricardo's understanding of the international adjustment process was the much-criticised proposition according to which a fall in the exchange rate could only be explained by a redundancy of currency.

8.3 The redundancy of money as the sole cause of fall in the exchange rate

Real and nominal variations in the exchange

At his time as in later literature, Ricardo has been often criticised for holding the "extreme Bullionist" position (Viner 1937: 106) according to which a fall in the exchange rate could only be explained by a redundancy of currency. When he was examined on 26 March 1819 by the Lords' Committee on the Resumption of Cash Payments, the author of the following questions had probably this kind of critique in mind, and the answers given by Ricardo might be unexpected in their denial of such a position:

> Question: Are not the rates of exchange affected by the balance of payments on all accounts?
>
> Answer: Yes, within the limits of the expence attending the transmission of gold.
>
> Question: Must not therefore a part of the depression of the exchange between any countries, be attributable to a cause independent of the amount of the circulating medium?
>
> Answer: Very frequently, but the real exchange would be in favour of the country, while the nominal exchange is against it.
>
> Question: Can you therefore conclude, from the degree to which the exchange is at any moment against any country, that the whole percentage of that unfavourable exchange is owing to the amount of its circulating medium?
>
> Answer: A part may be owing to other causes.
>
> (V: 448)

The possibility of a fall in the exchange to be explained by real causes – such as war transfers or extraordinary imports of corn following a bad harvest – as well as monetary ones had been contended in 1802 by Henry Thornton in *An Enquiry into the Nature and Effects of the Paper Credit of Great Britain* (see Chapter 1 above), and Ricardo had emphatically rejected it in the debate around the *Bullion Report* in 1810 (see Chapter 2 above). It is thus surprising that, in the quoted evidence of 1819, he might have acknowledged that "a part" of the unfavourable exchange "may be owing to other causes" than the redundancy of the currency. As Ricardo's second answer makes clear, his distinction between monetary and "other causes" had something to do with the distinction between the nominal and the real exchange rate.

His understanding of this distinction – hence of the question of the causes of an unfavourable exchange – is illustrated by correspondence raised at the end of the same year 1819 by the article "Exchange" written by John Ramsay McCulloch for the *Supplement to the Encyclopædia Britannica* (letter by Ricardo of 2 October, answered by McCulloch on 2 November, with a reply by Ricardo on 18 December). In his view, Ricardo's critiques were not of substance but of wording: "I think we agree in principle, I object to the language" (VIII: 93). They concerned McCulloch's use of the expressions "real par of exchange" and "real exchange".

On the real par of exchange, Ricardo objected to McCulloch's inclusion of the cost of transferring bullion in its calculation, which was a source of confusion:

> It is true that the expences of sending bullion from France to Poland may exceed the expence of sending it to England, but this circumstance will not alter the par, although it will allow of a greater deviation in the exchange from par between the more distant countries, before bullion moves to stop the rise

> or fall of the exchange. I cannot help thinking that the language of the Bullion Report is correct, and that it would introduce a new and less satisfactory definition if we were to allow of these expences in estimating the par of exchange between different countries. Suppose that the expence of sending silver from Poland to France or from France to Poland, to be 5 pct. it would in my opinion be correct to say that the exchange was at par when 100 ounces of silver in Poland would purchase a bill for 100 ounces of silver payable in France. According to your explanation I do not know whether you would estimate it to be at par when 105 ounces were given in Poland for a bill of 100 ounces payable in France or when 105 were paid in France for a bill of 100 ounces payable in Poland.
>
> (VIII: 89)

Ricardo thus insisted that the two factors constraining the variations in the exchange rate – the cost of transferring bullion from one country to the other, and the real par of exchange – should be clearly distinguished.

On the real exchange rate, Ricardo also objected to McCulloch. In his first letter he expressed doubts about the usefulness of this notion, before changing his mind:

> We mean the same thing, but I doubt whether there be any advantage in the distinction which is drawn between real and nominal exchange; by correcting the par, with every alteration in the bullion value of money, all would be clear.*
>
> Note* On further reflection there may I think be real use in the distinction drawn between the nominal and real exchange, but the distinction should be clearly defined.
>
> (ibid: 88)[21]

In his second letter Ricardo corrected McCulloch's exposition of his own ideas:

> If you substitute the words "real exchange" for "nominal exchange" you have exactly expressed my meaning, which I think agrees with the view I now entertain on this subject.
>
> (ibid: 141)

How should the distinction between the two notions "be clearly defined" and what was this "view" which Ricardo entertained "now" (in 1819)? The above note* continued as follows:

> The exchange may be said to be nominally affected to the amount of the difference between the market and mint prices of bullion, and be really affected by any deviation from par exceeding or falling short of this difference.
>
> (ibid: 88)

This explanation is made crystal-clear by inequalities (8.10) formalised above in Section 8.1 and which constrain the variations of the exchange rate. Let me recall them:

$$\overline{R_{GC}}\frac{1+m_G{}^P}{1-s_G{}^L}(1+c_{GM})\geq e\geq\overline{R_{GC}}\ \frac{1-s_G{}^P}{1+m_G{}^L}(1-c_{GX})\tag{8.10}$$

The exchange rate e might deviate from the legal par of exchange $\overline{R_{GC}}$ from above or below by two magnitudes. The first was the ratio which reflected the monetary factors (the cost s_G at which bullion was converted into coin at the mint and the cost m_G at which coin was converted into bullion in the melting pot, in each country) that limited the deviation of the real par of exchange R_G from the legal par $\overline{R_{GC}}$ produced by "the difference between the market and mint prices of bullion". Since, according to Ricardo's monetary theory (see Chapter 4 above), such difference (the depreciation or appreciation of money) was exclusively attributable to the state of the currency, "the exchange may be said to be nominally affected to the amount of" this difference: the cause of its fall (rise) was the redundancy (deficiency) of money. Second, the exchange rate e might also deviate from the legal par of exchange $\overline{R_{GC}}$ by the magnitudes in parentheses, that is, the cost c_{GM} or c_{GX} of transferring bullion either way. As mentioned above in Section 8.1, this factor was considered by Ricardo as "real": it depended on the characteristics of bullion as commodity and was independent of the state of the currency in each country. Consequently, the exchange rate was "really affected" in the limit set by this transfer cost, that is, by "any deviation from par exceeding or falling short" of the other (monetary) factor. This made room for real causes of change in the exchange rate.

This explains why for Ricardo, as illustrated by his answers during his evidence before the Lords' Committee, there was not one but two possible types of causes of deviation of the exchange rate from the legal par. One was "real", and it might affect the exchange in the limit set by the cost of transferring bullion from one country to the other, since this cost determined the threshold that triggered international arbitrage between the bullion and foreign-exchange markets. The other was "nominal" (monetary), and it might affect the exchange in the limit set by the minting and melting costs, since these costs determined the threshold that triggered domestic arbitrage between coin and bullion. These two types of causes were not alternative but operated at different levels: the balance of payments explained the "real" variations of the exchange rate between the bullion points calculated on the basis of the legal par of exchange, and the state of the currency explained the "nominal" variations beyond them but within the bullion points calculated on the basis of the real par. When the proportion by which the exchange rate was below the legal par was greater than the percentage cost of transferring bullion, the whole of the difference should be ascribed to the depreciation of the currency (see in Appendix 8 Ricardo's factual illustrations).

A matter of fact or of theory

It is thus inappropriate to blame Ricardo for ignoring the "real" causes of the fall in the exchange and contending that it could only be explained by the redundancy of the currency. His neglect for these real causes was rooted in the fact that, in normal times, the cost of transferring bullion from one country to the other was small and constant, so that the effect of the real causes on the exchange was insignificant and invariable. As Ricardo declared in a speech in Parliament on 24 May 1819:

> His [Ricardo's] own general opinion was, that an unfavourable state of exchange must always proceed from a redundant currency.
>
> (V: 16)[22]

But in extraordinary times such as the Napoleonic wars, Ricardo emphasised that the real causes could account for no less than 10 to 15 per cent of the fall in the exchange. The following extract of a quotation given in full in Section 8.1 above illustrates this point:

> The exchange in my opinion is, even in these turbulent times, rarely operated upon but by two causes: one, and that by far the most common is an alteration, or an apprehended alteration, in the relative prices of commodities in the two countries between which the exchange is estimated, and is in most cases to be traced to some augmentation or diminution in the amount of the currency of one of them. The other is an increased or diminished difficulty and expence, (or the anticipation of such) attending the transmission of money. The exchange with the continent has, I believe, for a length of time, not only been unfavourable to this country to the amount of the depreciation of our currency but considerably more, as much more probably as to 10 to 15 pc^{t}.
>
> (Letter to Horner, 4 January 1812; VI: 79)

This is the reason why the variation of the exchange rate was not as good an indicator of the state of the currency as the difference between the market price of bullion and the legal price of gold in coin: it could partly reflect a real cause which added to the monetary one.

Two conclusions about Ricardo's much-discussed contention that a redundancy of money was the sole cause of fall in the exchange rate may be derived from this analysis. First this contention allowed for the acknowledgement of the fact that the existence of a cost of transferring gold bullion from one country to the other made room for real causes of change in the exchange rate. This was a matter of fact, not of theory, and it was "no where disputed" (*Principles*; I: 230). Second, any divergence between the nominal exchange rate and the legal par of exchange beyond this allowance for the transfer cost of bullion was necessarily caused by the state of the currency, which made the real par (on the basis of which the actual bullion points should be calculated) differ from the legal par. This affirmation was a direct consequence of Ricardo's monetary theory, as embodied in the Money–Standard Equation, according to which the market price of gold bullion (the standard) could only be above (below) the legal price of gold in coin if the quantity of money was in excess (deficient). It was not a matter of fact but of theory.

Being grounded in his monetary theory, Ricardo's analysis of international adjustment reflected the characteristics of this theory. This is illustrated by his rejection of the price-specie flow mechanism.

8.4 Price-specie flow mechanism versus active management of the currency

In the Appendix to the fourth edition of *High Price*, Ricardo mentioned three ways an adjustment of the exchange rate could be made:

> An unfavourable exchange can ultimately be corrected only by an exportation of goods, by the transmission of bullion, – or *by a reduction in the amount of the paper circulation.*
>
> (*High Price*, Appendix to 4th ed.; III: 125; Ricardo's emphasis)

According to the price-specie flow mechanism, this correction occurred first "by the transmission [the export] of bullion", followed by "an exportation of goods" rendered cheaper by the "reduction in the amount of the paper circulation" associated with the export of bullion. One may ask how the two-stage international adjustment process described above fits this sentence, and inquire accordingly about the existence of a price-specie flow mechanism in Ricardo, in the same manner as in Chapter 7 above in which the analysis of the regulation of the quantity of convertible notes by the standard raised the question of the existence in Ricardo of a quantity theory of money. The answer is in both cases in the negative, and there is a good reason for that: a quantity theory of money is an integral part of the price-specie flow mechanism. However, one cannot be simply content with removing the quantity theory of money to conclude that the price-specie flow mechanism falls apart. There is also an important question involved, which is central in international economics: does international adjustment rely on changes in the balance of trade, that is, in the difference between aggregate exports and imports of commodities? This is the case with the price-specie flow mechanism, in which the balance of trade adjusts in response to changes in prices triggered by changes in the quantity of money. One may ask whether this second pillar of that mechanism is also to be discarded from Ricardo's theory. We will see that it should.

Already in the Bullion Essays Ricardo dissented with two common opinions on the balance of trade. First he objected to labelling "unfavourable" the balance of trade when gold bullion flew out:

> In return for the gold exported, commodities would be imported; and though what is usually termed the balance of trade would be against the country exporting money or bullion, it would be evident that she was carrying on a most advantageous trade, exporting that which was no way useful to her, for

> commodities which might be employed in the extension of her manufactures, and the increase of her wealth.
>
> (*High Price*; III: 54)

Not only a supposedly unfavourable balance of trade increased the wealth of the country (in terms of use-values) but also it did not correspond to any aggregate imbalance (in terms of values) between exports and imports: from the point of view of international trade, gold bullion was a commodity like any other, and when it flew out, aggregate exports were increased, causing an increase in aggregate imports, the balance between them remaining even. Second Ricardo also dissented with the idea that, after having flown out because it was in excess, gold money would again flow in when the ensuing fall in domestic prices would generate a "favourable" balance of trade. Although without mentioning Hume's inference from the competitive advantage procured by the fall in domestic prices – "In how little time, therefore, must this bring back the money which we had lost" (Hume 1752: 311; see Chapter 1 above) – Ricardo ironically observed:

> Is it to be contended that these results would not be foreseen, and the expence and trouble attending these needless operations effectually prevented, in a country where capital is abundant, where every possible economy in trade is practised, and where competition is pushed to its utmost limits? Is it conceivable that money should be sent abroad for the purpose merely of rendering it dear in this country [England] and cheap in another, and by such means to ensure its return to us?
>
> (*High Price*; III: 103)

We saw in Section 8.1 above that when money was in excess and the market price of gold bullion consequently rose above the legal price of gold in coin, bullion started to be exported when the exchange rate fell to the export bullion point, and this prevented any further fall in the exchange rate. This bullion-points mechanism was generally acknowledged as a matter of fact, because it was the consequence of the practice of international arbitrage. As shown by inequalities (8.10) this mechanism constrained the exchange rate within limits, but did not imply the return to the level before the monetary shock (equal, by assumption, to the legal par). It did not provide in itself an answer to the question: what happened next? In other words, what became of the bullion exported and what was the final outcome of the process? To answer these questions, one needed to complement the factual bullion-points mechanism with a theory. Its combination with the Quantity Theory of Money and with the assumed sensitivity of exports and imports to changes in money prices gave the so-called price-specie flow mechanism, according to which gold bullion flew in after having flown out and the final outcome was the return to the initial position which had been disturbed by the monetary shock.

This was not Ricardo's understanding of international adjustment. According to the two-stage adjustment process described above, *gold bullion went abroad and did not come back*. What flew in, *as a consequence of this export of gold bullion*, was another commodity (or several others). As for the final position, it depended on how the quantity of money adjusted and thus affected the market price of gold bullion. The international adjustment to an excess note issue was not implemented through the balance of trade but through the export of gold bullion: the structure of foreign trade was altered (bullion was exported and one or several new commodities were imported), but the balance of trade (the difference between aggregate exports and imports) remained even. Already in the bullion-points mechanism, the real par of exchange, defined as the ratio of the market prices of gold bullion in the two countries, was *not* a proxy of the purchasing power parity, as the market price of gold bullion was *not* a proxy of the general price level (see Chapter 3 above). But there was more: the return of the exchange rate e to the legal par $\overline{R_{GC}}$ was ensured by the return of the market price $P_G^{£}$ of gold bullion to the legal price $\overline{P_{GC}}^{£}$ of gold in coin, *not* by the return of the prices $P_{i \neq G}^{£}$ of all other commodities to their initial level before the monetary shock. As seen above when discussing the notion of par of exchange, the prices of the same commodity in any two countries, made comparable through the exchange rate, might permanently differ while the exchange was at par. The return to what Ricardo called "the equilibrium of money", that is, the equality of the exchange rate with the par – hence the equality of the purchasing power of domestic and foreign currencies in terms of the standard – did not ensure the purchasing power parity in terms of all other commodities.

In a monetary system endowed with a regulation of the note issue by the standard – the only system also endowed with external monetary stability – the domestic market for gold bullion was central, first through international arbitrage with its foreign markets, second through domestic arbitrage with the bank issuing convertible notes, because a change in the quantity of money affected the value of the standard by changing its market price, as illustrated by the Money–Standard Equation. It is worthwhile noting that international adjustment rested only on the stabilisation of the market price of gold bullion, not on the adjustment of domestic price levels and corresponding changes in the balance of trade (as in the price-specie flow mechanism). In a nutshell, according to Ricardo, international adjustment to a monetary shock resulted from the combination of the bullion-points mechanism with the Money–Standard Equation, in contrast with the price-specie flow mechanism in which the bullion-points mechanism was combined with the Quantity Theory of Money and the adjustment of the balance of trade.

The exact role of the exportation of bullion required, however, an important qualification: the domestic market for bullion was central in the international adjustment, not necessarily the exportation of bullion. This calls for an explanation. We saw in Chapter 7 that the adjustment of the domestic quantity of money depended on the monetary system. The dividing line was between convertibility and inconvertibility of the note into gold – that is, between the existence and the absence of a regulation of the note issue by the standard. When notes were inconvertible, the exportation of bullion corrected their excess issue generated by a once-for-all monetary shock, but nothing could prevent the Bank from expanding its issues indefinitely – hence repeating the monetary shock – so that the corrective effect came to an end when all coins had disappeared from domestic circulation. The final outcome was consequently not a self-adjustment but a change of monetary system, from a mixed system of coins and inconvertible notes to a circulation exclusively composed of inconvertible notes. When notes were convertible, the adjustment of the domestic quantity of money depended on the working of the market for gold bullion. The quantity of money was first reduced by the conversion of notes into coins to be melted with a view to exporting the bullion but this exportation ceased when the Bank of England started to purchase bullion in order to replenish its metallic reserve and thus triggered the Penelope effect, until its losses forced the Bank to contract the issue, restoring the situation before the monetary shock. Such a system was thus self-adjusting, but the self-adjustment eventually relied on the domestic limitation of the quantity of money, not the exportation of bullion. And it occurred after a lag depending on the behaviour of the Bank; in the meantime the whole economy (and not only the Bank) suffered from depreciation. It is the reason why, according to Ricardo, it was better to anticipate this forced reduction with an active management of the note issue. This was the object of the Ingot Plan.

8.5 The Ingot Plan and the gold-exchange standard

Leaving aside the cost of transferring gold bullion from one country to the other – which in normal times was small and constant – the range of variation of the exchange rate, as shown by inequalities (8.10), depended on the two magnitudes – the minting and melting costs – which limited the divergence of the market price of gold bullion from the legal price of gold in coin, hence, for a given state of the currency in the foreign country, the divergence of the real par from the legal par of exchange. Consequently, the exchange rate was all the more stable since the domestic monetary regime ensured the stability of the market price of the standard: for Ricardo, international monetary stability was the outcome of domestic monetary stability. The effect of the Ingot Plan on international adjustment should be envisaged from this point of view. Chapter 9 below will detail the reasons why it improved domestic monetary stability by changing radically the monetary system, in comparison with the pre-1797 (and post-1821) one. One may here somewhat anticipate this analysis and so justify why, in contrast with the usual interpretation in terms of an automatic mechanism, Ricardo's approach to international adjustment may rightly be inserted in the part of the present book devoted to policy. The institutional set-up and the policy rule that designed central banking à la Ricardo were also the ones which produced the best international monetary system in his view. Beyond the simple reduction of the range of variation in the exchange rate, they substituted, as driving force of adjustment, the domestic management of the note issue for international bullion flows, and they restricted to international payments the use of gold – what would later be called the gold-exchange standard.

The reduction of the range of variation in the exchange rate

As will be detailed in Chapter 9 below, the adoption in the Ingot Plan of convertibility both ways between money (the Bank of England note) and the standard (gold bullion) had the effect of stabilising as much as was desirable the market price of gold bullion, by narrowing its margin of variation around the legal price:

> That regulation is merely suggested, to prevent the value of money from varying from the value of bullion more than the trifling difference between the prices at which the Bank should buy and sell [bullion], and which would be an approximation to that uniformity in its value, which is acknowledged to be so desirable.
>
> (*Proposals*; IV: 67; *Principles*; I: 358)

Consequently, by comparison with the system in which the Bank of England note was convertible into coin and no obligation was imposed on the Bank to purchase bullion at a fixed price, the Ingot Plan eliminated the various costs associated with convertibility of bullion into coin and of coin into bullion, which, when the actual quantity of money differed from its conformable level, set the boundaries constraining the variations in the market price of gold bullion.

In the past, the extreme case had been obtained when, as at the time of the *Bullion Report*, the Bank of England note was inconvertible and had completely replaced coin in domestic circulation. As emphasised in Chapter 7 above, the absence of regulation of the note issue by the standard made the market price of gold bullion rise and the exchange rate of the pound fall without limit:

> The same cause which has produced a difference of from fifteen to twenty per cent. in bank-notes when compared with gold bullion, may increase it to fifty per cent. There can be no limit to the depreciation which may arise from a constantly increasing quantity of paper. The stimulus which a redundant currency gives to the exportation of the coin has acquired new force, but cannot, as formerly, relieve itself.
>
> (*High Price*; III: 78)

Since the domestic money – now the inconvertible Bank of England note – could not be converted into bullion with a view to exportation, in contrast with the situation when the note was convertible or when part of the domestic circulating money – the metallic one – was convertible into bullion, the situation was the same as if in a metallic regime rigorous laws had been enforced to prevent the exportation of the coin:

> Whenever the current of money is forcibly stopped, and when money is prevented from settling at its just level, there are no limits to the possible variations of the exchange. The effects are similar to those which follow, when paper money, not exchangeable for specie at the will of the holder, is forced into circulation. Such a currency is necessarily confined to the country where it is issued: it cannot, when too abundant, diffuse itself generally amongst

other countries. The level of circulation is destroyed, and the exchange will inevitably be unfavourable to the country where it is excessive in quantity: just so would be the effects of a metallic circulation, if by forcible means, by laws which could not be evaded, money should be detained in a country, when the stream of trade gave it an impetus towards other countries.

(*Principles*; I: 147)

This idea that "the level of circulation is destroyed" was reminiscent of a formula used by Ricardo in a letter to Malthus of 22 October 1811, when he referred to the former situation in which bullion could still be exported:

> If in any country there exists a dearness of importable commodities and no corresponding cheapness of exportable commodities money in such country is above its natural level and must infallibly be exported in payment of the dear commodities, – but what does this state of things indicate but an excess of currency, and it may surely be correctly said that money is exported to restore the level not to destroy it.
>
> (VI: 65)

Even when there were still coins in circulation, and also before 1797 when the Bank of England note was convertible into coin, the legal prohibition of melting and exporting the coin generated a cost that opened a margin of rise in the market price of gold bullion, hence of fall in the exchange rate. However this law was easily evaded and its effect was consequently weak; it is only under inconvertibility that the melting cost m_G was significant but for another reason: the growing scarcity of the coins to be gathered in circulation. Symmetrically, the delay with which the coins were delivered by the mint against bullion was responsible for a minting cost s_G that opened a margin of fall in the market price of gold bullion, hence of rise in the exchange rate.

The Ingot Plan eliminated these various costs which, according to (8.10), permitted the nominal exchange rate to vary when the quantity of money differed from its conformable level. The Bank of England note becoming convertible at no cost into exportable bullion, and bullion becoming convertible into the Bank of England note at a legal price only inferior by a slight margin b^L covering the management costs of the Bank, the margin of variation of the exchange rate was reduced. The legal par of exchange $\overline{R_G}$ became, with $\overline{P_G}^{£}$ the legal price of gold bullion in England:

$$\overline{R_G} = \frac{\overline{P_{GC}}^{F}}{\overline{P_G}^{£}} \tag{8.13}$$

The inequalities constraining the exchange rate consequently became:

$$\overline{R_G}\,\frac{1+m_G{}^P}{1-b^L}(1+c_{GM}) \geq e \geq \overline{R_G}\,(1-s_G{}^P)\,(1-c_{GX}) \tag{8.14}$$

If the principles of the Ingot Plan were also adopted in the foreign country, these expressions became:

$$\overline{R_G} = \frac{\overline{P_G^F}}{\overline{P_G^£}} \tag{8.15}$$

$$\overline{R_G}\,\frac{1}{1-b^L}(1+c_{GM}) \geq e \geq \overline{R_G}\,(1-b^P)(1-c_{GX}) \tag{8.16}$$

As emphasised by Marcuzzo and Rosselli, the Ingot Plan sped up international adjustment through gold flows, by narrowing the boundaries between which the exchange rate could vary before arbitrage was set in motion and stabilised it (for the distinction between "stable and unstable monetary regimes", and the classification of stable regimes according to the velocity of the adjustment mechanism of the quantity of money, see Marcuzzo and Rosselli 1991: 123–8). However, there was more than that, as shown by what happened if the same gold-standard system à la Ricardo was adopted in every trading nation: the stability of the international monetary system could be achieved without any international flow of gold. Not only would gold stop circulating inside each nation, but it would also stop moving from one nation to another, since the respective domestic quantities of paper money would endogenously adjust, without having to be corrected by the actual export or import of gold.The Ingot Plan radically changed the logic of the adjustment of the quantity of money – hence the monetary system itself – by substituting, as driving force of adjustment, the domestic management of the note issue for international bullion flows.

Domestic management of the note issue rather than international bullion flows

As was analysed in Chapter 7 above and recalled in the preceding section, in a system where the Bank of England note was convertible into coin, the adjustment to a monetary shock took the form of an exportation of gold bullion only as long as the Bank passively provided the coin demanded by arbitragers against its notes. As soon as the Bank purchased gold to replenish its reserves, the exportation of bullion was replaced by the Penelope effect. The adjustment of the quantity of money finally occurred when the Bank was compelled by its losses to contract its issues. Ricardo's Ingot Plan aimed at by-passing the intermediate steps of the exportation of bullion and of the Penelope effect to produce the required adjustment in the quantity of money. When, for whatever monetary reason – a discretionary change in the note issue or a change in "the wants of commerce" that made the existing quantity of notes inappropriate – the quantity of money was in excess (deficient), the market price of gold bullion rose above (fell below) its legal level, and this signal triggered the application of the policy rule that reduced (increased) the note issue, before the exportation (importation) of gold even started. Consequently, the adjustment of the quantity of money, hence of the exchange rate, was expected by Ricardo from the active behaviour of the issuing bank, not from the mechanical effect of the exportation or importation of gold. Rather than relying on the delayed adaptation of their behaviour by the directors of the Bank of England, Ricardo preferred subjecting it to a policy rule that immediately corrected discrepancies between the quantity of money issued and the (unknown) quantity of money required by the "wants of commerce".

It should be observed, however, that this active management of the currency, embodied in the Ingot Plan, only applied to such discrepancies, that is, to variations in the exchange having a domestic monetary origin. It did not apply to *any* variation in the exchange: according to Ricardo, the quantity of money should not be targeted by the exchange rate. During his evidence before the Lords' Committee on 26 March 1819 quoted in Section 8.3 above, Ricardo had acknowledged that "a part" of the unfavourable exchange "may be owing to other causes" than an excess quantity of money, and he added:

> There is no unfavourable exchange, which might not be turned in our favour, by a reduction in the amount of currency; it might not however be wise to make such a reduction.
>
> (V: 448)

This affirmation was just the consequence of the contention that the balance of trade was the effect of the state of the currency, not its cause. Already in *High Price* Ricardo had mentioned this practical consequence of such causality:

> It is only after a comparison of the value in their markets and in our own, of gold and other commodities, and because gold is cheaper in the London market than in theirs, that foreigners prefer gold in exchange for their corn. If we diminish the quantity of currency, we give an additional value to it: this will induce them to alter their election, and prefer the commodities.
>
> (*High Price*; III: 62)[23]

However, as testified by the last phrase in the evidence of 1819, this did not mean that, although possible, a monetary action on the balance of trade was desirable. If the quantity of money was in excess, its reduction should be implemented for its own sake – the elimination of domestic depreciation – the improvement of the exchange being a by-product. If the fall of the exchange was caused by real factors operating in the limit of the transfer cost of bullion, there was no reason to alter a situation of the currency which was not responsible for this fall: as quoted above, "it might not however be wise to make such a reduction". On many occasions Ricardo showed some indifference to the level of the exchange rate:

> The circumstance of the exchange being unfavourable, does not seem to me to be any disadvantage to us.
>
> (Evidence before the Lords' Committee, 26 March 1819; V: 442)

> To your second question whether I can point out distinctly an example or instance whereby one country gains and the other country loses by the rate of exchange between them? I answer that I believe the rate of exchange quite unimportant as it affects the interests of the two countries. Inasmuch it is sometimes a symptom of subsidies being paid, of unprosperous commerce &c., it is a subject of regret when it is unfavourable. In our transactions with Hamburgh for example I believe we should neither gain nor lose by the exchange being at 28 or 33 the relative prices of commodities in the two countries being raised or lowered in proportion to the rise or fall of the exchange.
>
> (Letter to Broadley, 14 June 1816; VII: 43–4)

Consequently, when variations in the exchange rate had a real cause, it was not appropriate to vary the note issue: gold flows triggered by arbitrage were in charge of the adjustment. With the adoption of the policy rule embodied in the Ingot Plan, international bullion flows would only correct the effect on the exchange rate of these real causes, and no longer that of the monetary ones. The signal to be used by the issuing bank to determine whether it should vary its issues when the exchange rate varied was simple and it derived from Ricardo's distinction between nominal and real effects on the exchange rate, as formulated in the quotation given earlier:

> The exchange may be said to be nominally affected to the amount of the difference between the market and mint prices of bullion, and be really affected by any deviation from par exceeding or falling short of this difference.
>
> (Letter to McCulloch, 2 October 1819; VIII: 88)

If the variation in the exchange rate was accompanied with a divergence between the market and the legal price of gold bullion, it had a monetary ("nominal") origin and called for intervention. If it was not accompanied with such divergence (or in the measure that it varied more than the market price of bullion), it had a non-monetary ("real") origin and the issuing bank should passively provide (absorb) the bullion demanded (supplied) by the arbitragers. Not being fuelled by the monetary shocks but only by real ones, these bullion flows would be small in importance:

> The most perfect liberty should be given, at the same time, to export or import every description of bullion. These transactions in bullion would be very few in number, if the Bank regulated their loans and issues of paper by the criterion which I have so often mentioned, namely, the price of standard bullion, without attending to the absolute quantity of paper in circulation.
>
> (*Proposals*; IV: 67; *Principles*; I: 357–8)

The corrective role of international bullion flows to variations in the exchange rate was thus restricted to those (exogenous) variations having a real origin; for the variations (endogenously) caused by the absence of conformity of the quantity of money to “the wants of commerce”, they should be corrected by the adaptation of the quantity of money itself, thanks to the policy rule of varying the note issue inversely with the difference between the market price and the legal price of the standard.

This distinction between two answers to variations in the exchange rate amounted practically to restrict the role of convertibility to the sole international payments. The monetary system was made a gold-exchange standard one.

A prototype of the gold-exchange standard

In a monetary system where the bank note was convertible into coin, as was the case in England before 1797 and again after 1821, this convertibility meant exchanging at a legal parity one circulating medium (the note) for another (the coin). This had two consequences. First, such conversion could occur for reasons linked to the state of domestic circulation, for example the debasement of the coin (see Chapter 6 above): then there was an internal drain of the metallic reserves of the issuing bank. Second, conversion with a view to exporting bullion – an external drain – required the melting of the coin, with its associated cost. In a monetary system designed according to the Ingot Plan, the bank note was convertible into gold bars (ingots) wearing a legal stamp but deprived of legal tender, hence which could not be used as circulating medium. This convertibility meant exchanging at a legal price a circulating medium (the note) for a special commodity (gold bullion) which was both the domestic standard of money and an international means of settlement. This had two consequences. First, such conversion could still be triggered by the state of domestic circulation – an excess issue of notes, which raised the market price of gold bullion above its legal price and made arbitrage profitable – but no longer by the characteristics of the metallic currency or for the purpose of internal circulation. Second, the only use of the bars obtained from the issuing bank was their exportation: the bank had only to face an external drain, and this increased the security of the monetary system (see Chapter 9 below).

Convertibility was thus *de facto* restricted to foreign payments, a feature that would later define a gold-exchange standard, in which the domestic currency is convertible into a foreign currency (itself convertible into gold) that cannot legally be used in domestic payments. Ricardo’s paternity of the notion of gold-exchange standard was acknowledged by Keynes in his book *Indian Currency and Finance*:

> Its theoretical advantages [of the gold-exchange standard] were first set forth by Ricardo at the time of the bullionist controversy. He laid it down that a currency is in its most perfect state when it consists of a cheap material, but having an equal value with the gold it professes to represent; and he suggested that convertibility for the purposes of the foreign exchanges should be ensured by the tendering on demand of gold *bars* (not coin) in exchange for

> notes – so that gold might be available for purposes of export only, and would be prevented from entering into the internal circulation of the country.
> (Keynes 1913: 22; Keynes's emphasis)

The relation with India was not fortuitous: the monetary system of this English colony had been reformed in the very first years of the twentieth century along the lines of the "Lindsay scheme" which explicitly referred to Ricardo's Ingot Plan.

Alexander Lindsay, who was an English banker in the Bank of Bengal, had stressed that the fall in the relative price of silver in terms of gold had depressed the exchange rate of the Indian silver rupee in terms of the British gold pound and consequently increased production costs in India through higher import prices. He was thus looking for a monetary scheme which would allow India to continue using the silver rupee for her domestic payments, while reducing the negative effects on her economy of the adoption of the gold standard in most industrialised countries. The solution was to adapt Ricardo's Ingot Plan to the situation of India. Mentioning Peel's bill of 1819, he observed that "this short trial is the only one ever given to Ricardo's scheme, and it passed through the ordeal satisfactorily" (Lindsay 1892: 6). For him, "in applying Ricardo's proposals to India, little modification is necessary either of the proposals or of Indian currency arrangements. The only change in the proposals will be the substitution of sterling money for gold bars, and rupees for paper money" (ibid: 8). Rupees would be convertible in India against drafts in pounds remitted to England and payable at a fixed price in notes by the Bank of England. The main consequences of this scheme would be to link the rupee to gold, hence to stabilise the exchange with gold-standard countries, and to guarantee the convertibility of the rupee for external reasons without gold having to enter Indian domestic circulation. Hence "gold will be the standard of value, though it will not be used in the internal circulation" (ibid: 12); the system had "a gold standard without a gold currency on the footing recommended by Ricardo in his celebrated scheme for 'A Secure and Economical Currency'" (ibid: 28).

In 1913 Keynes observed approvingly that "in the last ten years the gold-exchange standard has become the prevailing monetary system of Asia" (Keynes 1913: 25). As is well known, this system was extended to other countries in inter-war years, and later institutionalised, with qualifications, at Bretton Woods.

Appendix 8: The boundaries constraining the exchange rate

As shown in Chapter 8, the evaluation of the state of the exchange required, according to Ricardo, a disentangling of the margin of variation in the exchange rate opened by the cost of transporting bullion abroad, and the effect of the monetary conditions that might depreciate or appreciate the currency. How to do that was illustrated by Ricardo with two examples, one in his early letters to the *Morning Chronicle*, the other in *Principles*. This question was made more complex if the two countries were on a different standard.

1. The proportions in which the transfer cost of bullion and the depreciation of the note accounted for a fall in the exchange rate

In his letters of 29 August and 20 September 1809 to the *Morning Chronicle*, Ricardo showed that the greatest part of the fall in the exchange rate of the pound should be ascribed to the depreciation of the Bank of England note. To do that, he compared a situation in which the currency would be undepreciated and the observed situation at the time.

The cost of transferring gold bullion being given, the export bullion point determined the lowest level of the exchange rate which could exist when the domestic currency was undepreciated:

> If our circulation were wholly carried on by specie, I believe it would be difficult for this writer to convince us, that the exchange might be 20 per cent. against us. What could induce any person owing 100 l. in Hamburgh, to buy a bill here for that sum, giving 120 l. for it, when the charges attending the exportation of the 100 l. to pay his debt could not exceed 4l. or 5l.?
>
> (*The Price of Gold*; III: 24)

Someone in London having to pay a debt of £100 in Hamburg had the choice between two means of implementing this operation: either he bought in London a bill of exchange on Hamburg of the equivalent in *Mark banco* of £100 at the ruling exchange rate of the pound, or he purchased £100 in gold bullion in London and sent it to Hamburg where he sold it for *Mark banco* to discharge his debt. Knowing that in the second case the cost of the exportation of bullion was 4 or 5 per cent, he would not agree to paying for the bill more than £104 or £105. If in the London foreign-exchange market the price of such bill was £120, the difference could only be ascribed to the depreciation of the Bank of England notes paying for the bill of exchange, which lowered the exchange rate of the pound beyond the 4 or 5 per cent limit set by the transfer cost below the legal par:

> This is therefore the natural limit to the fall of the exchange, it can never fall more below par than these expences [of the transport of the metals]; nor can it ever rise more above par than the same amount. [...] Thus then it appears, that the exchange may not only fall to the limits which I have before mentioned, but also in an inverse proportion to the rise of gold, or rather the discount of bank notes. But these are the limits within which it is even now confined. It cannot on the one hand rise more above par than the expence of freight, &c. on the importation of gold, nor on the other fall more than the expences of freight, &c. on its exportation, added to the discount on bank notes.
>
> (ibid: 19–20)

In Chapter VII "On foreign trade" of *Principles* Ricardo repeated the argument according to which an exchange rate of 30 per cent below par might only be explained by the depreciation of the currency (hence an excess issue of notes), *not* by an autonomous cause of fall in the exchange rate:

> Those [like Ricardo] who maintained that our currency was depreciated during the last ten years, when the exchange varied from 20 to 30 per cent. against this country [England], have never contended, as they have been accused of doing, that money could not be more valuable in one country than another, as compared with various commodities; but they did contend, that 130*l*. could not be detained in England, unless it was depreciated, when it was of no more value, estimated in the money of Hamburgh, or of Holland, than the bullion in 100*l*.
>
> By sending 130*l*. good English pounds sterling to Hamburgh, even at an expense of 5*l*., I should be possessed there of 125*l*.; what then could make me consent to give 130*l*. for a bill which would give me 100*l*. in Hamburgh, but that my pounds were not good pounds sterling? – they were deteriorated, were degraded in intrinsic value below the pounds sterling of Hamburgh, and if actually sent there, at an expense of 5*l*., would sell only for 100*l*. With metallic pounds sterling, it is not denied that my 130*l*. would procure me 125*l*. in Hamburgh, but with paper pounds sterling I can only obtain 100*l*.; and yet it was maintained that 130*l*. in paper, was of equal value with 130*l*. in silver or gold.
>
> (*Principles*; I: 148–9)

The first part of the quotation illustrates the contention that the value of money, estimated in "various commodities", might differ from one country to the other. But this could not happen for the value of money estimated in bullion. Nobody would agree to "detain" £130 in England if their value in Flemish schillings were the same as £100 in bullion, unless the owner of the £130 knew that they had no more value than £100 in bullion, that is, that they were depreciated by 30 per cent. The exchange rate was a test of the depreciation, because it showed that the value of the £130 "detained", measured in Flemish schillings (130 e, with e the exchange rate of the pound in Flemish schillings), was the same as the value of £100 in bullion, also measured in Flemish schillings (hence 100 R_G, with R_G the real par of exchange). It amounted to the same to say that the proof of a 30 per cent depreciation of the pound was that the value of £130 was £100 in bullion, or that the rate of exchange e was below the par R_G by 30 per cent.

The second part of the quotation details what Ricardo meant in the first by "no more value, estimated in the money of Hamburgh, or of Holland, than the bullion in 100*l*". By "the pounds sterling of Hamburgh" he meant the quantity of pounds one might obtain in London by purchasing in Hamburg a bill on London and paying it with the quantity of money previously sent from London to Hamburg. The reasoning was based on the rationale of arbitrage. If the arbitrager decided to transport £130 from London to Hamburg – by the cheapest way, that is, in the form of bullion, at a cost of £5 – he expected to get £125, that is, an amount of Flemish schillings allowing him to purchase a bill of £125 on London, if his £130 were "good English pounds sterling". But then it did not make sense for him to purchase in London with £130 a bill payable in Hamburg a quantity of Flemish schillings that bought a £100 bill on London. Such operation did exist, however, as testified by the quotation of the exchange rate of the pound in Flemish schillings. This meant that the other operation was not more beneficial, hence that it did not produce £125 after deduction of the transport cost of bullion, but £100. In other words, this proved that the £130 were *not* "good English pounds sterling" but were "deteriorated", "degraded". The cause of this degradation was easy to find: the £130 pounds were not in metallic money but in depreciated paper.

2. The complications introduced by a difference in standard

As shown in Appendix 1 above, Ricardo criticised Vansittart in 1811 for wrongly ascertaining the state of the exchange in the year 1760, because Vansittart did not use the "real par of exchange" taking into account the difference in standard between London (gold bullion) and Hamburg (silver bullion). This real par R_{GS} obtained when, in the formula of the legal par computed on gold ($\overline{R_G} = \overline{P_{GC}}^{\text{Fs}} / \overline{P_{GC}}^{\text{£}}$), the lacking legal price of gold in coin in Hamburg was replaced by the price at which an ounce of gold bullion could be purchased or sold in the Hamburg market against silver bullion paid for at the legal price:

$$R_{GS} = P_{GS} \frac{\overline{P_S}^{\text{Fs}}}{\overline{P_{GC}}^{\text{£}}} \tag{1.3}$$

with $\overline{P_S}^{\text{Fs}}$ the legal price of silver bullion in Hamburg, $\overline{P_{GC}}^{\text{£}}$ the legal price of gold in coin in London, and the relative price P_{GS} of gold bullion in terms of silver bullion computed in the London market as a proxy of its level in the Hamburg market (because of arbitrage in the international bullion market):

$$P_{GS} = \frac{P_G^{\text{£}}}{P_S^{\text{£}}} = \frac{P_G^{\text{Fs}}}{P_S^{\text{Fs}}} \tag{8.17}$$

We saw that available historical data validate Ricardo's calculation of R_{GS}, hence his critique of Vansittart.

In inequalities (8.5) of Chapter 8 above, which state the limits of variation of the exchange rate computed on the basis of the real par on gold, R_G should now be replaced by the real par on gold and silver R_{GS}:

$$R_{GS}\ (1+c_M) \geq e \geq R_{GS}\ (1-c_X) \tag{8.18}$$

with e the exchange rate of one pound against Flemish schillings, and c_M and c_X the respective costs of importing or exporting bullion to (from) London from (to) Hamburg, supposed for simplicity to be identical for both metals.

From (1.3) and (8.18) one may deduce the boundaries constraining the exchange rate:

$$P_{GS}\frac{\overline{P_S}^{\text{Fs}}}{\overline{P_{GC}}^{\pounds}}(1+c_M)\geq e\geq P_{GS}\frac{\overline{P_S}^{\text{Fs}}}{\overline{P_{GC}}^{\pounds}}(1-c_X) \tag{8.19}$$

Applying (6.1) to the market price $P_G^{\pounds}$ of gold bullion in London and to the market price P_S^{Fs} of silver bullion in Hamburg gives their limits of variation:

$$\overline{P_{GC}}^{\pounds}(1+m_G{}^L)\geq P_G^{\pounds}\geq\overline{P_{GC}}^{\pounds}(1-s_G{}^L) \tag{6.1}$$

$$\overline{P_S}^{\text{Fs}}(1+m_S{}^H)\geq P_S^{\text{Fs}}\geq\overline{P_S}^{\text{Fs}} \tag{8.20}$$

with $m_G{}^L$ and $s_G{}^L$ respectively the melting and minting costs of the coin in London, and $m_S{}^H$ the commission charged by the Bank of Hamburg to pay accounts in *Mark banco* into silver bullion, the conversion of silver bullion into accounts in *Mark banco* being at no charge (see Chapter 1 above).

The upper boundary of the exchange rate e obtained when, in the first part of the definition of P_{GS} given by (8.17), $P_G^{\pounds}$ was at its maximum, and the lower boundary obtained when $P_G^{\pounds}$ was at its minimum, both given by (6.1). Inequalities (8.19) became then as follows:

$$\frac{\overline{P_S}^{\text{Fs}}}{P_S^{\pounds}}(1+m_G{}^L)(1+c_M)\geq e\geq\frac{\overline{P_S}^{\text{Fs}}}{P_S^{\pounds}}(1-s_G{}^L)(1-c_X) \tag{8.21}$$

In the second part of the definition of P_{GS} given by (8.17), e was also constrained by an upper boundary obtained when P_S^{Fs} was at its minimum and by a lower boundary obtained when P_S^{Fs} was at its maximum, making Inequalities (8.19) become as follows:

$$\frac{P_G^{\text{Fs}}}{\overline{P_{GC}}^{\pounds}}(1+c_M)\geq e\geq\frac{P_G^{\text{Fs}}}{\overline{P_{GC}}^{\pounds}}\frac{1}{1+m_S{}^H}(1-c_X) \tag{8.22}$$

Inequalities (8.21) and (8.22) determine for either direction of variation of e two thresholds triggering international arbitrage, respectively on silver bullion (depending on its market price in London) and on gold bullion (depending on its market price in Hamburg). The exchange rate was effectively constrained from above by the lower threshold (which triggered the import to London of the corresponding metal) and from below by the higher threshold (which triggered the export of the corresponding metal). The boundaries of the exchange rate were consequently given by:

$$\text{Min}\{\frac{\overline{P_S}^{\text{Fs}}}{P_S^{\pounds}}(1+m_G^L); \frac{P_G^{\text{Fs}}}{\overline{P_{GC}}^{\pounds}}\}(1+c_M) \geq e \geq$$
$$\text{Max}\{\frac{\overline{P_S}^{\text{Fs}}}{P_S^{\pounds}}(1-s_G^L); \frac{P_G^{\text{Fs}}}{\overline{P_{GC}}^{\pounds}}\frac{1}{1+m_S^H}\}(1-c_X) \quad (8.23)$$

A comparison between (8.10) and (8.23) shows the similarities and differences that existed in the international adjustment between a system in which the two countries had a standard in common and a system in which they were on different standards. In the first case, the exchange rate was constrained by fixed boundaries depending on the legal price of the common standard in each country (which determined the legal par of exchange) and on given parameters reflecting the conditions of convertibility both ways between the currency and the standard in each country and of the transfer of the standard from one country to the other. In the second case, in addition to these magnitudes, the boundaries constraining the exchange rate also depended on the market price in each country of the metal that was the standard in the other country. Consequently, the boundaries were no longer fixed but moved with the relative price of one standard in terms of the other, a magnitude which varied with the conditions of production of the two metals at the world level. In other words, the exchange rate was no longer constrained by a fixed "tunnel", exclusively determined by the monetary conditions in each country and the organisation of the world market of the metal acting as common standard, but by a "snake" which moved with changes in the production of gold and silver and whose "skins" were alternatively made of one metal or the other, as shown by the Min {…} and Max {…} operators in inequalities (8.23) (for a study of this "bimetallic snake" between London, Paris, and Hamburg from 1821 to 1873, see Boyer-Xambeu, Deleplace and Gillard 1997, 2013).

It should be observed that, although the boundaries constraining the exchange rate were not fixed in the case of two different standards, there were still boundaries: this was *not* a floating exchange-rate system. In contrast with the system based on a common standard, the price of the standard was not legally fixed in each country, the exchange rate adjusting to the legal par. Each of the two metals had now a fixed legal price in one of the two countries but only a variable market price in the other, where it was *not* the standard. However, this variable market price was itself constrained through arbitrage by the legal price of the same metal in the other country and by the level of the exchange rate. Inequalities (8.23) could be rewritten to show the boundaries constraining $P_S^{\pounds}$ with $\overline{P_S}^{\text{Fs}}$ and e being given, or P_G^{Fs} with $\overline{P_G}^{\pounds}$ and e being given. A complex dynamics constrained thus e, $P_S^{\pounds}$, and P_G^{Fs} together, thanks to arbitrage taking advantage of the monetary conditions in each country, the organisation of the world market of the two metals, and their conditions of production. This international bimetallism – which, it should be noted, did not require a legal domestic bimetallism in any country but simply a different standard in each – retained from the international monometallic standard the stabilising effect of the existence of a legal standard in each country and from domestic bimetallism the destabilising effect of the varying conditions of production of the metals, as had been emphasised by Ricardo (see Chapter 6 above).[24]

Notes

1 Cantillon's *Essai sur la nature du commerce en général* (Cantillon 1755 [1730]) was published in 1755 but probably written between 1728 and 1730. Cantillon disappeared mysteriously in 1734.

2 The first reference is to the 2015 edition of the original of Steuart (1767); the second reference is to the 1805 edition, reprinted in 1998. In both cases the roman figure indicates the volume in the edition.

3 At the time of Steuart, Paris quoted the exchange certain on London, while at the time of Ricardo London quoted the exchange certain on Paris. Leaving aside changes in the monetary units, the par of exchange was consequently at the time of Ricardo the reciprocal of that at the time of Steuart.

4 "How high the price of gold bullion may rise at London no man can say; but the highest it rose to, during the last war, was, I believe, 4*l.* 0*s.* 8*d.* *per* ounce standard" (Steuart 1767, II: 319; III: 343).

5 It is thus surprising to find in de Boyer des Roches (2007, 2008) the affirmation that the operation of the gold points was rejected by Ricardo. For a critique of this affirmation, see Rosselli (2008).

6 See also:

> If there were no expences whatever in sending bullion from one country to another the exchange would never deviate from par. It would be as invariable as the price of bullion is in countries where money is freely exchangeable for bullion on demand.
> (Letter to McCulloch, 2 October 1819; VIII: 93)

> Without any alteration in the quantity of metal in either, the relative value of their currencies may undergo a change, within the range of the expences of sending the metal from one to the other. If 10000 guilder were of the same intrinsic value as £1000, and the expence of sending money 2 pct., £1000 might for a considerable length of time purchase a bill for 10200 guilders at one period, and at another, for a considerable length of time also, it might only purchase a bill for about 9800.
> (Letter to Mill, 18 December 1821; IX: 129)

7 See also: "the par of exchange being calculated not on the value which the coin actually passed for in currency, but on its intrinsic value as bullion" (*Reply to Bosanquet*; III: 180).

8 As indicated by Sraffa in a footnote, "McCulloch assumes that the expense of conveying bullion from Rio Janeiro to London is 5 per cent".

9 This obviously should read "lower", although this mistake is not mentioned by Sraffa.

10 The incident phrase "supposing paper money not to be used" is explained by the fact that Ricardo here assumed a metallic circulation, so that a general rise in prices might only be produced by "an influx of money". If inconvertible paper money was also taken into consideration, the effects on the exchange were the same as in the case of obstacles to the international transfer of bullion; see Section 8.5 below.

11 This conclusion is apparently contradicted by the following quotation:

> It [the exchange] may also be ascertained by comparing it with some standard common to both countries. If a bill on England for 100*l*. will purchase the same quantity of goods in France or Spain, that a bill on Hamburgh for the same sum will do, the exchange between Hamburgh and England is at par; but if a bill on England for 130*l*., will purchase no more than a bill on Hamburgh for 100*l*., the exchange is 30 per cent. against England.
>
> (*Principles*; I: 147–8)

There is, however, no contradiction. The evaluation of the exchange concerned the English currency and the Hamburg currency, not the French or Spanish one. French or Spanish goods were only "some standard common to both countries" – any standard, not necessarily the standard of money – by which the parity of the pound and the Flemish schilling (Hamburg money) was ascertained. If one might pay in France for any given quantity of whatever commodity with a bill of £100 drawn alternatively on London or Hamburg, the exchange of the pound against Flemish schillings was at par. But if one had to draw a bill of £130 on London to be discharged of a payment one might do with a bill of £100 on Hamburg, the exchange of the pound against Flemish schillings was 30 per cent against the pound. This is no surprise: the fact that one might draw a £100 bill on Hamburg only meant that the bill in Flemish schillings drawn on Hamburg might purchase there a £100 bill on London. The exchange between the pound and the Flemish schilling was thus at par if it was indifferent to exchange French or Spanish money against pounds or against Flemish schillings then against pounds.

12 "Beside the improvements in arts and machinery, there are various other causes which are constantly operating on the natural course of trade, and which interfere with the equilibrium, and the relative value of money" (*Principles*; I: 141–2). "Although taxation occasions a disturbance of the equilibrium of money, it does so by depriving the country in which it is imposed of some of the advantages attending skill, industry, and climate" (ibid: 145).

13 For a denial of the existence of the purchasing power parity theorem in Ricardo, see also Marcuzzo and Rosselli (1991).

14 For simplicity, I suppose that international arbitrage ensures that the exchange rate quoted in London is equal to that in Paris.

15 This definition of the real exchange rate and its formal expression in (8.3) resemble what may be found in any modern textbook in macroeconomics under the heading "real exchange rate", with the general price level substituting for the price of gold bullion. As already emphasised in Chapter 3 above, this does not mean that for Ricardo the latter was a proxy of the former.

16 In the Appendix to the fourth edition of *High Price*, Ricardo quoted the author of the review of his book in the *Edinburgh Review* – Malthus – to criticise the contention that "the exportation of the 'precious metals is the *effect of a balance of trade*, originating in causes which may exist without any relation whatever to redundancy or deficiency of currency'" (III: 101; Ricardo's emphasis).

17 For a more sceptical view, and the suggestion that Ricardo in fact adhered to the description made by Thornton of the international transmission mechanism of an excess issue of notes, see Rosselli (2008: 77–8):

> Ricardo repeatedly states that it is a fall in the value of gold that determines its exportation, because he wants to stress that there is nothing that makes gold a special commodity, to be preferred to others to settle international debts. Yet, he does not feel the need to specify the sequence of steps by which an increase in the money supply determines the exportation of gold. Even in his later works, he will develop his theory of the value of gold, but will not feel the need for deepening this aspect of his analysis. A practical man, not particularly fond of putting in writing

his thoughts, he stresses only the points where his opinions are at variance with those of the others. Thornton had "considered this subject very much at large" and there was no need to repeat what was now common ground.

18 See also: "All trade is at last a trade of barter and no nation will long buy unless it can also sell, – nor will it long sell if it will not also buy" (Letter to Malthus, 26 June 1814; VI: 109). Sraffa mentions that "the phrase is Malthus's (*Observations on ... the Corn Laws*, 1814, p. 24)" (VI: 109 n1).
19 It is the reason why in his *Index* Sraffa mentions at the entry "Foreign trade": "principles of, in terms of barter, I, 133–6, in terms of money, I, 137–49; finally a trade of barter, I, 228, II, 154, IV, 214, VI, 109" (XI: 32). The pages in *Principles* are from Chapter VII "On foreign trade"; the other references are the ones quoted above in the text.
20 For a comparison of the various types of international adjustment in the literature on Ricardo, in the case of war transfers or abnormal importation of corn by Britain, see Marcuzzo and Rosselli (1991: 145–8), including their own view of the subject.
21 This hesitation about the usefulness of the notion of real exchange is surprising, since Ricardo had used it eight years before in *Reply to Bosanquet* (III: 213) and also six months before when he was examined by the Lords' Committee (see the above quotation from V: 448).
22 See also, in the first letter to McCulloch: "I cannot help thinking that in all cases an unfavourable exchange may be traced to a relative redundancy of currency" (VIII: 86).
23 This position was consistent with the affirmation, in *Reply to Bosanquet*, that the import of corn and the export of gold were voluntary – that is, governed by interest alone – even during a famine; they were *not* compulsory. Gold was exported neither because England was forced to import corn nor because foreigners refused to be paid in other English commodities:

> Mr. Bosanquet speaks as if the nation collectively, as one body, imported corn and exported gold, and that it was compelled by hunger so to do, not reflecting that the importation of corn, even under the case supposed, is the act of individuals, and governed by the same motives as all other branches of trade. What is the degree of *compulsion* which is employed to make us receive corn from our enemy? I suppose no other than the want of that commodity which makes it an advantageous article of import; but if it be a voluntary, as it most certainly is, and not a compulsory bargain between the two nations, I do still maintain that gold would not, even if famine raged amongst us, be given to France in exchange for corn, unless the exportation of gold was attended with advantage to the exporter, unless he could sell corn in England for more gold than he was obliged to give for the purchase of it. Would Mr. Bosanquet, would any merchant he knows, import corn for gold on any other terms? If no importer would, how could the corn be introduced into the country, unless gold or some other commodity were cheaper here? As far as those two commodities are concerned, do not these transactions as certainly indicate that gold is dearer in France, as that corn is dearer in England? Seeing nothing in Mr. Bosanquet's statement to induce me to change my opinion, I must continue to think that it is interest, and interest alone, which determines the exportation of gold, in the same manner as it regulates the exportation of all other commodities.
> (*Reply to Bosanquet*; III: 207–8)

These trade movements were consequent upon money being redundant in England, and gold rather than other commodities was exported because, as mentioned above in Section 8.2, it was "the cheapest exportable commodity".
24 For any pair of currencies, it can be shown that, at a moment of time, the "width" of the "bimetallic snake" was smaller than the range of variation of the exchange rate permit-

ted by an international monometallic standard, but through time changes in the relative price of the two metals made the "snake" oscillate, hence the exchange rate oscillated with it (see Boyer-Xambeu, Deleplace and Gillard 1997, 2013). The stabilising performance of international bimetallism thus depended on the respective force of these two effects. Econometric studies have shown that, on the period from 1821 to 1873, it was able to absorb several important shocks on the world gold / silver price, including the "gold rush" of the early 1850s; see Boyer-Xambeu *et al.* (2007a, 2007b).

9 Central banking and the euthanasia of metal currency

A currency is in its most perfect state when it consists wholly of paper money, but of paper money of an equal value with the gold which it professes to represent.

(*Principles*; I: 361)

The link between money and central banking is usually provided in the literature on Ricardo by the Quantity Theory of Money: it concerns the effects of an exogenous quantity of notes – issued discretionarily by the Bank of England – on the value of money. The attribution to Ricardo of a price-specie flow mechanism – according to which there is a mechanical adjustment of the domestic quantity of money thanks to international bullion flows and changes in the balance of trade – restricts the question of central banking to the rules that prevent the Bank of England from raising obstacles to this adjustment.

The object of the present chapter is to show that Ricardo's positions on central banking are better understood on the basis of the theory of money exposed in Chapters 3 to 7 above and of its consequences for international adjustment as analysed in Chapter 8. The starting point is Ricardo's conception of the public nature of paper money (Section 9.1), which is embodied in the two plans he designed for the monetary system, the Ingot Plan (Section 9.2) and the Plan for a national bank (Section 9.3). These plans aimed at managing the quantity of notes issued (Section 9.4) and at increasing the security of the monetary system (Section 9.5). They were an application of Ricardo's theory of money (Section 9.6). Appendix 9 compares five monetary systems endowed with a gold standard, the pre-1797 one, Ricardo's Ingot Plan, Peel's bill, Ricardo's Plan for a national bank, and the 1844 Bank Charter Act.

9.1 The public nature of paper money

Justice and security

In a letter to Jean-Baptiste Say of 24 December 1814, Ricardo still considered that "justice" and "security" were at variance on the question of the ownership of the bank of issue: the former object pleaded for public ownership (by "Government"), the latter for private one (by "a company of Bankers or merchants"):

> The plan for the currency of France which you have sent me to look over differs in no essential point from that which I recommended for our Bank of England [in the Appendix to the fourth edition of *High Price*], excepting that you propose Government to be the issuers, and to derive the advantages from the substitution of paper for metallic money. In all countries, I should think, there exists a repugnance to entrust to Government the power of issuing paper money, and when we consider that perhaps in no instance they have not abused such a power, it is not wonderful that such fears are prevalent. I am however so fully persuaded that the value of a currency depends on its quantity, and if your plan is adhered to there is such security against the quantity becoming excessive, that I cannot doubt of its success. My only doubt is whether Government will under all temptations rigidly abide by its own rules. In justice the public ought to derive the benefits which result from the substitution of a paper for a more valuable currency, but it has hitherto been given to a company of Bankers or merchants because they were more under the control of authority and could not with impunity use so formidable an engine to the injury of the public. At no time has the theory of money been so well understood as at present, and if the practice is conformable to it every thing respecting paper money will go on well.
>
> (VI: 165–6)

Eight months later, his commitment to justice was even greater, after the discovery of the "enormous profits" made by the Bank of England in its bargains with the government. At the request of Pascoe Grenfell, he was then completing the manuscript of *Proposals* ("late in September 1815", according to Sraffa 1951e: 46), which was first conceived as an attack at the Bank to be mounted in Parliament on this question. But he had also imagined a way to reconcile justice and security: the appointment of "Commissioners [...] independent of all ministerial control." In a letter to Malthus of 10 September 1815, he wrote:

> I think the Bank [of England] an unnecessary establishment getting rich by those profits which fairly belong to the public. I cannot help considering the issuing of paper money as a privilege which belongs exclusively to the state. – I regard it as a sort of seignorage, and I am convinced, if the principles of currency were rightly understood, that Commissioners might be appointed independent of all ministerial controul who should be the sole issuers of paper money. [...] In looking over the papers which have from time to time been laid before Parliament I think it might clearly be proved that the profits of the Bank have been enormous, – I should think they must have a hoard nearly equal to their Capital. By their Charter they are bound to make an annual division of their profits, and to lay a statement of their accounts before the Proprietors, – but they appear to set all law at defiance. I always enjoy any attack upon the Bank and if I had sufficient courage I would be a party to it.
>
> (VI: 268–9)

The idea of independent commissioners made its way in *Proposals*, which ended with a half-page outline of a public bank of issue, substituting for the Bank of England ("a company of merchants") when its charter would expire in 1833:

> The Bank are secure of their charter for seventeen years to come; and the public cannot, during that time, deprive them of the most profitable part of their trade. If indeed the charter were about to expire, the public might question the policy of permitting a company of merchants to enjoy all the advantages which attend the supplying of a great country with paper money; and although they would naturally look with jealousy, after the experience furnished by other states, to allowing that power to be in the hands of government, they might probably think that in a free country means might be found by which so considerable an advantage might be obtained for the state, independently of all control of ministers. Paper money may be considered as affording a seignorage equal to its whole exchangeable value, – but seignorage in all countries belongs to the state, and with the security of convertibility as proposed in the former part of this work, and the appointment of commissioners responsible to parliament only, the state, by becoming the sole issuer of paper money, in town as well as in the country, might secure a net revenue to the public of no less than two millions sterling. Against this danger, however, the Bank is secure till 1833, and therefore on every ground publicity [of its profits] is expedient.
>
> (*Proposals*; IV: 114)

It should be observed that the security of a public-note issue would not only be afforded by the political independence of the commissioners but also by "convertibility as proposed in the former part of this work", that is, convertibility of the note into bullion. Ricardo explicitly envisaged coupling the Ingot Plan – outlined in 1811 in the Appendix to the fourth edition of *High Price* and developed in 1816 in *Proposals* as applying to the Bank of England – and the public note issue. One may think that, in Ricardo's mind at that time, the Ingot Plan should be implemented for the Bank of England until the expiration of its charter (in 1833), and prolonged later under public ownership of the bank of issue. This conjecture is consistent with what may be found in *Principles*. In the first edition of 1817 and in the two subsequent editions of 1819 and 1821, the idea of a public bank was revived with the same arguments as in *Proposals*. After having shown that such bank would spare the interest on the loans made by the Bank of England to the government – hence the taxes levied on the public to pay for this charge of interest – he noted:

> I have already observed, that if there were perfect security that the power of issuing paper money would not be abused, it would be of no importance with respect to the riches of the country collectively, by whom it was issued; and I have now shewn that the public would have a direct interest that the issuers should be the State, and not a company of merchants or bankers. The danger, however, is, that this power would be more likely to be abused, if in the hands of Government, than if in the hands of a banking company. A company would,

> it is said, be more under the control of law, and although it might be their interest to extend their issues beyond the bounds of discretion, they would be limited and checked by the power which individuals would have of calling for bullion or specie. It is argued that the same check would not be long respected, if Government had the privilege of issuing money; that they would be too apt to consider present convenience, rather than future security, and might, therefore, on the alleged grounds of expediency, be too much inclined to remove the checks, by which the amount of their issues was controlled. Under an arbitrary Government, this objection would have great force; but, in a free country, with an enlightened legislature, the power of issuing paper money, under the requisite checks of convertibility at the will of the holder, might be safely lodged in the hands of commissioners appointed for that special purpose, and they might be made totally independent of the control of ministers.
>
> (*Principles*; I: 362)

In the perspective of the coming debate in Parliament on the resumption of cash payments by the Bank, Ricardo, on McCulloch's suggestion in a letter of 6 December 1818 (VII: 353), inserted in the second (1819) edition of *Principles* a four-page extract of *Proposals* containing the Ingot Plan. This insert remained in the third edition of 1821. Thus, these two editions of *Principles* contained the complete scheme of a paper money convertible into bullion and issued by a public bank. However, after the Ingot Plan, partly adopted by Parliament in 1819 as a transition to the resumed convertibility of the Bank of England note into coin, had been torpedoed by the Bank and abandoned in 1821 on the occasion of the return to the pre-war parity of the pound, Ricardo stepped back on convertibility into bullion, although introducing in the manuscript (1823) of his *Plan for a National Bank* an "expedient" provision that resurrected it (see below).

This latter plan again illustrated Ricardo's ongoing concern about the profits of the Bank of England, as shown in a letter to Malthus on 3 August 1823:

> I have been writing a few pages in favor of my project of a National Bank, with a view to prove that the nation would lose nothing in profits by abolishing the Bank of England, and that the sole effect of the change would be to transfer a part of the profits of the Bank to the national treasury.
>
> (IX: 325–6)

But above all it reiterated the view, already expressed in *Proposals* and deriving from his theory of money (see Chapter 4 above), that "paper money may be considered as affording a seignorage equal to its whole exchangeable value" (IV: 114)[1] and consequently should be issued by the State. In a letter to McCulloch on 8 August 1823 he wrote:

> I have written a short essay on the Plan of a National Bank, in which I have endeavored to shew that no one would be injured by such an establishment, but the Bank of England and the other issuers of paper money in the country

> who have no claim whatever to a profit which may be compared to that which is derived from the seignorage of money.
>
> (IX: 331)

The danger of "this great Leviathan, the Bank" for security

So far so good for justice. As for security, Ricardo did not only believe that a public power of issuing paper money could be prevented from being abused; he also contended that security was not on the side of "a company of merchants". It is striking that in the above quotation from *Principles* he mentioned the same argument – "a company would, it is said, be more under the control of law" – he had used in his letter to Say in 1814, but now he objected to it. The reason was that, as early as *Proposals*, Ricardo had emphasised that it had been unsafe to entrust the Bank of England with the power of regulating the currency, in the sense that it could vary the quantity – hence the value – of money at will:

> With the known opinion of the Bank directors, as to the rule for issuing paper money, they may be said to have exercised their powers without any great indiscretion. It is evident that they have followed their own principle with extreme caution. In the present state of the law, they have the power, without any control whatever, of increasing or reducing the circulation in any degree they may think proper: a power which should neither be intrusted to the State itself, nor to any body in it; as there can be no security for the uniformity in the value of the currency, when its augmentation or diminution depends solely on the will of the issuers. That the Bank have the power of reducing the circulation to the very narrowest limits will not be denied, even by those who agree in opinion with the directors, that they have not the power of adding indefinitely to its quantity. Though I am fully assured, that it is both against the interest and the wish of the Bank to exercise this power to the detriment of the public, yet, when I contemplate the evil consequences which might ensue from a sudden and great reduction of the circulation, as well as from a great addition to it, I cannot but deprecate the facility with which the State has armed the Bank with so formidable a prerogative.
>
> (*Proposals*; IV: 68–9; *Principles*; I: 359–60)

In a speech before the House of Commons on 12 June 1822 Ricardo would speak of "this great Leviathan, the Bank" (V: 202). According to him, the danger of "so formidable a prerogative" did not lie in the Bank issues being driven by interest or recklessness – "they may be said to have exercised their powers without any great indiscretion" – but in the fact that discounting bills – the very act by which the Bank issued notes – was decided on the basis of the quality of the bills, and not of the effect on aggregate circulation. In his "Notes on the Bullion Report" of 1810 Ricardo had already emphasised this point:

> The observations of Mr. Harman that the Bank never discount bills but for bona fide transactions cannot limit the quantity, – the same sum of money

> performs successively a great number of payments, – but a bill might be given for each of these payments for bona fide transactions and if the bank discounted them all we might have four or ten times the amounts of paper that is now actually in circulation.
>
> (III: 363–4)[2]

In modern parlance, the Bank's approach to the note issue was microeconomic – it relied on the characteristics of the commercial bill which was discounted – while it should have been macroeconomic – taking into account the state of the aggregate circulation, as signalled by the market price of gold bullion. The fact that the directors of the Bank of England persistently denied that their issues had any effect on the price of gold and on the level of the exchange rate was a proof of the danger to which their incompetence exposed the public. Indeed, there was a corrective mechanism – convertibility of the notes into coin – which eventually admonished them for their error. But in the interval before they were forced to adapt, "great distress would be suffered", as Ricardo observed before the House of Commons on 12 June 1822:

> His hon. friend [Mr. Haldimand, a Member of Parliament] had said, that whilst the Bank was obliged to pay its notes in gold, the public had no interest in interfering with the Bank respecting the amount of the paper circulation, for if it were too low, the deficiency would be supplied by the importation of gold, and if it were too high, it would be reduced by the exchange of paper for gold. In this opinion he did not entirely concur, because there might be an interval during which the country might sustain great inconvenience from an undue reduction of the Bank circulation. Let him put a case to elucidate his views on this subject. Suppose the Bank were to reduce the amount of their issues to five millions, what would be the consequence? The foreign exchanges would be turned in our favour, and large quantities of bullion would be imported. This bullion would be ultimately coined into money, and would replace the paper-money which had previously been withdrawn; but, before it was so coined, while all these operations were going on, the currency would be at a very low level, the prices of commodities would fall, and great distress would be suffered. Something of this kind had, in fact, happened.
>
> (V: 199–200)

Ricardo's solution to this problem was to adopt convertibility of the note into bullion instead of specie and to subject the Bank of England to the rule of varying its issues according to the spread between the market price of the standard and its legal price. This was the Ingot Plan.

9.2 The Ingot Plan

Many modern commentators simply ignore the Ingot Plan, for example Ahiakpor (1985, 2003), Perlman (1986), Peach (1993), Blaug (1995, 1996), de Boyer des

Roches (2007, 2008, 2013). When it is mentioned, it is often downplayed as being only a technical device – already to be found in Adam Smith – aiming at economising on gold by substituting paper money for metallic coins (see for example in the past Rist 1940 [1938]: 173, 176, and in modern times Laidler 1987: 293; Davis 2005: 155, 169, 194; Arnon 2011: 145; King 2013: 144). It is also often overlooked as a permanent system and reduced to a temporary device aiming at limiting the deflation involved by money supply contraction during the transition to convertibility at pre-war parity (see for example Hollander 1979: 494–5, 536). The genesis of this plan and the analysis of its content suggest that it was far more than that.

The 1811 outline

The idea of convertibility of the Bank of England note into bullion appeared in 1811 in the Appendix to the fourth edition of *High Price*:

> If the same benefits to the public, – the same security against the depreciation of the currency, can be obtained by more gentle means, it is to be hoped that all parties, who agree in principle, will concur in the expediency of adopting them. Let the Bank of England be required by Parliament to pay (if demanded) all notes above 20*l.* – and no other, at their option, either in specie, in gold standard bars, or in foreign coin (allowance being made for the difference in its purity) at the English mint value of gold bullion, viz. 3*l.* 17*s.* 10½*d.* per oz., such payments to commence at the period recommended by the Committee.
>
> This privilege of paying their notes as above described might be extended to the Bank for three or four years after such payments commenced, and if found advantageous, might be continued as a permanent measure. Under such a system the currency could never be depreciated below its standard price, as an ounce of gold and 3*l.* 17*s.* 10½*d.* would be uniformly of the same value.
>
> (*High Price*, Appendix to 4th ed.; III: 124–5)

One observes that the general motive of this plan was to guarantee for the monetary system the "security against the depreciation of the currency", by employing "more gentle means" which would:

> [P]revent the useless labour, which, under our system previously to 1797, was so unprofitably expended on the coinage of guineas, which on every occasion of an unfavourable exchange (we will not enquire by what caused) were consigned to the melting pot, and in spite of all prohibitions exported as bullion.
>
> (ibid: 125)

Ricardo did not take credit for this idea of convertibility into bullion, but had taken advantage of its implementation abroad for a long time, namely by the Bank of Amsterdam and the Bank of Hamburg (see Chapter 1 above).[3] However, the novelty was to marry this type of convertibility, which ensured the security of the monetary system (see Section 9.5 below), with the issuing of notes by discounting commercial bills, as the Bank of England did, which ensured the fulfilment of "the demands of commerce" (neither the Bank of Amsterdam nor the Bank of Hamburg issued notes or discounted bills).[4] Already in his "Notes on Bentham" written around Christmas 1810, Ricardo had mentioned these banks:

> The Bank of England is certainly not *quite* secure as a bank of deposit such as Amsterdam and Hamburgh, – but is infinitely more useful in making the whole capital of the country available. [...] In Holland and Hamburgh the advantages of the Banks is 1° in the use of paper instead of metals which has been admirably described by this author [Bentham], and 2° in having a uniform measure of value subject to no debasement or deterioration.
>
> (III: 288; Ricardo's emphasis)[5]

Ricardo's plan thus combined the advantages of the two systems:

> The plan here proposed appears to me to unite all the advantages of every system of banking which has been hitherto adopted in Europe. It is in some of its features similar to the banks of deposit of Amsterdam and Hamburgh. In those establishments bullion is always to be purchased from the Bank at a fixed invariable price. The same thing is proposed for the Bank of England; but in the foreign banks of deposit, they have actually in their coffers, as much bullion, as there are credits for bank money in their books; accordingly there is an inactive capital as great as the whole amount of the commercial circulation. In our Bank, however, there would be an amount of bank money, under the name of bank-notes, as great as the demands of commerce could require, at the same time there would not be more inactive capital in the bank coffers than that fund which the Bank should think it necessary to keep in bullion, to answer those demands which might occasionally be made on them. It should always be remembered too, that the Bank would be enabled by contracting their issues of paper to diminish such demands at pleasure. In imitation of the Bank of Hamburgh, who purchase silver at a fixed price, it would be necessary for the Bank to fix a price *very little below* the mint price, at which they would at all times purchase, with their notes, such gold bullion as might be offered to them.
>
> The perfection of banking is to enable a country by means of a paper currency (always retaining its standard value) to carry on its circulation with the least possible quantity of coin or bullion. This is what this plan would effect. And with a silver coinage, on just principles, we should possess the most economical and the most invariable currency in the world. The variations in the price of bullion, whatever demand there might be for it on the continent, or whatever supply might be poured in from the mines in America, would be confined within the prices at which the Bank bought bullion, and the mint price at which they sold it. The amount of the circulation would be adjusted

to the wants of commerce with the greatest precision; and if the Bank were for a moment so indiscreet as to over-charge the circulation, the check which the public would possess would speedily admonish them of their error. As for the country Banks, they must, as now, pay their notes when demanded in Bank of England notes. This would be a sufficient security against the possibility of their being able too much to augment the paper circulation. There would be no temptation to melt the coin, and consequently the labour which has been so uselessly bestowed by one party in recoining what another party found it their interest to melt into bullion, would be effectually saved. The currency could neither be clipped nor deteriorated, and would possess a value as invariable as gold itself, the great object which the Dutch had in view, and which they most successfully accomplished by a system very like that which is here recommended.

(*High Price*, Appendix to 4th ed.; III: 126–7; Ricardo's emphasis)

In spite of the rejection of the Bullion Report by Parliament (see Chapter 2 above), Ricardo tried to push his plan among political leaders. On 27 July 1811 he wrote to the Prime Minister and Chancellor of the Exchequer Spencer Perceval:

> Let the Bank be obliged to sell gold bullion, for their own notes, to any purchaser that shall apply for a quantity not less than 5 ounces, at the rate of £4.15 p[r] oz for standard bullion, and whatever the bullion so delivered by the Bank may arise from, whether from foreign coin, or from light guineas, let it be freely exportable at the will of the purchaser. An enactment to this effect would secure the public against any depreciation of the currency beyond that to which it has already reached.
>
> (VI: 43–4)

As shown by the price chosen for the conversion of the notes into gold bullion – the ruling market price of the latter at the time, 22 per cent above the mint price – the purpose of the measure was to stop the acceleration of depreciation, not to restore the currency to its original value. Such a proposal could not "in any way be considered as a hardship on the Bank", and "it would give the public complete security against the further depreciation of Bank notes" (ibid: 44–5), because the Bank of England would prevent any rise in the market price of bullion – hence any threat on its metallic reserves – by adjusting the amount of the note issue:

> Whilst the Bank have the power of limiting their issues of paper, they have the power of counteracting any tendency to a rise in the price of gold, whatever the demand for that article may be, either on the continent of Europe, or in any other part of the world.
>
> (ibid: 45)

The proposal was turned down by the Prime Minister, as mentioned by Ricardo ("He politely declined to follow my suggestions") on 11 December 1811 at the end of a letter to the Whig Opposition leader George Tierney, whom he also tried (unsuccessfully) to convince of the relevance of:

> [T]he means which might be advantageously adopted, first, to arrest the progress of the depreciation of our currency, and secondly to restore it to its standard value.
>
> (VI: 67)

The first object would be attained by the measure he had proposed to Perceval (the minimum quantity of bullion sold by the Bank "at a fixed price somewhere about the present market price" being now raised to "not less than 50, 100, or 200 ounces"; ibid: 67–8), the second by the gradual lowering, beginning six months later, of this fixed price by 6 or 9 pence (less than one per cent) each month, until after four or three years it was reduced to the mint price (£3. 17s. 10½d.). The restoration of the currency "to its standard value" was put by Ricardo in a larger perspective: the adoption of a permanent system of a circulation exclusively composed of notes convertible into bullion:

> When this desireable object should be attained it would be of little comparative importance to the public, whether the Bank were allowed to continue to supply the whole circulation, as they now do, with their notes, or whether they should be compelled to pay in specie. It is not money but money's worth that the holders of notes require, and it can be of little consequence to any reasonable man whether he goes to market with 20 guineas or £21 in notes, provided he can purchase precisely as much with one as with the other. If the public were secured against depreciation by possessing the power of exchanging their notes for bullion at the mint value of gold, I should prefer a circulation, such as ours, consisting wholly of paper, to any other, even as a permanent measure, as being more economical and possessing other obvious advantages.
>
> (ibid: 69)

Ricardo ended up by recalling the assumption on which his plan was based:

> It need not be observed that the whole of the above plan proceeds on the supposition that the Bank have uncontrouled power of regulating the rise or fall in the price of gold bullion, a point which was most satisfactorily proved during the late discussion on the report of the Bullion Committee.
>
> (ibid)

The 1816 plan

As shown in Chapter 7 above, Ricardo started with *Proposals for an Economical and Secure Currency* in 1816 to give a theoretical foundation to the assumption that the Bank regulated the price of gold bullion by its note issue. The pamphlet was originally conceived at the suggestion of Pascoe Grenfell as an attack at the

Bank of England on the high level and the distribution of the profits made by the Bank in its operations with the Government. It also contained the full development of what Ricardo would call in a letter of 5 March 1822 his "Ingot plan of payment" (IX: 176) and which is known in the literature as the Ingot Plan.

The two aims of the plan announced in the title of the pamphlet were summarised in the sentence opening the long passage of *Proposals* which would be quoted later in the second and third editions of *Principles*:

> To secure the public against any other variations in the value of the currency than those to which the standard itself is subject, and, at the same time, to carry on the circulation with a medium the least expensive, is to attain the most perfect state to which a currency can be brought.
>
> (*Proposals*; IV: 66; *Principles*; I: 356–7)

This passage continues with the proposed legal provisions which broke with the pre-1797 system:

> [A]nd we should possess all these advantages by subjecting the Bank to the delivery of uncoined gold or silver at the mint standard and price, in exchange for their notes, instead of the delivery of guineas; by which means paper would never fall below the value of bullion, without being followed by a reduction of its quantity. To prevent the rise of paper above the value of bullion, the Bank should be also obliged to give their paper in exchange for standard gold at the price of 3*l.* 17*s.* per ounce. Not to give too much trouble to the Bank, the quantity of gold to be demanded in exchange for paper at the mint price of 3*l.* 17*s.* 10½*d.*, or the quantity to be sold to the Bank at 3*l.* 17*s.*, should never be less than twenty ounces. In other words, the Bank should be obliged to purchase any quantity of gold that was offered them, not less than twenty ounces, at 3*l.* 17*s.* per ounce, and to sell any quantity that might be demanded at 3*l.* 17*s.* 10½*d.* While they have the power of regulating the quantity of their paper, there is no possible inconvenience that could result to them from such a regulation. The most perfect liberty should be given, at the same time, to export or import every description of bullion.
>
> (*Proposals*; IV: 66–7; *Principles*: 357)[6]

The first two legal changes in respect to the pre-1797 system introduced convertibility both ways (at fixed legal prices slightly different) between the Bank of England note and the standard (gold bullion). On the one hand, there existed before 1797 convertibility of the note into gold, but it was gold in coin, not in bullion, which could thus be obtained only by melting fraudulently the coin. On the other hand, the Bank of England was not in the past obliged to purchase all bullion offered to it at a fixed price, and it did that only discretionarily and at the market price. Convertibility of the note into bullion ensured that by arbitrage the market price of bullion would not rise much above the mint price when notes were issued in excess and money was depreciated. Symmetrically, convertibility of bullion into the note prevented the market price of bullion from falling too much below the mint price when the note issue was deficient and money was appreciated. The third legal provision – "the most perfect liberty [...] to export or import every description of bullion" – also broke with the pre-1797 system where melting and exporting the coin was prohibited. Here also, the object was to reduce the margin of variation of the market price of bullion triggering arbitrage, hence to facilitate the stabilisation of this price (see Section 9.5 below).

What may be called the ingot principle – convertibility of the note into bullion – was coupled by Ricardo with a provision which, although not legally binding, contributed, as quoted above, "to secure the public against any other variations in the value of the currency than those to which the standard itself is subject". This concerned the regulation of the quantity of notes issued, and may be called the management principle.

In the pre-1797 system as under inconvertibility, the issues of the Bank of England had an effect on the market price of gold bullion. As Ricardo put it in the letter to Tierney of 11 December 1811 quoted above: "the Bank have uncontrouled power of regulating the rise or fall in the price of gold bullion" (VI: 69). He would always criticise the Directors of the Bank for exercising this discretionary power while being ignorant on monetary matters. During the debate in 1819 in the House of Commons on the resumption of cash payments, a Director of the Bank of England having "denied the assertion of an hon. gentleman opposite [Ricardo], that they were not competent to the conduct of their own affairs", Ricardo bluntly replied:

> He meant no personal hostility to them as individuals, or as a public body; but he was of opinion, that they had taken wrong steps, and that they did not understand the subject of the currency.
>
> (V: 18)[7]

Being incompetent the Bank's discretion was dangerous to the public and it should be replaced by an explicit "criterion" of issuing which was also in the interest of the Bank because, by adjusting the market price of gold bullion to the legal price, it prevented profitable arbitrages from draining or flooding its metallic reserves:

> These transactions in bullion [at the Bank] would be very few in number, if the Bank regulated their loans and issues of paper by the criterion which I have so often mentioned, namely, the price of standard bullion, without attending to the absolute quantity of paper in circulation.
>
> (*Proposals*; IV: 67; *Principles*: 357–8)

The use of this "criterion" constituted "a judicious management of the quantity" of notes, which, by stabilising the market price of the standard at the level of the legal price, prevented money from being depreciated or appreciated:

> Besides, then, all the other advantages attending the use of paper money; by the judicious management of the quantity, a degree of uniformity, which is by

no other means attainable, is secured to the value of the circulating medium in which all payments are made.

(*Proposals*; IV: 57–8)

Referring to the Ingot Plan, Keynes (1930: 14) would go as far as speaking of "managed money": "If Ricardo had had his way with his ingot proposals, commodity money would never have been restored, and a pure managed money would have come into force in England in 1819." An evaluation of this affirmation would require discussing what Keynes meant by "managed money"; it will be enough here to ask whether the management principle may be understood as a discretionary monetary policy or as a rule of conduct by the Bank (see Section 9.4 below).

Implementing an "economical currency" was also one of the objects of the plan, as was recalled in *Principles*:

> The use of paper instead of gold, substitutes the cheapest in place of the most expensive medium, and enables the country, without loss to any individual, to exchange all the gold which it before used for this purpose, for raw materials, utensils, and food; by the use of which, both its wealth and its enjoyments are increased.
>
> (*Principles*; I: 361)

But there was far more than that, as James Bonar would justly emphasise in his "centenary estimate": "Ricardo had no idea of making his ingots masquerade as coins, 'money of a larger denomination', in the common meaning of the words. His complete Plan was to be the euthanasia of metal currency" (Bonar 1923: 298). Thirty years later, Richard Sayers also understood that Ricardo advocated external convertibility into gold rather than a domestic one: "Ricardo perceived that the essential condition of a gold standard is not gold coinage but convertibility into gold for international transactions" (Sayers, 1953: 38).

Although stamped to guarantee their weight and fineness, the bullion "ingots" in which notes were convertible were not money, because they were not legal tender: one could not legally pay in ingots. Convertibility of the note into bullion was consequently *not* convertibility of a money into another money *but* of the only money (the note) into its standard. Ricardo emphasised this aspect, and his plan assumed that the ingots would be assayed and stamped by the Bank itself, not to confuse them with "money of a large denomination". This was made clear in 1819 when, having not been followed on this point by the Commons' and Lords' Committees on the Resumption of Cash Payments, Ricardo resigned himself to this confusion because he thought it would damp the hostility of the Bank of England to the plan. In a letter to McCulloch of 8 May 1819 he wrote:

> The Committee have deviated in two points from the plan as originally suggested – they think that the bars of bullion delivered by the Bank, in exchange for notes, should be assayed, and stamped, at the Mint; and they have advised that after 1823, at the latest, we should revert to the old system of specie

> payments. Perhaps, in both instances, they have done right, for the Bank persisting in the most determined opposition to them, they were under the necessity of having the bullion stamped that it might be legally called money of a large denomination, and that the Bank might not raise a clamour against them for having imposed upon that corporation the obligation of paying in Bullion, from which they said their charter protected them.
>
> (VIII: 26–7)

Ricardo's wish to break with the old convertibility into coin was illustrated by his evolution about a provision which existed in the 1811 Appendix, leaving to the Bank the "option" of paying its notes "either in specie, in gold standard bars, or in foreign coin (allowance being made for the difference in its purity)" (III: 124). During the debates in Parliament in 1819 about his plan Ricardo first recommended such option before the Commons' and Lords' Committees (V: 379, 422) but he later opposed an amendment of this sort in the general debate in the House of Commons. According to Sraffa (1952b: 357):

> [P]erhaps Ricardo at first took it for granted that, Bullion payments being more advantageous to the Bank, the latter would not normally exercise the option of paying in specie; and later, when the reluctance of the Bank Directors to operate the plan became apparent, he thought it necessary to make Bullion payments obligatory.

Not being available at the Bank, gold coins could still be obtained at the mint, if it remained open to the public. *Proposals* did not pronounce on this point, although it showed Ricardo's preference for a circulation exclusively composed of notes. During the 1819 debates, he remained prudent and left the question open, only emphasising that the low-denomination notes (£1, 2, and 5), which had been issued by the Bank of England to substitute for the disappeared coins, should remain in circulation, and praising the 1816 reform having made silver coins a token currency. The logic of the Ingot Plan was, however, obvious: the gold coins still in circulation would progressively be carried to the Bank to be exchanged for notes, and the Bank of England note would become the sole currency. There was, however, a condition for that: the Ingot Plan should be made permanent and not just ensure the transition to the resumption of convertibility into coin.

A permanent plan

The letter of 8 May 1819 to McCulloch quoted above mentioned a second concession by Ricardo, on the temporary character of the Ingot Plan. But this concession was only tactical; his state of mind appeared at the end of the letter:

> In the second place they [the Committee] had to contend with public prejudice, and perhaps too with prepossessions which they themselves felt in

favour of coin. If no inconvenience is suffered from the working of this plan for the next 5 years, the Bank will be amongst the foremost in contending that it should be adopted as a permanent system.

(VIII: 27)

After the plan had been discontinued in 1821, mainly under the pressure of the Bank of England,[8] Ricardo retrospectively regretted that a chance had not been given to it for a fair try. In a letter to McCulloch of 3 January 1822 he wrote:

> All the friends of that bill [of 1819] had a right to expect that the Bank would make no preparation for specie payments till 1822, one year before the period fixed, and I for one flattered myself that if from 1819 to 1822 it were found that the system of bullion payments was a safe and easy one, specie payments would be still further deferred.
>
> (IX: 141)

This sentiment was publicly repeated in a speech before the House of Commons on 12 June 1822:

> That bill [of 1819] he had always considered as an experiment, to try whether a bank could not be carried on with advantage to the general interests of the country, upon the principle of not being called upon to pay their notes in coin, but in bullion; and he had not the least doubt that, if the Bank had gone on wisely in their preliminary arrangements – if, in fact, they had done nothing but watch the exchanges and the price of gold, and had regulated their issues accordingly, the years 1819, 1820, 1821 and 1822 would have passed off so well with the working of the bullion part of the plan, that parliament would have continued it for a number of years beyond the time originally stipulated for its operation. Such, he was convinced, would have been the course, had the Bank refrained from making those unnecessary purchases of gold which had led to so many unpleasant consequences.
>
> (V: 200)

Ricardo's consistent position from 1811 to 1819 thus shows that Bonar's evaluation was accurate: in Ricardo's mind, the Ingot Plan should lead to "the euthanasia of metal currency". In other words, it amounted to a demonetisation of gold in circulation: gold would remain the standard of money, but no longer money. Ricardo considered this achievement as a major progress in civilisation:

> A well regulated paper currency is so great an improvement in commerce, that I should greatly regret, if prejudice should induce us to return to a system of less utility. The introduction of the precious metals for the purposes of money may with truth be considered as one of the most important steps towards the improvement of commerce, and the arts of civilised life; but it is no less true that, with the advancement of knowledge and science, we

> discover that it would be another improvement to banish them again from the employment to which, during a less enlightened period, they had been so advantageously applied.
>
> (*Proposals*; IV: 65)

This new contribution to "the arts of civilised life" was, however, unfortunate.

The unhappy fate of the Ingot Plan

As adopted by Parliament on 25 June 1819 (and usually called Peel's bill after the name of the chairman of the Commons' Committee), the plan was incomplete and transitory. First, convertibility was only one way: the Bank of England was not obliged to buy any bullion offered to it at a fixed legal price. Second, Peel's bill stipulated in its second article:

> [T]hat it is expedient that a definite period should be fixed for the termination of the Restriction on Cash Payments; and that preparatory measures should be taken, with a view to facilitate and ensure, on the arrival of that period, the payment of the Promissory Notes of the Bank of England in the Legal Coin of the Realm.
>
> (V: 7)

Consequently the application of the plan was limited in time: after 1 May 1822, the Bank of England would have the choice of paying its notes in coin or bullion, and on 1 May 1823 convertibility into coin would be resumed. However, even if this was as a transitory device, the adoption of convertibility into bullion was a subject of satisfaction for Ricardo because, as seen above, he thought that the success of the experiment would lead to its prolongation. There were other reasons for him to be satisfied: the bill introduced the notion of decreasing scale he had suggested for the return to the pre-war legal price at which notes were convertible. The market price of gold bullion being £4. 2s. at the time of the bill, the legal price would be £4. 1s. from 1 February 1820, £3. 19s. 6d. from 1 October 1820, and finally the mint price of £3. 17s. 10½d. from 1May 1821. As also suggested by Ricardo, the prohibition of melting and exporting the coin was repealed.

In spite of the ambiguities noted above, the adoption by law of "the Ricardo system", as called in public by Alexander Baring (V: 92) and in private correspondence by Hutches Trower (VIII: 361), was considered by Ricardo as the "triumph of science and truth in the great councils of the Nation" (letter to Trower, 8 July 1819; VIII: 44). This triumph, however, did not last. The possibility for the Bank of England of choosing between paying its notes in coin or in bullion, programmed by Peel's bill for 1 May 1822, was advanced to 1 May 1821 on the occasion of the return to the pre-war parity of £3. 17s. 10½d., putting the Ingot Plan experiment to an end. The Bank of England had been instrumental in this sabotage, purchasing gold bullion and having it coined, before asking Parliament for permission to substitute coins for its low-denomination notes (see Chapter 5 above). The last time Ricardo evoked the advisability of implementing again the Ingot Plan was in a letter to Trower of 5 March 1822:

> If Cobbett's recommendation should again endanger the safety of the Bank of England in consequence of an extensive practice of hoarding sovereigns, which I by no means apprehend, it might become necessary to adopt the Ingot plan of payment once more.
>
> (IX: 176)

Even after his plan had been abandoned, Ricardo was accused of being responsible for the deflation that had occurred since 1819. He had to defend himself against this accusation, arguing that it was not his plan but the sabotage of his plan which had triggered an increase in the value of money – hence a general fall in prices – double what he had anticipated from the return to pre-war parity. The speech he delivered in the House of Commons on 12 June 1822 expressed his irritation:

> He [Ricardo] hoped the House would pardon this personal reference to his own opinion: he was very averse from intruding on their patience; but he was as it were put upon his trial – his plan had not been adopted, and yet to it was referred the consequences which were distinct from it; and he was held responsible for the plan that had been adopted, which was not his, but was essentially different from it.
>
> (V: 206)

I showed in Chapter 4 above that his defence on this occasion provided a factual illustration of his mature theory of money, as it is embodied in the Money–Standard Equation (see in particular my comments on the speech in the House of Commons on 11 June 1823 against Charles Western's motion).

Having measured the hostility of the Bank of England to the Ingot Plan, Ricardo prepared in the last months of his life another plan, which developed an idea going back to 1815 and aiming at transferring the power of note issuance from the Bank of England to a public institution (see Section 9.3 below). Nevertheless, according to his brother Moses, he always considered the Ingot Plan as his best practical achievement:

> In this pamphlet [*Proposals*], Mr. Ricardo suggested his plan for an economical currency. If there was any suggestion which emanated from him, upon which he seemed to pride himself more than any other, it was certainly this.
>
> (Moses Ricardo 1824: 10)[9]

Ricardo's Ingot Plan was resurrected by Alfred Marshall when he was examined by two Royal Commissions between 1886 and 1888, and in an article where he proposed a "currency scheme which [...] differs from his [Ricardo's] only by being bimetallic instead of monometallic" (Marshall 1887: 204), which was a puzzling difference, however (see Deleplace 2013b). As mentioned above in Chapter 8, Alexander Lindsay published in 1892 a pamphlet where he suggested to apply "Ricardo's Exchange Remedy" to the monetary system of India, making it "a gold standard without a gold currency on the footing recommended by Ricardo in his celebrated scheme for 'A Secure and Economical Currency'" (Lindsay 1892: 28). In his book *Indian Currency and Finance*, John Maynard Keynes credited Ricardo for having set forth the "theoretical advantages" of the gold-exchange standard which had in the meantime been adopted in India (Keynes 1913: 22). In the aftermath of World War I James Bonar observed that "in the winding up of the Treasury notes Ricardo's help, a century after his death, may be of some use, for our problems are still his problems, with their factors much magnified" (Bonar 1923: 300). "Ricardo's help" was finally welcome in 1925 when convertibility of the Bank of England note was resumed, not into coin but into bullion for the first time since 1819.

9.3 The plan for a national bank

The main provisions of the plan

In Section 9.1 above I described the genesis of this plan. Its main provisions were as follows. The note issue would be transferred from the Bank of England and the country banks to five independent commissioners having a monopoly all over England:

> Five Commissioners shall be appointed, in whom the full power of issuing all the paper money of the country shall be exclusively vested.
>
> (IV: 285)

The criterion for varying the issue would be the spread between the market price of gold bullion and the mint price:

> Regulating their issues by the price of gold, the commissioners could never err.
>
> (ibid: 293)

The method used to vary the note issue would no longer be discounting commercial bills – an activity left to non-issuing banks, including the Bank of England – but open-market operations on State securities (the term "open market" was used by Ricardo):

> If the funds of the Commissioners became so ample as to leave them a surplus which might be advantageously disposed of, let them go into the market and purchase publicly government securities with it. If on the contrary it should become necessary for them to contract their issues, without diminishing their stock of gold, let them sell their securities, in the same way, in the open market.
>
> (ibid: 284)

The other method used to vary the note issue was the purchase or sale of gold bullion:

> If, on the contrary, the circulation of London were too low, there would be two ways of increasing it – by the purchase of Government securities in the market, and the creation of new paper money for the purpose; or by the importation, and purchase, by the Commissioners, of gold bullion; for the purchase of which new paper money would be created. The importation would take place through commercial operations, as gold never fails to be a profitable article of import, when the amount of currency is deficient.
>
> (ibid: 297)

At the creation of the national bank, notes would be issued to discharge the government debt towards the Bank of England (equal to the capital of the Bank lent to the State plus part of the exchequer bills purchased by the Bank during the period of inconvertibility), sparing the taxes which had to be levied in order to pay the interest:

> On the expiration of the charter of the Bank of England, in 1833, the Commissioners shall issue fifteen millions of paper money, the amount of the capital of the Bank, lent to government, with which that debt shall be discharged. From that time the annual interest of 3 per cent. shall cease and determine. On the same day, ten millions of paper money shall be employed by the Commissioners in the following manner. With such parts of that sum as they may think expedient, they shall purchase gold bullion of the Bank, or of other persons; and with the remainder, within six months from the day above mentioned, they shall redeem a part of the government debt to the Bank, on exchequer bills. The exchequer bills, so redeemed, shall thereafter remain at the disposal of the Commissioners.
>
> (ibid: 285–6)

The national bank would "act as the general banker to all the public departments" (and to no other corporation or individual) (IV: 289) but would not lend to the State: the purchase of securities by the national bank could never be made directly from the government, so as to avoid a monetary financing of this debt:

> I propose also to prevent all intercourse between these Commissioners and ministers, by forbidding every species of money transaction between them. The Commissioners should never, on any pretence, lend money to Government, nor be in the slightest degree under its controul or influence. [...] If Government wanted money, it should be obliged to raise it in the legitimate way; by taxing the people; by the issue and sale of exchequer bills, by funded loans, or by borrowing from any of the numerous banks which might exist in the country; but in no case should it be allowed to borrow from those, who have the power of creating money.
>
> (ibid: 282–3).

The latter provision ensured the independence of the national bank from the State.

The question of the independence of the national bank

This independence was a quality that did not exist with the Bank of England, although it was private:

> Over Commissioners so entirely independent of them, the ministers would have much less power than they now possess over the Bank Directors. Experience shows how little this latter body have been able to withstand the cajolings of ministers; and how frequently they have been induced to increase their advances on Exchequer bills and Treasury bills, at the very moment they were themselves declaring that it would be attended with the greatest risk to the stability of their establishment, and to the public interest.
>
> (ibid: 282)[10]

Ricardo had already answered in *Principles* to the objection that a public note issue would soon become beyond control:

> Under an arbitrary Government, this objection would have great force; but, in a free country, with an enlightened legislature, the power of issuing paper money, under the requisite checks of convertibility at the will of the holder, might be safely lodged in the hands of commissioners appointed for that special purpose, and they might be made totally independent of the control of ministers. The sinking fund is managed by commissioners, responsible only to parliament, and the investment of the money entrusted to their charge, proceeds with the utmost regularity; what reason can there be to doubt that the issues of paper money might be regulated with equal fidelity, if placed under similar management?
>
> (*Principles*; I: 362–3)

This comparison with the sinking fund may be surprising in regard of the critique Ricardo made of the use of it, particularly in his article "Funding System" (1820):

> They [the ministers] considered the commissioners as their trustees, accumulating money for their benefit, and of which they knew that they might dispose whenever they should consider that the urgency of the case required it. They seem to have made a tacit agreement with the commissioners, that they should accumulate twelve millions per annum at compound interest, while they themselves accumulated an equal amount of debt, also at compound interest.
>
> (IV: 194)

According to Ricardo, "such pitiful shifts and evasions" (ibid: 195) were not the commissioners' fault – they "have faithfully fulfilled the trust reposed in them" (ibid: 191) – but the consequence of "ready compliance from Parliament" to authorise a partial repeal of the law each time the ministers asked for it (ibid: 193). The conclusion of Ricardo was that it was better to dispense with the sinking fund:

> It is, we think, sufficiently proved, that no securities can be given by ministers that the sinking fund shall be faithfully devoted to the payment of debt, and without such securities we should be much better without such a fund.
>
> (ibid: 196)

One might think that the same legislature, be it "enlightened" as Ricardo wrote in *Principles*, would no more resist in the future the demands by ministers to authorise the use of the note issue to finance current expenditure than it resisted in the past when the sinking fund was diverted from its professed use of paying the debt. Even in the third edition of *Principles*, one year after the article "Funding System", Ricardo did not change anything in the above passage, nor did he explain why a paper issue managed by commissioners would escape the evils denounced by him of a sinking fund also managed by commissioners. The question at stake was the possible interference between them and political power – whether Government or Parliament. On this point, as quoted above, Ricardo never suspected the commissioners of the sinking fund of any such interference (they "have faithfully fulfilled the trust reposed in them"; IV: 191) and it was for him legitimate to take them as an example for those who would manage the paper issue. This may explain why Ricardo did not think it necessary to refer to his previous article "Funding System" and to emphasise how his critique of that system did *not* disqualify commissioners for the management of the paper issue.

Nevertheless, even if the independence of its commissioners could be granted, this had not been enough to prevent the sinking fund from being diverted from its professed goal. One could hope that the legislature would be more "enlightened" in the future than in the past – Ricardo himself was busy in various attempts at reforming Parliament – but this was a bet which weakened the security of the proposed national bank. Although Ricardo did not mention it, there was, however, a substantial difference between the case of the sinking fund and that of a national bank, a difference that would prevent past evils of the former from being repeated with the latter. The independence of the commissioners was a necessary but insufficient condition for the sinking fund to work properly, while it was a necessary *and* sufficient condition in the case of a national bank – provided the commissioners were equipped with an appropriate criterion of note issuance.

In the case of the sinking fund, once it had been properly built by the commissioners, the later use of this dormant fund did not concern them, but ministers and Parliament; the independence of the commissioners in the building of the fund did not help in its later use. In the case of a national bank, the very act of issuing paper money was at the same time determining its use: purchasing gold bullion or government securities in the market. As explicitly stipulated in *Plan for a National Bank*, it could never be used to finance new government debt. The recent history of modern central banking, especially in times of liquidity crisis and/or sovereign debt crisis, suggests that, from a practical point of view, there is little difference for a central bank between purchasing securities directly from the government and purchasing them from banks in the secondary market, *while it liberally furnishes banks with liquidity to purchase them in the primary market*. In Ricardo's plan, however, the last proposition did not apply, since the national bank did *not* provide money to banks as the Bank of England did before by discounting bills. Open-market operations required government securities having been previously purchased by banks with money borrowed from the credit market, not from a central bank. Moreover, as quoted above, "the purchase [by the Commissioners] of Government securities in the market, and the creation of new paper money for the purpose" would be effectuated only when "the circulation of London were too low" (IV: 297), as indicated by the market price of gold bullion being below the mint price, but never, as in modern times, to provide liquidity to banks and/or finance to government.

Of course, there was always the risk that, as had been the case with the sinking fund, Parliament might violate its own law under the pressure of ministers; but this could only be done by forcing the commissioners to breach their duty, and not by wrongly using a fund built by commissioners according to their duty. In the terms used in *Principles*, this could happen "under an arbitrary Government" but not "with an enlightened legislature", all the more so since, as advised by Ricardo, "the commissioners should be appointed by government, but not removable by government" (IV: 290). An independent national bank strictly applying the management principle to the note issuance seemed to be enough for Ricardo to avoid "such pitiful shifts and evasions" as had been observed in the history of the sinking fund, even if his projects of reforming Parliament and making the legislature more "enlightened" were not to meet success.[11]

The ingot principle again

The role of the management principle in the Plan for a national bank suggests continuity with the previous Ingot Plan. This seems, however, not to be the case for the ingot principle, since convertibility of the notes into coin was enacted again:

> From the moment of the establishment of the National Bank, the Commissioners shall be obliged to pay their notes and bills, on demand, in gold coin.
> (*Plan for a National Bank*; IV: 289)[12]

It is not surprising that, after his Ingot Plan had been torpedoed by the Bank of England, Ricardo stepped back to convertibility into coin. This was, however, a tactical retreat only, because the new plan contained the following "expedient" provision:

> It might be expedient to oblige them [the commissioners] to sell gold bullion at 3*l*. 17*s*. 9*d*.; in which case the coin would probably never be exported, because that can never be obtained under 3*l*. 17*s*. $10^{1/2}$*d*. per oz. Under such a system, the only variations that could take place in the price of gold, would be between

> the prices of 3*l*. 17*s*. 6*d*. and 3*l*. 17*s*. 9*d*.; and by watching the market price, and increasing their issues of paper, when the price inclined to 3*l*. 17*s*. 6*d*., or under; and limiting them, or withdrawing a small portion, when the price inclined to 3*l*. 17*s*. 9*d*., or more; there would not probably be a dozen transactions in the year by the Commissioners in the purchase and sale of gold; and if there were, they would always be advantageous, and leave a small profit to the establishment.
>
> (ibid: 293–4)

This was the same scheme as in the Ingot Plan: the market price of bullion was constrained by arbitrage between two legal boundaries (see Section 9.5 below), the one at which the national bank sold bullion (£3. 17s. 9d.) and the one at which it purchased it (£3. 17s. 6d.). The variations in the market *price* of the standard – hence in the value of money, for a given *value* of the standard – were thus limited to 0.3 per cent. As for the mint price of £3. 17s. 10½d., it concerned gold in coin, not in bullion, the difference with the bank selling price of bullion (£3. 17s. 9d.) being enough to prevent arbitragers from demanding the coin with a view at its exportation ("the coin would probably never be exported") – the same effect as that expected from "a moderate seignorage" (see Chapter 6 above). As in the Ingot Plan, increasing (reducing) the note issue when the market price of bullion tended to its lower (upper) boundary stabilised this price even before arbitrage was implemented, so that "there would not probably be a dozen transactions in the year by the Commissioners in the purchase and sale of gold".

By prudence – and also because, as seen in Chapter 8 above, there might be variations in the exchange rate which had a real origin and should not give rise to a corrective change in the note issue – a metallic reserve should be kept by the national bank to satisfy demands by arbitragers for exportation and hence correct the exchange rate. The above quotation continued:

> As it is, however, desirable to be on the safe side, in managing the important business of a paper money in a great country, it would be proper to make a liberal provision of gold, as suggested in a former regulation, in case it should be thought expedient occasionally to correct the exchanges with foreign countries, by the exportation of gold, as well as by the reduction of the amount of paper.
>
> (ibid: 294)

The idea of separating domestic circulation and foreign payments, inherited from the Ingot Plan, was preserved in the Plan for a national bank that separated the management of the metallic reserve of the bank for its relations with foreign countries – which relied on the purchase and sale of gold bullion at fixed prices, as in the Ingot Plan – from its management for domestic circulation – which also relied on the purchase of gold bullion at a fixed price but on the sale of gold in coin at the mint price. This separation made the monetary system more secure (see below Section 9.5) and hence more economical because, according to Ricardo, it required a limited metallic backing of the note issue: at the creation of the bank the ratio of the reserve in bullion or in coin to note circulation would be between 17 and 28 per cent.[13]

9.4 The management of the note issue

A controversial question

The revolutionary character (theoretically and practically) of the Ingot Plan, fully recognised in old literature (see the above references to Marshall 1887, Lindsay 1892, Keynes 1913, 1930, Bonar 1923, Sayers 1953) has nearly disappeared in the modern one. When convertibility into bullion (as distinct from convertibility into coin) is not simply absent, it is considered as a technicality of secondary importance, aiming at economising on gold or at facilitating the return to convertibility into coin. The Plan for a national bank fares better, probably because it seems more appealing about the management of the note issue. However, in the recent literature on Ricardo, one may find on this question everything and the contrary, on the existence or not of a central bank, on the implementation or not of a discretionary monetary policy, on the presence or not of the lending-of-last-resort function. Some examples may illustrate this heterogeneity.

Davis (2005: 197) contends that:

> Ricardo's case for discretionary monetary policy appears in *Secure Currency* (1816) and in *Plan for a National Bank* (1824). By 'discretion' I refer to a central bank's role in stabilizing prices and correcting financial crises. The bank acts by altering its discount rate or by trading bullion and government bonds. [...] Discretion in this sense does not require a full-fledged countercyclical policy.

However:

> [D]oubts about Ricardo's ability as a monetary theorist have arisen because of the absence of any reference in his Plan for a National Bank to the role of the central bank as lender of last resort. [...] I submit that Ricardo never attributed to the central bank the role of lender of last resort because the Bank of England did not perform this function.
>
> (ibid: 208–9)

Diatkine (2008, 2013) argues that Ricardo advocated flexibility of the money supply but, even in the *Plan for a National Bank*, "this was not a discretionary policy, because the Bank's objective to regulate the value of money by only watching the price of gold, and not looking at other variables, was still at work" (Diatkine 2013: 139). Moreover, "the public bank was not a lender of last resort; it did not have to provide liquidity to banks. [...] In this respect, Ricardo's National Bank is not a central bank" (ibid: 141).

Arnon (2011) develops the idea, already put forward in a former publication, that, until nearly the end, Ricardo adhered to a Smithian notion of competitive banks and to an "anti-central banking position" (Arnon 1987: 275) – namely, a "free-banking position" (Arnon 2011: 260). However, in the last two months of his life (when he drafted his *Plan for a National Bank*), he converted himself to discretionary central banking, "in clear contradiction to Ricardo's earlier views" (ibid: 382). To sum up:

> Thus, in 1823, and for the first time since Ricardo started writing on monetary issues, he clearly rejects competition in issuing notes. [...] In his 1824 text, Ricardo discusses not only the responses to developments in the gold market, but also interventions aimed at influencing the quantity in circulation according to overall macroeconomic circumstances. [...] He openly recommends discretion.
>
> (ibid: 382–3; see also 149–50)

For King (2013: 142):

> [H]e [Ricardo] was a forceful critic of government policy in this area [money], and especially antagonistic towards the Bank of England. This led him to deny any role for active (counter-cyclical) monetary policy, and to anticipate twenty-first century political orthodoxy in his advocacy of an 'independent' central bank.

King "finds convincing [...] the standard Keynesian interpretation", as:

> [S]et out by R.S. Sayers, who regards Ricardo's strong support for the Quantity Theory of money as 'a major disaster' that committed him to the doctrine of the neutrality of money and hence forced him to deny any role for discretionary monetary policy. Sayers also attributes to Ricardo an unchanging refusal to advocate a lender of last resort function for the Bank, which is entirely consistent with his advocacy of Say's Law.
>
> (ibid: 147)

Sato (2013: 65) finds in Ricardo a "'discretionary' policy [which] means open-market operations that are performed considering the market price of bullion as a policy target and an active discount policy". In this sense, Ricardo advocated "a national bank independent of the government that could pursue a countercyclical policy" and perform "a central bank 'lender of last resort' function" (ibid: 66).

According to Otomo (2013: 170), "the idea of making the government the issuer of paper money was suggested in *Secure Currency*, further developed in *Principles*, and embodied in the *Plan* [for a National Bank]". In the latter, "the first measures for stabilizing the value of paper money – fixing the price of gold – remained unchanged, but the National Bank's management was changed through the control of securities and gold in the open market" (ibid).

Such heterogeneity in the evaluation of Ricardo's position on the management of the note issue, however, proceeds from a common conception of what may properly be called a central bank. For most of the commentators on this question, one may speak of a central bank if the bank of issue implements a monetary policy which: (a) is discretionary (in contrast with the mere application of a pre-determined rule), (b) takes into account "real" objectives (in contrast with monetary stability as the only concern), and (c) aims at influencing the interest rate (in contrast with varying the quantity of money). The differences between commentators then arise from the weight attributed to each of these characteristics and from various interpretations of Ricardo's writings in respect to them. The figure of Henry Thornton is often called for as a model of what at Ricardo's time a vision of a central bank could be: an institution which had to appreciate the situation before stepping in, considered the various threats faced by the general level of activity, particularly in the credit market, and varied the discount rate accordingly. Raising in this way the question of the management of the note issue in Ricardo inevitably exposes someone to difficulties, if not disappointment.

One reason is that the above features (a) and (b) do not necessarily overlap. As mentioned in Chapter 1 above, for Thornton the Bank of England had to appreciate the situation because the nature of its intervention should be different according to whether the cause of the disequilibrium was exogenous (a bad harvest or war transfers, both generating an adverse foreign balance) or endogenous (an excess note issue) to the monetary system: in the former case it should expand its issues, acting as a lender of last resort, while in the latter case it should restrict them. But this did not mean that Thornton favoured a monetary policy that would stimulate aggregate output: discretion was required only in times of crisis provoked by exogenous circumstances. To borrow the expression from Arnon (2011: 371), it was "defensive central banking" (note that Arnon attributes to Thornton an "active" central banking; ibid: 373). For Ricardo, as shown in Chapter 8 above, the bank of issue had nothing to do, when the cause of the variation in the exchange rate was "real", except providing or absorbing passively gold bullion. It should only intervene when the quantity of money was inappropriate, as testified by the divergence between the market price of gold bullion and its legal price. The bank of issue had consequently only to watch the price of gold: although, by difference with Thornton, there was no room in Ricardo for an appreciation of the situation, for both authors the objective was only monetary stability (extending in Thornton this notion to the credit market, because of a larger definition of money). In neither case was there discretion applied to boosting the economy.

Another reason why the above-mentioned definition of a central bank is misleading is that its features (a) and (c) do not overlap: a discretionary monetary policy is not necessarily one that aims at influencing the interest rate. As seen in Chapter 2 above, Thornton acknowledged in 1811 that the situation at the time called for the application of a note-issuing rule – the same as Ricardo's: "the Bank should regulate the issues of its paper with a reference to the price of Bullion, and the state of the Exchanges" (Thornton 1811: 327). This was not contradictory with the theoretical framework exposed in *Paper Credit* (1802): altering the discount rate was appropriate when the cause of the crisis was exogenous (as in 1795–1797), not endogenous to the monetary system (as in 1810–1811). However, even in the exogenous case, the discount rate should be *raised*, in order to attract foreign capital, domestic relief coming from enlarged discounts, not from lowering the discount rate. A rise in the discount rate certainly did not suit Ricardo, for whom bullion internationally traded was a commodity, not capital. But he had no difficulty in advocating enlarged discounts in cases of "embarrassed credit", since in such cases one did not have to fear a depreciation of money, as he emphasised in the letter to Tierney of 11 December 1811:

> If a greater circulation were required from the operation either of increased commerce, or of embarrassed credit, the bank might augment their issues without producing any effect whatever on the price of bullion, and consequently without exposing the Bank to any inconvenience, or depriving the merchants of that increased accommodation, which might be essential to their operations.
>
> (VI: 68)

Ricardo's conception of the management of the note issue thus raises the question of his understanding of the relation between bank issues and the rate of interest.

Bank issues and the rate of interest

The necessity to enlarge discounts by the Bank of England when credit was failing was evoked by Ricardo in reference to the crisis of 1793. Commenting on an extract of the Bullion Report,[14] he wrote:

> If the Bank had been more liberal in their discounts at that period, they would have produced the same effect on general credit as was afterwards done by the issues of Exchr. bills. It would appear that the bank would buy the exchr. bills but would not discount the merchants bills, – or rather they would not advance money to the merchants without the guarantee of Parliament. If the bank bought the bills it was then by an increase of circulating medium that public credit was ultimately relieved. If the public and not the bank purchased the bills then was a portion of the circulating medium of the country which had been withdrawn from circulation again brought forth by the credit of government being pledged for the parties requiring relief. Perhaps after all that confidence was on the point of being restored at the very moment that recourse was had to this boasted measure.
>
> (III: 349)

Here Ricardo acknowledged that in 1793 "more liberal" discounts by the Bank of England – in modern parlance lending of last resort – would have helped restoring confidence as the issuing of exchequer bills had done. But such "boasted measure" could have been dispensed with since confidence was "perhaps [...] on the point of being restored" by itself. That the issuing of bank notes could fill the void occasioned by a want of confidence between merchants in the credit market was emphasised by Ricardo in *Proposals*, and he stressed that notes could play this role quicker than metallic currency, and above all without harmful consequence for the value of money:

> Whenever merchants, then, have a want of confidence in each other, which disinclines them to deal on credit, or to accept in payment each other's checks, notes, or bills; more money, whether it be paper or metallic money, is in demand; and the advantage of a paper circulation, when established on correct principles, is, that this additional quantity can be presently supplied without occasioning any variation in the value of the whole currency, either as compared with bullion or with any other commodity; whereas, with a system of metallic currency, this additional quantity cannot be so readily supplied, and when it is finally supplied, the whole of the currency, as well as bullion, has acquired an increased value.
>
> (*Proposals*; IV: 58)

"More liberal" discounts by the Bank did not mean, however, lending at a discount rate below the market rate of interest. Indeed, Ricardo advised the Bank of England to discount its notes at a variable rate, provided it varied with the market rate, as he declared in Parliament on 19 March 1821:

> The rate of interest in the market had been invariably under 5 per cent since 1819. It would be a great advantage to the mercantile interests, that the Bank of England should discount the notes presented to them, not at one invariable rate of interest, but varying according to the alteration of the rate of interest in the market.
>
> (V: 97)[15]

According to Ricardo, the level of the market rate of interest could be approximated by the rate usually charged by the London discount banks, provided the Usury Laws did not interfere. Being examined on 30 April 1818 by a Commons Committee on the Usury Laws and asked "What is the criterion by which you judge the market rate of interest, or is there any criterion at all?" Ricardo discarded the discount rate when it was at the maximum level allowed by the Usury Laws (5 per cent) but added:

> When the market rate of interest is below 5 per cent, then I think that the discount given on a bill is a very good criterion of the market rate of interest.
>
> (ibid: 345)

During the discussion of the budget in the House of Commons on 1 July 1822 Ricardo rejoiced at the behaviour of the Bank of England which had decided to lower its discount rate, only regretting that it "should have done so long before", because of the then distressed state of the British economy. He observed that it was in the interest of the Bank itself:

> The country only required, and could only bear, a certain circulation; and when that amount of circulation was afloat, the rate of interest would find its wholesome and natural level. He [Ricardo] was glad that the Bank had determined to reduce its rate of interest to four per cent.; indeed, they would have done wrong in declining to do so, as by that means only could they bring their notes into circulation. If the Bank had not reduced its interest to four per cent. the country must necessarily resort to a metallic currency, or else notes must be issued from some other quarter, as it would be impossible for the Bank of England to put a single pound note into circulation.
>
> (ibid: 222–3)[16]

It appears thus that Ricardo always considered that the Bank had to adapt its discount rate to the market rate of interest and not to try to influence it. He criticised the Bank for having discounted bills at a lower rate than the market in order to "force" the circulation of its notes:

> The reason, then, why for the last twenty years, the Bank [of England] is said to have given so much aid to commerce, by assisting the merchants with money, is, because they have, during that whole period, lent money below the market rate of interest; below that rate at which the merchants could have borrowed elsewhere; but, I confess, that to me this seems rather an objection to their establishment, than an argument in favour of it.
>
> (*Principles*, I: 364)

The Bank of England had done wrong because its forced issues had depreciated the currency, without having a positive effect on the accumulation of capital:

> In another part of this work, I have endeavoured to shew, that the real value of a commodity is regulated, not by the accidental advantages which may be enjoyed by some of its producers, but by the real difficulties encountered by that producer who is least favoured. It is so with respect to the interest for money; it is not regulated by the rate at which the Bank will lend, whether it be 5, 4, or 3 per cent, but by the rate of profits which can be made by the employment of capital, and which is totally independent of the quantity, or of the value of money.
>
> (ibid: 363)

Ricardo thus contended that a variation in the bank issues – whether through discount lending by the Bank of England or open-market operations by the national bank – affected the market price of gold bullion (see Chapter 7 above) and not the market rate of interest. His monetary theory explained that any attempt by the Bank of England at forcing the circulation of its notes by lowering its discount rate below the market rate, or by the national bank at forcing by its open-market purchases the rate of interest on government securities below the ordinary level of the market rate, would raise the market price of gold bullion. In such a situation, if the Bank of England did not voluntarily follow what I called the management principle, convertibility of its notes constrained it to contract its issues (because of the Penelope effect). If the Ingot Plan or the Plan for a national bank was implemented, the Bank of England or the commissioners would apply the management principle, so that they would voluntarily contract the note issue whenever they observed a rise in the market price of gold bullion and were consequently warned of their error. In any case, no increase in the quantity of money above its conformable level could have a permanent effect on the market rate of interest.[17]

Nevertheless, does this mean that Ricardo discarded any management of the note issue? Being most of the time depicted as advocating a rule that would *restrict* the quantity of money, he seems to do so. However, watching the market price of the standard with a view at correcting the note issue was not only useful to detect an excess of notes but also their deficiency – a situation about which Ricardo was also concerned, particularly during the 1821–1823 debates on the depression.

Avoiding an undue contraction of the note issue

One thing was to contend that a monetary *expansion* could have no permanent effect on aggregate output and the accumulation of capital – a proposition that Ricardo certainly held – another to deny that an undue monetary *contraction* might have depressive effects. Avoiding such contraction was the second reason to compel the bank of issue to purchase at a fixed price any bullion offered to it – the first reason being to set a lower boundary to the variations in the market price of gold bullion (see Section 9.5 below). This provision guaranteed that, if the market price of bullion fell – which, according to Ricardo's theory, could only happen because the quantity of notes issued was deficient – bullion would be offered by arbitragers to the bank of issue, which could not refuse to purchase it with additional notes. This safeguard against a too restricted money circulation was already provided by the mint, where owners of bullion carried it to have it coined whenever the market price of bullion fell below the mint price. But the mint answered the need for money with a delay of two months for the fabrication of the coins, and in the interval general activity would be impaired. In contrast, the issuing of additional notes would be immediate, all the more so if, watching the fall in the market price of bullion, the bank applied the management principle and increased its issues even before bullion was carried to it.

This argument was exposed by Ricardo before the House of Commons on 24 May 1819 when he regretted that this provision had not been introduced in Peel's bill, because it would have prevented the Bank of England from reducing its issues too much:

> The Bank should reduce their issues cautiously; he only feared they would do it too rapidly. [...] He was only sorry that the Bank was not to be obliged

> by the resolutions to buy all the bullion offered to them at 3*l.* 17*s.* 6*d.* lest through excessive caution they might starve the circulation. The Mint, it was true, was to remain open to the public, who might coin the bullion which they obtained from the Bank. Mr. Mushett [...] had stated, that with a capital of 300,000*l.* the Mint could supply the public with 12,000,000*l.* a year. Yet a year was a long time to wait for twelve millions, and it might easily happen, that in the interim between the reduction of the Bank issues and the supply afforded from the Mint, the country might seriously feel the deficiency. It was on that account that he should have wished a resolution inserted, to compel the Bank to give its notes for bullion (at 3*l.* 17*s.* 6*d.*) on demand. With the exception of this omission, the plan was, in his opinion, perfectly safe and gentle.
>
> (V: 13)

As shown in Chapter 5 above, Ricardo's fear was justified, and on many occasions in Parliament in 1822 and 1823 he would retrospectively blame the Bank of England for having contracted its issues too much between 1819 and 1821 (to prepare for the return to convertibility of its notes into coin) and thus deepened the depression. This danger was eliminated both in the Ingot plan and in the Plan for a national bank. When general activity contracted or expanded, while the bank of issue did not change its issuing behaviour, the consequence was respectively an excess or a deficiency in the quantity of money, which was reflected by a positive or a negative spread between the market price of gold bullion and the legal price. One thus needed an instrument that linked real general activity and the note issue. In the Ingot Plan – which preserved the existence of the Bank of England as bank of issue – this link was provided by discount lending, in which the issuance of notes originated in commercial transactions. In the Plan for a national bank, the issuing bank no longer discounted commercial paper and there was a need for another kind of link between the real and the monetary sphere. This link was provided by open-market operations, at the initiative of the national bank. Open-market operations then substituted for discount lending as the appropriate instrument of monetary policy, with the same object in view: varying the note issue with the quantity of money needed by the real economy, as reflected by the sign of the spread between the market price of gold bullion and the legal price.

To conclude on Ricardo's "judicious management of the quantity" of notes, one may observe that the usual reading key "rules versus discretion" does not apply. The management principle did not fit this opposition in which both terms assume the exogeneity of the quantity of money, either fixed by a rule or discretionarily decided by the bank of issue. As quoted above, Ricardo's non-quantitative approach implied that "the Bank regulated their loans and issues of paper [...] without attending to the absolute quantity of paper in circulation" (*Proposals*; IV: 67; *Principles*; I: 357–8): as shown in Chapter 7 above, the quantity of notes should not be determined from outside but resulted endogenously from the fulfilment of the condition of conformity of money to the standard, that is, the equalisation of the market price of gold bullion with its legal price. In modern parlance,

Ricardo was not a "verticalist" – the quantity of money on the horizontal axis being exogenously given by a vertical line – but a "horizontalist" – a horizontal line intersecting the vertical axis and expressing the given level of an independent variable.[18] Of course, contrary to modern "horizontalists", this independent variable was *not* in Ricardo the rate of interest fixed by the monetary authorities but the legal price of the standard.

Of the two pillars of the Ingot Plan – the ingot principle and the management principle – it is as expected the latter, left unchanged in the Plan for a national bank, which was central for the question of the management of the note issue. The ingot principle, which, as seen above, was resurrected in a slightly modified form in *Plan for a National Bank*, was central for another question, illustrated by the title of *Proposals for an Economical and Secure Currency*: the security of the monetary system.

9.5 Increasing the security of the monetary system

The ingot principle and the management principle

The pamphlet *Proposals for an Economical and Secure Currency* was a turning point in Ricardo's theory of money, which was the outcome of two changes in Ricardo's inquiry about money. First, with the end of the Napoleonic wars in June 1815, the historical perspective was now the resumption of the convertibility of the Bank of England note. Consequently the question on the agenda was no longer the understanding of a monetary regime deprived of any standard but of one endowed with a standard. Second, this line of inquiry, formulated in 1816 in *Proposals*, now ran parallel to another line of inquiry on exchangeable values and the rate of profit, inaugurated in 1815 with the *Essay on Profits*. As a turning point *Proposals* designed what Ricardo's monetary programme would be until his death seven years later: the search for what he called "a perfect currency" that should fulfil three conditions:

> A currency may be considered as perfect, of which the standard is invariable, which always conforms to that standard, and in the use of which the utmost economy is practised.
>
> (*Proposals*; IV: 55)

The rationale of the first two conditions – the invariability of the standard and the conformity of money to this standard – has been analysed above in Chapters 3 to 7. It remains to study how Ricardo's plans for "a perfect currency" fulfilled these conditions, while adding the property that "in the use of [it] the utmost economy is practised".

As seen above, there were two principles on which the Ingot Plan was founded. First the ingot principle: the Bank of England notes had to be convertible into bullion (bars), instead of specie (coins) as they were prior to 1797. Symmetrically, these notes could be obtained from the Bank against bullion at a fixed legal price, slightly below the price of £ 3.17.10½ per standard ounce at which they were convertible. Second, the quantity of bank notes issued had to vary inversely with changes in the observed market price of bullion, instead of being left to the discretion of the Bank, as before. This provision constituted a "judicious management of the quantity" of paper money (*Proposals*, IV: 57); it was the management principle.

The specificity of both principles should be underlined. The ingot principle makes sense of the sentence in *Principles* (I: 354), that "it is not necessary that paper money should be payable in specie to secure its value": Ricardo was against the inconvertibility of notes, but he favoured another kind of convertibility than the one usually put forward before (and also after) him. The management principle meant that the issue of notes had to be modified according to an objective criterion – the market price of bullion – which in no way implied any judgement on the level of the stock of circulating notes or of the metallic reserves of the Bank. The object of these two principles was twofold: stabilising the market price of the standard, thus preventing the currency from being depreciated or appreciated; and preventing the drain of the Bank's metallic reserve. Let us look successively at these two goals.

Stabilising the market price of the standard

With convertibility of notes into bullion as into specie, arbitrage made the market price of bullion fluctuate with supply and demand between two fixed limits depending on the monetary regime; but the width of this margin was consequently not the same. As shown above in Chapter 6, the regime prior to 1797 was based on convertibility both ways between bullion and the gold coin and convertibility one way of the Bank of England note into full-bodied gold coin. This regime thus constrained the market price P_G of gold bullion between two fixed limits given by:

$$\overline{P_{GC}}(1+m_G) \geq P_G \geq \overline{P_{GC}}(1-s_G) \tag{6.1}$$

with $\overline{P_{GC}}$ the legal price of an ounce of gold in coin, m_G the melting cost of the coin (obtained at no cost from the Bank of England against its notes) into bullion, and s_G the minting cost of bullion into coin, equal to the rate of interest until the mint delivered the coins. Inequalities (6.1) illustrate the maxim enunciated by Ricardo in his letter to Grenfell of 19 January 1823:

> We all know that it is the melting pot only which keeps all currency in a wholesome state.
>
> (Deleplace, Depoortère and Rieucau 2013: 4)

Let me now call $\overline{P_G}$ the legal price of an ounce of gold bullion, which in the Ingot Plan substituted for the legal price $\overline{P_{GC}}$ of an ounce of gold in coin. The condition of conformity of money to the standard analysed in Chapter 3 above becomes:

$$V_M{}^* = \frac{1}{\overline{P_G}} V_G \tag{9.1}$$

which may be rewritten as:

$$P_G = \overline{P_G} \tag{9.2}$$

Equations (7.3) to (7.5) and (7.7) to (7.10) apply. Instead of (7.6), the combination of (7.5) and (9.1) determines the conformable quantity of money:

$$M^* = k\,\overline{P_G}\,\frac{Y}{V_G} \tag{9.3}$$

The limits imposed to the variations in the market price P_G of gold bullion were modified. With convertibility of notes into freely exportable bullion, the cost of melting fraudulently the coins obtained from the Bank disappeared, so that arbitrage ensured that P_G could not be permanently higher than the legal price. Symmetrically, the Bank was substituted for the mint in the issuing of the currency: notes were to be obtained from the Bank against bullion at a trifling cost b for the management of the issue, and this settled the lower limit to the variation of P_G thanks to arbitrage. In Ricardo's view, the application of a policy rule – the management principle – was preferable to actual conversion of notes into bullion or of bullion into notes by arbitragers. One way or the other the following inequalities applied:

$$\overline{P_G} \geq P_G \geq \overline{P_G}(1-b) \tag{9.4}$$

The comparison of (6.1) and (9.4) shows that the range of variation of the market price of gold bullion was reduced by the elimination of the melting cost (the Bank substituting for the melting pot to ensure the conversion of the currency into bullion) and the limitation of b to a level as low as was consistent with the private character of the Bank.[19] In Ricardo's terms:

> That regulation is merely suggested, to prevent the value of money from varying from the value of bullion more than the trifling difference between the prices at which the Bank should buy and sell, and which would be an approximation to that uniformity in its value, which is acknowledged to be so desirable.
> (*Proposals*, IV: 67; *Principles*, I: 358)

One object of the Ingot Plan was thus to ensure a higher stabilisation of the market price of bullion in normal times, hence, for a given value of the commodity chosen as the standard, a higher stabilisation of the value of money itself. Moreover, as mentioned above in Chapter 7, the circulation of notes could endogenously increase to accommodate the "wants of commerce" without the size of the reserve having to increase, while preserving the equality between the market price of bullion and its legal price (as quoted above, the Bank would not have to bother about "attending to the absolute quantity of paper in circulation"). Consequently, the working of the monetary system did not alter the world demand for gold bullion. The changes in the value of the standard were then limited to real causes. One may here recall the Money–Standard Equation established in Chapter 4 above in its simplified form:

$$\frac{\Delta V_M}{V_M} = \frac{\Delta V_G}{V_G} - \frac{\Delta P_G}{P_G} \qquad (4.8)$$

with $\Delta V_M / V_M$ the rate of change in the value of the pound in terms of all commodities except gold bullion, $\Delta V_G / V_G$ the rate of change in the value of an ounce of gold bullion in terms of all other commodities, and $\Delta P_G / P_G$ the rate of change in the market price of an ounce of gold bullion. In (4.8), not only the margin of variation in V_M induced by a change in P_G was limited to b but any domestic monetary cause of variation in V_G was eliminated.

There was an even more important object of the Ingot Plan: preventing the drain of Bank's reserves in case of monetary shocks.

Preventing the drain of the Bank's metallic reserve

Inequalities (9.4) were ruling in the normal course of events; but when the pressure on the currency became hard, the two sides of the inequalities were exposed to different threats. Whenever the Bank remained open to the public, it could absorb all the bullion which depressed the market; the only drawback imposed on the Bank by the Ingot Plan was to force it to accumulate a sterile asset. On the contrary, when the market price of bullion tended to increase, signalling a depreciation of the currency, this movement was hindered by arbitrage as long as the Bank had enough bullion reserves to ensure the convertibility of its notes. The suspension of cash payments decided in 1797 had shown that this could not always be guaranteed. The issue here at stake was no longer the range of variation in the value of the currency in normal times, but the security of the monetary system, which could be jeopardised by a drain of the Bank's metallic reserve. As the title of the 1816 pamphlet made explicit, convertibility into bullion was supposed to increase this security, as compared with convertibility into specie – but in precisely what way?

With convertibility into specie, one had to distinguish between three types of drain.

The panic

The first type of drain of the metallic reserve of the Bank of England was one caused by a panic, when notes were brought back to the Bank, not to melt the coin and export the bullion with profit, but to hoard the metal itself as a store of value:

> Against such panics, banks have no security, *on any system*; from their very nature they are subject to them, as at no time can there be in a Bank, or in a country, so much specie or bullion as the monied individuals of such country have a right to demand. Should every man withdraw his balance from his banker on the same day, many times the quantity of Bank notes now in circulation would be insufficient to answer such a demand.
>
> (*Proposals*, IV: 68; *Principles*, I: 358–9; Ricardo's emphasis)

This kind of run could then jeopardise the monetary system because notes issued through discounting of commercial bills were not backed by corresponding metallic reserves. This was the price to pay for issuing money to the benefit of owners of capital and not only of precious metals. For this kind of drain the Ingot Plan could not improve upon convertibility into specie because the threat to security was consubstantial with banking activity itself.

According to Ricardo, it was a panic which had forced suspension of the convertibility of the Bank of England note in 1797. The above quotation continues:

> A panic of this kind was the cause of the crisis in 1797; and not, as has been supposed, the large advances which the Bank had then made to Government. Neither the Bank nor Government were at that time to blame; it was the contagion of the unfounded fears of the timid part of the community, which occasioned the run on the Bank, and it would equally have taken place if they had not made any advances to Government, and had possessed twice their present capital. If the Bank had continued paying in cash, probably the panic would have subsided before their coin had been exhausted.
>
> (ibid)

This "probable" conjecture, made by Ricardo in 1816, about the outcome of the prolongation of convertibility, had it been decided in 1797, was at odds with the one he had made in 1810 in his manuscript notes on the Bullion Report:

> It has been contended, by some intelligent men, that in the year 1797 when there was a run upon the Bank for specie, – that the Directors would have upheld public credit and have put a stop to the demand for guineas by increasing their discounts, rather than by diminishing them. I am of opinion that the run upon the Bank in 1797 proceeded from political alarm, and a desire on the part of the people to hoard guineas. I was myself witness of many persons actually exchanging bank notes for guineas for such purpose, – therefore it is probable that the Bank could not have prevented the stoppage of payments

> to which they were obliged to have recourse. But a demand upon the bank for specie from fears of the solidity of its resources, or from political alarm, are very different from a demand arising from a high price of bullion and a low rate of exchange and must be differently treated. In the latter case it can proceed only from an excessive issue of paper, if the gold coin is not debased and can only be checked by calling in the excess. In 1797 the exchange was at 38 with Hamburgh and gold bullion at £3. 17. 6. – In 1810 the exchange is at 29 and gold bullion at £4. 13 –
>
> (III: 364–5)

Ricardo then commented on the answer given before the Bullion Committee by the Governor of the Bank of England to a question concerning the advisability of increasing the discounts "in order to support public credit" at a time when the market price of bullion was high and the exchange low. The Governor had given his "own opinion" according to which the discounts should neither be increased nor diminished, and he availed himself of "the experience of the years 1796 and 1797".[20] With this opinion Ricardo disagreed at two levels. First, at a factual one, he considered that the situation in 1796 and 1797 was not characterised by a failing public credit but by a panic; consequently, contrary to what "some intelligent men" (Henry Thornton, Walter Boyd) had contended in evidence, increasing the discounts would have been useless: "it is probable that the Bank could not have prevented the stoppage of payments to which they were obliged to have recourse". Second, at a theoretical level, the assumption made in the question – of a high price of bullion and a low exchange – disqualified the example of 1796–1797 (when the market price of bullion was below the mint price and the exchange with Hamburg high) and above all implied that the hypothetical situation was neither that of a panic or of a failing public credit, but of an excess note issue. In that case, according to Ricardo, discounts should be contracted. This was in fact the case in 1810, and the Governor of the Bank of England was consequently twice wrong, about the past and about the present.

Ricardo's attitude towards the panic gives rise to what John King calls a "residual question [...] more theoretical than factual" (King 2013: 119), which he borrows from Peach. For Peach, "to the extent that he [Ricardo] could make any sense of it [the distress] at all, its severity was attributed to blind irrationality on the part of the capitalist class" (Peach 1996: 30), and he quotes Ricardo's letter to Malthus of 9 October 1820:

> Men err in their productions, there is no deficiency of demand [...] we are guilty of some such folly now, and I can scarcely account for the length of time that this delusion continues.
>
> (VIII: 277–8)

King points to a contradiction in Ricardo: "Protracted episodes of 'great folly' and 'delusion' are indeed difficult to reconcile with Ricardo's belief that most people, in all social classes, are normally engaged in the rational pursuit of their own self-interest" (King 2013: 120). There is a contradiction only if one assumes, as King does, that there lies a "more theoretical than factual" question. But, as shown in what he wrote about the panic, Ricardo considered irrationality as a matter of fact, not of theory. For him, theory explained what should happen if people were rational, that is, behaved according to their interest, but he did not deny that it might happen that they were not. Theory was unable to explain that because it was out of its scope.

This does not mean that Ricardo neglected the role of confidence when he considered the design of the monetary system. As seen above, he acknowledged that the Bank of England might increase its discounts – hence the note issue – when in the credit market a lack of confidence resulted in difficulties for the borrowers. About money proper, when in 1811 he was pushing his plan of convertibility into bullion among political leaders, he stressed that such plan would improve confidence in the Bank of England note, at a time when it was envisaged to make it a legal tender, by guaranteeing against any further depreciation. Knowing that the Bank would be prevented by its own interest from issuing in excess, the public would be confident in the constancy of the future value of money, with a positive effect on contracts:

> If, Sir, you should deem it necessary, at the expiration of the bill which has just received the Royal assent, to make Bank notes a legal tender, a provision to the effect which I have suggested, would I am confident deprive such a measure of almost all its terrors, as it would give the public complete security against the further depreciation of Bank notes; without which they would have too much reason to fear, from their observations on the past, that the paper currency would continue progressively to sink in value. It is not necessary to point out the effects which will follow from such a conviction on all future leases and contracts.
>
> (Letter to Perceval, 27 July 1811; VI: 45)

> This would secure the public against any further depreciation of Bank notes, as the Bank would be obliged for their own safety to keep the amount of their circulation within the present limits whilst commerce and credit continued in its present state, to prevent such a rise in the price of bullion as would make it profitable to individuals to purchase it of them for exportation. [...] If no further measures were taken to approximate the currency to our ancient standard, the adoption of the one here recommended would alone give complete security as to the future: – the depreciation of our currency would be effectually checked, and the bank deprived of the alarming power which they at present possess, of diminishing, at their pleasure, the value of the monied property of every man in the kingdom. It would afford leisure too for the consideration of such further measures as might be necessary, without pledging Parliament to any particular course of proceeding. And if it should be thought expedient to make bank notes a legal tender, the knowledge which the public would have that though already depreciated more than 20 pct., the deprecia-

> tion of Bank notes would go no further, and that their value would no longer depend on the caprice or false theory of Bank Directors, would deprive that measure of all the alarm which without such security it is so much calculated to produce.
>
> (Letter to Tierney, 11 December 1811; VI: 68)

The design of the monetary system could thus affect positively the confidence of the public in money inasmuch as expectations about the rational – that is, interest-driven – behaviour of its issuer were concerned. It could do nothing against a panic generated by circumstances outside the monetary system itself.

The internal drain

A second type of drain was caused by the coexistence of coins and notes in the domestic monetary system; it was thus an internal drain. Old coins becoming light through debasement in one way or another while keeping their nominal legal value, the market price of bullion increased, and new full-bodied coins were demanded from the Bank (against notes) to be melted and sold in the market to pocket the difference (see Chapter 6 above). Facing a drain of its metallic reserve, the Bank had to purchase bullion in the market to have it coined, thus sustaining the market price above the legal price; this process (the Penelope effect analysed in Chapter 7 above) would go on, imposing losses on the Bank. In the Ingot Plan, notes convertible into bullion did not aim at complementing coins but at eliminating them altogether (as Ricardo wrote in *Principles*: "A currency is in its most perfect state when it consists wholly of paper money"; I: 361). The elimination of the metallic currency radically prevented this internal drain from occurring, by suppressing the defects which were attached to that kind of currency and caused the drain. There was an additional advantage: having no longer to guard itself against an internal drain, the Bank could hold a smaller reserve. The system was then more "economical" *because* it was more "secure".

The external drain

A third type of drain remained: the external one, when gold was obtained from the Bank to be exported. The security of the monetary system required that the metallic reserve of the Bank might not be threatened by an external drain. The second principle of the Ingot Plan – the management principle – was put to contribution to attain this goal. We saw in Chapter 8 above that, according to Ricardo, the monetary cause of a fall in the exchange rate – which led to an external drain when the exchange rate hit the export bullion point – should be handled by a contraction of the note issue, *before* the external drain even started. The management of the note issue was thus substituted for bullion flows as driving force of the international adjustment, and this eliminated the threat of external drain for this (monetary) type of causes. The corrective role of international bullion flows only subsisted for those variations in the exchange rate having a real origin – a type of cause which was acknowledged by Ricardo but could only generate small demands for bullion at the Bank, as compared with the demands triggered by a mismanagement of the note issue. As quoted above:

> These transactions in bullion would be very few in number, if the Bank regulated their loans and issues of paper by the criterion which I have so often mentioned, namely, the price of standard bullion.
>
> (*Proposals*; IV: 67; *Principles*; I: 357–8)

In the Ingot Plan, a small metallic reserve of the Bank would be amply sufficient to face this kind of real external drain, provided the ingot principle eliminated the risk of internal drain caused by the coexistence of coins and notes, and the management principle eliminated the risk of external drain caused by an excess issue of notes. In the Plan for a national bank, as seen above, "a liberal provision of gold" (between 17 and 28 per cent of the note issue) would be made "in case it should be thought expedient occasionally to correct the exchanges with foreign countries, by the exportation of gold, as well as by the reduction of the amount of paper" (*Plan for a National Bank*; IV: 294).

Both the Ingot plan and the Plan for a national bank aimed at increasing the security of the monetary system by limiting the need for a metallic reserve of the issuing bank to the occasional demand for bullion raised by non-monetary circumstances affecting relations with foreign countries.

9.6 An application of Ricardo's theory of money

On the question of central banking, the literature on Ricardo usually emphasises quantity rationing of the note issue and independence of the central bank. This is consistent with the attribution to Ricardo of a quantity theory of money. In contrast, his position on central banking is better understood as an application of his non-quantitative monetary theory (the Money–Standard Equation), in which the quantity of money is regulated by the standard.

According to Ricardo, two conditions were necessary and sufficient to achieve a "sound" (that is, "secure") state of the currency: convertibility of bank notes into bullion (ingot principle) and regulation of their issue so as to maintain the market price of bullion equal to its legal price (management principle). The first principle prevented an internal drain of the gold reserves of the issuing bank (except in the case of a panic, which no monetary system could guard from), and the second principle prevented an external drain for monetary reasons. These two principles ensured that the currency conformed to the standard (to eliminate monetary causes of instability in its value), although it was not issued through the monetisation of the standard but of capital (to ensure the fulfilment of the needs of trade). They testified to the fact that money was not subject to physical constraints: in Ricardo's system, the monetary standard is a specific commodity, but money is no commodity at all. No natural law explains changes in the value of money: such laws apply to one of their determinants (changes in the *value* of the standard), but not to the other (changes in the *price* of the standard, which entirely depends on the institutions ruling the monetary system). The quantity of money is not restricted by the available quantity of gold (whether at the level of the world as a whole or in the reserve of the issuing bank) but is adjusted to "the wants of commerce". The soundness of money only depends on the soundness of the plan designed for it.

The standard and the paper currency were thus two complementary but distinct features of Ricardo's ideal monetary system, and this complementarity is in no way trivial in the history of monetary thought and in the history of money as well. On the one hand, the Ingot Plan led to the demonetisation of gold in domestic circulation: gold was the standard of money but no longer money. On the other hand, Ricardo was the first to theorise the gold-exchange standard, by separating domestic circulation (of convertible notes) and foreign payments (in bills of exchange), though preserving a link through gold (which acted as domestic monetary standard and international means of settlement).

As seen above, *Proposals* was a turning point in Ricardo's theory of money, by stating the three conditions for "a perfect currency":

> A currency may be considered as perfect, of which the standard is invariable, which always conforms to that standard, and in the use of which the utmost economy is practised.
>
> (*Proposals*; IV: 55)

The Ingot Plan and the Plan for a national bank were the outcome of these conditions. Although the literature on Ricardo mostly emphasised the third one – the "economical" character mentioned in the title of the 1816 pamphlet – Ricardo was mainly interested by the first two, which gave the currency a "secure" character. The design of the monetary system could not do much for the invariability of the *value* of the standard, apart from avoiding any unnecessary demand for gold bullion by the bank of issue. But it was crucial to ensure the conformity of the currency to the standard, that is, the stabilisation of the market price of gold bullion at the level of its legal price.

The theoretical foundation of the Ingot Plan was not yet complete at the time of *Proposals*: as shown in Chapter 4 above, it would require the theory of value and distribution contained in *Principles*. But it was ready when the plan was discussed in Parliament in 1819 with a view to restoring the convertibility of the Bank of England note. The basis of the Ingot Plan was what I called the Money–Standard Equation, that is, the distinction between the two channels of variation in the value of money: variations in the value of the standard and variations in its market price. By eliminating gold from domestic monetary circulation and restricting its role to the function of standard of paper money, the ingot principle – convertibility both ways between the note and the standard – avoided the interference between the value and the price of the standard produced by the circulation of coins. As shown in Chapter 7 above, the demonstration that the quantity of money did not affect its value directly but indirectly, through the market price of the standard, gave a theoretical basis to the policy rule which Ricardo had advocated for long, namely varying the note issue inversely with the spread between the market price and the legal price of the standard. This was the management principle which allowed stabilising the value of money thanks to the stabilisation of the market price of gold bullion; this second pillar of the Ingot Plan was the second application of Ricardo's monetary theory.

Ricardo's conception of a monetary system based on a central bank was present as early as his Bullion Essays,[21] but it only acquired a theoretical foundation with *Proposals* and *Principles*. When in 1819 time came for a discussion and experimentation of "Ricardo's system", he was fully equipped both with a monetary theory and the applied institutions and rules deriving from it. This was not enough to overcome obtuse prejudices and vested interests.

Appendix 9: The Ingot Plan in perspective

Table 9.1 compares: (a) the monetary system as it existed before 1797 and was resumed from 1821 to 1844, (b) the Ingot Plan as embodied in *Proposals for an Economical and Secure Currency* (1816), (c) the transitory system adopted in Peel's bill in 1819 and discontinued in 1821, (d) the Plan for a national bank, as embodied in Ricardo's *Plan for the Establishment of a National Bank* (written in 1823 and published posthumously in 1824), and (e) the system embodied in the Bank Charter Act of 1844. Ricardo considered that, from 1797 (when the convertibility of the Bank of England note was suspended) to 1819 (when it was resumed), the monetary system had no standard (see Chapter 7 above); this period is consequently not included in Table 9.1.

Most of the legal provisions of the pre-1797 system were present in the system ruling from 1821 to 1844, with the exceptions of the Bank of England note becoming legal tender (in parallel with the gold coin) from 1833 on, and of melting and exporting the coin being authorised, as was the case since 1819. Discretion in the Bank of England issuance of notes evolved around 1830 (outside any legal provision): from 1828 on, the Bank committed itself to buy any bullion offered to it at a fixed price, and in the early 1830s it adopted the "Palmer rule" (after the name of the Governor of the Bank) for varying the issues (see Clapham 1944).

The provisions of the Ingot Plan, of Peel's bill and of the Plan for a national bank are detailed in Chapter 9 above.

The 1844 Bank Charter Act divided the Bank of England in an Issue department and a Banking department. The existing stock of notes at the time was backed around one half by the metallic reserve and one half by government securities. As for the additional issue, it was to be backed 100 per cent by an increase in the metallic reserve. The Banking department could lend the notes (by discounting bills) in the limit of the quantity issued by the Issue department (see Clapham 1944).

Table 9.1 Monetary systems with a gold standard

	Pre-1797 and 1821–1844	*Ingot Plan (1816)*	*Peel's bill (1819–1821)*	*Plan for a national bank (1823)*	*Bank Charter Act 1844 –*
Currency with unrestricted legal tender	Gold coin Bank of England note (after 1833)	Bank of England note	Gold coin	Gold coin National Bank note	Gold coin Bank of England note
Bank of issue	Bank of England	Bank of England	Bank of England	National Bank	Bank of England
Monopoly of note issue	Within a radius of 60 miles around the City Elsewhere: country banks	Unchanged	Unchanged	All over England	Within a radius of 60 miles around the City. Ceilings on country banks issues and transfer to Bank of England when lapsed
Mode of issuing notes	Discounting of commercial bills	Discounting of commercial bills. Convertibility of bullion	Discounting of commercial bills	Convertibility of bullion. Open-market operations on government securities	Discounting of commercial bills Convertibility of bullion
Note-issuing rule	None: discretion for *bona fide* bills	Expansion (contraction) when market price of bullion below (above) legal price	None: discretion	Expansion (contraction) when market price of bullion below (above) legal price	Issue department: expansion (contraction) when metallic reserve increases (diminishes)
Convertibility of circulating medium into the standard	Coin: melting and exporting prohibited (pre-1797), authorised (1821–1844) Note: into full-bodied coin	Note: into bullion	Coin: melting and exporting authorised Note: into bullion	Coin: melting and exporting authorised Note: into full-bodied coin (domestic) and bullion (for export)	Coin: melting and exporting authorised Note: into full-bodied coin
Convertibility of the standard into circulating medium	Coin: at the mint Note: none	Note: at the Bank of England	Coin: at the mint Note: none	Note: at the National Bank	Coin: at the mint Note: at the Bank of England

Notes

1 See also:

> It is on this principle that paper money circulates: the whole charge for paper money may be considered as seignorage. Though it has no intrinsic value, yet, by limiting its quantity, its value in exchange is as great as an equal denomination of coin, or of bullion in that coin.
>
> (*Principles*; I: 353)

2 On 9 April 1810 Mr. Harman, a Director of the Bank of England, had declared before the Bullion Committee: "I think if we discount only for solid persons, and such paper as is for real *bona fide* transactions, we cannot materially err" (III: 375).

3 When examined in 1819 on "Mr. Ricardo's plan" by the Commons' Committee on the Resumption of Cash Payments, the financier Alexander Baring confirmed this link with the Bank of Hamburg:

> The plan in question is, in fact, no other than that of the bank of Hamburgh, only substituting a currency of paper in lieu of a transfer of book debt; and the bank of Hamburgh has always been found, from long experience, the best institution for preserving the standard of value; the payments of the bank of Hamburgh are solely in silver bullion.
>
> (quoted in Sraffa 1952b: 358)

4 See Gillard (2004) on the Bank of Amsterdam and Achterberg and Lanz (1957–1958) on the Bank of Hamburg.

5 On Ricardo's notes on Bentham's manuscript "Sur les prix" see Deleplace and Sigot (2012).

6 As he explained in a footnote, Ricardo mentioned "uncoined gold or silver" because at the time of *Proposals* the pound was still legally on a double standard and the question of the choice of the standard was not yet settled. He himself opposed the double standard and at that time favoured the silver one; he would later prefer gold (see Chapter 2 above). In another footnote Ricardo observed that the Bank buying price could be fixed "a little above, or a little below" £3. 17s. and the minimum quantity of bullion to be obtained from or sold to the Bank could be made "ten or thirty" instead of twenty ounces. These were details: he wished only "to elucidate the principle" (*Proposals*; IV: 66n; *Principles*; I: 357n).

7 See the letter to Malthus on 9 July 1821: "they [the Directors of the Bank of England] are indeed a very ignorant set" (IX: 15).

8 One objection to the plan was that, aiming at eliminating the circulation of gold coins, it implied the issuance of low-denomination notes. The problem of forgery was put forward but the reluctance of the Bank of England to enlarge the circulation of its notes beyond the circle of merchants also played a role.

9 When in 1832 the question of the renewing of the charter of the Bank of England was raised, Moses Ricardo suggested to Ricardo's publisher, John Murray, to re-issue *Plan for a National Bank* with "a concise account of his plan for a secure and economical currency", that is, the Ingot Plan of 1816. As Sraffa observes, "nothing came of this suggestion" (Sraffa 1951f: 273).

10 See also the letter to Mill of 7 August 1823: "I have devoted a few days to the writing of a short tract to prove the practicability of the Government becoming the sole issuers of paper money. I feel fully assured that Commissioners might be appointed on such a plan, to manage the whole concern, that ministers would have much less influence over them, to make them swerve from their duty, than what they have possessed, and have indeed exercised over the Bk. of Engd" (IX: 329).

11 In the final version of his plan, Ricardo strengthened the independence of the commissioners from Parliament, as compared with the original MS in which they "should not be removable but in consequence of an address to his majesty by the House of Commons, or by both Houses of Parliament" (IV: 290n).
12 The bills were used for the relations between the London office of the national bank and its agents in the country.
13 The commissioners would issue £29 millions in notes, that is, 15 to reimburse the capital of the Bank of England, 10 to purchase gold or exchequer bills from the Bank of England, and 4 exchanged for the sums (in Bank of England notes) deposited by public departments at their bankers, for which the national bank would henceforth substitute. Ricardo envisaged two cases (IV: 291): £5 or 8 millions could be devoted to buy gold and respectively £9 or 6 millions to buy exchequer bills, giving a ratio of 17 or 28 per cent respectively.
14 "In this crisis, Parliament applied a remedy, very similar, in its effect, to an enlargement of the advances and issues of the Bank; a loan of Exchequer Bills was authorized to be made to as many mercantile persons, giving good security, as should apply for them; and the confidence which this measure diffused, as well as the increased means which it afforded of obtaining Bank Notes through the sale of the Exchequer Bills, speedily relieved the distress both of London and of the country" (III: 349).
15 Sraffa gives in a footnote the conclusion of the speech as it appeared in the *British Press*. It read:

> If I might advise the Bank, they would, instead of discounting at the invariable rate of 5 per cent. alter the rate of interest according to the changes of the market. During the war those merchants who could discount at the Bank, raised money at 5 per cent. whilst those who were not so favoured paid 7 per cent. for it. That was the case in the war, but at present it would be wise for the Bank to lower the rate of interest to 4 per cent.
>
> (V: 97n)

16 Sraffa gives two alternate reported versions of this part of Ricardo's speech; this is the second one, which is more detailed.
17 On the rate of interest in Ricardo see also Ahiakpor (1985), Panico (1988), Diatkine (2013), Pivetti (2015).
18 The distinction between "Horizontalists" and Verticalists" is borrowed from Moore (1988). For its role in modern post-Keynesian and Circulation approaches, see Deleplace and Nell (1996a).
19 In *Proposals* as in the extract of this pamphlet quoted in *Principles*, Ricardo mentioned £3. 17s. as a legal buying price of bullion by the Bank of England, which for a legal price of £3 17s. 10½d. at which bullion was provided by the Bank against notes gave for *b* a little more than one per cent. While the mint remained open to the public, *b* should be fixed a little lower than the rate of interest until the mint delivered the coins:

> The price of 3*l.* 17*s.* here mentioned, is, of course, an arbitrary price. There might be good reason, perhaps, for fixing it either a little above, or a little below. In naming 3*l.* 17*s.* I wish only to elucidate the principle. The price ought to be so fixed as to make it the interest of the seller of gold rather to sell it to the Bank, than to carry it to the mint to be coined.
>
> (*Proposals*; IV: 66n; *Principles*; I: 357n)

In his speech of 24 May 1819 before the House of Commons, Ricardo recommended £3 17s. 6d. as Bank buying price (V: 13), which gave for *b* a little less than 0.5 per cent.

20 This evidence reads as follows:

> [Question]: Suppose a case in which no demands were made upon the Bank by Government for unusual accommodations, but an unusual demand was made by merchants for increased facilities of discount, would the Bank in such a case consider itself as bound, in order to support public credit, to grant that increase of discounts, although there was a run upon it for Gold occasioned by the high price of Bullion and the unfavourable state of the exchange?
>
> [Answer by John Whitmore, Governor of the Bank of England]: I now consider my answer as my own opinion, not having the opportunity of consulting the Bank upon the question; in my opinion the Bank would not increase their discounts, nor on the other hand would it, I think, after the experience of the years 1796 and 1797, do well materially to diminish them.
>
> (III: 364–5)

21 This is testified by Ricardo's critique (around Christmas 1810) of Bentham's manuscript "Sur les prix". Comparing this manuscript and Ricardo's critique, Deleplace and Sigot (2012: 759–60) conclude:

> The confrontation of Bentham and Ricardo, as it appears in Ricardo's notes on Bentham's manuscript, highlights two lines of thought which coexist in classical monetary theory after Smith. In Bentham, a microeconomic theory of money focuses on the solidity of banks, whose primary role is to grant credit to private activity. In Ricardo, a macroeconomic theory of money focuses on a central bank, whose primary role is to regulate the aggregate quantity of money according to the value of the standard. Classical monetary theory, as illustrated by Bentham and Ricardo, then appears to be split in two variants: a banking system based on prudence and confidence *versus* a monetary system based on institutions and rules.

On Bentham on money see Sigot (2001) and Sigot and Deleplace (2012).

Afterword

Contrary to the widely shared opinion that Ricardo fared less well on monetary theory than in other fields and that he did not improve upon his early writings,[1] I have aimed in this book at showing that there is a coherent theory of money in Ricardo, integrated in his theory of value and distribution, and for this reason to be found in his mature monetary writings (from *Proposals* in 1816 onwards) rather than in the Bullion Essays of 1809–1811. The concept of standard of money is central in this theory and the adjustment of the market price of the standard (gold bullion) to the legal price of gold in coin (in the pre-1797 system) or in bullion (in Ricardo's Ingot Plan) plays a pivotal role in the channel of transmission of the quantity of money to its value. Indeed, as seen in Chapter 7 above, the description of the adjustment of the market price to the legal price of gold was already present in the Bullion Essays, and it remained valid in subsequent writings. But it was with *Proposals* that Ricardo shifted his theoretical interest from a situation in which money had no standard – since the suspension in 1797 of the convertibility of the Bank of England note – to a monetary system with a standard.

The analytical distinction (made in *Proposals*) between two causes of change in the value of money, on the one hand a change in the *value* of the standard, on the other hand a change in the *price* of the standard – a distinction embodied in what I have called the Money–Standard Equation – was coupled by Ricardo with the theory of value and distribution contained in *Principles* – a theory that applied to the value of the standard but not to its price – to elaborate a coherent theory of money. Ricardo's early understanding of the adjustment of the market price to the legal price of gold was thus introduced into a theoretical framework built in *Proposals* (for a money with a standard) and in *Principles* (for value and distribution), Ricardo being at his best with the consequences he derived in his writings and oral interventions between 1819 and 1823.

Ricardo did not ensure the coherence of his theory of money by submitting to the alleged "Ricardian vice" that concentrates on long-term positions and neglects short-term adjustments. On the contrary, a great part of this theory is devoted to the analysis of the adjustment of the domestic value of money, whether to a real change in the value of the standard (see Chapter 5 above) or to a monetary shock on metallic money (Chapter 6) or paper money (Chapter 7), and it also analyses the adjustment of the external value of money (the exchange rate) to a monetary shock (Chapter 8).

It may be useful to sum up the main results obtained in the book, before evoking the legacy of Ricardo's theory of money for today.

1. Results

Appendix 10 below gathers the main equations constituting Ricardo's model, which establishes results often at variance with what is affirmed in most of the literature that concentrates on the Bullion Essays. In the book I emphasise that Ricardo's mature theory of money is founded on the distinction between three notions: the value of money (in terms of all commodities except the standard), the value of the standard (in terms of all other commodities), and the price of the standard (in terms of money). This distinction leads to the main result of the book, which may be summed-up in four propositions: (a) the value of money varies positively with the value of the standard and inversely with its price (the Money–Standard Equation); (b) a change in the quantity of money relatively to the "wants of commerce" affects the value of money in the opposite direction, and it does so indirectly, through its effect on the price of the standard in the same direction; (c) for a given value of the standard, the quantity of money is endogenously determined through variations in the price of the standard; and (d) consequently, Ricardo's theory of money is *not* a quantity theory of money: the causal relation between the quantity of money and its value only applies to disequilibrium, not in the conformable state (when "money conforms to the standard") where the causality is the other way round.

Detailed results are (with the corresponding chapter where they are established):

- The value of money is defined by Ricardo, *not* as its purchasing power over the standard (gold bullion), *but* as its purchasing power over all commodities except the standard (Chapter 3).
- The question of the invariable standard is *not only* an integral part of Ricardo's theory of value and distribution *but also* of his theory of money (Chapter 3).
- There is in Ricardo *neither* inconsistency *nor* contradiction between an alleged commodity-theory of money and an alleged quantity-theory of money *but* an integration of a non-quantitative theory of money in the theory of value and distribution (Chapters 4 and 7).
- Changes in the value of money are *not* caused in the long run by changes in the value of the standard and in the short run by changes in the quantity of money, *but* always by the combination of the direct effect of changes in the value of the standard and of the indirect effect (through the market price of the standard) of changes in the quantity of money (Chapters 4 and 7).
- A discretionary change in the quantity of money does *not* cause an opposite change in its value directly, as in the Quantity Theory of Money, *but* indirectly, through a change in the market price of the standard. The transmission channel from the quantity to the value of money is the market price of the standard (Chapters 4 and 7).
- The discovery of a new gold mine does *not* lower permanently the value of metallic money because of an increased quantity of bullion produced *but* because of a fall in its cost of production (Chapter 5).

- A discretionary increase in the issuing of notes is *not* analogous with an increase in the quantity of metallic money following the discovery of a new gold mine *but* with a debasement of the circulating coins (Chapters 5 and 6).
- The effect of the debasement of the coins on the high price of gold bullion is another application of "the principle of limitation of quantity" according to which an excess quantity of money generates its depreciation (Chapter 6).
- For Ricardo a monetary system with a double standard was not only unstable because of the variability in the relative price of gold in silver but also because it increased the possibility for the issuing bank of varying the value of money at will (Chapter 6).
- In contrast with what happens under inconvertibility, the role of the export of bullion consequent upon an excess of convertible bank notes is only temporary in the adjustment, which eventually operates through a contraction of the note issue under the pressure on the metallic reserve of the bank (Penelope effect) (Chapter 7).
- Convertibility both ways between money and its standard prevents the value of money from diverging permanently from the value of the standard. However, convertibility of the note into coin and discretion in its issue made the adjustment process harmful and insecure. Although improving convertibility, the Ingot Plan aimed at ensuring the conformity of money to the standard without having actually recourse to it (Chapters 7 and 9).
- Because discretionary changes in the aggregate quantity of money only affect its value in disequilibrium and are corrected endogenously, Ricardo's mature theory of money, as it is embodied in the Money–Standard Equation, is *not* a quantity theory of money. Modern attempts at introducing real-balance effects or at linking Ricardo's alleged quantity theory of money and Say's Law are therefore irrelevant (Chapter 7).
- Contrary to the almost exclusive attention given to the Bullion Essays in the literature, Ricardo's mature theory of money does *not* apply to a money without a standard (such as inconvertible notes). Its only use for this question is to show that such a money is not viable (Chapter 7).
- The standard is neither a commodity like all others nor money: it has a unique character. As a commodity, gold bullion was produced in competitive conditions and its market price, in the gold-producing country, was regulated by its cost of production. In any country where it was used as the standard of money, its market price was regulated by a fixed legal price. This double regulation of the market price of the standard implies that it should be produced outside of the country in which it is used as the standard of money, the link being provided by the exchange rate (Chapters 5 and 7).
- Ricardo did *not* deny the possibility of a real shock on the exchange rate, but he distinguished between a real shock, which could only affect the exchange rate within the (narrow) limits set by the cost of the international transfer of bullion, and a monetary shock, which affected the exchange rate through a change in the real par of exchange (Chapter 8).
- The adjustment to a shock on the exchange rate is *not* through the domestic quantity of money, prices, and the balance of trade (the price-specie flow

mechanism) *but* through the international transfer of bullion if the shock is real or the management of the note issue if the shock is monetary (Chapter 8).
- When the cause of a fall in the exchange rate is monetary, the adjustment should not be left to the export of bullion, which forces the bank of issue to contract the quantity of notes only after a harmful delay, but it should result from a voluntary contraction of the issues by the bank, before arbitrage drains its metallic reserve (Chapter 8).
- The Ingot Plan was *not* a technical device for economising on gold *but* a radical change in the monetary system which demonetised gold in domestic circulation and separated domestic and foreign payments (a gold-exchange standard) (Chapters 8 and 9).
- There was continuity between the Ingot Plan and the Plan for a national bank on the two underlying principles of "a perfect currency" managed by a central bank: the ingot principle – convertibility of the note into bullion for foreign payments – and the management principle – varying the note issue inversely with the spread between the market price and the legal price of the standard (Chapter 9).
- The usual reading key "rules versus discretion" does *not* apply to Ricardo's "judicious management of the quantity" of notes: this quantity resulted endogenously from the fulfilment of the condition of conformity of money to the standard, that is, the equalisation of the market price of gold bullion with its legal price (Chapter 9).
- The combination of the ingot principle and of the management principle not only aimed at stabilising the market price of the standard – hence eliminating the monetary cause of variation in the value of money – but also at increasing the security of the monetary system, by preventing an internal or external drain of the metallic reserve of the central bank (Chapter 9).

2. The legacy of Ricardo's theory of money for today

A contribution to the modern theory of Classical prices

The publication in 1960 by Piero Sraffa of *Production of Commodities by Means of Commodities* showed that his masterly edition of Ricardo's *Works and Correspondence* not only offered a reappraisal of the latter's theory of value and distribution – providing an interpretation still hotly debated today in its own right – but also allowed the development of a modern theory of prices in the Classical tradition which constituted an alternative to the general-equilibrium approach grounded in the marginalist tradition. Leaving aside the sensitive question of whether Sraffian prices radically differ or not from neo-Walrasian prices, one may observe that both approaches face the same riddle: how to apply a "real" theory of the system of prices – that is, a theory that does not require money as a building block – to a monetary economy – that is, the economy of the "real world" in which commodities are not bartered against one another but traded against money. This so-called question of the integration of money in the theory of value has for long raised many difficulties in the general-equilibrium approach, and it cannot be avoided in the modern Classical one.

This question must all the more be faced because the *Sraffa Papers*, currently in a process of publication, do not leave any doubt about the fact that Sraffa viewed himself as part of an old tradition which considered that prices cannot be but money prices. In other words, although money is not among the determinants of the system of relative prices, it is nevertheless essential, in the sense that the only "real-world" economy to which this system applies is a monetary economy. However, such affirmation remains empty in the absence of a theory of the value of the circulating medium that allows deriving the money prices of the commodities from the system of their relative prices. To integrate Ricardo's conception of money as a pure means of exchange into a Ricardo–Sraffa system of relative prices, one cannot rely, as many modern advocates of this theory of prices do, on Sraffa's allusion to a causal relation between the money rate of interest and the rate of profit (Sraffa 1960: 33) – an allusion downplayed by Sraffa himself in his unpublished papers (see Deleplace 2014a).

To integrate money in the modern theory of Classical prices it seems appropriate to turn to Ricardo's monetary theory. Indeed, Ricardo may be considered as the author who introduced the method which would be later adopted by all economists interested in the working of a market economy: start with a theory of the real exchange values of commodities, abstracting from money, and then, since the implementation of exchange faces difficulties (as already emphasised by Adam Smith with the problem of the double coincidence of wants), introduce a theory of money as a solution to these difficulties. Ricardo was the first to build a consistent theory of (real) relative prices and – as the present book has shown – to develop a theory of money coherent with it, including the adjustment of the quantity of money in disequilibrium. This was the great posthumous victory of Ricardo in that field.

Unfortunately, the understanding of Ricardo's theory of money at his time and in the subsequent literature has been hindered by two obstacles, with which the integration of money in the modern theory of Classical prices is also confronted. One is the frequent confusion between money and the standard of money (gold bullion): since the standard is a commodity, this confusion leads to infer that a Classical approach is only consistent with a commodity-theory of money. In contrast, when money is carefully distinguished from its standard, it may be understood as a pure circulating medium designed in a way that makes it conform to the standard. The second obstacle is the specificity of the standard of money as a commodity being subject to a double determination of its price: by its difficulty of production (as all other competitively produced commodities) and by law (what makes it singular). The interpretation given here of Ricardo's theory of the value of money (the Money–Standard Equation) shows that this double determination is not contradictory but implies that the standard of money (gold bullion) be produced outside of the system of production of commodities that determines the relative prices and the distribution of income. By clarifying the specificity of the price of gold bullion, this interpretation also contributes to the modern theory of

Classical prices, since it shows the radical difference between Ricardo's standard of money (exterior to the economic system) and Sraffa's Standard Commodity (into which any given economic system may be transformed).

Ricardo's theory of money, as it is here interpreted, allows deriving the natural prices (in money) of the commodities from: (a) the system of (real) relative prices, and (b) the value of money in the conformable state, determined by the value of the standard (for a given legal price of the standard when transformed into money). In disequilibrium (strictly defined by the inequality between the actual and the conformable quantities of money), the value of money changes inversely with its quantity – hence the misleading resemblance with the Quantity Theory of Money – and this change triggers an endogenous adjustment of the quantity of money which restores the conformable state. The money prices of commodities are therefore completely determined in and out of the conformable state. The theory of money is thus integrated in the Ricardo–Sraffa theory of relative prices and distribution, although money itself is outside of the system of commodities and the determination of its value is *sui generis*.[2]

Two tours de force were performed by Ricardo in his theory of money. First, the adjustment of the actual quantity of money to its conformable level only depends on arbitrage in the bullion market, *not* on any adjustment in all other markets. Indeed the money prices in these markets are affected by the change in the market price for gold bullion, but this is only a consequence of this latter change, which does not play any role in the adjustment of the quantity of money. Second and consequently, a policy rule may be designed to enforce the conformable quantity of money better than by arbitrage in the bullion market, without having to know this conformable level but simply by comparing the observed market price of the standard with its legal price and adapting the note issue accordingly.

At the end of the present enquiry into the theory of money in Ricardo, one is, however, obliged to recognise a blind spot in it, when it is applied to the convertible bank note – that is, for Ricardo, the "most perfect" currency. On the basis of the indications given in his writings, it is possible to demonstrate that the actual quantity of notes adjusts to its conformable level thanks to arbitrage in the bullion market or, preferably, to Ricardo's policy rule. This adjustment is triggered by a variation in the market price of the standard (gold bullion) relative to its legal price. But this supposes that in the first place an inadequate quantity of money is reflected in such a variation. This assumption does not raise any difficulty for a metallic money: its excess can only be caused by a debasement of the coin (*not* by an increase in the production of bullion), which may be ascertained by a physical operation: weighing and assaying. When the trader in bullion fixes the price at which he agrees to sell it against debased coins, he knows how much of standard bullion the melting pot would extract from them, and how many undebased coins he could alternatively obtain by bringing his bullion to the mint. He can raise the selling price of his bullion accordingly, and the buyer is forced to pay more than the legal price in a proportion equal to the loss in metal he would suffer if he had his coins melted instead of using them to buy bullion in the market. The conditions of arbitrage thus explain that an excess quantity of money causes a rise in the market price of the standard.

There is nothing of the kind for convertible notes. No *physical* test allows measuring how much their quantity issued departs from its conformable level. In the contrary, convertibility into coins "fresh from the mint" (undebased) or into bullion (in Ricardo's Ingot Plan) testifies to the fact that the note fully "represents" the standard – that is, is neither depreciated nor appreciated. Convertibility of the currency into the standard, which in the case of metallic money is checked by the melting pot and provides the test to measure how much the currency is in excess, conceals the inadequacy of the quantity in the case of notes, by proclaiming that their value is equal to that of the legal weight of the standard that defines the monetary unit. How can the trader in bullion translate the excess or deficiency of the quantity of convertible notes into a divergence of the market price of his commodity from the legal price, when he has no physical way to know this inadequacy? To the best of my knowledge there is no indication in Ricardo about how to avoid this black box. In other words, the convertibility of paper money into a physical object (gold bullion) is the condition for the adjustment of the actual quantity of money to its conformable level, but it conceals what triggers this adjustment process. This limitation of Ricardo's theory of money reflects the (actual) mystery of the nature of a paper money convertible into a physical object (gold bullion).

This observation leads to another possible legacy of this theory for today: its contribution to a modern approach to money.

A contribution to a modern approach to money

It cannot be doubted that Ricardo's theory of prices and distribution reflected his general conception of society. And here one might be surprised at the gap between the market-oriented approach generally ascribed to him and his defence of a monetary system in which a central bank manages the currency in a way which practically deprives private arbitrage in the market for the standard of any role. There is, however, no contradiction.

Ricardo's tour de force was to define the value of money as its purchasing power over all commodities except the standard and to isolate the source of variability in this value that had a monetary origin (an inappropriate quantity of money issued) without having to consider the market prices of the commodities circulated with money. The clue was an explanation of the variations in the value of money which relied exclusively on the combination of the variations in the value and in the price of the standard (what I called the Money–Standard Equation). The variability in the value of money that had a monetary origin was exclusively located in the divergence between the market price of the standard as commodity (bullion) and its legal price when converted into money (coin or, in Ricardo's Ingot Plan, note convertible into bullion). The market price of the standard being regulated by the legal price through arbitrage permitted by convertibility (in the pre-1797 system) or thanks to Ricardo's policy rule (in his two plans), it was independent of the determination of the market prices of all other commodities (the so-called mechanism of gravitation).

This was not only important from a theoretical point of view but also from a political and practical one: an appropriate design of the monetary system allowed the monetary authorities to eliminate the variability in the value of money that had a monetary origin, by making the market price of the standard conform to its legal price. The intervention of a central authority – a central bank – to regulate the market price of the standard *and only this price* ensured the existence of "a perfect currency" which made any central intervention in all other markets unnecessary. Ricardo's centralised monetary system was thus the condition of the absence of central intervention in the markets for commodities. This conclusion that, even endowed with a commodity standard, a monetary system had to be centralised, is already a lesson for today. There is another one.

During the many years I spent on this book, I often heard the same question: intellectual archaeology is fine, but what is the use of inquiring about the theory of a money anchored to gold, something only few people still advocate today? And this enquiry may not even be useful to them: modern advocates of such system usually develop a laissez-faire approach to money, which is at odds with Ricardo's contention that stabilising the value of money requires a legal price of the standard – instead of the value of money being market-determined – and a central bank managing the quantity of money on the basis of the spread between the market and the legal prices of the standard – instead of the note issue being left to free banking. It may thus seem that any attempt at linking Ricardo's theory of money with modern inquiries into monetary questions is doomed to failure.

One may, however, ask the question the other way round. The main lesson of Ricardo's mature theory of money is that a monetary system cannot be stable if it is deprived of a standard. Of course, the variability of the value of the standard generates variability in the value of money, but this is the price to pay for avoiding a greater instability in the value of money, due to a poorly designed monetary system. Ricardo showed with the Ingot Plan that the value of notes issued through monetisation of capital (discounting of commercial bills) could be stabilised under the condition of being anchored to a standard and managed properly. If this analysis is considered as valid, the next step is to inquire into the standard that should be designed to obtain the same result in a modern economy. In the historical conditions of the time, Ricardo considered a metallic standard. While it had been recognised for long – probably the sixteenth century – that the legal price of the standard in coin should not be arbitrarily changed by the State, the Bullionist Controversy showed that debates were still raging about the conditions under which the market price of the standard could be stabilised so as to eliminate the causes of variability in the value of money that had a monetary origin. The merit of Ricardo was to clarify this issue by showing that convertibility between one circulating medium (the note) and the other (the coin) was not appropriate: "a sound state of the currency" required the euthanasia of metal currency and the implementation of the ingot principle – convertibility both ways between the sole currency (the note) and the standard itself (bullion) – coupled with the management principle – expansion or contraction of the note issue according to the market price of the standard being below or above its legal price.

These conditions for "a perfect currency" in no way require the standard to be metallic: any marketable asset that is legally convertible into money and into which money is legally convertible at a fixed price may play the same role, provided, as recalled above, that it does not belong to the system of production of commodities. Even more: the above-mentioned mystery of a paper money convertible into a physical object (gold bullion) might be lifted if convertibility were into a financial asset (the value of which is determined by the anticipation of future returns) instead of a physical commodity. Both conditions – being outside the system of production of commodities and being a financial asset – would be fulfilled by a public bond purchased and sold for money by a central bank at a fixed price and traded on a secondary market – a situation not far from that of our modern economies in times of deflationary crisis and non-conventional central bank policy. When, for example, the European Central Bank announced that it was prepared to purchase any amount of the sovereign debt issued by a given State, as long as the market interest rate on that debt stayed above a predetermined (although undisclosed) level – in other words as long as the market price of that debt stayed below a predetermined level – it did the same as Ricardo's central bank, which was to enlarge its note issue as long as the market price of gold bullion fell below its legal price. There are of course important differences – the benchmark interest rate remains secret and this non-conventional policy is supposed to be abandoned sooner or later – but it is a step in Ricardo's direction.

The substitution of a public-debt standard for the gold-bullion standard would marry the ingot principle of the currency adapted from *Proposals* with open-market operations suggested in the *Plan for a National Bank*, so that the note issue would vary according to the spread between the rate of interest on the secondary market for public debt and the legal rate of interest on this debt. The analytical condition for such an approach to central banking is of course to formalise the link between the quantity of central bank money issued and the price of public securities, a question at the heart of modern monetary theory.

Appendix 10: Ricardo's model of a monetary economy with a standard

The appendix gathers the main equations constituting Ricardo's model, with their numbers as they appear in Chapters 3 to 9, so as to allow the reader going to the relevant chapter for the explanation.

1. Domestic relations

Notations:

V_M and $\Delta V_M / V_M$: absolute level and rate of change in the value of one pound sterling in terms of all commodities except gold bullion.
V_G and $\Delta V_G / V_G$: absolute level and rate of change in the value of an ounce of gold bullion in terms of all other commodities.
P_G and $\Delta P_G / P_G$: absolute level (in £) and rate of change in the market price of an ounce of gold bullion.

$\overline{P_{GC}}$: legal price (in £) of an ounce of gold in coin (pre-1797 system).
$\overline{P_G}$: legal price (in £) of an ounce of gold bullion (Ingot Plan).
M^* and $\Delta M^*/M^*$: absolute level and rate of change in the conformable quantity of money, according to the "wants of commerce".
$\Delta M / M$: rate of change in the actual quantity of money.
Y and $\Delta Y / Y$: absolute level and rate of change of the aggregate value of commodities to be circulated.
k: ratio of the value of the quantity of circulating money to the aggregate value of commodities.
s_G: minting cost of bullion into coin, in percentage.
m_G: melting cost of coin into bullion, in percentage.
b: cost charged by the Bank of England when it purchases gold bullion against notes (in the Ingot Plan), in percentage.

Equations:

Condition of coherence of the price system:

$$V_M = \frac{V_G}{P_G} \tag{3.5}$$

Pre-1797 monetary system (mint and passive bank of issue)

Conformable state

Condition of conformity of money to the standard:

$$V_M{}^* = \frac{1}{\overline{P_{GC}}} V_G \tag{3.8}$$

which may be rewritten as:

$$P_G = \overline{P_{GC}} \tag{3.9}$$

Conformable quantity of money:

$$M^* = k\,\overline{P_{GC}}\,\frac{Y}{V_G} \tag{7.6}$$

Disequilibrium: definition of depreciation (or, if negative, appreciation)

$$d = \frac{V_M^* - V_M}{V_M^*} \tag{4.1}$$

which may be rewritten as:

$$d = \frac{P_G - \overline{P_{GC}}}{P_G} \tag{4.2}$$

Dynamics: the Money–Standard Equation:

$$\frac{\Delta V_M}{V_M} = \frac{\Delta V_G}{V_G} - \frac{\Delta P_G}{P_G} \tag{4.8}$$

Starting from $P_G = \overline{P_{GC}}$, any variation $\Delta M / M$ in the actual quantity of money and / or $\Delta M^* / M^*$ in the conformable quantity of money cause a variation $\Delta P_G / P_G$ in the market price of gold bullion given by:

$$\frac{\Delta P_G}{P_G} = \frac{\Delta M}{M} - \frac{\Delta M^*}{M^*} \tag{7.3}$$

hence:

$$\frac{\Delta V_M}{V_M} = \frac{\Delta V_G}{V_G} - \left[\frac{\Delta M}{M} - \frac{\Delta M^*}{M^*}\right] \tag{7.4}$$

Condition of permanence of conformable state:

$$\frac{\Delta V_M^*}{V_M^*} = \frac{\Delta V_G}{V_G} \tag{7.7}$$

hence:

$$\frac{\Delta M^*}{M^*} = \frac{\Delta Y}{Y} - \frac{\Delta V_G}{V_G} \tag{7.8}$$

Dynamics in disequilibrium:

$$\frac{\Delta V_M}{V_M} = \frac{\Delta Y}{Y} - \frac{\Delta M}{M} \tag{7.10}$$

Endogenous adjustment of M:

When V_M falls below $V_M{}^*$ – hence P_G rises above $\overline{P_{GC}}$ – notes are converted into coins and coins melted into bullion, and the Penelope effect forces the bank to contract its issues so that M is adjusted downwards to M^*. When V_M rises above $V_M{}^*$ – hence P_G falls below $\overline{P_{GC}}$ – coining of bullion and / or discounting of bills for notes adjust M upwards to M^*. Convertibility both ways limits the variations of P_G to:

$$\overline{P_{GC}}\,(1+m_G) \geq P_G \geq \overline{P_{GC}}\,(1-s_G) \tag{6.1}$$

Ingot Plan (active bank of issue)

The legal price $\overline{P_G}$ of gold bullion substitutes for the legal price $\overline{P_{GC}}$ of gold in coin. The condition of conformity of money to the standard is now:

$$V_M{}^* = \frac{1}{\overline{P_G}} V_G \tag{9.1}$$

which may be rewritten as:

$$P_G = \overline{P_G} \tag{9.2}$$

Conformable quantity of money:

$$M^* = k\,\overline{P_G}\,\frac{Y}{V_G} \tag{9.3}$$

The Money–Standard Equation (4.8) and equations (7.3) to (7.5) and (7.7) to (7.10) apply. However, in contrast with the pre-1797 monetary system, the management principle varying the quantity of notes inversely with the sign of the spread between P_G and $\overline{P_G}$ adjusts $\Delta M / M$ before convertibility is implemented, so that:

$$\overline{P_G} \geq P_G \geq \overline{P_G}(1-b) \tag{9.4}$$

2. International adjustment

Notations:

$P_{nG}{}^{p}$: natural price (in *pesos*) of an ounce of bullion in the gold-producing country.
$\overline{P_{GC}}{}^{£}$: legal price (in £) of an ounce of gold in coin in England (pre-1797 system)

$\overline{P_G}^{\pounds}$: legal price (in £) of an ounce of gold bullion in England (Ingot Plan).
$P_G^{\pounds}$: market price (in £) of an ounce of gold bullion in England.
$\overline{P_{GC}}^{F}$: legal price (in French *francs*) of an ounce of gold in coin in France.
$e^{\pounds/p}$: exchange rate of £1 against *pesos*.
$e^{\pounds/F}$: exchange rate of £1 against French *francs*.
$\overline{R_{GC}}^{\pounds/F}$: legal par of exchange of £1 against French *francs* (pre-1797 system).
$\overline{R_G}^{\pounds/F}$: legal par of exchange of £1 against French *francs* (Ingot Plan).
r: natural rate of profit in England during the time capital is invested in the importation and sale of bullion, in percentage.
s_G^L, s_G^P: minting cost in London and Paris respectively, in percentage.
m_G^L, m_G^P: melting cost in London and Paris respectively, in percentage.
b^L: cost charged by the Bank of England when it purchases gold bullion against notes, in percentage (in the Ingot Plan).
c_{GM}^{AL}: cost of transfer of bullion from the gold-producing country to England, in percentage.
c_{GM}^{PL}: cost of importation of gold bullion to London from Paris, in percentage.
c_{GX}^{LP}: cost of exportation of gold bullion from London to Paris, in percentage.

Equations:

Exchange rate with the gold-producing country:

$$\frac{1}{e^{\pounds/p}} P_{nG}^{p} (1 + c_{GM}^{AL})(1 + r) = P_G^{\pounds} \qquad (5.9)$$

The level of the exchange rate $e^{\pounds/p}$ depends on the natural price of gold bullion in the gold-producing country and on its market price in England (determined above), for a given rate of profit in England.

Exchange rate with France:

Pre-1797 monetary system

$$\overline{R_{GC}}^{\pounds/F} = \frac{\overline{P_{GC}}^{F}}{\overline{P_{GC}}^{\pounds}} \qquad (8.1)$$

$$\overline{R_{GC}}^{\pounds/F} \frac{1 + m_G^P}{1 - s_G^L}(1 + c_{GM}^{PL}) \geq e^{\pounds/F} \geq \overline{R_{GC}}^{\pounds/F} \frac{1 - s_G^P}{1 + m_G^L}(1 - c_{GX}^{LP}) \qquad (8.10)$$

Ingot Plan

$$\overline{R_G}^{\text{£/F}} = \frac{\overline{P_{GC}}^{\text{F}}}{\overline{P_G}^{\text{£}}} \tag{8.13}$$

$$\overline{R_G}^{\text{£/F}} \frac{1+m_G{}^P}{1-b^L}(1+c_{GM}{}^{PL}) \geq e^{\text{£/F}} \geq \overline{R_G}^{\text{£/F}}(1-s_G{}^P)(1-c_{GX}{}^{LP}) \tag{8.14}$$

In both cases, the variations in the exchange rate $e^{\text{£/F}}$ are constrained by boundaries depending on the characteristics of the monetary system in England and in France, and on the cost of transfer of gold bullion between the two countries. The margin of variation is smaller in the Ingot Plan than in the pre-1797 English monetary system.

Notes

1 This opinion is even shared by some of Ricardo's admirers. For example, the far-reaching albeit concise introduction written by Donald Winch in 1973 for the *Everyman's Library* edition of *Principles* illustrates how a most respectful evaluation of Ricardo may exempt money from the "intellectual aesthetics" (Winch 1973: xviii) embodied in this book. Emphasising that "the skill and tenacity with which he [Ricardo] pursued the task of constructing a deductive model capable of generating practical solutions excites admiration", (ibid) Winch nevertheless contends that the "three monetary pamphlets" which Ricardo published before writing *Principles* "were not markedly above the level of several other contributions to a distinguished debate" and concludes: "Indeed, as far as monetary analysis is concerned, Ricardo's stock has tended to decline rather than rise with the years" (ibid: vii).

2 Some scholars have recently advocated that the Ricardo–Sraffa tradition was not the only one inside the Classical theory of prices, and that another line of enquiry (mostly descending from Torrens and Marx) could be developed (see for example Benetti and Cartelier 1999, Benetti *et al.* 2015). In this approach, the money price of a commodity is determined in the same way in equilibrium and disequilibrium, namely as the ratio of the purchasing power (in money) spent on this commodity to the quantity of the latter brought to market ("the Cantillon Rule", after the eighteenth-century author who was the first to formulate it). The question may be raised whether Ricardo's theory of money, as it is here interpreted, may also fit this other Classical line of enquiry or is restricted to the Ricardo–Sraffa tradition.

References

Achterberg, E. and Lanz, K. (1957–1958) *Enzyklopädisches Lexicon für das Geld-, Bank- und Börsenwesen*, Frankfurt am Main: Knapp, 2 vols.

Ahiakpor, J.C.W. (1985) "Ricardo on money: the operational significance of the non-neutrality of money in the short run", *History of Political Economy*, 17(1): 17–30.

Ahiakpor, J.C.W. (2003) *Classical Macroeconomics. Some Modern Variations and Distortions*, London: Routledge.

Arnon, A. (1987) "Banking between the invisible and visible hands: a reinterpretation of Ricardo's place within the Classical School", *Oxford Economic Papers*, 39(2): 268–81.

Arnon, A. (2011) *Monetary Theory and Policy from Hume and Smith to Wicksell*, Cambridge: Cambridge University Press.

Baring, F. (1797) *Observations on the Establishment of the Bank of England & on the Paper Circulation of the Country: to Which is Added Further Observations*, New York: A.M. Kelley, 1967.

Baring, F. (1801) *Observations on the Publication of Walter Boyd*, London: Sewell, Cornhill, and Debrett.

Benetti, C. and Cartelier, J. (1999) "Market and division of labour: a critical reformulation of Marx's view", *Rivista di Politica Economica*, April–May: 117–39.

Benetti, C., Bidard, C., Klimovsky, E. and Rebeyrol, A. (2015) "Temporary disequilibrium and money in a classical approach", *Cahiers d'économie politique*, 69: 159–84.

Bidard, C. (2014) "The Ricardian rent theory two centuries after", Working Paper 2014-54, Economix-Université Paris Ouest Nanterre La Défense.

Blake, W. (1823) *Observations on the Effects Produced by the Expenditure of Government during the Restriction of Cash Payments*, London: John Murray and E. Lloyd & Son.

Blaug, M. (1995) "Why is the quantity theory of money the oldest surviving theory in economics?" in Blaug, M. *et al.* (eds), *The Quantity Theory of Money. From Locke to Keynes and Friedman*, Aldershot: Edward Elgar: 27–49.

Blaug, M. (1996) *Economic Theory in Retrospect*, fifth edition, Cambridge: Cambridge University Press.

Bonar, J. (1923) "Ricardo's Ingot Plan: a centenary estimate", *The Economic Journal*, 33, September: 281–304. Reprinted in Cunningham Wood J, (ed.), *David Ricardo. Critical Assessments*, London: Routledge, vol. IV, 1991: 25–43.

Bosanquet, C. (1810) *Practical Observations on the Report of the Bullion Committee*, London: Richardson.

Boyd, W. (1801) *Letter to the Right Honourable William Pitt on the Influence of the Stoppage of Issues in Specie at the Bank of England, on the Prices of Provisions and Other Commodities*, London: J. Wright.

Boyer-Xambeu, M.-T. (1994) "Henry Thornton et la Bullion Controversy: Au-delà des bornes, il n'y a plus de limites", *Revue économique*, 45(5): 1215–26.

Boyer-Xambeu, M.-T., Deleplace, G. and Gillard, L. (1986) *Monnaie privée et pouvoir des princes. L'économie des relations monétaires à la Renaissance*, Paris: Éditions du CNRS / Presses de la Fondation Nationale des Sciences Politiques.

Boyer-Xambeu, M.-T., Deleplace, G. and Gillard, L. (1994a) *Private Money and Public Currencies. The 16th Century Challenge*, Armonk: M.E. Sharp.

Boyer-Xambeu, M.-T., Deleplace, G. and Gillard, L. (1994b) "Régimes monétaires, points d'or et 'serpent bimétallique' de 1770 à 1870", *Revue économique*, 45(5): 1139–74.

Boyer-Xambeu, M.-T., Deleplace, G. and Gillard, L. (1995) *Bimétallisme, taux de change et prix de l'or et de l'argent. 1717–1873*, special issue of *Economies et Sociétés, Cahiers de l'ISMEA*, XXIX (7–8).

Boyer-Xambeu, M.-T., Deleplace, G. and Gillard, L. (1997) "'Bimetallic Snake' and monetary regimes: the stability of the exchange rate between London and Paris from 1796 to 1873", in Marcuzzo, M.C., Officer, L.H. and Rosselli, A. (eds), *Monetary Standards and Exchange Rates*, London: Routledge: 106–49.

Boyer-Xambeu, M.-T., Deleplace, G. and Gillard, L. (2010a) "Taux de change et prix de l'or et de l'argent à Paris, Londres et Hambourg, 1800–1873: le Système Bimétallique Européen", *Annuaire historique de la Banque de France*, www.banque-france.fr/la-banque-de-france/histoire/annuaire-historique.html, accessed 28 November 2016.

Boyer-Xambeu, M.-T., Deleplace, G. and Gillard, L. (2010b) "Exchange rates of the pound sterling with the French franc and the Hamburg mark banco, bi-weekly, 1800–1873", *Historical Financial Statistics*, Center for Financial Stability, http://www.centerforfinancialstability.org/hfs.php?, accessed 28 November 2016.

Boyer-Xambeu, M.-T., Deleplace, G. and Gillard, L. (2013) "Les arbitrages sur les changes et les métaux précieux entre Londres, Paris et Hambourg (1821–1873): les serpents bimétalliques", *Histoire et Mesure*, XXVIII(2): 205–41.

Boyer-Xambeu, M.-T., Deleplace, G., Gaubert, P., Gillard, L. and Olteanu, M. (2007a) "Mixing Kohonen algorithm, Markov switching model and detection of multiple change-points: an application to monetary history", *Lecture Notes on Computer Science*, 45(7): 541–50.

Boyer-Xambeu, M.-T., Deleplace, G., Gaubert, P., Gillard, L. and Olteanu, M. (2007b) "Combining a dynamic version of Kohonen algorithm and a two-regime Markov switching model: an application to the periodization of international bimetallism (1821–1873)", *Investigacion Operacional*, 28(2): 144–57.

de Boyer des Roches, J. (2007) "Cause and effect in the gold points mechanism: a criticism of Ricardo's Criticism of Thornton", *The European Journal of the History of Economic Thought*, 14(1): 25–55.

de Boyer des Roches, J. (2008) "Le rejet par Ricardo du mécanisme des points d'or", *Cahiers d'économie politique*, 55: 49–63.

de Boyer des Roches, J. (2013) "Prices, value and seigniorage in Ricardo's monetary economics", in Sato, Y. and Takenaga, S. (eds), *Ricardo on Money and Finance. A Bicentenary Reappraisal*, Abingdon: Routledge: 30–52.

Braudel, F. (1981–1984) *Civilization and Capitalism, 15th – 18th Century*, New York: Harper and Row, 3 vols.

Cannan, E. (ed.) (1919) *The Paper Pound of 1797–1821. The Bullion Report 8th June 1810*, London: King & Son, second edition (1925). Reprint: London: Frank Cass & Co, 1969.

Cantillon, R. (1755 [1730]) *Essai sur la nature du commerce en général*, Paris: INED, 1997.

Carr, J.L. and Ahiakpor, J.C.W. (1982) "Ricardo on the non-neutrality of money in a world with taxes", *History of Political Economy*, 14(2): 147–65.

Cartelier, J. (1994) "Étalon monétaire et mesure de la valeur: monnayage et systèmes de paiement", *Cahiers d'économie politique*, 23: 33–41.

Cartelier, J. (2015) "James Steuart: a neglected inspiration for an alternative economic theory", in Steuart, J. (1767) *An Inquiry into the Principles of Political Oeconomy*, edited by Longhitano, G., with Cartelier, J. and Deleplace, G., Napoli: Liguori Editore, vol I: XLI–LXVII.

Chipman, J.S. (1984) "Balance of payment theory", in Creedy, J. and O'Brien D.P. (eds), *Economic Analysis in Historical Perspective*, London: Butterworths: 186–217.

Clapham, J. (1944) *The Bank of England*, Cambridge: Cambridge University Press.

Davis, T. (2005) *Ricardo's Macroeconomics. Money, Trade Cycles, & Growth*, Cambridge: Cambridge University Press.

Deleplace, G. (ed.) (1994) *Monnaie et étalon chez David Ricardo*, special issue of *Cahiers d'économie politique*, 23.

Deleplace, G. (1996) "Does circulation need a monetary standard?", in Deleplace, G. and Nell, E.J. (eds), *Money in Motion. The Post Keynesian and Circulation Approaches*, Basingstoke: Macmillan: 305–29.

Deleplace, G. (1999) *Histoire de la pensée économique. Du "royaume agricole" de Quesnay au "monde à la Arrow-Debreu"*, Paris: Dunod, second edition: 2007.

Deleplace, G. (2001) "Does Ricardo's theory of money belong to the classical canon?" in Forget, E.L. and Peart, S. (eds), *Reflections on the Classical Canon in Economics. Essays in Honor of Samuel Hollander*, London: Routledge: 331–45.

Deleplace, G. (2004) "Monetary stability and heterodoxy: a history of economic thought perspective", in Arena, R. and Salvadori, N. (eds), *Money, Credit, and the Role of the State*, Aldershot: Ashgate: 45–62.

Deleplace, G. (2008) "Les deux plans monétaires de Ricardo", *Cahiers d'économie politique*, 55: 13–33.

Deleplace, G. (2013a) "The role of the standard in Ricardo's theory of money", in Sato, Y. and Takenaga, S. (eds), *Ricardo on Money and Finance. A Bicentenary Reappraisal*, Abingdon: Routledge: 115–23.

Deleplace, G. (2013b) "Marshall and Ricardo on note convertibility and bimetallism", *The European Journal of the History of Economic Thought*, 20(6), December: 982–99.

Deleplace, G. (2014a) "The essentiality of money in the Sraffa Papers", in Bellofiore, R. and Carter, S. (eds), *Towards a New Understanding of Sraffa. Insights from Archival Research*, Basingstoke: Palgrave Macmillan: 139–66.

Deleplace, G. (2014b) "An unorthodox genealogy on the relation between the markets for foreign exchange and credit in Steuart, Thornton, Tooke, and Keynes (1923)", communication to the 18th Annual Conference of the European Society for the History of Economic Thought, Lausanne.

Deleplace, G. (2015a) "Bullionist controversy", in Kurz, H.D. and Salvadori, N. (eds), *The Elgar Companion to David Ricardo*, Cheltenham: Edward Elgar: 41–55.

Deleplace, G. (2015b) "Papers on money and banking", in Kurz, H.D. and Salvadori, N. (eds), *The Elgar Companion to David Ricardo*, Cheltenham: Edward Elgar: 387–96.

Deleplace, G. (2015c) "Monetary theory", in Kurz, H.D. and Salvadori, N. (eds), *The Elgar Companion to David Ricardo*, Cheltenham: Edward Elgar: 344–56.

Deleplace, G. (2015d) "James Steuart: an unorthodox monetary approach to exchange and the foreign balance", in Steuart, J. (1767) *An Inquiry into the Principles of Political Oeconomy*, edited by Longhitano, G., with Cartelier, J. and Deleplace, G., Napoli: Liguori Editore, vol I: LXIX–XCVIII.

Deleplace, G., Depoortère, C. and Rieucau, N. (2013) "An unpublished letter of David Ricardo on the double standard of money", *The European Journal of the History of Economic Thought*, 20(1), February: 1–28.

Deleplace, G. and Nell, E.J. (1996a) "Introduction: monetary circulation and effective demand", in Deleplace, G. and Nell, E.J. (eds), *Money in Motion. The Post Keynesian and Circulation Approaches*, Basingstoke: Macmillan: 3–41.

Deleplace, G. and Nell, E.J. (eds) (1996b) *Money in Motion. The Post Keynesian and Circulation Approaches*, Basingstoke: Macmillan.

Deleplace, G. and Sigot, N. (2012) "Ricardo's critique of Bentham's French manuscript: secure currency versus secure banks", *The European Journal of the History of Economic Thought*, 19(4), October: 733–64.

Depoortère, C. (2008) "Quel modèle d'accumulation du capital chez Ricardo?", *Cahiers d'économie politique*, 55: 141–54.

Depoortère, C. (2013) "William Nassau Senior and David Ricardo on the method of political economy", *Journal of the History of Economic Thought*, 35(1), March: 19–42.

Depoortère, C. (2015) "Two unpublished letters by David Ricardo on a monetary pamphlet by Samuel Tertius Galton", *Journal of the History of Economic Thought*, 37(3), September: 341–61.

De Vivo, G. (1987) "Ricardo, David", in Eatwell, J., Milgate, M. and Newman, P. (eds), *The New Palgrave. A Dictionary of Economics*, London: Macmillan, vol. IV: 183–98.

Diatkine, S. (1994) "Offre de monnaie et politique monétaire chez Thomas Attwood", *Revue économique*, 45(5): 1271–88.

Diatkine, S. (2008) "La politique monétaire selon Ricardo: une comparaison avec l'École de la circulation", *Cahiers d'économie politique*, 55: 35–48.

Diatkine, S. (2013) "Interest rates, banking theory and monetary policy in Ricardo's economics", in Sato, Y. and Takenaga, S. (eds), *Ricardo on Money and Finance. A Bicentenary Reappraisal*, Abingdon: Routledge: 124–46.

Dome, T. (2004) *The Political Economy of Public Finance in Britain 1767–1873*, London: Routledge.

Dostaler, G. (2007) *Keynes and his Battles*, Cheltenham: Edward Elgar.

Feaveryear, A. (1931) *The Pound Sterling. A History of English Money*, Oxford: Clarendon Press.

Fetter, F.W. (1965) *Development of British Monetary Orthodoxy 1797–1875*, Cambridge: Harvard University Press.

Gilbert, G. (1987) "'A great national calamity': Ricardo's obituary in the *Morning Chronicle*", *The History of Economics Society Bulletin*, VIII(2): 21–6.

Gillard, L. (2004) *La banque d'Amsterdam et le florin européen au temps de la République néerlandaise (1610–1820)*, Paris: Editions de l'Ecole des Hautes Etudes en Sciences Sociales.

Glasner, D. (2013) "Monetary disequilibrium and the demand for money in Ricardo and Thornton", in Sato, Y. and Takenaga, S. (eds), *Ricardo on Money and Finance. A Bicentenary Reappraisal*, Abingdon: Routledge: 15–29.

Gootzeit, M.J. (1975) *David Ricardo*, New York: Columbia University Press.

Green, R. (1992) *Classical Theories of Money Output and Inflation*, London: Macmillan.

Green, R. (1998) "Money and banking", in Kurz, H.D. and Salvadori, N. (eds), *The Elgar Companion to Classical Economics*, Cheltenham: Edward Elgar, Vol. 2: 136–41.

Grubel, H.G. (1961) "Ricardo and Thornton on the transfer mechanism", *Quarterly Journal of Economics*, LXXV(2): 292–301.

Hansard, T.C. (1820–1830) *The Parliamentary Debates. Second Series*. 25 vols. London: T.C. Hansard.

Hayek, F.A. von (1939) "Introduction" to Thornton (1802 [1939]) *An Enquiry into the Nature and Effects of the Paper Credit of Great Britain*, London: George Allen and Unwin. Reprint: Fairfield: A.M. Kelley, 1991: 11–63.

Heertje, A. (1991) "Three unpublished letters by David Ricardo", *History of Political Economy*, 23(3): 519–26.

Heertje, A. and Weatherall, D. (1978) "An unpublished letter of David Ricardo: to Thomas Smith of Easton Grey, 27 April 1819", *The Economic Journal*, 88, September: 569–71.

Heertje, A., Weatherall, D. and Polak, R.W. (1985) "An unpublished letter of David Ricardo to Francis Finch, 24 February 1823", *The Economic Journal*, 95, December: 1091–2.

Henderson, J.P. (1997) *The Life and Economics of David Ricardo*, with supplemental chapters by J.B. Davis, Norwell: Kluwer.

Hollander, S. (1979) *The Economics of David Ricardo*, London: Heinemann.

House of Lords (1819) *Reports by the Lords Committees appointed a Secret Committee to inquire into the State of the Bank of England, with reference to the Expediency of the Resumption of Cash Payments; with Minutes of Evidence*. In *The Sessional Papers printed by order of The House of Lords* (1844), vol. 18.

Hume, D. (1752) *Political Discourses: Of the Balance of Trade*, in Miller, E.F. (ed.), *David Hume: Essays, Moral, Political, and Literary*, Indianapolis: Liberty Fund, 1985.

Keynes, J.M. (1913) *Indian Currency and Finance*, in *The Collected Writings of John Maynard Keynes*, London: Macmillan, vol. I, 1971.

Keynes, J.M. (1930) *A Treatise on Money. Volume 1. The Pure Theory of Money*, in *The Collected Writings of John Maynard Keynes*, London: Macmillan, vol. V, 1971.

Keynes, J.M. (1936) *The General Theory of Employment, Interest and Money*, in *The Collected Writings of John Maynard Keynes*, London: Macmillan, vol. VII, 1973.

King, J.E. (2013) *David Ricardo*, Basingstoke: Palgrave Macmillan.

King, P. (1803) *Thoughts on the Restriction of Payments in Specie at the Banks of England and Ireland*, London: Cadell and Davies.

Kurz, H.D. and Salvadori, N. (2015a) "Invariable measure of value", in Kurz, H.D. and Salvadori, N. (eds), *The Elgar Companion to David Ricardo*, Cheltenham: Edward Elgar: 205–11.

Kurz, H.D. and Salvadori, N. (eds) (2015b) *The Elgar Companion to David Ricardo*, Cheltenham: Edward Elgar.

Laidler, D. (1975) *Essays on Money and Inflation*, Manchester: Manchester University Press.

Laidler, D. (1987) "Bullionist controversy", in Eatwell, J., Milgate, M. and Newman, P. (eds) *The New Palgrave. A Dictionary of Economics*, London: Macmillan, vol. I: 289–94.

Leclercq, Y. (2010) *La banque privée supérieure. Une histoire de la Banque de France, 1800–1914*, Paris: Classiques Garnier.

Lindsay, A.M. (1892) *Ricardo's Exchange Remedy: A Proposal to Regulate the Indian Currency by Making it Expand and Contract Automatically at Fixed Sterling Rates, with the Aid of the Silver Clause of the Bank Act*, London: Effingham Wilson & Co.

Longhitano, G. (2015) "James Steuart: the political economy of the 'equal chance'", in Steuart, J. (1767) *An Inquiry into the Principles of Political Oeconomy*, edited by Longhitano, G., with Cartelier, J. and Deleplace, G., Napoli: Liguori Editore, vol I: IX–XXXIX.

McCulloch, J.R. (1818) "On *Proposals for an Economical and Secure Currency*, by David Ricardo, Esq.", *The Edinburgh Review*, Vol. XXXI: 53–80.

McCusker, J.J. (1978) *Money and Exchange in Europe and America, 1600–1775. A Handbook*, Chapel Hill: The University of North Carolina Press.

Malthus, T.R. (1811) "Review of the controversy respecting the high price of bullion", *The Edinburgh Review*, Vol. XVIII: 448–70.

Marcuzzo, M.C. (2014) "On the notion of permanent and temporary causes: the legacy of Ricardo", *Journal of the History of Economic Thought*, 36(4): 421–34.

Marcuzzo, M.C. and Rosselli, A. (1987) "Profitability in the international gold market in the early history of the gold standard", *Economica*, 54(215): 367–80.

Marcuzzo, M.C. and Rosselli, A. (1991) *Ricardo and the Gold Standard. The Foundations of the International Monetary Order*, London: Macmillan.

Marcuzzo, M.C. and Rosselli, A. (1994a) "The standard commodity and the standard of money", *Cahiers d'économie politique*, 23: 19–31.

Marcuzzo, M.C. and Rosselli, A. (1994b) "Ricardo's theory of money matters", *Revue économique*, 45(5): 1251–67.

Marcuzzo, M.C. and Rosselli, A. (1997) "Metallic standards and real exchange rates", in Marcuzzo, M.C., Officer, L.H. and Rosselli, A. (eds), *Monetary Standards and Exchange Rates*, London: Routledge: 81–105.

Marcuzzo, M.C. and Rosselli, A. (2015) "Natural quantity of money", in Kurz, H.D. and Salvadori, N. (eds), *The Elgar Companion to David Ricardo*, Cheltenham: Edward Elgar: 370–5.

Marshall, A. (1887) "Remedies for fluctuations of general prices", *Contemporary Review*, 51, March: 355–75. Reprinted in Pigou, A.C. (ed.), *Memorials of Alfred Marshall*, London: Macmillan, 1925: 188–211.

Martin, C. (2008) "Monnaie et reproduction du capital: un modèle pour aider un 'génie supérieur' ricardien", *Cahiers d'économie politique*, 55: 81–112.

Mason, W.E. (1957) "Ricardo's transfer mechanism theory", *Quarterly Journal of Economics*, LXXI(1): 107–15.

Mason, W.E. (1963) *Clarification of the Monetary Standard*, University Park: Pennsylvania State University Press.

Moore, B.J. (1988) *Horizontalists and Verticalists: The Macroeconomics of Credit Money*, Cambridge: Cambridge University Press.

O'Brien, D.P. (1975) *Classical Economics*, Oxford: Clarendon Press.

O'Brien, D.P. (1995) "Long-run equilibrium and cyclical disturbances: the currency and banking controversy over monetary control", in Blaug, M. *et al.* (eds), *The Quantity Theory of Money. From Locke to Keynes and Friedman*, Aldershot: Edward Elgar: 50–79.

O'Brien, D.P. (2007) *The Development of Monetary Economics. A Modern Perspective on Monetary Controversies*, Cheltenham: Edward Elgar.

Otomo, T. (2013) "Ricardo's theory of central banking. The monetary system and the government", in Sato, Y. and Takenaga, S. (eds), *Ricardo on Money and Finance. A Bicentenary Reappraisal*, Abingdon: Routledge: 147–76.

Panico, C. (1988) *Interest and Profit in the Theories of Value and Distribution*, New York: St. Martin's Press.

Patinkin, D. (1956) *Money, Interest, and Prices. An Integration of Monetary and Value Theory*, Evanston: Row, Peterson and Company.

Peach, T. (1993) *Interpreting Ricardo*, Cambridge: Cambridge University Press.

Peach, T. (1996) "Ricardo and Malthus on the post-Napoleonic distress: too many producers or a momentary lapse of reason?" in Corry, B. (ed.), *Unemployment and the Economist*, Cheltenham: Edward Elgar: 30–51.

Peach, T. (2008) "Ricardo, David (1772–1823)", in Durlauf, S.N. and Blume, L.E. (eds), *The New Palgrave Dictionary of Economics*, second edition, London: Macmillan.

Peake, C.F. (1978) "Henry Thornton and the development of Ricardo's economic thought", *History of Political Economy*, 10(2): 193–212.

Perlman, M. (1986) "The bullionist controversy revisited", *Journal of Political Economy*, 94(4): 745–62.

Pivetti, M. (2015) "Rate of interest", in Kurz, H.D. and Salvadori, N. (eds), *The Elgar Companion to David Ricardo*, Cheltenham: Edward Elgar: 427–31.

Plessis, A. (1982–1985) *La Banque de France*, Genève: Droz, 3 vols.

Porta, P.L. (1992a) "Introduction", in Porta, P.L. (ed.), *David Ricardo: Notes on Malthus's 'Measure of Value'*, Cambridge: Cambridge University Press: ix–xxi.

Porta, P.L. (ed.) (1992b) *David Ricardo: Notes on Malthus's 'Measure of Value'*, Cambridge: Cambridge University Press

Ricardo, D. (1809) *The Price of Gold. Three Contributions to the Morning Chronicle*, in Ricardo (1951–1973), vol. III, 1951: 13–46.

Ricardo, D. (1810–1811) *The High Price of Bullion, A Proof of the Depreciation of Bank Notes*, in Ricardo (1951–1973), vol. III, 1951: 47–127.

Ricardo, D. (1811) *Reply to Mr. Bosanquet's 'Practical Observations on the Report of the Bullion Committee'*, in Ricardo (1951–1973), vol. III, 1951: 155–256.

Ricardo, D. (1815) *An Essay on the Influence of a low Price of Corn on the Profits of Stock*, in Ricardo (1951–1973), vol. IV, 1951: 9–41.

Ricardo, D. (1816) *Proposals for an Economical and Secure Currency*, in Ricardo (1951–1973), vol. IV, 1951: 49–141.

Ricardo, D. (1817–1821) *On the Principles of Political Economy, and Taxation*, first edition: 1817, second edition: 1819, third edition: 1821, in Ricardo (1951–1973), vol. I, 1951.

Ricardo, D. (1824) *Plan for the Establishment of a National Bank*, in Ricardo (1951–1973), vol. IV, 1951: 275–300.

Ricardo, D. (1951–1973) *The Works and Correspondence of David Ricardo*, edited by Sraffa, P. with the collaboration of Dobb, M.H., Cambridge: Cambridge University Press, 11 vols.

Ricardo, M. (1824) "A memoir of David Ricardo", in Ricardo, D. (1951–1973), vol. X, 1955: 3–13.

Rist, C. (1940 [1938]) *History of Monetary and Credit Theory from John Law to the Present Day*, New York: Macmillan.

Rosier, M. (1994) "Être ou ne pas être smithien en 1804: le cas Lord Peter King", *Revue économique*, 45(5): 1227–50.

Rosselli, A. (2008) "Ricardo and Thornton on the 'unfavourable' rate of exchange", *Cahiers d'économie politique*, 55: 65–79.

Sato, Y. (2013) "Old and new interpretations of classical monetary theory", in Sato, Y. and Takenaga, S. (eds), *Ricardo on Money and Finance. A Bicentenary Reappraisal*, Abingdon: Routledge: 53–74.

Sato, Y. and Takenaga, S. (2013a) "Introduction. Ricardo's monetary thought 200 years on", in Sato, Y. and Takenaga, S. (eds), *Ricardo on Money and Finance. A Bicentenary Reappraisal*, Abingdon: Routledge: 1–11.

Sato, Y. and Takenaga, S. (eds) (2013b) *Ricardo on Money and Finance. A Bicentenary Reappraisal*, Abingdon: Routledge.

Sayers, R.S. (1953) "Ricardo's views on monetary questions", *Quarterly Journal of Economics*, 67(1), February: 30–49. Reprinted in Cunningham Wood, J. (ed.), *David Ricardo. Critical Assessments*, London: Routledge, vol. IV, 1991: 53–68.

Schumpeter, J.A. (1954) *History of Economic Analysis*, New York: Oxford University Press.

Shaw, W.A. (1895) *The History of Currency 1252–1894*, London: Wilsons and Milne.

Sigot, N. (2001) *Bentham et l'économie. Une histoire d'utilité*, Paris: Economica.

Sigot, N. and Deleplace, G. (2012) "From 'Annuity Notes' to Bank Notes: A Change in Bentham's Theory of Money", *History of Economic Ideas*, XX (1): 45–74.

Sinha, A. (2010a) *Theories of Value from Adam Smith to Piero Sraffa*, Abingdon: Routledge.

Sinha, A. (2010b) "A note on Ricardo's 'invariable measure of value'", *Cahiers d'économie politique*, 58: 133–44.

Smith, A. (1776) *An Inquiry into the Nature and Causes of the Wealth of Nations*, edited by Campbell, R.H. and Skinner, A.S., Oxford: Clarendon Press, 1976.

Sraffa, P. (1951a) "Introduction", in Ricardo, D. (1951–1973), vol. I: xiii–lxiv.

Sraffa, P. (1951b) "Prefatory note to volumes III and IV", in Ricardo, D. (1951–1973), vol. III: vii–viii.

Sraffa, P. (1951c) "Note on the Bullion Essays", in Ricardo, D. (1951–1973), vol. III: 3–12.

Sraffa, P. (1951d) "Note on 'Essay on Profits'", in Ricardo, D. (1951–1973), vol. IV: 3–8.

Sraffa, P. (1951e) "Note on 'Economical and Secure Currency'", in Ricardo, D. (1951–1973), vol. IV: 45–48.

Sraffa, P. (1951f) "Note on 'Plan for a National Bank'", in Ricardo, D. (1951–1973), vol. IV: 272–4.

Sraffa, P. (1952a) "Introduction to the speeches in Parliament", in Ricardo, D. (1951–1973), vol. V: xiii–xxxiv.

Sraffa, P. (1952b) "Notes on the evidence on the resumption of cash payments", in Ricardo, D. (1951–1973), vol. V: 350–70.

Sraffa, P. (1955a) "Addenda to the memoir", in Ricardo, D. (1951–1973), vol. X: 16–64.

Sraffa, P. (1955b) "Ricardo in business", in Ricardo, D. (1951–1973), vol. X: 67–106.

Sraffa, P. (1960) *Production of Commodities by Means of Commodities. Prelude to a Critique of Economic Theory*, Cambridge: Cambridge University Press.

Sraffa Papers, Cambridge: Trinity College, Wren Library.

Steuart, J. (1767) *An Inquiry into the Principles of Political Oeconomy*, edited by Longhitano, G., with Cartelier, J. and Deleplace, G., Napoli: Liguori Editore, 2015, 2 vols.

Steuart, J. (1767 [1805]) *An Inquiry into the Principles of Political Economy*, edited by Skinner, A.S., London: Pickering & Chatto, 1998, 4 vols.

Stigler, G.J. (1958) "Ricardo and the 93% labour theory of value", *American Economic Review*, 48: 357–67.

Takenaga, S. (2013) "Labour theory of value and quantity theory in Ricardo's economic theory", in Sato, Y. and Takenaga, S. (eds), *Ricardo on Money and Finance. A Bicentenary Reappraisal*, Abingdon: Routledge: 77–114.

Takenaga, S. (2016) "Introduction", in Takenaga, S. (ed.) *Ricardo and the Japanese Economic Thought. Selection of Ricardo Studies in Japan during the Interwar Period*, Abingdon: Routledge: 1–58.

Thornton, H. (1802) *An Enquiry into the Nature and Effects of the Paper Credit of Great Britain*, edited with an Introduction by von Hayek, F.A., London: George Allen and Unwin, 1939. Reprint: Fairfield: A.M. Kelley, 1991.

Thornton, H. (1811) "Two speeches of Mr. Henry Thornton on the Bullion Report", in Thornton, H. (1802 [1939]): 327–61.

Thuillier, G. (1983) *La monnaie en France au XIXe siècle*, Genève: Droz.

Viner, J. (1937) *Studies in the Theory of International Trade*, New York: Harper.

Weatherall, D. (1976) *David Ricardo. A Biography*, The Hague: Martinus Nijhoff.

Wheatley, J. (1803) *Remarks on Currency and Commerce*, London: Cadell and Davies.

Wicksell, K. (1934–1935 [1901–1906]) *Lectures on Political Economy*, London: Routledge and Kegan Paul, 2 vols.

Winch, D. (1973) "Introduction", in Ricardo, D. *On the Principles of Political Economy and Taxation*, London: J.M. Dent & Sons: v–xviii.

Name index

Occurrences of the name David Ricardo have not been listed. See the subject index for entries in relation to it.

Subject index

For Product Safety Concerns and Information please contact our EU
representative GPSR@taylorandfrancis.com
Taylor & Francis Verlag GmbH, Kaufingerstraße 24, 80331 München, Germany

www.ingramcontent.com/pod-product-compliance
Ingram Content Group UK Ltd.
Pitfield, Milton Keynes, MK11 3LW, UK
UKHW021023180425
457613UK00020B/1035

* 9 7 8 0 3 6 7 8 6 7 8 3 6 *